Scottish Fi.

An informed and irreverent guide for movie-lovers

MARK FURSE

Luath Press Limited

EDINBURGH

www.luath.co.uk

First published in hardback by Steamer Point Publishing, Glasgow 2024
This revised and updated edition first published 2025

ISBN: 978-1-80425-201-7

This book is made of materials from well-managed,
FSC®-certified forests and other controlled sources.

FSC
www.fsc.org

MIX
Paper | Supporting
responsible forestry
FSC® C011748

Printed and bound by
Ashford Colour Ltd, Gosport

Typeset in Sabon by
Main Point Books, Edinburgh

MARK FURSE, former Head of Law at Glasgow University, has embraced his passion for cinema post-retirement, delving into Scotland's film legacy with the meticulous detail of a scholar. Raised in diverse countries and educated across continents, Mark's journey in academia led him to an international career, eventually settling in Glasgow. This book reflects his deep love for film and dedication to cultural preservation.

Praise for *Scottish Films*

'Furse writes well and passionately, and there are constant reminders of films past ... [with] awesome attention to detail.'—SCOTTISH FIELD, review of first edition

'*Scottish Films* is an essential guide to the story of cinema in Scotland from the silent era to contemporary indie cinema. Mark Furse has done a heroic job researching films with Scotland at their heart. This will become an essential reference book for anyone interested in our cultural history.'—STUART COSGROVE, writer and broadcaster

'This is a marvellous book. Makes me proud to be Scottish and proud to love Scottish films. If you're either of these two it's well worth a bawbee. Well done Mark you deserve a Scottish BAFTA.'—DON COUTTS, director of *American Cousins* and others

'Exemplary in its encyclopaedic thoroughness and enjoyable to read, Mark Furse's labour of love provides an indispensable map of Scottish film from the silent era to the present day. *Scottish Films* is an invaluable resource for serious researchers and casual viewers alike.'—PROFESSOR DUNCAN PETRIE, author of *Screening Scotland*

'This is a brilliant new book referencing every film set substantially in Scotland – the result is stunning.'—NICK VARLEY, film producer

'This is a terrific compendium of Scotland's huge and rich film history. It's written with passion, an eye for detail, and a huge weight of knowledge by someone unafraid to throw in a deal of criticism too.'—KIRSTY WARK, journalist and broadcaster

Contents

Contents

Key to abbreviations and symbols

EIFF – Edinburgh International Film Festival

GFF – Glasgow Film Festival

GFT – Glasgow Film Theatre

MFB – *Monthly Film Bulletin*

NYT – *New York Times*

S&S – *Sight and Sound*

Film Title – Any film title in **bold italic** is the subject of an entry in this book and is Scottish within the definition I adopt throughout.

Film Title† – Any film title displayed like this is a film which is 'Scottish-adjacent'. On some lists these may appear as Scottish; their inclusion here will normally explain why I have *not* included them as Scottish.

Film Title – Film titles in *italic* only are neither Scottish nor Scottish-adjacent (although in a Scottish film's entry that film title is shown in *italic* throughout the entry).

→ – Entry out of date order, linked by theme, subject or person to the preceding main entry.

DOC – Documentary

How Scottish is it?
Films with entries in this book are assessed, fairly loosely, for how Scottish they are. All films are set substantially or entirely in Scotland. Beyond that the following criteria are used:

(1) substantially or wholly shot in Scotland

(2) Scottish creatives in key roles behind camera (e.g., director, screenwriter)

(3) Scottish actors in front of camera in significant roles.

S+ – Set in Scotland and one further criterion met – most often, but not always, this will be shot in Scotland.

S++ – Two further criteria met.

S+++ – Very Scottish: set and shot in Scotland, with significant Scottish creative input in front of *and* behind the camera.

How good is it? (see Appendix 1)
1 to 50 – For films ranked 1–50 an individual ranking is given.

T100 Films ranked 51–100.

W10 The worst ten films (1 being the worst).

Foreword

IT'S DIFFICULT TO explain a project as quixotic as the one which has led to this book: an examination of a genre which, officially, does not exist, through the prism of 427 films (all of which I have had to identify, track down and watch). I blame a mix of friends who enjoy arguments too much, alcohol (the two can make for interesting evenings), and *One Flew Over the Cuckoo's Nest* – the film (Milos Forman, 1975), not the book: watching this on rerelease in the late 1970s fundamentally changed my attitude towards cinema. I had been going to my local fleapit, where the carpets were so rank that your shoes were in danger of sticking to them and where you reeked of cigarette smoke after the film whether you smoked or not, as often as I could since moving back to England at the age of 11 (often sitting through the same film three times on a Saturday – because no one cared and you could). But until I saw *One Flew* I had pretty much treated cinema as a necessary diversion from life in an otherwise largely miserable suburban town in the Southeast of England. *One Flew* made me realise there was a difference between cinema, and good cinema (and I recognise that parts of the film may have aged badly). Good cinema admits us into the lives of others, raises questions, can challenge and change attitudes and is worth going to whether or not one lives in miserable suburbia.

Since the late 1970s I have seen *a lot* of films at the cinema – thousands of them. I ran a film society at my first university, took a course at the BFI when I lived in London, and self-educated at any available cinema, chief among them London's BFI Southbank and the Prince Charles Cinema, and Scotland's Glasgow Film Theatre and the Edinburgh Filmhouse (the welcome rebirth of which is underway as I write this). I have read far too much about cinema (as much, if not more, than I have about the subject which elevated me to a Professorship at the University of Glasgow). Predictions of its demise notwithstanding, I continue to believe cinema remains, at its best, a potent cultural force with the power to entertain *and* to matter – as a fair few films in this book do. There are, of course, also films covered here which neither entertain nor matter, but someone had to watch them to work that out and warn others.

Because this book is about films related to a place, rather than to a genre, person, year or era, the range covered is hugely diverse. There will be films discussed here you have not heard of which are worth digging out and I would be beyond astonished if any reader has seen every film I treat as Scottish.

This revised and expanded edition of *Scottish Films* consists of all entries contained in the first book (minus *Shadowland*, Simon David Kay, 2021, which was not shown in cinemas), as well as 52 additions: 17 are new releases, 17 are films I had not previously identified as Scottish, and 18 I was previously unable to find have been tracked down. I have also reorganised some of the material and corrected a small number of mistakes. Notwithstanding the application of a research skillset developed at universities over decades and my determination to eliminate – at least here – many of the errors littering online reports and discussions about some of the films discussed, it is inevitable that some mistakes will remain. These are my responsibility alone. If you alert me to any I will be grateful and correct them should a future edition be forthcoming. While I am reasonably confident that I have now identified all films falling within my definition of 'Scottish', there's the possibility that some have slipped past me – particularly films made in a foreign language. If you think I have missed a film from this edition please let me know, although do bear in mind the inclusion criteria set out in the introduction.

Putting together a book about films with the distinction of being substantially set in Scotland has turned out to be a far heftier exercise than I had first imagined. In my naivety I had thought at the outset of this project – which has now consumed nearly four years – there might perhaps be at most 100–125 entries; this book covers 427 films falling within my definition of 'Scottish', and roughly 12–15 are being released each year.

Mark Furse,
Glasgow, June 2025

INTRODUCTION

'Scottish' film

FORMALLY, FOR ALMOST all purposes, almost all the time, there is no such thing as a 'Scottish' film. I know this sounds absurd; after all, the book you are now reading is called '*Scottish* films', and I think we'd all agree that *Local Hero* is Scottish. Film nationality raises questions which are answered in multiple ways depending on what question is being asked and who is asking it. It is rare for those questions to require answers below the level of the nation state – in our case of the UK. For the Oscars, film nationality is determined by the place where artistic control rests – typically, although not exclusively, with the country in which the lead production company has its seat. The Internet Movie Database (IMDb), as close to an industry standard as we get, attributes film nationality based on funding sources, and may confer multiple nationalities on the same film. *Breaking the Waves* has, according to IMDb, 13 countries of origin. Throughout this book every film in **bold italic** is the subject of an entry: I define *Breaking the Waves* as Scottish for the purposes of this book (which does not mean that it is not simultaneously Danish, Swedish, Dutch or any of the other ten nationalities given on IMDb), but *never* on IMDb is a film 'Scottish' – even if the funding flows significantly from Screen Scotland, this is classed as UK funding.

The only body which defines a Scottish film (and Scottish filmmakers) is the British Academy of Film and Television Arts (BAFTA) in Scotland. A key question driving its definition is in essence that of 'to whom, and for what, should we give awards'? The Scottish arm of the BAFTA has existed since 1986 and has been presenting the BAFTA Scotland awards since 2008. The eligibility criteria for consideration are that two of the following apply: (1) the production company has a substantive business and production base in Scotland; (2) at least 50 per cent of the production budget must be spent in Scotland, or on Scottish talent; and (3) Scots must have significant creative involvement (if you make a low-budget film in the US, manage to persuade Tilda Swinton to be in it, permit her to ad-lib, and blow 51 per cent of the budget on her, you've made a Scottish film!). Individuals are considered Scottish based on place of birth, or residency, or self-identification combined with spending a considerable time in Scotland. These criteria, which are eminently reasonable in the context of BAFTA Scotland's aims, have resulted in the inclusion of films which audiences are unlikely to recognise as 'Scottish', notwithstanding the funding and production history and those involved with the film. This was the case for example when the excellent *Starred Up* (David MacKenzie, 2013) was awarded Best Film.

If you're having a rambling conversation in the pub after several pints with friends and someone asks, 'What's the best Scottish film?', your approach is unlikely to be that taken by BAFTA Scotland. You might argue in favour of *F9: The Fast Saga*† (Justin Lin, 2021) (any film title followed by † relates to a 'Scottish-adjacent' film, but not one which is Scottish for the purposes of this book) which a piece in *The Scotsman* remarkably suggested was the best film set in Edinburgh, while your friend might go for **Under the Skin**, but most likely no one is going to ask the question, 'What do you mean by Scottish?'. Here, I have *had to* define 'Scottishness' (other definitions are available and are equally valid), and have done so in response to the questions which interest me and which have driven this book over the three-plus years of its creation: 'How are Scots, and Scotland, depicted on film – what does cinema have to say about us and our country?', and 'Is there such a thing as a Scottish national cinema?' In wondering to what extent films reflect Scotland as it is, or perpetuate myths and stereotypes ranging from the mildly amusing to the obnoxious, I was almost certainly influenced by Raymond Durgnat's *A Mirror for England: British Movies from Austerity to Affluence* (think about how Scotland is treated in that title for a second...), a once-significant work of film criticism published in 1970, which I read as a teenager: are Scottish movies a mirror for Scotland?

The approach I take is audience-centric, rather than finance- (IMDb), or creative control- (the Oscars) centric: *we* get to say whether a film is Scottish or not, and who's to say that we're wrong? More specifically, in this book, using my definition, *I* get to say whether a film is Scottish or not. You are quite free to say that I am wrong, but at least my criteria will be moderately clear. In Appendix 2, I set out films which I believe hit my criteria, but which I have not been able to watch, which is to say that I *have* watched every film which is the subject of an entry in this book. I have therefore been able to avoid many errors which crop up repeatedly online in comments about some of the more obscure films (it is somewhat frustrating to read a critique of a film and then to realise that the writer has clearly never seen it). I have also ruled out some films which feature in the many lists of Scottish films; these lists can be good, but some are junk. Just because a film features Scotland Yard does not mean that it is set in Scotland (unless that film happens to be **Das indische Tuch**); and just because a film is set on a British island does not necessarily mean we are in Scotland – there are *other* islands, both real and imaginary, in the UK. *Retreat*† (Carl Tibbetts, 2011) for example, is an interesting film with an exceptional cast and appears on many lists of Scottish films. This is set on an island which, based on the establishing shot alone, may lie to the west of Scotland (as of March 2025 it's available on Netflix, and the short description there states that 'Blackthorne' island is in Scotland). But, that one shot aside, there is *nothing* in the film which locates it as being set in Scotland – no accents, no dialogue reference to Scotland; it was not shot in Scotland.

What is a Scottish film?

All the films covered in this book turn their gaze, or purport to do so, significantly on Scotland. For the purposes of *this* book, a film is classed as Scottish if it fulfils the following criteria.

(1) *It is set in whole or in substantial part in Scotland, whether or not filmed in Scotland.* **Dog Soldiers** is an effective horror film which is set in a convincingly portrayed Scottish Highlands, although for reasons of finance the film was largely shot in Luxembourg. **Brigadoon** recreates Scotland (or more accurately something purporting to be Scotland) entirely in a Hollywood studio. Both films are covered in this book. Documentaries are included, and their numbers are rapidly rising as digital filming and distribution democratises filmmaking.

In early January 2025 the BBC news website featured an article, 'How did Scotland become a Hollywood hotspot?', leading with a photograph of Glen Powell, in Scotland for the filming of Edgar Wright's remake of *The Running Man* which will be released late in 2025. One thing we can be sure of is that *The Running Man* will not be set in Scotland (the 1987 Schwarzenegger vehicle, directed by Paul Michael Glaser, was set in a TV studio in the US). With increasing frequency Scotland is being employed as a set for films the content of which has no, or only minimal, connection to Scotland (see, eg: *World War Z*†, Marc Foster, 2013; *The Batman*†, Matt Reeves, 2022; *Indiana Jones and the Dial of Destiny*†, James Mangold, 2023). Screen Scotland has stated that film and TV production in Scotland added over £600m to the Scottish economy in 2021 (the last year for which a figure is available at the time of writing). A separate study released in 2024 showed that 35 per cent of European visitors to Scotland are influenced in their choice of destination by having seen a film or TV show set in Scotland. But even if they are shot here, films set somewhere else don't reflect Scotland

and are not covered in this book. Films focusing on Scots *outside* Scotland are also not covered here.

I exclude the *Harry Potter* franchise†. Clearly, the train that Harry and his wizarding and witching chums take from Platform 9¾ in London to Hogwarts follows a route through Scotland, passing over the Glenfinnan Viaduct (itself a motif overused to denote 'Scottishness' – see for example *Stone of Destiny*), arriving somewhere on the northwest coast. Beyond identifiable geographic features shown on screen there is no claim that the films represent Scotland, and they do not tell a Scottish story; at the very best they represent an alternative universe in which a different Scotland exists. Many films in this book feature an alternative reality (arguably every work of fiction creates an alternate reality), but one in which we are in a version of Scotland like the one we live in. Women from Mars do not land in Scotland seeking men to assist with a population shortfall (***Devil Girl from Mars***), and aliens do not (I hope) cruise the streets of Glasgow looking for humans to harvest (***Under the Skin***), but in both films, allowing for the twist on our reality, there are attempts – wonky in ***Devil Girl***, authentic in ***Under the Skin*** – to portray Scotland as it is or might be. Applying this principle to *The Open*† (Marc Lahore, 2015), a fascinatingly distinctive sci-fi film, leads to its exclusion. It was shot in a recognisable Scotland, on Lewis and Harris, and then deliberately lifted *out* of political geography; the only place names given are fictionalised (and based on celebrated tennis players).

A similar fate befalls *Where the Skin Lies*† (Michael Boucherie, 2017), a horror film with a strong premise, which *was* shot in Scotland. However, unless you recognised a particular small rural road and a ruined building, you would be able to make only a stab at the location. Apart from a short shot of the drive to a house, the film is set inside the house. There are no other signifiers of Scotland (influenced perhaps by the lack of funding from Scotland, which might have come with conditions – the money came from Belgian tax breaks and crowdfunding). This really could be anywhere in the UK. I also had to think carefully about whether to include *Tornado*† (John Maclean, 2025). Some reviewers have identified the location as England. Peter Bradshaw's *Guardian* review was headed 'windswept samurai western set in apocalyptic Scotland'; Nikki Baughan's *Screen Daily* review is more nuanced: 'In the unforgiving landscape of 1790s Britain...' which gels better with the film's text. Certainly, the film was shot in Scotland, but never is Scotland otherwise identified as being the location. The film opens with the words: 'The British Isles – 1790'. Maclean (who directed the exceptional 2015 film *Slow West*†, which at its start is *expressly* set in Scotland – the lead character, played by Kodi Smit-McPhee, is the son of a Scottish laird who follows his lost love to the US) was kind enough to speak to me after a GFF screening. I asked him whether he was wedded to a view of the film as being 'Scottish'. His response was that while the film was shot in Scotland, he was determined to show that by the 18th century *Britain* was home to people from all over the world. With apologies to Maclean, I take this as licence to exclude his entertaining western-samurai British mash-up from this book.

Films set only *in part* in Scotland, but which fail to clear my 'substantial' hurdle are excluded – a great many more films than those covered here contain scenes set in Scotland, whether these be a fleeting visit, or a more extended stay. My approach is a matter of judgement, not science, although the following examples may explain my approach, which is largely, but not exclusively, driven by the proportion of the film spent in Scotland. In *The Da Vinci Code*† (Ron Howard, 2006), our two heroes, played by Tom Hanks and Audrey Tatou, visit Rosslyn Chapel. However, the time spent in Scotland is but a small fraction of a much longer film. *Salmon Fishing in the Yemen*† (Lasse Halström, 2011), which crops up on several lists of 'Scottish' films online, required that significant scenes be shot in Scotland, making use of the Ardverikie Estate, near Laggan, but again the Scottish scenes are not, in the context of the whole, substantial. The same fate befalls both *Skyfall*† (Sam Mendes, 2012) and *Casino Royale*† (Val Guest et al, 1967). In *Skyfall* some 30 minutes of the total running time are spent in Scotland (and these were in part shot in England); in *Casino Royale* the 'Scottish' scenes run for 21 of the film's 131 minutes, and those were shot largely in Ireland. *The Private Life of Sherlock Holmes* just scrapes in, with 50 minutes of its 125-minute running time set in Scotland.

(2) *The film is feature-length, being at least 70 minutes long, or, in the case of a silent film, over 4,000 feet in length.* A line must be drawn somewhere, and I've drawn it here (for the purposes of the Oscars a 'feature' film must be 40 minutes plus, but that is clearly absurd). I recognise that this perhaps unfairly excludes short films. I have made a single exception, in respect of the **Bill Douglas Childhood Trilogy**, which I have treated as a single entry (it would have been a travesty to omit it).

(3) *The film must have had a cinema screening, even if only at film festivals.* This is a low bar to clear, but films made wholly for TV and not shown at any cinema are thus excluded (a clutch of victims of this policy are the made-for-TV Christmas films set in Scottish castles and country houses).

(4) *The film must have been released or been screened by the end of July*

2025 and must have been available to watch. The oldest film covered is **Kidnapped** (1917); the most recently released in the UK is **Harvest,** from July 2025. In total, 427 films are covered.

Approach and structure

This book is the first to approach Scottish cinema through an atomistic approach, looking at the films which might make up Scottish cinema. Earlier books are more discursive, and I have relied in part on the following general texts.

Colin McArthur (ed), *Scotch Reels* (1982)
Forsyth Hardy, *Scotland In Film* (1990)
Eddie Dick (ed), *From Limelight to Satellite: A Scottish Film Book* (1990)
Duncan Petrie, *Screening Scotland* (2000)
Colin McArthur, *Brigadoon, Braveheart and the Scots* (2003)
David Martin-Jones, *Scotland: Global Cinema* (2009)
Jonathan Murray et al (eds), *Scottish Cinema Now* (2009)
Jonathan Murray, *The New Scottish Cinema* (2014)
Christopher Meir, *Scottish Cinema Texts and Contexts* (2015)
John Caughie et al (eds), *Early Cinema in Scotland* (2018)

I have brought together material from a wide range of other sources, including books about specific films, people and studios, more general books about British and international cinema, or genres, as well as reference works. Numerous journal and magazine articles have been read, as have many of the original reviews, as well as press reports from both specialist and general sources. I have sometimes given the 'rating' a film attracts on the review aggregator site Rotten Tomatoes, which provides a rough proxy for a film's critical reception, although this is far from perfect (I've often drawn from reviews *not* listed on Rotten Tomatoes). The Internet has of course been a rich route to information (although not always entirely reliable). I cannot possibly list all websites visited, or all contributors to them, but I am grateful to all. To the best of my ability all facts and quotes are correct, and all quotes not directly from the film discussed are attributed, although full references are not given – this is intended to be a readable book (albeit an accurate one).

As the only factor linking the films covered in this book is their 'Scottishness', there is, in all other respects, a wide variety. They range over more than a century, covering intimate Scottish-made dramas (*The Party's Just Beginning*) to British wartime propaganda (*I Know Where I'm Going!*), to Franco/German science fiction (*La Mort en Direct*), to Hollywood epics (*Braveheart*), to British soft-core pornography (*Come Play with Me*), and from animation (*L'Illusionniste*) to documentary (*Scheme Birds*) and mockumentary (*Death of a Vlogger*). Even Italian *giallo* makes an appearance (*Seven Deaths in the Cat's Eyes*).

I have not been able to include *every* film which meets my definition of Scottish. First, while I have spent considerable time identifying relevant films and have received emails suggesting others, there remains the thin possibility that I missed some, even when these are in English. It is more likely that I have missed some which are not in English, although this edition of the book adds films from Poland, Russia and Indonesia. Second, I have only included as entries films I have been able to see. Sadly, in some cases, you are unlikely to be able to get hold of these (I make it clear where there are serious problems with accessibility), but you should be able to access nearly all the films covered here, although you might need to expand your streaming subscriptions, or resort to second-hand DVDs. In Appendix 2 I set out a list of films I am confident meet my definition, but which I have not yet been able to track down. In some cases this might simply be because I missed a one-off screening, and the film has not, at the time of writing, been made more widely available. Accessibility is a variable. For this edition of the book 18 films which were featured in the first version of Appendix 2 back in 2024 are included, sometimes simply because a copy has been randomly uploaded to YouTube.

Films are covered in date order unless it appeared appropriate to group entries together (typically when they hold a director or subject in common – the first such grouping goes with the first entry in this book, *Kidnapped*, 1917). Where entries are grouped the text appears at the place of the date of release of the first film covered in that group. An entry appearing out of date order, linked to a previous entry or entries, is indicated with an arrow: →. For the basic data I have consulted IMDb but have occasionally modified this considering the film's credits in the version that I have watched. Occasionally I note, and explain, inconsistencies in the data. Although I have spent a considerable amount of time clearing up mistakes others before me have made, I recognise, sadly, that I will have made some of my own, my best efforts notwithstanding. Feel free to bring these to my attention.

Unless otherwise stated the primary language of all the films covered is

English. I have given alternative titles only where these are widely used in English-language reference sources (as is the case, for example, in respect of *Whisky Galore!* (1949) which was released in the US as *Tight Little Island*).

All the opinions I offer in this book (unless clearly attributed) are mine and mine alone. You're free to disagree, and almost certainly will, and your opinion is equally valid. I have given a top 100 but have only ranked films 1–50; in essence there is then a shared second group of 51–100. Film rankings are highly subjective, and I struggle with the concept of reducing a work of art to a score. I have made it clear whether I think a film is great, good, indifferent, or downright bad; I have also highlighted what I believe to be the worst 10 films in the book.

How Scottish is it?

Every film covered in this book, apart from documentaries, has been subject to a playful measure of a film's 'Scottishness', based on four criteria: (1) the story and its location (*every* film passes this criteria or it would not be included); (2) the *actual* filming location; (3) the creative team, with particular emphasis given to the director and screenwriter; and (4) the cast. I make no claims to scientific rigour, consistency, or fairness. The HSII? rating appears as S+ to S+++, and has *nothing* to do with quality: there are, sadly, S+++ films which are rubbish, and films only set in Scotland (but which are neither filmed here nor involve Scottish creatives and actors) which are very good. While Scottishness and quality are not correlated, there is at least *some* correlation between Scottishness and content – very broadly, the more Scottish a film is, the more likely it is that the reel Scotland will approximate the real Scotland.

Spoilers ahead!

Each entry, unless the film is a documentary, starts with a short description of the plot. Spoilers may also appear in the remaining paragraphs. If you wish to watch a film without spoilers, do so before reading the relevant entry – you can then have the pleasure of disagreeing with me. It's easy to do.

Kidnapped (1917)　　　T47

Directed by Alan Crosland
Screenplay by Charles Sumner Williams
Leading cast: Raymond McKee (David Balfour);
    Joseph Burke (Ebenezer Balfour); Robert Cain
    (Alan Breck); William Wadsworth (Rankeillor)
B&W (tinted), 4 reels, US

The young David Balfour inherits the House of Shaws estate following the death of his father, but must overcome the attempts of his avaricious uncle, Ebenezer, to remove him. With the assistance of outlaw Alan Breck, he succeeds.

Robert Louis Stevenson's novel *Kidnapped*, published first in serial form (with a *much* longer title) in the magazine *Young Folks* in 1886, was first filmed in 1917 for Thomas Edison's Conquest Pictures. Publicity material asked: 'Lives there a man or boy who has not thrilled to the famous story…?' *Kidnapped* then became a cinematic staple. At the time of writing, this feature-length adaptation of Stevenson's novel is available in a version restored by the US Library of Congress. It's an engaging film and stays close to the novel's story. Although set entirely in Scotland, the film was most likely shot, according to the American Film Institute, in the Bronx, at Edison's Decatur Avenue studio. The production values are strong, with well-crafted interiors. Exteriors convince as snow-covered rural scenery, but not as the Highlands. McKee, from Iowa, was 26 when the film was made but looks younger on screen (although not the 17 that Stevenson's David is). He was only four years younger than Cain, although the age difference appears greater: while Breck tells David that he loves him like a brother, the relationship is closer to that of father and son. There is verve in the scenes in the old tower as Ebenezer tries to engineer David's death. The film moves along quickly and is worth a watch.

→ Kidnapped (1938)

Directed by Alfred L Werker
Screenplay by Sonya Levien and Eleanor Harris
Leading cast: Warner Baxter (Alan Breck);
    Freddie Bartholomew (David Balfour); Arleen
    Whelan (Jean MacDonald)
B&W, 90 minutes, US

The key elements above are retained, but the story's focus is on Breck, and his romance with Jean. At the film's end Breck exhorts his Scottish followers to peace and unity before embarking on exile with Jean. David has played a key role in securing this outcome.

'Scotland for Ever!' is the last line of this freewheeling adaptation, the first made in the sound era. It is, however, wrote Frank Nugent in *The NYT*, 'about as Scottish as a hot-dog stand'. This version of *Kidnapped* has an oblique relationship with Stevenson, and is more the film of Alan Breck, his derring-do and romance. David's story is reduced, and there is less tension and threat in his interactions with Ebenezer than is the case in the source novel. The tower scene is perfunctory and has little of the atmosphere

Freddie Bartholemew as David

the cinematographer who shot *Citizen Kane* (Orson Welles, 1941), although there is little evidence here of his later genius.

The extensive changes to the story made by Levien and Harris were not to everyone's taste. Nugent wrote: 'There is just enough Stevenson left in the piece to give the producer technical immunity from prosecution for fraud'.

→ *Kidnapped* (1948)

Directed by William Beaudine
Screenplay by Scott Darling
Leading cast: Roddy McDowall (David Balfour);
   Houseley Stevenson (Ebenezer); Roland
   Winters (Capt. Hoseason); Dan O'Herlihy
   (Alan Breck); Sue England (Aileen Fairlie)
B&W, 81 minutes, US

Retains the story of the novel, subject to the addition of a romance between David and Aileen, the daughter of a duplicitous inn-owner, who helps Breck and David escape.

of the 1917 film. This too was shot in the US, at the 20th Century Fox Studios and in the hills of Laurel Canyon. The set-designer's knowledge of what is authentically Scottish was clearly challenged: ten minutes in, as David sets out on his walk to Edinburgh, he passes a road marker indicating that 'Edinboro' is 43 miles away.

Freddie Bartholemew was 13 when the film was shot. His poise is such that this does not show to any significant extent. This was his ninth feature, but – at least in the judgement of David Thomson – his career was already in decline. So too was Warner Baxter's; few of his films have lasted (but see *42nd Street*, Lloyd Bacon, 1933). His unathletic Breck is subdued, for all the bravado he shows. The role of Jean came at the start of Whelan's career – less than a year after she was first put under contract at Fox. Director Alfred Werker was brought in to replace Otto Preminger, sacked after his explosive temper got the better of him following a confrontation with Darryl Zanuck. The most significant person to be credited on *Kidnapped* is the legendary Gregg Toland,

Roddy McDowall was 19 when *Kidnapped* was filmed but had been appearing in films since the age of ten. In the same year that *Kidnapped* was made, he appeared as Duncan in *Macbeth* (1948), which also features O'Herlihy. Twenty years later McDowall directed *The Ballad of Tam Lin*. This version of *Kidnapped* has little to distinguish it, save perhaps the remarkably *un-Scottish* Californian scenery substituting for the Highlands and a set of extremely dodgy accents – although McDowall, who was also credited as co-producer, is the most convincing as a Scot. Even at a relatively short 81 minutes *Variety*'s reviewer thought the film lagged: 'Beaudine's direction has kept the action slow and missed on injecting sufficient swash and buckle'. The *MFB*'s reviewer thought it would at least 'appeal to children'. Clearly filmmakers were uncertain as to what *Kidnapped* needed in addition to the story provided by Stevenson. In the 1938 version romantic interest was added for Breck; in this version it is David who falls for Aileen, while Breck remains unencumbered (in *Schüsse unterm Galgen* the filmmakers clearly thought they'd nailed it with romance for both David and Breck, *and* a lion).

→ *Kidnapped* (1959)   S+

Directed by Robert Stevenson
Screenplay by Robert Stevenson
Leading cast: Peter Finch (Alan Breck Stewart); James MacArthur (David Balfour); Bernard Lee (Captain Hoseason); John Laurie (Ebenezer Balfour); Miles Malleson (Mr Rankeillor)
Colour, 97 minutes, UK/US

Retains the story of the 1917 version and is close therefore to the novel.

Disney's 1959 adaptation has the virtue of being moderately faithful to the original novel. It also marks the first big-screen appearance of Peter O'Toole, in the role of Rob Roy's son, Robin MacGregor – which leads to a gloriously ridiculous scene in which, to settle an argument, O'Toole

and Finch hold a bagpipe playing contest. O'Toole comfortably wins. If anyone was born to write and direct a version of a Robert Louis Stevenson novel, it was surely Robert Stevenson, who had directed his first film, *A Blonde Dream* in 1932, but who is best known as the director of *Mary Poppins* (1964). He made several films for Disney in the second part of his career.

Maclean's review of *Kidnapped* was more positive than not: 'a robust and sometimes highly diverting comedy-drama, weakened by an excess of flamboyant overacting on the part of John Laurie as the wicked uncle who betrays young David... Peter Finch zestfully depicts a Scottish soldier of fortune who teams up with the boy.' In the *MFB* there was praise for the fidelity to the novel, and for the use of Scottish actors (Currie, for example had previously appeared in *The Brothers* and *The Edge of the World*; Laurie had a raft of credits to his name, including *The 39 Steps, The Edge of the World, I Know Where I'm Going!* and *The Ghost of St Michael's*). But there was also criticism: the 'action itself seems tempered in its excitement, and occasionally verges on dullness. The screenplay is verbose and confused'.

The use of Scottish actors was not, of course, to everyone's taste. *Variety*'s reviewer liked the locations which 'pay off richly, with an authentic flavour', but not the 'accents as thick as Scotch oatmeal.' While several of the cast are Scottish, the two leads, Finch and MacArthur (who played Dan Williams in over 250 episodes of *Hawaii Five-O*, 1968–1979), are not;

neither was Lee, who after a very long career became better known as the first 'M' in the James Bond films.

→ *Schüsse unterm Galgen (Shots Under the Gallows)* (1968)

Directed by Horst Seeman
Screenplay by Wolfgang Held, Horst Seeman
Leading cast: Werner Kanitz (David Balfour); Thomas Weisgerber (Alan Breck); Alena Procházková (Catriona)
B&W, 107 minutes, East Germany, German

Retains the basic story of the 1917 version and novel, save for the fact that David falls in love, rescues the girl from his uncle, and rides away to fight for freedom alongside Breck. There's also a lion.

This version of Robert Louis Stevenson's *Kidnapped* was made in East Germany by the prolific DEFA (Deutsche Film AG), in widescreen 'Totalvision' format, and distributed only behind the Iron Curtain. The film was a commercial success: with its mix of adventure, evil Englishmen, plucky Scots, secret doors and passageways, shipwreck, romance, a lion and an ending that sees David and Catriona passionately embracing in the foam on a beach, this is not surprising. It is the most entertaining of the versions of *Kidnapped* covered here – even if it would have RLS turning in his grave. In 2022 the film was digitally restored in a version available at the Deutsche Kinemathek, in Berlin, but a good version (German-language only) is available online.

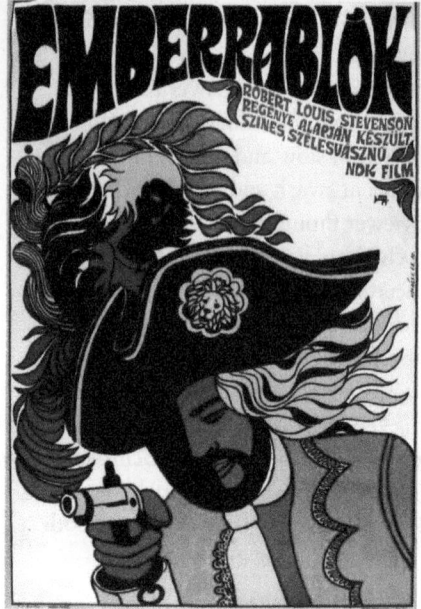

Hungarian poster for the East German production of a Scottish classic

→ *Kidnapped* (1971)   S+

Directed by Delbert Mann
Screenplay by Jack Pulman
Leading cast: Lawrence Douglas (David Balfour); Michael Caine (Alan Breck); Donald Pleasence (Ebenezer Balfour); Jack Hawkins (Capt. Hoseason); Vivien Heilbron (Catriona Stewart); Trevor Howard (Lord Advocate Grant)
Colour, 100 minutes, UK

Expands on the basic story of Kidnapped *with the inclusion of material from* Catriona. *After securing his inheritance David seeks to fight injustice, while establishing his relationship with Catriona*

Stewart, daughter of a man wrongly accused of murder. Breck is the real killer and surrenders himself after a confrontation with Catriona.

This version of *Kidnapped* is, from the outset when the film opens on the bloody battlefield of Culloden, the most obviously lavish production. It has in Michael Caine an actor who makes for a robust Breck (in fact here the problem is that, as Richard Combs pointed out in the *MFB*, 'the contrast between David and the cavalier Breck has swung decisively in Breck's favour'), and an excellent supporting cast, including the Scottish stalwart, Gordon Jackson. As Catriona, Vivien Heilbron, born in Glasgow in 1944, was in her first film; later she was to play Chris Guthrie in the three TV series based on *The Scots Quair* trilogy. The film also has the great advantage of having been largely shot in Scotland (with some interiors in Pinewood). Much use is made of Mull, and Stirling Castle stands in for Edinburgh.

The film is distinctive in making clear in the opening credits that it is not simply a version of Stevenson's *Kidnapped* – it is based both on Stevenson's titular novel, and on *Catriona* (aka *David Balfour*, published in 1893 after appearing in serial form in *Atalanta*). This picks up the story immediately after the ending of *Kidnapped*, and introduces the character of Catriona MacGregor Drummond, the granddaughter of Rob Roy, providing a love interest for David. It deals with David's attempt to secure justice in relation to James Stewart,

Lawrence Douglas and Donald Pleasence

wrongly charged with murder. Here the capitulation of Ebenezer occurs only 60 minutes into the film and is but one part of a larger story, which includes a more considered treatment of Scotland and the Union. There is particular emphasis on Highland/Lowland tensions, encapsulated in the relationship between Lowlander David and Highlander Breck. As noted in the *Independent Film Journal*'s review: 'Jack Pulman has turned out a very literate screenplay that is always two-dimensional in its approach to the problems the main character, David… faces. Since some of these problems are thoughtful questions of justice and politics, a nice counterbalance is struck between these scenes and the film's adventure action sequences'. Notwithstanding a murder plot and a duel, the last 40 minutes lack the urgency and drive of the first hour but offer a richer framing of the film in its Scottish context than is the case where the story focuses on David's attempt to secure his rightful inheritance.

The Pride of the Clan (1917)

Directed by Maurice Tourneur
Screenplay by Elaine S Carrington and Charles E
  Whittaker
Leading cast: Mary Pickford (Marget MacTavish);
  Matt Moore (Jamie Campbell)
B&W, 7 reels, US

*In the west of Scotland Marget MacTavish
assumes leadership of her clan after
the death of her father. After romantic
complications, and peril, she marries the
son of a noble family.*

Hollywood's idea of 'Scottish' in 1917

Shot largely in Massachusetts in 1916,
The Pride of the Clan, which remains

extant, was made by Mary Pickford's
production company when she was
one of the most famous women on the
planet. A contemporary review in *The
Billboard* tells us most of what we now
need to know, with Pickford's Marget
being 'a character that will move her
devotees to tears and smiles in alternate
waves of emotion as they watch the little
Scotch lassie'. The story is ridiculously
sentimental, although *Variety*'s reviewer
thought it 'thoroughly satisfactory'.

The Man Beneath (1919)

Directed by William Worthington
Screenplay by LV Jefferson
Leading cast: Sessue Hayakawa (Dr Ashuter);
  Helen Jerome Eddy (Kate Erskine); Pauline
  Curley (Mary Erskine); Jack Gilbert (James
  Bassett)
B&W, 5 reels, US

*A celebrated Indian doctor and man-of-
science visits a friend in Scotland and falls
in love with his sister. He plays a key role
in saving his friend from the clutches of
a Black Hand secret society, but racial
barriers prevent his marriage to the sister.*

Made over 100 years ago, *The Man
Beneath* is underpinned by racism, which
both it, and the novel on which it was
based, challenge, although that challenge
only went so far. A product of its time,
it remains riddled with racist tropes and
stereotypes – particularly of 'The mystery
of the Far East' (one of the intertitles).

The novel, *Only a N----r*, was published in 1901 by the Glaswegian-born author Edmund Mitchell (1861–1917). A journalist (including for the *Glasgow Herald*, and the *Times* of India) and extremely widely travelled, he later settled in the US and died in New York. Much of the film is set in Scotland, but it's not a Scotland anyone familiar with the country would recognise (everything was shot in California). However, there was local interest, and the film was certainly exhibited in Scotland – at the least it was shown at Helensburgh's La Scala cinema in 1920.

The Man Beneath stars one of the most remarkable figures of the silent era, Sessue Hayakawa, credited in *Variety* with giving 'a really clever performance... holding to the character at all times and winning the sympathy of the audience'. While Hayakawa is now best known for playing Colonel Saito in *The Bridge on the River Kwai* (David Lean, 1957), his career extended from 1914 through to 1967. In the silent era he was a bona fide sex symbol – something utterly exceptional for an actor of Japanese origin, and his parties were legendary. He even formed his own production company, Haworth Pictures, which made *The Man Beneath* (see Carla Valderama, *This Was Hollywood*, 2020).

In *The Man Beneath* Hayakawa plays 'a Hindoo' – racially appropriate casting was not a major issue in 1919 – and his role is circumscribed by racist convention. He could not be shown kissing a white woman, and, laudable

Mitchell's anti-racist novel adapted by a Japanese born American star

though the intentions of Mitchell, and later Jefferson and Worthington were, he was required both to be a better man than his Scottish counterpart, and to accept gracefully as his reward an unrequited love. As *Variety* notes, the film's ending is 'rather unsatisfactory... and in balance with the picture'. Hayakawa's co-star, John Gilbert (credited as Jack Gilbert), was building his career in 1919, on his way to being a superstar by the mid-1920s before being destroyed by alcohol.

The Man Beneath's intertitles were criticised even at the time of release as being something of a mess, and if you now seek out this curious museum piece, things are going to get even more problematic. The only copy which appears to be readily available is held by an archive in the Netherlands. It's freely accessible online, but the titling is (a) erratic, and (b) in Dutch.

The Little Minister (1921)   S+

Directed by Penrhyn Stanlaws
Screenplay by Edfrid A Bingham
Leading cast: Betty Compson (Lady Babbie);
  George Hackathorne (Gavin); Edwin Stevens
  (Lord Rintoul)
B&W, 6025 feet, US

Thrums, Scotland. Weavers have been impoverished by a reduction in wages. Babbie (daughter of the local laird, appearing in disguise) helps them, and offers support to the local 'little' Minister, Gavin. They fall in love.

The first full length adaptation of Barrie's kailyard bestseller

The Little Minister was based on a cloyingly sentimental novel by JM Barrie (one of the authors now derided as a member of 'the Kailyard') first published in 1891. Although Barrie himself was unhappy with the book, it was a rampant commercial success and adapted for stage six years later. Filmed on multiple occasions, with silent versions released in 1913, 1915, 1921 and 1922, it is not to modern taste.

In June 1922, *Kinematograph Weekly*, working on the basis that 'most people know the story', encouraged exhibitors to: 'Exploit the author's name and dwell on the popularity of *The Little Minister* both as story and stage play. Advertise as a typical Barrie romance of whimsical humour, pathos and dramatic force'. On release, the same magazine described the film as 'refreshing, charming, interesting, and... has got the Scotch atmosphere of Thrums wonderfully well'. The film

was expensive to shoot, with the Scottish scenes (filmed in the US) requiring 'the construction of numerous expensive street scenes' (*Kinematograph Weekly*, 1921).

There is an infectious humour to the film, and inventive touches – notably when the little Minister turns to his Bible to find the face of Babbie staring up at him. The film is also not quite as mawkish as the 1934 version (see below), and the action moves swiftly to an improbable, albeit wholly predictable conclusion. For Lord Rintoul it would be a disgrace for his daughter, the *Lady* Barbara, to marry a lowly village Minister; for the deacons, previously plotting to remove Gavin, this is a matter of delight, such that the penultimate scene plays out as high comedy. There is, however, a sour undertone to the film, a central premise of which is that gypsies are 'thieves and spies'. Gavin stands condemned because he consorts with one, and all ends well only because Babbie is in fact *not* a gypsy, but a Lady of high standing (and therefore, axiomatically, of good moral character). The plot turns on the principle of marriage *per verba de praesenti* (marriage by words alone), which remained valid in Scotland until 1940. Director Stanlaws was born in Dundee in 1877.

→ *The Little Minister* (1934)

Directed by Richard Wallace
Screenplay by Jane Murfin, Sarah Y Mason and
  Victor Heerman
Leading cast: Katherine Hepburn (Babbie); John
  Beal (Gavin); Frank Conroy (Lord Rintoul)
B&W, 110 minutes, US35

Plot as above, although there is significant variation in detail.

This version, made by RKO studios, was shot on the RKO lot and at locations in California. In *The Saturday Review* Mark Forrest tempered a generally positive review with strong critique of the scenery: 'so plainly a product of the studio that the cardboard effect obtrudes itself to the detriment of the whole picture'. *The Scotsman*'s critic was more forgiving: 'Hollywood's efforts to re-create a Scottish atmosphere are commendable'.

This was the sixth film to feature four-time Oscar winner Katherine Hepburn (27 years old when *The Little Minister* was released in December 1934), who had had a huge hit two years earlier with *Little Women* (George Cukor, 1932). Although *The Little Minister* was not a

John Beal as the Little Minister and Katherine Hepburn as the laird's wayward daughter

success, it was significant in establishing the public image of Hepburn as a woman with a strong independent spirit. As William J Mann puts it in his biography of Hepburn (*Kate: The Woman Who Was Hepburn*, 2006) 'what [*The Little Minister*] told us about Kate was... that she was a lurking insurrectionist... Her gypsy woman even dares to sing on Sunday... she stands accused of desecrating the Sabbath – an extremely tenuous position in this cautious, conservative era'.

Reviewing the film on its release in *Maclean's*, Ann Ross was moved by the sentimentality: 'Hardened movie-goers sniffed and blew their noses, and weak sentimentalists just broke down and had a good cry'. Sentimentality of the sort on evidence here is not however the current fashion.

The Little Minister is not all bad. The score, by legendary film composer Max Steiner, is strong, as is the cast, and although thin on Scots, the accents adopted are passable. One Scottish actor of note *is* featured: the local policeman is played (for laughs) by Andy Clyde, who was born in Blairgowrie in 1892. He started his career in the music halls in Scotland, before moving to Hollywood and accumulating nearly 400 credits in film and television, most notably as the genial sidekick California Carlson in many of the *Hopalong Cassidy* westerns.

Rob Roy (1922)   S+

Directed by WP Kellino
Screenplay by Alice Ramsey
Leading cast: David Hawthorne (Rob Roy MacGregor); Sir Simeon Stuart (Duke of Montrose); Gladys Jennings (Helen Campbell)
B&W, 6,000 ft, UK

Inversnaid, home of the MacGregors. Rob Roy is proclaimed Clan Chieftain. He pledges allegiance to the Marquis of Montrose (the Duke), who is angered when Rob and Helen, whom Montrose covets, elope. Montrose and his factor, Killearn, plot the downfall of Rob, and he is declared a rebel. He fights back, taking inspiration from the story of Robert the Bruce. Rob and Helen launch an elaborate plot and defeat the Duke; Rob kills Killearn and retakes possession of Inversnaid.

Rob Roy (attr. Arthur Vivian, 1911) was the first three-reel (ie, feature) film made in the UK. It was produced by a Glasgow-based company, The United Films Ltd, but, sadly, is believed lost (see Caroline Merz, 'Rob Roy: Britain's First Feature Film', in John Caughie et al, *Early Cinema in Scotland*, 2019). Rob Roy's story was also the subject of several shorter films. The 1922 feature-length version covered here, made by prolific English director Kellino, for Gaumont, remains extant, and accessible. In *The hunt for Rob Roy: the man and the myths* (2004) David Stevenson argues there are two Rob Roys: an historical figure who was a cattleman, lost his property, feuded with Montrose, was imprisoned and eventually pardoned, dying peacefully at the age of 63; and the man of myth, which began with the publication of *The Highland Rogue* in 1723 (authorship is sometimes attributed to Daniel Defoe, but this is disputed), and was fostered by Walter Scott in his 1817 Waverley novel, *Rob Roy*.

The opening intertitle for the 'romance' *Rob Roy* makes clear the romanticised/fetishised approach the film is going to take: 'To Scotland, not to Scott, did we go... There amid the mountain lochs and glens, Nature made Peace, and Man made War. It was a primitive existence, almost barbaric in its roughness; a life of perilous adventure – feuds, fighting, marauding, hunting (and hunted) – that was joy to the sturdy men of the Clan MacGregor'. It is also made clear that liberties are taken with history. The film is the first in this book to make use of the oft-repeated shots of Highland cattle, although at least here they are not superfluous – cattle trading being central to the story. It is also the first in this book to be shot in Scotland, around Aberfoyle. *Kinematograph Weekly* reported that a contract, the first of its kind in Scotland, was placed with Cowieson & Co of Glagsow to build sets including the baronial castle erected by the Duke at Inversnaid, the church around which the final conflict is fought, and other buildings. Kellino originally planned to shoot market scenes in Oban: with dismay, the *Oban Times* reported that attempts to film there were defeated by poor weather.

The result is that the film is convincing in its settings. Some scenes are strong: the burning of Inversnaid is particularly effective (Kellino liked this scene so much that it is repeated as Helen relays the tale of woe to Rob). There are other effective set pieces, particularly when the effete Killearn, who takes snuff, is mocked by Rob who mimics his habits while relieving him of the rent he has collected from downtrodden tenants (this scene too is replayed). Overall, however, as *Kinematograph Weekly*'s reviewer noted in October 1922, 'it is a tale of missed opportunities, for a great deal more could have been made of such an exceptionally strong and romantic theme. The general effect is one of efficient workmanship, but throughout any real inspiration is lacking'. Kellino was accused of under-directing his cast, but a strong box office was anticipated given that Rob Roy 'is a romantic figure [who] appeals to the imagination of everybody'.

→ *Rob Roy: The Highland Rogue* (1953)   S+

Directed by Harold French
Screenplay by Lawrence Edward Watkin
Leading cast: Richard Todd (Rob Roy MacGregor); Glynis Johns (Helen Mary MacPherson MacGregor); James Robertson Justice (John Campbell, Duke of Argyll); Michael Gough (Duke of Montrose); Finlay Currie (Hamis MacPherson)
Colour, 81 minutes, UK

In this version Rob is positioned as first and foremost a Jacobite rebel, continuing the fight. Argyll is sympathetic to his cause, and there is a long wooing of Helen. Rob is ultimately pardoned by the King in London, who has read Daniel Defoe's The Highland Rogue.

The Disney production *Rob Roy: The Highland Rogue* plays loose, if not always fast, with its source material. It is a good-looking adaptation of the story, but its focus is wayward. Much time is spent on a comic wooing of Helen (while her garrulous father plays the bagpipes) and the subsequent wedding. Time is also spent in the rooms of power in London. The film relies heavily on the charm of Richard Todd (see also *Flesh and Blood, Why Bother to Knock*), and on James Robertson Justice's Argyll, but lacks the bite of the later 1995 version. There was some location shooting in Scotland.

→ *Rob Roy* (1995)   S+   T100

Directed by Michael Caton-Jones
Screenplay by Alan Sharpe
Leading cast: Liam Neeson (Robert Roy
   MacGregor); Jessica Lange (Mary); John Hurt
   (Montrose); Tim Roth (Cunningham); Eric
   Stoltz (McDonald); Brian Cox (Killearn)
Colour, 139 minutes, UK/US

Plot substantially as for the 1922 version, except that Rob's wife is raped by Cunningham, and bears a child, which Rob eventually accepts as his own.

This film cleaves more closely to myth than to history, although the setting is broadly accurate. The result is largely satisfying, if perhaps in need of a little pruning.

   Rob Roy was released in the US on April 14, 1995; *Braveheart* was released 40 days later, whereupon *Rob Roy* became lost in its shadow. Time however has been kinder to *Rob Roy* than to *Braveheart* (*Rob Roy* was at least shot in Scotland and is not drenched in quite as much 'blood-and-soil' nonsense). Reviewing the film

BAFTA-award winner Tim Roth is terrific as Cunningham

on release, Janet Maslin in *The NYT* (who seemed peculiarly fixated on men in kilts) emphasised the strength of Neeson's performance: 'the film doesn't convey much sense of why [Rob Roy] should matter to modern viewers, who may know less about Rob Roy the folk hero than Rob Roy the drink. Which is why it's handy that Mr Neeson strides so impressively, acts so forcefully and towers over every other man in sight'. However, the real star turn – and this in a cast which has exceptional strength in depth – is Roth, who is terrific as Cunningham, by turns a smirking fop, lethal cold killer, and flamboyant debaucher. He was nominated for the Oscar and Golden Globe as Best Supporting Actor, won the BAFTA and makes a perfect foil for Neeson's Rob. Double Oscar winner Lange (one of them from 1995, for *Blue Sky*, Tony Richardson, 1994) as Mary has one of the strongest scenes in the film after her character has been raped.

   Caton-Jones was born in Scotland, and had previously directed three films, starting with *Scandal* (1989). His most recent completed film at the time of writing was *Our Ladies*. David Manderson's book *Directed by Michael Caton-Jones: Rob Roy 1995* (2009) discusses the film.

Annie Laurie (1927)

Directed by John S Robertson
Screenplay by Josephine Lovett
Leading cast: Lillian Gish (Annie Laurie); Norman
    Kerry (Ian MacDonald); Creighton Hale
    (Donald)
B&W and tinted, 97 minutes (9 reels), US

In the Highlands, the Campbells and the
MacDonalds feud. Ian MacDonald woos
Annie, the daughter of the King's Governor,
who at first prefers his effete brother,
Donald. By subterfuge the MacDonalds
are persuaded to house Campbell troops;
Annie's intervention saves the MacDonalds,
confirming her new allegiance.

Lillian Gish as the titular Annie Laurie

Receiving its premiere in New York in May 1927, *Annie Laurie* was a major MGM production, featuring one of the leading stars of the silent era in Gish (born in 1893, she made her first film in 1912, and her last in 1987). It was neither the first time nor the last the Scottish song (the original authorship of which is disputed) was the inspiration for a film: the first attempt in 1913 was set in the American civil war, the song serving to melt the heart of an obstinate father standing in the way of a marriage; in a British 1939 film of the same name directed by Walter Tennyson, only the song's title was appropriated. Robertson's 1937 film does not follow closely either of the main versions of the song but is at least authentic in placing the story in Scotland in the 17th century.

Annie Laurie was not, at least in the US, a success. *Variety* reported that one San Francisco cinema pulled it before it had got to its first weekend. There was even talk of relaunching the film under a different name, '*Ladies from Hell*', as the studio believed that audiences stayed away in the mistaken belief that *Annie Laurie* was a 'costume' rather than historical action picture. Reviewing the film after its New York premiere – for which the final section was heavily (and from the sounds of it, garishly) tinted – Mordaunt Hall wrote in *The NYT*: 'It lacks the atmosphere of Bobby Burns's land. It is a story seen through the glens and dales of Culver City, [California], as something that ought to belong to Scotland. But you cannot make a Scotsman by merely putting a man in a kilt'.

The film's reception in Scotland may perhaps have been a little more positive,

and Scots a little more forgiving of the artifice than Hall. This was certainly the case at
Kirkcaldy's Rialto (which eventually became
the Odeon, before burning down in 1974).
Here, the manager went to great pains to
promote the film, decorating the cinema
with heather, dressing the staff in tartan, and
adding a live performance before screenings.
Kinematograph Weekly reported: 'With
the tartan, the heather, the dancing and
singing, and the fact of being Scotch... [the]
picture, needless to say, was a great success'.
Watched now, *Annie Laurie* holds scant
appeal. The 'Scotland' shown is, obviously,
not Scotland – and while artificiality may
not always be fatal, it is when the 'action'
is either dull, or ludicrous. *Annie Laurie*'s
action is, at different times, both.

Gold (1934) [and *L'or* (1934)]

Directed by Karl Hartl
Screenplay by Rolph E Vanloo
Leading cast: Hans Albers (Werner Holk);
    Friedrich Kayßler (Prof Achenbach); Michael
    Bohnen (John Wills); Brigitte Helm (Florence
    Wills)
B&W, 120 minutes, Germany, German

*Prof Achenbach is killed when sabotage
destroys his German laboratory while he
attempts alchemy. With the support of
Wills, an avaricious English businessman,
the work is continued by Achenbach's
protégé Holk at 'Dunby Castle, Scotland'.
Knowing Wills to be responsible for the
sabotage, Holk seeks revenge, while Wills'
daughter, Florence, falls in love with him.*

Gold, and its near-identical twin *L'or* (Serge
de Poligny and 'Charles Hartl'), were beat-
en to the punch only by *The Cohens and
the Kellys in Scotland* (Albert DeMond and
John McDermott, 1930) for the prize of being the first feature film made in the sound
era to be substantially set in Scotland. I have
not been able to track down *The Cohens...*
and there is a possibility that it is not
extant. This makes *Gold* the oldest readily
available sound film to feature in this book
(its shoot began well before that of *The
Secret of the Loch*). *Gold* and *L'or* are
both German productions, with the French
version being shot alongside the German
(an approach used to deal with the sound
era's new language barriers to distribution).
While the language and names change in
L'or – including even the name of the German co-director – the two are in essence the
same film, albeit with some cast changes,
and it is *Gold* which forms the basis for this
entry. *Gold* is one of four German-language
films featured in this book and is certainly
the best of a very mixed bunch.

There are good reasons to be sceptical
about a prestige film made at UFA
(Universum-Film Aktiengesellschaft –
where Hitchcock made *The Blackguard*
in 1924) after the Nazi Party had
assumed power in Germany and asserted
ownership of the studio. At the time
Gold was made however, the Party had
not established the domination over
film production that was to come later,
and the film is short on nationalistic
ideology. Part thriller, part science fiction
(although not at the level of Fritz Láng's
1927 *Metropolis*, in which *Gold*'s Brigitte

Helm played Maria), *Gold*'s villain is a perfidious Englishman, but the real battles here are not nation versus nation, but scientific research versus exploitative acquisition, virtue versus vice.

Gold was shot entirely in Germany and was, even by UFA standards, a lavish production. Unable to resist the pun, *The NYT* reported that UFA 'spent a huge amount of marks for the purpose of making cinema gold'. Its review of the New York run of the German-language version at the 86th St Casino Theatre was laudatory, with no hint of political concern: 'a remarkable display of thrilling scenes involving excellent views of some fearful and wonderful machinery'. So lavish and long was the production that lead actor Albers sued UFA, demanding an increase in salary, although he lost the case. His career ran from silent cinema through to the 1950s (and included a role in the first German sound production). In the immediate post-war period he was permitted to continue working as he had consistently distanced himself from the Nazi regime, but his career nevertheless suffered. In *Gold* he is a strong and effective leading man.

There is, unsurprisingly, nothing authentically Scottish in the film, but *Gold* is at the minimum an interesting piece of film history; as a thriller/sci-fi film it's more than halfway decent.

The Secret of the Loch (1934)

Directed by Milton Rosmer
Screenplay by Billie Bristow, Charles Bennett
Leading cast: Seymour Hicks (Professor Heggie); Nancy O'Neil (Angela Heggie); Gibson Gowland (Angus); Frederick Peisley (Jimmy Anderson); Eric Hales (Jack Campbell)
B&W, 78 minutes, UK

Jimmy Anderson, a reporter for the Daily Sun, stays at the Glendonald Hotel, near Loch Ness, investigating reports of a monster in which Professor Heggie, who lives nearby, has an interest. Jimmy falls in love with Heggie's daughter Angela, proves the existence of the monster, and wins Angela's hand.

There are 11 films in this book which play with the theme of Nessie, a subject which sometimes brings out the worst in filmmakers, and she (I'll play along with the nonsense) is also referenced in *Lassie*. You'd be forgiven for thinking the film *Nessie & Me* (Jim Wynorski, 2016) might be Scottish; fortunately (it's very bad) it is set in North America. In *The Private Life of Sherlock Holmes* Nessie is a machine designed to keep the inquisitive away; in *Nessie, das verrückteste Monster der Welt* she is both a robot TV prop *and* a 'real' Nessie looking like a bizarre cuddly toy; in *Loch Ness* 'she' is a family of dinosaur hybrids; in *Beneath Loch Ness* she is evil personified; and in *Incident at Loch Ness* she is a metaphor.

TSOTL sits at the beginning of the modernisation of the global myth of the Loch Ness monster and is the first film to feature Nessie – here, an iguana, very clearly *not* the diplodocus the Professor claimed the monster to be. The film producers had moved quickly. It was only in 1933 that Loch Ness became firmly embedded as home to the monster, following the publication of an article in the *Inverness Courier*. In December 1934, *Kinematograph Weekly* reported that the 'famous scientist' J Williamson, a noted underwater photographer, had attended a screening of the film because he hoped to 'go up to Loch Ness with his photographic diving bell apparatus in an attempt to secure pictures of the Monster underwater'. The legend of the Loch Ness Monster, surviving somewhere in the nearly 7.5 billion cubic metres of water in the loch, has its roots in the dim past, but cannot be taken seriously – save by those promoting the local tourist economy.

The Scotsman reported in February 1934 that work had begun on filming *The Secret of the Loch* with the arrival of a production crew, staying at the hotel in Foyers (on the southern shore of the loch). Only establishing shots were taken and no actors were present. *TSOTL* is most readily available as part of a DVD set of Ealing Films, which is misleading – it is *not* an Ealing film. The production company, Wyndham Productions, was but one of many independent British outfits which rented space at Ealing's large production studios. *TSOTL* was edited by one of the greatest British film directors, David Lean (born in 1908). Note that IMDb incorrectly names Jimmy Anderson as Jimmy Andrews.

TSOTL is fundamentally an English film (the four lead actors were born in Jersey, Durham, Sydney, and London), which projects onto Scotland a metropolitan perspective in which there is cliché, but where Scotland is not *that* different from England. As David Martin-Jones puts it in *Scotland: Global Cinema* (2009), the film 'confirmed pre-existing views of Scotland as England's wild pre-modern other and simultaneously disavowed Scotland's supposedly pre-modern status'. As was to happen later in *I Know Where I'm Going!*, a key plot line results in the union by marriage of Scotland and England.

Contemporaneous reviews of *TSOTL* are not abundant. *Kinematograph Weekly*'s anonymous reviewer wrote: 'that there are dramatic and directorial shortcomings is not denied, but these in no way mitigate against the film's merits as a novelty item'.

→ *What a Whopper* (1961) S+

Directed by Gilbert Gunn
Screenplay by Terry Nation
Leading cast: Adam Faith (Tony); Sidney James (Harry); Carole Lesley (Charlie); Terence Longdon (Vernon); Charles Hawtrey (Arnold); Marie France (Marie)
B&W, 90 minutes, UK

Tony Blake, a frustrated author whose book on the Loch Ness Monster has been rejected, concocts a scheme to fake a sighting of the monster, assisted by his friends, to boost interest in the subject. At

Adam Faith, Marie-France and Nessie

Loch Ness the group becomes entangled with a salmon poaching operation, inept local policemen, a father pursuing his daughter whom he believes to be eloping, and a French hitchhiker. Chaos ensues. At the end, the 'real' Nessie appears, winks, and says 'What a Whopper'.

What a Whopper is a now badly dated film which was, on release, an attempt to cash in on the star power of singer Adam Faith (described in his *Variety* obituary as 'dashingly handsome'), who provides the title song. In this, it follows the grand British tradition of basing films around the appeal of popular entertainers (eg, Dame Vera Lynn, George Formby and Sir Cliff Richard), and by 1960 producers were reaching for the teenage market (Cliff Richard had appeared in his first film in 1959). Faith, born in 1940, had a string of chart hits from 1960 onwards before moving into acting, most notably taking the lead in the later TV series *Budgie* (1971–1972). He had the recognition to secure *What a Whopper*'s release in some European territories, and

the film also played in the US. There's a plethora of British acting talent on show here, including in minor roles Clive Dunn and Spike Milligan.

This is as much an extended bedroom farce (or, as the *MFB* put it, 'an unsubtle British comedy routine') as it is a film about faking a sighting of the Loch Ness Monster. Lazy sexist 'jokes' abound, and no opportunity is passed up to show a girl in her underwear. The film is also littered with England/Scotland jokes and unimaginative caricature (although the owner of local inn, 'The Claymore', is the very English Sidney James who is also in **The 39 Steps**, 1959, and **Crest of the Wave**). Even the great Terry Nation had to start somewhere – this was his first dramatic script to be filmed. The best thing that the *MFB* could find to say about *What a Whopper* was that 'the Scottish locations are pleasing'. One to pass by.

→ *The Private Life of Sherlock Holmes* (1970)　T100

Directed by Billy Wilder
Screenplay by Billy Wilder, IAL Diamond
Leading cast: Robert Stephens (Sherlock Holmes); Colin Blakely (Dr Watson); Christopher Lee (Mycroft Holmes); Geneviève Page (Gabrielle Valladon); Irene Handl (Mrs Hudson)
Colour, 125 minutes, UK/US

An episodic complex plot interweaves different threads, which tie up at Loch Ness as Sherlock Holmes uncovers a secret project to develop a submersible craft and plays a part in thwarting a German plot to seize this.

While many suggest that *The Private Life of Sherlock Holmes* is one of Billy Wilder's lesser films (the winner of six Oscars, Wilder directed, among others, *Double Indemnity*, 1944, *Sunset Blvd*, 1950, and *Some Like it Hot*, 1959), some critics have fiercely argued that it deserves much greater appreciation. Kim Newman has suggested that it 'is the best Holmes movie ever made and sorely underrated in the Wilder canon'. Butchered by the studio from an intended cut of over three hours to its present length, time has been good to it – viewed now, the film is at the very worst interesting, and at its best a bold (perhaps even radical), well-written and elaborately constructed reinterpretation of the Sherlock Holmes myth.

An extended opening section clews, as Vincent Canby suggested in *The NYT*, to one of Wilder's common themes: 'That is, sex. To put it bluntly, and profanely, were Holmes and Dr Watson… lovers?' The sexual comedy of manners remains in the background through the film. It is easy

Colin Blakely and Robert Stephen explore Loch Ness

to make the longer section of the film sound ridiculous. Its plot encompasses missing midgets, Trappist monks, the Loch Ness Monster, and Queen Victoria; but little is as it seems, and the mystery is a coherent one. It also becomes clear that the two sections are adroitly tied together. Stephens makes a great Sherlock, possibly better even than Basil Rathbone. Nearly half the film is set and shot in Scotland, most of this around Inverness and Loch Ness (Nairn train station plays its part, being passed-off as Inverness).

→ *The Loch Ness Horror* (1982)

Directed by Larry Buchanan
Screenplay by Larry Buchanan and Lynn Shubert
Leading cast: Sandy Kenyon (Professor George Sanderson); Miki McKenzie (Kathleen Stuart); Barry Buchanan (Spencer Dean); Eric Scott (Brad)
Colour, 89 minutes, us

Professor Spencer Dean comes to Loch Ness to investigate Nessie. He works with local professor George Sanderson. In addition to containing Nessie, the loch also conceals the wreck of Luftwaffe B97, which the military blow up, killing Nessie in the process. Local lass Kathleen, with whom Spencer flirts, has a Nessie egg, and she and Spencer put this back into the loch. A voice-over says that there is 'new evidence on the existence of a population of large animals in Loch Ness', and that the stigma of 'crackpot' has been removed.

Director and co-writer Larry Buchanan (it

took *two* people to write this nonsense?) published his autobiography, *It Came from Hunger: Tales of a Cinema Schlockmeister*, in 1996. His is one of the truly maverick careers in filmmaking. Sadly, even within the genre and limits in which he worked, *The Loch Ness Horror* is something of a low point. Made for virtually no cost (Buchanan cast his son as Dean, and his daughter in a smaller role to save money), and with absolutely no attempt to make California look like Scotland, this is nearly the worst of all the Nessie films covered here (and there is stiff competition for that title). There are some laughs to be had at this tosh, but certainly there is no horror. Scenes in which Nessie – who is of course 'real' in this film – interacts with people (exclusively by munching them) are out of the bottom drawer of the special effects department.

The approach to all things Scottish *is* hilarious. Get the bagpipes in early is the approach taken here – as they play over the opening credits. Aye, we *must* be in Scotland. The accents are risible, as, before there was the ability to Google, are some of the salient facts offered during the film. Inhabitants of Drumnadrochit would be delighted to know that the train from London stops there; they might be less delighted to know that the nearest airport is Prestwick (although that's not far down the road – at least according to Professor Sanderson); and perhaps they would be tempted by the renowned fleshpots of Inverness. So bad it's bad.

→ *Nessie, das verrückteste Monster der Welt (Nessie, the Craziest Monster in the World)* (1985)   W9

Directed by Rudolf Zehetgruber
Screenplay by Rudolf Zehetgruber
Leading cast: Britta Pohland (Deborah 'Debbie' Campbell); Oliver Rohrbeck (Dan McKenzie); Denise Gorzelanny (Gina Campbell); Christian Rode (Sir Charles Desmond); Delia Behpour/ Miriam Behpour (Vanessa 'Nessie' Campbell)
Colour, 83 minutes, German, West Germany

A bizarre (and only barely comprehensible) story with a mix of familial intrigue involving fake kidnappings and murder attempts, a TV prop fake Nessie, and the 'real' Nessie.

This German production, which appears to have had a release only in Germany and which can only be seen in German (a version on YouTube can be played with auto-translate subtitles, but these are garbage), is one of the most bizarrely bad films in this book. As German reviewer, Oliver Noeding, put it: did the filmmakers

DAS UNGEHEUER VON LOCH NESS – EIN UNGEHEUERlicher FILM!
NESSIE *Das verrückteste Monster der Welt*

This lobby card from a truly terrible film shows the 'real' Nessie 'realise, with dismay, that they had created a… film that was so broken, botched and deranged that, to protect humanity, it had to be burned, or, better still, encapsulated and shot into space?' The various story-threads barely come together in anything approaching coherence. The opening scene, in which Debbie's car is shunted off the road, appears to have come straight out of *Duel* (Steven Spielberg, 1971); while Nessie – the 'real' one, not the TV prop – appears to have been bought in a cuddly toy store. To be watched only if you speak German and have a taste for the ludicrous.

→ *Loch Ness* (1996)   S+

Directed by John Henderson
Screenplay by John Fusco
Leading cast: Ted Danson (Johnathan Dempsey); Joely Richardson (Laura); Kirsty Graham (Isabel); Ian Holm (water bailiff); James Frain (Adrian Foote)
Colour, 101 minutes, UK/US

American academic, Dempsey, tries to save his career by proving the non-existence of Nessie. He stays in the Moffat Arms, run by Laura, a single mother with a cute daughter.

Loch Ness was shot in Scotland, which allows us, while on Loch Ness, to spend time admiring the beautiful scenery of Loch Torridon, and the splendid view of Eilean Donan. It trots out tired tropes of quaint Scotland: the obligatory ceilidh occurs after ten minutes; it takes only 19 minutes until whisky is drunk before lunchtime; both

Laura and daughter Isabel are redheads; Isabel is gifted with something approaching second sight; and in the wee shop the local hicks will believe any nonsense they are told. In *Empire* Rob McCabe described it as 'at its best a pleasant enough movie that more subdued, narcoleptic children might well enjoy. At its worst, it's really rather dull'. He's being a little generous. *Loch Ness* is pedestrian nonsense. Henderson also directed *The Adventures of Greyfriars Bobby*.

→ *Beneath Loch Ness* (aka *The Evil Beneath Loch Ness*) (2001) S+

Directed by Chuck Chomisky
Screenplay by Shane Bitterling, Justin Stanley
Leading cast: Patrick Bergin (Blay); Lysette Anthony (Elizabeth); Brian Wimmer (Case Howell); Vernon Wells (constable)
Colour, 96 minutes, UK

Following a death in Loch Ness, adventurer and TV presenter Case Howell is sent to uncover the truth. Local ne'er-do-well Blay lost his son on the loch 17 years ago and seeks revenge. Case and Blay dive to take on Nessie, while local coastguards depth-bomb the loch (yes, they do have bombs).

'Sixty feet of prehistoric terror' is the tagline used on the DVD, bearing the title *The Evil Beneath Loch Ness*. Anthropomorphism is not the only thing wrong with this. There is little terror on display in this silly, predictable, but not entirely un-charming B-movie. What *is* on display are copious shots of the area around Loch Ness, but this is second unit footage; as was the case with *The Loch Ness Horror,* the primary production did not leave California. The underwater footage and scenes on the loch – from which identifying features are absent – were shot at Castaic Lake. This might explain the ability to pay in dollars in the local bar, inappropriate flora, and the sketchy approach taken to matters such as police uniforms, accents, and Scottish vernacular.

There's quite a bit of pseudo-science bandied around, with talk of saline levels and sea fissures, but while our lead team consists of university researchers, including a marine biologist, there's actually very little science. Neither is there a huge amount of action, but, in part because no one involved really appears to take this all *too* seriously, there is just enough to move things along. *Beneath Loch Ness* is deeply derivative. While the progenitor of *Beneath* may be *Lake Placid* (Steve Miner, 1999), there are more obvious rip-offs. The local constable, played by Australian actor Wells, will not 'quarantine the loch' because 'this is our tourist season. This is the busiest time of the year for us. It doubles our business'. If this sounds like a familiar line to take, that's because it is the approach taken by Larry Vaughan, as the mayor of Amity, in *Jaws* (Stephen Spielberg, 1975). *Jaws* is not the only film to inspire Chomisky and co. For the climactic crucial fight-to-the-death scene we have shifted firmly into *Aliens* territory (James Cameron, 1986). Blay squishes giant eggs as Nessie rouses herself for one final stand (Ripley standing off against

the Alien queen, flamethrower in hand, it ain't). Silly, but fun.

→ *Incident at Loch Ness* (2004) S+

Directed by Zak Penn
Screenplay by Zak Penn
Leading cast: [All as 'self'] Zak Penn; Werner
 Herzog; Kitana Baker; Gabriel Beristain; Russell
 Williams II
Colour, 94 minutes, UK

Film director Wener Herzog travels to Loch Ness to shoot a documentary, dealing with 'a figment of our fantasy'. All is not as it seems.

This is *not*, heavens be praised, another film about Nessie as such. *Incident at Loch Ness* is in part about documentary film-making. Somewhat like a nested Russian doll, it is a work of fiction in the form of a mockumentary containing within it a further documentary. Mostly it is about the maverick, erratic, and sometime brilliant, independent director Werner Herzog, who came to prominence as part of the New German Cinema (*Neuer Deutscher Film*) movement in the 1970s. *Incident* is peppered with in-jokes and references, which are unlikely to be picked up by, or be of interest to, someone without good knowledge of Herzog's career. As Walter V Addiego put it in the *San Francisco Chronicle*: 'This is mandatory viewing for Herzog fans. It's an inside joke, but for those who get it, it's loose, funny and, in its own way, Herzogian.' At the end of the film Penn says 'it was epic, it was, honestly, like

Zach Penn goes Herzog on Herzog

something out of a Werner Herzog film'.

Herzog made his first short film in 1962. With the feature *Even Dwarves Started Small* (*Auch Zwerge haben klein angefangen*) (1970), he began to attract an international arthouse audience. Far more successful was 1972's *Aguirre, the Wrath of God* (*Aguirre, der Zorn Gottes*). This began an artistically rich, and personally tempestuous, working relationship with lead actor Klaus Kinski (it is alleged that during filming Herzog pulled a gun on Kinski during an argument), with whom he also made his masterpiece *Fitzcarraldo* (1982), in which a steamboat is pulled over an isthmus between two Amazonian rivers. While Herzog's feature films established his international reputation, he has made documentaries for film and TV throughout his career – significantly outnumbering his fictional output – and has himself been the subject of documentary (most notably in Les Blank's *Burden of Dreams*, 1982, chronicling the making of *Fitzcarraldo*). His only Oscar nomination came in 2009 for the documentary *Encounters at the End of the World* (2007). For a

whistle-stop introduction to Herzog, read his 'Minnesota Declaration' (which is very short and readily available online), ideally the version including the 2017 addendum. This is not Herzog's only film in this book – he also appears in *Mister Lonely*.

It is easy to forget while watching it that *Incident* is a scripted work of fiction. Writer-director Penn became a celebrated figure when, at the age of 23, he sold the story for *Last Action Hero* (John McTiernan, 1993). He has accumulated writing and story credits on superhero films and provided the screenplay for Steven Spielberg's *Ready Player One* (2018). *Incident* was his first film as director.

In *Incident*, Herzog, *playing* Herzog, says, 'I've always been interested in the difference between fact and truth, and I've always sensed that there is a deeper truth that exists in cinema, and I would call it the ecstatic truth'. There are, in *Incident*, layers upon layers of fictions and truths. These are extended on the DVD commentary, where the fiction is continued through the commentary. This makes the film an enjoyable, playful, tease. It's also the only film in this book to feature the world's coolest man, Jeff Goldblum, who makes an appearance at a dinner party thrown by Herzog.

→ *The Water Horse* (2007) S+

Directed by Jay Russell
Screenplay by Robert Nelson Jacobs
Leading cast: Alex Etel (Angus MacMorrow);
  Emily Watson (Anne MacMorrow); David
  Morrissey (Capt. Hamilton); Brian Cox (Old
  Angus); Ben Chaplin (Lewis Mowbray)
Colour, 112 minutes, New Zealand/UK/Australia

Two tourists in a bar in the Scottish Highlands are told 'the true story' of the Loch Ness Monster by Old Angus. As a child during WWII he found an egg which hatched into the water horse of Celtic legend. With the help of his sister and a handyman he raised, released, and then saved 'Crusoe' when she was threatened by the military. He never saw Crusoe again, but as he finishes his story a young boy finds an egg on the local shore.

The legend of Nessie gets a thorough reworking in *The Water Horse*, which is *very* loosely based on Dick King-Smith's 1990 novel of the same name (he also wrote the much more successful *Babe*).

There's some depth (no pun intended) to this, with Angus' father presumed dead (he accepts at the end that his father will not come back), and the family struggling to rebuild itself. As Anne says, just before she too sees Crusoe, 'There's no monster, and there's no magic... There's just this war, and death'. *The Water Horse* is satisfyingly predictable – we know that when Anne says 'there's no magic', she will come face to face with Crusoe. There's enough in the film to entertain (it carries a score of 74 per cent on Rotten Tomatoes), although at 112 minutes some of the pacing is a little slow. *The Guardian*'s Peter Bradshaw is not cited on Rotten Tomatoes for this film, but would lie in the 26 per cent, dismissing it in two short paragraphs, starting with: 'A sentimental retelling of the Nessie legend with a monster that's a lot more convincing than the RADA accents'. More typical is Jennie Kermode in *Eye For Film*: 'The Water Horse ticks all [the usual] boxes but also has a more complex backstory, interesting characters, and a refreshing absence of mawkishness'.

There is some pitting of England v Scotland here, although everything appears resolved at the end: Morrissey's English Captain has not seen front line service and is uptight; Chaplin's Lewis is 'a hero of sorts', who has seen service, believes in magic, and helps bring Angus out of his shell. Captain Hamilton's approach to Angus is to treat him as a squaddie, forcing him to parade, and to work. Yet they work together to save Crusoe at the end. *The Water Horse* was shot primarily in New Zealand (Lake Wakatipu stands in for the Scottish loch), although there was some location work in Scotland, and the effect is moderately convincing if one ignores specifics of geography. Establishing shots at the start give us the ever-trusty Eilean Donan, mountains, glens, and red deer.

→ *Loch Ness: They Created a Monster* (2023) DOC

Directed by John MacLaverty
Colour, 91 minutes, UK

MacLaverty's engaging 'lochumentary' (sadly this is his joke, not mine) focuses on the media attention courted by a rag-tag mix of characters, ranging from the nefarious to the engagingly bonkers, who devoted time, money, and mental health, in the search for Nessie in the 1970s through to the early 1980s.

→ *Nessie* (2023) S+++

Directed by Robbie Moffat
Screenplay by Tim Churchill, Robbie Moffat and Catherine O'Reilly
Leading cast: John Michie (Jimmy); Jason Harvey (Geordie); Edith Glad (Alice); Tanya Fear (Heather); Patrick Kilpatrick (Taylor Bradley Campbell)
Colour, 96 minutes, US/UK

'Loch Ness village': as locals go about their gentle lives, and the local hotel struggles, Jimmy, chair of the village council, receives a letter stating that the village has been left $50m by an American millionaire, who had as a child spent time in the village and seen Nessie. His son, estranged from his father, contests the will. Heather, a trainee solicitor, devises a scheme to secure the money and the son's investment in the future of the village.

To understand better the place of the indefatigable Robbie Moffat in modern British and Scottish filmmaking see the larger set of entries starting with *Love the One You're With*. On the basis of those entries you'd be forgiven for thinking his films, while made with undoubted enthusiasm, are, to be charitable, rudimentary. *Nessie* however is a significant step up both in budget and quality. The film benefits from actors with substantial experience, including leads Tanya Fear (*Kick-Ass 2*, Jeff Wadlow, 2013), John Michie (73 episodes of *Taggart*) and Patrick Kilpatrick, an American who has an extremely long CV. Best known of all is Stephanie Beacham (see also *The Ballad of Tam Lin*) who plays a London lawyer (albeit her three scenes could have been shot in a single day).

Nessie has a charm which is lacking in *Loch Ness*, with which tonally it shares quite a bit in common. It also has more bite: like *The Maggie, The Ghost Goes West*, and *Local Hero*, *Nessie* sees down-to-earth Scots seeking to pull the wool over the eyes of sophisticated, rich, Americans. That the locals in *Nessie* don't complete their dastardly mission lies only in the most disappointing of plot twists in the film (although one you will certainly see coming). *Nessie* is far from perfect: the set-up to the battle of wits takes more than half the film; the soundtrack is intrusive; and there is – presumably to satisfy a potential American audience – a little too much of the cliché (whisky at four minutes, Highland cattle at 13, bagpipes at 32), but it is competently made, warm-hearted, and at times fun.

Bonnie Scotland (aka *Heroes of the Regiment*) (1935)

Directed by James W Horne
Screenplay by Frank Butler, Jefferson Moffitt
Leading cast: Stan Laurel (Stanley McLaurel); Oliver Hardy (Oliver Hardy); June Lang (Lorna McLaurel); Vernon Steele (Col. Gregor McGregor); William Janney (Allan Douglas); James Finlayson (Sgt. Maj. Finlayson)
B&W, 80 minutes, US

This poster makes very dubious claims

Stanley travels to Scotland believing he is going to benefit from a relative's will. He is left only a set of bagpipes, and a snuff box. Events become complicated, and he and Ollie end up on the Indian frontier, involved in a local war.

Although *Bonnie Scotland* was made when Laurel and Hardy were at the height of their career, watching it is not a satisfying experience. After the opening section in Scotland, the film descends into incoherence. Even die-hard Laurel and Hardy enthusiasts struggle with the film. Laurel and Hardy Central (*laurelandhardycentral.com*), run by ardent fans, has little good to say about *Bonnie Scotland*: 'overburdened with half a dozen impossible-to-follow subplots… it is the first 30 minutes that are about the only worthwhile minutes in this film'. Fortunately, it is those 30 minutes (35 in the version I watched) that are set in Scotland.

Beyond the bagpipes and kilts, there's little attempt at authenticity – which after all was not really the point when it came to Laurel and Hardy capers. The film was shot entirely in California. Accents are all over the place (the *Variety* critic called them 'pretty sour'): Australian-born Daphne Pollard plays a maid with an 'orrible cockney accent; American June Lang makes a stab at Scottish in the early scenes but gives up the ghost in India; New York native William Janney makes no discernible attempt. James Finlayson, born in Larbert, does provide a genuine Scottish voice. He first appeared on film in 1918, after abandoning a degree at Edinburgh University, and by the time of his death in 1953 had appeared in over 250 films.

The two best jokes appear in the Scottish segment. In the most technically inventive scene, Ollie falls (predictably) into a river after Stan blows the contents of the snuff box into his face. Underwater he continues to sneeze, sending jets of water into the air, until the river is dry. Best of all though is the fish-cooking scene. This is a classic Laurel and Hardy set piece, as Ollie maintains his pretence at dignity and sophistication, creating a table out of an upturned drawer balanced across chairs, while the fish 'cooks' using the bedsprings as a grill, with a candle underneath. Of course, it all goes horribly, and entertainingly, wrong.

Many of the original posters, and the pressbook, advertised *Bonnie Scotland* as providing '60 minutes of joy'. Even in its opening week in the us different versions ran for 90 minutes and 70 minutes. One is left wondering whether the tag line constituted a recognition that at least some of the film is not joyous, or was an attempt to sucker audiences into thinking that they only had to endure this for an hour. The original British poster used the even more misleading line, 'Their masterpiece of laughter'.

The Ghost Goes West (1935) T17

Directed by René Clair
Screenplay by René Clair, Eric Keown, Geoffrey Kerr, Robert E Sherwood
Leading cast: Robert Donat (Murdoch Glourie/ Donald Glourie); Jean Parker (Peggy Martin); Eugene Pallette (Mr Martin)
B&W, 95 minutes, UK

In the 1700s Murdoch Glourie, a charming womaniser, is killed on the battlefield while hiding from the fight. He haunts the family castle, moving with it when it is dismantled and taken to the US, having been bought by a millionaire. His modern-day descendant falls in love with the millionaire's daughter.

Equal parts comedy, farce, and ghost story, it would be easy, watching this piece of delightful nonsense, to forget that its French director, René Clair, had already made the extremely well-regarded *Sous Les Toits de Paris* (*Under the Roofs of Paris*, 1930), and *À Nous La Liberté* (*Freedom for Us*, 1931) before he was contracted to an English two-picture deal by Alexander Korda. The film is, for all its silliness, engaging, in places hilarious, and notwithstanding the obvious artifice involved in set construction, design and cinematography, looks great (David Thomson is less impressed by Clair's approach, referencing a 'prettiness that now seems a crucial handicap'). The British public embraced the film, voting it film of the year in the *Film Weekly* poll for 1936. Like them, Ingmar Bergman may have held it in some regard. My friend James, who was lucky enough to spend time at the Bergman estate on Fårö, found a copy of the vHs recording in Bergman's library. At the time of writing the film boasts a 100 per cent fresh score on Rotten Tomatoes (although based on only eight reviews).

The plot requires Robert Donat to play both Murdoch and Donald Glowrie – as romantic complications are required, and these arise from a feisty Peggy mistaking the ghost for live flesh-and-blood. The role was originally intended to go to Charles Laughton. At that point the film was going to be called *Sir Tristram Goes West*, and the ghost was to have no live counterpart. But Clair had seen Donat in *The 39 Steps* which had been released earlier that year, and was happy with the change in approach. Donat is delightfully light in the dual roles, convincing both as a congenital coward playing his part,

Robert Donat and Hay Petrie star in a sparkling film

presumably – although the film is decidedly non-specific in historical detail ('Scotland in the 18th century' is all that appears on a title card just after the credits) – in the events following the '45 Jacobite Rebellion, and as a singularly inept estate owner.

Reviewing the film at the time of its release, Graham Greene wrote that its satire is 'at the expense of rich and tasteless Americans', and it is this aspect that continues to delight today. The absolute highlight occurs when a grand party is held at the reassembled castle with Peggy's somewhat gauche millionaire father Eugene Pallette pulling out all the stops to create a 'Scottish' extravaganza. The 'Scottishness' on display must be seen to be believed. I howled with laughter when watching this for the first time. As Duncan Petrie puts it in *Screening Scotland* (2000) 'the central opposition between Scotland and America, old and new, tradition and vulgar materialism is handled with considerable subtlety'.

The film is only tangentially Scottish. A contemporary reviewer writing in the *MFB*

noted, somewhat generously, that 'the Scottish accents vary'; there is an online claim that the film 'apparently featured' Eilean Donan Castle. I doubt this, and IMDb lists only the Denham Studios in England as the location, although there are genuine exterior shots. In *The Observer* CA Lejeune wrote about the shoot after visiting the Denham set: 'Built on a clear bit of meadow by the river was the lower half of a medieval Scottish castle. The upper half of the castle was suspended in miniature from a platform in front of the cameras, and looking through the lens… you saw a complete castle, perfect and whole'. Most of the action is, however, set in Scotland.

The 39 Steps (1935)   T15

Directed by Alfred Hitchcock
Screenplay by Charles Bennett, Ian Hay
Leading cast: Robert Donat (Richard Hannay); Madeleine Carroll (Pamela); Godfrey Tearle (Professor Jordan); Lucie Mannheim (Annabella Smith)
B&W, 86 minutes, UK

Richard Hannay, an engaging and resourceful 'colonial', is dragged into a plot involving a secret organisation determined to sell key British military secrets to an unspecified enemy power. Initially suspected of murder, he is chased across the UK by the police and the gang before triumphing.

More has probably been written about Hitchcock than any British director. The French *nouvelle vague* director François

Hitchcock's film remains a classic

Truffaut led the charge with his series of interviews conducted in 1962 (*Hitchcock*, rev'd edn 1983). This contains a section on *The 39 Steps,* as does Donald Spoto's *The Art of Alfred Hitchcock* (rev'd edn 1992). Mark Glancy has written *The 39 Steps* in the British Film Guide series (2003).

The 39 Steps treads a skilful balance between Boys' Own adventure, with Donat able to manoeuvre his way out of seemingly any situation, and a screwball romance in the spirit of *It Happened One Night* (Frank Capra, 1934). It was important in the development of Hitchcock's work, and his public recognition, particularly with American critics. Spoto called it his 'first indisputable masterpiece [marking] a major shift in his style'. It was also an attempt by studio Gaumont-British to increase production values in the hope of making an impact with American audiences, who saw British cinema as second rate.

John Buchan's novel was heavily modified in the screenplay. There is no romantic interest in the original, and Hannay is given a Scottish background, although presented more as 'a colonial'. The novel was written in the early days of World War I. The film was shot in 1935 when Hitler had assumed power in Germany, and war seemed a strong possibility. No specific enemy is named – this would not have been tolerated by the British censors – but for the audience there would have been an understanding that this might well be Germany. Hitchcock was a great admirer of Buchan and his 'understatement of highly dramatic ideas' (Truffaut). The film moves at breakneck speed, with Hitchcock using 'one idea after another and eliminating anything that interferes with the swift pace' (Truffaut). It is this remarkable pace of action, with Hannay rising to every challenge, which carries *The 39 Steps.* But it is the panache and lightness of touch with which this is done, and the charm Donat and Carroll bring to their roles, which have ensured its longevity. It 'stands alone in the genre as a survivor of time and fashion' (Spoto).

There are elements in *The 39 Steps* which are echoed in Hitchcock's later films: the cool blonde, and the double hunt in which the hero must evade both the police and the villains (meaning he has no easy out; this element is present too in Buchan's novel). A pursuit by helicopter transmutes into one of the most recognisable of Hitchcock's scenes as Cary Grant is threatened by the crop-spraying plane in *North by Northwest* (1959).

The *39 Steps* has been filmed on a further two occasions, by Ralph Thomas in 1959, and by Don Sharp in 1978 (as *The Thirty Nine Steps*) – see below. A BBC TV film was made in 2008 (James Hawes), although this takes great liberties with the source material. Although it finds its way onto many 'Best Scottish Films' lists, *The 39 Steps* did not require its cast at any point to be in Scotland. A second unit shot exteriors in the country, which were matched to first unit material shot in England.

→ *The 39 Steps* (1959)   S+

Directed by Ralph Thomas
Screenplay by Frank Harvey
Leading cast: Kenneth More (Richard Hannay);
  Taina Elg (Fisher); Barry Jones (Professor Logan)
Colour, 93 minutes, UK

The story is as above, although updated for the nuclear age.

This, the second film version of John Buchan's novel, is a remake of Hitchcock's 1935 film, rather than a reinterpretation of the novel. It is however updated for the period, with the plot focusing on

ballistic missiles. The chase in Scotland sees Hannay hitching a lift (Sidney James is the driver), then falling in with a cycling party. A different, and perhaps more believable, explanation is given for Hannay's competence. He works 'for the Government, in a sort of way. Political warfare I'd suppose you'd call it'. More was 44 when *The 39 Steps* was shot (making him 15 years older than Elg), and his Hannay is less vigorous and more cerebral than either Donat, or Powell (who was 35 when the 1978 version was filmed). Some scenes are taken directly from Hitchcock, although the frisson of the hotel room scene, which remains very faithful to the original, is not as potent as it would have been in 1935, and there is less chemistry between Elg and More than between Carroll and Donat.

Taina Elg aside, Ralph Thomas' film presents a plethora of British talent (including an uncredited Peter Vaughan, in his first film role), alongside the two strong leads. Elg was born Finnish and was a world-class ballerina before injury forced her to change her career. More's career was very well established, and he was on a strong run with a BAFTA in 1955 for *Doctor in the House* (1954), also directed by Ralph Thomas, and BAFTA nominations in both 1956 (*The Deep Blue Sea*, Anatole Litvak, 1955) and 1957 (*Reach for the Sky*, Lewis Gilbert, 1956). There was substantial location shooting in Scotland, mainly around Edinburgh and Stirling, including at the Brig o' Turk Tea Room, which remains a going concern, and is to this day popular with cyclists.

Miss Fisher is reading *Anatomy of a*

Murder (John D Voelker, 1958) on the train when Hannay kisses (assaults) her. Otto Preminger's film adaptation of that novel was released in the UK nine months after *The 39 Steps*, and is a far superior film. Critics who reviewed *The 39 Steps* were broadly happy with it, but preferred the original.

→ *The Thirty Nine Steps* (1978)
S+

Karen Dotrice and Robert Powell

Directed by Don Sharp
Screenplay by Michael Robson
Leading cast: Robert Powell (Richard Hannay);
   David Warner (Sir Edmund Appleton); Eric
   Porter (Lomas); Karen Dotrice (Alex); John
   Mills (Scudder)
Colour, 102 minutes, UK

The basis of the story is as above, although with some changes, particularly in the final scenes.

There was some excitement in my third year English class when *The Thirty Nine Steps* came to our local cinema in 1978. It features, albeit in a fairly small role, Ronald Pickup, whose brother, David, was our English teacher. The film had the drive – spies, murders, threat, chases and love interest – to keep the 14-year-old me thoroughly entertained on a Saturday afternoon. The adult me would prefer better plot development, and less comic-strip freneticism.

The Thirty Nine Steps shares with Hitchcock's film the common origin of Buchan's novel and a freewheeling approach to its adaptation. The British

agent, Scudder (giving John Mills one of the strongest roles in the film), replaces Lucy Mannheim's mysterious woman. The central Scottish section, which extends to only fractionally less than half the total running time, encompasses the same mix of chase, peril and escapade; or, as Martyn Auty put it in the *MFB*, Hannay is propelled 'from one contrivance to the next'. The film introduces, much later than Hitchcock, a romantic interest (Karen Dotrice appears also in in *The Three Lives of Thomasina*, in which she plays the young Mary McDhui). In this version the placement of the 39 steps at Big Ben leads to 'the best Hitchcock pastiche to date' (*S&S*), as onlookers stare aghast at Hannay dangling precariously from the clock's hands.

Powell is a more ferocious and threatening Hannay than Robert Donat, although he does not match Donat's level of charm. The cast was a who's who of British acting at the time, although the lack of recognisable international stars (John Mills aside) reduced the film's marketability. Director Don Sharp had a strong track record at Hammer Films.

Many scenes were shot in Dumfries and Galloway, including at Drumlanrig and Morton castles.

Mary of Scotland (1936)

Directed by John Ford
Screenplay by Dudley Nichols
Leading cast: Katherine Hepburn (Mary Stuart); Fredric March (Earl of Bothwell); Florence Eldridge (Elizabeth Tudor); Douglas Walton (Lord Darnley); John Carradine (David Rizzio)
B&W, 123 minutes, US

In 1561, Mary returns to Scotland to resume her rightful place as its Queen, threatening Elizabeth I in England, as Mary has a strong claim to her throne. Elizabeth foments dissent among the Scottish Lords. Mary's personal life is tumultuous. Her secretary, David Rizzio, is murdered, on the orders of her husband, Lord Darnley. Later, after she gives birth (further threatening Elizabeth), Darnley is murdered, and her son kidnapped by her brother Moray. Mary remarries, to the Earl of Bothwell, but Moray leads the Scottish Lords in rebellion. Bothwell is exiled, and Mary becomes a puppet. She flees to England, anticipating the support of Elizabeth, but is detained, and later executed.

Mary first featured on film as early as 1895 (*The Execution of Mary, Queen of Scots*, Alfred Clark), which ran to less than one minute (there remains disagreement as to whether Mary is played by a man or a woman). Mary was the subject of several silent films.

In September 1936, *Kinematograph Weekly* reported *Mary of Scotland* had been 'a triumph' in New York. It was one of only five films to have played to full houses for three weeks in the Radio City Hall, New York's largest cinema. In its first week the film took the then colossal sum of $103,000 (it was also phenomenally expensive to make, being one of a small number of productions the budget of which exceeded $1m). The film opened in the UK at the Empire, Leicester Square, in late August.

Reviewing the film eight months earlier, the *MFB* had hailed it as 'a dignified and painstaking dramatisation of the life of Mary, Queen of Scots', praising the film for its historical accuracy. The film is not the dramatisation of Mary's life, sharing a common feature of the four films covered here in focusing almost exclusively on the last 25 of her 44 years, beginning with her arrival in Scotland. There was less praise in the *MFB* for the film's ability to engage. It was, indeed, judged to be a 'failure as dramatic entertainment'. At 123 minutes the film was very long for its time and, for the *MFB* reviewer, lagged continually. This is certainly the case: the film is based on a stage play by Maxwell Anderson (over-lauded by *The NYT* as 'the finest play of the season and one of the finest pieces of writing in the collected works of the American drama'), and there are points at which the action is interrupted for wordy history lessons, or for filling in the story beyond that shown. Some of

Katherine Hepburn

these longueurs are substantial, leading Frank Nugent in *The NYT* to point to a 'blend of excellence and mere adequacy in the... new picture'.

Mary of Scotland was directed by John Ford (and shot at the RKO studios in Hollywood), with whom Hepburn was smitten. While *Mary* was shooting, Ford won an Oscar for *The Informer* (1935) (one of the four he won over his career), and he was at the top of his game. Hepburn's previous film, *Sylvia Scarlett* (George Cukor, 1935) had been a disaster, and she badly needed a hit. The Radio City box office was inflated by a heat wave, driving people into air-conditioned theatres; reviews were mixed, and the box office was ultimately a disappointment. The film was not the multiple award winner RKO had hoped for. Indeed, the only award it won was a special nomination for John Ford at the Venice Film Festival (where it was also nominated for 'the Mussolini cup' for the Best Foreign Film – the award going to the German western, *Der Kaiser von Kalifornien*, Luis Trenker, 1936).

An issue all versions of the film face is the passage of time. They have in common that they cover a period of at least 25 years (longer in the case of the 2013 version); in this version Hepburn (who was 29 when the film was made) appears barely to age, and in the absence of any dates being given during the film, the viewer is, some attempts at historical accuracy notwithstanding, likely to believe that the action occupies a much shorter period than it did. This is not a poor film, although its pacing is at times painfully slow. Forsyth Hardy (*Scotland in Film*) has suggested that the fact that Hepburn could trace her ancestry back to the Earl of Bothwell may have influenced her decision to take on the role. He found her performance to be 'strident' and 'hoydenish'; it 'did not suggest for a moment someone brought up in France at the court of Henry II and Catherine de Medici'.

→ *Mary, Queen of Scots* (1971)
S+ T45

Directed by Charles Jarrott
Screenplay by John Hale
Leading cast: Vanessa Redgrave (Mary, Queen of Scots); Glenda Jackson (Queen Elizabeth); Ian Holm (David Riccio); Timothy Dalton (Henry, Lord Darnley); Trevor Howard (William Cecil); Patrick McGoohan (James Stuart)
Colour, 128 minutes, UK/US

Follows the conflict between Mary and her cousin, Elizabeth, through to Mary's execution.

This version of Mary's life after acceding to the Crown is a mainstream 'safe' stroll through the same territory occupied by the other three films covered here, none of which is without fault. *Mary, Queen of Scots* was a lavish conventional production by a director and writer with a track record in this sort of stuff. It benefits from an outstanding cast, pitting two of England's best actors – Vanessa Redgrave (who was 34 when the film was shot), and Glenda Jackson (35) – against each other, with support coming from the well-established (Trevor Howard – who was in *Kidnapped* in the same year – Daniel Massey, Patrick McGoohan), and the up-and-coming (Timothy Dalton, Ian Holm). Jarrott and Hale had already worked together on another historical feature, *Anne of the Thousand Days* (1969), which scooped six Oscar nominations (with one win, for Margaret Furse's costumes – she also worked on *Mary* and, amongst many others, *Madeleine*, *Kidnapped* (1959), and *The Three Lives of Thomasina*; as far as I am aware, I am not a relation).

The film was nominated for multiple Oscars and Golden Globes in 1971 but was passed over at the BAFTAS. Glenda Jackson did win the Best Actress BAFTA in 1972, but, in a sign of the changing times, this was for *Sunday Bloody Sunday* (John Schlesinger, 1971; which also garnered the awards for Best Film, Director, and Actor). The 'New Hollywood' was gaining ground in the US, and in the UK the 'kitchen sink' dramas were achieving the same effect; staid, traditional, Hollywood

epics were in decline, and films like *Mary, Queen of Scots* became unfashionable. Paradoxically, television became the place for historical epics, repackaged as TV series – they didn't have the production values, or expense, of their Hollywood counterparts, but they had the luxury of time. Mary herself crops up in *Elizabeth R* (1971), in which Glenda Jackson again played Elizabeth.

Critical response to the film was at best warm. In the *MFB* Richard Combs wrote that Hale's screenplay 'is coolly literate and precise... but it provides almost no interpretation of the characters as individuals and unfortunately [Jarrott's] direction goes little further... There is a complete failure to present the conflicts visually'. Vincent Canby in *The NYT* was

Vanessa Redgrave and Glenda Jackson on the set at Shepperton

brutal: 'all it's doing is touching bases, like a dull, dutiful student', and 'It's just solemn, well-groomed and dumb'. For Roger Ebert, the central problem was that 'it cherishes a soap-opera approach to history, condensing several decades of pretty complicated diplomacy into an account of Mary's three marriages, her second husband's bisexuality, Elizabeth's quirky affair with her Master of Horses, and so on'.

There was some limited shooting in Scotland: Mary gives birth to James at Hermitage Castle, but most of the film was shot in England.

→ *Mary Queen of Scots* (2013)

Directed by Thomas Imbach
Screenplay by Thomas Imbach, Andrea Staka
Leading cast: Camille Rutherford (Mary); Mehdi
 Dehbi (Rizzio); Sean Biggerstaff (Bothwell);
 Aneurin Barnard (Darnley); Edward Hogg
 (Moray); Tony Curran (John Knox)
Colour, 119 minutes, Switzerland/France,
 French/English

Set in flashback from the night before her execution, the film charts Mary's life from her birth through to her imminent death, narrated through a series of letters from Mary to Elizabeth.

An article by Dalya Alberger in *The Observer* in August 2013 discussed the ongoing fascination Mary, Queen of Scots, holds for filmmakers. At that time two UK productions were under way (one was abandoned, the other is discussed in the following entry). But,

as Alberger noted, Thomas Imbach had beaten both UK films to the punch. Unfortunately, Imbach's film, which was shown at the GFF in 2014 is a very mixed bag. Some of the visuals are great, but the many failures mar the result. Two artificial devices power the film: the first the letters Mary writes to Elizabeth (who is never seen in the film); the second the symbolism flowing from the use of puppet theatre, in which Mary and Elizabeth, manipulated by Rizzio, provide a commentary on the events.

Mary Queen of Scots is undoubtedly ambitious, and it looks very good indeed. Imbach also acted as the cinematographer of landscapes, although, that the film was shot outside Scotland is occasionally noticeable in that some of the architecture does not match (notwithstanding that there is some very limited use made of exterior shots from Scotland, including of Dunottar Castle). The real problem however is that the film's construction, in which so much is internalised, places huge demands on its cast, particularly on Rutherford's Mary, and Barnard's Darnley. Both flounder. Interviewed before the film was shown at the GFF, Rutherford said: 'It's still absurd to me as a 21-year-old French girl making this film about Mary, Queen of Scots so long ago in Scotland, and it's filmed in Switzerland... I hope [the Scots] like it'. Unfortunately, the relatively inexperienced actor is not able to deliver the emotional depth Imbach's approach demands. Dehbi's Rizzio and Biggerstaff's Bothwell are strong, but the film needs more.

→ *Mary Queen of Scots* (2018) S+

Directed by Josie Rourke
Screenplay by Beau Willimon
Leading cast: Saoirse Ronan (Mary Stuart);
  Margot Robbie (Queen Elizabeth I); David
  Tennant (John Knox); Jack Lowden (Henry
  Darnley); Brendan Coyle (Earl of Lennox); Guy
  Pearce (William Cecil); Ismael Cruz Cordova
  (David Rizzio); Martin Compston (Lord
  Bothwell)
Colour, 124 minutes, UK/US, English/French/
  Gaelic

*With some time shifts, covers the period
between Mary's arrival in Scotland, and her
execution, including a meeting between her
and Elizabeth.*

With lead actors offering name recognition
(Ronan is also in **Death Defying Acts** and
The Outrun), and a female director with
a background in theatre, this is the most
recent version of Mary's life to be committed
to cinema. *Mary Queen of Scots* is Josie
Rourke's only feature at the time of writing
(she was attached to *The Nan Movie*,
Catherine Tate, 2022, but her name did not
appear in the final credits for this critical
flop). Her background in theatre may
explain her welcome willingness to cast, at
least in part, without reference to colour.
It also explains why so much in the film is
theatrical – particularly the staged scenes
in the courts of both queendoms, and why
there is substantial reliance on explanatory
conversations. This frustrated several
reviewers; Matthew Norman in the *London
Evening Standard* for example, referred to a
'stiflingly expository screenplay'.

The unalloyed strengths of the film are
James Merifield's design, Max Richter's
score, and its costumes, by Alexandra
Byrne (who was both Oscar and BAFTA
nominated). The most distinctive element
of the film is the attempt to refocus it
on the two women, ruling in a world
dominated by men, but both of whom
are cleverer than most of the men who
surround them. In this context, for
example, Knox's invective against Mary
is as much based on misogyny as it is on
religious bigotry. I only wish the approach
were *more* successful. To quote Deborah
Ross in the *Spectator*, 'the film wants to
make the point that the women might have
reached some kind of accord had they been
spared the bearded men... But this is so
clumsily achieved it is even spoken out loud
all the time.' Most reviews were positive,
although rarely unequivocally so, and some
really did not like the film. In *The Atlantic*
David Sims was not at all happy: '...this
movie is little more than a vibrant-looking
tableau, a two-dimensional take on an
intricate piece of history'.

Saiorse Ronan

Auld Lang Syne (1937)

Directed by James A FitzPatrick
Screenplay by WK Williamson
Leading cast: Andrew Cruickshank (Robert
 Burns); Christian Adrian (Jean Armour);
 Richard Ross (Gavin Hamilton)
B&W, 72 minutes, UK

An episodic life of Robert Burns.

In early 1937 the *MFB* ridiculed this
quota-quickie biopic: 'naïve almost beyond
belief... Andrew Cruickshank gives a
portrait of the poet which would not be
recognised as such by students of his life
and work'. Time has not improved the
film, and the best biopic of Burns currently
available is Robbie Moffat's **Red Rose**.

The Edge of the World (1937)
S++ T46

Directed by Michael Powell
Screenplay by Michael Powell
Leading cast: John Laurie (Peter Manson); Belle
 Chrystall (Ruth Manson); Eric Berry (Robbie
 Manson); Niall MacGinnis (Andrew Gray); Finlay
 Currie (James Gray)
B&W, 74 minutes, UK

*Titles read: 'The slow shadow of death is
falling on the outer isles of Scotland. This is the
story of one of them – and all of them...' On
the island of 'Hirta' the small community leads
a fragile existence. Finally, the crofters ask for
the laird's help in evacuating to the mainland.*

The first of three films in this book directed
by Michael Powell, *The Edge of the
World* is often discussed in relation to St
Kilda, but was shot on Foula, lying to the
west of Shetland Mainland. Powell was
inspired to write the story for the film after
reading about the evacuation of the final
36 residents of St Kilda which had taken
place seven years earlier, in 1930. Foula
itself had a population of 118 in 1931.
Powell paid the owners of Foula £200 for
the right to film there, after he was refused
permission to shoot on St Kilda. He wrote
in his autobiography (*A Life in Movies*,
1986), that Foula 'was more rugged and
inhospitable even than St Kilda'. Powell
envisaged the film as 'a *Drama*! An *Epic*!
About People!!'. But he wanted to make
the film on location, and to incorporate
local people into the cast for authenticity.
 Laurie's career prospects were
significantly enhanced after *The 39 Steps*
(1935) was released, and Powell thought
'he had the potential of a great actor'.
With his strikingly stern physiognomy,
he is terrific as the factor trying to cling
to old ways. Currie, who hailed from
Caithness, played the other patriarch (he
also appears in a lead role in *The Brothers*).
Of the younger leads, MacGinnis was
Irish, and Chrystall English, as was Berry.
All other parts were cast in Scotland. In
some respects, *The Edge of the World* is a
conventional story of families in opposition
to each other, which are ultimately, after
tragedy, united by love. The film is also
conventional in contrasting tradition and
the past with modernity and the future.
The crofters' existence is governed by the

inhospitable environment and by reverence to God and the Kirk. The contrast here is *not* with England (to which Scotland was more likely to be compared in earlier films), but to the Scottish mainland, which provides a (then) modern trawler fleet, employment and – crucially – life-saving medicine.

In 1978 an expanded version of the film was released, incorporating a short film financed by the BBC, *Return to the Edge of the World*, providing 23 minutes of contextual material (directed by Powell), about the experience of making the film. Powell also published *200,000 Feet on Foula* (Faber, 1938), which is no longer in print, and continued to regard the film as a significant turning point throughout the remainder of his career.

→ *The Spy in Black* (aka *U Boat 29*) (1939)   T33

Directed by Michael Powell
Screenplay by Emeric Pressburger
Leading cast: Conrad Veidt (Captain Ernst Hardt); Valerie Hobson (the school mistress); Sebastian Shaw (Ashington)
B&W, 77 minutes, UK

1917. U-boat 29 takes Captain Hardt to Orkney where he will report to a German agent and lead a plot to destroy the British fleet. He is foiled.

The Spy in Black, set during World War I, was conceived when a new war with Germany seemed inevitable. It was released in August 1939; war was declared the following month. In October, events caught up with the film; a German submarine torpedoed the Royal Navy's *Royal Oak* in the Scapa Flow, and interest in the film grew. *The Spy in Black*'s significance to film history is that this was the first time that Michael Powell and Emeric Pressburger – arguably the most important creative team in British cinema – worked together. The result is an exceptional film which maintains a Rotten Tomatoes score of 100 per cent. Although set in Orkney, filming there was limited to three days, with most of the film shot in Alexander Korda's monstrous vanity project, Denham Studios in London.

The German actor Conrad Veidt received lead billing. He had achieved international recognition with the expressionist masterpiece *The Cabinet of Dr Caligari* (Robert Wiene, 1920), and the Nazi regime was reluctant to lose him, but his wife, who was in part of Jewish descent, was in the UK, and he was permitted to leave. He did not return to Germany, and died in 1943, one year after the release of *Casablanca* (Michael Curtiz), in which he played Strasser. Powell was not happy with the first script, which followed closely the source novel by Scottish author J Storer Clouston. In *A Life in Movies* (1986) Powell cites Pressburger: 'the object of the exercise was to provide a stunning part for a great star [Veidt] and... no such part existed. It was also necessary to provide an intriguing part for Miss Hobson, who was no dummy'. Hobson started her career as a dancer before switching to acting, making

Wendy Hiller's journey ends in love and understanding

her first (uncredited) appearance in 1932. The third actor on whom the film depends, Shaw, had his first film credit in 1930, and in 1983 was Anakin Skywalker in *Star Wars: Episode VI – The Return of the Jedi* (Richard Marquand).

Everything about the film is good, but its foundations are a strong subtle script and three great performances. The film eschews a crude good/evil approach. Hardt will not take off his uniform, as he is a military officer, not a spy (a device replicated in *The Eagle Has Landed*, John Sturges, 1976); believing Ashington to be a corrupt traitor, he holds him in contempt. Both audiences and critics loved it.

→ *I Know Where I'm Going!* (1945) S+ T1

Directed by Michael Powell, Emeric Pressburger
Screenplay by Michael Powell, Emeric Pressburger
Leading cast: Wendy Hiller (Joan Webster); Roger Livesey (Torquil MacNeil); George Carney (Mr Webster); Pamela Brown (Catriona); CWR Knight (Col. Barnstaple)
B&W, 91 minutes, UK

Joan is 25. A voice-over tells us she 'knows where she's going'. She is the fiancée of 'one of the wealthiest men in England', owner of a large chemicals company. She journeys to the Western Isles for the wedding. There,

*she falls in love with Torquil, a naval officer
and Laird of 'Kiloran'.*

IKWIG is a masterpiece, that would
likely be even better known were it not
somewhat in the shadow of other great
films made by Powell and Pressburger
in the same purple period (*The Life and
Death of Colonel Blimp*, 1943 – which
also starred Roger Livesey; *A Canterbury
Tale*, 1944; *Black Narcissus*, 1947; *The
Red Shoes*, 1948). On its face it is a simple
and predictable love story but it is told
with panache and is a film that Martin
Scorsese loved; he was 'fascinated by how
romantic it was, and how mystical it was'.

Not content with simply telling a story,
Powell and Pressburger tell it inventively,
revelling in what cinema can achieve.
On the overnight sleeper to Glasgow, an
elaborate dream sequence – its rhythm
and sound synchronising with the wheels
on the track – has Joan literally marrying
'Consolidated Chemical Industries';
at Glasgow Central Train Station the
station-master's top hat appears to emit
steam as we cut to a steam train's funnel.
Throughout the film is visually ravishing.

I Know is not just a love story – it is
domestic propaganda, subtly so, but made
during World War II for that purpose.
Joan is English, Torquil is Scottish, so
their joining at the film's end suggests
national unity and 'togetherness'. He is
on leave and of course will have to return
to the war whatever happens with Joan.
Catriona's husband is English, and he
is fighting overseas. Similarly, the film
promotes cultural and economic unity.

Joan's middle-class Mancunian, who at
first appears to be simply chasing wealth,
is seduced by more honest, down-to-earth
values represented by the islanders. There
are significant conversations about money:

JOAN: People around here are very
poor I suppose.
TORQUIL: Not poor, they just haven't got
money.
JOAN: It's the same thing.
TORQUIL: Oh no, it's something quite
different.

Joan's wealthy fiancé is criticised and
mocked by the locals: he has salmon
shipped in, when there is plenty to catch
on Kiloran (he has expensive fishing
tackle, but the fish 'don't know him'); and
is having a swimming pool built when
there are the sea and a loch to swim in.
Pamela Brown's Catriona, who first puts
Joan and Torquil up for the night, returns
with rabbits she has shot, a self-reliance
which many people in rural Britain
adopted in World War II. Joan finds this
seductive, realising she does *not* want to
marry for money and *would* rather catch
her own salmon and swim in the sea.

The renaming of Colonsay to Kiloran
aside, this is so Scottish that I am
informed by my friend James the literal
translation of the Swedish title is *It
Happened in Scotland*. Much is made of
the Mull locations, and it *matters* that
Scotland, and local culture, are in the
foreground (this serves the propaganda).
The longest scene takes place at a ceilidh
held to celebrate a diamond wedding

anniversary. Not only does the solidity of the marriage relationship throw into relief Joan's uncertain position, but the joyful traditions – Scottish dancing and music – the use of Gaelic and the strong sense of community all serve to persuade the city-dwelling Englishwoman of the value of another local culture.

Late in 2023 *IKWIG* was re-released in a version restored by the BFI as part of a wider Powell and Pressburger season; audiences and critics alike continued to respond with accolades.

Said O'Reilly to McNab (1937)
S+ T100

> Directed by William Beaudine
> Screenplay by Leslie Arliss, Marriott Edgar and Howard Irving Young
> Leading cast: Will Mahoney (Colonel Timothy O'Reilly); Will Fyffe (Malcolm McNab); Robert Gall (Jock McNab); Jean Winstanley (Mary McNab)
> B&W, 80 minutes, UK/US

New York: con man and chancer Colonel Reilly stays one step ahead of the law. Scotland: Reilly's son, Jock, proposes to McNab's daughter, Mary, but her father is disenchanted by Jock's Irishness and lack of prospects. Jock invites his father, who has 'millions', to Scotland. O'Reilly and McNab spar. Police eventually catch up with O'Reilly, but McNab comes to his rescue.

A light and genuinely funny comedy, *Said O'Reilly* relies for its humour on the disparate approaches to money taken by Reilly, a profligate chancer, and McNab, a caricature of the careful Scot, whose mantra is 'the secret of success is not so much in earning money, as in keeping it'. Both share one thing: a love of golf. Our introduction to McNab starts with a shot of his 1937 trophy for the 'St Andrews Golf Club Championship', although he first represents himself to O'Reilly as being rubbish at the game. Opening in New York, the film, shot in London's Gainsborough studios, moves swiftly to Scotland where the battle of wills between O'Reilly and McNab takes place. The battle climaxes, unsurprisingly, on the golf course.

There's plenty to enjoy here. Beaudine's script is sharp, and the two leads spark well off each other. For *Picturegoer*'s Lionel Collier, the 'interplay of these two makes for really good fun, for while it is broadly farcical the human touch is not forgotten and the character traits in each are emphasised'. *Variety*'s reviewer noted that 'Fyffe is a pleasure to watch from start to finish'.

Said O'Reilly is the only film in this book to feature Dundee-born Will Fyffe in a leading role, although he has an uncredited role in **Bonnie Prince Charlie** and a minor role in **The Brothers**. He was a renowned music hall performer, and made his first film in 1914, at the age of 19.

Storm in a Teacup (1937)

Directed by Ian Dalrymple and Victor Saville
Screenplay by Ian Dalrymple and Donald Bull
Leading cast: Vivien Leigh (Victoria Gow); Cecil
  Parker (Provost William Gow); Rex Harrison
  (Frank Burdon)
B&W, 87 minutes, UK

*The provost of 'Baikie', a small town on
the 'Scottish west coast', battles with a
local journalist, who falls in love with the
provost's daughter.*

The engaging rom-com *Storm* is based,
indirectly, on a German play by Bruno
Frank. The film provides the opportunity
to see both Vivien Leigh (two years away
from achieving stardom with *Gone with
the Wind*, Victor Fleming, 1939) and
Rex Harrison early in their careers. Cecil
Parker would have been more familiar
to British audiences, and he is superbly
pompous as the local provost looking
to move onto the national stage by
embracing calls for Scottish independence.
The best turn however belongs to Sara
Allgood (whose dog the provost will
not reprieve from a destruction order).
The *MFB*'s reviewer wrote that 'the fun
becomes fast and furious', and the film,
shot in the studio, is a light pleasure.

Marigold (1938)   S+

Directed by Thomas Bentley
Screenplay by Dudley Leslie
Leading cast: Sophie Stewart (Marigold Sellar);
  Patrick Barr (Lt. Archie Forsyth); Phyllis Dare
  (Mme Marly); Edward Chapman (Mordan);
  Nicholas Hannen (Major Sellar)
B&W, 74 minutes, UK

*The 1840s: vivacious Marigold lives with
her aunt, the minister's wife Mrs Pringle,
and is engaged to a pompous church
elder. She wants to view the visit of Queen
Victoria to Edinburgh Castle, but is told
that's out of the question. Defiantly she
accepts an invitation to the event from Lt
Forsyth, a dashing soldier with whom she
falls in love. Her father catches up with
her but a brief intervention by the Queen
ensures all's well that ends well.*

If you were to rely on the scant few plot
summaries of *Marigold* available online
you would be forgiven for thinking that this
would be a dour film unleavened by light
touches. Nothing could be further from the
truth. The play *Marigold*, a Scottish romantic comedy/drama written by L Allen Harker
and FR Pryor, was first produced in 1927 and
was a hit. Later, in a cut-down 25-minute
version, it became the first play to be publicly
broadcast by the BBC on its new regular –
then 'high definition' – service in 1936. The
TV version featured Scottish lead actress,
Sophie Stewart (1905–1977; also in **Devil
Girl from Mars**) who had performed the
role over 1,000 times on stage. Two years
later the play was made into a feature film

by the Associated British Picture Corporation, with Stewart again taking the lead. The film was able to expand on the stage-setting, making use of external shots in Edinburgh, its castle, and the surrounding countryside, although the first month's primary shooting took place in Elstree and notwithstanding the attempts to open things out, the film's origins in the theatre are clear.

It's possible that the review in the *MFB* may be the first time (it's far from the last) viewers were patronisingly warned, in relation to cinema, 'Scottish accents may present occasional difficulties to Southern ears' (the accents are largely authentic, but not broad); on the plus side the *MFB*'s reviewer noted the 'exceptionally charming' settings. There is, as *Picturegoer*'s Lionel Collier pointed out, 'rather too much dialogue and not enough action' and even at its short running time the film is occasionally languid, but it retains charm as a period piece, and as a depiction of Victorian moral values: scenes in which Marigold and her fiancé let books of etiquette dictate their actions and responses are entertaining, as are plot elements at the end bordering on farce. *Marigold* may contain the first depiction of Queen Victoria (here young and attractive and played by Pamela Stanley) in the sound era. Unfortunately, *Marigold* is now something of a rarity and, I regret, you are unlikely to be able to track it down: I was able to watch this only at the BFI Mediatheque in London on a VHS transfer.

Hoots Mon (1940)

Directed by Roy William Neill
Screenplay by Roy William Neill, Jack Henley and John Dighton
Leading cast: Max Miller (Harry Hawkins); Florence Desmond (Jenny MacTavish); Davina Craig (Annie)
B&W, 77 minutes, UK

'England's funniest comedian', Harry Hawkins, determines to conquer Scotland in response to a challenge from impersonator, Jenny MacTavish, whose act includes Harry. He flops in Glasgow, both in the theatre, and in the fiercely nationalist Thistle Club where after a performance he requires hospitalisation. The ending sees a reconciliation and shared show for charity with MacTavish.

A Warner Brothers-produced quota quickie, shot at Middlesex's Teddington Studios, *Hoots Mon* capitalised on the fame of Max Miller, one of England's greatest comedians. If the film is rarely discussed in the context of Scottish cinema, that is because, settings aside, little about this is Scottish. *Hoots Mon* is little more than wartime propaganda combined with a vehicle exploiting the acts of Miller and Desmond. Miller's act was toned down for cinema, lacking the ribaldry he brought to music hall, but when he is on stage in the film he still engages. Desmond was a superb impressionist (her work in the film includes Bette Davis: 'I've won the Academy Award so many times they're thinking of renaming it and calling it the Davis Cup'). Writing in *S&S* in 1993 Geoffrey McNab argued that there was little to enjoy in the off-stage scenes which dominate the film, although acknowledges that 'as soon as [Miller] has his audience, he is transformed'.

Given the film was shot shortly after the outbreak of World War II it was essential that, despite highlighting tensions between England and Scotland, the film results in a coming together and partnership – a necessity for the successful war effort. There is no coincidence in the fact that the key charity performance by Hawkins and MacTavish takes place on 2 September 1939. While *Hoots Mon* may lack the sophistication of the later *I Know Where I'm Going* or the tension of *Cottage to Let*, there is plenty here to enjoy.

Hoots Mon had no pretensions and was well received on release. The *MFB's* reviewer was more than satisfied: 'For those who like dialogue that flickers like lightning, magnificent fooling and broad humour this is definitely a picture to see'. *Kinematograph Weekly*'s reviewer enjoyed the 'knockabout fare in which Cockney and Scottish humour play equal parts'.

Cottage to Let (aka *Bombsight Stolen*) (1941)

Directed by Anthony Asquith
Screenplay by Anatole de Grunwald and JOC Orton
Leading cast: Leslie Banks (John Barrington); Jeanne De Casalis (Mrs Barrington); Alastair Sim (Charles Dimble); John Mills (Flt. Lt. Perry)
B&W, 90 minutes, UK

In World War II, at a cottage converted into a military hospital on a Scottish estate, a local inventor develops the perfect bombsight. A German plot to steal it is thwarted.

Leslie Banks and a young George Cole

Filmed early in 1941 in the Gaumont London studios, *Cottage to Let* fails to make the most of its setting, which provides the plot's required remoteness, but otherwise adds little apart from the adoption of some dodgy accents. As the *MFB* put it, 'the Scottish atmosphere was never realistic'. That aside, there is plenty to enjoy in a tightly plotted spy/

mystery thriller, with some good set pieces and humour. Central to this is 15-year-old George Cole (Arthur Daley in the long-running TV series *Minder*; also in *The Bridal Path*) in his first screen role. His cheeky London evacuee, Ronald, is sharp and has a Sherlock Holmes fixation. Successful in the UK, *Cottage to Let* received a later release as *Bombsight Stolen* in the US in 1943.

The Ghost of St Michael's (1941)

Directed by Marcel Varnel
Screenplay by Angus MacPhail and John Dighton
Leading cast: Will Hay (Will Lamb); Claude Hulbert (Hilary Tisdaile); Felix Aylmer (Dr Winter); Charles Hawtrey (Percy Thorne)
B&W, 82 minutes, UK

An exclusive school is relocated from Kent to a castle in 'Dunbain' on Skye. Lamb, a new, inept teacher, contending with authority and rebellious pupils, is instrumental in unmasking an enemy spy plot.

Heavily reliant on the charm of Will Hay (the MFB's review was succinct: 'If you like Will Hay's humour, you will like this film'), *The Ghost of St Michael's* is a lesser Ealing Studios production. It was shot in late 1940 under full wartime conditions and is entirely set-bound. The 'Scottishness' however is emphasised in the mythology surrounding the 'castle', complete with harbingers of doom in the form of ghostly bagpipe music.

Like *Cottage to Let* the film features precocious evacuee children (the precocity aided by the fact that Charles Hawtrey, who is excellent, was signed up to play the lead schoolboy at the age of 25). Hay's attempts at teaching are mildly amusing. Ralph Denton in *Picturegoer* wrote, 'as farcical comedy, *The Ghost of St Michael's* is good. Regarded as a sign of Mr Hay's return to his former eminence, it is first rate'. Hay aside, the remainder of the cast is strong, with John Laurie providing authentic, if overblown, Scottish atmosphere.

Old Mother Riley's Ghosts (1941)

Directed by John Baxter
Screenplay by Arthur Lucan, Geoffrey Orme and Con West
Leading cast: Arthur Lucan (Mrs Riley); Kitty McShane (Kitty Riley); John Stuart (John Cartwright)
B&W, 82 minutes, UK

After being sacked as a char-lady at Cartwright manufacturing, Mother Riley inherits a Scottish castle (at 'Auchterarder in the county of Ecclefechan'!). She moves in along with her daughter and a young inventor she has taken under her wing. Industrial spies attempt to steal the inventor's design but are defeated by Mother Riley.

Arthur Lucan had success with the Mother Riley character across music hall, film and light entertainment for nearly 20 years, making 17 films, in which, with the single exception of *Old Mother Riley's Ghosts*, he always appeared only in his female alter-ego. In *Ghosts* he also appears as a perfidious male plotter, able to double as Mother Riley. When Lucan was 28 he married 16-year-old Kitty McShane, and the mother-daughter double act on display in *Ghosts* was born.

The film, of which almost exactly half is set in the Scottish castle, combines a thin plot, physical comedy routines, broad humour, and a scant regard for Scottish geography or authenticity. The latter is supplied only by John Laurie, who appeared in **The Ghost of St Michaels** in the same year. Here he hams things up even more than he did in **St Michaels**, but it's what the film called for. Director John Baxter later made the much more significant **The Shipbuilders**.

Shining Victory (1941)

Directed by Irving Rapper
Screenplay by Howard Koch and Anne Froelich
Leading cast: James Stephenson (Dr Paul
  Venner); Geraldine Fitzgerald (Dr Mary
  Murray); Donald Crisp (Dr Drewett)
B&W, 80 minutes, UK

Forced by the duplicitous Professor von Reiter to leave a position in Vienna, English researcher Dr Venner moves to Scotland to research a cure for dementia precox, working with his assistant Dr Murray. They begin a passionate affair.

Shining Victory's promotion relied heavily on the fact that it was based on a play by Scottish author AJ Cronin (who also provided the source material for **Hatter's Castle** and **The Green Years**, and who later created television's Dr Finlay). Cronin's *The Citadel* (1937) had been a publishing sensation, the first adaptation of which for the screen had been a hit for King Vidor (*The Citadel*, 1938). While *The Citadel* has been filmed on multiple occasions (most notably as *Tere Mere Sapne*, Vijay Anand, 1971, a neo-realist Indian film with the addition of song and dance numbers), the Scottish film **Citadel** has *nothing* to do with the novel, which is set in the Welsh mining valleys, where Cronin had worked while practicing medicine.

Shining Victory was filmed at the Warner Brothers studios in Burbank. 'Hopewell Towers Sanitorium' is, we are told, in Scotland, and is a (set-constructed) Gothic pile, but otherwise nothing in the film is notably authentic. The result is worthy, but dull; *Variety*'s critic wrote, as 'a straightforward exposition of the avenues of clinical research [*Shining Victory*] might appeal to very limited audiences; but entertainment factors are missing'.

London-born Donald Crisp (1882–1974) appears in five other films in this book, from 1917 (**The Little Minister**), to 1961 (**Greyfriars Bobby: The True Story of a Dog**). His career spanned the silver and golden ages of cinema working alongside almost every actor of note, and with many great directors. He even played General Ulysses S Grant in *The Birth of a Nation*

(DW Griffith, 1915), arguably one of the most significant films ever shot (notwithstanding it is a piece of racist filth). Bette Davis has an uncredited appearance in *Shining Victory*'s opening scenes: a friend of Rapper, who was directing his first film, she dressed as a nurse for the first day of shooting, inserting herself on the set without Rapper noticing (*Kinematograph Weekly*, April 1941).

Back-Room Boy (1942)

Directed by Herbert Mason
Screenplay by Joc Orton, Val Guest and
 Marriott Edgar
Leading cast: Arthur Askey (Arthur Pilbeam),
 Googie Withers (Bobbie), Vera Frances (Jane),
 Joyce Howard (Betty)
B&W, 82 minutes, UK

Arthur, who presses the button which sends out the time pips on the BBC, rebels after being jilted by Betty, and taps out a syncopated rhythm at midnight. He is sent to a meteorological station on 'Orry', a remote lighthouse island near Orkney. He, and a group of models who have been washed ashore, thwart a Nazi plot.

Arthur Askey and Googie Withers were both British wartime stars. Askey was an 'everyman' with whom working-class audiences would relate, his diminutive size, and apparent ineptitude never preventing him winning through. The film is, as noted in the *MFB*, 'farcical', but it was never meant to be anything else. The plot is ridiculous, and gentle fun is poked

at the Scottish in a ten-minute scene in the (presumably Orcadian) hotel on the trip to Orry where a love of whisky, a belief in the powers of the local kelpie (improbably named Brunnhilde), and nearly impenetrable accents, dominate. Having professed to Bobbie (the first model to be washed ashore), 'I hate your sex. I loathe women, all of them', Arthur is required to mend his ways ('united we stand') as everyone – men, women, Scottish and English – come together to defeat the Nazi plot to mine a shipping channel. A product of its time and of very limited interest now, *Back-Room Boy* was made by Gaumont and Gainsborough Studios and shot entirely in London.

Hatter's Castle (aka *A J Cronin's Hatter's Castle*) (1942) S+

Directed by Lance Comfort
Screenplay by Paul Merzbach and Rudolph
 Bernaeur
Leading cast: Robert Newton (James Brodie);
 James Mason (Dr Renwick); Deborah Kerr
 (Mary Brodie); Emlyn Williams (Dennis)
B&W, 102 minutes, US

In 'Levenforth', James Brodie is the local hatter. He is tyrannical, unliked, and engaged in an illicit affair. His mistress persuades him to give a job to her step-brother, who seduces Mary, James' daughter. Tragedy envelops the family.

The second of three films in this book based on source material from Scottish author

James Mason and Deborah Kerr

AJ Cronin, *Hatter's Castle* was an adaptation of his first novel, a melodrama (or, as *Kinematograph Weekly* put it, 'sordid, but realistic'). The film retains the Tayside setting but was shot in Denham Studios, and Scotland fades into the background. Most of the accents in the local pub, 'The Winton Arms', are English, and we are spared local 'colour'. The greatest problem with the film is that Newton's Brodie is detestable and played with only this one note (although the *MFB*'s reviewer praised the performance – the film 'is made by Robert Newton's character study'); the viewer has no choice as to where sympathy lies. The drama is rooted more in Victorian patriarchal harshness than in the 1940s; writing from the set, *Kinematograph Weekly*'s reporter watched the shooting of a scene in which Brodie expels Mary from the family home, noting 'I should have been glad to quit such a household of ponderous Victorian trappings.'

This was Deborah Kerr's fourth film appearance (it would have been her fifth, but her debut scenes in Michael Powell's

Blackout, 1940, were left on the cutting-room floor), and it is the only film in this book in which the great Glasgow-born actor appears. She had a phenomenal career, most notably in *Black Narcissus* (Michael Powell and Emeric Pressburger, 1947) for which she received one of her six Oscar nominations (eventually she was recognised with an honorary award in 1994), *From Here to Eternity* (Fred Zinnemann, 1953) and *Bonjour Tristesse* (Otto Preminger, 1958).

Nightmare (1942)

Directed by Tim Whelan
Screenplay by Dwight Taylor
Leading cast: Diana Barrymore (Leslie Stafford); Brian Donlevy (Daniel Shane); Gavin Muir (JB Abbington)
B&W, 81 minutes, US

In London, gambler Daniel assists Leslie with the removal of a dead body from her house; the two flee to 'Abbington' in North Scotland, and become instrumental in thwarting a Nazi sabotage ring led by Leslie's cousin.

There is much about *Nightmare* which is reminiscent of **The 39 Steps** (and its remakes): a charming and resourceful foreigner (here, an American) becomes entangled in a complex plot involving a hostile foreign power (in this case very explicitly Nazi Germany) while being hunted by the police, and flees with a strange woman to Scotland. *Nightmare* has been largely lost in the shadow of the earlier (and better) film. When it does attract attention, this is because it was one of only six features to star Diana Barrymore, daughter of Hollywood legend John Barrymore, whose tragic life merits at least a footnote in film history.

Nightmare was released late in 1942, at a time when Hollywood was fully geared up to support the US war effort and its allies. The propaganda is blunt to say the least. The perfidious Abbington, owner of the 'Highland Bell' distillery, is working with the Nazis, and professes admiration for their ideology ('for all their faults the Germans understand the value of biology'). Thankfully, Leslie explains, 'he isn't Scotch; he was adopted... at the age of 12' – from Germany of course, where, according to Daniel, 'they catch them young and train them early'.

The story on which the film was based was written by Philip MacDonald, the London-born grandson of Scottish author George MacDonald. This explains the setting in Scotland, where only the presence of a distillery and some accents denote Scottishness. The script's understanding of UK geography is, to say the least, sketchy, and the film was shot entirely at Universal Studios in California.

The Shipbuilders (1943)

Directed by John Baxter
Screenplay by Gordon Wellesley, Stephen Potter and Reginald Pound
Leading cast: Clive Brook (Leslie Pagan); Morland Graham (Danny Shields); Nell Ballantyne (Mrs Shields)
B&W, 90 minutes, UK

Pagan's Yard, the Clyde, 1931: as a ship is launched, the yard's owner, Leslie Pagan, is concerned that there are no more orders and although the workers express faith in him they are, to his distress, laid off. Time passes: Leslie Pagan is shown struggling to secure orders, Danny Shields, a riveter, is shown bearing up under his vicissitudes. Hitler rises to power, and ships are required again.

Opening with a paeon to British shipbuilders, who riveted the way to the creation of 'the greatest commonwealth of nations the world has ever seen', *The Shipbuilders* is very obviously a product of wartime. The film builds on Greenock-born George Blake's 1935 novel about the fate of Scotland's industrial workers in the depression, expanding the story through to the yard's recovery as rearmament reinvigorated British shipbuilding. Notwithstanding the difficulties faced by Shields, a proxy for all the laid-off workers, a shared struggle is emphasised, and class conflict effaced: Pagan's efforts to reopen the yard are intercut for most of the film with Shields' struggles, and Pagan helps Shields when his son is arrested and tried for a crime he did not commit.

Blake's novel was distinctive in focusing on Scottish industrial workers at a time when, in literature, Scotland was more often constructed as a rural idyll and a place of myth. The film too is unusual for its time in focusing on Scottish industry, although the vision it offers is idealised: Shields maintains his dignity and optimism throughout the long years of unemployment, even when his wife leaves him, and Pagan's concern and support for his workers is virtue personified. He is, as has been pointed out elsewhere, a variation on a paternalistic country squire (Brook directed and appears in *On Approval*). But this sense of a shared enterprise is what the Government wanted from filmmaking in World War II.

While the obvious propaganda – most blatantly on show in montage sequences blending Hitler's ascent with Britain's response, and in wartime developments – firmly anchors the film to its context, it remains 'a fascinating portrayal of working-class life and domestic conflict' (Petrie, in *Screening Scotland*). As Hardy put it in *Scotland on Film*, the 'warmth of Glasgow life found expression even in the dereliction and gang ridden streets'. Given the film was shot entirely in the studio, it convinces surprisingly well as a portrait of the industrial Clyde. *Floodtide* and *On a Clear Day* expand on the theme of Clydeside shipbuilding.

On Approval (1944)   S+ T48

Directed by Clive Brook
Adapted for the screen by Clive Brook
Leading cast: Clive Brook (George, 10th Duke of Bristol); Beatrice Lillie (Maria Wislack); Googie Withers (Helen Hale); Roland Culver (Richard Hulton)
B&W, 80 minutes, UK

1890s London: George, a charming bachelor, is pursued by Helen. His friend Richard courts Maria, who tells him that in Scotland they 'shall spend a month together as married people' – 'on approval'. After a series of farcical events both couples arrive at Maria's house; shenanigans follow. Neither relationship survives: George and Maria marry, as do Richard and Helen.

Time Out quotes director Lindsay Anderson (*This Sporting Life*, 1963; *If...*, 1968) hailing *On Approval* as 'the funniest British comedy ever made'. While this is hyperbole there can be no doubt that *On Approval* is an effervescent comedy of the highest order. Based on a successful stage play, the film is presented – with clever bookending – in two acts. The first takes place in George's London house; the second, and longer, in a baronial-style house on an island (not named as Skye) within rowing distance of the mainland at the Kyle of Lochalsh. English writer/director/lead actor Clive Brook had a successful career spanning over 40 years (including the lead in *The Shipbuilders*), the highlight of which was probably his performance opposite

The US poster for *On Approval* emphasising the film's daring nature

1944 (and would have been unthinkable in the 1890s). The *New York Daily News'* critic, Danton Walker, called *On Approval* 'the most daring comedy of the decade'. But, if you are going to break conventions, Scotland is obviously the place in which to do this. Unless of course, you happened to *be* Scottish – Maria's housekeeper is scandalised when the four turn up but is at first persuaded to stay; when a maid reveals that Helen has a see-through night dress all the serving staff immediately depart.

Although the latter two-thirds of the film are set in Scotland, it was shot in the studio in London. The action is very largely interior-based and constrained to the four leads. We are spared therefore the usual Scottish clichés, but the script does veer at one point into a parody of dialect. It's a minor sin in 'a classic of frivolity' (Dwight Macdonald in *Esquire*).

The Body Snatcher (1945)   T26

Directed by Robert Wise
Screenplay by Philip MacDonald, Carlos Keith (Val Lewton)
Leading cast: Boris Karloff (Cabman John Gray); Bela Lugosi (Joseph); Henry Daniell (Dr Wolfe 'Toddy' MacFarlane); Russell Wade (Donald Fettes); Sharyn Moffett (Georgina Marsh); Rita Corday (Mrs Marsh)
B&W, 78 minutes, US

Edinburgh, 1831. Dr MacFarlane procures corpses from Cabman John Gray, with Fettes, a medical student,

Marlene Dietrich in *Shanghai Express* (Josef von Sternberg, 1932). Frederick Lonsdale, better known as a writer of musical theatre, wrote the play which opened in New York in 1926, later transferring to London. The influence of Oscar Wilde is evident – the play's structure allows it to consist of a barrage of witticisms. The dialogue is continually sharp, and very often hits the target.

The basic set-up, testing a relationship by acting as if married, to determine whether the contemplated marriage would in fact be desirable, was very risqué for

*as the intermediary. Gray acquires the
corpses through murder. He is blackmailed
by Joseph (MacFarlane's servant) and
kills him. MacFarlane confronts Gray
and in turn kills him. During a storm
MacFarlane and Fettes steal a body from a
country churchyard. MacFarlane becomes
convinced it is Gray, loses control of his
carriage and plunges to his death.*

Many sources state that *The Body Snatcher*
is based on the Burke and Hare murders of
1838. It is not, although they are related.
Robert Louis Stevenson's short story, 'The
Body Snatcher', was published in *The
Pall Mall Gazette* in 1884 and referenced
those killings. *The Body Snatcher* picks up
the story when Burke and Hare are 'dead
and buried'. Gray gave testimony at the
trial which exonerated MacFarlane, then
assistant to Dr Knox (who was supplied
by Burke and Hare), and Gray now has
a hold over him. The Burke and Hare
murders have often provided fodder for
film and TV makers. Five films are covered
here; *The Doctor and the Devils*† (Freddie
Francis, 1985) is omitted, being set in an
anonymous English city.

Legendary Hollywood producer Val
Lewton was behind *The Body Snatcher*
and co-wrote the film under one of his
several *nom de plumes*. His influence is all
over it: he was a producer who exercised
very strong creative control. As Alexander
Nemerov puts it, 'Lewton ran the show.
He came up with the story ideas, cast
actors and actresses, and described settings
and costumes, paying finicky attention to
historical accuracy in the case of period

dramas' (*criterion.com*).

This is a studio production, filmed
over less than a month at the RKO Ranch
and studios in Los Angeles. There is an
attempt at historical authenticity, but
minimal cultural authenticity. The first
voice we hear is Wade, with a distinctly
Oklahoman way of pronouncing 'Edin-
burr-ow'. Daniell was a noted English
actor renowned for playing screen villains,
Karloff an English actor who had begun
his career before 1920, and who became
renowned for playing Frankenstein's
monster (*Frankenstein*, James Whale, 1931;
The Bride of Frankenstein, James Whale,
1935; *Son of Frankenstein*, Rowland V
Lee, 1939). As Gray, Karloff is the central
character and is excellent. Lugosi was born
in what was then Hungary, now Romania,
and like Karloff was associated with horror,
although famously his final appearance was
in Ed Wood's *Plan 9 From Outer Space*
(1957), which was distinctly *unhorrific*.
In *The Body Snatcher* he has little to do,
save to explain that he comes from Lisbon
(which explains his curious accent, and
gives Gray a chance to relate to him the
Burke and Hare story) and be killed.

The film really belongs to Lewton and
director Robert Wise, a four-time Oscar
winner making only his third credited
film. Wise and Lewton had previously
worked together on *The Curse of the
Cat People* (Gunther von Fritsch and
Robert Wise, 1944). One of the main
challenges filmmakers faced at the time
was to circumvent the Production Code,
which imposed strict moral and content
standards on American cinema. The

Karloff and Lugosi tenuously brought together to promote *The Body Snatcher*

result of this is that much of the horror in *The Body Snatcher* happens out of sight. Best of all is the exceptionally lit scene in which a street singer is killed. Gray has eyed her up, she walks down the street disappearing into a dark alley, and Gray follows, also passing into dark. Her song continues, then suddenly stops. The Production Code also required that MacFarlane be 'punished', so the audience knew he *was* going to either be arrested or meet a very sticky end. The brilliance in Lewton and Wise is how they pull this off, in a fitting ending to a very strong film.

→ *The Greed of William Hart* (aka *Horror Maniacs*) (1948)

Directed by Oswald Mitchell
Screenplay by John Gilling
Leading cast: Tod Slaughter (Hart); Henry Oscar (Moore); Patrick Addison (Hugh Alston); Anne Trego (Janet Brown); Aubrey Woods (Jamie Wilson)
B&W, 80 minutes, UK

Hart and Moore secure corpses for Doctor Cox from the cemeteries, for which they are paid ten Guineas, although there are rumours 'about the bodies that never reach the cemeteries'. Alston, a ship's doctor, becomes concerned about Mary Paterson, who is killed by Hart and Moore, and investigates. Jamie, a well-liked local lad, is killed. This is Hart and Moore's undoing; they're forced to kill another woman, Mrs Docherty, and the pub locals are worried about Jamie. Alston and a police Sergeant find Jamie's body, and Moore is arrested. Hart agrees to turn King's evidence but is taken by the mob.

Tod Slaughter (tagged 'Mr Murder') has been described as providing 'a bridge between the Victorian blood and thunder melodramas and the gore and flash of Hammer Studios in the early 50s' (Terry Sherwood, *spookyisles.com*). This is certainly a good explanation as to where *The Greed of William Hart* sits; John Gilling, who supplied the screenplay (and later directed *The Flesh and the Fiends* – which to all intents and purposes is a remake of *TGOWH*) later became influential at Hammer.

Reviewed on release, the *MFB* noted that: 'Effective lighting and camerawork do much to build up a suitably grim and gloomy background to the bloodcurdling story, which is worked up to a terrific climax of suspense and horror', but even as late as 1986 the *MFB* was describing *TGOWH* as 'excessively lurid'. But horror film has moved on and has left *TGOWH* behind. It is certainly not as effective as *The Body Snatcher*, nor as entertaining as *The Flesh and the Fiends*.

The most interesting thing about

TGOWH is the way in which Hart and Moore's names are overdubbed. In the original they were named as Burke and Hare, and this is how the film was shot. The British censors reacted strongly to horror films based on British history and required all mentions of Burke and Hare to be removed from the film (the censors had earlier required the removal of a verse recited by Boris Karloff referencing Burke and Hare from *The Body Snatcher*). The cost of doing this was such that the producers could not afford music for the film.

Edinburgh is barely mentioned and is certainly never seen. There is little Scottish, fakery and story-origin aside, about this early entry in the Burke and Hare canon.

→ *The Flesh and the Fiends* (aka *Mania*) (1960) T100

Directed by John Gilling
Screenplay by Leon Griffiths
Leading cast: Peter Cushing (Dr Robert Knox); Donald Pleasence (William Hare); George Rose (William Burke); June Laverick (Martha Knox); Dermot Walsh (Dr Geoffrey Mitchell); John Cairney (Chris Jackson); Billie Whitelaw (Mary Patterson)
B&W, 94 minutes, UK

Edinburgh, 1828: 'resurrectionists' Burke and Hare supply corpses to Dr Knox, who rails against curbs on medical research. Burke and Hare turn to murder but are eventually exposed; Burke is hanged. Dr Knox is exonerated by his peers.

In 1998, Martin Scorsese wrote an article for *Film Comment* with the tantalising title: 'Guilty Pleasures'. As he put it, 'these films are not good. They're guilty. But there are things in them that make you like them, that make them worthwhile.' *The Flesh and the Fiends* is on his list, and it is indeed worthwhile. Best of all is the cinematography by the co-producer Monty Berman, with the strong cast a close second. The cast is led by Cushing, who provides 'his usual polished performance' (*MFB*), with excellent support from Pleasence, Whitelaw, and Walsh. But the film does have its failings. The many scenes set in 'society', or in the anatomy theatre (with Cushing denouncing limitations on medical research), and courtships, lie alongside, but do not fit well with, the milieu inhabited by Burke and Hare, and by Mary.

The Flesh opened in London to a strong box office in February 1960. A racier version was distributed to the continent, which included more risqué, although still mild, erotic scenes (some DVD releases contain both versions). This is the first film, *formally*, to tell the story of Burke and Hare (*The Greed of William Hart* – see above – does tell the story; note that Gilling provided the screenplay for the earlier film). The opening title makes the following claim: 'This is the story of lost men and lost souls. It is a story of vice and murder. We make no apologies to the dead. It is all true.' In broad outline, although not in all details, the film is accurate and, for its time, is effective horror, unusually shot in widescreen format in the French

John Cairney and Billie Whitelaw

anamorphic Dyaliscope (misspelt on the film titles) format.

The producers (Monty Berman and Robert S Baker) had had success the year before with another film based in British true-life crime, *Jack the Ripper*, which they both produced and directed for Mid Century. For *Flesh*, Gilling was brought in as director, and production moved to Triad. There was no location shooting in Scotland, the film being made entirely at the Shepperton Studios. As the *MFB* noted, 'the studio sets fail to capture the grim atmosphere pervading many of Edinburgh's closes even today'.

Critics were less kind to the film on its release than many now are. *S&S* was dismissive: 'Gratuitously gruesome account... tricked out with love interest and a prostitute. Makes one pine for Karloff and

Val Lewton, who did it all years ago, with so much more nicety'. Much more recently, Michael Barrett in *PopMatters* put *Flesh* on a list of 15 'classic horror films that just won't die', describing it as 'a richly grim historical film laced with shudders and witty dialogue.' It's certainly worth revisiting.

→ *Burke and Hare* (1972)

Directed by Vernon Sewell
Screenplay by Ernle Bradford
Leading cast: Darren Nesbitt (Burke); Glynn
  Edwards (Hare); Harry Andrews (Dr Knox);
  Alan Tucker (Arbuthnot); Françoise Pascal
  (Marie); Yutte Stensgaard (Janet)
Colour, 94 minutes, UK

'Gentlemen' are entertained in a brothel. In Hare's lodging house a man dies, and Hare and Burke start selling corpses to Dr Knox, quickly turning to murder. They are brought to justice by the efforts of medical student Arbuthnot, who acts after seeing the body of Marie, a prostitute with whom he was in love, in Dr Knox's lecture.

Comedy trio The Scaffold (Mike McGear, Roger McGough and John Gorman – best known for their hit 'Lily the Pink', 1968) provide the jaunty song 'Burke and Hare', which plays over the opening credits (the first words of which are 'In the land of bonnie Scotland, it's not so bonnie today'). This sets a tone somewhat at odds with the film's subject matter – although the film is, to say the least, inconsistent: this is Burke and Hare, the gratuitous nudity version. In 1968

Yutte Stensgaard (who plays prostitute Janet, and who also starred in Hammer's notorious *Lust for a Vampire*, Jimmy Sangster, 1971) told a Danish newspaper that 'all the British films being made now have nude scenes... If not people won't bother to see them... so sooner or later I'll probably have to jump on the bandwagon'. It's a bandwagon that Burke and Hare embraces. The telling of the Burke and Hare story is competently done, but it is intercut with extended, and largely redundant, brothel scenes where plenty of kink and female nudity, but little horror, are on display. Apart from establishing the relationship between Arbuthnot and Marie, these scenes add only titillation. *The Flesh and the Fiends*, released almost exactly 12 years earlier, lingered in the memory of reviewers of Burke and Hare. In the MFB, David Pirie wrote: 'It's sad to see the talents of Vernon Sewell... being frittered away on a project as incoherent as this one. Unlike [The Flesh and the Fiends], Ernle Bradford's screenplay seems less concerned with Dr Knox's character than with presenting a series of anaemic fetishistic interludes in the local brothel'.

The influence of Hammer and Amicus films hangs heavy over *Burke and Hare*, although director Sewell started his career working on *The Edge of the World*, as skipper of the supply vessel – a very far cry from the lurid *Burke and Hare*. He was a prolific director of 'B' movies, but 'never capitalised fully on either his pictorial skills or his capacity for creating a tightly suspenseful narrative' (S Chibnall and B McFarlane, *The British 'B' Film*). He did, however, thoroughly enjoy filmmaking and his career, and had no desire to graduate to larger studio productions.

Any attempts to recreate 19th-century Edinburgh are at best half-hearted. Some of the cast make no attempts at a local accent; others 'are somewhat on the level of Home Counties amateur dramatics' (Pirie). The film was shot in the studio, although it is clearly positioned in Edinburgh.

→ *Burke & Hare* (2010)   S+

Directed by John Landis
Screenplay by Piers Ashworth, Nick Moorcroft
Leading cast: Simon Pegg (William Burke);
  Andy Serkis (William Hare); Isla Fisher (Ginny
  Hawkins); Tom Wilkinson (Dr Robert Knox)
Colour, 91 minutes, UK

Edinburgh, 1828. Burke and Hare are Irish labourers who realise that there is money to be made in selling cadavers to anatomy professors. They are arrested. Burke confesses and is hanged; Hare goes free.

Told as a dark comedy (which is how *Burke & Hare* was marketed), the story of the two murderers has promise, and the two leads (joined by a plethora of British talent, including Bill Bailey as a hangman narrating the beginning and end of the film, Vincent Price, Stephen Merchant, and Paul Whitehouse) would, on paper, appear perfectly cast. Unfortunately, the film ponderously misfires, and its few laughs are insufficient to compensate for the prevailing dullness. The problem lies not with the casting, but with the script and the

direction. Best of all is Ronnie Corbett as the captain (and later colonel) of the militia, who commands incompetent soldiers, but solves the crime, and 'picks up the best of the laughs' (Philip Kemp in *S&S*). But when a minor character who receives 18th billing in the credits draws all the attention something has gone wrong.

Director John Landis had an extremely successful early career, but *Burke & Hare* was his first feature film for 12 years, and as of 2025 it remains his last. There are sly visual gags, although these tend to be stretched out too long. I laughed at first when, in Greyfriars Churchyard as Burke and Hare attempt to rob a grave, we see a wee dog sitting patiently on the grave of John Gray, but the gag becomes laboured and heavy-handed. This fate befalls many of the best jokes. One cannot help wondering how much better *Burke & Hare* might have been had it been penned by Simon Pegg, who by this point had co-written *Hot Fuzz* (Edgar Wright, 2007) and *Run Fatboy Run* (David Schwimmer, 2007). *Burke & Hare* was neither a critical nor a commercial success. It took under $5m at the global box office, and at the time of writing holds a score of 32 per cent on Rotten Tomatoes.

Although the events of the film take place wholly in Edinburgh, the city was in part, effectively and inventively, recreated in the grounds of Stirling Castle.

The Green Years (1946)

Directed by Victor Saville
Screenplay by Robert Ardrey and Sonya Levien
Leading cast: Charles Coburn (Alexander Gow); Tom Drake (Robert Shannon); Beverly Tyler (Alison Keith); Hume Cronyn (Papa Leckie)
B&W, 127 minutes, US

Orphaned Robert Shannon, brought up Catholic, moves to Scotland where he is raised by his Presbyterian penny-pinching grandparents. He forms a close bond with his great-grandfather who is supportive of a career in medicine.

The Green Years was a prestige production for MGM studios – a long, slow family drama based on the successful formula AJ Cronin had revisited in his 1944 bestseller. Cronin's name featured heavily in publicity and the book was still selling well when the film was promoted. Shot at the MGM studios in California, no effort is spared to flag the Scottish location. There are robust, if variable, attempts at accents and tartan aplenty (a feature in *Picturegoer* archly captions an image of Coburn 'in his more than Scottish Sunday suit').

The film gave rise to a three-year libel case in the London courts, *Turner v Metro-Goldwyn-Mayer Picture Ltd*. Following a negative review of the film by the BBC's E Arnot Robinson, MGM wrote to the BBC, alleging that the critic was 'completely out of touch with the tastes and entertainment requirements of the picture going millions'. She was barred from future press screenings and the BBC was asked to take her off the air. The allegation was repeated elsewhere, and Robinson sued (using her married name of Turner). Robinson's review was not flattering: 'when will Hollywood learn that to make everything larger, louder and lumpier than life is simply to diminish its effect?', but MGM were defensive of their product, and irritated by the approach of British film critics in particular (see Melanie Selfe, '"Intolerable Flippancy"…' (2011)). The case dragged through the courts, with MGM the ultimate 'winners' (although the cost to both sides was considerable). Other critics were more supportive of the film. *Variety*'s reviewer catches the general tone: the performances were strong, the relationship between Alexander and Robert 'well developed', the production 'top drawer'. The only cavil was 'a tendency to overlength which makes for an occasional slowness'.

The strong cast includes Dean Stockwell, in his fourth film, Jessica Tandy and Richard Haydn. Coburn was Oscar-nominated as Best Supporting Actor. Cinematographer George Falsey was also nominated in the black and white category. In America the film was voted the second-best of the year in the annual National Board of Review of Motion Pictures young reviewers' poll.

The Silver Darlings (1947) S++

Directed by Clarence Elder
Screenplay by Clarence Elder
Leading cast: Helen Shingler (Catrine); Murdo
  Morrison (adult Finn); Clifford Evans (Roddie)
B&W, 84 minutes, UK

Caithness, following the Clearances: after her husband, a herring fisher, is pressganged by the Royal Navy, Catrine sets about surviving wtihout him. She forms an attachment with a herring fisher, and her son determines to become one.

Taken chronologically, *The Silver Darlings* is only the second film in this book to carry a S++ rating (ie, it is really quite Scottish): the director and screenwriter were both Scottish (as they are the same person, this is perhaps not noteworthy; however, the novel on which the film was based was written by Neil M Gunn, also a Scot), and the film is set, and exteriors were shot, in Scotland. *Kinematograph Weekly* reported as early as April 1943 that the producers were heading to the north of Scotland in 'a further round-up of authentic Highland crofters and fisher-people'; they ended up shooting in and around Thurso and across the entire north coast. Only one of the leading actors, Morrison, was a Scot, being born on Lewis (where he also died in his 60s); he also appears in *I Know Where I'm Going!*. The production company was the patriotically named Holyrood Films (short lived, this was its only film).

The Silver Darlings should therefore, perhaps, be better known. That it is not must lie partly in the fact that it is, even at a relatively tight 84 minutes, a little ponderous and had limited traction on release. *Variety*'s review was dismissive: 'Romantic drama of Scottish fishermen limited in appeal' (that's the *entire* review). The *MFB* took a different tack however, praising the emphasis on 'an unusual and well-treated subject', and it is this distinction, along with moderate authenticity – shared at the time only with *The Edge of the World* – which merits interest today.

Bonnie Prince Charlie (1948) S+

Directed by David MacDonald
Screenplay by John C Mather and James
  Eastwood
Leading cast: Hugh McDermott (Michael); Hazel
  Court (Ellen); Peter Reynolds (Albert); Joseph
  Tomelty (Professor Hennessy); Adrienne Cori
  (Doris); Patricia Laffan (Nyah)
Colour and B&W, 77/117 minutes, UK

'His Majesty', King James II, dreams of his restitution. BPC is despatched to Scotland to secure this. He fails.

The answer to the question 'What do you get if you film a historical epic, leave out all the action, and put in only the boring bits?' is *Bonnie Prince Charlie*. On release *BPC* was both a critical and commercial flop of epic proportions. In the first of David Niven's two autobiographies, *The Moon's A Balloon* (1971), he writes about *BPC*. It 'was one of those huge florid extravaganzas that reek of disaster from the start.' The film went through the hands of three directors, and Niven sent a cable to legendary studio head Samuel Goldwyn: I HAVE NOW WORKED EVERY DAY FOR FIVE MONTHS ON THIS PICTURE AND NOBODY CAN TELL ME HOW THE STORY ENDS STOP ADVISE

One of the film's marketing taglines reflects the paucity of imagination from all involved: 'The bonniest hero of them all!'. Following previews and early screenings BPC was substantially cut to the now standard version of 98 minutes, with some colour scenes being replaced with black and white for commercial, not artistic, reasons (the version I have watched runs to 117 minutes and is wholly in colour). The film was poor when made and has not aged well. It abounds with Highland clichés and is tedious, although David Niven is extremely convincing at playing David Niven. It opens with classic establishing shots of Highland scenery, closing in on the ever-scenic Eilean Donan Castle (which by 1745 had in fact been substantially destroyed by the British navy). This opening aside, the first 20 minutes are static, full of words and devoid of action: an introduction to history, politics, persons and clans is interminable, and the early Jacobite successes are simply recapped in yet another talking heads scene. This is not, as might be hoped, merely a context-setting prelude. Most of the film takes place indoors or against painted backdrops, featuring people sitting and

David Niven in one of the film's more action-packed moments

talking, standing and talking, or at really exciting moments, walking and talking. Even the battle of Culloden is elided. This is strange; Niven recounts the shooting of action scenes and there was substantial on-location time spent in Scotland.

There are express nods to the film in both *Castle in the Air* and *The Decoy Bride*, testament to the continuing whiff of its ordure. A silent film, *Bonnie Prince Charlie* (Charles Calvert, 1923) featuring Ivor Novello is believed lost. Would that BPC had met the same fate...

Hills of Home (aka Master of Lassie) (1948)

Directed by Fred M Wilcox
Screenplay by William Ludwig
Leading cast: Edmund Gwenn (Dr William MacLure); Donald Crisp (Drumsheugh); Tom Drake (Tammas Milton); Janet Leigh (Marget Mitchell)
Colour, 97 minutes, us

In the glens of California – sorry, Scotland – Lassie accompanies Dr MacLure on his rounds, and is a useful test dummy for medical procedures. MacLure saves the life of young Tammas Milton, who then trains as a doctor. MacLure falls off his horse; Lassie organises a valiant rescue attempt, overcoming her aquaphobia in the process, but MacLure later dies. Milton returns to pick up the local practice.

When *Master of Lassie*, as it was titled in the UK, played in Glasgow in late 1949 the manager of the Mayfair cinema (in Sinclair Drive before being demolished in 1980) awarded a cup to the winner of an essay writing competition for the under-15s, with the title 'If I were Master of Lassie' (*Kinematograph Weekly*, January 1950). The essay – the contents of which are unrecorded – may have been better than the book on which the film was based.

There was a time when works by Ian Maclaren were wildly popular. He is now however disparaged as one of the key representatives of the 'kailyard school'. Maclaren was born John Watson in Essex in 1850, went to Edinburgh University,

became a minister of the Free Church of Scotland before switching allegiance to the Presbyterians, and then moving to the us, where he died in 1907. While not his most popular work, *A Doctor of the Old School* (1895) was successful enough to come to the attention of Hollywood, providing the inspiration for the fourth of the Lassie films.

Hills of Home came early enough in the successful and long-running series for Lassie still to be played by Pal (who also features in the sixth film in the series, *Challenge to Lassie*). There is no doubt we are in Scotland: the opening credits play out on a thistle-bordered tartan before the film moves into a mix of painted backdrop and Californian hills where the small town of 'Drumtochty' is set, amongst 'the riches of the glen'. All that the locals need can be found 'in ourselves, except for two things: the collie dogs of Scotland to tend our flocks, and a doctor to keep us hearty'. Just shoot me now...

'Scottish' accents do the rest of the heavy lifting (that of Drake, a New Yorker, is particularly egregious). *Variety*'s reviewer was however pleased that Lassie was 'not weighted down with the ostentatious makeup of some of the Scottish characters', and found the 'death-bed scene, burial and cemetery visitation are effective enough to please the most jaded'.

Gwenn also appears in *Challenge to Lassie* (as does Donald Crisp). He was born in London, and won a Best Supporting Actor Oscar in 1948, not for *Hills of Home*, but for *Miracle on 34th Street* (George Seaton, 1947).

...because California looks just like Scotland

→ *Lassie* (2005)

Directed by Charles Sturridge
Screenplay by Charles Sturridge
Leading cast: Peter O'Toole (The Duke);
  Samantha Morton (Sarah Carraclough); John
  Lynch (Sam Carraclough); Peter Dinklage
  (Rowlie)
Colour, 100 minutes, US/France/Ireland/UK

*The late 1930s, Yorkshire: in financial
desperation, Lassie's loving family sell her
into a life of misery. After being taken to
Scotland, she escapes and makes her way
home, facing perils and finding kindness
along the way.*

A superb cast (which includes Kelly
Macdonald), stunning landscapes (and
a fleeting glimpse of the Loch Ness
Monster!), bring lustre to a rote, but slick,
Lassie vehicle. The majority of *Lassie*,
which begins and ends in Yorkshire, is set
in Scotland, but filmed in Ireland. The later
film *Challenge to Lassie* is covered below –
it's really a Greyfriars Bobby film.

Macbeth (1948)

Directed by Orson Welles

Screenplay by William Shakespeare (adapted by Orson Welles)

Leading cast: Orson Welles (Macbeth); Jeanette Nolan (Lady Macbeth); Dan O'Herlihy (Macduff); Roddy McDowall (Malcolm); Edgar Barrier (Banquo)

B&W, 107 (89) minutes, US

Orson Welles in his strikingly designed Macbeth

An adaptation of Shakespeare's text in which Macbeth murders his way to becoming King of Scotland. He is defeated by Macduff, and the crown returned to the rightful heir, Malcolm.

The Scottish play has been filmed several times – three versions are covered in this book. The 2021 Coen Brothers adaptation, *The Tragedy of Macbeth†*, is omitted, on the grounds that it is set in a construct, with no attempt to ground it in a 'real' (or even mythical) Scotland; also missing is Akira Kurosawa's *Throne of Blood* (*Kumonosu-jō*) (1957), which transposes the story to Japan. Orson Welles' version of *Macbeth*, which was only the fourth Shakespeare play to be adapted in Hollywood in the sound era, had a troubled history. It was originally completed as a 107-minute version, but Welles was forced to recut and redub the film, taking it down to a more acceptable 89 minutes stripped of the more robust attempts at Scottish accents. The restored full-length version is widely available and is the one I watched.

Welles had originally wanted to make

Othello (which he was able to do three years later), and struggled to raise the funding for *Macbeth*, which was shot on a limited budget, on second-hand sets, and which was compared very unfavourably to Laurence Olivier's more respectful (and better) *Hamlet* (1948), which won the Golden Lion at the Venice Film Festival. Ahead of a planned screening of *Macbeth* at Venice, Welles fell out with the Italian media. At a press conference he had been dismissive of neo-realism, and he kept digging (see Simon Callow, *Orson Welles: One Band Man*, 2015). He decided simply to withdraw his film from the festival, being convinced that it would find no favour, and that all the attention would go to the Olivier film. Welles, who is not credited with the screenplay for *Macbeth*, made significant editorial changes to the Shakespeare original (and is recognised as having, at least, 'adapted' the original). These changes were controversial at the time, as too was the approach of shooting significant passages as a soliloquised voice-over, rather than as on-screen dialogue (which may have contributed to the ability to shoot the film in only 23 days).

There is, however, much to admire in the full-length version, notwithstanding variable performances, and it has its advocates. Samm Deighan, in *Diabolique* in 2016, wrote: 'Welles essentially turned *Macbeth* into an expressionist horror film… it is precisely *Macbeth's* cheap artifice that Welles uses to his advantage, creating an eerie backdrop for a tale of witchcraft, murder, rebellion, and damnation.'

If anything, the Welles version is more suited to modern taste than it was on release. It's dark, and the horror of the play is foregrounded. The full-length version is well worth watching.

→ *Macbeth* (1971)   T38

Directed by Roman Polanski
Screenplay by Roman Polanski and Kenneth Tynan
Leading cast: Jon Finch (Macbeth); Francesca Annis (Lady Macbeth); Martin Shaw (Banquo); Terence Bayler (Macduff); Nicholas Selby (Duncan)
Colour, 140 minutes, UK/US

Shakespeare's play, with edits, strong bloody violence, and nudity.

The elephant in the room as regards this, the best of the three productions of Macbeth covered here, is that it was directed by Roman Polanski. In 1977 the then 43-year-old was arrested after having sex with a 13-year-old child; he

pled guilty, spent 42 days in gaol, then fled the US before sentencing – and has remained a fugitive from justice ever since. He cannot come to the UK without fear of extradition (explaining why *Tess*, 1979, was shot in France). He has also made some exceptional films, both before and after 1977 (*Chinatown*, 1974; *The Pianist*, 2002 – for which he won the Oscar as Best Director, although in 2018 he was expelled from the Academy). He also suffered the loss of his pregnant wife, Sharon Tate, when she was murdered by followers of Charles Manson in August 1969 – *Macbeth* was the first film he made after this.

There's been a huge amount written about Polanski's *Macbeth*, including the book, *Macbeth* (Rebekah Owens, 2017). As Agnieszka Rasmus wrote in 2018, *Macbeth* caused controversy from the outset: 'its bloody imagery, pessimism, violence and nudity were often perceived as excessive or at least highly controversial, earning it an 'X' rating' ('What bloody film is this? *Macbeth* for our time'). Added controversy was provided by the fact

Francesca Annis and Jon Finch

that funding flowed from Hugh Hefner's *Playboy* empire, which was attempting to make a break into film production: *Variety* reported in August 1970 that the production would be 'youth slanted'.

Many have drawn parallels between Polanski's interpretation and presentation of *Macbeth*, and his tumultuous personal life. John Coleman, in the *New Statesman*, put the hullabaloo to one side, turning his 'attention instead to… an honourable and intelligent, occasionally inspired reworking of *Macbeth* for the big screen'. In *Positif*, Michael Ciment was disappointed that the claustrophobic horror of Polanski's *Rosemary's Baby* (1968) was missing from *Macbeth*: 'Rosemary's troubled sleep… logically led to Macbeth's nightmare and claustrophobia. But the real horror, despite the outward signs, is not there this time'.

The casting of Jon Finch and Francesca Annis was certainly a pitch for an anti-establishment approach, one 'in sync with the youth-oriented tone of Sixties pop culture' (David Sterritt, in *Cineaste*). One of the issues often discussed in relation to almost *any* version of Shakespeare, is the actors' ability to speak the language; those in this production can. In *Cineaste* in 1998 Polanski said, 'I worked with English actors and almost all actors in England have had theatrical training. At some time in their lives they went on the road and played Shakespeare'.

The location shooting for *Macbeth* took place in Northumberland and Wales, but looks good throughout.

→ *Macbeth* (2015)　　　S+ T49

Directed by Justin Kurzel
Screenplay by Todd Louiso, Jacob Koskoff, Michael Lesslie
Leading cast: Michael Fassbender (Macbeth); Marion Cotillard (Lady Macbeth), Paddy Considine (Banquo), David Thewlis (Duncan), Jack Reynor (Malcolm)
Colour, 113 minutes, UK/France/US

Broadly sticks to Shakespeare, but with some variation.

Kurzel's film plays to contemporary taste better than the Welles or the Polanksi versions (yet I prefer the Polanski). It is very violent, although much of this is stylised (comparisons have been drawn with *300*, Zach Snyder, 2006), and in significant part was shot in Scotland. The film does, of course, have its detractors – people can become extremely puritanical about Shakespeare, and protective of a particular reading of the play. The film makes changes to the text, as anyone who knows the play would immediately pick up: the witches will meet again 'upon the battlefield' (*not*, 'upon the heath'). Some of these are simple editorial choices, but some of the reworking is significant. This is the case in respect of Macbeth himself, 'an embodiment of the psychological damage of warfare under conditions of modern armament' (Ari Mattes, *The Conversation*), damaged when the story begins, not the virtuous man whose moral descent the play tracks.

Macbeth was only the second film from the Australian director, who started

Michael Fassbender in Kurzel's visceral *Macbeth*

his career in theatre set design (late 2024 saw the release of his excellent third film *The Order*). In *The Guardian* he discussed the tribulations of filming in the Highlands in winter: 'It was brutal. But I understood it… you're surrounded by this vast landscape you know isn't yours, so you're always intimidated. You expect to vanish up a mountain or get eaten by the ground. Which is kind of what happened in Scotland.' Fassbender, who had made *The Centurion* five years previously, already had experience of filming in the Highlands. The cast serve Kurzel well, but the real strength of the film lies in its design. It is a film 'of pummelling beauty' (American critic, Kimberly Jones), in which there is a thin line between the real and the unreal – a world of dreams and visions, of mists and blood red skies in which the real stars are Adam Arkapaw's cinematography (winning the American Society of Cinematographers Spotlight Award, in 2016) and the score by the director's brother, Jed (who also scored *The Babadook*, Jennifer Kent, 2014).

The Swordsman (1948)

Directed by Joseph H Lewis
Screenplay by Wilfrid H Pettitt
Leading cast: Larry Parks (Alexander MacArden); Ellen Drew (Barbara Glowan); George Macready (Robert Glowan)
Colour, 80 minutes, us

In the late 17th century, the MacArdens and the Glowans feud. But Romeo and Juliet is repurposed as, once all hurdles are overcome, the two clans are united by young(ish) love.

The Swordsman was made at the time when films signified Scottishness early on, the credits appearing on a tartan background (see also **Hills of Home**), and when, in US productions (the film was made by Columbia), Californian hillsides served as a substitute for Scottish glens. Somewhat oddly, the film looks at first more like a western, as a stagecoach is chased down, and anyone looking for anything more than light-hearted, fast-paced nonsense here would be looking in the wrong place. In the UK's *Picturegoer* some concern was expressed that *The Swordsman* 'bears little resemblance to reality'. But its critic was won over by the 'carefree romp, refreshingly naïve and spectacular'. In response (or perhaps in agreement), a gentleman from Gourock wrote to the journal some months later, also referencing the debate around **Bonnie Prince Charlie**, saying 'we go to the cinema for entertainment. Not to sit worrying about [history]'.

Challenge to Lassie (1949)

Directed by Richard Thorpe
Screenplay by William Ludwig
Leading cast: Lassie (Lassie); Edmund Gwenn (John Trail); Donald Crisp ('Jock' Gray); Alan Webb (James Brown); Geraldine Brooks (Susan Brown); Reginald Owen (Sergeant Davie)
Colour, 76 minutes, US

Edinburgh, 1860: in the High Court, John Trail pleads for Lassie's life, telling the story of her devotion to her deceased master – she sleeps at his grave every night in Greyfriars Churchyard – and the extent to which she has touched lives, including those of local children. The Lord Provost reprieves Lassie, granting her the freedom of the city.

MGM's audacious shoehorning of their star Lassie (played by 'Pal', in the sixth film in the Lassie franchise) into the story of Greyfriars Bobby largely works – if, that is, you can accept that Bobby is called Lassie, is a rough collie (not the Skye terrier of the novel), and that Californian countryside and a Hollywood studio pass muster as Scotland and Edinburgh. A short review in the *MFB* is dismissive of this 'heart-rending canine drama', to which a satisfactory conclusion was essential and therefore predictable. This did not prevent *The Hollywood Reporter* being concerned that younger viewers might find the maudlin tone of the film too much to bear. Lassie, played by Pal, also appears in **Hills of Home**.

Like the two later Greyfriars Bobby films (the first of which also featured Donald Crisp), *Challenge to Lassie* is based on Eleanor Stackhouse Atkinson's 1912 novel. The faithful-to-the-grave Skye terrier is referenced in both **The Body Snatcher** (in which he is perfunctorily bumped off) and **Burke and Hare**.

→ *Greyfriars Bobby: The True Story of a Dog* (1961) S++ T100

Directed by Don Chaffey
Screenplay by Robert Westerby
Leading cast: Donald Crisp (James Brown);
   Laurence Naismith (Mr Traill); Alex Mackenzie
   (Auld Jock); Gordon Jackson (farmer)
Colour, 87 minutes, US

Laurence Naismith and Bobby

'This is the true story of a dog who lived almost a century ago': a Skye terrier follows its master, Auld Jock, when he makes the 20-mile trip to Edinburgh. Jock dies, and Bobby stays with his grave in Greyfriars Churchyard. He is eventually granted the freedom of the city, a story reported by The Scotsman, on 2 May 1867.

This is Disney at its finest, and the best version of the story committed to film. As was noted in *S&S*, 'Chaffey brings a warm-hearted, Victorian gravity to the slender story… which is both endearing and exactly in character'. Chaffey's best-known films are the Ray Harryhausen stop-motion masterpieces *Jason and the Argonauts* (1963) and *One Million Years B.C.* (1966); he also directed another Disney cute-animal film in this book, *The Three Lives of Thomasina*.

Even hard-bitten critics bowed to the emotional power of the film. *Variety*'s review is typical: 'Patiently and brilliantly trained, Bobby wraps up the stellar honours for himself… nevertheless, there are some very effective pieces of thesping, largely by Scottish actors.' While the two leads were not Scottish, there is a wealth of Scottish acting on display in the film, which was shot

in Edinburgh and at Shepperton Studios.

Duncan Macrae plays the angular, somewhat threatening, police officer who is responsible for the case coming to court. He also features in, amongst others, *You're Only Young Twice*, *The Brothers*, *Whisky Galore!*, *Kidnapped* (1959) and *Tunes of Glory*. He was a schoolteacher in Jordanhill (and plays a schoolteacher in *Geordie*) before becoming an actor. Mackenzie was Captain MacTaggart in *The Maggie* and appears in seven more films in this book. Andrew Cruickshank, the kindly Lord Provost, born in Aberdeen in 1907, did a lot of TV work, and was in *Kidnapped* (1959) and *El Cid* (Anthony Mann, 1961).

Whether the story of Greyfriars Bobby as told in the film is true – as the longer title would have us believe – is another matter altogether. The myth certainly has legs, but does not appear, in many particulars, to survive robust analysis. 'Grave dogs' were common in European cemeteries, and Bobby appears to have had a *very* long life.

→ *The Adventures of Greyfriars Bobby* (2005)   `S+`

Directed by John Henderson
Screenplay by John Henderson, Richard
   Matthews and Neville Watchurst
Leading cast: Thomas Lockyer (Constable John
   Gray); Greg Wise (Minister Lee); James Cosmo
   (James Brown); Oliver Golding (Ewan Adams);
   Christopher Lee (the Lord Provost); Ardal
   O'Hanlon (Coconut Tam)
Colour, 104 minutes, UK

Largely sticks to the legend, although not based on the novel. Bobby is a West Highland White Terrier; John Gray a policeman; the local minister crusades for social justice in the face of the terrible living and working conditions of the Old Town.

Where the earlier two films were grounded in rural traditions, this dreary version is located firmly in an industrialised Scotland, where economic injustice is rife. As *The Scotsman* put it, this is 'an important social tract outlining how Auld Reekie finally got – wait for it – new drains!'.

Variety's critic, Derek Elley, preferred Disney's 1961 version (me too): '…in contrast this new version ambles along in a chummy, very British way but lacks warmth and any strong character hooks.' The best thing about the film is the welcome, if brief, appearance from Christopher Lee as the kindly Lord Provost. Ardal O'Hanlon plays a real-life Edinburgh 'worthy', Coconut Tam, who is somehow shoehorned into the film. Bobby is played by a cute, but unnamed, West Highland White Terrier (inevitably some complained about him being the wrong breed). He received a 'special mention' from that year's Palm Dog Awards (presented annually alongside the Cannes Festival, since 2001).

The original treatment for the film was provided by Scottish writer Ross Smith, who detailed his experiences in the industry in *See You at the Premiere: Life at the Arse End of Showbiz* (2021). Interviewed in the *Scottish Express* he explained that *Greyfriars Bobby*, which was shown in just 77 cinemas in the UK, 'never had a chance against your Marvel superheroes, Wallace & Gromit, and others like that'. The film bombed at the box office. There is some location shooting in Edinburgh, but more use is made of Stirling.

Floodtide (1949)   `S++`

Directed by Frederick Wilson
Screenplay by George Blake, Donald B. Wilson,
   Frederick Wilson
Leading cast: Gordon Jackson (David Shields);
   Rona Anderson (Mary Anstruther); John Laurie
   (Joe Drummond); Jack Lambert (Anstruther);
   Elizabeth Sellars (Judy)
B&W, 90 minutes, UK

'The Clyde – cradle of shipbuilding': after leaving his family farm, David's work ethic and virtue see him progress in the shipyard. Having averted a disaster, he is free to marry the shipyard director's daughter.

Ten years before *Floodtide* was made, shipbuilding on the Clyde was the focus of the Gracie Fields vehicle *Shipyard Sally†* (Monty Banks, 1939), set in 1934. Most of that film is set in London, with an extended opening sequence set (but not shot) in Clydebank. The film, buoyed by Fields' vivacity, and some cracking songs, is a joy. The same cannot be said of *Floodtide*, which is 'conventional and often absurd' (*MFB*), and an 'external construction of Scotland and the Scots, produced by London' (David Pirie). It is however of some interest. The film is remarkable for its representation of late 1940s Glasgow, and for its approach to – and assumptions about – class, wealth and power. One of the screenwriters, Blake, was deeply critical of the Kailyard School, and had previously written the novel *The Shipbuilders*, on which the 1943 film of the same name was based (see above). But *Floodtide*, like *The Shipbuilders*, remains deeply conservative, preaching social cohesion and harmony with a quiet fervour; social/class mobility is enabled if the virtuous working class educate themselves and work hard.

It helps that the film was made when the Clyde was in its pomp, and when Britain had recently been on the winning side of the war. As David's uncle Joe says: 'you're working on the Clyde boy, and that's an honour in itself if you had the sense to see it... Take away the Clyde and Britain would be sunk in any war we'd ever have to fight.' David's father, seeking to hold David to the land, is less sanguine – at least about Glasgow, which he describes as 'a Sodom and Gomorrah'. Take away the political and social interest (*more* interesting now than on release) that flows from this period piece and there is not much left. The drama, or perhaps melodrama, really *is* absurd. This is particularly true of the love story, although in real life, Jackson and Anderson married after the film was completed, staying together until Jackson died in 1990.

Gordon Jackson is reliable in the lead role, while required to do little beyond be earnest. Born in Glasgow in 1923, he first appeared on film in 1942. *Floodtide* provided his first lead role, although fame came later with **Whisky Galore!**. Jackson's last appearance was in a TV play broadcast posthumously in 1991. He features in 13 films covered in this book, including **The Prime of Miss Jean Brodie**, which also featured Anderson. He is supported by several Scottish actors in *Floodtide*, including John Laurie (also in **The 39 Steps, The Edge of the World, Madeleine** and **The Brothers**), who despite his many roles in good films will always be better known as Pte. Frazer in *Dad's Army* (1968–1977).

The Secret of St Ives (1949)

Directed by Phil Rosen
Screenplay by Eric Taylor
Leading cast: Richard Ney (Anatole de Keroual);
  Vanessa Brown (Floria Gilchrist); Henry Daniell
  (Maj Edward Chevenish)
B&W, 75 minutes, US

1813, Edinburgh Castle: French troops captured in the Napoleonic wars are imprisoned. Anatole, Viscount of St Ives, is among them. Maj Chevenish, Commander of the Castle, and Anatole both love Floria, who regularly visits Anatole. The love triangle, an escape, a contested inheritance, a duplicitous lawyer and Maj Chevenish's skullduggery give rise to plot twists and a predictable conclusion.

One of many films in this book to be based on the works of Robert Louis Stevenson (in this case, loosely, on his unfinished novel *St Ives*, later completed by Arthur Quiller-Couch), *St Ives* belies its title – St Ives not being the town in Cornwall, but a French aristocrat, imprisoned in the 'impregnable castle that towers high on a cliff overlooking the countryside'. We don't see much of the countryside in this B feature, as the film is set largely, and ploddingly, in interiors, permitting Columbia Pictures and journeyman director Rosen (making his last film in a career which began in the silent era) to make the film cheaply, and avoid the infliction of an overly fake version of Scotland on the audience (we do *not* avoid the imposition of hilariously

bad fake-French accents from the prisoners, which give anything in TV's *'Allo 'Allo!* a run for its money). The cost-cutting is evident and was noted in contemporary reviews.

St Ives has left few ripples on the fabric of cinema history. It is rarely shown and hard to locate. Copies *can*, with effort, be obtained, but doing so may not be worth it. The script is long on dialogue and short on action: as *Variety* put it, 'some derring-do action… would have made it more passable'. Most of the film is set in Scotland, although some later scenes are London-based; the shoot barely left the Columbia lot in Hollywood.

Whisky Galore! (aka *Tight Little Island*) (1949)   S+++ T35

Directed by Alexander Mackendrick
Screenplay by Angus MacPhail and Compton
  Mackenzie
Leading cast: Basil Radford (Captain Paul
  Waggett); Catherine Lacey (Mrs Waggett);
  Bruce Seton (Sergeant Odd); Gordon Jackson
  (George Campbell); Gabrielle Blunt (Catriona
  Macroon); James Robertson Justice (Dr
  Maclaren); Joan Greenwood (Peggy Macroon);
  Wylie Watson (Joseph Macroon)
B&W, 82 minutes, UK

On the island of 'Todday', in the Outer Hebrides, the locals combine to frustrate and humiliate Waggett, who is determined to track down a cargo of whisky which has been rescued from a shipwreck.

Original *Whisky Galore!* poster

Based on Compton Mackenzie's novel of 1947 (the author plays a small role in the film) and adapted in part by him, *Whisky Galore!* was unusual for its time in being filmed entirely on location on Barra. CA Lejeune, in *The Observer*, wrote that Barra was 'so much an integral part of the texture of the film that you can almost taste the salt and feel the crunch of the sand and the spring of the turf'. This, plus the large, engaging cast and strong writing, have ensured the film's enduring popularity.

The short review published in the *MFB* on the film's release remains a good place to start: *Whisky Galore!* 'has been produced and directed with a refreshing sense of comedy and an understanding of Anglo-Scots relationships. The central joke may soon be tired of, but the situations it illuminates have a variety of their own, and a talented cast sees to it that no island character study shall go unnoticed'. What that review does not comment on is the deliciously cruel treatment of Waggett, which underpins the film's humour.

While *Whisky Galore!* may appear superficially light and frothy, Charles Barr, the leading chronicler of Ealing's output, has recognised that '*Whisky Galore!*, like its characters, is cruel and clever'; Todday 'does not represent an indulgent fantasy of escape from modern pressures... it is a community in whose capacity for survival we can believe [embodying] an ancestral Celtic shrewdness and toughness, from which we should learn' (*Ealing Studios*, 1993). The best comedy is very often cruel, and Ealing had turned the recognition of this into something of an art form in another great film from 1949, *Kind Hearts and Coronets* (Robert Hamer).

In 1951 Michael Balcon, the producer who led Ealing Studios, was asked to sum up the state of play in British cinema for *S&S*. He wrote, in part: 'A newcomer to feature direction is Sandy MacKendrick. His first venture in this field was *Whisky Galore* – one of a series of comedies in which some erudite periodical found "nothing to laugh at", although fortunately for us, the public in this country, in France [nb – in France the film was released under the charming title, *Whisky A Gogo*] and in the United

States had the crassness to disagree with this judgment'. In the US the film performed well in the arthouse market. In the UK it has become much loved (and, disappointingly, remade).

→ *Rockets Galore* (aka *Mad Little Island*) (1958) S+++

Directed by Michael Relph
Screenplay by Monja Danischewsky
Leading cast: Jeannie Carson (Janet Macleod);
   Donald Sinden (Hugh Mander); Ian Hunter
   (Air Commodore Watchorn); Roland Culver
   (Capt. Waggett)
Colour, 94 minutes, UK

Todday's islanders are again triumphant, this time in frustrating the building of a rocket site.

Rockets is a sequel of sorts to *Whisky Galore!* The novel was written by Compton Mackenzie ten years after *Whisky Galore*, incorporating many of the same characters. But appearances and personnel aside, *Rockets* is not an Ealing Studios film, being made after Ealing shut down, and is not nearly as good as its predecessor (Charles Barr calls it a 'feeble reincarnation'). *Rockets* tries to be two things at once and is not wholly successful at either: one, a gentle story of London/England/officialdom being outwitted by Todday/Scotland/community; the other a critique of the Cold War arms race.

Until the appearance/creation of a rare bird, however, all the islanders' attempts to frustrate the development of the rocket base have come to nought, with the result that what we really have is a series of vignettes of island charm – often involving whisky and 'Celtic' music; and acts of petty sabotage playing out as short sketches, none of which pack a punch or are particularly funny. The one genuinely funny sequence comes in the final ten minutes in which TV news, current affairs programmes (featuring commentators such as historian AJP Taylor), and newspaper headlines report on the significance of the rare bird. Headlines include the *Daily Sketch*: 'It's Ours! Britain has pink gull before Russia'. Here we have a touch of *Dr Strangelove or: How I Learned to Stop Worrying and Love the Bomb* (Stanley Kubrick, 1964); like *Strangelove*, *Rockets* also features a German rocket scientist – although Kubrick and Peter Sellers push the insanity and satire much further. There are also some similarities with *Local Hero*, but the latter is a far, far better film than *Rockets Galore*.

→ *Whisky Galore* (2016) S+++

Directed by Gillies MacKinnon
Screenplay by Peter McDougall
Leading cast: Kevin Guthrie (George Campbell);
   James Cosmo (MacAlister); Eddie Izzard (Capt.
   Waggett); Naomi Battrick (Peggy Macroon);
   Ellie Kendrick (Catriona Macroon)
Colour, 98 minutes, UK

Story is as for the original.

A dull remake of a better original.

Madeleine (1950)

Directed by David Lean
Screenplay by Stanley Haynes, Nicholas Phipps
Leading cast: Ann Todd (Madeleine Smith);
    Norman Wooland (William Minnoch); Ivan
    Desny (Émile L'Angelier)
B&W, 101 minutes, UK

7 Blythswood Square, Glasgow, the 1850s. Madeleine, the daughter of a prosperous family, murders Émile, with whom she had an affair, when he blackmails her with letters she wrote. She is tried for murder; the case becomes a public sensation.

The distributors were not sure how to position the film

The opening lines of *Madeleine*, spoken in the present day (1950), are these: 'In this great city of Glasgow there is a square, Blythswood Square... there is one house in this square which is exceptional, for it has an interest which time can never change. Number 7, which still remains, was the home of Madeleine Smith...' The camera pans over the square, up to no 7, which still stands today. The rest of the film, establishing shot aside, was made at Buckinghamshire's Pinewood Studio.

In 1857 Madeleine Smith was tried for murder, having been accused of poisoning her ex-lover, Émile, when he blackmailed her following the end of their affair. The jury returned the verdict, distinctive to Scotland, of 'not proven'. This explains the most used tag line on the various posters: 'Can you decide what no jury ever could?' Variations on this question were used in an extensive marketing campaign for the film in the UK.

Madeleine was made at the urging of Ann Todd (whose father was Scottish), who had married Lean in 1949 and had performed the role of Madeleine on stage. Even before the film's release in the UK (in February 1950), Lean told the *Daily Express* that he did not like *Madeleine*: making it was a 'miserable' experience. The critical reception was, at best, lukewarm. The film speaks more to Victorian morality than to anything distinctly Scottish. In *David Lean* (2014), Melanie Williams argues that this is the lens through which the film should be read. She quotes the pressbook published to accompany the film, which stated that

Madeleine was 'born out of her time... Her letters to her lover would have been outstanding today. In the muffled age in which she lived, they were a sensation'. Unfortunately, Lean was not heavily invested in telling this sensational story. From the director who had earlier given us *Brief Encounter* (1945) and *Great Expectations* (1948), and who was later to make one of the best British films of all time, *Lawrence of Arabia* (1962), *Madeleine* is for the most part lacklustre.

The Gorbals Story (1950) S+

Directed by David MacKane
Screenplay by David MacKane
Leading cast: Russell Hunter (Johnnie Martin);
   Roddy McMillan (Hector); Betty Henderson
   (Peggie); Isobell Campbell (Nora Reilly);
   Howard Connell (Willie Mutrie)
B&W, 74 minutes, UK

Artist Johnnie Martin remembers Glasgow, where he was born and was a 'poor newspaper boy'. In flashback, the film depicts a short period in his life as a young man living with Hector and Peggie in their tenement in the Gorbals. At the film's end he asks: 'all those other youths who still remain, how long will they endure environments like that? How long will these things remain painted in drab and dirty colours, sullying the canvas of our social conscience?'

The Gorbals Story is based on Robert McLeish's 1946 play, which had a remarkable impact when first performed by the left-wing Glasgow Unity Theatre, notwithstanding that, according to *The Scotsman* a few weeks into the first run, 'it was not a good play, and had many faults'. However, it 'dealt with the topical problem of housing, which everybody felt'; the paper reported that 60–70 per cent of the audience had never seen a straight play before. Many of the original Unity cast transferred to the film production. *The Scotsman*'s London critic (who liked the play) was disappointed in the film: 'Never could one grasp the sordid slum atmosphere which pervaded the play; never could one escape from the feeling that the Unity Players were scared of the camera.' The result now is that if *The Gorbals Story* is of interest it is as a cultural artefact or historical document; it is *not* riveting cinema – in fact, it is dull. The *MFB* provided only short comment at the time of the film's release. This might have been just as well. Its entry in full is: 'Life in the tenements of a Glasgow slum. The naïvely written story (adapted from a play) is presented in theatrical rather than cinematic style, generally amateurish but with some accomplishment here and there. One respects its aims'. *Picturegoer*'s reviewer had very similar complaints, also referring to the film as 'amateurish', and lauding the good intentions: 'It could have been a tremendously moving human essay, but it rarely rises above an emotional staginess'.

It is possible, although not certain, that *The Gorbals Story* did not receive its first screening *in* the Gorbals until 2015, when it was screened as part of the Southside Film Festival (see *The Guardian*, 'The

Gorbals Story – landmark film finally premieres in the Gorbals', October 2015). There is an extensive discussion of the film by John Hill in Chapter 7 of *Scotch Reels*.

The film was shot in the Merton Park Studios, in London, with minimal establishing shots of Glasgow.

Flesh and Blood (1951)

Directed by Anthony Kimmins
Screenplay by Anatole de Grunwald
Leading cast: André Morell (Dr Marshall); Richard Todd (Charles Cameron/Cameron Sutherland); Ursula Howells (Harriet Marshall); Joan Greenwood (Wilhelmina Cameron); Glynis Johns (Katherine)
B&W, 102 minutes, UK

Glasgow, the 1860s: Charles Cameron, a genius and philanderer, dies of TB. Harriet, his mistress, later gives birth to Wilhelmina. She grows into a beautiful but wilful young woman, is accused of murder, has a child, and dies by suicide. Her son, Cameron, is dissolute as a youth, but qualifies as a doctor, distinguishes himself in World War I, is saved by the love of a good woman, Katherine, and defeats a serious epidemic.

Flesh and Blood was directed by Kimmins immediately after **Bonnie Prince Charlie** (later he directed **The Amorous Mr. Prawn**). He was not required to be in Scotland for *Flesh and Blood*, which was shot in the Teddington studios in Middlesex. Apart from being set in Scotland and in small part in Italy, *Flesh and Blood* and **Bonnie Prince Charlie** have something else in common: they are both tediously messy (**The Amorous Mr. Prawn** is by far the best of the three films). *Flesh and Blood* was based on *A Sleeping Clergyman* (1933) by the Scottish playwright and doctor James Bridie (see also **Storm in a Teacup** and **You're Only Young Twice**), who co-founded the Citizens Theatre in Glasgow, and who worked on three films with Alfred Hitchcock.

The play, set between the 1860s and the 1930s, examined the nature of hereditary evil, with two generations – Charles and daughter Wilhelmina – both breaking from conventional morality. The question was whether the lineage could be redeemed by virtue in the third generation. In the film, this gives rise to plenty of melodrama and a relatively high death count. It also gives rise to abrupt shifts between the three periods, and rushed storytelling as far too much is packed in. The *MFB*'s reviewer noted that 'the first two episodes... are dealt with in a somewhat perfunctory manner. Characters are killed off before they have time to develop, theatrically melodramatic scenes follow one another rapidly.' A consequence of this is that none of the characters are rounded. Todd was praised in *The Hollywood Reporter* for his 'moving and sincere performance in a dual role', but even he is unable to develop either of these fully. Todd can also be seen in **Rob Roy: The Highland Rogue**; the first eight minutes of *A Man Called Peter*† (Henry Koster, 1955), 'the story

93

of a man and his close relationship with God', are also set in Scotland, but the rest of the film is not. *Flesh and Blood*'s strong cast includes George Cole (also in **Cottage to Let** and **The Bridal Path**), Michael Hordern and Patrick Macnee.

Happy Go Lovely (1951)

Directed by Bruce Humberstone
Screenplay by Val Guest
Leading cast: David Niven (BG Bruno); Vera-Ellen (Janet Jones); Cesar Romero (John Frost)
Colour, 97 minutes, UK

At the Edinburgh International Festival a desperate producer mistakes a chorus girl for the girlfriend of a Scottish multi-millionaire (and potential backer). She is promoted to the lead role; many misunderstandings, dancing, and the inevitable romance follow.

One might have thought that David Niven would be reluctant to return to Scottish subject matter after the disaster that was **Bonnie Prince Charlie**. But the aspirations of the musical/rom-com *Happy Go Lovely* were less ambitious, and the shoot did not require the cast to leave the Elstree studios in Hertfordshire (some establishing shots of Edinburgh are used). Niven plays 'the richest man in Scotland'; Gordon Jackson and John Laurie both appear. Vera-Ellen (who is the star of **Let's Be Happy**) was a sensational dancer, who had worked on Broadway and appeared on film alongside, amongst others, Danny Kaye, Gene Kelly

and Fred Astaire. The result is inoffensive inconsequential nonsense. As Alan Warwick put it in *Picturegoer*, the plot is 'a bit thin', there are 'several cinematic clichés, but *Happy Go Lovely* remains entertaining. The Scottish and Festival settings are of very limited significance.

The Man from Planet X (1951)

Directed by Edgar G Ulmer
Screenplay by Aubrey Wisberg and Jack Pollexfen
Leading cast: Robert Clarke (John Lawrence); Raymond Bond (Prof. Elliot); Margaret Field (Enid Elliot); William Schallert (Dr Mears)
B&W, 71 minutes, US

As Planet X moves swiftly towards Earth, an emissary lands on the Scottish island of 'Burry', near the home of Professor Eilliot and his daughter, Enid, while John, an American newspaperman, investigates.

There is very little Scottish about *The Man from Planet X* save for an artificially rendered low-budget attempt to represent Scottish moors, and some accents adopted by supporting characters. Enid even makes the dreaded mistake of correcting John's use of the American 'drugstore' by saying, 'it's "chemist" in England'. The script tells us that we are in Scotland because the island of 'Burry', where all but the opening sequence is set, is the closest place on Earth to Planet X's route, but any remote spot would have done the job just as well.

Made on a shoestring budget reported to

Margaret Field encounters a UFO in the Highlands

be less than $50,000 (with the consequence that the effects can barely be called 'special'), and shot on a tight schedule, *The Man from Planet X* is nevertheless beloved of hardcore sci-fi fans. Ulmer's direction is effectively tight (*Box Office* wrote that 'the offering opens wide the throttle in trying for fantasy, hokum and chills'). *The Man from Planet X* beat classics such as *The Day the Earth Stood Still* (Robert Wise, 1951) and *The Thing from Another Planet* (Christian Nyby, 1951) to the punch in dealing with alien invasion.

This does not have the gloriously camp quality of the later ***Devil Girl from Mars*** but there is sufficient silliness to satisfy, and for genre fans with Scottish inclinations would make a good double bill with the domestically produced ***X the Unknown***. Even critics at the time, often dismissive of genre productions, found some merit in the film: the *MFB* praised it as 'considerably more entertaining than the previous heavy-handed semi-serious interplanetary productions… the action is fast and the dialogue has been limited to a near-minimum'. Margaret Field, who has little to do, was 28 when the film was shot.

At the time she was mother to the four-year old Sally who would go on to win the Best Actress Oscars for both *Norma Rae* (Martin Ritt, 1979) and *Places in the Heart* (Robert Benton, 1984).

The Brave Don't Cry (1952) S++

Directed by Philip Leacock
Screenplay by Montagu Slater
Leading cast: John Gregson (John Cameron);
  Meg Buchanan (Margaret Wishart); Andrew
  Keir (Charlie Ross); Fulton Mackay (Dan
  Wishart); John Rae (Donald)
B&W, 89 minutes, UK

New Cumnock, Ayrshire, 1950: a cave-in at a coal mine leads to disaster, and intense rescue efforts.

The Knockshinnoch Castle Colliery disaster of September 1950 was at the time widely covered in both domestic and international media. Rescuers worked three days to bring out 118 trapped miners (sources differ as to this number, but the normally reliable British Pathé historical collection site references 118 – original newsreels are readily available to stream); 13 could not be reached and died (a part of the story somewhat glossed over in the film). There is today a memorial at the site. *The Brave Don't Cry* is one of the films, possibly the best, produced by the Government-backed 'Group 3' initiative, an 'underfunded and fudged attempt by the ailing Labour administration to breathe new life into the British film industry' (Simon Popple, 'Group

Three: A lesson in state intervention?', 1996). Group 3 was also responsible for *You're Only Young Twice* and *Laxdale Hall.* The membership of Group 3's board included Sir Michael Balcon and John Grierson, sometimes dubbed 'the father of documentary'. He is credited as executive producer on *The Brave*, and Popple wrote that it 'was Grierson's favourite film'. The film is realist in tone, verging on documentary. Indeed, Duncan Petrie has suggested that the film 'itself can be regarded as a rare exercise in British neo-realism' (*Screening Scotland*, 2000). There is little to distinguish Pathé news clips of those waiting outside the colliery from footage in the film. This was the first drama film for director Leacock, who had previously worked on documentaries.

What is most remarkable about the production was its use of a large group of actors who had no prior training in film, being taken from the ranks of Glasgow's Citizens Theatre. To acclaim, the film opened the 1952 EIFF. Unfortunately, industry politics were such that it received only a limited UK release. Petrie wrote that 'it proved to be one of Group 3's rare critical and commercial successes'. The film was not in fact a commercial success, but it did attract a positive critical response. The *MFB*'s reviewer wrote: 'in its semi-documentary, semi-impersonal way *The Brave Don't Cry* is an estimable achievement... sketching its characters with directness and a refreshing absence of mannerisms... In its genre, though, the film stands quite high, and it gains greatly from the use of unfamiliar players.'

Margaret Rutherford, Barbara Kelly and David Tomlinson

Castle in the Air (1952)

Directed by Henry Cass
Screenplay by Edward Dryhurst and Alan
Melville
Leading cast: David Tomlinson (Earl of
Locharne); Helen Cherry (Boss Trent); Barbara
Kelly (Mrs Coldfelter Dunne); Brian Oulton
(Arthur Phillips)
B&W, 89 minutes, UK

*An impoverished Scottish Earl plots to sell his
decrepit haunted castle to the highest bidder.*

Castle in the Air treads very similar
ground to **The Ghost Goes West**, both
dealing with the sale of a run-down
haunted castle by a Scottish nobleman to
an American. The earlier film, however,
has more wit and sparkle than *Castle*,
which all too readily betrays its origin
in Alan Melville's play. Here the joke
is not on the American heiress, who
knows exactly what she is getting, and
whose purchase of the castle for £90,000
liberates the Earl and permits him to
propose marriage to his estate manager,
Boss. Instead, the joke is on Philips, a
socialist civil servant working for the Coal
Board, which permits plenty of digs at the
Government of the day and bureaucracy.
Layered into this is an irrelevant turn
from Margaret Rutherford playing (as
she often did) a dotty old lady, this time
obsessed with genealogical nonsense. She
labours under a mistaken belief that the
Earl may be the rightful King of Scotland,
permitting plenty of twaddle about the
'45, and the local Jacobite society, all of
which ultimately amounts to nothing.
Tomlinson was 12 years into his 40-
year career, and would go on to greater

things, most notably playing Mr Banks in *Mary Poppins* (Robert Stevenson, 1964). Gordon Jackson appears as one of a group of visitors being shown around the castle. He has nothing to say. The film was shot in the Elstree studio.

You're Only Young Twice (1952)
S++ T100

Directed by Terry Bishop
Screenplay by Lindsay Galloway and Reginald Beckwith
Leading cast: Duncan Macrae (Prof. Hayman); Edward Lexy (Lord Carshennie); Diane Hart (Ada Shore); Joseph Tomelty (Dan McEntee); Robert Urquhart (Sheltie); Charles Hawtrey (Adolphus Hayman)
B&W, 81 minutes, UK

Ada arrives at the 'University of Skerry-vore' and is taken for the Principal's new secretary, although she is in fact niece to the porter. He in turn arrived years ago to be appointed as Professor of Gaelic Literature, but was mistakenly given the better-paid porter role.

When *You're Only Young Twice* was made there were but four universities ('the Ancients') in Scotland, but the film, which was shot largely at Glasgow University, added a fifth. It is doubtful whether any of the Ancients would have been flattered by the film's gently chaotic satirising of the peculiarities of academic life. Based on a play by Glaswegian-born James Bridie (also responsible for *Storm in a Teacup*),

YOYT is an insubstantial but amusing enough comedy, although it pushes the bounds of credibility, particularly when McEntee (Tomelty – as well known as a playwright and novelist as a character actor), the porter, is revealed to be not only a former General in the Irish Republican movement, but a holder of PhDs from Oxford and Harvard, and a Nobel Laureate, leading *Picturegoer*'s reviewer to conclude 'it is all so incredibly farcical that it fails to register'.

YOYT was a Group 3 production (see also *The Brave Don't Cry*) which, although supported by the British Government, was financially weak and therefore focused on 'films made on a very modest budget' (Michael Balcon, in *Variety*), but quickly established a track record in promoting new talent. Despised by the UK's commercial distributors, their films struggled to find audiences. *YOYT* gave Ronnie Corbett (see also *Rockets Galore* and *Burke & Hare*) his first on-screen appearance.

Laxdale Hall (aka Scotch on the Rocks) (1953) S+ T100

Directed by John Eldridge
Screenplay by Alfred Shaughnessy and John
  Eldridge
Leading cast: Ronald Squire (General Matheson);
  Kathleen Ryan (Catriona Matheson); Raymond
  Huntley (Samuel Pettigrew MP); Sebastian Shaw
  (Hugh Marvell MP); Fulton Mackay (Andrew
  Flett)
B&W, 77 minutes, UK

A Whitehall delegation, led by Pettigrew, an industrialist and MP, travels to Laxdale, a remote village in the Highlands to evaluate whether, in light of local protests and refusals to pay road tax, a new road and pier should be built. The villagers also battle Glaswegian salmon poachers. All is satisfactorily resolved.

Laxdale Hall, which shares an origin with Welsh author Eric Linklater's 1951 novel of the same name (the novel was developed first as a film treatment), is one of the delights among the earlier films covered in this book. The film is similar in spirit to **Whisky Galore!** (1949) and **Rockets Galore** (indeed, it was first intended that it be an Ealing film), but is more generous in its tone, and a little more subtle in its treatment of the difference between the remote Scottish community and London. This was not, however, the view of the reviewer in the *MFB*, who wrote that 'the film makes an indifferent, rather amateurish-looking, addition to [an overworked] screen genre'. *Kinematograph Weekly* was more generous

– 'satire... highlights the homely, heather-carpeted shenanigans', as was *Picturegoer Weekly* – 'Beautiful scenery and heart-warming comedy'.

The conflict in *Laxdale Hall*, which is gently and smoothly resolved, is not so much one between Scotland and London, as it is between modernity and tradition. After railing about the lack of amenity in Laxdale, Pettigrew is told by a local 'no doubt the 20th century could learn a thing or two from Laxdale'. At a public meeting (which mirrors that in **Rockets Galore**) Pettigrew is bemused that the locals are not attracted by his offer of life in a new factory town and blunt in his appraisal of the community's value: 'In your present mode of life you're not an asset to Great Britain. You're a liability'. The reasons behind his conversion remain a little opaque, although whisky is certainly involved. Of his two colleagues, one is likely to return to Laxdale (drawn by love); the other has suggested that the daughter of the General (and local laird) leading the protests joins him in London, although this appears unlikely to happen.

Like **The Brave Don't Cry** (in which Fulton Mackay also appears), *Laxdale Hall* was a Group 3 production, with John Grierson acting as executive producer. The commercial cinema industry, which had a near stranglehold on UK distribution, was hostile to the State-sponsored Group 3, and although *Laxdale Hall* did very well commercially in Scotland, it failed to secure any traction with English distributors. In early 2012 a pristine print, held by a private collector, was unearthed.

Prior to that the only copies available were badly damaged. This in turn led to a DVD release and to significant media coverage, given that *Laxdale Hall* provided Rikki Fulton with his first on-screen appearance (as 'First Poacher'; it's a minor role, although he is instantly recognisable). In his autobiography, he wrote about his £20 salary for the film and the daily commute by bus up to Applecross, where the location shooting took place. The Bealach na Ba pass features in the film, in a considerably worse state than it is today. The film also gave Prunella Scales, as the young schoolteacher, her first role in a feature.

For reasons beyond understanding – as the film is clear as to geography (there's even a map pointed at during the delegation's first briefing) – it has entered the lore that Laxdale is on a Hebridean Island. This error has been repeated in a great many sources. Laxdale is, very clearly, on a peninsula on the mainland, opposite Skye.

The Master of Ballantrae (1953) S+

Directed by William Keighley
Screenplay by Herb Meadow
Leading cast: Errol Flynn (Jamie Durie); Anthony Steel (Henry Durie); Roger Livesey (Col. Francis Burke); Beatrice Campbell (Lady Alison)
B&W, 90 minutes, UK/US

1745: Scotland. Jamie Durie, the Master of Ballantrae, supports Bonnie Prince Charlie while his brother, Henry, remains loyal to King George, in an arrangement designed to secure the family fortunes. Jamie becomes a fugitive after defeat at Culloden, and falls in with Irishman, Colonel Burke. They flee Scotland, become pirates, and return to Ballantrae with riches. They are captured, and sentenced to death, but engineer an escape with the help of Lady Alison, with whom Jamie is in love. The three ride off together.

Like **Kidnapped** (multiple versions) and **The Body Snatcher**, The Master of Ballantrae is based on a work by Robert Louis Stevenson (*The Master of Ballantrae: A Winter's Tale*, published in 1889). But this film is at least as far removed from the novel as is **Schüsse unterm Galgen** from *Kidnapped*, although it is not as funny in its deviations. It does, however, have the strong benefit of a lead actor, Errol Flynn, who was one of the true greats of the Hollywood golden age, even though by the time *Ballantrae* was made he was, as David Thomson writes, 'going out of fashion'. *Ballantrae* is not nearly as 'lamentable' as Thomson would have us believe. Reg Whitley, in the *Daily Mirror* praised Flynn's 'smashing performance... in his element in a fighting role'. The film moves at pace, covering the Jacobite rebellion, smuggling, piracy, a final capture and escape, and multiple romances, in a very brisk 90 minutes. For *The NYT* the film had 'plenty of good old-fashioned muscularity crowding a highly pictorial Technicolor frame' and 'at least three-fourths of [*Ballantrae*] makes a rousing, spectacular outlet for a pair of estimable adventurers'. Donald Hunt,

Although ageing, Errol Flynn still had the charisma to carry this film

in a double-page spread in *Picturegoer* described Flynn as 'still at the top of the line'.

There was some shooting in Scotland, and much use of tropes which were already clichés by 1953: Eilean Donan is Ballantrae castle, Highland cattle play a part, and there are the obligatory bagpipes and Highland dancing (or something roughly like it). The good news here is that there is little attempt at Scottish accents; there is none from Flynn, and Livesey (also in *I Know Where I'm Going*) slips in and out of an approximation of Irish brogue. Clearly however, there was some attempt at veracity. *The Hollywood Reporter* noted that in the shooting of *Ballantrae*, the closest Flynn came 'to a flare up... was when Errol wanted to wear a kilt for close-ups of his riding into battle. He liked himself in a kilt, and it took considerable persuasion to reconcile him to the fact that the Scots did not ride to war like that'.

The Maze (1953)

Directed by William Cameron Menzies
Screenplay by Daniel B Ulman
Leading cast: Richard Carlson (Gerald MacTeam);
 Veronica Hurst (Kitty Murray); Katherine
 Emery (Edith Murray)
B&W, 80 minutes, US

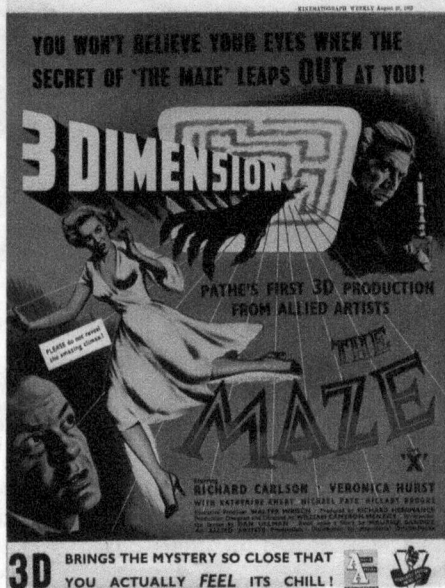

UK Trade advertisement for *The Maze*

While celebrating his engagement to Kitty in Cannes, Gerald is summoned to the family home of 'Craven Castle' in Scotland. His fiancée, having not heard from him for some time, visits the castle with her aunt. They find Gerald aged. This is not the only mystery to be uncovered.

'It occurred in Scotland. In a remote and distant castle in the Highlands': these are the words spoken, straight to camera, by Katherine Emery early in the film. It is the isolation, and the aura of myth (the film flirts with folk-horror), which drives the setting, recreated on a Californian sound stage. Unfortunately, other than in specialist screenings (or if you have an exceptional TV and the right Blu-ray recording), *The Maze* cannot now be watched as it was intended to be – in glorious 3D (albeit in black and white and with a 1.37:1 aspect ratio).

Hollywood veteran Menzies, whose last feature this was, is credited with direction *and* design. He was the first winner of the Oscar for art direction, for *The Dove* (Roland West, 1927) and *Tempest* (Sam Taylor, Lewis Milestone and Viktor Tourjansky, 1928). His stellar career included an honorary Oscar for colour design work on *Gone with the Wind* (Victor Fleming, 1939), and shortly before *The Maze* was shot, he directed sci-fi B-movie classic *Invaders from Mars* (1953). *The Maze* was made at the high point of Hollywood's first serious flirtation with 3D, which lasted only from 1952–1954; widescreen formats, which were simpler to use (3D required the projection of two film strips, making the process cumbersome to say the least), offered the spectacle that Hollywood was looking for in its attempts to fight off the threat of TV. Many of Menzies' design elements for *The Maze* are driven by the possibilities offered by 3D, with depth of field exaggerated to thrust the action into the audience – an element clearly at play in the maze itself.

Strip out the novelty, and there remain

reasons to revisit *The Maze*. Its taut running time ensures that the plotting is tight, and Menzies builds a strong atmosphere of menace, notwithstanding the design's artifice. The cast is strong and watching Carlson – who was in a purple period – is always a pleasure. Just before *The Maze* he appeared in *It Came from Outer Space* (Jack Arnold, 1953); the following year he was in *Creature from the Black Lagoon* (Jack Arnold, 1954). If, however, you are searching for an authentically Scottish experience, the film has little to offer.

Brigadoon (1954)

Directed by Vincente Minnelli
Screenplay by Alan Jay Lerner
Leading cast: Gene Kelly (Tommy Albright); Van Johnson (Jeff Douglas); Cyd Charisse (Fiona Campbell); Elaine Stewart (Jane Aston); Hugh Laing (Harry Beaton); Barry Jones (Mr Lundie)
Colour, 108 minutes, US

In the Scottish Highlands, the village of Brigadoon wakes up, as it does for one day every 100 years. Vacationing New Yorkers, Jeff and Tommy, arrive, and Tommy falls in love with Fiona. Later, back in New York, Tommy is unhappy. He and Jeff fly back to Scotland. Tommy's love is so strong that he is admitted to Brigadoon, and to Fiona's arms.

Brigadoon carries a weight of opprobrium that few films should be expected to bear. It has become for some the poster child for Scottish cliché and misrepresentation,

its title a code word for all that is bad about Scottish cultural stereotyping (the opening title is shown over a background of tartan, and Highland cattle make an appearance in the first two minutes). McArthur has written that *Brigadoon* 'has come to be seen... as the very nadir of mawkish Tartanry and Kailyard [and a] shorthand for all that is twee and regressive', but advocated in support of the film (*Brigadoon, Braveheart and the Scots* (2003)). I have sat in the GFT on a dreich Sunday afternoon, with an audience which I presume to be largely Scottish, enjoying almost every minute of it. It is, of course, true that *Brigadoon* presents a ridiculous version of Scotland, in which *nothing* is authentic, but at least – unlike **Braveheart** – it makes no claims to authenticity or truth; it would be tough work to pin a political platform or ethical position to it. *Brigadoon* is pure hokum (notwithstanding a dark streak running through it) and was never intended to be anything but. As a musical it is not perfect, but that is a different matter.

Cyd Charisse and Gene Kelly dance in the studio-shot *Brigadoon*

On the original musical's stage debut, *The NYT* theatre critic, Brooks Atkinson, was fulsome: 'In a fantasy about an imagined Scottish village it has fulfilled an old theatre ideal of weaving music, dancing and story into a single fabric of brightness and enchantment'. As MGM geared up towards the film's release, distributors were teased with a *Variety* advert that promised even more: 'Hoot Mon, It's Better Than The Broadway Success'. On release however not all critics were convinced. The *MFB* reviewer wrote that 'in view of its credentials... *Brigadoon* amounts to a sizeable disappointment... the tenuous romantic fantasy is slackly developed'. Here there is pertinent criticism. Both as choreographer and as an actor Gene Kelly's most inventive days were behind him when *Brigadoon* was made; the high point of his career was 1952's *Singin' in the Rain* (Stanley Donen, Gene Kelly) and the ballet choreography he brought to *Brigadoon* was by then somewhat over-familiar and passé.

Against Minnelli's protestations, *Brigadoon* was filmed in the MGM studio with no attempt to disguise painted backdrops. Even on its release critics were concerned by the caricature of Scotland. McArthur cites reviews in Scottish newspapers, including the Glasgow's *Evening News* whose reviewer wrote of 'the laughable sights of Hollywood studio sets of the Scottish Highlands'. To modern audiences the obvious artificiality of the film perhaps adds to its charm. Of all film genres, musicals are, along with animation, the most artificial; if the story hums along and songs are good, that's enough. It does, and for the most part they are.

Crest of the Wave (aka *Seagulls Over Sorrento*) (1954)

Directed by John Boulting and Roy Boulting
Screenplay by Hugh Hastings, Frank Harvey and Roy Boulting
Leading cast: Gene Kelly (Lt. Bradville); John Justin (Lt. Roger Wharton); Bernard Lee ('Lofty' Turner); Jeff Richards ('Butch' Clelland); Sidney James (Charlie Badger)
B&W, 92 minutes, UK

'An island off the west coast of Scotland – called ironically by its naval inhabitants, "Sorrento"': following the death of the lead British naval scientist working on the development of a torpedo system, Bradvile, an American, is brought in to assist.

Made by the Boulting brothers (who were a significant force in British filmmaking from the late 1940s through to the early 1960s, with productions such as *I'm All Right Jack*, John Boulting, 1959 and *Lucky Jim*, John Boulting, 1957), in co-production with MGM, *Crest of the Wave* reached for an international audience with the casting of Gene Kelly as the American brought in to assist the British in a post-war military project. The film was based on Hugh Hasting's long-running stage play, which opened in London in 1950 (at one point featuring Gordon Jackson), but the Boultings opened up the action with substantial exteriors. That this was filmed in the Channel Islands reduces the Scottish element to simply one of a professed, but not evidenced, location.

Set largely in a naval testing station, there are tropes familiar from war films as a motley group's tensions (grounded in class, experience, and nationality) are resolved; above all there are Anglo–American tensions – both personal and professional – to be overcome. The film's realistic depiction of the humdrum nature of much military service is an unusual strength. Gene Kelly was not playing to type here (his role in **Brigadoon** being more typical) but is 'quietly effective and convincing' (the *MFB*). The film also gives a reminder that Sidney James was a fine dramatic actor.

Devil Girl from Mars (1954) S++
T36

Directed by David MacDonald
Screenplay by John C Mather and James Eastwood
Leading cast: Hugh McDermott (Michael); Hazel Court (Ellen); Peter Reynolds (Albert); Joseph Tomelty (Professor Hennessy); Adrienne Cori (Doris); Patricia Laffan (Nyah)
B&W, 77 minutes, UK

Something falls to Earth and Professor Hennessy investigates, staying at the local pub in the Highlands. A flying saucer lands, carrying Nyah, who is intent on capturing strong Earthmen to take them to Mars, where a war of the sexes has left women in charge, men in decline. The motley crew in the pub work together to defeat her.

Scottish-born MacDonald, who began his career working in the US under Cecil B DeMille, was an extremely prolific director in the late 1940s through to the mid-1950s, a time when British cinemas were obliged to show a certain percentage of homegrown output, and cheap films – 'quota quickies' – were made to satisfy this requirement. He had, however, nearly destroyed his career with the disaster that was *Christopher Columbus* (1949). It was in this period that he directed the utterly bonkers *Devil Girl from Mars*.

'If one could choose one film to represent British trash cinema of the 1950s and 1960s, it would be cult favourite *Devil Girl from Mars*. An adaptation of a play, it is a deliciously camp tale of an interplanetary dominatrix on the prowl in rural Scotland' (IQ Hunter, *British Trash Cinema*, 2013). Note that almost certainly, contrary to the opening credits and almost every commentary about the film, it was *not* based on a play (stating that it was inflated the pay of the screenwriters). You either love trash movies, or you don't. I do, and find just as much to enjoy in the better ones as I do in anything by François Truffaut. If you're a fan of *The Rocky Horror Picture Show* (Jim Sharman, 1975), and haven't seen *Devil Girl*, you should – and I defy you not to wonder whether Richard O'Brien had also watched the film and taken inspiration from it.

Devil Girl is close to being an 'anywhere' film; it would be just as much at home on Exmoor or in Snowdonia. However, there is, as Hunter points out, something bathetic about Nyah's landing in the Scottish Highlands, and it permits the film to operate as a 'comic encounter between Britain and modernity, as if modernity itself were alien'. That modernity is decidedly wonky; Nyah's ray-gun is impressive, as is her power of mind control, but robot Johnnie looks more like a walking hot drink dispenser and was *clearly* a guy in a box.

There is something wonderfully daring about *Devil Girl*. In *The British 'B' Film* (2009), Steve Chibnall and Brian McFarlane point out that: 'Clad as a dominatrix in leather cap, cloak and stiletto boots, [Nyah] is a genuinely shocking figure in the staid world of British filmmaking of the time'. *Devil Girl* is not *really* a B-movie; it was always intended to be a standalone feature, opening in London cinemas in May 1954. It's hard to believe that the director of this tight, bizarre masterpiece was the same gentleman who directed *The Brothers* (see below). He could clearly turn his hand to anything.

It has been pointed out that the contemporaneous review in the *MFB* is an early example of a recognition of the delight to be found in cinematic nonsense (in essence, of camp cult): 'This primitive effort at British science fiction is quite enjoyably ludicrous, mainly on account of Patricia Laffan's splendid Nyah'. The review in *Picturegoer,* however, illustrates the general disdain for genre cinema at

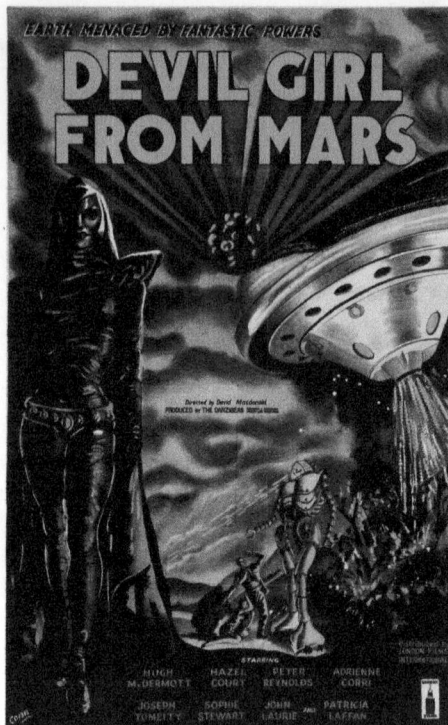

A strong poster for a gloriously bonkers film

the time, starting with the words: 'Gather round, juveniles – here's a space-ship melodrama which is going to intrigue you'. Notwithstanding this dismissive start, the review is positive and ends: 'The destruction of the Devil Girl supplies requisite tension without being too flamboyant'. But the film *is* flamboyant. I suspect it is one of the lesser-known films in this book. It deserves not to be.

Note that self-anointed schlockmeister, Larry Buchanan (see *The Loch Ness Horror*) made *Mars Needs Women* in 1968 – he at least had surely seen *Devil Girl from Mars*.

→ *The Brothers* (1947) S+++ W8

Directed by David MacDonald
Screenplay by Muriel Box, Sydney Box
Leading cast: Patricia Roc (Mary Lawson); Will
  Fyffe (Aeneas McGrath); Maxwell Reed (Fergus
  Macrae); Finlay Currie (Hector Macrae);
  Duncan Macrae (John Macrae)
B&W, 91 minutes, UK

Spring, 1900, Skye: Mary Lawson arrives to be taken in by Hector Macrae, whose wife has died. He has two sons, John and Fergus. This leads to much melodrama, interleaved with a tale of illicit whisky production, and two executions by geese.

Excitement was high in Edinburgh on Sunday 17 August 1947, when the stars of *The Brothers*, including English glamour queen Patricia Roc (closely associated with the Gainsborough Studio melodramas), attended a charity premiere of the film at the New Victoria Picture House on Clerk Street (later the Odeon, before closing in 2003). The film was unusual for its time in being shot largely on location in Scotland, on Skye. It was directed by Scottish-born MacDonald, and many Scots actors were among the cast. Roc was later described by fellow actor Dulcie Gray in the following terms: 'couldn't act for toffee apples, but she was beautiful' (in Matthew Sweet's magisterial *Shepperton Babylon*, 2005). When interviewed by Sweet, Roc had little to say about *The Brothers*, other than a brief comment about Will Fyffe, who, although born in Dundee, is ineffably linked with Glasgow following the success of

his song 'I Belong to Glasgow': 'He was a character. He committed suicide didn't he? Threw himself through a window'. It is, in fact, more likely that Fyffe's fall from a hotel window at the age of 62 was accidental.

On its release the *MFB* reviewer wrote of *The Brothers* that it 'has a beautiful photographic background; but despite its setting there is no refreshment to be found in its dealings with sex, hatred, superstition and murder', and that Roc 'is too glamorous... and weakens what otherwise appears to be the realism of the film'. Bosley Crowther of *The NYT* wrote that Roc 'is lovely in form and grace, but her hair-dos, her dresses and her expressions smack more of Elstree than of the Hebrides'. The film was not successful on release.

There are certainly problems with *The Brothers*, which is based on English author LAG Strong's 1932 novel of the same name, although considerable licence was taken by the screenwriters. Crowther noted that it 'is a sketchy and choppy affair and quite a considerable truncation of the novel... it is full of non sequiturs, and its suddenly happy ending is as fake as some indoor studio scenes'. Note that Crowther was reviewing the American version of the film, which differed from that released in the UK in some respects (particularly in its introduction of a happy, if somewhat illogical, ending). There are truly ridiculous elements to *The Brothers*, the highlight of which occurs following the conviction of an excise informer by a kangaroo court, based in part on 'immortal testimony' presented by Laurie's Dugald, who is believed to have visions. In a scene revisited at the very end, the hapless informer is executed by a goose (really!). A scene involving an invisible conger eel and a do-it-yourself amputation runs this close. Skye and Roc, however, look great in 1940s black and white.

The Maggie (1954) `S++` `T100`

The one film to make more than clichéd use of highland cattle

> Directed by Alexander Mackendrick
> Screenplay by William Rose, Alexander Mackendrick
> Leading cast: Paul Douglas (Calvin B Marshall – the American); Alex Mackenzie (Captain MacTaggart – the skipper); Tommy Kearins (Dougie – the wee boy); Hubert Gregg (Pusey)
> B&W, 92 minutes, UK

The Maggie, a 'puffer' of which MacTaggart is the skipper, comes into port at Glasgow. It is a run-down boat, with a motley crew, but serendipitously secures a contract to take a cargo owned by American businessman, Marshall, to 'Kitarra'. Things do not go well.

If the plot of *The Maggie* seems familiar, it may be because the similarities to Ealing's *The Titfield Thunderbolt* (Charles Crichton, 1953) are so strong. *The Maggie*'s story was provided by William Rose, an American who worked in England for ten years, making a speciality out of portraying the old and quirky in the UK (he was responsible in part for *Genevieve*, Henry Cornelius, 1953, and *The Smallest Show on Earth* – aka *Big Time Operators* – Basil Dearden, 1957). He also wrote *The Ladykillers*, which

Mackendrick directed the year after making *The Maggie*. Towards the end of his career, having returned to the US, Rose penned the much-lauded *Guess Who's Coming to Dinner* (Stanley Kramer, 1967) for which he won an Oscar. As Charles Barr points out in *Ealing Studios* (1993), Ealing comedies had by this point met with some success on the US arthouse film circuit. The studio recognised the commercial benefit in introducing direct American elements into its films.

Like **The Ghost Goes West**, *The Maggie* targets an American, although in this case the director's sympathies were with Marshall. *Time* magazine drew attention to the cruel treatment meted out to Marshall, who is a defeated man at the film's end. Mackendrick responded, writing that he 'saw the story very much from the viewpoint of the American'; for him, the 'savagely unfair' treatment of Marshall was 'part of the flavour of the joke'. The credits signal the element of caricature. Douglas is simply 'the American'; Mackenzie 'the Skipper'. Even before the action has started the audience would have anticipated conflict – and indeed, be hoping for it.

While Marshall is deserving of sympathy, *The Maggie* still skews heavily towards the Scots. A newspaper reporter following the story tells Marshall: 'These old puffers are public characters in Scotland, they're very popular ... people like them, they've affection for them... They've got a touch of tradition Mr Marshall, of the old simple "live and let live", of human values'. A scene in which Marshall attends a 100th birthday party late in the film is *very* similar to one in *I Know Where I'm Going!* where Joan attends a celebratory ceilidh and at first appears to serve almost the same purpose, drawing Marshall into the local charm. But Mackendrick pulls back from this, pivoting instead into the most savage phase of the conflict when the *Maggie* is not underway the next morning.

Actor Alex Mackenzie was born in Glasgow in 1885. *The Maggie*, made when he was nearly 70, was his first film, but after this success he went on to feature in, amongst others, seven further films covered in this book, including *Geordie, Kidnapped* (1959) and *The Battle of the Sexes*. Douglas had a long and varied career in the US, succeeding on Broadway, as a radio sports announcer, and as a Hollywood star.

The location shooting, in gorgeous black and white, takes in scenes on the west coast, including lovely shots of Bowmore, on Islay. I've noted elsewhere the irritating habit of dropping in Highland cows to emphasise Scottishness. In *The Maggie* a long scene on a pier makes the most inventive, funny, and thoroughly unobjectionable, use of the beasts in any film in this book.

Trouble in the Glen (1954)

Directed by Herbert Wilcox
Screenplay by Frank S Nugent
Leading cast: Margaret Lockwood (Marissa Mengues); Orson Welles (Sanin Cejador y Mengues); Forrest Tucker (Maj. Jim 'Lance' Lansing); Margaret McCourt (Alsuin)
B&W, 91 minutes, US

Sanin is, by inheritance, the local laird but offends the locals and has little sympathy for them. Jim, an American pilot in the war, confronts him and falls in love with his daughter, Marissa. Travellers steal cattle, and bloodshed is avoided only when Jim and Marissa work together. Sanin mends his ways.

This is not an easy film to find material about, but I was not going to pass up the opportunity to include an Orson Welles vehicle. Perhaps the most remarkable thing about *Trouble in the Glen* now is that in Simon Callow's exhaustively definitive biography of Welles (which currently runs to three volumes; a fourth is anticipated) it receives no mention, beyond inclusion in a list of Welles' works. It is justifiably forgotten, being predictable, and overly sentimental. It was a poor attempt to cash in on the success of *The Quiet Man* (John Ford, 1952): the poster hailed 'Here's the Riot Man! From the author of "The Quiet Man"' (an alternative graphic used the line 'The glen is not the only thing in trouble!'). There are, in fact, two authors involved here. Both films have their source in fiction by Maurice Walsh, and were adapted by the same screenwriter, Frank S Nugent, who started his career as a crime reporter for *The NYT* and became one of its most influential critics.

I suggest you do *not* watch *Trouble in the Glen*. Welles' introduction, delivered in his richly sonorous voice, is the following, and really tells you all you need to know: 'The trouble in the glen began, I'm afraid, when I came here. This is Glen Echan, we're high in the Highlands, or Heelands, in an area infested with hostile tribes of savages known as Scotsmen and situated a good many degrees north of civilisation'.

A letter published in *Box Office* in 1953 by the manager of the Astra Cinema in what was then Kitwe Nkana in Northern Rhodesia suggested that if *Trouble in the Glen* was 'as good as *The Quiet Man*' it might lead to Scots living in the area repatriating, as he said had been the case after one Irishman took his family home having seen the earlier film. He need not have worried. Here are highlights from the *MFB* review: 'heavy-handed regional comedy'; 'cloying sentimentality'; 'the whole tone of the film is as synthetic as its remarkable picture of the Highlands'; 'accents remain defiantly Irish'; 'the scenery, in Trucolor, takes on an equally unfamiliar appearance, the predominant colour being an acid shade somewhere between yellow and green'. It's not an easy film to track down. My advice is, don't bother.

Geordie (aka *Wee Geordie*) (1955) S+

Directed by Frank Launder
Screenplay by Sidney Gilliat, Frank Launder
Leading cast: Alastair Sim (the laird); Bill Travers (Geordie MacTaggart); Doris Goddard (Helga)
Colour, 93 minutes, UK

'THE PLACE: Scotland; THE TIME: Yesterday and Today – with a wee peep at Tomorrow'. Geordie puts considerable effort into gaining size and strength via a correspondence course. He ends up competing in the hammer, at the Melbourne Olympics, and successfully woos the girl of his dreams.

Scottish-born author David Harry Walker began to write while imprisoned during World War II in Colditz. He was liberated in 1945, and after moving to Canada became a prolific author, publishing many short stories and novels, including *Geordie* (1950) – on which the film is based (the book was reissued as *Wee Geordie* to coincide with the film) – and *Come Back, Geordie* (1966). *Geordie* is inoffensive and pleasantly trivial, although at places leaden. It lacks the energy of Launder and Gilliat's better-known work, the original run of *St Trinian's* films.

Variety hailed Bill Travers (also in *Ring of Bright Water* and *The Bridal Path*) as 'an impressive newcomer to stardom'. This was Travers' 16th film; he achieved real fame with *Born Free* (James Hill and Tom McGowan, 1966). More praise was given by *Variety* to Scottish actor Paul Young, playing young Geordie. He was 11 years old when *Geordie* was released in September 1955, and went on to appear in, amongst others, **Another Time, Another Place** and **The Girl in the Picture**. As of 2019 he was still acting, taking the recurring role of Shug in the series *Still Game* (2002–2019).

Reviewing the film on its UK release, *Variety* hailed it 'another fine example of the teamwork of Launder and Gilliat... the very naivete of the principal characters gives the subject the necessary warm human values and right degree of sentiment'. The *MFB*'s reviewer was less comfortable with the 'sentiment': 'it is sentimental where it should be tender and commonplace where it should be discerning. The rhythm of the film is slack, the Highland backgrounds are photographed in colour sometimes reminiscent of Raphael Tuck postcards'.

The bulk of the film was shot at Shepperton Studios, with some location shooting in Scotland, largely around Stirling and the south Trossachs.

The Flying Scot (aka *The Mailbag Robbery*) (1956)

Directed by Compton Bennett
Screenplay by Norman Hudis, Jan Read and Ralph Smart
Leading cast: Lee Patterson (Ronnie); Kay Callard (Jackie); Alan Gifford (Phil)
B&W, 80 minutes, UK

Scotland, Tuesday: Ronnie and Jackie, a 'just married' couple, board the night-train to London. They are joined by Phil

and rob the train of mailbags holding £500,000. We cut back to the planning, as Ronnie insists nothing can go wrong – but a detail lets them down...

While *The Flying Scot* takes place on a train travelling from Scotland to London, the film's construction means that the bulk of the action takes place north of the border – qualifying this short, taut, heist thriller for entry here. None of the three leads were British – Patterson and Callard were Canadian, Gifford American. The director *was* British, although he had spent time attempting to establish himself in Hollywood. *The Flying Scot* is considered one of the highlights of a largely lacklustre career.

The film was shot in the studio, with some stock footage of a moving express, giving rise to some irritation to train buffs who have pointed out that the train mysteriously changes carriages mid-journey and arrives and departs at the same station; there are also some day/night continuity errors. However, the film holds the tension skilfully; the *MFB*'s reviewer praised it as 'an ingenious and entertainingly developed thriller'.

X The Unknown (1956)

Directed by Leslie Norman
Screenplay by Jimmy Sangster
Leading cast: Dean Jagger (Dr Adam Royston);
  William Lucas (Peter Elliott); Leo McKern
  (Inspector 'Mac' McGill)
B&W, 81 minutes, UK/US

'*Lochmouth Atomic Energy Establishment*', *Scotland: Dr Royston, an American scientist, and Inspector McGill battle X, a blobby mass which has broken through the Earth's crust, with a hunger for radioactive material.*

X the Unknown is a Hammer sci-fi film, released as the lower part of a double bill with *Les Diaboliques* (Henri-Georges Clouzot, 1955), which attempted to capitalise on the unexpected success of the similarly themed Hammer sci-fi hit *The Quatermass Experiment* (Val Guest, 1955), to which it was originally intended to be a direct sequel. We are in the nuclear age, which has reached Scotland: if unchecked, X will head to the nuclear power station near Inverness, threatening the entire city. Here, the power of science (and scientists) is recognised and Royston, at least, is seen as a force for reason and good. He is challenged only by his boss, who does not recognise his genius, and by the father of a dead boy, who tells him 'you're a scientist, not a doctor. You don't look after the sick. You meddle with things that kill, like they killed my boy in there. You should be locked up... locked up with others like you who build bombs they can't control'. Ultimately X

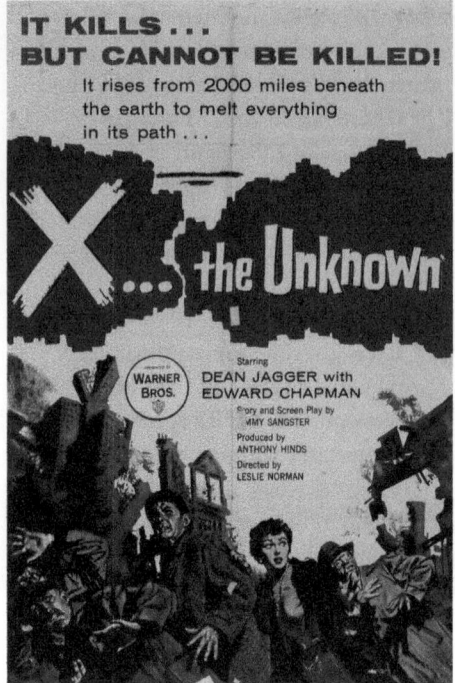

The one film to make more than clichéd use of highland cattle

is shown to be a force of nature, to which Royston's science provides the cure.

Although not credited, American director Joseph Losey (*The Servant*, 1963; *Modesty Blaise*, 1966; *The Go-Between*, 1971 etc) started work on *X the Unknown* but was on the House Un-American Activities Committee (HUAC) blacklist, which would have prevented Hammer securing a US distribution deal for the film, and he bowed out. Norman directed only nine feature films, including Ealing's *Dunkirk* (1958), before turning to TV. His direction of *X the Unknown* was criticised in *Variety* – 'Norman's direction is not able to rise above [the weak script] handed him'.

While McKern and Jagger form a likeable paring, the film has its problems, particularly with special effects. X is not shown for a long time into the film (with the consequence that there are a few too many shots of people looking in terror at something we cannot see). When X is, finally, revealed it looks, as the *MFB* put it, like 'a type of rolling rubber mattress, disappointingly unhorrific in content and appearance'. The *MFB*'s conclusion was that 'enthusiasts may find [it] rather tame when compared with the more grisly experiments of Professor Quatermass'. *Variety*'s critic was not a fan either: the film was static, the script weak. The film is discussed in Denis Meikle's *Hammer: The Haunted House of Horror* (2017).

Let's Be Happy (1957)　　S+

Directed by Henry Levin
Screenplay by Diana Morgan and Dorothy Cooper
Leading cast: Vera-Ellen (Jeannie MacLean); Tony Martin (Stanley Smith); Robert Flemyng (Lord James MacNairn)
Colour, 107 minutes, UK, English (with limited other European languages)

Heatherdale, Vermont: Jeannie sings 'Loch Lomond'. With a $5,000 inheritance she sets off for Scotland and the Edinburgh Festival, and is sat next to fellow American Stanley on the plane. He follows her to Edinburgh. Running out of money, while staying in a lavish room, Jeannie is mistaken for a millionaire by an impoverished Scottish Lord, and wooed. Stanley fights back, leading to the inevitable happy ending.

Four musicals are featured in this book. Two of them star Vera-Ellen, who is also in 1952's *Happy Go Lovely,* similarly set during the Edinburgh Festival and which was also a UK musical seeking to boost its credentials by hiring an established American star (both films also have in common the very Scottish Gordon Jackson). The source material for *Let's Be Happy* was an old stage comedy, *Jeannie*, by the Glasgow-born playwright and screenwriter Aimée Stuart, which was itself filmed in 1941 (that version depicts a Scottish girl using her inheritance to tour continental Europe and is not, for the purposes of this book, a Scottish film).

Shot in rich Technicolor and 2.55:1 widescreen (reduced to 2.35:1 on the DVD I watched), *Let's Be Happy* is sumptuous to look at. *Variety* commended the 'background of the Edinburgh Festival' and 'colourful panoramas of Scottish beauty spots' (eg the Old Course at St Andrews); *Kinematograph Weekly*'s writer noted that 'seldom if ever, has a wide screen colour brochure of Scotland been so compelling or so lush'. For the cast however, most of the four-month shoot was at Elstree studios for the interiors.

Despite its source pedigree, the Cinderella story is occasionally charmless, losing its way through a long, staid middle section. *Variety*'s review was positive, but the more rigorous *MFB* was less content: 'when the story moves to Europe it becomes laborious and is tricked out with production numbers which are for the most part vulgar in conception and undistinguished in execution'. If, however, richly artificial 1950s musicals are your thing, this one is for you.

The Bridal Path (1959)   S++

Directed by Frank Launder
Screenplay by Frank Launder and Geoffrey
  Willans
Leading cast: Bill Travers (Ewan McEwan); Fiona
  Clyne (Katie)
Colour, 95 minutes, UK

On the Island of 'Beigg' in the Hebrides, Katie has been living as Ewan's housekeeper. She loves Ewan, but is his cousin, and leaves for the mainland after marriages between cousins are prohibited. Seeking a wife, Ewan also leaves, but over the course of three days a series of mistakes leads to him being hunted by the police, and rowing back to Beigg, where Katie has returned. They agree to marry – on Mull.

The second of three films in this book to be built around the star appeal of Bill Travers (see also **Geordie** and **Ring of Bright Water**), who appears to tower over those around him and, in this film at least, to be irresistible to women. *The Bridal Path* is a slight but amiable fish-out-of-water comedy detailing the travails of an islander seeking a wife on the mainland. The film's strengths are its Technicolor on-location shooting (or, as Richard L

Coe put it, in *The Washington Post*, it's 'one of those gentle comedies in which the charm of its setting far outweighs the surrounding fictions') and a plethora of Scottish and British supporting actors, including Gordon Jackson, George Cole, Duncan Macrae and a young Terry Scott (in his fourth film, playing a policeman for the fourth time).

The film is based on Nigel Tranter's 1952 novel of the same name. Tranter was a wildly prolific Glasgow-born author, whose output included nearly 40 novels (including westerns written under a pseudonym) and many non-fiction works, almost all of which took Scotland as their subject. He was also active in the Scottish Convention and a strong advocate for devolution.

The film has charm, but it is very slight. As *Variety* put it, 'the joke wears a shade thin'. AH Weiler in *The NYT* was a little more generous, noting that the cast were 'expertly spinning one small joke and slightly telegraphing their punch line'; CA Lejeune in *The Observer* took a similar line: '*The Bridal Path* is really quite gentle, pleasant and a little staid'.

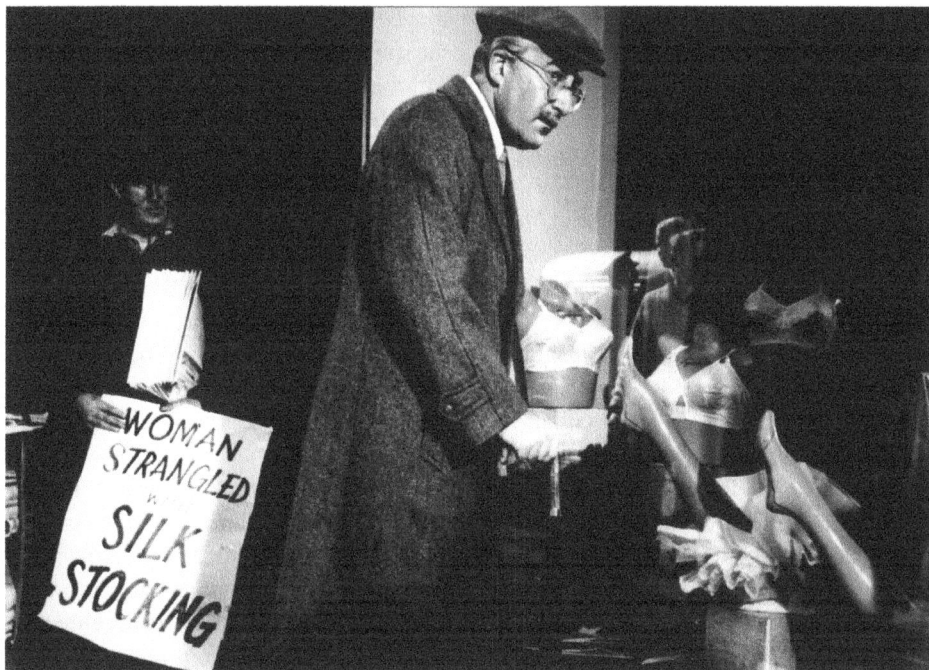

Does Peter Sellers get away with murder in Edinburgh?

The Battle of the Sexes (1960) S+

Directed by Charles Crichton
Screenplay by Monja Danichewsky
Leading cast: Peter Sellers (Mr Martin); Robert
  Morley (Robert Macpherson); Constance
  Cummings (Angela Barrows); Donald Pleasance
  (Irwin Hoffman)
B&W, 84 minutes, UK

In the US, Mrs Angela Barrows' colleagues scheme to send her somewhere far away and wild: Scotland. In Edinburgh, the 'House of Macpherson', a family tweed business, changes hands. New owner Robert commissions Angela to update the business. She clashes with traditionalist accounts manager Mr Martin.

The Battle of the Sexes (the German title is better: *Mr Miller ist kein Killer*) was based on a James Thurber short story, 'The Catbird Seat', published in *The New Yorker* in 1942. There had been several attempts to bring it to the screen before *Battle* was made, but none had been successful (the film has nothing to do with a famous tennis match).

There can be no doubt that *Battle* is dated. It is very fine in parts, and funny, but occasionally leaves a sour taste. It opens with a reference to a 'timeless struggle for supremacy between man and woman'. *Battle* is not only about conflict between the sexes, but about conflict between the new, America, and the old, in this case Scotland (a theme also addressed in, amongst others, *The Maggie, The Ghost Goes West* and *A Shot at Glory*). Where the film comes unstuck is in its conflation of the two conflicts. In doing so it elicits sympathy for Mr Martin's ultimately successful campaign of persecution based on Mrs Barrow's failure to understand local traditions and culture. The audience is clearly meant to find satisfaction in the sight of a woman (who has been set up to appear to be having a breakdown) being bundled out of her workplace by a group of men. She is dismissed casually by Robert: 'Such breakdowns are perfectly common with women who undertake the burden of business life'. When the 'battle of the sexes' slides into the background, there is much fun to be had in the new/old, America/Scotland, innovative/conservative tensions on show.

It is no surprise that *Battle* was compared to Ealing comedies in contemporaneous reviews; Crichton and Danichewsky both worked at Ealing, and Sellers himself was an Ealing alumnus (*The Ladykillers*, Alexander Mackendrick, 1955). *The Spectator*'s reviewer Isabel Quigly found aspects of the film to be outdated, although thought it 'a neat and highly enjoyable film, with some brilliant timing... and the sorts of scorings-off that will appeal to everyone'. For AH Weiler in *The NYT*, it provided a 'gentle,

tongue-in-cheek ribbing that cleaves to the spirit, if not entirely to the letter, of Thurber's lampoon... with charm and a few belly laughs'. The *MFB*'s reviewer was less satisfied: 'the few good moments fail to atone for stretches of flatness and repetition, emphasised by Charles Crichton's surprisingly slack handling'.

The cast is very strong. American émigré Cummings is given a thankless task but performs it with gusto. Both Sellers and Morley are excellent: the former adopts a convincing Scottish accent, and there is a Chaplinesque air to his resilient timidity (it was because of this performance that Stanely Kubrick cast Sellers in *Lolita*, 1926); Morley is always watchable. The Edinburgh exteriors are superb in 1950s black and white, although studio-based interiors constitute the bulk of the film.

Tunes of Glory (1960)   S++   T34

Directed by Ronald Neame
Screenplay by James Kennaway
Leading cast: Alec Guinness (Major Jock Sinclair); John Mills (Lt. Col. Basil Barrow); Dennis Price (Major Charles Scott); Susannah York (Morag Sinclair); Gordon Jackson (Capt. Jimmy Cairns)
Colour, 106 minutes, UK

Shortly after World War II, Oxford-educated Barrow takes over command of a Scottish battalion. He clashes with Sinclair, a Glaswegian who rose through the ranks. Barrow is fragile, broken by the war, and dies by suicide. Sinclair is put in charge

*of the funeral, ordering a ceremonial
procession, with 'all the tunes of glory'.*

Auchterarder-born James Kennaway, who
died at the age of 40, published *The Tunes
of Glory*, his first novel, in 1956, later
adapting it into the film's screenplay. His
second novel, *Household Ghosts* (1961),
was subsequently filmed as **Country Dance**.
Tunes pits two men against each other:
while Mills' Barrow has seniority, class,
and both family and military tradition on
his side, the battle is an unequal one. He
is 'a stickler for detail' (there are echoes of
Humphrey Bogart's Captain Queeg, in *The
Caine Mutiny*, Edward Dmytryk, 1954)
and suffers a brittleness which may flow
from his time as a tortured prisoner of war
in the Far East. This ensures he is no match
for Guinness' robust Sinclair, whose only
stint in captivity was in Glasgow's Barlinnie
gaol. Only after the death of Barrow, when
Sinclair turns on the officers, saying 'it
was murder, and I may be the murderer,
but you are the accomplices', does Sinclair
break down (and this is his least convincing
moment).

Neame, who later directed **The Prime
of Miss Jean Brodie**, marshals his forces to
great effect in *Tunes*. Following a screening
at the Venice Film Festival, *Variety*'s
reviewer wrote that his 'crisp and vigorous
direction keeps the main spotlight on the
two central characters, and no director
could be better served by his stars'. The
strength of the film lies in its capturing
of traditions in a Highland regiment, in
the two central performances, and in the
strong supporting cast. The romantic and

Alec Guiness dominates the officers' mess

family relationships – Sinclair/Morag,
Morag/Fraser and Sinclair and an actress
(Kay Walsh) – detract from the central
focus, adding little (the *MFB* critic also
found these distractions annoying). At
the centre Guinness and Mills are superb,
playing the roles somewhat contrary to
type. Previous work would have suggested
that Guinness would take on the role
of the educated traditional army officer.
Indeed, there are reports that he was first
offered this, but turned it down in favour
of Sinclair, suggesting that Mills play
Barrow. Guinness had two years previously
won an Oscar for his role as Colonel
Nicholson in David Lean's *Bridge on the
River Kwai* (1957) and may have felt that
the role of Barrow would be too similar.

The scenes in the mess (interiors were
shot in England's Shepperton Studios),
and the military scenes shot in Stirling
Castle, ring very true. I grew up in the
bosom of the army, and as my father was
at one point stationed in Edinburgh, I
had a passing familiarity with a Scottish

officers' mess, although many Scottish regimental traditions have now been lost following army reorganisation. Barrow draws on a tradition extending back 200 years; his great-grandfather and grandfather were both colonels of the battalion. Sinclair makes his own traditions, exploiting Barrow's reverence for history as he manoeuvres Barrow into dropping a formal investigation into the conduct of battalion members, suggesting that what will be hurt will be 'the idea of the battalion, the living and the dead altogether, the regiment. That's what suffers most'. By the end of the film, although Sinclair is now in charge of the battalion, it has indeed been harmed. *Tunes of Glory* is amusingly referenced in *Long Shot*.

Don't Bother to Knock! (aka *Why Bother to Knock*) (1961)

Directed by Cyril Frankel
Screenplay by Denis Cannan and Fritz Golfurt
Leading cast: Richard Todd (Bill); Nicole Maurey (Lucille); Elke Sommer (Ingrid); June Thorburn (Stella)
Colour, 89 minutes, UK

Edinburgh: Bill, a philandering travel agent, hopes to marry Stella. After she rejects him he gallivants across Europe, then runs into problems when too many of the girlfriends he has picked up along the way descend upon his Edinburgh flat.

I hate to disappoint, but this is not *Don't Bother to Knock* (Roy Ward Baker,

1952) starring Marilyn Monroe and Richard Widmark; instead, you get Elke Sommer and Richard Todd (titles apart, there's no relationship between the two films). While the opening title proclaims that we are in Edinburgh – establishing exteriors confirm this – the city and country are largely incidental to the unamusing plot, save for the fact that the Edinburgh International Festival sits in the background.

Todd was a dramatic actor (*Flesh and Blood*; *Rob Roy: The Highland Rogue*) and a producer on *Don't Bother*, which was born of a longstanding desire to see British films match American successes in Europe. For *Don't Bother* he secured actors from France (Maurey) and Germany (Sommer), with Sommer already having had significant exposure in Italy where her first films were made (she was able to work in German, Italian, French, Spanish and English). *Kinematograph Weekly* described the production as 'a perfect example of a "natural" international subject'. Unfortunately, Todd was simply not suited to play the Lothario in a light farce and comes off as a slightly creepy and desperate older man intent on seducing younger women (there was a 21-year age gap between he and Sommer), while still desiring the quiet life with an overly-patient fiancée. The *MFB*'s reviewer sums things up well: 'Despite an elegant wardrobe, pretty faces, and the contemporary trappings of an unusually chic and sunny Edinburgh, this isn't even one of sophisticated comedy's poor relations.'

The Amorous Prawn (aka The Amorous Mr. Prawn) (1962) S+ T100

Directed by Anthony Kimmins
Screenplay by Anthony Kimmins and Nicholas
  Phipps
Leading cast: Ian Carmichael (Cpl. Sidney Green);
  Joan Greenwood (Lady Dodo Fitzadam); Cecil
  Parker (Gen. Sir Hamish Fitzadam); Dennis
  Price (Prawn – Mr Vernon)
B&W, 89 minutes, UK

In the large country house the army provides for Dodo and her husband, the General in command of the Military Headquarters Northwestern District, near Oban, Dodo concocts a scheme to make money by hosting American salmon fishers when the General is sent overseas for two months. Farce ensues. The General returns unexpectedly and is roped into the scheme. More farce ensues. The Secretary of State for War turns up as a guest with his 'wife'. Cue even more farce.

The Amorous Prawn betrays its origins as a stage play, also by Anthony Kimmins (whose previous experiences with Scottish subjects were the disastrous **Bonnie Prince Charlie** and the somewhat better **Flesh and Blood**), which opened in London in 1959 (at which point *Variety* noted that though 'far from perfect, it is amusing enough to get by'). Firmly in the tradition of farce, the film starts slowly but gains pace as events spiral out of control. The increasingly frantic antics spill from room to room, and there's plenty of the staples of the genre: frequent misunderstandings and equally frequent costume changes as the staff switch rapidly between military and civilian attire. By the final scenes the film descends into chaos (or, as the *MFB* put it, 'a glorious romp'). It is, as *Variety* sums up, 'non-demanding light entertainment'.

John Barry provided the score; there is some location shooting in Oban, and Scottish stalwart Finlay Currie (*The Edge of the World, The Brothers, I Know Where I'm Going!* etc) plays Lochaye.

Maciste all'inferno (The Witch's Curse) (1962)

Directed by Riccardo Freda
Screenplay by Oreste Biancoli and Piero Pierotto
Leading cast: Kirk Morris (Maciste); Vira Silenti
  (Martha Gaunt); Angelo Zanolli (Charley Law)
Colour, 91 minutes, Italy

As Martha Gaunt is burned as a witch in Scotland in 1550, she curses the ground. 100 years later a descendant and namesake arrives in the village as a new bride, and is seized by the locals who continue to suffer under the curse. Maciste arrives to save the day, but must descend into Hell to do so.

Like **Lo Spettro**, and the later giallo film **Seven Deaths in the Cat's Eyes**, it would be possible to treat *Maciste* as a foreign language film, but for the fact that dialogue was recorded post-shooting, and that multiple versions of Italian films at the time could be released depending on a film's international appeal; arguably all versions are equally authentic. The film is now of only ephemeral interest as part of the Italian populist 'peplum' (or 'sword-and-sandal') genre. Its strapping hero, Kirk Morris – who arrives on the scene in Scotland with no explanation whatsoever – was born Adriano Bellini, became a gondolier, and rebranded after winning a body-building contest. The character of Maciste, with striking similarities to Hercules, was created in part by Gabriele D'Annunzio (an utterly remarkable man – albeit with some distasteful views – about whom a biopic really should be made), and featured in a long series of films in the 1910s and 1920s, before being revived in the 1960s. Morris played him in two films, but a number of other actors also had a stab at the role in the same period.

There is *nothing* about *Maciste all'inferno* which is in any way an authentic portrayal of Scotland – the shoot was entirely in Italy, with the scenes in Hell being filmed in the Castellana Caves. Everything is thrown at Maciste in the Hell sequence, which includes, in the words of Kim Newman, 'encounters with Moon Men, Toto, the Cyclops, the Sheikh, a tsar, and the denizens of King Solomon's Mines'. In the English-language version, some actors fail in the attempt to replicate Scottish accents. But almost exactly half the film is set in Scotland (which also provides the doorway to the Hell in which Maciste spends the other half), so it's in this book. Director Riccardo Freda also made *Lo Spettro*, both films being made by the same production company, Panda Film.

Das indische Tuch (The Indian Scarf) (1963)

Directed by Alfred Vohrer
Screenplay by Harld G Petersson and Georg Hurdalek
Leading cast: Heinz Drache (Frank Tanner); Corny Collins (Isla Harris); Hans Clarin (Lord Edward Lebanon); Klaus Kinski (Peter Ross)
B&W, 93 minutes, West Germany, German

In a remote castle in Scotland, cut off by a storm, relatives gather following the death of the castle's owner. A murder mystery unfolds...

One of a successful series of films in Germany based on the works of Edgar Wallace, made in stylish black and white by Rialto Film. In a country house, relatives of Lord Lebanon, hoping to inherit his estate, are serially murdered. *The Frightened Lady,* a novelisation in 1933 of the original play (first performed in 1931), places 'Mark's Priory' as being close to Horsham (in West Sussex). This was twice filmed in Britain: *The Frightened Lady* (T Hayes Hunter, 1932) and *The Case of the Frightened Lady* (aka *The Frightened Lady*) (George King, 1940). Those films are not set in Scotland.

Vohrer's adaptation changes the story substantially, with the characters being isolated in the cut-off castle. That isolation is explained by a radio announcement of a heavy storm in the west of Scotland (I suspect the German translator may have been misled by references in the original to police from Scotland Yard!). Be that as it may, it was at least the belief of the director that the multiple murders and resultant sleuthing in *Das indische Tuch* took place in Scotland... The action is exclusively set inside the house, so there is, in fact, nothing else about this which makes it Scottish. Available only in German, without subtitles.

Lo Spettro (*The Ghost*, aka *The Spectre*) (1963)

Directed by Riccardo Freda
Screenplay by Oreste Biancoli and Riccardo Freda
Leading cast: Elio Jotta (Dr John Hichcock); Barbara Steele (Margaret Hichcock); Peter Baldwin (Dr Charles Livingstone)
Colour, 97 minutes, Italy

Scotland, 1910: in his large Gothic country house Dr Hichcock, who is disabled and married to Margaret, dabbles in the occult. He is murdered by Dr Livingstone, with whom Margaret is having an affair. The two lovers are then trapped in a web of uncanny events, and both die.

The pace of filmmaking in 1960s' Italy was so rapid that Freda had directed four films between the similarly Scottish-set *Maciste all'inferno* and the release, just one year later, of *Lo Spettro*. The approach to international marketing was sufficiently flexible that Freda directed *Lo Spettro* under the pseudonym Robert Hampton, while fellow screenwriter Biancoli, with whom Freda had worked on *Maciste*,

adopted the pen-name Robert Davidson. Freda had directed the English actor Barbara Steele, who has an uncredited bit-part in the 1959 version of *The Thirty Nine Steps*, and who appeared in many Italian films during this period, in *The Horrible Dr Hichcock* in 1962, but there is no narrative link between the two films.

Like many other Italian films of the period *Lo Spettro* has much in common with Hammer's output (although Italian films were first to the punch in a gothic revival) but, as Kim Newman pointed out in a survey of Italian exploitation films in 1986, 'the luridness of [*Lo Spettro*'s] subject matter (necrophile adultery) would have made [it] unproduceable in Britain'.

Set entirely in Scotland, and shot entirely in Italy, the location matters little: as the *MFB*'s reviewer put it, this is a 'Gothic, skull-festooned and highly unlikely Scotland'. But *Lo Spettro* has its strengths in Barbara Steele's performance, design and strong set pieces, and is one of the better gothic horror films of the period.

Horror icon Barbara Steele in *Lo Spettro*

Patrick McGoohan and Susan Hampshire

The Three Lives of Thomasina (1963) S+

Directed by Don Chaffey
Screenplay by Robert Westerby
Leading cast: Multiple cats (Thomasina);
  Patrick McGoohan (Andrew McDhui); Susan
  Hampshire (Laurie MacGregor); Karen Dotrice
  (Mary McDhui); Elspeth March (voice of
  Thomasina)
Colour, 97 minutes, UK/US

'Inveranoch', Scotland, 1912. A cat, Thomasina, introduces the story, which is 'all about me'. She's adopted by Mary, the daughter of the local vet, Andrew, who fails to save Thomasina when she 'dies'. She is saved by the 'Witch up in the Glen', Laurie. Mary contracts pneumonia and is also saved by Laurie; Andrew and Laurie marry.

Although the credits state that Thomasina was filmed at Pinewood Studios in London, there was in fact substantial on-location shooting in Scotland, with a part of the film being made in Inverary, on Loch Fyne. Thomasina could have been set pretty much anywhere but Disney retained the original novel's 'rugged and picturesque Scottish Highlands' location. The film is based on Paul Gallico's

Thomasina, the cat who thought she was God, published in 1957 (Gallico also wrote the Mrs Harris series of novels, most recently filmed as *Mrs. Harris Goes to Paris*, Anthony Fabian, 2022). Some use is made of Scottish colour, but not cloyingly so; the one bagpipe incident is moderately engaging, occurring when Mary and her friends stage a funeral for Thomasina (mistakenly believing her to be dead) – with Mary noting later that 'Jamie McNab can play Mackintosh's Lament on the pipes with only nine mistakes'. Karen Dotrice also features in *The Thirty Nine Steps* (1978).

As with all Disney films of this ilk there are conflicts to be neatly resolved. Here we have tensions between the Highland residents of Inveranoch (who note that Andrew McDhiu is '*not* a Highlander') and their expectations as to community service, and Andrew's attempt to bring progress and science to 'these people here'. There is also a personal conflict between Andrew's rational, somewhat cold, nature, and Laurie's empathetic kindness. Yet they are both outsiders. To quote Susan Hampshire, Laurie 'had a life of her own, she sang in Gaelic, she spoke Gaelic... lived on her own in the woods and [didn't] do the normal thing'. There can, therefore, be no doubt that the two, complementing each other perfectly, will marry. This is, after all, a Disney film, and its values are writ large: Christianity, community, and the nuclear family.

Your ability to tolerate *Thomasina* will depend on your tolerance of saccharine schmaltz. The *MFB* dismissed the film as 'glutinously sentimental – even for Disney'. Within the twee there is one truly bizarre cat-dream sequence which, it is now suggested, constitutes 'the trippiest cat video on the entire internet' (*dangerousminds.net*).

Das Rasthaus der grausamen Puppen (*The Devil's Girls*) (1967)

Directed by Rolf Olsen
Screenplay by Rolf Olsen
Leading cast: Essy Persson (Betty Williams); Erik Schumann (Bob Fishman)
B&W, 96 minutes, Italy/West Germany, German

In Glasgow, Betty and Bob screw up a robbery and Bob kills a policeman. He flees, while Betty is sent to gaol. She escapes with four other prisoners and flees to the Highlands. The police catch up with them at the end.

Confusion about this highly entertaining piece of German trash cinema abounds. The film is known by various titles: a direct translation could be *The Inn of the Cruel Dolls*; in the US it appears to have been released in a dubbed version (which I can find no trace of) as *The Devil's Girls*. The original release is available on a German DVD, in German only. The opening words of the film's description on the DVD cover are: 'a wet and cold night in London'. Ignore that: the film starts with one word on screen – 'GLASGOW', and it is set in its entirety in Scotland; first in Glasgow as

Betty and Bob mess up a straightforward smash-and-grab, killing a policeman in the process, then in something purporting to be a Scottish 'women's penitentiary', then in the Highlands.

There are some attempts to ground the location (someone reads 'The Glasgow Telegraph' – while the headline is in English, the text below is German; a travelling salesman is implausibly called Lupus McIntosh etc), but these are so patchy and thin as to be laughable – vehicles are variously left- and right-hand drive, and the Highlands scenes were shot in northern Italy. The action too is risible with the film teetering on a tightrope between outright titillation (as when the female governor attempts to seduce Betty), and Edgar Wallace-type police drama (see **Das indische Tuch**, above). But the treatment of sexuality and the abuse of prisoners was radical for its time and, as the body count rises and events lead towards the inevitable denouement, there is great fun to be had here. There's an excellent review of the film on the 'Girls with Guns' website, where it is named *Inn of the Gruesome Dolls*.

Fantômas contre Scotland Yard (*Fantomas vs. Scotland Yard*) (1967)

Directed by André Hunebelle
Screenplay by Jean Halain and Pierre Foucauld
Leading cast: Jean Marais (Fantômas etc); Louis de Founès (Le commissaire Juve); Mylène Demongeot (Hélène); Françoise Christoph (Lady Dorothy MacRashley); Jean-Roger Caussimon (Lord Edward MacRashley)
Colour, 100 minutes, France/Italy, French

Notorious criminal mastermind Fantômas decides to extract money from wealthy Scots and is pursued by Juve. The battle of wits is fought out in a 'Scottish' castle.

The popular Fantômas character was created by Marcel Allain and Pierre Souvestre in 1911. It took only two years for him first to appear in film, although the dominant image now derives from the trilogy made between 1964 and 1967 (influenced by *The Pink Panther,* Blake Edwards, 1963, *A Shot in the Dark,* Blake Edwards, 1964 and by the Bond films) in which *Fantômas contre Scotland Yard* was the last instalment. There are opening shots in Scotland, but almost all the film was shot in France. Dastardly crime, high-jinks, shenanigans and complex plotting abound. The Fantômas films were popular on release and are available on Blu-ray.

Ring of Bright Water (1969)   S+

Directed by Jack Couffer
Screenplay by Jack Couffer, Bill Travers
Leading cast: Bill Travers (Graham Merrill);
   Virginia McKenna (Mary MacKenzie); Peter
   Jeffrey (Colin Wilcox)
Colour, 107 minutes, UK/US

Graham acquires a pet otter, Mij, and moves from London to an 'old world cottage' on the west coast of Scotland. He forms a relationship with local doctor, Mary. Mij meets an untimely death, but not before siring pups. Graham writes The Ring of Bright Water.

Gavin Maxwell's memoir, *Ring of Bright Water,* was published in 1960, and became a bestseller – I refused to read it, because my mother took me to the film when it came out, which traumatised me. If you have the slightest interest in films about otters, the one you otter watch is not this passionless effort, but the 2024 documentary *Billy & Molly: An Otter Love Story. Ring of Bright Water* may look good, but it is not good drama. There are long sequences in which we simply watch Mij cavort; much of what remains is an overly literary voice-over adapted, very loosely, from Maxwell's book, or is Graham talking to Mij. A bigger problem with the film is that there is more chemistry between Mij and Graham than there is between him and Mary. This is surprising – the two leads had worked together before (*Born Free,* James Hill and Tom McGowan, 1966) and were husband and

wife. Bill Travers appears also as the lead in *Geordie* and in *The Bridal Path*. But Mij was popular with both families and with critics, more so than the human leads.

Howard Thompson, in *The NYT* was delighted by Mij, notwithstanding the fact that the film was 'the mildest of yarns': 'The otter is the sleekest, funniest and most beguiling trouper in years, stealing every scene and scooting across the terrain as though he owned Scotland.' Not everyone was so taken. In *Film Quarterly* David Denby was much less generous: 'I guess it's for children, or at least for those who won't be impatient with its remarkable laziness and irresolution'. The *New Statesman* was even harsher: 'a long, lame travelogue about the West Highlands… Cute, meaningless.'

The film was largely shot on location, with the main village and home to Graham and Mij being Ellanabeich, on Seil Island, to the southwest of Oban. Oban itself provided the fish market where Graham buys food for Mij. A shark hunt was filmed on the Firth of Lorne.

I did not anticipate I would get the chance to write the words 'Val Doonican' in this book. He supplied the title song.

Sinful Davey (1969)

Directed by John Huston
Screenplay by James R Webb
Leading cast: John Hurt (Davey Haggart); Ronald
  Fraser (MacNab); Pamela Franklin (Annie);
  Nigel Davenport (Chief Constable Richardson);
  Robert Morley (Duke of Argyll)
Colour, 95 minutes, UK/US

A flamboyant frolicsome retelling of
David Haggart's memoirs, which takes
great liberties with Haggart's story.

Sinful Davey was John Hurt's first
starring role. His previous film was the
comedy *Before Winter Comes* (J Lee
Thompson, 1968), which may have
convinced the producers of *Davey* that he
would be able to carry the film. Director
John Huston was one of the Hollywood
greats (*The Maltese Falcon*, 1941; *The
Treasure of the Sierra Madre*, 1948 etc),
but by the late 1960s his career had
slumped: he had shot some of *Casino
Royale* (1967), which stank to high
heaven; *Reflections in a Golden Eye*
(1967), which was weak; and then went
on to *Sinful Davey*, which lies somewhere
between the two in terms of quality. The
last film he completed was *The Dead*
(1987), which is close to perfect.

How then, can one explain *Sinful
Davey*? The source material is strong
and deserved better. David Haggart lived
only a short life. He was born in 1801
and became an eclectic criminal (the
Dictionary of National Biography states
that he was a 'thief and homicide') whose
brief career ended when, shortly after his

21st birthday, he was executed. Prior to
his execution he dictated his memoirs to a
phrenologist. The book was subsequently
published, although there is disagreement
as to its veracity. The film is based on
the book, but consistently downplays the
severity of Davey's criminal activity. In
the film no one is killed, and the fruits
of the main heist are returned to the
victims. The Duke of Argyll finds Davey
so diverting that he pleads for a lesser
sentence at the trial, furnishes his cell
with luxuries, and celebrates his escape.
The cast is strong and, as John Coleman
notes in the *Spectator*, they all 'appear
to enjoy their bits'. There is something
rather entertaining about watching Robert
Morley – far from strapping – appear
to toss the caber as the Duke opens the
Highland games at Inverary. The real
problem lies with the script. I cannot do
better than to quote Jonathan Coe in
S&S: 'The structure is both rambling and
repetitive; typically a scene will begin on
a calm enough note... Davey will come
along to disrupt things... hey presto, we're
off on one of the film's extended chases'.

The film was shot almost entirely in
Ireland. John Huston could leave the set
and be in New York for dinner. Quoted in
The Guardian he stated that: 'Our story
must appear to be happening in Scotland.
The only reason we have for filming it
in Ireland is that I like to be here and my
associates, who know this, are humouring
me'.

Maggie Smith and Pamela Franklin

The Prime of Miss Jean Brodie (1969) S+ T8

Directed by Ronald Neame
Screenplay by Jay Presson Allen
Leading cast: Maggie Smith (Jean Brodie); Robert Stephens (Teddy Lloyd); Celia Johnson (Miss Mackay); Gordon Jackson (Gordon Lowther); Pamela Franklin (Sandy); Diane Grayson (Jenny); Jane Carr (Mary McGregor)
Colour, 116 minutes, UK

Edinburgh, 1932 to 1936. Jean is a teacher at the Marcia Blaine School for Girls. All her pupils are 'the crème de la crème, and she is in her prime, but her attitudes bring her into conflict with the school authorities. Tragedy strikes, and she is sacked.

The Prime of Miss Jean Brodie is rightly lauded for the towering performance delivered by 34-year-old Maggie Smith, acting alongside her then husband, Robert Stephens. Smith had been Oscar-nominated as Best Supporting Actress in 1966 for her role in *Othello* (Stuart Burge, 1965) and won as Best Actress for *Jean Brodie* in 1970 (she also won the BAFTA). It's understandable that a performance of such power should be remembered, but this should not overshadow the magnificent ensemble cast.

Both Muriel Spark's novel (1961) and Jay Presson Allen's play (1966) were successful, but the film performed better with the critics than it did commercially. While Smith's performance as Jean is admirable, Jean herself is deeply flawed: she is selfish, vain, and silly; her political naivety is bottomless, and she is a panderer. The consequences of her actions include the death of her pupil Mary, and the seduction of another, Sandy, by her (married) teacher, Teddy. But it takes time for Jean's darkness to be revealed as the layers of self-constructed veneer are skilfully peeled away. Her adulation of Mussolini, whom she first praises for ensuring pavements are clean, later extends to Franco. Even after Mary has been killed in Spain, Jean clings to her convictions: 'Mary died a heroine... it was her intention to fight for Franco against the forces of darkness'. Yet perhaps even more troubling is her pushing for her place in Teddy's bed to be taken by 16-year-old Sandy. Summing up the girls' attributes she describes Sandy as the one with insight, and turning to Jenny says, 'in years to come... Jenny will be famous for [*pause*] sex'.

It is Teddy and Sandy (with her 'insight') who, finally, speak the truth. TEDDY: 'You're not in your prime Jean, you're a frustrated spinster taking it out in idiot causes and dangerous ideas; you're a *schoolmarm*'. SANDY: 'I didn't betray you. I simply put a stop to you... you are dangerous and unwholesome, and children should not be exposed to you'.

Jean Brodie was shot largely on location in Edinburgh, including at the Edinburgh Academy, and extensive use is made of the Old Town.

The McKenzie Break (1970) T100

Directed by Lamont Johnson
Screenplay by William W Norton
Leading cast: Brian Keith (Capt. Jack Connor); Helmut Griem (Kapitan Willi Schluetter); Ian Hendry (Maj. Perry)
Colour, 108 minutes, UK/Ireland

Led by Schluetter, 600 German prisoners of war, held in the McKenzie camp in Scotland rebel, then there is a mass escape. Schluetter's foil is Connor, an unorthodox officer. Connor finds the escapees making their way to a German submarine, which evades a British torpedo boat. Most prisoners escape, but Schluetter is left behind.

The McKenzie Break is based on Sidney Shelley's novel *Bowmanville Break* (1968), set in Canada, which itself was based loosely on two separate Canadian incidents. The film's action is relocated to Scotland, but little about the film is Scottish. Most of it was shot in Ireland. There is no recorded instance of an effective escape from any of the several POW camps in Scotland during World War II.

While there are several films fictionalising or celebrating real WWII POW escape attempts, *The McKenzie Break* is unusual, but not unique (see, eg, *The One That Got Away*, Roy Ward Baker, 1957) in focusing on an escape attempt by Axis prisoners from an Allied POW camp. In *The NYT* Roger Greenspun had little but praise for the film, which he found 'so greatly superior to most recent war movies, adventure movies, escape movies and action movies generally that it seems almost unfair to raise the objection that it is not quite as good as it sets out to be'.

As an escape drama the film is gripping. Tension is effectively built, and the outcome remains in doubt until the very end. However, *The McKenzie Break* follows well-established tropes, and it remains clear where our sympathies should lie. Griem, a German actor with a long career (the high point being Maximilian in *Cabaret*, Bob Fosse, 1972), is charismatic as Schluetter and, for the first ten minutes of the film, he may have our sympathy. It quickly becomes clear however that he is a 'bad' German: a Luftwaffe prisoner will have no part in his riot, which is contrary to the Geneva Convention; he is antisemitic and homophobic; he has probably murdered the previous senior German officer, casually orders the murder of a prisoner and is responsible for the deaths of others. Hendry's Maj. Perry, referred to dismissively as 'the headmaster', is ineffective, lacking the wiles to spar with Schluetter, for whom the deadly foe is Connor. As the brusque, roguish Irishman Keith is effective (accent slippage notwithstanding). As Mark Cunliffe puts it, 'Keith manages to depict the bullish, insolent nature of the man whilst maintaining a level of charm' (*Letterboxd*). The final scene has Schluetter and Connor staring at each other, each of them having partly succeeded and partly failed, in seemingly mutual respect.

The Ballad of Tam Lin (aka *Tam Lin*, aka *The Devil's Widow*) (1970) S+ T14

Directed by Roddy McDowall
Screenplay by William Spier
Leading cast: Ava Gardner (Michaela Cazaret); Ian McShane (Tom Lynn); Richard Wattis (Elroy); Stephanie Beacham (Janet Ainsley)
Colour, 106 minutes, UK

Tom is a member of Michaela's coterie of beautiful young things and is her lover. They spend time in a baronial house in the Scottish Borders. Tom falls in love with Janet and determines to leave Michaela. Later he is hunted by Michaela's 'creatures'; if they catch him, they will tear him to pieces. With Janet's aid, Tom survives.

Tam Lin is a weird trip into folk-horror. It is tempting, and would be wholly consistent with *Tam Lin*'s style, to write this entire entry in a late-1960s Californian hippy commune patois, but I shall resist. Every film is a product of its time, but few set a cultural moment in aspic. *Tam Lin*, notwithstanding its Scottish setting, and its source in a folk ballad dating to at least the first half of the 16th century, perfectly captures the period in which flower-power and psychedelia intersected. The film might as well be set in a Californian commune. While that may seem incongruous in the setting of the Borders (*Tam Lin* was shot in part at Traquair House and around Peebles), it was filmed partly in what appears to have been a glorious July in

1969. Beautiful women in diaphanous gowns, and beautiful men – sometimes in tailored suits, sometimes bare-chested – elegantly waft through the house, or decorate the garden. They are constantly at play – appearing to have little else to do – and in one bizarre moment bounce along on space hoppers. There are stylistic directorial/editing quirks too which are redolent of the late '60s, including the use of tinted shots, and of arrested action and stills. One month after the Scottish shoot, the Summer of Love came to a crushingly brutal end. Manson's followers committed their murders in August 1969 and, in December, Hells Angels killed a black concertgoer at the Altamont Free Concert, but McDowall could not have predicted the future. One cannot help wondering how much darker *Tam Lin* might have been had it been made even six months later.

As it is, *Tam Lin* at least intersects with horror (the credits include a list of members of the 'Second Coven'). The source ballad, which the film *very* cleverly follows, with a strong degree of fidelity to the story essentials, tells of a man rescued from the Queen of the Fairies by his one true love. It references abortion, and includes nightmarish hallucinations, and the chase to near death at the end.

Tam Lin also merits attention because of those involved in its production. This was Roddy McDowall's only film as a director. As an actor he was prolific (best known for the original *Planet of the Apes* films, he plays David Balfour in the 1948 version of *Kidnapped*). Hollywood legend Ava Gardner's career at this point remained

A film in sore need of rediscovery

strong. Her films either side of *Tam Lin* were *Mayerling* (Terence Young, 1968) and *The Life and Times of Judge Roy Bean* (John Huston, 1972). Ian McShane was on his way to wide recognition; Stephanie Beacham was in only her second film role. Also appearing are a young Joanna Lumley, Madeline Smith (who has the line: 'I'll swallow anything as long as it's illegal') and Bruce Robinson, who later directed the greatest British comedy film ever made, 1987's *Withnail and I*. Unfortunately, the film's production company's struggles resulted in the release being delayed. When *Tam Lin* 'finally reached the screens in limited release in 1972 it received next to no attention' (Kendra Bean and Anthony Uzarowski, *Ava: A life in movies*, 2017).

Tam Lin would make a perfect late-night companion to *The Wicker Man*; it is not a great film, but it is a fascinating one and has in recent years witnessed something of a resurgence. October 2022 saw the release of a superb Blu-ray edition replete with extra material (released as *The Ballad of Tam-Lin*).

Country Dance (aka *Brotherly Love*) (1970)　T100

Directed by J Lee Thompson
Screenplay by James Kennaway
Leading cast: Peter O'Toole (Sir Charles Ferguson ('Pink')); Susannah York (Hilary Dow); Michael Craig (Douglas Dow)
Colour, 112 minutes, UK/US

In rural Perthshire Hilary's marriage appears to be collapsing. She attempts to support her mentally ill brother, Charles, whose love for her verges on the incestuous. Charles is committed to a psychiatric hospital, and Hilary returns to her husband.

Tunes of Glory and *Country Dance* have in common both a writer – Kennaway (in the case of *Country Love* he first turned his novel, *Household Ghosts* (1961), into a play, before adapting it for the screen), and actor Susannah York. *Tunes* is the better film. *Country Dance* opens with the tiring signifier of Scotland – a lone piper plays on a random hillside (as,

in the movies only, they often do), but this hillside is in Ireland, where the film was shot. True to the source, the setting remains a Perthshire farm estate, with forays into Dundee, but little is made of the Scottish background, although the country dance of the title is a ball-cum-ceilidh to support the local Conservative association. The film was given an X (adult) certificate on release (which has not been revised). This would have been driven by the issues the dark script dealt with: alcoholism, mental illness, suicide and, *very* obliquely, incest. The language is theatrically ornate, as if Pink takes refuge in the one last dignity open to him as he presides over the terminal decline of a minor aristocratic lineage. O'Toole (also in *Kidnapped*, 1959 and *Lassie*, 2005) who was drinking heavily when the film was shot, is magnificent in a difficult role, and is matched step-by-step by York.

When Eight Bells Toll (1971)　S+

Directed by Etienne Périer
Screenplay by Alistair MacLean
Leading cast: Anthony Hopkins (Philip Calvert); Nathalie Delon (Charlotte); Corin Redgrave (Roy Hunslett); Jack Hawkins (Sir Anthony Skouras)
Colour, 94 minutes, UK

Agent Calvert puts his nautical skills to use to take on a criminal gang raiding boats carrying bullion. The gang's centre of operations is near 'Torbay' (Tobermory, on Mull).

When Eight Bells Toll was intended by the producers to plug a gap in the market after it was announced that Sean Connery would be quitting as James Bond. But this is Bond-lite. Hopkins was 33 when *Bells* was made and had some feature films under his belt but did not at this point have the presence of Connery, and the film did not have the production budget or resources to match the Bond franchise, although the inclusion of Nathalie Delon (who had divorced Alain Delon in 1969) added a touch of European glamour of the sort on display in the Bond films. Everyone in the film is competent in their roles, but the always-reliable Robert Morley (see also *Sinful Davey* and *The Battle of the Sexes*) as *Bells'* equivalent of 'M', is the most watchable, and this is not meant to be the case in a spy/action movie. Although the film performed reasonably at the UK and European box-offices, its performance in the US was weak, and it did not do as well financially as its backers had hoped. Bond was revived, and no Carver franchise was forthcoming.

Vincent Canby, the influential *NYT* reviewer, was dismissive: 'the movie collapses in a heap of failed attempts to be both plausible and stylish – the first being beyond Mr MacLean's interest, and the second being beyond the talents of Etienne Périer, a director whose every shot and cut is predictable'. There is no verve whatsoever to the film. It moves from one scene to the next in much the same way as an escalator moves – with reliable, steady, and unexciting routine. Périer had made one English-language film before *Bells*, the

Spanish/French production *The Day the Hot Line Got Hot* (1968), and there was little in his short career to indicate that an English-language action film would play to his strengths. Over 45 years he accrued 28 director credits, none of which stand out as notable successes.

Where Bond had made much of international locations, offering audiences views of global exoticism, the action in *Bells* is limited to Scotland's western islands. Much of the film was shot on Mull, and Duart Castle makes a substantial appearance. There is good aerial footage covering swathes of both Mull and Skye, as well as Staffa and Fingal's Cave.

The Bill Douglas Childhood Trilogy: My Childhood (1972), My Ain Folk (1973), My Way Home (1978) S+++ T2

Directed by Bill Douglas
Screenplay by Bill Douglas
Leading cast: Stephen Archibald (Jamie);
   Hughie Restorick (Tommy); Jean Taylor Smith
   (grandmother); Paul Kermack (Jamie's father);
   Helena Gloag (Jamie's father's mother); Joseph
   Blatchley (Robert)
B&W (with minimal colour in My Ain Folk),
46/55/71 minutes, UK

[MC] *A Scottish mining village in 1945. Tommy and Jamie live with their gran, who dies, leaving them adrift.* [MAF] *Their gran dead, the brothers fend for themselves before Tommy is taken into State care. Jamie's father leaves and, after*

Jean Taylor Smith, Hughie Restorick and Stephen Archibald in *My Childhood*

his grandfather dies, Jamie too is taken into State care. [MWH] Jamie, who aspires to become an artist, has been living in a care home in Edinburgh, where he later works. Later still he is a young conscript in the RAF in North Africa.

The remarkably singular *Childhood Trilogy* is usually categorised as being both autobiographical and part of the very strong British tradition of social realism. Douglas himself is quoted as saying the 'childhood of the title is literally my childhood and the incidents I recount are with a few variations things that actually happened to me'. Douglas sent a draft of the screenplay of *MC* to director Lindsay Anderson (*This*

Sporting Life, 1963; *If ….*, 1968; *O Lucky Man!*, 1973) – who is thanked in the closing credits – and was shocked when Anderson quickly identified the film as autobiographical, suggesting the final title, rather than Douglas' proposed *Jamie*.

There had been nothing like this made in Scotland when *MC* was completed in 1972 – arguably there has *still* been nothing like this made in Scotland, although Loach's *Sweet Sixteen*, Mullan's *Neds* and Ramsay's *Ratcatcher* come close. An even closer analogy might be Margaret Tait's *Blue Black Permanent*, not that Tait's film is in the social realist tradition, but that it is a singular vision by an artist made with no prospect of commercial success, because the writer/director had something they needed to say. The closest two British films I can think of in tone to *The Childhood Trilogy* are Terence Davies' *Distant Voices, Still Lives* (1988) and Richard Billingham's *Ray & Liz* (2018). So different to anything else was the trilogy that the book *Scottish Reels* (ed, Colin McArthur, 1982) was later criticised for ignoring Douglas' work, which did not conform to the narrative and argument of the book (a critique of 'kailyard' representations of Scotland), in that it was too distinctively the work of a Scottish auteur and too grounded.

In his introduction to the BFI Blu-ray/DVD set, Peter Jewell (who in *MWH* is represented as 'Robert') suggests that the trilogy 'is far from straightforward autobiography, and [Douglas'] films are not as much "social realism" as "poetic realism"'. He references in support of this the scene in *MWH* in which Robert teaches Jamie how to eat kippers, something which in fact happened later when the two shared a flat. There is poetry throughout the trilogy in the economy of the language (the written scripts would reduce to a small number of pages), and in the visual imagery. Even when confined to the three houses – one opposite the other two – in which most of the events in Newcraighall take place, there is an austere beauty to the photography. This reaches its apotheosis in a scene in *MC* when Tommy stands on a railway bridge above a train, swathed in its smoke. There is also a glorious absurdity to some of the scenes in the RAF station in Egypt, a small British island surrounded by

a sea of sand, and itself largely consisting of sand, which at one point Jamie is required to sweep smooth.

Archibald, who plays Jamie and had no experience of acting yet, is terrific. He met Douglas at a bus stop in Edinburgh and was picked on the spot. His life too was hard; Douglas said that 'I'd just look into his eye, and I could see that he knew exactly what I was talking about'. His life after the trilogy remained difficult; he spent some time in prison and died at the age of 39. Restorick (Tommy) also died young, by suicide, in 1990. Douglas died aged 57, having directed only one further film, *Comrades* (1986). *The Childhood Trilogy* is a very powerful legacy. Fortunately, his stature has grown in recent years, his significance is recognised in *Bill Douglas: A Film Artist*† (Amelia Watts and Phil Wickham, 2022).

Madame Sin (1972)　S+

Directed by David Greene
Screenplay by Barry Oringer and David Greene
Leading cast: Bette Davis (Madame Sin); Robert Wagner (Anthony 'Tony' Lawrence); Denholm Elliott (Malcolm De Vere); Gordon Jackson (Commander Cavendish); Catherine Schell (Barbara)
Colour, 75 minutes, UK

Tony, an unemployed American 'agent' with a tragic history, becomes ensnared by master criminal 'Madame Sin' while thwarting a plot to hijack a Polaris submarine. This is merely a setback for Madame Sin, who emerges triumphant.

Madame Sin is a pale attempt to emulate the pizazz of the James Bond series (*Time Out* notes it has 'lots of exotic sets and outlandish secret weapons, just a pity it's all rather old hat Bond stuff') and is set and filmed substantially on Mull (here simply 'the island', although it is firmly positioned on the west of Scotland); most interiors were shot at Pinewood. It is as likely that the film was influenced by *The Man from U.N.C.L.E.*, which ran on TV through 105 episodes from 1964–1968, as it was by Bond. The production values of *Madame Sin* betray the fact that it was intended to be a pilot for a TV series – the lead production company was the UK's Incorporated Television Company Ltd (ITC), and of the director's 90 directorial credits the vast majority are for TV. No series was forthcoming, and after a 1972 network broadcast in the US, *Madame Sin* received theatrical releases in a limited number of territories.

Were it not for the fact that Madame Sin was played by double Oscar-winning Hollywood legend Bette Davis there would be little to save the film from total obscurity, and there is little reason now to seek this out. The decision to bump Robert Wagner off in the penultimate scene results in both a very downbeat ending, and the viewer wondering how things would have continued. If the plan was to run a series based around Madame Sin herself, perhaps with Elliott continuing to play her chief henchman, things might have been interesting. Otherwise, she does not have to do much more than stand around looking mildly threatening. Elliott is the

only person who endows the film with life. The plot, such as it is, is both ridiculous (although at the time this was not fatal) and very thin (which probably was). The review in the *MFB* is on the nail: 'the film is defeated by the trite mechanics of the plotting… overall a dull script, a wooden hero and an abysmal ending'.

La morte negli occhi del gato (*Seven Deaths in the Cat's Eyes*) (1973)

Directed by Antonio Margheriti
Screenplay by Antonio Margheriti and Giovanni Simonelli
Leading cast: Jane Birkin (Corringa); Hiram Keller (Lord James MacGrieff); Françoise Christophe (Lady Mary MacGrieff)
Colour, 95 minutes, Italy/France/West Germany

Dragonstone castle, Scotland: a series of murders take place while Corringa visits her mother, Lady Alicia, and her aunt, Lady Mary, who owns the castle. Corringa's cousin, Lord James, is the heir to the estate. He is suspected of the murders (as are others) and is believed to be dangerously unstable.

Seven Deaths straddles gothic and *giallo*, being rooted firmly in the former, but with many tropes of the latter, including the gruesome murders and the basic 'whodunnit' structure (it also followed Dario Argento's two films from 1971 in having both an animal and a number in the title). The one thing which *Seven Deaths* is

The German poster for an Italian Giallo film set
in Scotland

the actor to look out for here is Luciano
Pigozzi (playing Angus – while credited
as 'Alan Collins'), known as the Italian
Peter Lorre (the resemblance is striking),
who appeared in some seminal *giallo* films,
including *Blood and Black Lace* (Mario
Bava, 1964) and *Baron Blood* (Mario
Bava, 1972).

Although this is available on free
streaming services, the quality is better on
the Blu-ray and DVD releases.

Nothing But the Night (aka *The Resurrection Syndicate*, aka *The Devil's Undead*) (1973)

Directed by Peter Sasdy
Screenplay by Brian Hayles
Leading cast: Peter Cushing (Sir Mark Ashley);
  Christopher Lee (Colonel Bingham); Diana
  Dors (Anna Harb); Georgia Brown (Joan
  Foster); Fulton Mackay (Cameron)
Colour, 90 minutes, UK

*Trustees of the Van Traylen orphanage, at
'Inver House' on the island of 'Bala', are
serially murdered. Pathologist Sir Ashley,
Colonel Bingham, and a reporter, Joan,
investigate. All is not as it seems…*

not iparticularly Scottish, notwithstanding
that it is set in a Scottish castle and its
grounds (in reality, the Castello Massimo
in Arsoli). There are Scottish names (but
not Scottish actors), some attempts in the
English dubbed version at accents and, at
the funeral of Lady Alicia, bagpipes. But
I wasn't going to pass up the opportunity
to include here a film with more than a
passing relationship to *giallo*, featuring
both Jane Birkin and (in a supporting
role) Serge Gainsbourg. There is also,
somewhat randomly, a gorilla (potentially,
given references to Freud, a manifestation
of ego but this is almost certainly reading
too much into the film). For *giallo* fans,

An impish pub-quiz question might be:
'which 1973 film gave Michael Gambon
his first credit, stars Christopher Lee, is
set on a Scottish island, and ends with a
bonfire and death?' The correct answer is,
of course, the almost completely forgotten
Nothing But the Night. It's forgotten for
two reasons: first, it has been powerfully

Georgia Brown and Peter Cushing

by British horror writer John Fenwick Anderson Blackburn, doesn't carry the film. The end is much better than the beginning, but a good punchline is not enough. The cast list, however, is strong, with London-born Georgia Brown (who began her career as a blues singer, before moving into musical theatre and then TV and film) standing out.

overshadowed by Lee's next film, *The Wicker Man*; and second, it's not good. As Joe Dante says in an introduction to the film on YouTube, 'sometimes the magic works, and sometimes it doesn't. In the case of [*NBTN*]... the magic doesn't work'. Lee had formed Charlemagne Productions, responsible for the film, intending that he have more control over his career and a bigger share of the money he'd been earning for others (Hammer in particular). The result was a commercial failure, and no further films were made.

The film moves from London to the Scottish island 'Bala' about 30 minutes in and stays there. However, harbour scenes were shot at Dartmouth in Devon, and the island exterior scenes on Dartmoor. Notwithstanding the presence of Fulton Mackay as the local police commander there is very little here which is convincingly Scottish.

While Sasdy was building a reputation as a strong director of horror, with *Countess Dracula* and *The Hands of the Ripper* (both 1971) under his belt, the script for *NBTN*, based on a novel

The Wicker Man (1973)   S+   T5

Directed by Robin Hardy
Screenplay by Anthony Shaffer
Leading cast: Edward Woodward (Sergeant Howie); Christopher Lee (Lord Summerisle); Ingrid Pitt (librarian); Britt Ekland (Willow); Lindsay Kemp (Alder MacGreagor); Diane Cilento (Miss Rose)
Colour, 88 minutes (original release), UK

Police sergeant Neil Howie, a devout Christian, arrives by seaplane at Summerisle in the Hebrides to investigate the disappearance of a young girl. He stays at the local inn, where the landlord's daughter Willow exudes sexuality. He encounters resistance and obfuscation from the islanders. When seeking permission to exhume the body of the missing girl, whose grave he has located, Lord Summerisle explains the importance of the 'old gods' to life on the island. Howie is pursued and becomes trapped in a gigantically constructed wicker man; he is sacrificially burnt alive.

The Wicker Man belongs to a select group of films in that it is both more lauded *and*

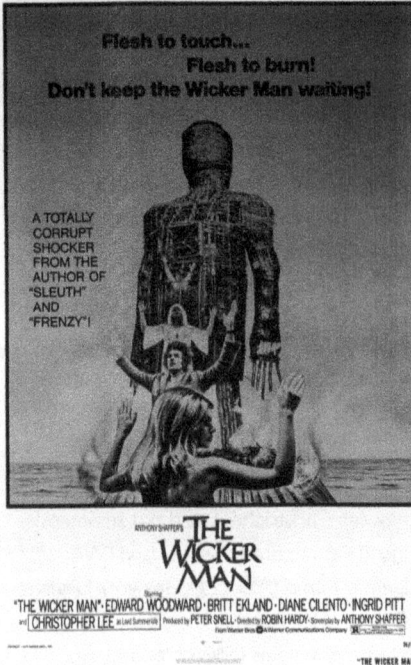

US one-sheet poster

complexity of its distribution history (which has resulted in three different versions of the film existing, and the original negatives being almost certainly destroyed), and the rivalries and enmities which continued to exist between the film's creators years after its release.

Famously, in 1977 *Cinefantastique* magazine described *The Wicker Man* as 'the Citizen Kane of horror movies'. Whether it is, in fact, a horror film is a matter of some debate. Certainly, it was the winner of the Saturn Award for the Best Horror Film in 1977, but Lee disputes the label: '*The Wicker Man* was in the end horrifying, but not what I call a horror film'. What is clear is that *The Wicker Man* played a key role in the ascendancy of British folk-horror cinema, a genre which to this day continues to be popular (for a robust analysis of the relationship between the film, folk myth, and the development of film genre see *The Quest for the Wicker Man*, B Franks et al, 2006). Whether it is horror, science fiction (the case can be made), or a thriller is perhaps moot. If anything, it is the difficulty in easily pigeon-holing the film that has fed into its cult status.

What is certain is that *The Wicker Man* is a powerful film, although this is only fully revealed in either of the longer cuts of 96 or 102 minutes which emerged in the US after significant detective work and restoration, and which are now available on DVD and Blu-ray. Cut twice originally, first for content, then for length (in his foreword to Brown's book, Woodward refers to the film 'being slashed in the cutting room'), the original release is a

more popular now than it was on its first, botched, release. It featured in volume two of Dan Peary's *Cult Movies* (1983) – the second of a trilogy that gave definition and life to the cult movie phenomena – and has its own chapter in Justin Smith's *Withnail and Us: Cult Films and Film Cults in British Cinema* (2010). More significant are Allan Brown's excellent book, *Inside the Wicker Man: How not to make a cult classic* (rev edn 2010) and John Walsh's *The Wicker Man: The Official Story of the Film* (2023). Brown explores the complicated story of the film's making (which resulted in a rushed location shoot in the wrong season); the byzantine

In The Wicker Man modernity is defeated by tradition

little *too* taut and truncated. It omits the layered complexity of Howie and Lord Summerisle's relationship, encapsulated in their views as to the role of God, gods, and religion. This in turn diminishes the power of their final confrontation.

That *The Wicker Man* is a beloved film is either despite or because of its flaws. Woodward and Lee (wig notwithstanding) are excellent, but the cast is not uniformly so. While Pitt was clearly having the time of her life (Brown quotes her as saying: 'To be a librarian is a wonderful thing. To be a nymphomaniac as well is broadening the scope of the role considerably'), Ekland was not, and her performance was later overdubbed, so the voice we hear is not hers. Kemp has acknowledged that his casting as the innkeeper was a curious choice, and that he struggled with the accent. But somehow everything comes together – perhaps it is simply that the

atmosphere of threatening strangeness which pervades the film is enhanced, rather than damaged, by the off-kilter dynamics on screen.

Location tourism is vibrant – the film was shot almost entirely in Dumfries and Galloway, and many of the original locations remain recognisable from the film (see the appendix to Brown's book). The film is referenced in *Shallow Grave*, as Alex is shown watching it on TV, and its echoes reverberate through *Calibre*. It is also interwoven into Rupert Russell's engaging 2024 documentary *The Last Sacrifice*, which draws a connection between a gruesome Cotswolds murder, 1960s counterculture, witchcraft and folk-horror film. Note that another film from 1973, *Nothing But the Night*, also ends on a Scottish island with Christopher Lee, and a bonfire.

→ *The Wicker Tree* (2011) S+

Directed by Robin Hardy
Screenplay by Robin Hardy
Leading cast: Brittania Nicol (Beth Boothby);
   Henry Garrett (Steve Thomson); Graham
   McTavish (Sir Lachlan Morrison)
Colour, 96 minutes, UK

'Tressock', in the Borders: Texan evangelists Beth and Steve, who have come to convert the natives, are welcomed by Sir Lachlan. Things go badly wrong.

Robin Hardy directed **The Wicker Man**. Nearly 40 years later he made this wretched attempt (described directly as 'the sequel to *The Wicker Man*' by the film's second unit director, Adrian Mead – see **Night People**) to cash in on the earlier film's success. It did not. Even Sir Christopher Lee is dragged into this rubbish, making a fleeting appearance as an 'Old Gentleman'. Like **Gregory's Two Girls**, this should never be watched, lest it forever corrupt your view of an earlier, better-beyond-belief film. Reviews are almost entirely dismissive. *Time Out*'s Joshua Rothkopf had this to say: 'a hee-haw slam on ugly Americanism, a vast reduction of the original's notion of unravelling civilisation'; for Allan Hunter in *Screen International*, the film suffered from 'ropey dialogue, rhubarbing extras, hammy performances and tired horror movie clichés. To add insult to injury, the film was screened in Scotland, while the rest of the UK was spared.

The Great McGonagall (1975) S+

Directed by Joseph McGrath
Screenplay by Joseph McGrath and Spike
   Milligan
Leading cast: Spike Milligan (William
   McGonagall); Peter Sellers (Queen Victoria)
Colour, 95 minutes, UK

Dundee, 1890: William Topaz McGonagall, a truly awful 'poet' and performer dies. A picaresque life story is then relayed, most of this shown on stage in a music hall.

William McGonagall, who claimed to be born in Edinburgh, but was most likely born in Ireland, achieved notoriety and popularity as a poet and performer in Victorian Scotland although he was destitute when he died in Edinburgh in 1902 (not, as the film suggests in its opening scene, in Dundee in 1890); the verses recited by Milligan in the film are all written by McGonagall.

The Great McGonagall is a challenging film to explain to anyone too young to remember the BBC radio programme *The Goon Show* which, like *TGM*, was largely written by Spike Milligan and which too starred Peter Sellers (also in **The Battle of the Sexes**). Whereas *The Goon Show* was extremely influential on British popular culture, smashing staid conventionality, *TGM* disappeared largely without trace, notwithstanding the high profile of its two lead actors. Like *The Goon Show* the film lacks coherent structure, and frequently verges on the surreal. It includes jokes contemporary to its production, which now have little resonance and the film is at times offensively racist. Director McGrath, who was born in Glasgow, had worked extensively with The Beatles, and in 1968 had directed a short TV show featuring The Goons. The film was shot entirely in London over a period of three weeks during a production that was at times as chaotic (Sellers proving to be very unreliable) as is the result. Pointless nudity was demanded by producer David Grant, who made the film as a tax write-off.

Come Play with Me (1977)

Directed by George Harrison Marks
Screenplay by George Harrison Marks
Leading cast: Kelly the forger (Alfie Bass);
  Clapworthy (George Harrison Marks); Lady
  Bovington (Irene Handl); Rodney (Jerry
  Lorden)
Colour, 94 minutes, UK

Bovington Manor Health Farm at 'Garloch' in the Highlands is turned first into a sex club, then a forgery centre.

Come Play with Me is possibly the most unlikely film to be covered in this book. It's not the worst film here, but it is certainly the most notorious. It earned the distinction of the longest continuous run at a cinema of any film in British history when, from its release in 1977 until 1981 it ran at the Moulin Cinema on Soho's Great Windmill Street. Later it went on to be a bestseller on VHS. The film says more about the peculiar British attitude

to sex and censorship than it does about Scotland, where most of the 'action' is, for no apparent reason whatsoever, set. The improbably named 'Bovington Manor' is, in fact, Weston Manor in Oxfordshire.

There is not, really, a plot; there is some pretence of one, but it verges on the incoherent. In short, Come Play with Me is a soft-porn film (with allegations made at the time that some scenes were shot 'hard'), with David Sullivan, later the founder of the Sunday Sport, as an executive producer. Tonally Come Play with Me is all over the place, ranging from something akin to Donald McGill's saucy seaside postcards up to the boundaries of what was then permitted by the BBFC. Happily embracing any publicity, Sullivan told the News of the World, which ran a feature after actors had complained they were misled as to the film's pornographic nature, 'nothing is simulated... the film will make Linda Lovelace look like Noddy'. It doesn't (Lovelace was the lead performer in Deep Throat, Gerard Damiano, 1972; a poster advertising the film can be seen in a Soho street scene in Come Play with Me). There's a good piece on the production on *marymillington.co.uk*.

Obviously, you should not watch this retrograde, sexist, nonsense, not because doing so will make you a bad person, but because it is rubbish; it even fails to be erotic. If, however, you ignore my advice, you will find, 37 minutes in, what must surely be one of the most bizarre scenes in a British film, when – for no reason whatsoever, and with little obvious talent – Kelly and Clapworthy break into a musical number, with backing from the Manor's resident strippers (I confess, I laughed out loud at the sheer craziness of this).

Come Play with Me's place in British cultural history is secured not only by its record-breaking run, but by featuring, in a small role, Mary Millington. But the film did *not*, as a later poster claimed, make her a star. Born in 1945 (as Mary Ruth Quilter), she became a glamour model before turning to hardcore pornography, the distribution of which was at the time unlawful in the UK. She met David Sullivan in 1974, and was heavily promoted by him, appearing regularly in his soft-core publications, such as *Whitehouse*, which Clapworthy is seen 'reading' in *Come Play with Me*. Later she opened her own sex shop. In the legal and moral climate of the time she regularly had run-ins with the law, and died by suicide in 1979, before the release of the Sex Pistols' film, *The Great Rock and Roll Swindle* (Julien Temple, 1980), in which she had a small part. It is remarkable then that the film also stars Irene Handl, the well-respected English character actor, who only eight years earlier had worked with Hollywood legend Billy Wilder (see *The Private Life of Sherlock Holmes*). She plays the owner of Bovington Manor, and apparently threatened to walk off the set once she realised the nature of the production.

The only thing Scottish about *Come Play with Me*, apart from its alleged location, is the name of the porter, McIvor. In a late scene he is in full Scottish regalia.

Long Shot (1978)   S+ T100

Directed by Maurice Hatton
Screenplay by Eoin McCann
Leading cast: Charles Gormley (Charlie); Neville Smith (Neville); Ann Zelda (Anne)
B&W/Colour, 85 minutes, UK

Charlie, a producer, and Neville, a screenwriter, attempt to pitch a film at the EIFF.

Long Shot is a film about the attempt to raise a production budget for the making of a Scottish film. The first 50 minutes are set (and were shot) at the 1977 EIFF ('the longest continually running film festival in the world'), before the 'action' moves to London and, in a final scene, Hollywood. In another era this might have been called a mockumentary, but it precedes *This is Spinal Tap* (Rob Reiner, 1984) by some six years. *Long Shot* is a remarkable time capsule, which is more likely to be loved by those who can relish the filmic and Scottish references (and indeed, Scottish/filmic; the scene involving Susannah York is glorious but relies in part on familiarity with *Tunes of Glory* and '60s and '70s British film) and the cameo performances (the very best of which comes from Alan Bennett). To take only directors, the film includes John Boorman, Wim Wenders, Stephen Frears and Maurice Bulbulian. That these riches were available to the makers of a film with a limited budget demonstrates the goodwill filmmakers had for the project.

Although the film deals with the trials and tribulations of hard-pressed independent filmmakers, and would be of general interest, it has added value in the framework of this book by being addressed specifically to Scottish cinema. In this context the key discussion is that between Charlie, pitching a co-production deal, and Quebecois producer/director Bulbulian, who says: 'You want to have a national cinema here? You want to say things with the film that you are making? You have to find a way right here to do these things. You don't have to rely on others to make cinema. You have to rely first of all on yourself.' This might have been a manifesto for the development of Scottish cinema. Gormley was himself trying to break through into directing and later wrote and directed both *Living Apart Together* and *Heavenly Pursuits*.

Some critics found the film *overly* self-referential. The *Time Out* review began with the following: 'An incestuous, half-hoax docu-farce, largely set against the background of the Edinburgh Festival, on the travails of setting up a British feature film' but concluded with 'its hard-knocks humour probably succeeds in carrying it beyond an in-joke.' *Long Shot* does not have the depth of *Sunset Boulevard* (Billy Wilder, 1950) or *The Player* (Robert Altman, 1992), but it is, for Scottish cinephiles, a delight.

That Sinking Feeling (1979) S+++
T16

Directed by Bill Forsyth
Screenplay by Bill Forsyth
Leading cast: Robert Buchanan (Ronnie); Billy Greenless (Wal); Alan Love (Alec); John Hughes (Vic)
Colour, 93 minutes, UK

In Glasgow, Ronnie organises a raid on a sink factory, co-opting his group of singularly inept friends.

That Sinking Feeling is, without a doubt, one of the most important Scottish films made. In the five years preceding the release of *TSF* four films are covered here, **The Great McGonagall, Come Play with Me, The Thirty Nine Steps** (1978) and **Long Shot**, (which, it should be noted, is about the difficulty of making a film in Scotland); you then have to go back to 1973 for **Seven Deaths in the Cat's Eyes** and **The Wicker Man**. In the five years after *TSF*'s release there are 11 entries (admittedly three of these are by Forsyth); more importantly there is a notable shift in *who* begins making 'Scottish' films, and what these films are about – in short, more are made by Scots, and speak to authentic Scottish experiences. If you were to plot out a family tree of Scottish cinema, a great many of the lines would lead back to *TSF* and Forsyth. There was a brief period in the early 1980s when, to quote Duncan Petrie, 'Forsyth not only established himself as the pre-eminent Scottish filmmaker of his generation [but] was also for some critics the most important figure in the short-lived revival in British cinema' (*Screening Scotland*, 2000).

An opening title card reads: 'The action of this film takes place in a fictitious town called GLASGOW. Any resemblance to any real town called GLASGOW is purely coincidental' which is, of course, untrue. Later, when first pitching the heist to his inept gang of friends (the word 'gang' is inappropriate in this context, as it suggests organisation and threat, neither of which are to the fore), Ronnie asks: 'What's this area famous for?' The answers given are: 'drunks', 'murders', and 'multiple social deprivation'. Ronnie insists it is famous for 'sinks'. These illustrations reflect the general tone of a sharp, witty, inventive and made-on-a-shoestring film. It is also evident that Forsyth loved cinema: there are, at least, references to Charlie Chaplin (in the way Ronnie eats his breakfast cereal on a park bench before fastidiously cleaning up) and *Some Like it Hot* (Billy Wilder, 1959; in the scenes of Vic and Wal in drag). Crucially for its critical reception and longevity, *TSF* oozes charm, and there are strong gags, some verging on the surreal.

For Forsyth this was the first film of four which dominated Scottish cinema through to the mid-1980s. For many of the cast *TSF* was a first, and only, film. Buchanan appeared in *Gregory's Girl* and had a small role in *Comfort and Joy*; Greenlees' last appearance was in *Comfort and Joy*; and Love only appeared in one more film, *Gregory's Girl*. John Gordon Sinclair, who played Andy, went on to bigger roles in *Gregory's Girl* and *The Girl in the Picture*,

and continues to act; he also writes well-regarded crime fiction.

TSF received its world premiere at the EIFF, before securing a limited UK release later that year. It was reported that it was the cheapest UK-made film ever to be released. The BFI Flipside double-format DVD/Blu-ray release comes replete with extras, including commentaries, interviews, documentaries, and an analysis of the film's shoestring budget.

→ *Gregory's Girl* (1980) T10 and *Gregory's Two Girls* (1999) S+++

Screenplay by Bill Forsyth
Leading cast [GG] John Gordon Sinclair (Gregory Underwood); Dee Hepburn (Dorothy); Clare Grogan (Susan); Robert Buchanan (Andy); Jake D'Arcy (Phil Menzies) [G2G]: John Gordon Sinclair (Gregory Underwood); Dougray Scott (Fraser Brown); Maria Doyle Kennedy (Bel); Carly McKinnon (Frances); Hugh McCue (Douglas)
Colour, 91 minutes, UK; Colour 116 minutes, UK/Germany

[GG] Gregory hangs out with his friends, and inexpertly pursues Dorothy, who joins his football team.

Many who have seen *Gregory's Girl* might forget that Gregory's girl is his younger sister, Madeline (Allison Forster). In the penultimate scene, after his first successful date, she interrogates Gregory and says: 'It's hard work being in love, eh? Especially

Dee Hepburn and John Gordon Sinclair

when you don't know which girl it is... who's going to be Gregory's girl?'. He tells her she is. This is symptomatic of the gentleness which underpins this coming-of-age-in-Cumbernauld delight, resulting in it being one of the most loved entries in this book. With *That Sinking Feeling* the year before, Forsyth had demonstrated that it was possible to make a film in Scotland with a low budget and local talent; with *Gregory's Girl* he showed that it was also possible to do so and end up with a breakout hit.

Very little happens in *Gregory's Girl*: a boy in fourth year (ie, about 15 years old), pursues girls and plays football, and is rubbish at both. He hangs out with friends who are equally inept (the girls, older boys, and younger boys all seem *more* sophisticated than Gregory and his friends). That by the film's end he has

kissed a girl, Susan, is the result of *her* machinations – aided by other girls who work together (because, as Susan explains, 'girls do that') – and is an achievement for which he can take virtually no credit, save for the fact that he is quite charming in an awkward teenage sort of way. This makes the film extremely easy to relate to. Being an awkward teenager is a near-universal experience, which probably feels roughly the same whether you are in Cumbernauld, London, Los Angeles, or indeed Caracas (to which Gregory's friend Alan wants to move, as women outnumber men by eight to one – or so at least he has read).

The film is not really about the casual sexism of the early 1980s, or the uphill battle facing an athletic schoolgirl who believes it is her right to play in the school team. But these are present, and to an audience now some elements may be uncomfortable: Gregory and his friends are, after all, peeping Toms at the start of the film. While parents are all but absent from the film (there is only a short interaction between Gregory and his father), schoolteachers are not, and there are two suggestions of sexual attraction between teachers and pupils (this is more likely to jar if you have also seen *Gregory's Two Girls*).

Some of the cast had already appeared on film – notably in *That Sinking Feeling* (for example, Sinclair, Buchanan and Billy Greenlees). This was the first film for both Hepburn and Grogan. Hepburn has since appeared in a small number of episodes of the TV series *Maggie* (1982) and *Crossroads* (1985–1988) but has been seen only once more at the cinema, as Mary Bruce in *The Bruce*. Grogan was about to hit the big time, as the frontwoman for the band Altered Images, whose career burned briefly and brightly between 1981 and 1983. She features in *Comfort and Joy* and *The Wee Man* and continues to act; she makes a voice appearance in *My Old School*.

Gregory's Girl secured Forsyth the 1982 BAFTA for Best Screenplay, and the critical response was overwhelmingly positive. In the *MFB* John Pym praised its 'notably fresh comedy' and 'delicacy and inconsequentiality', noting that: 'Even the most absurd characters… have a sort of possessed, dignified fervour in their ineffectual efforts to make contact with the opposite sex'. *Variety*'s critic thought it would struggle with general audiences in the US, who were more used to the vulgarity of films such as *Porky's* (Bob Clark, 1981), but that it had the 'freshness

and quirky charm' to succeed in more specialist cinemas. Writing nearly 20 years later, Duncan Petrie compared *Gregory's Girl* with *That Sinking Feeling*, noting that like the earlier film it 'also relies heavily on a surface wit and charm, although this time with a greater underlying complexity and intelligence'. Sadly, complexity and intelligence are entirely lacking from the follow-up, *Gregory's Two Girls*.

[G2G] Gregory, *now a teacher at his old school, develops a crush on a pupil, and helps her social activism.* [W5]

If you love *Gregory's Girl*, do not, under any circumstances, watch *Gregory's Two Girls*, which may ruin forever the pleasure to be found in the first film. *Gregory's Two Girls* was the last of Forsyth's eight feature films. Following *Comfort and Joy*, he made three films in America (*Housekeeping*, 1987; *Breaking In*, 1989; and *Being Human*, 1994). His return to Scottish filmmaking resulted in a horribly misjudged film which has been largely forgotten, although not by Sinclair, who in 2020 admitted this was a misstep. That Gregory is now a teacher, working at his old school, who develops a crush on a pupil does not help matters – that the opening scene is a (wet) dream does not redeem it. There might have been merit in a story of local activists taking on an evil corporation, but the layering in of an extremely uncomfortable 'rom-com' element is excruciating. It is possible to successfully make a sequel to a much-loved original (see eg, *T2: Trainspotting*), but *Gregory's Two Girls* fails to do this. At the time of writing, *Gregory's Girl* has an audience rating of

81 per cent on Rotten Tomatoes, its sequel stands at a very generous 7 per cent. Both films are discussed by Jonathan Murray in *Discomfort and Joy: The Cinema of Bill Forsyth* (2011).

→ *Local Hero* (1983) S+++ T100

Directed by Bill Forsyth
Screenplay by Bill Forsyth
Leading cast: Peter Riegert (Macintyre); Burt Lancaster (Felix Happer); Denis Lawson (Urquhart); Peter Capaldi (Oldsen); Jenny Seagrove (Marina); Fulton Mackay (Ben)
Colour, 111 minutes, UK

Mac (Macintyre) is despatched from Texas to negotiate the purchase of 'Ferness Bay' on the north-west coast of Scotland. He is both charmed, and outwitted, by the local community, and falls in love.

With *Local Hero*, Forsyth consolidated a winning streak which had begun with *That Sinking Feeling* and continued with *Gregory's Girl*. Somewhat regrettably, it is arguable that *Local Hero* was the last good film he made. Still, if this was to be the summit of his career as a writer/director, it's a damn fine summit; an entry on the 'Recommends' section of the BFI website claims 'Bill Forsyth's *Local Hero* could very well be the best Scottish film ever made. Its themes on the value of the natural world and Scotland and its people are as relevant today as they were in 1983.' It won Forsyth the 1984 BAFTA for Best Director, and two American critics' awards for the screenplay.

LOCAL HERO

A beautiful coastline...
A rich oil man wants to develop it.
A poor beach bum wants to live on it.
An entire town wants to profit by it.
And a real-live mermaid wants to save it...
Only one of them will get their way.

Local Hero US release poster

It was also a hit with audiences.

The central joke in *Local Hero* has much in common with the premise of several Ealing films, including *Whisky Galore!* in that it is the (not so) naïve and innocent locals who are pulling the fast one over the sophisticated outsider. Except for Ben, they are keen to sell, and contemplate how they will spend their millions (an engaging conversation discusses the respective merits of a Rolls-Royce or a Maserati for transporting sheep). It's a good gag but the punchline could be stronger. There is no revelatory moment when Mac realises he is being outmanoeuvred. It is also hard to reconcile what viewers are expected to accept as a happy ending with what the locals wanted the ending to be. This works only if for the locals it is a win/win game – they'd love the financial wealth flowing from the deal but are also in love with their current lifestyles (as appears to be the case); a drunken Mac makes clear that *he* is falling in love with that lifestyle, as he offers to switch places with Urquhart. He may be drunk, but the offer appears serious.

Critical reaction to the film was almost universally positive. In *S&S* Nick Roddick wrote: 'Forsyth's screenplay and direction, Chris Menges' stunning camerawork and a series of nicely judged performances… achieve the almost forgotten ideal of a British film that is thematically dense, deals with serious issues, is funny, has well-developed characters, can handle running gags and gives off a general sense of confident control'. This however was in response to the first half of the film. Like me, Roddick finds the conclusion to the set-up less satisfying: 'the whole mixture, for all its enormous skill, topples back into the clutches of a certain kind of British cinema'. Gary Arnold, in *The Washington Post* had no such concerns: 'A feast of comic grace notes, *Local Hero* is bound to strike one that scores a decisive hit'. Forty years after its release, *Local Hero* maintains a perfect 100 per cent score on Rotten Tomatoes.

Glasgow-born Mark Knopfler, of Dire Straits, provided the soundtrack for *Local Hero* (one I still regularly play), as well as for *Comfort and Joy*. Another connection between the two films is Chris Menges'

cinematography. He later went on to shoot the Roland Joffé masterpieces *The Killing Fields* (1984) and *The Mission* (1986), winning Oscars for both.

Local Hero is referenced slyly in **Soft Top, Hard Shoulder**, and directly quoted in **You've Been Trumped**. A short book about the film is available: *Directed by Bill Forsyth: Local Hero (1983)* (David Manderson and Alistair Scott, 2011). In 2022 Jonathan Melville's excellent *Local Hero: Making a Scottish Classic* was published.

→ *Comfort and Joy* (1984) S+++

Directed by Bill Forsyth
Screenplay by Bill Forsyth
Leading cast: Bill Paterson (Alan); Eleanor David (Maddy); Clare Grogan (Charlotte); Alex Norton (Trevor); Roberto Bernardi (Mr McCool)
Colour, 106 minutes, UK

Glasgow, in the run-up to Christmas. Radio presenter Alan's relationship ends. He becomes entangled in fierce rivalry – including violence – between two branches of a family selling ice cream but manages to negotiate a solution.

Comfort and Joy is the fourth of the films that Forsyth made in Scotland before his move to American production. There is progression through the first three films, but with *Comfort and Joy* Forsyth steps backwards. Tom Milne in *S&S* wrote that: 'Like people as much as Bill Forsyth seems to, and there is always the danger that you will fall into the Ealing trap of making cosily patronising little comedies about their foibles'. In an interview, Forsyth stated of *Comfort and Joy* that 'I just set out to make a slightly more serious film... emotionally serious, about a more serious kind of human situation, and I just kind of kept the jokes in it'. The result however has none of the panache of the earlier films, although it would suffice on a dreich afternoon.

On 11 September 1984, *Variety* ran a report headlined: '"Comfort and Joy" Plot Mirrors Glasgow Trial'. It reported that in the week the film premiered in London, a 'trial began in Glasgow in which four men are charged with setting fire to the house of ice-cream van driver, killing its occupants'. Two men were wrongly convicted of murder, and it took nearly 20 years before they were successful in having their convictions quashed. While *Comfort and Joy* does not reference this serious crime, the background of tension in the ice cream trade in Glasgow was public knowledge when the film was made.

La Mort en Direct (*Death Watch*, aka *Deathwatch*) (1980) S+ T11

Directed by Bertrand Tavernier
Screenplay by David Rayfiel, Bertrand Tavernier
Leading cast: Harvey Keitel (Roddy); Romy Schneider (Katherine Mortenhoe); Harry Dean Stanton (Vincent Ferriman); Max von Sydow (Gerald Mortenhoe)
Colour, 117 minutes, France/Germany

Katherine is told she is dying and agrees that what remains of her life will be filmed by NTV. She then attempts to hide, but Roddy, a journalist with a camera implant, finds her, and a bond is formed. She is being filmed without her knowledge. Later, Roddy goes blind, filming stops, and Katherine uncovers his role. NTV race to find them: Katherine has been misdiagnosed – it is the medicine she is taking which will kill her. In her ex-husband's house, NTV catch up as Katherine overdoses and dies.

French director Bertrand Tavernier, who died in 2021, had a prolific and varied output, his best-known film outside France being his paean to jazz, *'Round Midnight* (1986). *Death Watch* was his fifth film, his first in English, and the only one in which he flirted with science fiction, although now the world has moved on this looks less like SF and more like acute social commentary. The novel on which the film is based, *The Continuous Katherine Mortenhoe* (DG Compton, 1973), continues to be held in high regard, and is available in the SF MASTERWORKS collection.

Dee Hepburn and John Gordon Sinclair

In the world of *Death Watch* 'nobody's dying anymore – not from sickness'. But Katherine Mortonhoe is, and is paid 'to die young, in public'. The film addresses continually the issue of narratives, representation, humanity, and alienation – it is not just that *we* are watching a screen, but that characters *within* the film do the same. For some critics the film was too self-referential and obsessed with the screen. Writing in the *MFB* Richard Combs questioned Tavernier's sci-fi sensibilities: 'His vision of the future is a thoughtless mélange of present-day urban blight and a few half-baked notions of persecution by the media'. Now, these criticisms appear misplaced. *Death Watch* asks the questions: what do we see, how do we see it, and how are *we* seen? The world as portrayed is neither truly dystopian, nor anti-utopian, but one which has become, in part at least, recognisable. Other reviewers were more positive, although the dour film, which offers no easy pleasures, struggled to find an audience and is not widely available.

The vision of the city (Glasgow) is one in which much is wrong with the world – a homeless shelter run by an uncaring priest, tenement squalor, brawlers, casual police violence, and protesters – while the rural west of Scotland (including Mull) offers a more humanised terrain. Glasgow is not named in the film, which could have been shot in any large city struggling to transition to a post-industrial identity with a rich, built, and in parts crumbling, landscape. But there is little attempt at anonymisation, and with outstanding cinematography by Pierre William Glenn, this is a superb record of how large parts of the city looked in 1980.

Austrian-born Romy Schneider was 42 years old when the film was made and died just two years later. While her performance was rightly singled out for praise, Keitel and Stanton are both excellent. Robbie Coltrane appeared fleetingly in his first film.

Released 19 years before the first season of TV's *Big Brother* was broadcast, and 43 years before the emergence of ChatGPT, *Death Watch* is more relevant now than on its release. Katherine is a 'computer author', pitching narratives to her machine, 'Harriet'; frustrated and angry, she asks Harriet 'are we too exhausted from building you to make up our own stories?' Harriet answers: 'Affirmative'. Katherine challenges NTV producer Vincent: 'There are private things.' 'Are there? Why?' Questioned about the show, Vincent admits that '37 per cent find it offensive and stay with us... because it's real'. Faced with her NTV contract, hounded and fetishised, Katherine feels the only option open to her is to take her own life.

North Sea Hijack (aka *ffolkes*) (1980)

Directed by Andrew V McLaglen
Screenplay by Jack Davies
Leading cast: Roger Moore (Ffolkes); James
    Mason (Admiral Brinsden); Anthony Perkins
    (Kramer)
Colour, 95 minutes, UK

A misogynistic genius, Ffolkes, leads his irregular but highly trained Ffolkes Ffusiliers to thwart a plot to extort £25m from the British Government by threatening the destruction of two North Sea oilrigs.

A taut, albeit entirely predictable, thriller relying heavily on the star power of the then-Bond, Roger Moore. There's little Scottish about *NSH*, save for a faked-up castle, plenty of whisky, and the North Sea oilrig setting (reached from an Aberdeen we never see). The discrepancy in the budgets available to the Bond franchise and *NSH* shows in the technical weaknesses in the sea-set scenes. The focus therefore is not on big set pieces, but on the game of cat-and-mouse between gangster Kramer (he rejects the term 'terrorist', as he has 'no politics') and the maverick Ffolkes; but the winner can never be in doubt. The film was released, unsuccessfully, as *ffolkes* in the US. The final scene is a delight.

A Sense of Freedom (1981) S++

Directed by John Mackenzie
Screenplay by Peter McDougall
Leading cast: David Hayman (Jimmy Boyle)
Colour, 86 minutes, UK

Glasgow, 1960s: violent gangster Jimmy Boyle is found guilty of murder and sentenced to life imprisonment. In prison he is violent, and violence is perpetrated on him, in a seemingly unbreakable vicious circle. Eventually the authorities try a different approach and, in 1974, he is sent to Barlinnie.

A Sense of Freedom is based on the book by Jimmy Boyle, published in 1977, which was written while he was held in the special unit at Barlinnie Prison. It was made for the UK television network STV but was released to cinemas in the US in an edited version (hence the shorter 81 minutes running time shown on IMDb) and has been shown at the EIFF on at least two occasions. In Scotland the story told would have been fairly well known in 1981, and viewers would have been able to set the film in context. To an audience without this knowledge, further explanation would help. It is not until after the final production credits that the key information is given: Boyle was given a life sentence in 1967, sent to Barlinnie in 1974 (which is when the film ends), returned to an ordinary prison in 1980, and was released in October 1981. He is now an artist and author.

In a 1980 Parliamentary debate (roughly contemporary to the film's production, but before its broadcast) on the Barlinnie Special Unit penal experiment Boyle was discussed by Russell Kerr MP: 'A graduate of the Gorbals slums in Glasgow, Boyle had a most unenviable record as a Glasgow hoodlum and stand-over man – and a murderer to boot. Moreover, rumour had it that he was an "agent" of the notorious Kray brothers, a "hit man" in the modern terminology. Today, the unquestioned moving spirit of the Barlinnie special unit is the same Jimmy Boyle – cultivated, charming, intelligent and with some impressive works of sculpture to show to the visitor he escorts around the unit.' There was however a concern that the 'quite fantastic publicity' which Boyle's book and art had attracted was not welcomed by the Scottish Office and the Scottish Prison Service (although Boyle is not the only ex-inmate of the unit to write a book about his experiences). The authorities did not cooperate in the making of *Freedom*, so the prison-based scenes were shot in Kilmainham Prison in Dublin. The special unit, opened in 1973, was closed in 1994, 'in the face of relentless public criticism'. It's an unusual facet of the film that it barely shows us Barlinnie, yet it *is* about the special unit, which lies just out of sight on the other side of the mirror, and in basing the film on Boyle's book, it celebrates an achievement of the unit.

Not all aspects of *Freedom* are as strong as Hayman's central performance – he dominates the film and is mesmerising and convincing – but when first shown on TV it would have been sensational. Edinburgh-born Mackenzie had demonstrated a commitment to social justice through earlier work (and he later directed *The Long Good Friday*, 1980), and *Freedom* is clear as to its position: while Boyle is in prison – most of the film – repression begets brutality which begets repression, and no one wins. As a prison officer says to Boyle, 'I don't know whether we've turned you into what you are, or you've turned us into the kind of people you imagine that we are'. While this is the point, it is, *as a story*, somewhat unsatisfying. There is no real trajectory towards change (there are two very brief hints of this, but they are not developed), and the film ends at the point where redemption begins.

→ *Silent Scream* (1990) S+++ T43

Directed by David Hayman
Screenplay by Bill Beech, Jane Beech
Leading cast: Iain Glen (Larry Winters); Anne Kristen (Mary Winters)
Colour, 85 minutes, UK

September 1977: HM Prison Barlinnie. Larry Winters, who has a psychotic illness, is incarcerated. He takes drugs, and under their influence his life is shown in fractured flashbacks, interspersed with fantasy sequences. He dies at the age of 34.

Director David Hayman is better known as a prolific actor who has been working since the late 1960s. He appears in many films in this book, including *A Sense of Freedom* (above), with which *Silent Scream* has a thematic and contextual relationship. It too

Iain Glen is terrific in Silent Scream

features the Barlinnie Special Unit in which Jimmy Boyle was incarcerated. *A Sense of Freedom* ends with the transfer of Boyle into the unit. *Silent Scream*, although it contains many flashbacks, is centred around the time that Winters spent in the unit as a contemporary of Boyle, whose sculptures are shown, and may be positioned as a companion piece to the earlier film, although tonally it is very different. Hayman had directed for television before making this, his first film, and has made two further feature films: *The Hawk* (1993) and *The Near Room* (1995). The opening credits attribute the screenplay to Bill Beech (the closing credits expand this to encompass Jane Beech), an art student who was taken to the Barlinnie Special Unit by his then tutor to work with the prisoners, where he met Larry Winters, an inmate who was

writing, discussing with him the possibility of making a short film about his life.

Silent Scream is an occasionally exceptional film, on its face sitting within the British tradition of gritty realist cinema. Formally, the film begins with Mary Winters about to visit Larry and ends with her being told of his death. Yet from within this framing the film billows out through time in a complex structure. Hayman projects cinematic flair onto the prosaic setting; non-realist elements include fantastical scenes and animated sequences, speaking to the interior monologue of Winters, played by a young Iain Glen (now perhaps best known for his long-running role in HBO's epic *Game of Thrones*, 2011–2019; see also *Man to Man*). At the Berlin International Film Festival in 1990, Glen was awarded the Silver Bear for Best Acting Performance; Hayman won the OCIC award. The film itself won the Scottish BAFTA and EIFF Best Film awards – accolades which are not reflected on IMDb.

Variety's reviewer thought (rightly) that *Silent Scream* would struggle to find an audience, but that it was in parts very impressive: 'Hayman doesn't make it easy on the audience as he jumbles memories, fantasies and reality. Audiences may find this style unsettling… when the device works, it works brilliantly'. In the *MFB* Julian Petley noted that the film was 'nothing like British prison movies in the realist vein'. He concluded: 'The end result is that the distinction between "objective" and "subjective" reality is broken down, in much the same way as *Silent Scream*'s sophisticated visual language tests the boundaries between the prison drama and "art" film'.

Silent Scream was shot at Glasgow's Blackhat Studios and on location; Hayman later directed another Scottish film with dark currents, *The Near Room*.

→ *The Wee Man* (2013)   S+

Directed by Ray Burdis
Screenplay by Ray Burdis
Leading cast: Martin Compston (Paul Ferris);
John Hannah (Tam McGraw); Patrick Bergin
(Arthur Thompson); Laura McMonagle (Anne
Marie)
Colour, 106 minutes, UK

The turbulent life of Glasgow hard man Paul Ferris, encompassing crime, prison, and reform.

The weakest of the 'Glasgow hard-men' films

Three films focus on Glasgow hard men, the first two being **A Sense of Freedom** and **Silent Scream**. *The Wee Man* is one too many. The subject of this film is Paul Ferris, who came to prominence a generation later than Jimmy Boyle and who, after two prison sentences and successfully defending a charge of murder, became an author and consultant. The film is therefore at least grounded in the real. It is, according to the opening credits, '*based* on a true story' (my emphasis), while Burdis has said that 'most of the events in the film are factual'. The film is at best pedestrian, with several critics taking the view that it is in fact rather poor: Charles Gant, in *Variety* – 'a banal biopic'; Peter Bradshaw in *The Guardian* – 'a clumsy, clichéd crime thriller… forgettable'; Allan Hunter, in *Screen Daily* – 'just another swaggering, shouty, true-life crime story'. The overly complex flashback structure is unnecessary and obscures the story. So does the attempt, understandable given both the source and that Ferris advised on the film, to cast Ferris in the best possible light. The first violent act we see him perpetrate occurs when his victims are assaulting a woman; he respects his mum and dad (played respectively by Clare Grogan and Denis Lawson); and is outraged when 'civilians' are targeted.

The strong cast lends some weight to the film, but the makers of *The Wee Man* have little of significance to say. In *A Sense of Freedom* there is a genuine attempt to look at the effects of imprisonment on both the prisoner and the gaoler; *The Wee Man* lacks this depth. The film's shooting location further weakens it. Burdis did not enjoy the experience of trying to make the film in Glasgow, with the result that much of the location shooting took place in London's East End. He said: 'We got a letter from the police saying we weren't welcome to shoot in Glasgow because of the subject matter. The police also wanted to see a copy of the script, which I'd never come across in more than 40 years in the business. The whole thing was like something out of Nazi Germany' (*The Scotsman*, 2013). While this may pass unnoticed by anyone who does not know Scotland, to a Glaswegian audience it screams artifice, although this did not stop the film enjoying some box office success in Scotland on its release: *Variety* reported it took £239,000 in its first ten days.

Eye of the Needle (1981)   S+

Directed by Richard Marquand
Screenplay by Stanley Mann
Leading cast: Donald Sutherland (Faber); Kate Nelligan (Lucy Rose); Christopher Cazenove (David Rose); Ian Bannen (Godliman)
Colour, 112 minutes, UK

London, 1940: ruthless German spy, Faber (codename 'the Needle'), steals military secrets and heads to 'Storm Island', where he will be picked up by a U-boat. He stays with Lucy and David, seducing Lucy and killing her husband, before being shot by Lucy.

Eye of the Needle, based on a Ken Follett novel, is a flawed thriller, shot in large part on Mull. It is one of three films in this book (**The Spy in Black, The McKenzie Break**) to involve rendezvous with German submarines off the coast of Scotland. Director Richard Marquand made his first feature film, sub-par horror *The Legacy*, in 1978. He followed up a year later with *The Birth of the Beatles*, then made *Eye of the Needle*. It is surprising that, on the basis of this film, Marquand was chosen to direct *Star Wars: Episode VI – The Return of the Jedi* (1983) (with a strike in the US limiting available directors, he was selected in part because he was willing to bow to Lucas' vision for the film). He died at the early age of 49, having made only three more films, including the blockbuster hit *Jagged Edge* (1985).

In *Eye of the Needle* the pacing is off – it takes a long time to set up the

Kate Nelligan

dynamics failing to conceal an underlying lack of direction'.

Sutherland's angular edginess, and convincing air of nervous intelligence, made him an ideal actor to play a spy (but not to play an avuncular Roman as he does in *The Eagle*). He had done so to good effect five years earlier in *The Eagle Has Landed* (John Sturges, 1976), a better film in which it was possible to feel sympathy and empathy for his character. In *Eye of the Needle* it is not. While Canadian actor Kate Nelligan's role is central to the film, her character is underdeveloped, her motivations unconvincing.

Hero (1982)   S+++

Directed by Barney Platts-Mills
Screenplay by John Francis Campbell and Barney Platts-Mills
Leading cast: Derek McGuire (Dermid O'Duinne); Caroline Kennell (Princess Grannia); Alastair Kennell (Finn MacCumhail); Stewart Grant (O'Shin)
Colour, 92 minutes, Gaelic and English, UK

The Highlands in the medieval period: swords and sorcery abound.

key sequence between Lucy and Faber, and the film teeters at this point between fast-paced thriller and more considered psychological combat. There is an unpleasantness, perhaps a product of its time, in the interactions between Faber and Lucy, particularly in the scene in which Lucy sleeps with him to maintain the pretence that she does not know who, or what, he really is. Reviewers who claim that Faber falls in love with Lucy seem to miss the point – she may briefly fall in love with him, but he is simply using her. A potential confrontation with Godliman (solidly played by Ian Bannen), is avoided, somewhat negating any investment the viewer makes in the chase. Writing in the *MFB*, Robert Brown's verdict was that 'the plot is a straightforwardly galumphing affair, and the film remains as faceless and unpleasant as its Nazi hero, its aggressive

Hero deserves a place in Scottish film history as the first film to be shot almost entirely in Gaelic (a few scenes only are in English). Picked up by Channel 4 after it was made, *Hero* was shown at the Venice Film Festival but did not secure a UK release. From Venice, *The Guardian* reported it 'totally puzzled everybody, including the jury, because there were no subtitles to elucidate its Gaelic dialogue'. It was for some time believed to be lost but is now available on the BFI Player, where the introduction states 'the film is now waiting to be eagerly discovered afresh by a new generation of *Game of Thrones* enthusiasts'. Any *GOT* fan who watches *Hero* is going to be in for serious disappointment. The film's production values are low, verging on the non-existent, and the amateur cast (young people from Drumchapel) are inept.

But there was a method behind the ramshackle. Platts-Mills grew up with privilege (his father was a Labour MP and a barrister, who defended the Krays) and was given a job at Shepperton Studios when he was just 15. He was 22 when he set up his own production company, and at 25 directed *Bronco Bullfrog* (1970), a minor classic of British working-class cinema. By the time *Hero* was made Platts-Mills was working independently, and focusing on projects which benefited disadvantaged youth, saying 'I would rather see the video stumblings of a schoolkid or any amateur than the technically polished output of film school alumni'. This explains the approach to *Hero* but is unlikely to convince a general viewer that there is any significant merit to the film. Robert Hanks in the *Independent on Sunday* wrote 'Platts-Mills said, "I regard everything of mine as a failure," but *Hero* was clearly more of a failure than most: native Gaelic speakers who saw it didn't realise it was in Gaelic. But: "The kids loved making it," which was the main thing.'

Living Apart Together (1982) S+++

Directed by Charles Gormley
Screenplay by Charles Gormley
Leading cast: BA [Brian Alexander] Robertson (Ritchie Hannah); Barbara Kellerman (Evie Hannah); Judi Trott (Alicia)
Colour, 93 minutes, UK

Glaswegian rock musician Ritchie Hannah breaks a tour to return to Glasgow following the death of a friend. His personal life is a mess, his marriage precarious.

Living Together Apart was denied wide distribution, although it did have a charity premiere at the Scala in Glasgow on 5 May 1983, and *The List* suggests there were at least some Scottish screenings, but there are no contemporaneous reviews. The IMDb entry suggests *LAT* runs to 140 minutes, but this is surely an error. In 2013 it was digitally restored by Park Circus and shown at the GFF. It was then released on DVD. This restored version runs to 93 minutes. The unrestored version is available to stream. The combination of this troubled history is that *LAT* remains largely forgotten and while the Glasgow-set film 'remains a culturally significant record of both the time and the city, effectively capturing and conveying [its] spirit and tone' (The Arts Shelf), and is worth a watch for that alone, it is, alas, not a gem.

LAT was shot in Glasgow in 1981, when Glasgow-born Robertson was extremely popular. His single 'Bang Bang' had climbed to no. 2 in the UK charts in

1979, and he had two further top ten hits in 1980. His greater success came as a songwriter for others, including Cliff Richard, but most notably with Mike Rutherford of Mike and the Mechanics, leading to the global hit 'The Living Years', released in 1988. Of his experience making the film, which he has stressed was *not* autobiographical, Robertson has said: 'It's true I may not be Scotland's greatest acting export, but I... was OK enough not to completely piss off pros like Dave Anderson and Barbara Kellerman.' Robertson may have had no experience as an actor (and in one key scene when he and Evie first fight this shows), but it is vitally important that he is convincing as a musician and singer, and of course he is. Best of all is the ensemble filling out the smaller roles. *LAT* briefly features Peter Capaldi in his first credited performance (it is he with whom Evie has her affair), and John Gordon Sinclair is a barman in a 'blink-and-you'll-miss-it' performance.

Scottish writer/director Gormley, who is the main protagonist of *Long Shot*, made four years earlier, died in Glasgow in 2005. He worked with Bill Forsyth at Tree Films and was involved in making short documentaries in the 1970s, but is best known for his second, and final, film *Heavenly Pursuits*.

→ *Heavenly Pursuits* (aka *The Gospel According to Vic*) (1986) S+++

Directed by Charles Gormley
Screenplay by Charles Gormley
Leading cast: Tom Conti (Vic Mathews); Helen Mirren (Ruth Chancellor); David Hayman (Jeff Jeffries)
Colour, 92 minutes, UK

Vic, a teacher at Glasgow's Blessed Edith Semple School, achieves strong results with committed teaching, and comes to the attention of the media when it is claimed that he is the beneficiary of miracles and may be able to work them.

Four years after making *Living Apart Together*, Charles Gormley made *Heavenly Pursuits* (for which BA Robertson, star of the earlier film, composed the music), also set and filmed in Glasgow. For *Heavenly Pursuits* he had two lead actors who were becoming established, and a strong supporting cast. Paisley-born Conti had started his career in the late 1950s and although better known as a stage actor, had achieved some prominence following roles in *Merry Christmas Mr. Lawrence* (Nagisa Ōshima, 1983) and *Reuben Reuben* (Robert Ellis Miller, 1983) for which he received Golden Globe and Oscar nominations. Mirren, whose name comes second on the opening credits, was also on the up, having been memorable in *The Long Good Friday* (John Mackenzie, 1980) and having had two significant roles in 1984, in the excellent *Cal* (Pat O'Connor),

Tom Conti and Helen Mirren

and the not quite so good *2010: The Year We Make Contact* (Peter Hyams). With support including David Hayman (*A Sense of Freedom*, *Rob Roy*, *Regeneration* etc), Dave Anderson (*Restless Natives*), a young Ewen Bremner in his first role (as one of the pupils making 'miraculous' progress), and a cameo from Scottish stalwart Gordon Jackson as a TV presenter, things must have looked extremely promising for *Heavenly Pursuits*. The result is a film which treads a path between satire, comedy and romantic comedy, but which is a little too comfortable, as a result of which the satire loses some force.

In the Vatican office responsible for assessing the evidence of sainthood, Father Cobb (Brian Pettifer) makes the case for the Blessed Edith Semple and is rebuffed, but Cobb is worried about the state of faith in his Scottish church: 'every year the congregation gets older, and the young don't understand. Scotland's a hard-headed country when it comes to believing'. Under his very nose however, in the school of which he is the chaplain, miracles *are* happening, in the form of achievements by pupils who have been relegated to a remedial class and who are benefitting from diligent and inspirational teaching by Vic. Media interest however, lies not in hard-won results, but in supposed divine intervention – something even Vic briefly gives credence to. For *Time Out*: 'Treated with tongue-in-cheek seriousness, the resulting confusion of cross-purposes as the media jump on the band wagon treads a delicate path through the morass of cynicism, gullibility and wishfulness'. The film would be stronger if the satire had more bite, or if the potential for black comedy were exploited. The addition of a hastily resolved romantic entanglement detracts from the central argument, but the film remains a light pleasure.

Another Time, Another Place (1983) S++ T100

Directed by Michael Radford
Screenplay by Michael Radford
Leading cast: Phyllis Logan (Janie); Giovanni Mauriello (Luigi); Paul Young (Dougal)
Colour, 118 minutes, UK

An army lorry carries Italian POWs; we are in rural Scotland, and it is late summer. Three POWs are put up in the bothy at Janie's home which she shares with older husband Dougal. Janie enters into a sexual relationship with Luigi, and must disclose this when he is wrongly accused of rape.

Based on a novel by Scottish author Jessie Kesson, *Another Time, Another Place* was shot on the Black Isle. *ATAP* is less about national identities and their differences and similarities (although it is, in part, about this), and more about individual difference and identity. The landscape of the film is wide, and open, although bounded by the sea and woods (the sea to look out on, the woods to have assignations in). Amid this openness, the key characters are prisoners.

Luigi and his compatriots are prisoners of war; Janie is also a prisoner, trapped in a marriage in which there appears to be little love. The perfunctory marital sex she does not enjoy contrasts strongly with later scenes of lovemaking with Luigi. In fact, Luigi's future appears to be less constrained than Janie's. Frustrated and angry he asks, 'when bloody war finished? When?' But he knows it will finish, and he will be able to return to his home in Naples (although he does not know what he will find there).

Notwithstanding the language barriers – which are sustained for the audience; there are no English subtitles – and the difference in circumstances, Janie can, to some extent, bond with Luigi and the prisoners. Yet both language and circumstances make Luigi's first attempts at seduction at best clumsy, at worst aggressive. On almost their first encounter, after showing her the few photographs and small touches (including a homemade shrine to the Madonna) the POWs have added to the bothy, he asks: 'You like me. Is possible please we, we make jigi jigi?'. Throughout there is doubt as to the nature of the relationship. Is it one of burgeoning love, or is it in fact merely transactional – both using sex as an escape? Certainly, Janie's increasingly free attitude, reflected in part in her choice of dress, is noted: 'Good God, she's all dolled up for planting tatties'.

There is an 'aura of predictability' (Gilbert Adair, *MFB*) about the film which weakens it: there can be no doubt that Janie and Luigi will have an affair, and no doubt that the affair, like the war, must come to an end (although there may be doubt as to Janie's future). This notwithstanding, there are two ingredients which elevate *ATAP*. Phyllis Logan is outstanding in her first film. Vincent Canby, in *The NYT*, found the film 'ordinary', Logan 'luminous'. She was rewarded with the BAFTA for Most Outstanding Newcomer to Film in 1984.

Also making a first feature film was Roger Deakins, credited as 'lighting cameraman/camera operator'. He is now a double Oscar winner, for *Blade Runner 2049* (Denis Villeneuve, 2017) and *1917* (Sam Mendes, 2019), with a further 14 nominations. *ATAP* is beautifully shot. When open landscapes are used, they can be sumptuous, although more often the film closes in. Throughout, vertical planes impose a sense of physical and emotional imprisonment, and separation. Scenes are shot through closed windows (both looking out and looking in) or framed through doorways, from light into dark, and from confined to open space. The final shot of the film has Janie, having confessed her sin, standing outside a friend's door. Having been invited in, the film ends with her hovering on the threshold (a clear reference to *The Searchers*, John Ford, 1956). Will she enter, returning to her old community and life, or will she walk away?

Ill Fares the Land (1983)   S+++

Directed by Bill Bryden
Screenplay by Bill Bryden
Leading cast: David Hayman, Fulton Mackay, Paul Scofield (narrator)
Colour, 102 minutes, UK

A dramatic reconstruction of the year on St Kilda leading to the evacuation of the remaining 36 inhabitants in August 1930.

The existence, and demise, of the remote community on St Kilda has proved a source of fascination since at least 1698, when Martin Martin wrote *A Late Voyage to St Kilda*. The island maintains an exceptional UNESCO status, recognised both for its natural and cultural heritage. *Ill Fares the Land* deals with the last year of the islanders' lives, before, at their own request, they were evacuated to the mainland. They are shown eking out a precarious life, being treated like exotic zoo specimens by tourists, debating in their parliament, attending church, and in death and grief.

Ill Fares the Land remains Scottish theatre director Bill Bryden's only film. He explicitly rejected the 'docu-drama crap' and described the film as 'fiction based upon fact'; he also said, 'most of what happens in the film happened'. The authenticity of *Ill Fares the Land* may be challenged (see Ian Spring, 'Lost land of dreams – representing St Kilda', 1990), but it does have the advantage of being at least partly shot on St Kilda, something Michael Powell failed to achieve (see *The Edge of the World*). However, it proved impossible to shoot scenes with actors on the island, and sets were constructed on the mainland west coast, near Applecross. The film is slow and dour – but then so was the tenuous, and ultimately untenable, life of the islanders. The film was made for Channel 4, but received some distribution, and was shown at the London Film Festival where it was nominated for the Outstanding Film award. It can be tricky now to find, but copies do from time to time appear on YouTube.

The Girl in the Picture (1985) S++

Directed by Cary Parker
Screenplay by Cary Parker
Leading cast: John Gordon Sinclair (Alan); Irina Brook (Mary); David McKay (Ken)
Colour, 84 minutes, UK

Glaswegian photographer Alan and his girlfriend Mary, a student at Glasgow University, break up and get back together again.

By 1985, when *The Girl in the Picture* was released, John Gordon Sinclair had become reasonably well known to British audiences. *That Sinking Feeling* (1979) introduced him to the Scottish public, *Gregory's Girl* (1980) had been a breakout hit in the UK (and had been shown abroad), and *Local Hero* (1983) met with international success. *TGITP* rests very much on his shoulders, and his inherent likeability – it is in other respects a somewhat slender film. Alan is thinly fleshed out, Mary is merely a cipher,

the muse around whom Alan revolves; but French actress Irina Brook, making her first feature film, does as well as can be expected with slim material. It's not a waste of celluloid, but neither is it likely to have lingered long in the memory of those who saw it back in 1985. It's a simple story, as old as the trees: boy has girl, boy loses girl, boy gets girl back – and there can be little doubt as to the fact that this is what the trajectory will be. In two parallel and linked narratives, the younger member of the 'Smile Please' photography studio team, Ken, after simply fantasising about the girls in the photographs he develops, gets a girl, and the couple whose engagement photographs are taken at the beginning get married (although there must be doubt as to their prospects for wedded bliss).

All of this plays out against the backdrop of Glasgow, most of it in the West End; the university is featured extensively. There is nothing much wrong with *TGITP*; it is competently made and at times entertains. Walter Goodman was harsh in *The NYT* – 'boring'; *Time Out*'s reviewer was more generous: 'an engaging debut… a classy light comedy with a firmer hold on reality than most of its American teenage counterparts'. *TGITP* suffered from unfavourable comparisons – inevitable given location and lead – with the films of Bill Forsyth. Unusually, American writer/director Parker has no other credits listed on IMDb, although he continues to work in the arts.

Restless Natives (1985) S++ T100

Directed by Michael Hoffman
Screenplay by Ninian Dunnett
Leading cast: Vincent Friell (Will); Joe Mullaney
(Ronnie); Bernard Hill (Will's father); Anne
Scott-Jones (Will's mother); Ned Beatty
(Bender); Teri Lally (Margot)
Colour, 90 minutes, UK, English/Japanese

Ned Beatty confronts Scottish folk heroes

*Ronnie and Will, from Edinburgh, become
modern-day highwaymen, holding up
coach parties of tourists, becoming folk
heroes, and part of the tourist experience.
But they are hunted by the police,
supported by Bender from the 'American
Central Intelligence Bureau'.*

While writing this book, many people
have told me how much they love
Restless Natives, which received funding
after the screenplay won a competition
run by the Oxford Film Foundation. I'm
not one of them, although I recognise
it has charm and some wit. But there
is substantial padding and resort to
caricature, particularly in relation to
the cohort of better-known actors who
provide cameos (Mel Smith's local
gangster; Nanette Newman's oblivious
tourist). There are times when the film
feels more like an extended advert for
Scottish tourism than a Forsyth-inspired
socially grounded comedy (which is
clearly what was intended). There is little
suggestion that Scotland has more to
offer than tourism: as the police officer
in charge of the investigation explains
after the arrest of Ronnie and Will, 'I had

a telex from the Secretary of State for
Scotland, the Scottish Secretary. It seems
tourist spending has gone up 15 per cent
since the start of these activities. You're
bigger than the Loch Ness monster.'

A sequence of films explains the
decision to make *Restless Natives*, which
was filmed in the autumn of 1984:
Gregory's Girl (1980), *Local Hero* (1983)
(like Mac, Bender spends a lot of time on
the phone to the US), and *Comfort and
Joy* (1984). It would be all but impossible
to have any meaningful discussion about
Restless Natives without referencing Bill
Forsyth, and the difficulty is that while
on the face of it there is much in common
between the films, *Restless Natives* has
neither the depth, nor the charm, of
Forsyth's best work.

It *did* matter that in the mid-1980s
someone other than Forsyth was making
films like this. At the minimum it helped
to develop a critical mass of Scottish talent
and experience and provided employment
for actors and technicians. The three
Scottish leads maintained acting careers,
albeit of varying longevity. This was
Friell's first film, and he later appeared in

Trainspotting (as Diane's father) and *The Angels' Share*. Mullaney has no credits after 1994. Lally, who also had a small role in *Comfort and Joy*, appeared in over 100 episodes of *High Road*.

Highlander (1986)   S++

Directed by Russell Mulcahy
Screenplay by Gregory Widen, Peter Bellwood, Larry Ferguson
Leading cast: Christopher Lambert (Connor MacLeod); Sean Connery (Ramirez); Roxanne Hart (Brenda Wyatt); Clancy Brown (The Kurgan); Beatie Edney (Heather MacLeod)
Colour, 116 minutes, UK

From 16th-century Scotland to the present day (1985) MacLeod battles 'immortals' for 'the prize'. MacLeod prevails ('there can be only one'), winning the ability to read the minds of everyone on the planet and help them.

Highlander, shot in significant part in Scotland, is preposterous, cheesy fun. It remains of interest: in 2020 Jonathan Melville published *A Kind of Magic: Making the Original Highlander*, written with affection and rigour; see also 'How we made Highlander: Connery opened his homemade whisky on the plane' (*The Guardian*, 2016).

Highlander is the only film in this book to feature the late Sir Sean Connery in a live-action role, and he plays an immortal *Spanish/Egyptian*. American/French actor Christopher Lambert, hot off the heels of the uber-cool *cinéma du look* showpiece

Subway (Luc Besson, 1985) but cast based on his role in *Greystoke: The Legend of Tarzan, Lord of the Apes* (Hugh Hudson, 1984), plays the *Scottish* Highlander. Prior to making *Highlander*, Lambert had been billed as Christophe. For *Highlander* he gained an 'r', but not a credible Scottish accent. Director Mulcahy said that 'the fact that he couldn't speak English didn't really matter' (Melville).

It is hard now to appreciate how successful *Highlander* was on release in Europe (it was badly marketed in the US and did not perform well). It is however easy to appreciate how well it captures the 1980s aesthetic, which is not surprising given that this had in significant part been created by Mulcahy, *the* pre-eminent maker of music videos in the early–mid 1980s (it was he

French actor Christopher Lambert plays the immortal Scot

who shot the first video played on MTV: 'Video Killed The Radio Star'). Mulcahy had also directed the extremely quirky (and now cult favourite) *Razorback* (1984).

There is broadly a split in the opinions of critics between reviews published on the film's release, and those written later. On release, more were inclined to agree with *The Washington Post*'s Paul Attanasio whose hilarious review includes the following: 'It's all here, folks: fancy wipes, expressionistic angles, quick-cut close-ups, stylized backlighting, camera moving in endless illogic. It's as if a 15-minute history of film technique had been compiled by a psychotic.'

And yet, in 1986 the words 'My name is Connor MacLeod, of the Clan MacLeod, AND I AM IMMORTAL', and 'There

can be only one' rang out across school playgrounds in the UK (and from me, at the tender age of 22, walking home from the cinema). Somehow the film caught the wave, and its fandom has endured. To quote one of the cast, James Cosmo, 'it was a ground-breaking film. It used rock music, the camera never stayed still, it was a wonderful mix [of genres] and the ideas were terrific. It really was a seminal piece of work' (Melville). That *Highlander* has endured so well is because it is 'really a lot of fun to watch as a camp classic' (cast member Jon Polito, also in Melville). Although some derided the film it spawned two direct sequels of declining quality (*Highlander II: The Quickening*, Russell Mulcahy, 1991; *Highlander III:*

The Sorcerer (aka *Highlander: The Final Dimension*), Andrew Morahan, 1994), three further films, and a TV series which ran for 119 episodes. As of early 2025 Jersey-born ex-Superman Henry Cavill is slated to play Connor MacLeod in a franchise reboot, to be directed by Chad Stahelski of *John Wick* fame.

Osobisty pamiętnik grzesznika przez niego samego spisany (*Memoirs of a Sinner*) (1986)

Directed by Wojciech Has
Screenplay by Michal Komar
Leading cast: Piotr Bajor (Robert); Jan Jankowski (Gustaw); Maciej Kozlowski (the stranger)
Colour, 114 minutes, Poland, Polish

Scotland: the Day of Resurrection, and corpses climb out of graves. One, Robert, tells his story before being taken away for final judgment. Illegitimate, but acknowledged as the second son of a mill owner in 18th-century Scotland, his life changes when he forms a bond with a mysterious stranger. Robert takes the stranger for 'an angel of light', while many see him as the Devil. Their connection leads to sin and Robert's death.

It would be easy to watch *Memoirs* without thinking of Scotland – the language is Polish, the rural location *looks* like central Europe and the film was shot in Poland. There are however just enough touches in design and soundscape to suggest that Wojciech Has retained the setting of Scottish author James Hogg's novel, *The Private Memoirs and Confessions of a Justified Sinner* (published anonymously in 1824). Robert's hair is red, there are Scottish elements in the interior designs (particularly in the heraldry in stained-glass windows), and the music is Scottish-ish. In screening the film as part of a 2024 Has retrospective, Film at Lincoln Centre described *Memoirs* as being 'set in Scotland', and as a 'delirious and beautifully crafted adaptation'.

The argument made by Robert is that his sins do not necessarily disqualify him from redemption at the Last Judgment; his graveside audience is unable to decide, declaring the judge will determine his fate. The source novel is far from straightforward, dealing with Calvinist theological arguments and being told from two perspectives, but as David Cairns has pointed out, Has had a history of being willing to tackle difficult sources.

At one time Bill Douglas (*The Childhood Trilogy*) had intended to make his own version of the novel, but the attempt died with him. For Cairns, the Polish version 'maintains [the novel's] central weirdness' but is 'oddball' and 'muddies the point'. Certainly, the film *looks* great (although not as a plausible representation of 18th-century Scotland), and there is much to admire. *Memoirs* is difficult to track down; I was able to watch this in a high-quality version, with subtitles, only through a Russian social media site.

Play Me Something (1989)   S++

Directed by Timothy Neat
Screenplay by John Berger and Timothy Neat
Leading cast: John Berger (stranger); Tilda
   Swinton (hairdresser)
Colour, 72 minutes, UK

*On Barra a group of strangers are delayed
while waiting for a plane to Glasgow. The
stranger tells a story, based in part in Venice.
Having told his story, the stranger leaves,
and the plane lands.*

'It is', wrote Julian Petley in the *MFB*, 'difficult not to approach [*Play Me Something*]
as anything other than a John Berger text'.
Berger is best known as the author of the
hugely influential *Ways of Seeing* (1972), itself based on a series of TV essays broadcast
the same year. The film is based on a Berger
short story, and his arresting voice dominates. Storytelling is at the heart of *Play Me
Something*: as the stranger begins to speak,
he says, 'any story is like an open ticket,
across the sea, to any place in the world'.
His story is disrupted by the other travellers, who interject and participate, just
as the film itself is disrupted by multiple
aspect ratios and image qualities. *Play Me
Something* wears its intellectual argument
lightly and Berger's voice is captivating, his
narrative compelling. But this is, by design,
very far from mainstream narrative cinema.
   The inclusion of this film here is margin-
al: while IMDb gives its running time as 72
minutes, the British Film Institute, which
provided my route to the film, records a time
of 69 minutes.

Venus Peter (1989)   S+++ T100

Directed by Ian Sellar
Screenplay by Ian Sellar and Christopher Rush
Leading cast: Ray McAnally (grandfather); David
   Hayman (Kinnear); Sinéad Cusack (Miss
   Balsilbie); Gordon R Strachan (Peter)
Colour, 94 minutes, UK

*Peter grows up in Stromness with his
mother. His grandfather is a fisherman, and
Peter wants to go out with him on his boat
'Venus', after whom Peter is nicknamed.
Peter has a strong imagination, fuelled by
poetry. The catch brought in by Peter's
grandfather dwindles continually; unable to
maintain payments to the bank, the boat is
repossessed. Peter's father comes to see him
– he is not a sailor. He will pay for Peter to
go to boarding school.*

Venus Peter was filmed on Orkney over
a period of eight weeks, generating
huge local interest, and significant wider
media attention. The *Sun* reported:
'Film crew sparks AIDS fear on island'. A
more balanced report from Orkney was
published in *S&S*. Nicholas Kent pointed to
the film's portrayal of Peter's world: 'riven
by the conflict between the bleak reality of
a dying fishing community progressively
impoverished by the diminishing hauls of
the few remaining fishermen, and his own
pure romanticism'. The romanticism on
display is semi-autobiographical, although
geographically relocated. Christopher
Rush's book, *A Twelvemonth and a Day*
was published in 1985 and optioned by
producer Chris Young, notwithstanding

its lack of a conventionally plotted story, because 'it was full of interesting images', and he wanted to make 'a film that wasn't based on social realism but on something as mythical as the sea'.

Financing the film was not easy, particularly given this was Sellar's first feature. *The Guardian*'s critic, Derek Malcolm, reported that Young sold shares to friends in the screenplay for £50, promising them £80 if the film went into profit. It did. Malcolm was more than content with the outcome, which, as he noted, 'represented Britain very honourably at Cannes': 'no one has tried to sentimentalise the story... It is *Venus Peter*'s toughness, as well as its nostalgia for lost times, that one remembers'. Director of photography Beristain had previously shot Derek Jarman's *Caravaggio* (1986) and his cinematography on *Venus Peter* was widely praised: the *MFB* drew attention to the film's 'astonishing golden tones'. In *Incident at Loch Ness* Beristain 'plays' himself.

The performance of Strachan is crucial to the success of the film. Determined that he be played by a local boy, Sellar told Nicholas Kent they simply saw 'every possible child in the Orkney isles'. This is Strachan's only credit. McAnally, playing his grandfather, died shortly after the film's shooting was completed.

The Big Man (aka *Crossing the Line*) (1990) S+

Directed by David Leland
Screenplay by Don MacPherson
Leading cast: Kenny Ireland (Tony); Liam Neeson (Danny Scoular); Joanne Whalley (Beth Scoular); Billy Connolly (Frankie); Ian Bannen (Matt Mason); Hugh Grant (Gordon)
Colour, 93/112/116 minutes, UK

Danny, previously a striking miner facing the police, turns to bare-knuckle fighting to support his family. He fights on behalf of Mason, a gangster who bets on Danny. Danny turns his back on Mason after learning that his last fight was held simply to determine which of two gangsters would pay for the killing of a third.

William McIlvanney's father had been a miner, and two of McIlvanney's novels, *Docherty* (1975) and *The Big Man* (1985), deal directly with mining and its legacy in Scotland (McIlvanney's sports journalist brother, Hugh, published *On Boxing* in 1982). In *The Big Man*, Danny Scoular fights to support his family, and to recapture his identity and pride. The adaptation is not perfect but is better than the Rotten Tomatoes score (20 per cent at the time of writing) would suggest.

The Big Man (shot on location in Coalburn and in Glasgow) was heavily edited for the American market and the film exists in various lengths. American reviews of the film may do director David Leland and co. an injustice. Vincent Canby in *The NYT* concluded: '*Crossing the*

Liam Neeson and Joanne Whalley

Line means to be a wicked commentary on the state of Britain under Prime Minister Margaret Thatcher... Much of the climactic fight is photographed in such lovely slow-motion that the blood and the sweat look phony, which, in turn, suggests that everything else is suspect.' The fight sequence runs to some 11½ minutes; it may be 'suspect', but it is also brutal, and graphic in its violence and depiction of injury.

The moral position taken by the film is clear: the coal miners were in the right, standing up for principle. As Danny puts it at a job interview, he was imprisoned 'for politics'. The arranged fight, however, is not a matter of principle. But Danny does stand by his principles when he steals Mason's money to give to his (now blind)

opponent, who exonerates him from any blame for the fight's outcome. Like the novel, the film really asks the question what is it that makes 'a big man' – physical, or moral stature? It comes down firmly on the side of courage, resolve and integrity.

Geoff Andrew, in *Time Out*'s (non-contemporaneous) review is more positive than Canby: 'as a portrait of one man's desperate struggle to survive against all odds, the film is tough, taut and intelligently critical of the man's world it depicts.' *The Big Man* was the first film to provide a role for Douglas Henshall.

Tickets for the Zoo (1991) S+++

Directed by Brian Crumlish
Screenplay by Christeen Winford
Leading cast: Alice Bree (Carol); Tom Smith
  (George); Micky McPherson (Pogo)
Colour, 94 minutes, UK

Edinburgh: brother and sister Carol and George turn 18 and are required to leave the social care home where they live. They struggle to survive. Carol becomes pregnant, and later dies by suicide.

Duncan Petrie (*Screening Scotland*) described *Tickets for the Zoo* as a 'didactic television film [which was] an interesting attempt to inform the audience about how easily vulnerable members of society can fall into destitution'. It was made after 12 years of Conservative government and focuses on an issue in respect of which problems were all too obvious, while support and solutions were minimal to the point of cruelty. Any right-minded person watching the film in 1991 should have been angry, but neither Carol nor George rail at the system. This makes the film stronger – here we have two people determined to make the best of things as honestly as they can, yet they are *still* screwed.

Crumlish and Winford had made a trilogy of documentaries focusing on homelessness for Channel 4 before turning to *Tickets for the Zoo*. The film received limited cinema showings, but through festivals won international awards. In the UK it was most notably screened on Channel 4 as part of its 'Gimme Shelter'

strand. *Tickets* was shot entirely in Edinburgh, on a low budget, with a cast of largely unknown actors; Alice Bree convinces as Carol. The film also gave Ashley Jensen (see *The Legend of Barney Thomson*) her first role. Crumlish, who died in 1994, was described in an obituary in *The Herald* as 'another of that small group of ragged-trouser pioneers [who] got Scottish film-making going'.

Blue Black Permanent (1992) S++ T100

Directed by Margaret Tait
Screenplay by Margaret Tait
Leading cast: Celia Imrie (Barbara Thorburn);
  Jack Shepherd (Philip Lomax); Gerda
  Stevenson (Greta Thorburn); James Fleet (Jim
  Thorburn)
Colour, 86 minutes, UK

Barbara, a photographer, recalls her life, and that of her mother, Greta, as told to her. Her grandmother drowned in the sea in Orkney, and Greta also drowned, although there is ambiguity as to whether she sleepwalked into the sea or died by suicide.

Blue Black Permanent stands out as the first feature film made in Scotland to be directed by a woman. Margaret Tait was in her 70s when she made this, her only film. Tait was born in Orkney, but after studying film in Rome began her career making experimental and short films in Edinburgh in the mid-1950s, later moving back to Orkney. It is notable that *BBP* spans both locations, with Greta being an Orcadian living in Edinburgh. Place, rather than action, is central to *BBP*. Little happens over the four timeframes the story occupies, and if everything is unpacked and rearranged the story is a simple one. But to Barbara 'It's not just a story to me, because you see I knew her, and it's my story too'. Greta was clearly more at home in Orkney, and it is there that she dies. Barbara, however, is her 'father's daughter – landswoman, townie'.

Tait creates homes and hearths which are almost tactile – Greta revels in the sensuality of her toes digging into a sheepskin rug. Referencing the breakfast she shares with her father, Robert Yates in *S&S* notes that 'Tait could be inviting us to feel [its] texture'. The details of Andrew's studio and Barbara's home are similarly, and lovingly, pored over; but this is not the case in respect of Greta's family home in Edinburgh. Symbolically, on Orkney Greta finds some small flowers which, we are told, will grow nowhere else ('when transplanted it dies'); Greta then says, 'I love it so much' and cries.

The success of *BBP* is not to be measured in terms of box office receipts, or widespread reviews, but in the conviction with which Tait's artistic intent is realised on screen. The film continues to be discussed and is recognised as holding an important place in Scottish cinema. Duncan Petrie writes about *BBP* in *British Rural Landscapes on Film* (ed Paul Newland, 2016), suggesting it leaves the audience 'not with a sense of resolution… but rather with the (reassuring) idea that the world

continues to turn, nature endures, and place remains fundamentally connected to concepts of identity, life and death. As such [*BBP*] provides [an] emphatic example… of the interconnection between people and place'.

Soft Top Hard Shoulder (1992) S++

Directed by Stefan Schwartz
Screenplay by Peter Capaldi
Leading cast: Peter Capaldi (Gavin Bellini); Elaine Collins (Yvonne)
Colour, 91 minutes, UK

Gavin undertakes a road trip from London to Glasgow to attend his father's 60th birthday party. He is an aspiring artist; his family make and sell ice cream in Glasgow. On the way he meets Yvonne, and a series of mishaps ensue.

Glasgow-born Peter Capaldi became a star in the UK with his role as the foul-mouthed Malcolm Tucker in the TV series *The Thick of It* (2005–2012) but is better known internationally as The Doctor in *Doctor Who* (2013–2017). In addition to these not inconsiderable achievements, he is an Oscar and BAFTA-winning writer-director for the short film *Franz Kafka's It's a Wonderful Life* (1993). *It's a Wonderful Life* was directed by Frank Capra in 1946; 12 years previously, Capra helmed *It Happened One Night* (the first film to win the Oscar 'big 5'). This, in turn, is an obvious source of influence on *Soft Top Hard Shoulder*. In Capra's film Clark Gable and

Claudette Colbert end up as unlikely travel companions, resort to hitchhiking, and share a hotel room together; Gavin and Yvonne are unlikely travel companions, resort to hitchhiking, and share a B&B room together. In *Time Out* Geoff Andrew found the influence of *It Happened* 'rather too strong' but took some pleasure from the script's 'fair share of engagingly offbeat one-liners' and found the characters 'deftly sketched'; David Parkinson, for the *Radio Times*, wrote that 'virtually everything about this odd couple comedy... is ill-judged'. Others were more positive.

There is at least one reference to *Local Hero* (a rabbit appears destined to be roadkill), Capaldi's second film (after *Living Apart Together*, which was released in the UK some four months before *Local Hero*). But those who suggest that the ice cream family background has its roots in Forsyth's *Comfort and Joy* miss the point: Capaldi is (in part) of Italian descent, his parents did own an ice cream business, and he did study at the Glasgow School of Art.

British road movies (see also *Hold Back the Night*) don't work as well as they do in the US, where scale is in their favour (although Capaldi understands this, and references to America deliberately puncture any impression of grandiosity). It helps, as in *STHS*, if the route taken is the scenic one, and it helps that Gavin and Yvonne are likeable, and their relationship believable (Capaldi and Collins have been married since 1991). The greatest strength in the film lies in its convincing depiction of the joy to be found in returning home after a time in exile (even where that

is self-imposed). Another road movie, *Aberdeen*† (Hans Petter Moland and Tony Spataro, 2000), has its journey's end in Scotland, but most of the journey takes place outside Scotland, and in road movies it is the journey, not the destination, which counts (in reverse the same is true of the documentary *Make it to Munich*†, Martyn Robertson, 2025).

Year of the Comet (aka *A Very Good Year*) (1992) S+

Directed by Peter Yates
Screenplay by William Goldman
Leading cast: Penelope Ann Miller (Margaret Harwood); Tim Daly (Oliver Plexico); Louis Jordan (Philippe); Art Malik (Nico)
Colour, 91 minutes, US

An extremely rare bottle of wine is discovered on an estate on Skye; acting for different parties, Margaret and Oliver attempt to recover it while falling in love. Other more nefarious parties also give it a go.

It is remarkable that a combination of a script by Goldman – who also wrote *Butch Cassidy and the Sundance Kid* (George Roy Hill, 1969) and *The Princess Bride* (Rob Reiner, 1987) – and direction by Yates (*Breaking Away*, 1979 and *The Dresser*, 1983), could have resulted in such an appallingly bad film (carrying a zero rating on Rotten Tomatoes). But as Goldman once famously quipped, 'in Hollyood no-one knows anything'. My vote for the worst line goes to: 'The glorious aura of sex emanates from your perfect body.' The 50 minutes spent in Scotland don't come close to redeeming this.

As an Eileann (aka *From an Island*) (1993)   S+++

Directed by Mike Alexander
Screenplay by Douglas Eadie
Leading cast: Ken Hutchison (MacAlasdair); Iain
   F MacLeod (Calum); DW Stuibhart (Coileon);
   Wilma Kennedy (Janet)
Colour, 99 minutes, Gaelic (majority) and
   English, UK

'*Carraig*', *on a Scottish island: Calum is destined for university and is tutored by MacAlasdair, former headmaster of the now-boarded up local school. MacAlasdair begins an affair with a former pupil which ends when her fiancé returns from Texas. Calum leaves for Aberdeen.*

As an Eilean is one of only four films covered in this book which are substantially in Gaelic. Where Gaelic is partially used in other films this is usually to signal difference and separation or exclusion. In *As an Eilean* Gaelic is the primary language of the community within which the film is set. *As an Eilean* focuses on two characters: MacAlasdair and Calum, linked by intelligence and a love of learning. Both are apart from their community, but on different trajectories: MacAlasdair arrived as an outsider to become the local school's headmaster, staying on after the death of his wife

and closure of the school, while Calum is about to leave the island. Calum has a brief relationship with local girl Kirsty, who is going to Glasgow University; Calum's mother, whom Calum accuses of being a snob, bemoans the fact that all the bright women leave the island – if they leave, the bright men, like Calum, will not come back. Calum's difference from his family (and the rest of his community) is signalled in a myriad of ways. He is, uniquely, being tutored by MacAlasdair, and is singled out in school. He is irritated by his mother's interruptions while trying to watch the 'great film' *The Battle of Algiers* (Gillo Pontecorvo, 1966) on TV. A key conversation with MacAlasdair signals to Calum what lies in wait if he stays on, or returns to, the island. MacAlasdair explains that his wife, who was a very good musician when they met, 'lost it while here, of course'. Calum asks why 'of course'? There is no answer, but the film leaves spaces, in which the seeds can grow.

The Scottish Kailyard writers of the late 19th and early 20th centuries created literature in which local ministers and schoolteachers had agency, making decisions to which the community deferred. *As an Eilean* challenges this; MacAlasdair and the local minister are both flawed. MacAlasdair is bitter after the death of his wife and is prepared to begin a potentially destructive affair; the minister is fundamentalist, superstitious, and ignorant.

As an Eilean is based on the novel *The Last Summer* (1969) and the story *The Hermit* (1977), by Iain Crichton Smith. *The Last Summer* is set in World War II but is effectively transposed in the film to the early 1990s, and *As an Eilean* has a quality of timelessness (or being *out* of time). It remains worth watching, although may be a little hard to track down.

Chasing the Deer (1994)   S+

> Directed by Graham Holloway
> Screenplay by Bob Carruthers, Steve Gillham,
>   Jerome Vincent
> Leading cast: Mathew Zajac (Alistair Campbell);
>   Lewis Rae (Euan Campbell); Brian Blessed
>   (Major Elliott); Fish (Angus Cameron);
>   Dominique Carrara (Charles Edward Stuart)
> Colour, 95 minutes, UK, English/Gaelic

1745: to save his son, Euan, Alistair joins the Jacobite army. Euan escapes and is taken in by British officer Major Elliott. Alistair and Euan meet on the Culloden battlefield, Alistair tending to his wounded son before himself being killed.

Chasing the Deer is more celebrated for the ingenuity with which the funding for the film was put in place, than for the result. Reports at the time were that the film was made for £460,000, much of this raised from small investors. The film *aims* at epic but misses the target. Geoffrey Macnab, reviewing the film in *S&S*, concludes that it 'offers a heritage-museum vision of the Jacobite uprising'. *Time Out* was harsher: 'truly lamentable'. The film is not awful; it is merely bad. For the size of its budget, it is at times remarkable, with cinematographer Alan M Trow working miracles. While

the cinematography is to be lauded, the direction is not, and the screenplay is leaden. Director Graham Holloway was a documentary maker, and this his first feature film; it was also his last. The camera is rarely fluid – action moves into and out of the frame, rather than the frame following the action. For a film based on a dramatic, if ultimately futile, military campaign, far too much time is spent on talking-head exposition (relatively cheap to shoot) betraying an insecurity in the director's ability to 'show, not tell'. Much of the acting is inexpert; both Dominique Carrara and Lewis Rae have this as their only feature film acting credit.

Chasing the Deer was largely shot on location in Scotland, at Kingussie, the Cairngorms and Fort George. The soundtrack features Scottish Celt-rockers Runrig (along with material from Fish, formerly lead singer of Marillion). Apart from the scenery, the best thing in the film is Blessed's performance; his Major Elliott is, for the most part, a sympathetic character – 'He's no like you'd expect an Englishman to be. He could very near be a Scotsman himself' says one of the Scots militiamen supporting the English army.

Online sources often confuse the film with *Culloden 1746 – The Last Highland Charge* (1993), a reconstruction of the battle, narrated by Brian Blessed. *Chasing the Deer* was retitled for VHS and DVD release as *1746: The Last Highland Charge*. Confusion is unavoidable. *Chasing the Deer* is not easy to find. Dutch and German DVDs have English soundtracks but are poor transfers from VHS.

Shallow Grave (1994) S++

Directed by Danny Boyle
Screenplay by John Hodge
Leading cast: Kerry Fox (Juliet Miller);
  Christopher Eccleston (David Stephens); Ewan
  McGregor (Alex Law); Ken Stott (DI McCall);
  Keith Allen (Hugo)
Colour, 89 minutes, UK

The flatmates contemplate their future...

In Edinburgh (a voice-over tells us 'this could have been any city – they're all the same'), Juliet, David and Alex offer Hugo ('a novelist') a room in their shared flat. When Hugo dies, the flatmates find a bag of money; they decide to keep it and dispose of his body. Events spiral out of their control as they become the targets of gangsters, and under suspicion by the police.

Shallow Grave is a remarkable film, establishing first-time director Boyle as a vibrant force in British cinema. It was the most successful British film of 1995, as *Trainspotting* was in 1996, and secured a slew of awards for Boyle (including, for he and producer Andrew Macdonald, the Alexander Korda Award for Best British Film at the BAFTAs). It provided the first role of note for McGregor, who had had a recurring role in the TV series *Lipstick on Your Collar* (1993) but whose only film work had been a small role way down the credits in one of Bill Forsyth's 'American' films, *Being Human* (1994) – in which Ken Stott also appeared. Given that *Being Human* sank at the box office, and was panned, McGregor was probably grateful

to have *Shallow Grave* released later the same year.

As important as *Shallow Grave*'s impact was on the careers of those involved, its impact on the standing of Scottish cinema – even though, as the opening voice-over makes clear, the film could be set in *any* city – was more significant. As Mark Browning writes: 'Prior to *Shallow Grave*, the popular perception of Scottish cinema was dominated by certain key figures... The establishment of the Scottish Film Production Fund in 1982 laid the groundwork for the provision of institutional support... but Boyle's work also acted as a catalyst for a doubling of Scottish-based production through the 1990s' (*Danny Boyle Lust for Life*, 2011). The claim has been made that *Shallow Grave* did more than enliven Scottish cinema, and that it rejuvenated *British* cinema. Boyle himself has indicated that the aims of the production team were more modest: 'We were ingénues making it up as we went along, trying to get away with it. All we were trying to do was make a highly entertaining, decent first film' (*Creating Wonder – Danny Boyle in Conversation with Amy Raphael*, 2013).

On that benchmark – and indeed on pretty much any benchmark – the film was wildly successful.

There is a similarity in the openings of *Shallow Grave* and *Trainspotting*. Both start with a voice-over and fast movement – in the former, a road surface from a car (intercut with two detours into the woods – presumably where the shallow grave of the title is going to be found) and, in the latter, a run through the streets. In *Shallow Grave* the voice-over is provided by Eccleston: 'I'm not afraid to declare my feelings. Take trust for instance, or friendship. These are the important things in life. These are the things that matter, that help you on your way. If you can't trust your friends, well what then?' In the nearly 90 minutes that follow, friendship and trust are dismantled, piece by inexorable piece, as greed and paranoia take over (in a manner not dissimilar to *The Treasure of the Sierra Madre*, John Huston, 1948). Money really *is* the root of all evil.

Many critics have commented on the fact that none of the central characters are likeable, with the result that they don't hold our sympathy. This has the consequence, as Anthony Lane argued in *The New Yorker*, that *Shallow Grave* becomes 'a frosty exercise in logic. But the director, Danny Boyle, does wonders with a small budget, and the suave, dense-hued look of his movie stays with you long after the horror has evaporated.'

Braveheart (1995)

Directed by Mel Gibson
Screenplay by Randall Wallace
Leading cast: Mel Gibson (William Wallace); Brian Cox (Argyle Wallace); Sophie Marceau (Princess Isabelle); Patrick McGoohan (Edward I); Angus Macfadyen (Robert the Bruce); Catherine McCormack (Murron)
Colour, 178 minutes, US, English/French/Gaelic/Latin/Italian

Scotland, 1280. Edward I of England claims the throne of Scotland, and Wallace leads the resistance. Denied vital support by the Scottish Lords notwithstanding his successes, Wallace is captured, tortured and executed.

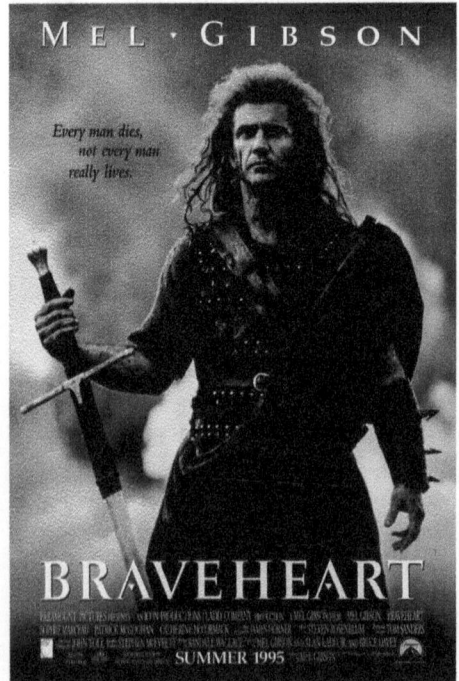

Braveheart is an extremely slick and well-made Hollywood epic. It was both a commercial and critical success – Box Office Mojo records that on a budget of $72m the film took over $213m. It won five Oscars including Best Picture and Best Director; a further 33 awards are listed on IMDb. I have interviewed students in East Asia seeking to study in Scotland because they have seen *Braveheart* (I did not tell them that it was largely shot in Ireland). Yet it is a deeply problematic film.

Mel Gibson's Wallace is the virtuous centre throughout

No film covered in this book has generated as much debate as *Braveheart* has, and it remains hugely divisive. As Colin McArthur pithily puts it: 'A project more calculated to create a "ferrets in a sack" situation in contemporary Scotland could not be imagined' (*Brigadoon, Braveheart and the Scots – Distortions of Scotland in Hollywood Cinema*, 2003). In a very different, and far less rigorous book, *Braveheart* is described as: 'Culturally and politically the most significant film of the nineties' (Lin Anderson, *Braveheart From Hollywood to Holyrood*, 2005). It isn't.

The past is immutable, but history and historiography – how we discuss and relate to the past – is not. That *Braveheart*'s relationship to the past would be complex was evident from its very conception. The 15th-century balladeer Blind Harry, who is believed to have composed *The Wallace* some 175 years after Wallace's death, provided the source material for *Braveheart*. Screenwriter Randall Wallace is quoted by Anderson: 'I decided to write about William Wallace... they say that nothing is known... Is *Blind Harry* true?

I don't know. I know that it spoke to my heart and that's what matters to me, that it spoke to my heart'. In other words, truth be damned.

The historical inaccuracies and distortions in *Braveheart* are legion – simply listing them has become reductive. But whether it matters that a Hollywood film is historically inaccurate depends on the nature of the inaccuracies: no film can tell the whole truth, and historical films *must* lie. Like McArthur I find the approach of Robert Rosenstone, an historian who has advised on feature films, persuasive. He argues that there is a key distinction between an invention which is consistent with the truth as we know it ('true invention'), and one which is inconsistent ('false invention'). *Braveheart* is littered with 'false inventions'. The film gives an illusion of 'truth' (screen titles with dates, places etc, informative exposition), but departs from it to a significant degree. It does so in ways which consistently skew the representation of Wallace as a heroic figure in a world without moral shade. He is a man of the people – a 'commoner', but one who is literate and speaks fluent Latin and French! – inspirationally leading a rebellion against a perfidious tyrant ('the most ruthless king ever to sit on the throne of England') who rules over a nation of sexually inadequate Englishmen. *Every* artistic choice – from the screenplay, to shot composition, to editing, to music (James Horner's unsubtle soundtrack is clichéd and cloying) – positions Wallace as the virtuous centre of a wicked frame. Randall Wallace and Mel Gibson inadvertently created in *Braveheart* a film which was readily adopted by white supremacists. It was also appropriated by the Scottish National Party, in a move which is now largely recognised to have been a mistake; the film's blood-and-soil posturing was wrongheaded when *Braveheart* was shot, and is now simply obnoxious.

The Near Room (1995)   S+++

Directed by David Hayman
Screenplay by Robert Murphy
Leading cast: Adrian Dunbar (Charlie Colquhoun); David Hayman (Dougie Patterson); Julie Graham (Elise Gray); Andy Serkis (Bunny); Emma Faulkner (Tommy Stirling)
Colour, 90 minutes, UK

Returning to Glasgow after an absence of 17 years, reporter Charlie is dragged into an investigation involving the sexual exploitation of minors, corruption, politics and power. The daughter he abandoned when he was 16, Tommy, is involved.

After directing *Silent Scream*, Hayman made *The Hawk* (1993), set in England, before returning to Scotland two years later for *The Near Room*, a gritty noir thriller which 'starts dark and gets darker before fading into pitch black' (*The Scotsman*). The film was compared to an obvious influence, *Taxi Driver* (Martin Scorsese, 1976) by Tom Tunney in *S&S* and elsewhere to *Se7en* (David Fincher, 1995). Although not in the same class as either, *The Near Room* is nearly very good. The noir atmosphere is strong, and Hayman makes the best possible use of Glasgow, although style sometimes trumps substance. But as *The Scotsman*'s critic put it: 'While a tad self-conscious at times and very brutal for a lot of the time, *The Near Room* is compelling and taut'.

The film's grim subject matter led to difficulties securing a distributor: after its completion, and a premiere at the EIFF, it took a further 18 months to come to cinemas, notwithstanding strong receptions on the festival circuit. This led Hayman to accuse the British film industry of being weak and lacking courage. *The Near Room* gave Serkis his second screen role, and McAvoy his first. *Newsweek* reported later that Hayman had been to talk at his school. McAvoy said: 'He'd done loads of movies and worked with f--ing Schwarzenegger, and as a young kid I was like, "Oooh, that's interesting"'. He offered to 'make the tea or run errands' on Hayman's next film but was instead given an audition.

Iain Robertson in *Small Faces*

Small Faces (1995)   S+++ T31

Directed by Gillies MacKinnon
Screenplay by Billy MacKinnon, Gillies
  MacKinnon
Leading cast: Iain Robertson (Lex Maclean);
  Joe McFadden (Alan Maclean); Steven Duffy
  (Bobby Maclean); Kevin McKidd (Malky
  Johnson); Laura Fraser (Joanne Macgowan);
  Clare Higgins (Lorna Maclean); Garry Sweeney
  (Charlie Sloan); Mark McConnochie (Gorbals)
Colour, 108 minutes, UK

*Glasgow, 1968: 13-year-old Lex, older
brother Alan (who aims to go to art
school), and eldest brother Bobby live with
their mother, Lorna, in Govanhill. Their
father is dead. Over a period of a few days
their lives intersect with two rival gangs,
leading to tragedy.*

You know *Small Faces* is going to be
good by the end of the opening credits
sequence. This plays out over a riotous
map of Glasgow being drawn by Lex. This
comment on the Glasgow of 1968 has
gangland territories and events marked
out; it shows the place of Lex himself
in 'oor hoose' (a comfortable sandstone
tenement in Govanhill), along with Bobby
(angry and wielding a hammer), and Alan
(with angel's wings and a halo), but it also
shows what lies on either side. To the east,
Sloan and 'Glenland'; to the west, 'Bad

179

Malky' and 'Tongland' (in the earlier *That Sinking Feeling*, the graffito 'Tongs OK' can be briefly seen spraypainted on a wall). Bodies with daggers in them bob along the Clyde, and a man plummets off a bridge. There are also Glasgow landmarks – north of the river there is the 'Sarry Heid' (the now-closed Saracen's Head). The film then breathes life into, and shows death in, these spaces. Although shot in the mid-1990s the late-'60s atmosphere is convincing; John de Borman's cinematography is terrific.

As Duncan Petrie noted in *Screening Scotland* (2000), *Small Faces* treads a well-balanced line between mythologising the violence in Glasgow at the time and revealing its horrors. Certainly, neither of the gang leaders, McKidd's Malky and Sweeney's Sloan, are given the clichéd 'he was good to his ma' treatment. Malky is an erratic and dangerous psychopath – it is notable that his end comes not via gang violence, but through the actions of his own step-brother/victim Gorbals (who tells Lex at their first meeting that he will have no part in gang activity). Sloan is initially portrayed a little more sympathetically; the first time Lex and Alan help him it is for Alan to insert his face into a painting hung in a gallery. This veneer quickly rubs off; Alan's friend is badly beaten for being in the wrong place at the wrong time, and Lex is headbutted by Sloan without reason. Interviewed in *The Scotsman*, screenwriter Billy MacKinnon (credited alongside his brother), said that: 'On one hand we are dealing with the optimism, madness and restlessness of the Sixties; in the other, the destruction of the slums and resettlement where areas that had once had their own working-class culture lost any sense of community and became a bewildered mess.'

By a twist of fate, *Small Faces* was made before *Trainspotting*, but received its UK release two months later, and was overshadowed by it. Reviewers however were positive. In *Empire*, William Thomas took the view that it did not suffer in comparison: 'a tough but humorous tale of brotherly rivalry and gangland warfare which can proudly rank alongside… *Trainspotting*'. *Small Faces* changed lives. It was the first film for Robertson, Fraser, McFadden and McKidd. Robertson was 15 when *Small Faces* was released. After winning the 1996 Scotland BAFTA award for Best Performance he said in *The Herald*: 'It just goes to show that a wee naebody fae Govan kin dae good'. He's maintained an acting career (most notably in *River City* (2017–2022)) and appears in *The Debt Collector*. Fraser has gone on to have a rich career (see also *16 Years of Alcohol, Beats, Nina's Heavenly Delights* and *The Flying Scotsman* etc). McFadden played the lead in the TV adaptation of Iain Banks' *The Crow Road* (1996) and was in nearly 150 episodes of *Holby City* (2014–2020). McKidd was next in *Trainspotting* and is also in *The Acid House, Dog Soldiers,* and *16 Years of Alcohol*. He hit the financial, if not the artistic, jackpot with over 300 episodes of *Grey's Anatomy* (2008–2022).

In March 2023 it was reported that a sequel was to be made, with the main cast, and MacKinnon, on board.

Breaking the Waves (1996) S+ T9

Directed by Lars von Trier
Screenplay by Lars von Trier, Peter Asmussen
Leading cast: Emily Watson (Bess McNeill);
    Stellan Skarsgård (Jan Nyman); Katrin Cartlidge
    (Dodo McNeill); Adrian Rawlins
    (Dr Richardson)
Colour, 159 minutes, Denmark/Sweden/France/
    Netherlands/Norway/Iceland/Spain/UK

In church, Bess explains to old men suspicious of 'outsiders' her desire to marry Jan, who works on the oil rigs. They marry, there is a party and, for Bess, her first sex. Bess's mental health is fragile, and after Jan is seriously injured, she engages in sexual encounters with random men so that she can tell Jan about it. Jan's health improves. The encounters become increasingly horrific. When Jan relapses Bess sacrifices herself for him. He recovers, and Jan and his friends smuggle her body to the oil rig and consign it to the sea. Celestial bells ring out over the rig.

Emily Watson makes a stunning debut in
Breaking the Waves

Breaking the Waves is a film of remarkable power dealing with big themes: community and family; the Church, God, faith, sacrifice, and miracles; marriage, love, and sex; and mental and physical health. It made a huge critical impact on release, winning multiple awards, including the Grand Prix at Cannes in 1996 (although it missed out on the Palme d'Or, which went to Mike Leigh's *Secrets and Lies*, 1996), and in 1997 the French César for Best Foreign Film. At the 1997 Danish film awards (the Roberts), it won pretty much everything. The first time I saw it, at the Phoenix cinema (now the Picturehouse) in Oxford, I had to remain in my seat through to the lights coming up. Considering it to be one of the best films I had seen I also vowed never to watch it again (and yet I find that it keeps on dragging me back).

It's hard to know to whom the biggest plaudits belong: von Trier, or Watson. I cannot imagine anyone else in the role of Bess. Watson was in her late 20s when *Breaking the Waves* was shot. It was her first film and catapulted her to international recognition. Peter Travers in *Rolling Stone* offered this paeon: 'Look closely at the actress in the photo below. Her name is Emily Watson. She is 29, British and a former member of the Royal Shakespeare Company. This is her first movie, and her knockout performance heralds one of the most extraordinary film debuts in ages.' Watson was Oscar and BAFTA nominated (losing out to Frances McDormand and Brenda Blethyn respectively), but she did take home the European Film Award for Best Actress. Watson also appears in *The Water Horse*.

Two minutes into *Breaking the Waves* Bess is asked to leave the church and take a seat outside. In tight close-up she turns, looks directly at the camera, and smiles. This is followed by the first of eight titles: 'Bess Gets Married', and the first of the extradiegetic songs which serve as punctuation points (Mott the Hoople's 'All The Way From Memphis'). What an introduction to Watson that early look is! We might expect Bess to be cowed and nervous, oppressed by old men with the power to determine her fate. But there is that smile, and with it a recognition that she is, at least for now, in control and happy. Buffeted by the vicissitudes of fate and frail mental health she does not remain in control. The chapter titles chart the story: (2) life with Jan; (3) life alone; (4) Jan's illness; (5) doubt; (6) faith; (7) Bess' sacrifice; (8) the funeral. *Breaking the Waves* is not an easy film; the trials that Bess goes through are horrific, but in the film's logic-defying end there is hope and joy. It would have been easy to package Bess' suffering and actions as exclusively a mental health

issue – to deny faith. To reposition this as a matter of miraculously rewarded faith, without inviting ridicule, is a masterful achievement by von Trier.

Together with fellow Dane Thomas Vinterberg, von Trier launched the Dogme 95 manifesto shortly before *Breaking the Waves* was made. It is something of a paradox that his greatest film does not adhere to the rules set out in the manifesto. *Breaking the Waves* is the first film in the Golden Heart trilogy, so called because the films focus on women who maintain their beliefs and innocence in the face of tragedy (*The Idiots*, 1998, and *Dancer in the Dark*, 2000). It is the best of these.

The Bruce (1996)   S+

Directed by Bob Carruthers and David McWhinnie (Brian Blessed – additional scenes)
Screenplay by Bob Carruthers
Leading cast: Sandy Welch (Robert the Bruce); Brian Blessed (Edward I); Dee Hepburn (Mary Bruce); Richard Brimblecombe (Edward II); Oliver Reed (Bishop Wisharton); Pavel Douglas (John 'Red' Comyn)
Colour, 107 minutes, UK

A monk writes the Bruce's history. With Scotland in disarray and under the yoke of the English, Robert the Bruce attempts to unite the Scottish nobility in opposition to King Edward I. He is betrayed by John 'Red' Comyn, and defeated by Edward I. The Bruce kills Comyn, is crowned King of Scotland, rebuilds his forces and defeats the English at the Battle of Bannockburn.

Like *Chasing the Deer* (for which Carruthers provided the screenplay), *The Bruce* was made on a wing and a prayer; the budget of less than £500,000 was secured with the backing of many 'associate producers', some of whom appear in the film. In *Empire* Darren Bignall wrote: 'this is a flat, half-baked fling at the events leading up to the historic battle of Bannockburn, seen squarely from the viewpoint of Robert The Bruce'. It is remarkable that a film with aspirations as limited as are on show here would vie for space in cinemas after the release of *Braveheart* (much as I loathe the film, it does have the one merit of being exceptionally well made). *The Bruce* feels more like something from the 1980s 'straight to video' era than it does a film from the late 1990s. It would certainly have been improved by giving up any attempt to film battle scenes – these are appallingly inept.

Historian Andrew E Larson wrote an entertaining piece about *The Bruce* on his blog: 'It feels very much like some enthusiastic Scottish history re-enactor wanted to prove that it was possible to make an historically-accurate movie about Scottish history that was still a really good film, and then only managed to get the first half of the job done.' As others have pointed out, the film is so poorly explained, that you'd have to have a decent grasp of Scottish medieval history to follow the events. After the first battle in the film, which did *not* happen, the events are moderately close to history, although there are many anachronisms. As Larson writes: 'we get lots of Highlanders in kilts three hundred years too early. And guys playing bodhrans, which won't be invented

for about half a millennium. Oh, and brace yourself for gratuitous modern bagpipes. They had a piper, and they were gonna get damn good use out of him.'

Brian Blessed is, of course, fun to watch. He clearly didn't take this nonsense too seriously. Dee Hepburn as the Bruce's wife is wasted, and Michael Van Wijk (who at the time might have been the best-known cast member in the UK – he was Wolf in the hit TV series *Gladiators*) as Henry de Bohun is hilarious.

→ *Outlaw King* (2018) S++ T100

Directed by David Mackenzie
Screenplay by Bash Doran, David Mackenzie, James MacInnes
Leading cast: Chris Pine (Robert Bruce, Earl of Carrick); Stephen Dillane (King Edward I of England); Florence Pugh (Elizabeth Burgh)
Colour, 121 minutes, UK/US

Scotland, 1304: Wallace's rebellion against Edward I of England, who has taken control of the country is put down. Scottish lords, including Robert Bruce, swear fealty to Edward. Bruce rebels and is declared an outlaw. Crowned King of Scots at Scone he is defeated in battle, fleeing to Islay. His wife and daughter are captured and taken to England. Bruce and his men begin to fight back. The English army rides out and is defeated at Loudoun Hill by a much smaller Scottish force.

Outlaw King has neither the scale nor the emotional pull of *Braveheart* but is,

Chris Pine as The Bruce

in important ways, better. It helps that the film was shot entirely in Scotland (as Mackenzie put it, 'according to the borders of 1305'), that the bombast of *Braveheart* is absent, and that it provides a better proximation of the past. As narrative, the films would work well as a double bill; tonally there would be a substantial disjunct. When released it was the most expensive feature film to be made in Scotland. Unfortunately, being picked up by Netflix, its cinema release was limited. Reviews were broadly positive, if not entirely gushing with praise.

Scottish writer-director David Mackenzie, co-founder of Glasgow-based Sigma films, came to *Outlaw King* with a strong track record. In addition to helming *Young Adam, Perfect Sense* and *Hallam Foe*, he also made the superb American-set *Hell or High Water* (2016), which also stars Chris Pine. He works regularly with producer Gillian Berrie, whose list of credits, starting with *My Name is Joe* and *Ratcatcher*, is outstanding.

The accuracy of *Outlaw King* has, of course, been picked over; if this is not with quite the same degree of vigour as is the case with *Braveheart* it is because the film does not raise the same issues in relation to its distortions (and was not as commercially successful). In *The Hollywood Reporter* Mackenzie said: '[Braveheart] was made 20 years ago and had a certain perspective, and if you look at it now, you might be quite worried by some of that blood-and-soil stuff... The historical accuracy of what Bruce was doing is something we've tried a lot to delve into in our film. Some things are conflated, but essentially these narrative beats are things that happened.' The events shown in *Outlaw King* extend over a period of five years, starting with Bruce's submission to Edward I in 1302 (the year in which he married Elizabeth Burgh) and ending in May 1307 with the Battle of Loudoun Hill – the triumphant and brilliantly filmed set piece ('a spectacular final battle scene shot with flair by the cinematographer Barry Ackroyd' – Peter Bradshaw, in *The Guardian*). What is missing in the film is any strong sense of the complexities of Bruce himself – we see the key events, but not *the man*; if anything Elizabeth is more strongly realised. The large supporting cast is strong.

The choice of Chris Pine as Bruce generated some discussion. But he has the charisma required, and someone with a high profile was necessary to secure financing. Florence Pugh (*The Falling*, Carol Morley, 2014; *Lady Macbeth*, William Oldroyd, 2016 – see also *Malevolent*) had begun her path to recognition as one of the best actors of her generation before *Outlaw King* was made and after this went on to lead roles, including in *Midsommar* (Ari Aster, 2019), *Black Widow* (Cate Shortland, 2021) and *Dune: Part II* (Denis Villeneuve, 2024). She was nominated as Best Actress in the 2019 BAFTA Scotland Awards.

→ *Robert the Bruce* (2019) S+

Directed by Richard Gray
Screenplay by Eric Belgau, Angus Macfadyen
Leading cast: Angus Macfadyen (Robert the Bruce); Diarmaid Murtagh (James Douglas); Anna Hutchison (Morag)
Colour, 124 minutes, UK/US/Australia

Scotland, 1306: The country is in turmoil after the death of King Alexander III. Robert the Bruce murders English sympathiser John Comyn but becomes King in name only. Wounded, in the winter wilderness, he watches a spider spin its web. He is protected by Morag and reunited with those who have remained loyal. End titles tell of the Bruce's later success.

The normally excellent Jared Harris, who plays John Comyn, gets off lightly. He is killed within the first 25 minutes of this laborious snooze-fest. Made well over 20 years after he played the Bruce in *Braveheart,* Macfadyen reprises the role, in a film he co-wrote, which picks up where *Braveheart* ended. By a bizarre turn of events, the film was shot largely in Montana, although Macfadyen told *The Scotsman*: 'I defy anybody to tell when we're in Montana and when we're in Scotland.' There are scenes where the difference is clear. There was *some* shooting in Scotland, Macfadyen believing that it would not be politic to make the entire film in Montana.

RTB was beaten to the punch by *Outlaw King*, which was released seven months before *RTB*. As well as being a superior film with bigger (and better) production values and a bigger star in the lead, it slaked the market's thirst for Robert the Bruce biopics. In June 2019 *The Herald* reported that Macfadyen, along with actor Tim Robbins and local politicians, were campaigning to persuade Cineworld to reverse a decision not to show the film at any of its Scottish venues. Box Office Mojo reports a global take of $23,425. *Variety*'s Owen Gleiberman went for the jugular – the film is a 'staid, morose, and achingly pedestrian historical drama... it's "Braveheart: The Polite Domesticated Streaming Version." The film is dunked in a lukewarm bath of doubt and regret.'

Trainspotting (1996) and *T2: Trainspotting* (2017) S++ T3

Directed by Danny Boyle
Screenplay by John Hodge
Leading cast: Ewan McGregor (Renton/Mark); Ewen Bremner (Spud); Jonny Lee Miller (Sick Boy/Simon); Kevin McKidd* (Tommy); Robert Carlyle (Begbie); Kelly Macdonald (Diane); Anjela Nedyalkova (Veronika)† [* not in T2; † T2 only]
Colour, 93/117 minutes, UK

[Trainspotting] *Renton, Sick Boy and Spud take heroin. Renton tries to quit. Later he quits quitting, and Tommy too becomes addicted. Spud is jailed; Renton enters rehab, but relapses later. He tests HIV negative; Tommy is HIV positive. Renton moves to London. Begbie, wanted for armed robbery, and Sick Boy later stay with him. They return to Scotland for*

Tommy's funeral. A drug deal nets them £16,000, which Renton steals, leaving Spud £4,000. Renton is 'choosing life'.

[T2] *20 years later Mark returns to Edinburgh from Amsterdam. Begbie escapes gaol; Spud attends a drug users' meeting; Simon is a pimp and blackmailer. Their lives intersect: Mark, Simon and Spud work on building a sauna/brothel, with an EU grant. Spud begins to write. Begbie sees Mark and attempts to kill him. In a final fight Spud knocks Begbie out, and he is returned to gaol. Spud's stories find a title, and will be published...*

The film's iconic poster

'Doubtless, more has been written about *Trainspotting* than any other British film of the past twenty-five years.' So begins the discussion of the film by Justin Smith in *Withnail and Us* (2010). Murray Smith has written a book on the film for the BFI series Modern Classics, and in 2021 Coattail Publications produced its sumptuous (and sumptuously expensive) *Trainspotting: 25th Anniversary*, by Jay Glennie (available

A sense of urgency is never far away in *Trainspotting*

only in a limited edition of 1,000).

Irvine Welsh's novel, his first, was published in 1993, when Scottish writing was experiencing something of a renaissance: established authors such as William McIlvanney and Alasdair Gray were joined in the 1980s and 1990s by new writers. James Kelman published his first novel, *The Busconductor Hines* in 1984; Janice Galloway's *The Trick is to Keep Breathing* appeared in 1989; and Jeff Torrington's *Swing Hammer Swing* was published in 1992. Reviewing *Trainspotting* on publication, Brian Morton in *The New Statesman & Society* described it as 'a tense, urgent chronicle of

addiction', and wrote of Welsh's characters that: 'Theirs is a kind of Burroughs-like junk language, grossly and intimately performative. It expresses a society-outside-society, but... it still somehow insists on a place in the old everyday world of mam and dad, home, school and university.' In the *Sunday Times*, in 2017, anticipating the release of *T2*, Scottish author and broadcaster Stuart Cosgrove was quoted: 'I can't think of another piece of Scottish literature that has come out in my lifetime that has had the same level of pop cultural impact or resonance for young people. It was common to see people with *Trainspotting* in their bag or reading it on

Older, and somewhat wiser – Ewan McGregor and Ewen Bremner

the train wherever you went in the world.'

The film, too, had a massive impact. *Trainspotting* made stars out of some of its cast and its director, although, except for Macdonald, all had at least some experience and recognition before *Trainspotting* (McKidd had been only in *Small Faces* made the year before but it received general release in the UK two months after *Trainspotting*). It was Macdonald's first film. To *The Guardian* in 2022 she said: 'I remember getting on the bus after my final audition. It was a screen test and I left their makeshift studio that we filmed in on Alexandria Parade (*sic*), and I waited for the bus and I sat on the top deck. And I knew it was between me and one other person. And I sort of knew I'd got it. I had a feeling: "This is my life starting now". It was a clear fork in the road.'

If *Shallow Grave* is Britain's *Reservoir Dogs* (Quentin Tarantino, 1992) then *Trainspotting* is Britain's *Pulp Fiction* (Quentin Tarantino, 1994). It is remarkable that in both cases they were the directors' debut and sophomore films (albeit Tarantino made the unreleased *My Best Friend's Birthday* in 1987). Over their careers Boyle has shown that he is a more rounded director with a greater range.

Trainspotting opens fast and maintains its momentum – helped along by an effective use of voice-over (which often, but *not* here, flags that a film is in trouble), and an exceptional curated soundtrack. In the opening scene, Iggy Pop's 'Lust for Life' plays; Renton and Begbie are chased, and one of the most recognisable opening speeches in British cinema starts, with the words 'Choose life...' (Mark riffs on this in *T2*). Renton and his friends choose 'not to choose life' and, as Renton says, 'who needs reasons when you've got heroin?'. Renton serves as a guide, pulling the audience along and securing empathy, as choices are explained. There is pace, humour, and horror – and real power in some scenes (particularly the baby's death and the response to it). The slowest period is the London interlude, when Renton is enjoying the height of Thatcherism: 'There was no such thing as society, and even if there was, I most certainly had nothing to do with it'. This, however, is clearly deliberate – a calm before the storm of Tommy's funeral, the deal, Renton's betrayal, and Begbie's subsequent meltdown. Boyle's direction is remarkably inventive. The 'toilet diving scene', which starts less than ten minutes into the film is perhaps the defining moment. The painstaking construction of this scene is laid out in detail by Glennie.

Between *Trainspotting* and *T2* Boyle had a string of successes, including *28 Days Later* (2002), *Slumdog Millionaire* (2008), which won him the Best Director Oscar, and *Steve Jobs* (2015). He also directed the opening ceremony for the London 2012 Olympics. While *T2* lacks the spectacular imagination of its predecessor, it is, like its characters, director, and presumably its audience, slower and more mature. *T2* constantly references *Trainspotting,* and the two films are best watched back-to-back. By the end of *T2* Spud is in the ascendant;

he is clean, he helps Veronika steal the grant money and, in a 'meta' move, it is his writing which becomes the source for both the films. Together they form a unified and exceptional piece of work.

→ *The Acid House* (1998) S+++

Directed by Paul McGuigan
Screenplay by Irvine Welsh
Leading cast: Stephen McCole (Boab); Maurice Roëves (God); Tam Dean Burn (Alec); Kevin McKidd (Johnny); Michelle Gomez (Catriona); Gary McCormack (Larry); Ewen Bremner (Colin 'Coco' Bryce); Martin Clunes (Rory); Jemma Redgrave (Jenny)
Colour, 111 minutes, UK

[1] *'The Granton Star Cause': Boab's life is turning bad. God tells him he is an insect, and a 'lazy dirty pest'. [2] 'A Soft Touch': Johnny and Catriona marry, she treats him appallingly, they part, then reunite. [3] 'The Acid House': Coco and a baby switch consciousnesses after being struck by lightning. The body-swap is later reversed.*

The Acid House was McGuigan's first film and was based on Welsh's short story collection of the same name, published in 1994, one year after *Trainspotting*, and one year before *Marabou Stork*. At the 1998 Stockholm Film Festival, McGuigan won the FIPRESCI prize for *The Acid House* by virtue of 'its originality in presenting a crass Scottish everyday world in a surreal, almost hallucinogenic light, very true to its author and its adventurous visual style.' But there are problems with this portmanteau film: the three stories do not tie up. A consequence of this is that the whole is *not* greater than the sum of the parts. The extent to which you will like the film will depend in part on whether your judgement is more skewed by the segment you prefer, or the segment you most dislike. If, of course, you enjoy all of them you're minted.

The original intention of the film's producers was that each segment be directed by someone different. The film was greenlit after the phenomenal success of *Trainspotting*. Alongside source, context, and some themes, the two films have in common the presence of Bremner, whose segment gives the film its name. This is not the strongest segment (Xan Brooks, in *S&S*, argued that it was 'both the most ambitious and the least satisfying') – that honour goes to 'The Granton Star Cause', which clearly riffs on Franz Kafka's *Metamorphosis* (1915).

In *The Hollywood Reporter* Frank Scheck drew the link with *Trainspotting* (as almost every critic did), noting that *The Acid House* 'displays the same mixture of scabrous humour, brutality and surrealism… only less skilfully and entertainingly'. That is a fair summation.

→ *Filth* (2013) S+++ T32

Directed by Jon S Baird
Screenplay by Jon S Baird
Leading cast: James McAvoy (Bruce); Jamie Bell (Lennox); Eddie Marsan (Bladesey); Imogen Poots (Drummond)
Colour, 97 minutes, UK

The run-up to Christmas in Edinburgh. Bruce is a Detective Sergeant vying for promotion. Following the death of his wife he has psychotic episodes, before being demoted, and dying by suicide.

Filth was published in 1998. The film, which came 15 years later, is, like the novel, challenging. It deals with a very serious topic – a collapse in mental health leading to suicide – with a framing which is frenetic, outrageously vulgar, and disconcertingly witty. While the ending may force the viewer to re-read the film, this is followed by a jaunty Christmas tune, and an animated credits sequence which cuts across the severity of what has come before. McAvoy (whose first film, **The Near Room** is discussed above) gives a bravura performance, in some measure similar to his David Percival in the highly entertaining *Atomic Blonde* (David Leitch, 2017), which also features Eddie Marsan. Deborah Ross in the *Spectator* also liked McAvoy: 'one of those actors who can, by some process – I don't know what the technical name for this is, but it could be "brilliant acting" – bring depth to emptiness… McAvoy offers us sufficient glimpses of the guilt and shame and

"... brilliant acting ..." James McAvoy

self-loathing that drive him and, oddly, we begin to care what happens to him.'

In *The NYT* Stephen Holden found much to like in the direction: 'Baird's visual imagination is more Terry Gilliam-goes-to-the-circus than the inside-the-toilet realism of Danny Boyle's *Trainspotting*.' These imaginings include a scene in which Bruce, dressed as Carole (his dead wife), fantasises being chauffeured by David Soul, who sings 'Silver Lady' to him. However, Holden was not persuaded that the film worked: 'After a certain point, watching it is like listening to the ravings of an increasingly incoherent and abusive drunk.'

Filth is throughout deliberately and outrageously politically incorrect. Perhaps this flows from Bruce's illness. A racist outburst *is* explained as a response to his wife's departure driven by his mental illness. But this may also simply be a comment on modern policing, and as Bruce's boss (John Sessions) says, 'this is *Scotland*!'. More generally, the line between delusion, and just plain bizarre, is not well-defined in *Filth*. But maybe life's like that.

The first words we hear Bruce say, as he walks down Castlehill in Edinburgh, are: 'Scotland. This nation brought the world television, the steam engine, golf, whisky, penicillin, and of course, the deep-fried Mars bar. It is great being Scottish. We are such a uniquely successful race'. This is immediately undermined by a shot of ne'er-do-wells lounging against a wall, but *Filth* does not carry us along on a journey specific to Scotland; although it may appear parochial through a narrow lens, its story is universal.

Mrs Brown (aka *Her Majesty, Mrs Brown*) (1997)   S+

Directed by John Madden
Screenplay by Jeremy Brock
Leading cast: Judi Dench (Queen Victoria); Billy Connolly (John Brown); Geoffrey Palmer (Henry Ponsonby); Antony Sher (Disraeli)
Colour, 101 minutes, UK/Ireland/US

1864, Balmoral: three years after the death of Queen Victoria's husband she remains in mourning, becoming reliant on John Brown, a 'devoted outdoor servant' to Prince Albert. Four years pass, and she is eventually persuaded to rejoin public life. In 1883, Brown, who has continued to serve the Queen, dies of pneumonia.

This is one of two films exploring an unconventional (for the time) friendship involving Queen Victoria, the other being *Victoria & Abdul* (Stephen Frears, 2017). Both star Dench as Victoria. For *Mrs Brown* she received her first Oscar nomination. She won the following year after playing a different Queen in *Shakespeare in Love*, which, like *Mrs Brown*, was directed by Madden. Of the three films *Mrs Brown* is clearly the strongest, not perhaps because Dench's performance is the stronger, but because the character of Brown is so well fleshed out by Brock's screenplay and by Connolly's performance.

The allure of wallowing in grief in the stunning setting of Balmoral is clear, and *Mrs Brown* is of tangential interest in illustrating, although not expressly exploring, Victoria's romanticisation of Scotland and the impact this had on the creation of a new Scottish mythology in the late 19th century. In summoning Brown, Ponsonby's voice-over references 'the Queen's sentimental, though deeply held view, that all Highlanders are good for the health'. Reference too is made to Victoria's book *Leaves from the Journal of Our Life in the Highlands* which was published first in 1868, selling over 20,000 copies. In the Balmoral scenes, which extend for the greater part of the film, we are treated to much tartan, Scottish music, and views of the Highlands.

The critical response to *Mrs Brown* on release was very positive. Anthony Lane's review in *The New Yorker* is not untypical, writing that Madden 'could have set this up as a minor tragedy, but he has the wit, especially in the first half, to play it cool and droll... Connolly offers a portrait of devotion so fierce that it verges on the mad; and Sher is a riot – he has the air of a man who finds the whole affair vastly entertaining. And he's right.' *Mrs Brown* marked the first screen appearance of Gerard Butler (see **Dear Frankie** and **The Vanishing**).

Regeneration (aka *Behind the Lines*) (1997)   S+++

Directed by Gillies MacKinnon
Screenplay by Allan Scott
Leading cast: Jonathan Pryce (Capt. William
  Rivers); James Wilby (2nd Lt. Siegfried
  Sassoon); Jonny Lee Miller (2nd Lt. Billy Prior);
  Stuart Bunce (2nd Lt. Wilfrid Owen); Dougray
  Scott (Capt. Robert Graves)
Colour, 109 minutes, UK/Canada

World War I, Craiglockhart Hospital: poets Sassoon and Owen, along with other soldiers, are treated by Dr Rivers for mental health issues brought on by combat in the trenches of France.

On publication, Pat Barker's *Regeneration* Trilogy (*Regeneration*, 1981; *The Eye in the Door*, 1993; and *Ghost Road*, 1995) was lauded; the final instalment winning the Booker Prize. Only *Regeneration* has been adapted for the screen. After the explosive *Small Faces*, MacKinnon made *Trojan Eddie* (1996), which had a mixed reception, then, with a £1m grant from the National Lottery, he turned to *Regeneration*. The film was picked up for distribution by arthouse company Artificial Eye, leading *The Scotsman* to report that the producers would have to settle for critical, rather than commercial, success. Modest critical success was indeed forthcoming, although some pointed to the fact that the individual narratives do not fuse well into a coherent whole. The strengths however are on clear display. A strong ensemble cast lends emotional depth to each narrative, while Owen's words blend superbly with the cinematography of Canadian Glen MacPherson. As Stella Bruzzi wrote in *S&S*, if 'some of the narrative flow and the detail of Barker's novel have been lost in translation, *Regeneration* the film still retains many of the imaginative depths of those who experienced the Great War which the book plundered'.

Although the Edinburgh location of Craiglockhart Hospital (Dumbarton's Overtoun House) is emphasised, its location is incidental. But the film does come with a supporting cast consisting of several Scottish actors, including David Hayman, Kevin McKidd and, in his second feature, James McAvoy. For the US release the film was recut, retitled, and reduced to 96 minutes.

The Slab Boys (1997) S+++ T100

Directed by John Byrne
Screenplay by John Byrne
Leading cast: Robin Laing (Phil McCann); Russell
  Barr (Spanky Farrell); Bill Gardiner (Hector
  McKenzie); Louise Berry (Lucille Bentley); Anna
  Massey (Miss Elsie Walkinshaw)
Colour, 97 minutes, UK

Paisley, 1957: three young men – the slab boys – grind dyes in a workshop. Hector, who is bullied by the other two, dreams of inviting the office siren, Lucille, to the upcoming works dance. Spanky dreams of going to the United States, and Phil aspires to be an artist.

I first saw John Byrne's semi-autobiographical play *The Slab Boys* at the Old Red Lion Theatre in London somewhere around 1990. In a small, intimate theatre there was a fierce intensity to the production which is missing from the film. A 1983 off-Broadway production of the play starred Kevin Bacon, Val Kilmer and Sean Penn. In a particularly harsh review of the film, *Variety* pointed out: 'It's that kind of star power the movie desperately needs to complement its bold, brash and colourful design, which goes for a studio-based artificiality bolstered by a soundtrack of rerecorded period songs'. The songs in question are provided by Scottish artists Edwyn Collins (Bobby Darin's 'Dream Lover'), Pat Kane, Lulu, The Proclaimers (Chuck Berry's 'No Particular Place to Go') and Eddi Reader. The 1950s design of the film, from Teddy Boy outfits and quiffs to an American-style café, complete with jukebox, is a treat – and is moderated with Paisley wit.

AL Kennedy, writing for *S&S*, visited the set of *The Slab Boys* at Glasgow's Westbridge House. She noted that the 'studio is a gift for anyone anxious to be fooled by detail, or seduced by craftsmanship... It will also be a timely reminder that Scottish films need not be trapped in the marketable clichés between Grim-and-Gritty-Northern and Whimsical-Hamish-McBrigadoon.' Unlike the *Variety* reviewer, I did not find that 'a good 50% of [the] dialogue is ear-strainingly incomprehensible'. While this is a lazy complaint, regularly made by American reviewers who find non-standard English

and American accents difficult, our own Allan Hunter, in a generally positive review for *Screen International* noted that 'the plethora of broad Scottish accents may also prove a disincentive for some viewers'. The film, which was moderately expensive to make, performed poorly at the box office.

There is a weakness in the lack of experience of the central actors playing the slab boys, none of whom possess strong charisma. This is not true of Louise Berry, who was literally approached on the street by Byrne and invited to audition.

The Winter Guest (1997) S++ T100

Directed by Alan Rickman
Screenplay by Sharman Macdonald, Alan Rickman
Leading cast: Phyllida Law (Elspeth); Emma Thompson (Frances); Sheila Reid (Lily); Sandra Voe (Chloe); Gary Hollywood (Alex); Arlene Cockburn (Nita)
Colour, 108 minutes, UK/US

Winter in a small coastal town, and the sea is frozen over. Four pairs interact, and death hangs over the scene.

Shot in Fife, in the winter of 1996, *The Winter Guest* is endowed by *cinematographer* Seamus McGarvey with a cold, painterly beauty which, as Duncan Petrie has pointed out, is reminiscent 'of Scandinavian masters such as Carl Theodor Dreyer and Ingmar Bergman' (*British Rural Landscapes on Film*, ed Paul Newland, 2016). The 'winter guest' of the title is clearly death, which has taken Frances' husband, lurks waiting for Elspeth, and is ever-present for Lily and Chloe. Roger Ebert was not convinced by *The Winter Guest*: while he admired the film's 'look and tone', it left him 'feeling strangely hollow', and 'at the end there is an emptiness, like stepping into air, or like a play interrupted after the first act'. Alan Rickman, better known as an actor ('And call off Christmas!') only directed two films, this and 2014's *A Little Chaos* (a chamber piece about two gardeners constructing the grounds at Versailles). He died in 2016, in his early seventies, and it is to be regretted that he did not have the opportunity to direct more.

The Winter Guest is set over one day (Nita asks: 'What if there's only this day left to us. Out of all our lives, this one day?'). The dynamic within each pair is strong, but the lack of interaction between each pair is limiting. They face different futures with different levels of fear or hope. Lily and Chloe's routine of going to funerals surrounds them with death. Tom and Sam face the uncertainties of puberty and manhood, and are naïve. Frances does not know how to reorder her life following the death of her husband, but what she really wants is a way to 'leave him behind'. Her mother 'needs to be needed' and hopes that Frances will need her, as at the end of the day it appears she does. Alex is both eager and timid in the early stages of forming a sexual relationship (perhaps for the first time), and finds the presence of his father, in photographs prominently displayed in the house, intimidating – their

relationship does not appear to have been a strong and supportive one.

Some scenes – Alex and Nita sharing intimacy before an open fire; Lily and Chloe in a tea-room – reflect the origins of the film in Glasgow-born Sharman Macdonald's play (which Rickman had directed for the stage in Leeds and London). While the dialogue is somewhat theatrical, there are many silences in which the camera does the talking, and the relationship between Phyllida Law and Emma Thompson, real-life mother and daughter, is convincing. The result is a strong film.

The Governess (1998)   S+

Directed by Sandra Goldbacher
Screenplay by Sandra Goldbacher
Leading cast: Minnie Driver (Rosina da Silva);
  Tom Wilkinson (Mr Charles Cavendish);
  Florence Hoath (Clementina Cavendish);
  Jonathan Rhys Meyers (Henry Cavendish);
  Harriet Walter (Mrs Cavendish)
Colour, 115 minutes, UK

The mid-19th century: following the death of her father, Rosina (who is Jewish) is hired as a governess to a Scottish family living in a baronial pile on Skye. She enters into a passionate affair with Charles, her employer, a pioneer in the photographic arts.

Minnie Driver had achieved prominence by the time *The Governess* was made, having already featured in *Grosse Pointe Blank* (George Armitage, 1995) and *Good*

Minnie Driver

Will Hunting (Gus Van Sant, 1997). Here she carries the film, more than holding her own against Wilkinson, as Rosina moves from a relatively cloistered existence in a tight-knit London Jewish community, to an equally, if differently, cloistered existence on Skye (the actual location shooting was on Arran). On her carriage journey through Scotland, Rosina writes to her sister: 'green, green and even more green; anodyne hostile countryside. How I detest it'. Her destination conjures up for her 'the gothic' – and this is the world into which *The Governess* plunges us.

Rosina must lie to avoid discrimination, changing her name and misrepresenting her background. But her upbringing, natural intelligence and inquisitiveness ensure that she is the intellectual equal of Charles, unlike his wife; while this adds to her attraction, it is also more than he can really bear. *The Governess* offers therefore a fertile bed for drama, in which, to quote Roger Ebert, 'there are rich underlying ironies, not least that by denying their assigned places in society (he as a husband, she as a Jew), they are able for a time to

function freely just as two people happy to be together in mind and body'.

It might be thought that the Skye location exists simply to impose isolation and contrast with Rosina's London background. But for Goldbacher (making her second and last feature), there was probably more to it than this: her father was an Italian Jew, and her mother was born on Arran.

My Name is Joe (1998) S+++ T100

Directed by Ken Loach
Screenplay by Paul Laverty
Leading cast: Peter Mullan (Joe Kavanagh);
    Louise Goodall (Sarah Downie); Gary Lewis
    (Shanks); David McKay (Liam); Annemarie
    Kennedy (Sabine); David Hayman (McGowan)
Colour, 105 minutes, UK/Germany/France/Spain

Joe, an alcoholic, runs an amateur football team. He enters a relationship with Sarah, a health worker, who becomes pregnant. To save a friend, Liam, from the clutches of McGowan, a local gangster, Joe agrees to transport drugs for McGowan. Sarah leaves him. Joe stops working for McGowan; Liam hangs himself. After Liam's funeral, Joe and Sarah walk away side by side.

My Name is Joe is the first of three films from Laverty and Loach which constitute what the BFI website calls 'an informal trilogy'. It is followed by *Sweet Sixteen* and *Ae Fond Kiss*, although the duo also later made *The Angels' Share*. Before all

Peter Mullan at his very best

these, Laverty and Loach made *Carla's Song*† (1996), starring Robert Carlyle and Oyanka Cabezas, whose characters meet in Glasgow, and then travel to Nicaragua, where the majority of the film is set. *Riff Raff*† (1991) had also starred Robert Carlyle, as Stevie, who returns to Glasgow for his mother's funeral (Mullan also had a role in this film). In *Ken Loach: The Politics of Film and Television* (2011), John Hill discusses what he calls Loach's 'Scottish turn'. Loach began working with Laverty, human rights lawyer turned screenwriter, on *Carla's Song*, seized the opportunities for funding available in Scotland, valued the authenticity in Laverty writing about his own nation, and saw in Scotland a more radical working-class environment than was the case in the England of New Labour. In 2016 the importance of this body of work was recognised by BAFTA Scotland with an outstanding achievement award being given to Loach, Laverty, and long-time producer Rebecca O'Brien.

In October 2019, *The Guardian* ranked Loach's films, taking the view that this was 'the finest of Loach's Scotland-set films. Mullan plays the classic Loachian male: struggling with demons, hoping to be redeemed by love but dragged down by misplaced loyalties. It's Mullan's charisma that puts this one over the top, both ferocious and tender as the film requires it.' The film won Mullan the Best Actor award at Cannes in 1998, and the British

Newcomer award at the London Critics Film Circle Awards in 1999 (given that Mullan had his first film role in **Big Man** in 1990 and had been in both **Shallow Grave** and **Trainspotting** that's a generous interpretation of 'newcomer'). Interviewed in *Cineaste* at the time of the film's release, Loach stressed the importance of Mullan's connection to Glasgow: 'He absolutely has Glasgow in his bones, he's a lad from a local working-class family. Everybody from that area knows all about alcoholism'.

→ *Sweet Sixteen* (2002) S+++ T100

Directed by Ken Loach
Screenplay by Paul Laverty
Leading cast: Martin Compston (Liam); William Ruane (Pinball); Michelle Coulter (Jean); Gary McCormack (Stan)
Colour, 106 minutes, UK/Germany/Spain

Liam and Pinball are teenage hustlers in Greenock. Liam's mother is in gaol, and he attempts to raise the money to buy a caravan for her to live in after her release. He starts to work for a gangster and drug merchant. Pinball burns out the caravan, and Liam's mother moves in with Stan, who is abusive. Liam stabs Stan, and on his 16th birthday stands alone on the shore, wanted by the police.

Sweet Sixteen was conceived while Laverty was writing **My Name is Joe.** He has said: 'I remember writing *My Name is Joe* and what often happens when you're writing a script is a lot of characters try and claim attention, and they say "Me, me, me! You must tell my story!" And there was a couple of rowdy teenagers who demanded attention and one who, in my mind, is now Liam.' Set in Greenock, *Sweet Sixteen* is, like **My Name is Joe**, a film in which the protagonist appears hemmed in by circumstances. As he approaches his sixteenth birthday, Liam's behaviour is not that of a child. In his wheeling and dealing, which moves from the petty to the criminally serious, he shows maturity beyond his years. It is only in his naïve optimism regarding his ability to help his mother on her release from prison that there is the slightest hint of childhood. This is obliterated on his birthday.

In *Cineaste* Roger Bromley wrote that Loach 'shows us the hidden injuries and brutalities of class in the early days of the new century... There are no simple answers; the movie does not end but pauses, and on that pause we reflect upon the absences and the silences'. The absences in *Sweet Sixteen* ring loudly. The film raises the question as to how it is, in a wealthy welfare-state-based economy, people can be so left behind. In **My Name is Joe** Sarah's health care worker suggested at least the possibility of beneficial (if occasionally ineffective) state support. In *Sweet Sixteen* the welfare state is all but invisible.

Sweet Sixteen was Compston's first film role. He told the BBC in 2022 he secured the role after a teacher stopped him in his school corridor saying that a film crew was looking for children to appear in a film: 'I think you're exactly it. I think you should go meet them'. Compston is excellent in it and has gone on to have considerable success. He is in a further nine films in this book, including **Red Road, Donkeys** and *The Legend of Barney Thomson*. There was some controversy over the 18-certificate awarded to the film; one result of this was that Compston was too young legally to watch it.

→ *Ae Fond Kiss...* (2004) S+++ T21

Directed by Ken Loach
Screenplay by Paul Laverty
Leading cast: Shabana Akhtar Baksh (Tahara Khan); Atta Yaqub (Casim Khan); Eva Birthistle (Roisin Hanlon); Shy Ramzan (Hammid)
Colour, 104 minutes, UK/Italy/Germany/Spain/Belgium

Glasgow Southside: Casim, an accountancy graduate, meets Roisin, a teacher. To his family's opposition they form a relationship which jeopardises Roisin's job as she teaches at a Catholic school.

Ae Fond Kiss takes its name from a song by Robert Burns, 'a well-known drunken fornicator', according to one of the less tolerant teachers in the school where much of the action is set. Loach and Birthistle both came away with awards for the film, including wins at the Berlin Film Festival, and the 2005 French César for Best European Film. In the context of Scottish cinema, there is a distinctive focus on a family of Pakistani-Muslim origin living in Glasgow's Southside

(Casim's sister, Tahara, describes herself at a school debate as 'a Glaswegian, Pakistani, teenager, woman, of Muslim descent who supports Glasgow Rangers in a Catholic school'). It is also, for a Loach film, remarkably buoyant (as I write this, I am aware that my cultural background shapes my perception of the ending). That Casim's relationship with Roisin survives the pressures brought to bear by his family, and that Tahara determines, in the face of family opposition, to pursue her dream of being a journalist and study at Edinburgh University (her siblings have studied in Glasgow) is, for me, very satisfying. Loach and Laverty certainly appear to intend the ending to be positive. John Hill writes that they had 'moved in a new direction and produced, possibly as a result of earlier criticisms of their work, a considerably more upbeat account of contemporary Scotland' (*Ken Loach: The Politics of Film and Television*, 2011).

Identity can be a very simple matter ('my identity is whatever I say it is'); it can also be wildly complex. As Tahara says at the film's start: 'Take my family. My sister considers herself as a Muslim first and, because she has a political streak, calls herself black. My dad's been in this country for over 40 years and is 100 per cent Pakistani, or so he thinks' (her own statement of identity is quoted above). In *Ae Fond Kiss*, although the temptation may be to focus on Casim, it is important that both he *and* Roisin, an Irish Catholic, are from immigrant backgrounds – in both cases linked to countries subject to British colonial oppression. The fact that

Casim is in many respects *more* Scottish than Roisin (he was born, raised, and educated in Scotland) obliges the viewer to think carefully about the issues of identity raised by the film, which *are* complex, and skilfully handled.

Casting *Ae Fond Kiss* was difficult, as Loach explained to the *Independent*: 'We had a very specific hoop to jump through. We had to find actors for the roles of Casim and his sisters who spoke pure Glaswegian, and for his parents, individuals whose accents were a combination of Glaswegian and Punjabi... We couldn't have chosen a more difficult group to pick a family from.' Yaqub, from Glasgow's South Side, trained as a social worker, and had signed on with a modelling agency when he was cast. He recognised the importance of the film's approach to the central relationship Casim forms with Roisin. He said later that 'Ken Loach told a story where a guy who was Muslim fell in love with a girl who was Catholic. And these things happen. We can encourage more of that understanding...' (*The Argus*, 2017). He has a small role in *T2: Trainspotting*, and also appears in *Con Men, Isolani, Wild Rose* and *The Defender* (Gary J Hewitt, 2024).

Ae Fond Kiss premiered at the EIFF in August 2004. It was well received and maintains a score of 89 per cent on Rotten Tomatoes at the time of writing.

→ *The Angels' Share* (2012) S+++ T18

Directed by Ken Loach
Screenplay by Paul Laverty
Leading cast: Paul Brannigan (Robbie); Siobhan Reilly (Leonie); John Henshaw (Harry); Scott Kyle (Clancy); Gary Maitland (Albert); Jasmine Riggins (Mo); William Ruane (Rhino)
Colour, 101 minutes, UK/France/Belgium/Italy

Robbie performs community service, under the supervision of Harry, who loves whisky. Robbie becomes a father. He hatches a plan to steal (without anyone noticing) some exceptionally rare and valuable whisky. He works with friends he has made who are also under Albert's supervision, and the theft is (partly) successful.

'The angels' share' is a phrase which anyone who has taken a distillery tour will have heard. It refers to the loss of a cask's contents through evaporation. The film deals with whisky, is set in part in the Highlands, features men (and a woman) in kilts, Edinburgh Castle, and The Proclaimers' '(I'm Gonna Be) 500 Miles', *twice*! But the genius is that it's the perfect *antidote* to Scottish clichés, which Laverty and Loach have great fun lampooning. Robbie has *never* tasted whisky before Albert gives him a dram to wet the baby's head; on the visit to Edinburgh, Mo is astonished by 'that big thing on top of the hill' – he has never seen Edinburgh Castle (Albert asks him 'have you never seen a tin?'); Robbie has no idea how to

THE
ANGELS'
SHARE

DIRECTED BY
KEN LOACH
SCREENPLAY BY
PAUL LAVERTY

FOUR FRIENDS.
ONE MISSION.
LOTS OF SPIRIT.

ENJOY RESPONSIBLY

The Angels' Share gives us the lighter side of Ken Loach

pronounce 'ceilidh'; and towards the end even *Braveheart* gets a direct mention.

The Angels' Share is by some way the lightest of the four Loach/Laverty films covered here – it is a comedy, played for laughs notwithstanding its firm grounding in social realism, violence, and its strong social message. That we are in for a good time is clear from the start. Albert, clearly no genius, stands wobbling on the edge of a deserted train station platform. Through the Tannoy he is instructed to stand back, as a train is coming through. He does so, promptly falling onto the tracks. In desperation, the speaker on the other end of the Tannoy raps out: 'This is God calling… GET OFF THE FUCKIN' TRACK!'. The violence that does occur in the running confrontation between Clancy and Robbie is therefore all the more shocking for its realism.

This was the first film role for Brannigan, who is perfect as Robbie. He has since appeared in, amongst others, *Under the Skin* and *Sunshine on Leith*, albeit in supporting roles. Aiming to achieve accuracy, Loach hired whisky luminary Charles MacLean (author of leading guides to whisky) as a consultant; it is he who plays the role of the expert leading the tasting session in Edinburgh and presiding over the opening of the rare cask the night before the auction.

Orphans (1998) S+++ T22

Directed by Peter Mullan
Screenplay by Peter Mullan
Leading cast: Douglas Henshall (Michael); Gary Lewis (Thomas); Stephen McCole (John); Rosemarie Stevenson (Sheila); Malcolm Shields (Duncan); Frank Gallagher (Tanga)
Colour, 101 minutes, UK

Glasgow, April 1997: three sons, Thomas, Michael and John, and a daughter, Sheila – who relies on a wheelchair – surround their mother's coffin. The film then follows the events of the night before her funeral.

Orphans is the first of three films to be directed by Peter Mullan, who remains better known as an actor – with a recent cv including large roles in TV series *Ozark* (2017–2018), *Westworld* (2018–2020) and *The Lord of the Rings: The Rings of Power* (2022–2024). Fourteen of his many film appearances are covered in this book. His second film as director, *The Magdalene Sisters* (2002), is set in Ireland; his third, **Neds**, has its own entry below. *Orphans* is a strong film, albeit a little rough around the edges, and remains vibrant.

There is in *Orphans* something of a Greek tragedy, or epic, as three of the four siblings make their way through Glasgow's night, buffeted by a storm, while Thomas waits by their mother's coffin.

Odysseus-like, Michael even ends up passed out on an abandoned pallet, adrift on the Clyde. The structure of the film allows for the creation of a rich tapestry of vignettes of Glasgow life, along with punchy wit and dialogue (Tanga to John: 'Stabbing your brother the night before you bury your ma? That's a very killable offence.')

Orphans won awards and acclaim, although its release history was over-complicated: Mullan scooped up four awards at the 1998 Venice Film Festival and the Most Promising Newcomer award (as director) at the Evening Standard British Film Awards in 2000. FilmFour had provided £750,000 finance for the film, but chose not to release it (it was released instead in the UK by Downtown). Interviewed in *S&S* Mullan explained the position: 'When Orphans didn't get to Berlin I got a phone call saying C4 would not be distributing it. After *Trainspotting*, the attitude was money, money, money, and they thought *Orphans* would be too hard to sell. What angered me was the hypocrisy – I could have told them from the start the film wouldn't make money, but they said, make your own film, make your own art. Then after C4 dumped it, distributors saw *Orphans* as yet another failed Scottish film, but because it won four awards at the Venice Film Festival, attitudes changed.' Channel 4 attracted further fury from Mullan when it inadvertently, blaming a 'systems error', destroyed the unused footage; when Mullan was preparing the DVD release only limited extra material was available.

Outside Scotland *Orphans* faced a problem familiar to Scottish film: accents. A positive review by Justine Elias in *Film Comment*, in which Mullan is praised for not 'creating a movie that's a genteel showcase for performers', for pushing his actors and securing strong performances, raises the language issue, and explains the approach taken in the US: 'Mullan's bold storytelling runs up against an almost insurmountable barrier: the actors' often impenetrable Glaswegian accents... *Orphans* has been completely subtitled – and the result is... a rewritten, sanitised, de-Scottishised film. When an enraged John yells at a passer-by, "Nobody gives a fuck!" the subtitles render this as "Nobody cares"'. Echoing Tanga, Elias labels this 'a killable offense'.

In *S&S* Edward Lawrenson enjoyed *Orphans*' 'quietly assured surrealist slant' and was won over by its ambition, notwithstanding that it was in places 'rough'. The film does not deserve its very low Rotten Tomatoes rating.

→ *Neds* (2010)   S+++ T100

Directed by Peter Mullan
Screenplay by Peter Mullan
Leading cast: Conor McCarron (John); Joe Szula (Benny)
Colour, 124 minutes, UK/France/Italy

Glasgow, 1972. We follow the trajectory of John, whose father is an abusive alcoholic. When the film begins John is a cherubic star pupil at primary. He changes, and becomes a violent ned, before things take a turn for the better.

For any reader not familiar with Scottish slang, *urbandictionary.com* offers this definition of 'neds': 'Non Educated Delinquents, have a habit of standing around on street corners drinking 98 per cent of the world's supply of Buckfast, wearing enough cheap gold to make a prostitute blush whilst thinking that tucking their shell suit bottoms into their socks is the height of fashion'. *Neds* secured Mullan the Best Writer and Director awards at the Scottish BAFTAs in 2011, and the Evening Standard British Film Award for Best Film in the same year. On Rotten Tomatoes it holds a highly creditable score of 94 per cent.

Given the similarities in background between John and Mullan, the writer/director faced questions as to the extent to which the film was autobiographical. In *S&S*, he was clear where the boundaries lay: 'this is easily 90 per cent fiction, albeit very much influenced by things I saw, heard about and experienced. There were tiny bits of pressure, way back – people saying it would sound better if it's "a true story". But it's not a true story, so it felt more honest to say so, in advance'. It was not planned that Mullan would play the role of the father. He stepped in as a plan B as money ran out, although the casting director – his brother Lenny – was concerned. Mullan 'knew it was just a character – it was not my dad – and playing him was ridiculously easy. Funnily enough, if I'm honest, every word that he says in the film is verbatim from my own experience. My father did say those things, and do those things. But it was not a case of working out issues with my dad, but presenting that kind of behaviour as starkly as I could.'

One of the most considered reviews of the film on its release was provided by Jonathan Murray in *Cineaste*, who concluded with the following: 'Mullan's third feature marks him out as one of the most audacious, ambitious, and accomplished directors working in Britain today'. The review which precedes this does however raise questions, particularly in relation to Mullan's not entirely successful attempt to avoid social realism. Murray is also concerned by the extent to which John's fate appears to be out of his hands – his path seems entirely predetermined, his agency having been stolen.

Postmortem (aka *Obit*) (1998) S+

Directed by Albert Pyun
Screenplay by John Lowry Lamb, Robert McDonnell
Leading cast: Charlie Sheen (James McGregor); Michael Halsey (DI Ballantyne); Ivana Milicevic (Gwen Turner)
Colour, 105 minutes, US

James is a troubled American detective of international renown, staying (and drinking) in Glasgow. He is dragged into a murder investigation, both as suspect and as investigator.

Directed by US-born B-movie legend Pyun, *Postmortem* barely hits the criteria set for entry in this book – it received a cinema release only in Japan, going straight to video in other markets. The trailer for the VHS release is worth a watch. The voice-over positions the action: 'In a peaceful Scottish town American ex-cop James McGregor thought he left the violence behind… it hadn't even started'. *Peaceful Scottish town*??? Glasgow is my home city, and I love it, and *never* should it be thus described. However peaceful Glasgow was at the start of filming it was certainly made less so by the presence of the lead actor (credited as 'Charles Sheen'). The Scottish *Daily Record* ran one edition with its front-page headline: 'Star's Scots Shame: Charlie Sheen in cocaine bender'. It was reported that Sheen had 'spent £1000 on the drug with a prostitute and her pimp in Easterhouse', then stopped off in a convenience store to buy tinfoil, baking soda and a teaspoon. He was only actually in Glasgow for six days of the ten-day shoot. Sheen has some charisma but, somewhat surprisingly, in *Postmortem* he is more convincing playing sober than he is playing drunk. He's not *hugely* convincing as either. Ivana Milicevic, playing the beautiful local police officer (who would later feature in *Casino Royale*, Martin Campbell, 2006), attempts to adopt a reasonably convincing local accent. But it's Irish, or rather, *Oirish*.

Pyun is a hugely prolific genre director with a buccaneer approach. He's the sort of figure about whom books should be written. One has been – *Radioactive*

Dreams: The Cinema of Albert Pyun
(Justin Decloux, 2019). A very short
synopsis of his career might simply read:
'He favoured quantity over quality'. The
influence of the greatly superior *Manhunter*
(Michael Mann, 1986) is all over
Postmortem, but James is no Will Graham
(for that matter, Sheen is no William
Petersen). *Postmortem* looks and feels like
a made-for-TV movie, lacking the richness
and complexity of feature film design and
cinematography. Given this is at heart a
noir detective story, the main problem is
that there is little attempt to build mystery.
There are no red herrings, and the killer's
identity is entirely predictable. *Postmortem*
is not, ultimately, so bad it's good, but
neither is it good.

Urban Ghost Story (1998)S+ T100

Directed by Geneviève Jolliffe
Screenplay by Geneviève Jolliffe and Chris Jones
Leading cast: Heather Ann Foster (Lizzie Fisher);
   Stephanie Buttle (Kate Fisher); Jason Connery
   (John Fox)
Colour, 82 minutes, UK

*Twelve-year-old Lizzie 'dies' in a car
accident; when she is revived something
may have followed her back. Life with
her mother and younger brother becomes
increasingly difficult as the family struggles
financially, in their run-down council flat.*

Adapting one of the key premises of
Flatliners (Joel Schumacher, 1990) – that a
retreat from the white light of death brings

with it passengers – *Urban Ghost Story* is
by some way the better film. Rather than
the shiny glamour that Schumacher and
his cast of bright-young-things brought
to the proceedings, *UGS* is set in a more
downbeat Glasgow estate (filming took
place in the London studio for the interiors,
and Glasgow for exteriors) and blends social
realism into its story, raising the question
of whether Lizzie's phantoms are the result
of the near death experience, or of living
in increasingly precarious circumstances.
In *Fangoria*, Alexandra Heller-Nicholas
celebrated the film a few years after its
release as, 'the rarest of things: ... one of
the most authentically rendered '90s horror
films about the poor, lower-class world
which its cast of central characters inhabit'.
UGS's blend of the psychological, social,
and paranormal menace gives rise both to
a slow build of social horror, and genuine
jump scares.

Jolliffe was just 26 when *UGS*, her first
feature, was completed (she held the record
for the youngest British film producer,
being only 19 when her first film was
made). Connery had a well-established
career and was by far the best known
of the cast. Here he plays a sleazy local
journalist, who attempts to capitalise on the
family's predicament and expose the alleged
paranormal activity as a hoax. Billy Boyd
appears in his first feature as a menacing loan
shark (see also **On a Clear Day**, **The Flying
Scotsman** and **Stone of Destiny**). Foster was
in her first, and to date only, film.

Billy Connolly as reformed con-turned-sculptor Nickie Dryden

The Debt Collector (1999) S+++

Directed by Anthony Neilson
Screenplay by Anthony Neilson
Leading cast: Billy Connolly (Nickie Dryden);
  Ken Stott (Gary Keltie); Francesca Annis (Val
  Dryden); Iain Robertson (Flipper)
Colour, 109 minutes, UK

Nickie is now an acclaimed sculptor, but was formerly a violent debt collector, arrested once on suspicion of murder by Keltie, who years later still pursues Nickie. A young hoodlum models his career on Nickie's, and events spiral out of control.

Ostensibly a film about rehabilitation, law, culture, and civilised behaviour, *The Debt Collector*, the first (and still only) film from Edinburgh-born playwright Anthony Neilson, fails to deliver on its lofty themes and is poor. As Richard Kelly wrote in *S&S*, 'one just can't believe that Neilson gave this debate much more than ten minutes' thought before sitting down to pen this grisly, suspense-free shocker'. Before the deadly fight between the two protagonists Nickie asks Keltie, 'Why?' – a question most viewers of the film will also have. Keltie has no answer. Speeches from him about the promise to uphold law and order, to protect people, and the failure to deliver on this obligation do not explain the peculiarly obsessive nature of his personal vendetta against Nickie. Unless, that is, we are merely asked to believe that Keltie's obsession flows simply from a belief that Nickie now is being rewarded, rather than punished, for the sins of his past.

The starting point for *The Debt Collector* can only ever have been the true-life story of Glasgow hardman Jimmy Boyle (see *A Sense of Freedom*). Boyle was a violent criminal who spent significant time in prison, wrote a book and became a successful sculptor. Nickie is portrayed as a violent criminal who… well, you get the point. According to contemporaneous reports however there was no acknowledgement of this source of inspiration in the production notes. Richard Kelly has been quoted above. The concluding paragraph of his review includes the following: 'Today, when the adjectives "dark" and "psychological" modify "thriller" they are intended to denote a higher purpose. What they actually denote is that a series of stabbings will be performed, a fetid air of sexual frustration will pervade, and a "flawed" servant of the law will pronounce solemnly on the evil that men do.' In *Variety* Derek Elley longed for more ruthless editing: 'Some scenes… simply hold up the action; others go on past their prime; and the long-awaited climax wobbles perilously close to farce.' *The Debt Collector* is set in Edinburgh but was filmed in both Edinburgh and Glasgow – a requirement of the assistance of the Glasgow Film Fund. It had only a limited release.

Hold Back the Night (1999) S+

Directed by Phil Davis
Screenplay by Steve Chambers
Leading cast: Christine Tremarco (Charleen); Stuart Sinclair Blyth (Declan); Sheila Hancock (Vera)
Colour, 104 minutes, UK

Charleen, whose father is sexually abusive, leaves home. She meets Declan, and later Vera, who has a camper van, and who wishes to see the Ring of Brodgar before she dies. The subsequent road trip permits Charleen to find the strength to return home and confront her father.

Hold Back the Night is one of only two films directed by Phil Davis (better known as an actor – he plays the lead in *Quadrophenia*, Franc Roddam, 1979). *HBTN* deals with difficult themes of sexual abuse, survivor trauma, and healing. In an interview in *Uncut*, Davis said his mission was to make 'radical, difficult dramas which you can still see in the multiplexes'. It is hard to remain optimistic through *HBTN*. Charleen's history is horrific, and she is, for very good reason, angry, but the expression of that anger requires her to maintain one note through most of the film. Of Declan we learn very little; he is not much more than a cipher, and it is Vera who fleshes out the film with humour, compassion and complexity.

The film's treatment of Scotland is yet another tired example of the country being used as somewhere 'other', in this case where issues are resolved at the end of a, for the UK, very long road trip. Reporting in *The Guardian* from the EIFF, Brian Logan wrote: 'Davis has made a road movie about the restorative powers of the Scottish landscape.' Peter Bradshaw was more critical: 'Yet another shrill British film about child abuse... *Hold Back the Night*... is maladroit, and bafflingly without the conviction, sophistication or production values you would expect from the most ordinary television drama.'

The Match (1999) S+++ W6

Directed by Mick Davis
Screenplay by Mick Davis
Leading cast: Max Beesley (Wullie Smith); Richard E Grant (Gorgeous Gus); James Cosmo (Billy Bailey); Bill Paterson (Tommy); Laura Fraser (Rosemary Bailey); Ian Holm (Big Tam); Neil Morrissey (Piss Off); Alan Shearer (Alan Shearer)
Colour, 95 minutes, UK

In 'Inverdoon', a bet has been running for 100 years between L'Bistro (now owned by Gus) and Benny's Bar. The winner of the final football match played between teams representing each venue will determine who owns both.

Featuring a largely wasted wealth of acting talent, along with blink-and-you'll-miss-them cameos from Alan Shearer and Pierce Brosnan, *The Match* is one of three films covered in this book (*A Shot at Glory* and *Gregory's Girl*) to be based around football (even if only partly, as in *Gregory's Girl*),

and is the worst by a Highland mile.

The *Match*'s script, by Glaswegian writer/director Mick Davis, is trite and predictable, overstuffed with 'characters', perhaps because, as Derek Elley suggested in *Variety*, the central outcome 'could be spotted by a drunken Scot on a foggy night'. Indeed, the outcomes to all the conflicts outlined in a heady rush of introductions are all too obvious (one – between Billy and his ex-wife and daughter, is simply ignored). It is difficult to see what could have attracted the producers to the film, and the inclusion of Hollywood's Tom Sizemore (as an ex-pat drunk American living in what appears to be an abandoned set of Nissen huts), presumably an attempt to gain traction with American filmgoers, seems wildly optimistic. Grant has little to do but to play the pantomime villain, have his nose broken by Brosnan, and be urinated on by a small dog (according to *The Scotsman* the intention was that the dog would be 'rather affectionate with his leg', but the training failed).

At least most of the film is inoffensive, although there is one scene which would now be swiftly cast aside in any script review: in Benny's, a 'kilted Scottish nutter' (as described by Allan Hunter in *The Scotsman*) seems to have the ability to smell an Englishman coming from a hundred yards away, leading to the bar emptying to drive him away on the street. Hunter was particularly harsh: '*The Match* is a charmless, strangely atavistic enterprise... it has all the humanity and sparkling wit of an obsolete computer programme.' The best Scottish film to feature football remains *Gregory's Girl*.

My Life So Far (1999)   `S+`

*In the comfort of 'Kiloran Estate', in the
1920s, the life of an eccentric Scottish
family is disrupted by the arrival of a
beautiful young Frenchwoman.*

The memoir of a childhood in the beautiful
'Craigielands' house near Moffat, *Son of
Adam* (1990), by Sir Denis Forman, the
former Chair of the Board of Governors of
the British Film Institute, is here translated
into a British period drama, pedestrian
albeit somewhat strengthened by its strong
cast. After a showing outside competition
at Cannes, *Variety*'s Todd McCarthy wrote
'small insights are the best *My Life So
Far* can manage, and the minor incidents
that fill the film's brief running time will
hardly make a deep impression on modern
audiences'. In *The NYT*, Stephen Holden
noted 'it suggests Ingmar Bergman's *Fanny
and Alexander* [(1982)] with all its demons
comfortably subdued'.

   Director Hugh Hudson, who had been
Oscar-nominated for another, better, period
piece, *Chariots of Fire* (1981), was not at
a good point in his career; *My Life So Far*
was not well received and did not secure
a UK release. The film was shot largely at
Ardkinglas House, on the shores of Loch
Fyne (also the primary location for *Then
Came You*); Kelly Macdonald was in her
early 20s but playing well below her years.

Ratcatcher (1999)   `S+++` `T7`

*Glasgow, 1973: as James and Ryan play by
the canal, Ryan drowns. There is ambiguity
as to James' culpability. Glasgow is
blighted by a bin-collectors' strike; the
tenement in which James' family lives is not
fit for habitation. The family are rehoused.*

Sitting firmly within the British social
realist tradition and clearly influenced
by *The Bill Douglas Childhood Trilogy*
(although with one fantastical interlude
involving a white mouse, space travel, and
the moon), *Ratcatcher* is a very good film
indeed. It is all the more remarkable that
it was shot with a largely untrained cast,
was made on a tiny budget, and was writer-
director Ramsay's first feature-length film
(she had previously made only two shorts,
Small Deaths, 1996 and *Gasman*, 1998,
both of which feature on the Pathé DVD
of *Ratcatcher*). In the 23 years since, her
output has been small: *Morvern Callar*,

We Need to Talk About Kevin (2011), *You Were Never Really Here* (2017) and *Die, My Love* (2025), but has sustained a quality which proves that *Ratcatcher* was not a first-film fluke. It is one of only two films in this book to be the subject of a BFI Film Classics book, by Annette Kuhn (2008) (*Trainspotting* is the subject of a BFI Modern Classics book).

In *Fifty Key British Films* (eds Sarah Barrow and John White, 2008 – *Ratcatcher* is one of only three films in this book which feature there) Barrow wrote 'it is the emotional impact of *Ratcatcher* that sets it apart, and the sheer beauty of its cinematography that makes it extraordinary'. The director of photography, Alwin Küchler, worked with Ramsay again on *Morvern Callar*. As Barrow suggests, if one was looking for reference points to *Ratcatcher* they might lie in Bill Douglas (*The Bill Douglas Trilogy*), Ken Loach (*Ae Fond Kiss, Sweet Sixteen* etc), whose 1969 film *Kes* is a very obvious forerunner to *Ratcatcher* (James plays at being a bird – although it is Kenny who is obsessed with animals), and Terence Davies (*Distant Voices, Still Lives* (1988); see also *Sunset Song*).

Ratcatcher was nominated for many awards. Amongst others, Ramsay won the BAFTA's Carl Foreman Award for Most Promising Newcomer, the Grand Prix at the Bratislava International Film Festival, and the Best Director Silver Hugo at the Chicago International Film Festival. On Rotten Tomatoes the short summary offered by the site's editors is: 'Critics find *Ratcatcher* to be hauntingly

William Eadie in the seminal Ratcatcher

beautiful, though its story is somewhat hard to stomach'. The rating given there is 85 per cent. Amongst 'top critics' there is only one negative review, from Charles Taylor, of *Salon.com* (an American outlet). He found the film to be simultaneously impressive *and* frustrating: 'The trouble is, she doesn't do anything to bring her characters close to us... both the characters and the actors who portray them serve as vehicles for Ramsay's stylistic flourishes.' More representative is Elvis Mitchell in *The NYT*, who called *Ratcatcher* a 'brilliant directorial debut [with] a gorgeous blend of beauty and squalor, packed with imagery that will play over and over in your head for weeks'. In the US the film was released with subtitles.

Unlike *That Sinking Feeling, Sweet Sixteen* and *Trainspotting*, *Ratcatcher* did not launch the careers of any of its young cast, and it stands apart as an inspired piece of individualistic filmmaking.

→ *Morvern Callar* (2002) S++ T100

Directed by Lynne Ramsay
Screenplay by Lynne Ramsay, Liana Dognini
Leading cast: Samantha Morton (Morvern
    Callar); Kathleen McDermott (Lanna)
Colour, 97 minutes, UK/Canada

*At Christmas, Morvern's boyfriend dies by
suicide. Rather than reporting the death,
she buries the body herself, and heads
to Spain for a holiday with her friend
Lanna. Her boyfriend has left Morvern the
manuscript of a novel he has completed.
She sells this to a publisher for £100,000,
and after a short return home, packs and
leaves.*

Like **Our Ladies**, *Morvern Callar* is based
on a novel by Scottish author Alan Warner.
Writing in *S&S*, Xan Brooks urged his
readers to ignore the synopsis that came
just before his review. As Brooks puts it:
'Judged on actions alone, Morvern Callar
is an amoral monster. And yet one of the
marvels of this opaque, haunting picture is
that we never quite see her that way'. The
disjunct between bald iteration of plot, and
its delivery, relies on four factors: Ramsay's
direction; Alwin Küchler's cinematography;
a remarkable performance from Samantha
Morton; and a strong sense of place, which
grounds the action in the real.

    As she did in **Ratcatcher**, Ramsay uses
non-professional actors in some roles.
This included McDermott, although
she later went on to appear in shorts,
films and TV shows. But everything in
Morvern Callar hangs on Morton, twice

Oscar-nominated, who has shown she is
exceptional throughout her career. Here
she delivers an 'uncanny performance as
the half dead, half hopelessly alive Morvern
– a fiercely resourceful and ultimately
sympathetic creature' (Kristin Marriott
Jones, in *Film Comment*). Conventional
morality would suggest that an audience
would not be siding with Morvern. She
is, after all, going to walk away with a
fraudulently gained £100,000, and at no
point takes responsibility for, or faces, what
should be inevitable consequences of her
actions. And yet, it is all but impossible not
to at least question whether she is, after all,
acting out of love, compassion and hope. In
this context it is relevant that the final song
(of a superb playlist – music is ever-present
in the film) is The Mamas and the Papas'
'Dedicated to the One I Love', and that the
manuscript she passes off as her own was
dedicated to her, with love, by her boyfriend.

Women Talking Dirty (1999) S+

Directed by Coky Giedroyc
Screenplay by Isla Dewar
Leading cast: Helena Bonham Carter (Cora);
    Gina McKee (Ellen); Eileen Atkins (Emily Boyle);
    James Nesbitt (Stanley); James Purefoy (Daniel);
    Richard Wilson (Ronald)
Colour, 97 minutes, UK

*Edinburgh: Ellen, a married graphic
designer, and Cora, a university dropout
and young mother, become unlikely
friends. Cora has a second child by Ellen's
husband, Daniel.*

Premiered at the Toronto International Film Festival, *Women Talking Dirty* ostensibly had much going for it, boasting a strong British cast, a focus on female friendship, a director whose previous film was the well-received *Stella Does Tricks*† (1996; in which a young Glaswegian prostitute – Kelly Macdonald – moves to London), and an Edinburgh setting. But *Women Taking Dirty* belied its promise. In *Variety*, Derek Elley wrote that it was 'an embarrassing sophomore stumble... and overall about as believable as [Bonham Carter's] Scottish accent' (which is pretty unbelievable). Philip French in *The Observer* was similarly unimpressed: 'the plotting is as chaotic as the film's handling of Edinburgh's geography, but the performances keep it afloat.'

The fundamental problem lies in the screenplay (by Isla Dewar, based on her own 1996 novel), which is a mess. A flashback structure flowing from Ellen's divorce party lacks clear structure, so the narrative becomes patchy. Characters are thinly fleshed out, and Cora comes close to being the manic pixie dream girl to the more organised Ellen; a token gay couple, who care for Cora's children, are thin stereotypes. The soundtrack is strong, and Brian Tufano's cinematography makes the most of the location.

A Shot at Glory (2000) S++

Directed by Michael Corrente
Screenplay by Denis O'Neill
Leading cast: Robert Duvall (Gordon McLeod); Michael Keaton (Peter Cameron); Ally McCoist (Jackie McQuillan); Kirsty Mitchell (Kate McQuillan); Brian Cox (Martin Smith)
Colour, 114 minutes, UK/US

Troubled football star Jackie McQuillan is given a chance at redemption at League 2 Kilnockie FC. He takes it, and in the process secures the club's future.

This much-ridiculed film holds a surprisingly high (and overly generous) critics' score of 67 per cent on Rotten Tomatoes, although McCoist is still often ribbed about his performance. He does a decent job in the role, which, personal circumstances and Kilnockie aside, cleaves close to his successful career, if not his affiliations. It also means that his participation in the games shown is convincing – until, that is, the final penalty shoot-out, which is very ropey. The story is even constructed to ensure he has had a break from football, with commentators noting that he is out of shape and has lost pace.

What is most remarkable about *A Shot at Glory* is that a film with such a parochial focus was directed and written by Americans, with much of the push coming from Duvall. Corrente had made three previous films; his first, *Federal Hill* (1994), was well received. O'Neill had one previous writing credit, for the strong Meryl Streep adventure film *The River Wild* (Curtis Hansen, 1994). Three universal stories are in play in *ASAG*. First, a pitch-based David and Goliath contest, as the team in what was then the third tier of Scottish football goes on its successful cup run. Second, we have another tension reminiscent of **The Battle of the Sexes** or **Local Hero**, as the local resource (the club) is threatened by American economic power. Third, we have the classic comeback story, as Jackie redeems himself both professionally and personally. More awkwardly, there is also some attempt to graft on a serious theme about sectarianism, which is raised in the opening voice-over delivered by Andy Gray, and which we return to when Jackie saves a young Rangers fan from a beating after defacing a Celtic graffito. This theme, however, remains in the background and underdeveloped.

A *Shot at Glory* was filmed in part in the picturesque harbour town of Crail, in Fife, with additional scenes in Glasgow, and at various football stadia. 'A Shot at Glory revisited' (YouTube) provides an entertaining hour-long discussion with McCoist, Duvall and other cast members.

Beautiful Creatures (2000) S++

Directed by Bill Eagles
Screenplay by Simon Donald
Leading cast: Rachel Weisz (Petula); Susan Lynch (Dorothy); Iain Glen (Tony); Alex Norton (DI Hepburn)
Colour, 86 minutes, UK

Dorothy's abusive boyfriend, Tony, leaves her. She later saves Petula from her abusive partner, who dies in the process. They're

left with a body, a local policeman who sees a route to riches, the return of Tony, and the corpse's brother, to contend with.

Good lead actors are wasted in
Beautiful Creatures

Beautiful Creatures is set in Glasgow, and was filmed in the city and in Bo'ness, but in such a way that its locations are all but effaced. It is only the presence of a strong support cast of Scottish actors and, in the final scenes, Bank of Scotland £100 notes, which make the setting clear. All too obviously influenced by *Thelma & Louise* (Ridley Scott, 1991), and *Lock, Stock and Two Smoking Barrels* (Guy Ritchie, 1998), *Beautiful Creatures* has limited ambition but, given its tight 86 minutes, entertains. The relationship between Susan and Petula develops well and there are some decent gags, but the vulgarity could have been pushed even further, and the all-too-tidy resolution is a cop-out.

Complicity (aka *Retribution*) (2000)

S++

Directed by Gavin Millar
Screenplay by Brian Elsley
Leading cast: Jonny Lee Miller (Cameron Colley);
  Brian Cox (Inspector McDunn); Keeley Hawes
  (Yvonne); Bill Paterson (Wallace Byatt)
Colour, 99 minutes, UK

Edinburgh and the Highlands, the late 1990s, and flashbacks. While high-profile murders take place, Colley, a left-wing crime reporter for the Caledonian newspaper, is fed material by a mole in connection with 'Project Ares', relating to the supply of munitions to Iraq. Colley is arrested for the murders, which relate to his past, but is exonerated.

There have been two TV series based on novels by Scottish author Iain Banks, who wrote science fiction as Iain M Banks (no one has dared yet to take on the challenge of filming his magisterial series of *Culture* novels): *The Crow Road* (1996), also directed by Gavin Millar and written by Brian Elsley (and with which *Complicity* shares some cast members), and *Stonemouth* (Charles Martin, 2015). *Complicity* is the only film based on his books. The book is extremely violent, with Colley existing in a frenzy of indignation, anger, sex, and drugs. In common with several of Banks' novels, it links childhood/ early adulthood events, loves, and traumas, with events in later adulthood.

  Complicity would be stronger were it given much more room to breathe,
allowing time for the two threads of the story to come together, or were it shorter, tighter, more focused and more violent and extreme than it already is. Miller is not given the licence to dial up Colley to 11; he's fine, but his Sick Boy in *Trainspotting* suggests he could have been great in this role. Playing against type, Hawes is exciting, but her role underdeveloped – here she is simply a sexpot and there should be more to her character than that. The local colour of Scotland at the time is good insofar as it is shown, but again there needs to be either *more* or *less* of this. While *Time Out*'s reviewer wrote 'it has clearly been made with love, as well as respect for the source material', I take the same position as Kim Newman who, in *S&S*, preferred the novel: 'the film still feels like a polite, careful literary adaptation, which ironically disarms much of the book's calculated disreputability.'

The Little Vampire (2000)

Directed by Uli Edel
Screenplay by Karey Kirkpatrick, Larry Wilson
Leading cast: Jonathan Lipnicki (Tony
  Thompson); Rollo Weeks (Rudolph Sackville-
  Bag); Richard E Grant (Frederick); Jim Carter
  (Rookery); John Wood (Lord McAshton)
Colour, 95 minutes, Germany/Netherlands/US

A young boy, Tony, helps to protect a family of vampires from a vampire hunter, and in lifting an ancient curse.

The Little Vampire is based on a successful

series of over 20 books, beginning with *Der kleine Vampir* (1979), by German author Angela Sommer-Bodenburg. The film relocates the action to Scotland, which, with its baronial castles, provides a suitably Gothic location. Dunimarle Castle in Fife stands in for the Thompsons' house; Dalmeny House in South Queensferry as McAshton's seat.

Vampire films can be magnificent, but *The Little Vampire* has only a slight charm, and there is insufficient 'smart' content to satisfy any adult required to watch along. More importantly there is an uneasy tonal range to the film, which struggles to balance horror, comedy, and cute. Flying vampire cows with glowing red eyes will either scare the bejesus out of a young viewer or have them in stitches; while the romantic adulation expressed by Anna to Tony is awkward. There was a lot of talent involved in the making of *The Little Vampire*. German director Uli Edel has an erratic record, ranging from the very good (*Last Exit to Brooklyn*, 1989), to the awful (*Body of Evidence*, 1992). British actors Richard E Grant, Alice Krige (the Borg Queen in *Star Trek: First Contact*, Jonathan Frakes, 1996; see also *She Will*) and Jim Carter have all been in better films and are all required – as is often the case in films aimed at children – to overact their socks off. Lipnicki's first role was as Renée Zellweger's cute son, Ray, in *Jerry Maguire* (Cameron Crowe, 1996), and he is rather good as Tony. Unfortunately, Rollo Weeks does not have the same charisma.

An animated version of *The Little Vampire* was released direct to streaming in 2017 as *The Little Vampire 3D*, directed by Karsten Kiilerich and Richard Claus (who was a producer on the 2000 film), while a further animated version was made in 2020 as *Petit vampire* (*Little Vampire*, Joann Sfar). This has resulted in some confused commentaries on the film(s).

Love the One You're With (2000)   S+++

Directed by Robbie Moffat
Screenplay by Robbie Moffat
Leading cast: Paul Cunningham (Charlie Grant); Hazel Ann Crawford (Gina MacKenzie); Niall Sutherland (Colin Patterson)
Colour, 92 minutes, UK

Glasgow. Over the May Day bank holiday weekend, Charlie, a successful businessman, finds himself on the streets with only the homeless to help him. He forms a relationship with Gina, and is instrumental in bringing down a corrupt and murderous policeman.

Glasgow-born Robbie Moffat is a phenomenon of contemporary British filmmaking, who, along with regular collaborator Mairi Sutherland, appears to have developed an entire ecosystem. You almost certainly have not heard of him, nor of any of the nine films discussed here (the most recent Scottish film from Moffat, *Nessie* is discussed above along with other films featuring the 'monster'). It would have been easy simply to dismiss his output as too 'fringe' and to have omitted

his work from this book. But that would
be a grievous injustice; he has made more
'Scottish' films than any other director, and
if they are neither high-concept nor high-
budget, nor shown in multiplexes, well,
chapeau!

Moffat began making films with the
Glasgow-set *Love the One You're With*,
and has since directed nearly 30 further
films, ranging from documentary (*Walking
with Elephants*, 2019), to *I Know What
I'm Doing* (2013) – a reimagining of *I
Know Where I'm Going*, set wholly in
England. Seven further films by him are
discussed below, along with one directed
by Sutherland, all of which, Robbie assures
me, have been shown in cinemas at least
once (*Rain Dogs*, 2004 is Scottish but I was
not able to track it down). *Nessie*, Moffat's
best film, is dealt with above in the set of
entries related to the Loch Ness Monster. I
haven't separately dealt with the engaging
Got to Run† (2011), in which less than
half of the film is set in Scotland. If it was
by another director, I might have included
it, but there are plenty of entry points here
to Moffat's work.

Love the One You're With opens
with Charlie concluding a property deal
in Glasgow and being given a cheque
for £500,000. After a one-night stand
he awakes to find his beloved bright-
yellow Porsche Boxster impounded (with
his wallet in the glove box) and is then
mugged. Events have placed him amongst
society's dispossessed (although there is
an easy solution, which when employed
towards the end of the film is dealt with
so cursorily that we might wonder why

this wasn't invoked on the first morning).
Charlie must now navigate a world very
different to the one he is used to, amongst
people he would normally look through
(if, that is, he deigned to notice them at
all). The film's heart may be in the right
place but *Love the One You're With* is not
good. The acting is variable (Crawford,
who was also in **Postmortem**, is one of
the more polished cast), the script trite.
For 90 minutes the emphasis is on the
decency of the homeless people with whom
Charlie interacts (as he puts it, 'it's the
first time in my life I've actually been with
a bunch of people I like'), and how they
are continually let down by 'the system',
but – Patterson's comeuppance and Gina's
'rescue' aside – the situation remains
unchanged at the end of the film. Charlie
regains his material possessions, his power
and status, and drives away with the girl –
a Porsche in the 21st century substituting
for a white stallion. We can but hope he
has had an epiphany and will now work
for the good of others rather than for
himself.

→ *The Hawk and the Dove* (2002) S+++

Directed by Robbie Moffat
Screenplay by Robbie Moffat
Leading cast: Jon-Paul Gates (Harry John Gillespie); Joanna Kate Rodgers (Ebony); Ian Stirling (Bingo)
Colour, 90 minutes, UK

Bookkeeper Harry steals from his criminal clients, and hides out in Tarbert with Ebony, an Edinburgh sex worker. Events spiral to a tragic conclusion.

There's no getting away from the fact: *The Hawk and the Dove* is terrible with no redeeming features. It's the sort of film which Alistair Harkness probably had in mind when he wrote (of **Fast Romance**) that some films are 'rubbish in a way that only low budget Scottish movies seem able to manage'. No one is likely to describe Moffat's extensive output as accomplished, but he has made films which are far better than this.

Gates and Rodgers both appear in another Moffat film, *Nudes in Tartan* (2011) which, sadly, is not covered here, as it is set in London.

→ *The Winter Warrior* (2003) S+++

Directed by Robbie Moffat
Screenplay by Robbie Moffat
Leading cast: James Watson (Fingal); Victoria Pritchard (Jessica); Jon-Paul Gates (Ida)
Colour, 99 minutes, UK

573 AD. Angles raid weakened Celtic territory. Fingal, a Celt and mercenary once in the pay of the Roman army, kills a raider, freeing the slave Jessica. Fingal's wife is taken and killed by Angles led by Ida, who seizes Jessica. Fingal hunts the group down, frees Jessica and marries her.

If **Centurion** and **The Eagle** belong in this book, so too does *The Winter Warrior* trilogy (see also **The Bone Hunter** and **Axe Raiders**) all of which are set in what is, today, Scotland, pitching the Celts against wicked Angles. The film, made with a cast of 15 and a tiny budget, tells a simple story, and relies heavily on Watson and Pritchard, and Scottish scenery, for its appeal. There is perhaps too much of walking Angles being 'pursued' by a walking Fingal – some trimming would have been welcome – and the actors and budget struggle with the fight scenes, but it's hard to knock a film which delivers so much from so little.

Lead actor James Watson, born in Glasgow, is also to be seen in *Ratcatcher* (as a bus driver), in *Perfect Sense* (as a 'crying bus driver'), and in *A Woman in Winter* (where he is promoted to taxi driver). Ilaria D'Elia, who plays his murdered wife, was also in Martin Scorsese's **Gangs of New York** (2002). Both

D'Elia and Pritchard reappear in a later Moffat film, *Finding Fortune*, but D'Elia is sadly absent from the rest of the trilogy.

→ *The Bone Hunter* (2003) S+++

Directed by Robbie Moffat
Screenplay by Robbie Moffat
Leading cast: James Watson (Fingal); Gary Taylor (Domal); Linsey Baxter (Henini); Oliver Cotton (Regulus)
Colour, 88 minutes, UK

573 AD: North of Hadrian's Wall. Henini, a widow and bride-to-be is escorted north by Celts who are attacked by Angles, kidnapping Henini. She is carrying a precious Christian relic. Fingal sets out to rescue her, securing the assistance of Domal and the monk, Regulus.

Moffat could probably make 1,000 films on the budget of *The Eagle*, and, if you simply accept it for what it is, *The Bone Hunter* is more fun (there are no 'sulky slabs' here). Notwithstanding that there are fights to be fought and a quest to be quested, there's a welcome lightness of touch: Regulus' is shortened to the much more prosaic 'Reg', and he carries the sword of Conan the Barbarian!

Note that Moffat's own site gives the date for the action as AD 575, which leads on to other sites copying the error; the opening film titles have this as AD 573 (which means the action follows on very soon after that in *The Winter Warrior*). Pedantry aside, nothing turns on this difference.

→ *Finding Fortune* (2003)   S++

Directed by Robbie Moffat
Screenplay by Robbie Moffat
Leading cast: Ilaria D'Elia (Helen); Victoria Pritchard (Sylvia); Jason Harvey (Davie)
Colour, 108 minutes, UK

Londoners Helen and Sylvia attempt to track down Helen's missing husband in the Highlands. Sylvia picks up Davie along the way. An incoherent plot involves Buddhists, a mysterious pursuer, a gun, murder, and the police.

Referencing DW Griffith, Jean Luc Godard famously said, 'all you need to make a movie is a girl and a gun'. *Finding Fortune* proves he was wrong.

→ *Red Rose* (2004)   S+++

Directed by Robbie Moffat
Screenplay by Mairi Sutherland
Leading cast: Michael Rodgers (Robert Burns); Lucy Russell (Jean Armour); Rebecca Palmer (Maria Riddell)
Colour, 107 minutes, UK

The complicated life of Robert Burns from 1790 to his death in 1796.

If you want a biopic of Robert Burns – and who doesn't? – this is the film for you. *The Life of Robert Burns*, a silent film from 1926, directed by Maurice Sandground, long believed lost, is extant but all but impossible to see (an expert in the life of Burns, quoted by *Biopic* on the film's release, suggested the best approach to the film was to cut out 50 per cent, and burn the remainder). 1937's **Auld Lang Syne** is terrible. Almost all attempts to make a modern biopic have failed, notwithstanding that Johnny Depp (!) and Gerard Butler have both been linked to the role – and David Hayman was reported in 1997 to be trying to raise funds to make a biopic, with the hope that either Ewan McGregor or Johnny Lee Miller would play the role. All attempts, bar one... With *Red Rose*, Moffat has made the best biopic of Burns available.

Red Rose is a bold effort to make a historical biopic on a limited budget, with a reasonable degree of accuracy as to key events. For the most part this works – although there is only so much that clever camera angles can hide (the sight of, eg, dormer windows can lift one out of the period). Decently acted (Palmer picked up a Best Actress award from the Monaco International Film Festival), and a story engagingly told.

→ *Cycle* (2006)   S+++   W7

Directed by Robbie Moffat
Screenplay by Robbie Moffat
Leading cast: Marnie Baxter (Isla); Andreas
   Beltzer (Brendan/Robert Linden); Rachel Rath
   (Pearl)
Colour, 89 minutes, UK

Walking from the Bridge of Orchy to the Kingshouse Hotel, then to the Clachaig Inn, five Stirling University students are murdered by a cycling psychopath who eats brains.

If a psychopathic serial killer tells his victim 'I'm going to suck your brains out', this *must* be followed by the act. If brains are outside the budget, my wife, a consultant neurologist, suggests tofu might work. But in *Cycle* this is not the case, and the film simply sucks, delivering neither horror nor tension, committing the ultimate sin of just being dull, without toppling into bonkers/fun territory.

→*Axe Raiders* (2007)   S+++

Directed by Robbie Moffat
Screenplay by Robbie Moffat
Leading cast: Rachael Sutherland (Ethne); Gary
   Taylor (Domlech); Marnie Baxter (Melangall);
   Jon-Paul Gates (Aeric)
Colour, 90 minutes, UK

577 AD: Caledonia. Conflict between Celtic Christians and 'land-hungry Angles' is rife. Fingal has been killed by an Angle leader Aeric; his daughter, Ethne, seeks revenge.

Axe Raiders ('The Axe Raiders' in the film's opening titles) is the weakest of the three entries in Moffat's *The Winter Warrior Trilogy*, possibly because it lacks a key ingredient: Fingal. On the other hand, the focus on a female hero (who allies with another forceful woman, Melangall), provides Moffat the opportunity to give the film a strong, if historically implausible, feminist slant. As with the rest of the trilogy there's little attempt at historical accuracy. Glasgow is referred to under that name some 600 years before any recorded use of 'Glasgu', and it is the language above all that pulls one out of the period; but this must be deliberate. While at the start the Angle leader is given a poetic mode, for the rest of the film the characters speak as if they are talking in the 21st century.

→ *Going Green* (2012) S++

Directed by Mairi Sutherland
Screenplay by Robbie Moffat and Mairi
  Sutherland
Leading cast: Rachel Rath (Amber); Darren
  Enright (Nigel); Amy Dawson (Liberty); Jon-
  Paul Gates (Jet); Suzanne Kendall (Crystal);
  Louise Hawthorne (Dreamcatcher)
Colour, 92 minutes, UK

In London, Amber and Nigel face the repossession of their house and decide to take an extended break in Scotland; later their daughter Liberty joins them, followed by Amber's father. Their lifestyle changes completely – for the better.

Unlike the other films in this section, *Going Green* is directed by Sutherland, but the close collaboration between Sutherland and Moffat is such that the film is consistent with the others. *Going Green* has left virtually no trace. The scenery is beautiful; the story simple; the message cheering.

→ *The Right Bus* (2021) S++

Directed by Robbie Moffat
Screenplay by Robbie Moffat
Leading cast: Ed Ward (David Gregson);
  Suzanne Kendal (Connie Renton); Edan
  Hayhurst (Danny Renton); Edith Glad (Louisa
  Renton)
Colour, 93 minutes, UK

David and Connie separately inherit parts of an estate in Scotland, near Oban. Connie's complicated family history and life in America make her resistant to taking up the estate, but she travels there with her children. She and David meet.

The Right Bus is, unusually for a Robbie Moffat film, based on a novel; in this case a first novel, with little footprint, by Glenn Ward. This straightforward romantic drama in which the importance of serendipity is to the fore ('it may be luck, it may be chance, but you have to be aware the right bus awaits; it's just a matter of recognising it') is a more polished production than most of the earlier films covered here, the only clumsy note being a ponderous voice-over narration provided by English actor Ward. Kendall, also English, was previously in **Going Green** and other Moffat/Sutherland productions.

One Life Stand (2000)　S+++

Directed by May Miles Thomas
Screenplay by May Miles Thomas
Leading cast: Maureen Carr (Trise Clarke); John
　Kielty (John Paul Clarke); Gary Lewis (Jackie
　Clarke)
B&W, 119 minutes, UK

*Single mother Trise attempts to secure
her son John Paul work with a modelling
agent. The agent sets him up with older
women as a sex worker. Trise attempts to
save their relationship. After arguing with
his mother, John Paul moves in with one of
his clients.*

One Life Stand attracted significant critical
acclaim but did not secure a cinema release
after being shown at the Edinburgh and
Bergen international film festivals. As
Jonathan Romney put it in *Film Comment*:
'This taut, intimate, nervily acted piece
doesn't waste a second, and makes
maximum use of claustrophobia-inducing
shooting conditions. Not surprisingly,
British distributors have so far reacted with
utter indifference'. The film is, as Duncan
Petrie noted in *Cineaste*, directly influenced
by Pier Paolo Pasolini's *Mamma Roma*
(1962), in which Anna Magnani plays an
ageing prostitute who attempts to rebuild
her relationship with her son. In *One
Life Stand*, the roles are reversed. Petrie
described *One Life Stand* as 'a profound
engagement with small moments of human
contact, hope, and despair'.

The film won the Scottish BAFTAs for
Best Drama, Director, Writer and, for
Scottish actor Maureen Carr, a very richly
deserved award for Best Performance. On its
release the film attracted as much attention
for the method of its production (it was the
first British feature to be made digitally) as
it did for its smart content. Glasgow-based
May Miles Thomas is served well by a
strong central cast, but she must take the
lion's share of credit for the film's success:
she is credited with screenplay, director of
photography, editor (the film was edited on
Thomas' PC), and director.

Glaswegian Gary Lewis appears in many
films in this book, beginning with his first
film role in **Shallow Grave**, running up to
Stella. John Kielty has had a small number
of roles in television but has not appeared
in another feature. Thomas followed
One Life Stand with **Solid Air** (2003), an
excellent neo-noir also set in Glasgow; for
The Devil's Plantation see below.

→ Solid Air (2003)　S+++

Directed by May Miles Thomas
Screenplay by May Miles Thomas
Leading cast: Brian McCardie (Robert
　Houston); Kathy Kiera Clarke (Nicola Blyth);
　Gary Lewis (John Doren); Laura Harvey
　(Leena)
Colour, 115 minutes, UK

*A game of poker: Robert, a compulsive
gambler, loses his car, and returns home
for his father's funeral. Finding that his
father made a claim for an asbestos-related
industrial injury, Robert attempts to pursue
the case, working with Nicola, a lawyer,*

while, driven by excessive gambling, his personal life implodes.

Opening with the jazz standard 'You Don't Know What Love Is', a card game and a voice-over, Glasgow-set *Solid Air* creates a neo-noir vibe from the outset; initially the palette tends to black and white, but the film is shot in washed-out colour and widescreen (May Miles Thomas explained to me 'the photography… was a very conscious decision on my part; a dark, autumnal, desaturated look that I tested two years before the film was made', achieved with the aid of colourist Perry Gibb). It is more conventional than *One Life Stand*, and one would have anticipated that it would gain some traction. In fact, although *Solid Air* played at the EIFF and won awards at the Tróia International Film Festival, it did not secure a distribution deal and has slipped into obscurity. It is, sadly and unjustifiably, extremely difficult to watch: until I requested access, the Moving Image Archive had not needed to create a digital copy of the film (my request at least makes the film a *little* more available for others).*

As Robert's trail takes him through the underside of Glasgow there are echoes of one of the all-time great films, *Chinatown* (Roman Polanski, 1974), where the main villain is corporate greed at a level socially far removed from its victims (as one character cuttingly says, the asbestos-caused mesothelioma 'is a poor man's disease'). *Solid Air* is not as good as *Chinatown* (few films are), but it *is* good. In keeping with the noir vibe, moral ambiguity abounds: a lawyer says 'civil cases aren't about justice, they're really only about money', while Robert behaves more like the inveterate gambler he is, than an aggrieved pursuer, when he says 'all in' while instructing his lawyer to continue the case. However, it is clear at the end of the legal process that Robert has been driven by more than his need for money, and the film maintains a clear emphasis on the victims of economic and institutional injustice.

Solid Air is firmly rooted in Glasgow; everything here is authentic, and a strong cast of Scottish actors lends the film added veracity. May Miles Thomas has told me of the production difficulties in getting the film made, and the challenges she faced when changes at a key distributor resulted in support for the film being removed. She was told London-based distributors believed *Solid Air* was 'too long, too dark, and too Scottish'. With public financial support, a strong cast, solid production values and a smart script the film does not deserve to have been cast aside after only two screenings in the UK.

* The National Library of Scotland Moving Image Archive, at Glasgow's Kelvin Hall offers many free services, including viewing facilities. It's well worth checking out. The feature film collection is focused on films which have received Scottish public funding.

→The Devil's Plantation (2013)

S+++

Directed by May Miles Thomas
Screenplay by May Miles Thomas
Leading cast: Gary Lewis (narration); Kate Dickie
(narration)
B&W, 93 minutes, UK

*A film essay and 'psychogeographic
journey' through Glasgow.*

The Devil's Plantation (which is the
traditional name for the Bonnyton Mound,
near Eaglesham) was the culmination of
an online project supported by Creative
Scotland. It presents, according to *The
Herald*, an 'arresting [and] contemplative'
unique portrait of Glasgow, interweaving,
through Lewis' and Dickie's narration,
the work and theories of Harry Bell,
and the post-incarceration life of Mary
Ross. Bell was an amateur archaeologist
who published *Glasgow's Secret
Geometry* in 1984, suggesting that the
city's development followed prehistoric
communication lines. Mary Ross, who
was committed to a psychiatric hospital
in 1959, was discharged to a Glasgow she
did not recognise in 1992. Her subsequent
life in the city, and Bell's research, map
different but overlapping perspectives,
presented in beautifully austere imagery
with a pace which verges on the hypnotic.
Interviewed in *The Scotsman* prior to the
film's showing at the GFF, Thomas said 'I'm
asking people to sit very passively looking
at scenes of Glasgow where the streets are
empty and not very much happens. But it's

not just that, they're being told a wonderful
story. For me this is almost like a fairytale,
I've tried to give it that aura.' Following
The Devil's Plantation, Thomas made
Voyageuse† (2018) (which intersects in part
with Scotland), a documentary essay about
her mother-in-law, who was born in 1933
and fled the Austro-Hungarian border in
Nazi Europe for England (Peter Bradshaw:
'an engrossing cine-memoir... one of the
most enjoyable documentaries of the year').

Strictly Sinatra (2000)

S+++

Directed by Peter Capaldi
Screenplay by Peter Capaldi
Leading cast: Ian Hart (Toni Cocozza); Kelly
Macdonald (Irene); Brian Cox (Chisolm); Alun
Armstrong (Bill)
Colour, 97 minutes, UK

*Glasgow: nightclub performer Toni
Cocozza, who sings Frank Sinatra covers,
is taken up by local gangster Chisholm,
who has spent time in Las Vegas and has
met Sinatra. Cocozza becomes increasingly
ensnared in the criminal underworld,
jeopardising his relationships with
accompanist Bill and Irene.*

Receiving its Scottish premiere at a charity
gala in Glasgow in October 2001, Peter
Capaldi's only feature as director has, like
Soft Top Hard Shoulder (which he wrote
and stars in), a strong dose of Americana
and nostalgia. Here a young Glasgow
singer, failing to move on to bigger things,
is *strictly* Sinatra (until required by

Chisholm to sing a cover of Elvis Presley's 'In The Ghetto'), and finds his life possibly mirroring Sinatra's in an increasing entanglement with organised crime.

Strictly Sinatra has a strong initial set-up, nicely atmospheric Glaswegian scenes and, in Hart (also in *Mary Queen of Scots*, 2018), an engaging central performance. Also good is Armstrong, who stepped in only when Ian Bannen died early on in production. There's enough here to please, but the film teeters between the engaging milieu of the nightclub and Hart's attempts to break onto a bigger stage, and the harsher world of the gangsters. *S&S*'s Edward Lawrenson was among the critics thrown by the changes in mood, noting the 'dour Glasgow hardmen, particularly Brian Cox's menacing Chisolm, who seem to have strolled from the pages of a William McIlvanney novel, throwing the jokey tone of the rest of the movie off balance'. Ken Eisner, in *Variety*, enjoyed the 'winsome effort', but felt that the 'lovely premise, great Glasgow atmospherics and pungent performances are gradually overtaken by routine gangland plot'.

Late Night Shopping (2001) S++
T100

Directed by Saul Metzstein
Screenplay by Jack Lothian
Leading cast: Luke de Woolfson (Sean); Kate Ashfield (Jody); James Lance (Vincent); Enzo Cilenti (Lenny); Heike Makatsch (Madeline Zozzocolovich)
Colour, 91 minutes, UK/Germany

Four friends meet in a Glaswegian café 'most nights, before and after their night shifts' to 'sit around, drink coffee and pass the time'. The friends help Sean solve a relationship crisis.

It doesn't sound like a great pitch: four aimless 20-somethings who work night shifts in Glasgow spend their time together in an all-night café drinking milkshakes and coffee. Yet there is something inconsequentially delightful about *Late Night Shopping*, the first feature film from Glasgow-born Metzstein. The success of the film relies on the chemistry between the four somewhat inexperienced leads. Woolfson was making his first film; Cilenti his second. Ashfield had been in films since 1994; Lance (who has the biggest challenge of making womaniser Vincent more than merely disgusting) had the longest CV. Now, the most recognisable member of the cast is probably Makatsch. Two years after *Late Night Shopping* she played the role of Mia, the vamp PA to Alan Rickman's Harry, in *Love Actually* (Richard Curtis, 2003). It is odd, however, that for a film set in Glasgow there are virtually no Scottish

The four friends take a road trip to Ayrshire

accents to be heard. The film won the BAFTA Scotland awards for Best Film, and Best Director.

There are risks to films which consist of friends sitting around talking. One of the challenges is to open things up. Until they take a road trip in the final third of the film almost all the interaction between the characters is set within the all-night café. But each is shown in their workplaces, although the focus is on Sean and Vincent. Jody is less well served. Lenny is shown at work, failing to connect with a co-worker on whom he has a crush. Sean has his apparently deserted flat and searches for clues as to whether Madeline still lives there. His job in the hospital also leads to sex with the girlfriend of a comatose patient (the result of which is to convince him he loves Madeline). Vincent engages with a colleague, who subsequently dies of a heart attack, and we see his womanising. He gets many of the best lines, although the best of all is probably that written by Jody on a napkin in the final act when the four are in the Melbourne Café in 'Light Haven' (Saltcoats). Echoing an earlier comment from Vincent, she sets out her plan for when she returns to the city: 'Get a job. Get a life. Then what?'

The most engaging sequence in the film is the road trip to Ayrshire. There is a running gag in which the car radio cannot be switched from a channel playing '80s classics; a shot of a crazy golf course looks like it walked straight out of a Wes Anderson film. Ultimately, however, Jody's t-shirt ('On The Road – Jack Kerouac') serves as an ironic comment on the limits of the group's horizons.

Pyaar Ishq aur Mohabbat (2001) S+

Directed by Rajiv Rai
Screenplay by Shabbir Boxwala and Rajiv Rai
Leading cast: Kirti Reddy (Isha Nair); Arjun
Rampal (Gaurav Saxena); Sunil Shetty (Yash
Sabharwal); Aftab Shivdasani (Tajinder
Bharadwaj)
Colour, 168 minutes, India, Hindi/English

Isha, a beautiful medical student, obtains a scholarship to study at the world-renowned University of Glasgow. She is pursued across Scotland and Europe by three men of different circumstances and character who covet her.

A Bollywood film in Hindi and English, shot largely in Scotland, with some side-action in Switzerland, *PIM* received its world premiere in Govan, recognising in part the emphasis placed on the city by the film. Isha arrives at Prestwick (presumably having taken an idiosyncratic route) 35 minutes into the film – and much of the next 130 minutes is spent in Scotland. Unsurprisingly, Isha ends up with the right man. See 'Bollywood: Non-Resident Indian-Scotland', in David Martin-Jones, *Scotland: Global Cinema*.

Dog Soldiers (2002) T28

Directed by Neil Marshall
Screenplay by Neil Marshall
Leading cast: Sean Pertwee (Wells); Kevin
McKidd (Cooper); Emma Cleasby (Megan);
Liam Cunningham (Ryan)
Colour, 105 minutes, UK/Luxembourg

In the Scottish Highlands a squad of soldiers engage in a training exercise. Things spiral out of control when they are attacked by werewolves, and a fight to the death in a farmhouse ensues.

In the closing credits of *Dog Soldiers*, the following appears: 'Filmed on location and in studios in the Grand Duchy of Luxembourg...' There is, in other words, very little Scottish about the film apart from its Highlands location, although the lead role of Cooper is played by *Trainspotting* alumnus McKidd (who appears also in *Small Faces, The Acid House, 16 Years of Alcohol, The Rocket Post* and *Brave*). This has not stopped this extremely effective, and occasionally very funny, horror film from being taken to heart. In 2020 it formed part of the programming of my local Odeon in Glasgow for Halloween in a brief respite between Covid-19 lockdowns and was well-attended.

The action in *Dog Soldiers* moves from open forest and countryside to a claustrophobic farmhouse as the options facing the soldiers close in – by the very end we are in first a bathroom, then a kitchen, and finally a cellar. The sets themselves

Soldiers battle werewolves to highly entertaining effect in 'the Highlands'

were constructed on a small scale to require the actors playing the werewolves to contort. *Dog Soldiers* was Neil Marshall's first film; his next was *The Descent*† (2005) in which the action is almost *entirely* confined to tightly enclosed spaces (this has a short opening scene in Scotland, then moves to the Appalachian mountains). Marshall also made ***Doomsday*** and ***Centurion*** (see below).

The screenplay is very snappy ('We were attacked. By huge fuckin' howlin' things'). It is a pity then that Megan gets one speech which, while drawing laughs in the screening I attended, verges on misogynistic – echoing in part some of the earlier banter between the soldiers. The most quoted line is probably the single word 'sausages', as Wells is plied with alcohol (acted by a genuinely inebriated Pertwee) before his stomach is glued back together. In *The Hollywood News* in 2020 Marshall spoke about this scene: 'Bob Keen was making the werewolves for us and he mentioned in conversation somewhere about superglue being invented for the Vietnam war to stitch back soldiers on the battlefield... that was too interesting to not have in the script... That's the kind of thing that people remember. The fact that Sean is just so hilarious in that scene... he was a little bit tipsy and it comes off.' Janine Pipe took this as the inspiration for the title of her book, *Sausages: The making of Dog Soldiers*, published in 2022.

Dog Soldiers is so good it gets its own

entry in Christopher J Olson's *100 Greatest Cult Films* (2018) – he calls it 'one of the all-time great werewolf movies, as well as a true cult classic'. The film has also generated a faltering afterlife: a proposed TV series, *Dog Soldiers: Legacy* (2011) failed to get off the ground, with only one episode directed; at the time of writing IMDb lists *Dog Soldiers: Fresh Meat* as 'in development'. Marshall was not attached to either of these initiatives. A restored version of the film was presented by Marshall at *FrightFest* in 2022.

Rhona Mitra battles the Scottish who have degenerated in *Doomsday*

→ *Doomsday* (2008)   S+

Directed by Neil Marshall
Screenplay by Neil Marshall
Leading cast: Bob Hoskins (Bill Nelson); Rhona Mitra (Eden Sinclair); Alexander Siddig (Prime Minister John Hatcher); David O'Hara (Michael Canaris); Craig Conway (Sol); Malcolm McDowell (Kane)
Colour, 105 minutes, UK/US/South Africa/Germany

2035: 27 years after an epidemic devastates Scotland, leading to its isolation and total collapse, the disease is found in London. A team, led by Sinclair, is sent to Glasgow to track down survivors who might hold the key to a cure.

The vision of a post-apocalyptic Scotland offered here is not encouraging: within less than 30 years of an epidemic's outbreak, and Scotland's isolation, society has collapsed. Survivors are either vicious feral cannibals ('This is our city. Whoever they send here, we're gonna catch 'em, we're gonna cook 'em, and we're gonna eat 'em!') or have reverted to a medieval castle life (scenes being partially shot at Blackness Castle), knights in armour included.

Doomsday is one giant rip-off: first, of *28 Days Later* (Danny Boyle, 2002), then – even more blatantly – of *Mad Max 2* (aka *The Road Warrior*, George Miller, 1981), and *Mad Max Beyond Thunderdome* (George Miller and George Ogilvie, 1985), with some riffs from *Aliens* (James Cameron, 1986) thrown in for good measure. As Gregory Kirschling wrote in *Entertainment Weekly*, 'you have to wonder how [Marshall would] like it if someone ripped off *The Descent* so egregiously'. To be fair, Marshall also rips off himself, borrowing from **Dog Soldiers** and *The Descent*: he clearly likes combat in tight spaces.

The plot is ridiculous, the octane levels high. Were you to get home late after a good night out on the Tennents (which the film suggests has a shelf life of over a quarter of a century) and fancy something loud, visceral, and fast, *Doomsday* would fit the bill. You might not notice the ridiculous implausibility, the plot holes, and the wasted tee-ups which go nowhere, and you could admire the strong cast, which includes alumni of *Dog Soldiers* (Sean Pertwee, Craig Conway and Emma Cleasby amongst others), and the rendering of a derelict and overgrown Glasgow.

The Last Great Wilderness (2002) S+++

Directed by David Mackenzie
Screenplay by Michael Tait, Alastair Mackenzie and Gillian Berry
Leading cast: Alastair Mackenzie (Charlie); Jonny Phillips (Vincente); Ewan Stewart (Magnus); David Hayman (Ruaridh); Victoria Smurfit (Claire)
Colour, 95 minutes, UK/Denmark

Two unlikely travel companions, Charlie and Vincente, on a road trip to Skye, are forced to stay at a retreat lodge in the Highlands populated by a motley group who engage in rituals in the local woods. People hunting Vincente catch up with him, and he dies. Charlie stays with the lodge community for some time, then leaves.

David Mackenzie's (see **Young Adam, Hallam Foe, Perfect Sense** and **Outlaw King**) *TLGW* was funded under a scheme run by Scottish Screen to promote films which embraced experimental storytelling. Its Danish co-production places the film within the Dogmac output (see **Wilbur**

(Wants to Kill Himself), below). The film's set-up tells us very clearly what we are going to get: Charlie and Vincente, first by accident, and then apparently by coercion, are required to stay in the lodge where there are hints of ghosts, and strange goings on.

It is clear that we are heading into gothic territory, with a strong dose of *The Wicker Man* thrown in. Except this is not how things go – the film is more *The League of Gentlemen* (1999–2017), although a build to comedy is disrupted by the brutality meted out on Vincente – but this is *not* by the residents of the lodge. As Andy Richards put it in *S&S*, 'As the inclusion of a raucous cross-dressing party scene confirms, the Lodge is less a site of Gothic entrapment than a locus of liberation and transformation'. Or, as Derek Elley more pithily put it in *Variety*, *TLGW* 'turns from a 'putative road movie… into a weirdo comedy'.

The tonal shifts however are somewhat jarring. To quote Elley again: 'It's in the delayed second act that the problems mount, and the tone starts to swing all ways'. The script is somewhat wayward, and the lurch in mood is disconcertingly abrupt. However, there is enjoyment to be had in a film playing so robustly and knowingly with genre expectations.

Wilbur (Wants to Kill Himself) (2002) S+++ T100

Directed by Lone Scherfig

Screenplay by Lone Scherfig, Anders Thomas
  Jensen

Leading cast: Jamie Sives (Wilbur); Adrian
  Rawlins (Harbour); Shirley Henderson (Alice);
  Lisa McKinlay (Mary); Mads Mikkelsen (Horst);
  Julia Davis (Moira)

Colour, 109 minutes, UK/Denmark/Sweden/
  France

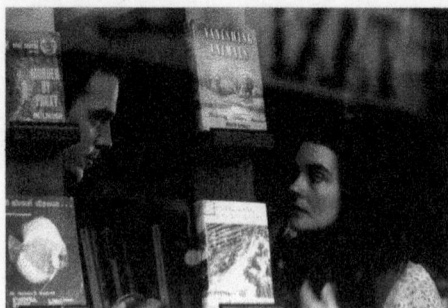

Jamie Sives and Shirley Henderson in Glasgow

Glasgow: Wilbur and his brother run a second-hand bookshop. Wilbur attempts suicide and is treated for depression. Wilbur's brother, Harbour, marries Alice, and a ménage à trois ensues. Harbour dies by suicide after ignoring a potentially fatal illness. Wilbur, Alice, and her daughter visit Harbour's burial site.

Given *Wilbur* deals with suicide, with no less than three different people attempting this (Harbour successfully), and with terminal illness, it is no small wonder that it manages to avoid almost any trace of being maudlin. It is, given its content, remarkably life-affirming, and pulling that off is a neat trick. *Wilbur* was a co-production involving Glasgow's Sigma Films, and Copenhagen's Zentropa Entertainments. This was one of several Scottish/Scandinavian co-productions which had a significant impact on the landscape of Scottish cinema in the early 2000s (see also *Skagerrak* and *Donkeys*). A fuller discussion of what is sometimes termed 'Dogmac' may be found in *The New Scottish Cinema* (Jonathan Murray, 2015).

Danish director Scherfig told *S&S* that she 'would have liked the film to be more realist and to be set more on the streets of Glasgow'. That it is not was commented on by several reviewers. In *S&S*, Philip Kemp, who did not like the film, wrote that although *Wilbur* is 'set in Glasgow, and was indeed partly shot there... there's very little sense of Scottishness about it. The relentlessly quirky characters seem to float in a social limbo'.

It is not easy to like Wilbur. His repeated attempts at suicide go beyond cries for help, and even his doctor, Horst, has given up on him. It takes the entry of Alice into his life for things to begin to turn, with the creation of a *ménage à trois* accepted by his brother. The key signal of change is that when Wilbur returns home one evening soaked to the skin it is not because he has attempted to drown himself in the Clyde, but because he has saved someone else from that fate. Unlike Wilbur's various attempts at suicide, Harbour's is successful, triumphant (defeating a painful death by cancer), and an act of self-sacrifice; his illness is terminal, and his death comes only after he has commanded Wilbur to treat Alice and Mary as best he can. Harbour's death facilitates the creation of a new nuclear family and is consistent with his constant sacrifice up to that point; he has continually placed the needs of others before his own. It is this which endows the film with life.

16 Years of Alcohol (2003) S+++ T100

> Directed by Richard Jobson
> Screenplay by Richard Jobson
> Leading cast: Kevin McKidd (Frankie); Laura Fraser (Helen); Susan Lynch (Mary); Stuart Sinclair Blyth (Miller); Jim Carter (director)
> Colour, 102 minutes, UK

In an Edinburgh bar, Frankie, in voice-over, says, 'This is a story about hope'. In flashback we follow Frankie's life leading to this moment. His family home is unstable, and he starts drinking at an early age. He and his friends are violent. After joining AA, he rebuilds his life and enters a relationship with Mary. This has only recently ended – we are back in the bar, he decides to embrace hope and phones Mary, but is pursued by Miller, a former friend.

This is the first of four films in this book to be directed by Richard Jobson, former frontman of the band *Skids*, which had some success from 1977, when formed in Dunfermline, to 1980. The band's best-known single, 'Into the Valley', and the 1980 album, *The Absolute Game*, broke

into the top 10. As founder members drifted away, the band finally broke up in 1982 (although reformed sporadically to play gigs, eventually releasing a new album in 2018: see *The Skids: Revolution*). In 2005, *The Herald* described Jobson as 'the closest Scotland has to a film auteur in the mould of Woody Allen or Mike Leigh'.

Writing in *The Guardian* in 2004, music journalist and author Sean O'Hagan described *16 Years* in the following terms: 'It is an unashamed art movie, a semi-autobiographical account of [Jobson's] violent childhood... slow and meditative at first, then fast and violent... It is also undeniably moving and, in places, soul-bearingly honest.' *16 Years*, Jobson's first film, was made for the small sum of £400,000. A higher budget was contemplated, but Jobson has said that backers fell away as the unconventionality of the film was revealed; they were particularly deterred by the extensive use of voice-over.

Interviewed by the BBC, Jobson said that 'I didn't want the film to be in the tradition – which is a fine tradition – of British social realism. I like those films very much, but it's not what I was interested in making... I wanted it to be much more fragmented, like a dream, and I wanted Edinburgh to be like a character in the film.' In this Jobson succeeds. He referenced Wong Kar-wei in the same interview, and *16 Years* is closer in spirit to Kar-wei's *As Tears Go By* (*Wong Gok ka moon*, 1988) than it is to *Neds* or *Small Faces*, with which it has been compared on the basis that, like them, it is a semi-autobiographical film set in a

Scottish city and like them there is more focus on violence than on alcohol.

While Jobson was trying to do something somewhat distinctive in the British cinema of the time, *16 Years* was not unique in employing visual lyricism while dealing with a topic grounded in social reality (see, eg, *Trainspotting*, made seven years earlier). The attempt was widely praised. After a showing at the Locarno Film Festival in August 2003, *Variety* reported that 'the highly directed film adopts a semi-impressionistic approach more European than British in flavour, aided by a terrific central performance by Kevin McKidd and painterly lensing by John Rhodes.' While many admired Jobson's attempt to break out of a 'miserabilist' approach to social realism (the film maintains a score of 70 per cent on Rotten Tomatoes), there was at the same time widespread criticism of the script, which as delivered largely by McKidd has a poetic quality verging on the hypnotic but is riddled with cliché. Trite lines are an irritant in an otherwise interesting film.

→ *The Purifiers* (2004) S+++

Directed by Richard Jobson
Screenplay by Richard Jobson
Leading cast: Kevin McKidd (Moses); Gordon Alexander (John); Rachel Grant (Li); Dominic Monaghan (Sol); Amber Sainsbury (Frances)
Colour, 85 minutes, UK

In a dystopian Glasgow, The Purifiers, led by John, protect people in their territory. Invited by Moses to a meeting of all the city gangs, they decline to join the others in controlling the city, leave the meeting, and are hunted through the night.

If, by 12 minutes into *The Purifiers*, you are not shouting at the screen 'It's *The Warriors*!' (Walter Hill, 1979), you should be. And if you haven't seen *The Warriors*, then put that on instead of watching Richard Jobson's extremely puzzling second film. At the minimum the film must have looked good enough on paper to attract funding from Screen Scotland, and to secure the participation of McKidd and Monaghan (Merry, in *The Lord of the Rings*), actors of some repute. But in execution this is a mess. The message might be: don't make a film based on karate without a cast, and stunt performers, capable of delivering good fight sequences (and if this is your thing, then see instead *Unleashed*, where Jet Li *does* deliver). Some of the cinematography makes night-time Glasgow look great, but that's about the best that can be said of this.

→ *A Woman in Winter* (2006)

S+++

Directed by Richard Jobson
Screenplay by Richard Jobson
Leading cast: Jamie Sives (Michael); Julie Gayet
(Caroline); Brian Cox (Dr Hunt)
Colour, 100 minutes, UK, English/limited French

*In Edinburgh, theoretical physicist
Michael and Caroline, who is French,
enter a relationship. The beginning of the
film is also its end: standing on a bridge
parapet, Caroline spins and falls. Michael's
investigations into time and space, and
the film's structure, suggest linearity has
been abandoned, and his relationship with
Caroline bridges two realities. Michael's
experiences are either inconsistent with the
central story, or are unlikely coincidences.
At the end Michael is dead, but Caroline
feels his presence, and tells him she loves
him.*

Early on in *A Woman in Winter*, Jobson's
third film after *16 Years of Alcohol* and *The
Purifiers*, one of Michael's astrophysicist
colleagues, sceptical of Michael's more
outré theories, says 'without causality,
there's only chaos'; towards the end of the
film, she says 'time is only nature's way of
preventing everything from happening at
once'. These are perhaps the clearest signals
as to what *may* be happening in *A Woman
in Winter*, where time's arrow might not
be so linear after all. On the other hand, it
would be possible to read the film literally.
Michael has attempted suicide in the past
and had a breakdown after parts of his

work were shown not to be viable. What
he sees may be fantasy and, as Dr Hunt
says, as a physicist he really should believe
in coincidence.

The evidence however is strong that
Jobson is trying to do more than tell a
story linearly and literally, and that the
film is an experiment in causality and love.
But significant demands are made on the
viewer to draw conclusions, such that the
question to be asked is whether *A Woman
in Winter* is an ambitious failure, or merely
incoherent. For *Variety* it appeared to be
a bit of both: 'Unstinting in ambition but
impoverished in realisation, *A Woman
in Winter* is so intent on pushing the
boundaries of regular British cinema that it
forgets to take its audience along.'

In January 2005, shortly after *A Woman
in Winter* was shot, *The Herald* reported
that Jobson was going to stop making
films in Scotland (he didn't), having been
turned down for funding by Scottish
Screen, although the film *was*, in part,
funded by the UK Film Council (based in
London). *The Herald* quoted a brutally
frank Scottish Screen representative: 'He
put forward his script for *A Woman in
Winter* for consideration in October 2003.
It was unanimously rejected by the readers'
panels... the script was mostly style over
substance... the project needed more
development work.'

Kevin McKidd, who had been in both
of Jobson's first two films, was originally
slated to be in *Woman in Winter* but was
replaced by Jamie Sives (also in *On a
Clear Day*, *Hallam Foe* and *Wild Rose*),
alongside French actor Julie Gayet (who

cropped up in a couple of episodes as herself in TV's *Call My Agent* (*Dix pour cent*, 2015–2020)). It is after a screening of a French film which his girlfriend finds inexplicable (Michael is accused of being pretentious because he liked it), that Michael first sees Caroline; the next time he sees her she is holding a book about Truffaut. Perhaps Jobson really is trying to tell us that he wanted to break away from an uncinematic British approach to filmmaking. Unfortunately, the result does not convince and might reasonably be accused of being a little pretentious.

→*New Town Killers* (2008) S+++

Directed by Richard Jobson
Screenplay by Richard Jobson
Leading cast: James Anthony Pearson (Sean MacDonald); Dougray Scott (Alistair Raskolnikov); Alastair Mackenzie (Jamie Stewart); Liz White (Alice MacDonald); Charles Mnene (Sam)
Colour, 100 minutes, UK

Financial analyst Alistair, and his new colleague Jamie, hunt Sean through the streets of Edinburgh over the course of a single night. If Sean is caught, he will be killed; if he survives, he will be paid. Sean turns the tables on the hunters.

Like *16 Years of Alcohol* and *A Woman in Winter*, *New Town Killers* is also set, and filmed entirely, in Edinburgh. The result, however, is unconvincing tosh, although occasionally effective in building tension.

Dougray Scott

It lies in the sub-genre of horror films in which people hunt people, which stretches back to *The Most Dangerous Game* (Irving Pichel and Ernest B Schoedsack, 1932). More specifically it lies in the further refined sub-sub-genre in which the rich hunt the poor and is therefore to be read as an indictment of capitalism, or as Alistair puts it when Sean asks, 'why me?': 'it's only natural, it's just the way it is. I win, you lose.' Audience satisfaction requires that Alistair does *not* win (although his ultimate defeat in no way threatens to bring down systemic exploitation). Interviewed in *The Herald*, Scott said that *NTK* 'deals with issues that mean something to me and which I respond to – how people just pay lip service to the underclass and the difficulties they face and their lot in life, and the opportunities they have to get out of that.' But the film only deals with one side of that equation, and Raskolnikov is a terminally one-dimensional caricature; wealth and class replace character. The point is rammed home through two encounters Sean has with the police. Early on he and Sam are told to 'stay away from here' (the New Town) and 'get back down the hole youse came from'. Later, when he is driving the bankers' Maserati, the same police politely point out that a shirt (worn by a corpse) is hanging out of the boot and then move on.

NTK marked the first film credit for Karen Gillan, as 'young girl in bus station', who is a part of the unexplained, and frankly unbelievable, web of entrapment which the bankers have woven around Sean. The more recent film *Get Duked!* is thematically similar but leavens the threat with a very large dose of wit and is a better watch.

3 (aka *iii*) (1995)　　　S+++

Directed by Morag McKinnon
Screenplay by Morag McKinnon
Leading cast: Tam Dean Burn (the elder); Niall Greig Fulton (Carl); Jackie Joyce (Sri)
Colour, 74 minutes, UK

On a rocky coast a young man, Carl (a graphic designer), is wasted after a party. He's picked up by his friend Sri, a musician, who takes Carl back to her flat in Edinburgh. Carl and Sri hang out, and at work he is given a big new contract, but he has visions, is confused, and feels disassociated. He invites Sri back to the beach 'where this all started', having previously declared his love for her.

3 (a title which renders the film opaque to online search tools) was the first feature film made by Scottish director McKinnon (who later directed the Scottish BAFTA-award-winning *Donkeys*). Her more recent output consists of short films and documentaries. A significant piece in the history of indigenous Scottish filmmaking, and one of the few feature-length Scottish 'art' films, *3* is now little known. It is not discussed in any detail in the few works about Scottish cinema (even when *Donkeys* is discussed; in *Screening Scotland* McKinnon's name is misspelt), and it is extremely hard to find any comment in a standard source. This may be because watching the film will be a challenge aesthetically to many potential viewers, and physically to almost all, unless that is you have access to the National Library of Scotland Moving Image Archive at Kelvin Hall in Glasgow, where a rather poor VHS copy is available. The film's IMDb entry is incomplete and inaccurate. The film was, however, screened at the EIFF from where it received a three-line review in *The Herald*, with William Russell harshly decrying the acting and the script ('which, when it is not unspeakable, is highfalutin rubbish'), but recognising that for all its weaknesses *3* is 'visually astonishing'.

3 is either a straightforward love story, behind which lies an art film, or an art film hiding within it a straightforward love story – which option you pick may say something about your taste in film. It is not entirely successful, its ambition outstripping the result, and is hampered by inexperienced actors. An opening sequence, set on the shore where Carl wakes up, shows a primitive society engaged in ritualistic dance, celebrating birth and growth (carrying echoes of the 'dawn of man' sequence from *2001: A Space Odyssey*, Stanley Kubrick, 1968).

Throughout, Carl is troubled by magic-realist visions – he tells Sri, 'everywhere I go the places and the people are the same, but everything feels different... I'm getting confused' (a feeling some viewers may also experience). An 'Elder' who comes to Carl in visions warns him 'when a soul is alone it can easily be broken', telling him that two souls together are stronger. Having been haunted, prompted and pushed by the Elder, Carl declares his love for Sri, and they may be presumed to be together at the end.

3 never had any prospect of commercial success, although the very limited information available suggests it was made for a mere £40,000, but it did win one festival audience award.

AfterLife (2003) S+++

Directed by Alison Peebles
Screenplay by Andrea Gibb
Leading cast: Lindsay Duncan (May Brogan);
  Kevin McKidd (Kenny Brogan); Paula Sage
  (Roberta Brogan); James Laurenson (Professor
  Wilkinshaw); Shirley Henderson (Ruby)
Colour, 100 minutes, UK

Kenny, a journalist working in London, has the chance to secure a position with a major network in the US. In Scotland, his mother and sister Roberta, who has Down syndrome, need his help. Kenny is unreliable in his efforts, but in the face of his mother's diagnosis of terminal cancer, realigns his priorities.

Three Scottish films in three years were written by Andrea Gibb: *AfterLife*, **Dear Frankie**, and **Nina's Heavenly Delights** (a ten-year hiatus followed the latter, and her more recent work has been for TV, including five episodes of *Call the Midwife*, 2017–2021). All three films deal with fractured families and healing. In *AfterLife*, Kenny's father has died some time ago, his mother devotes herself full time to the care of Roberta, fatally neglecting her own health in the process, and Kenny is largely absent, and unreliable when present (his mantra being 'I'll just be two minutes'). **Dear Frankie** is the best of the three.

AfterLife tees up a debate on assisted suicide and euthanasia (the AfterLife of the title is a barely disguised proxy for Dignitas) but, even though May chooses to die by suicide rather than painfully by cancer, intending (and failing) to euthanise Roberta at the same time, and a running thread sees Kenny securing an interview with the controversial Professor Wilkinshaw, who advocates for assisted suicide, the film barely scratches the surface of the issue. After a screening at the London Film Festival, Khalid M Ali in the *British Medical Journal* praised *AfterLife* for making 'astute, yet unsentimental observations about the doctor-patient relationship', but his focus was on the relationship between May and her GP, and between them suicide is not mentioned.

At heart, *AfterLife* is a conventional heart-warming tale (with too many echoes of *Rain Man*, Barry Levinson, 1988) of Kenny's growth, and Roberta's growing independence. This was sufficient to secure the audience award at the EIFF in 2003.

By far the best thing in the film is the performance of Paula Sage, a Scottish actor with Down syndrome, who also appeared in *The Party's Just Beginning*.

American Cousins (2003) S+++ T100

Directed by Don Coutts
Screenplay by Sergio Casci
Leading cast: Danni Nucci (Gino); Shirley
 Henderson (Alice); Gerald Lepkowski
 (Roberto); Russell Hunter (Nonno); Dan
 Hedaya (Settimo); Stephen Graham (Henry);
 Russell Hunter (Nonno)
Colour, 115 minutes, UK

Glaswegian/Italian café owners, Roberto and his grandfather Nonno, become involved with the American offshoot of their family, who are gangsters. Mayhem ensues, leading to a satisfactory conclusion.

American Cousins is a delightful film which crosses genre boundaries, taking a surprisingly breezy approach to crime. As in *Unleashed*, Glasgow becomes home to violence perpetrated by cosmopolitan criminals, but much more is made of the city, its culture, and its history. This Glasgow is a vibrant community, built in part by immigrants. Roberto's grandfather and his brother drew lots to see who would emigrate to Scotland, and who to the US; whoever made the most money would later be joined by the other, but the war and families intervened. When the American Gino says that, had the lots been drawn differently, he would be in Glasgow,

Roberto points out that he now is, and at the film's end he stays.

In what David Martin-Jones described as a 'savvy marketing move' (*Scotland: Global Cinema*, 2009) the promotion for *American Cousins* emphasised romance over violence. In this respect at least, the film is predictable; there is no doubt that by the end Alice, the café's waitress, and Roberto will be together, even though she is briefly tempted by the prospect of moving to America with Gino. However, the journey to this end is an entertaining one.

In *Variety* Eddie Cockrell wrote that Coutts 'has captured some Bill Forsyth magic in *American Cousins*, a sly and self-assured dramatic comedy.' Edward Lawrenson in *S&S* wrote, 'if *American Cousins* never quite manages the effortless whimsy of Forsyth (forgetting, perhaps, the darker edge present in the best of his work)... the movie has its share of low-key pleasures. This is in large part thanks to the relaxed performances of the cast.'

Don Coutts is a Scottish filmmaker, with extensive TV credits, including the TV series *Katie Morag* (2013–2015); *American Cousins* is his only fiction feature film as director; he also directed the documentary *Heading West: A Story About a Band Called Shooglenifty*. Shirley Henderson, perhaps still most memorably Moaning Myrtle in *Harry Potter and the Chamber of Secrets* (Chris Columbus, 2002) and *Harry Potter and the Goblet of Fire* (Mike Newell, 2005), also appears in, amongst others, *Trainspotting, Wilbur (Wants to Kill Himself), Filth* and *T2: Trainspotting*. She also plays the role of

Vincent D'Onofrio's sister in *Salt on Our Skin*† (aka *Desire*) (Andrew Birkin, 1992), which has significant scenes set in Scotland, amounting to about one-fifth of the film's running time.

The Devil's Tattoo (aka *Ghost Rig*) (2003)

Directed by Julian Kean
Screenplay by Sally Charlton, Graeme Clapperton, Bill Dale and Julian Kean
Leading cast: Noel Fitzpatrick (Crawford); Jamie Bamber (Tom)
Colour, 90 minutes, UK

Seven environmental activists occupy an abandoned oilrig due to be scuppered. They encounter a supernatural entity and are, serially, killed; one survives.

The Devil's Tattoo is only marginally Scottish. The first clue as to its location occurs in the opening production credits which include Scottish Screen. The next does not occur until 50 minutes in, when found footage (*The Blair Witch Project*, Daniel Myrick and Eduardo Sánchez, 1999, has a lot to answer for) reveals that the original oil rig crew had strong Scottish accents. The film features Rory McCann, who had completed season two of TV's Glasgow-based *The Book Group* (2002–2003) when *The Devil's Tattoo* was shot. He is now much better known as Sandor Clegane ('The Hound') in *Game of Thrones* (2011–2019). He is the first crew member to be despatched. English actor

Jamie Bamber found fame more quickly; shortly after this nonsense was shot, he moved to the role of Lee Adama ('Apollo') in the excellent *Battlestar Galactica* reboot (2003–2009).

Notwithstanding its four script writers, nothing about *The Devil's Tattoo* is ambitious. It draws from *Alien* (Ridley Scott, 1979 – one shot is a direct *Alien* rip-off), and more closely from *The Thing* (John Carpenter, 1982), but while the key plot premise is original, not enough is made of this until the very end, and the film has none of the suspense or terror of its more illustrious progenitors. The special effects, such as they are, hint at a low budget.

Man Dancin' (2003)   S+++

Directed by Norman Stone
Screenplay by Sergio Casci
Leading cast: Alex Ferns (Jimmy Kerrigan); Tom Georgeson (Father Gabriel Flynn); James Cosmo (Donnie McClone); Kenneth Cranham (DI Pancho Villers)
Colour, 113 minutes, UK

Glasgow: hard man Jimmy Kerrigan attempts to go straight after serving a nine-year prison sentence. Required to take anger management classes led by Father Flynn, he takes part in the church passion play; life mirrors art.

In *The Scotsman*, director Norman Stone described *Man Dancin'* as 'a film of hope and humour', noting that 'Glasgow has taken a big step forward since the 1960s, and the even darker period before that'; he was not looking to make a film to stand alongside *A Sense of Freedom* or *The Silent Scream*. Screenwriter Casci had previously written another unconventional Glasgow-set gangster film, **American Cousins**, for which he was both a BAFTA nominee and a BAFTA Scotland winner. Unlike the earlier film, however, the thematically more ambitious *Man Dancin'* struggles to blend two different approaches.

Variety reported that *Man Dancin'* was shot on 16mm and then blown up to 35mm, giving the film its grainy look. This, coupled with Mike Fox's cinematography, provides the Glasgow-set film with a gritty feel, which is betrayed as the story moves, somewhat clunkily, from a standard gangster-going-straight plot to something more allegorical. Andy Richard in *S&S* took this to be a strength: 'What could easily have been a predictable slice of hardboiled Glasgow noir turns out to be a quirky take on the "putting on a show" sub-genre – only with the Clydeside mafia to contend with rather than sprained ankles.' My view is closer to that of Derek Elley, who noted that the film's final act was 'phony and borderline silly'.

Uncredited on IMDb, there are cameo roles in the film for both Sally Magnussen (Stone's wife), and artist Peter Howson. The film gave Ferns his first feature lead. The Lennoxtown-born actor had appeared in only one film, but his casting guaranteed publicity; he was well known, having played wife-beater Trevor in over 100 episodes of *EastEnders* (2000–2002). He received the Best Actor award at the

Cherbourg Film Festival. *Man Dancin'* received its premiere in Glasgow (Stone wrote that he was surprised to see Kris Kristofferson in attendance) but was not successful on release in the UK.

Skagerrak (2003)   S++

Directed by Søren Kragh-Jacobsen
Screenplay by Anders Thomas Jensen and Søren Kragh-Jacobsen
Leading cast: Iben Hjejle (Marie); Bronagh Gallagher (Sophie); James Cosmo (Robert); Scott Handy (Roman); Helen Baxendale (Stella); Martin Henderson (Ian/Ken)
Colour, 104 minutes, English/Danish, Denmark/Sweden/UK/Spain/German/France/Switzerland

Marie and Sophie arrive by boat in Peterhead. On a night out their money is stolen. Marie agrees to act as a surrogate mother, for £40,000. Sophie dies in a car crash. Marie goes to Glasgow to find Sophie's boyfriend, but he is already dead, and she becomes embroiled in a scheme by his ex-employees to relieve her of her money. A complicated chain of events ends with her giving birth. Four years later she lives with two of the men she met in Glasgow, and with three children.

Before directing *Skagerrak*, which is a mess of a film, Denmark's Søren Kragh-Jacobsen had made the much more highly regarded *Mifune* (*Mifunes sidste sang*, 1999), which also starred Iben Hjejle, who received an Outstanding Young Actress honourable mention for the role at the Berlin Film

Iben Hjejle

Festival. Outside of Denmark, Hjejle is best known for her role as John Cusack's girlfriend (leaving him early on) in *High Fidelity* (Stephen Frears, 2000). Hjejle, and co-star Bronagh Gallagher, are the only highlights of *Skagerrak*, which tries to do a lot, but is unable to deliver because the script is terrible.

Reviewing the film on release in *FILM-DIENST*, Claus Löser could not contain his frustration: 'boredom quickly sets in, and the hectic hustle and bustle on the screen leaves the viewer completely cold… Unbelievable characters and hair-raising events are sold as fairytale narratives that lack any hint of subtext and real metaphysics'. It is clear Kragh-Jacobsen *was* trying to tap into something greater

than a simple story about two young women adrift, one of whom makes money through surrogacy. If nothing else, Marie's name is a giveaway: we *are* meant to draw the obvious connection. This is reinforced by the *three* mechanics with whom she spends time in Glasgow, although they don't come bearing gifts. All elements of fable are overwhelmed in the chaos and utterly improbable coincidences which (very poorly) tie the characters together. Or, as Gunnar Rehlin put it in *Variety*, 'despite stellar performances [the] plot-heavy pic's story stretches credulity and signals the outcome well before it should'.

In 2002 *Variety* carried a feature on Scandinavian filmmaking, which was increasingly relying on an English-language market, noting that several of the original signatories of the Dogma manifesto, including Kragh-Jacobsen, had gone on to make films in English, with bigger budgets than would be available for Danish or Swedish language productions. Peter Aalbaek Jensen, the CEO of Zentropa Entertainment, the production company behind *Skagerrak* and *Wilbur (Wants to Kill Himself)*, said: 'It is impossible to package a film with a budget exceeding $3 million if you insist on shooting it with Danish dialogue. It takes international funding, and foreign financiers are not placing their money in a Danish-language film'. It was always intended that *Skagerrak* be set in Scotland and shot in English, but the international co-production (which included the participation of the BBC, Scottish Screen, and the Glasgow Film Office) meant that the budget could be pushed to $4m.

The decision to set the action in Scotland was driven, said Kragh-Jacobsen, by the need to place the action outside Denmark, 'where the girl could be away from protective Danish society. Setting [the film] in Denmark would make the drama of the story impossible' (quoted by Jonathan Murray in *The New Scottish Cinema*). Leaving aside the fact that the drama remains implausible even when in Scotland, the approach then taken is, as is all too often the case, simply to position Scotland as 'the other'. As Murray notes, '*Skagerrak* needs only its opening five minutes to make crystal-clear its central characters' lack of personal interest in Scotland', and the film is not 'a work substantively "about"

Scotland'. It is noteworthy that the central three characters are not Scottish. As an exemplar of the Dogmac output, *Skagerrak* is of some interest. It is of little value as entertainment.

The Ticking Man (2003) S+++

Directed by Steven Lewis Simpson
Screenplay by Steven Lewis Simpson
Leading cast: Alan McCafferty (Peter); Harriet Hunter (Marianne); Ian Hanmore (Hitman); Gavin Marshall (Barry); David Wilde (North)
Colour, 85 minutes, UK

Marianne and Peter witness the execution of a drug dealer. North hires the Hitman to kill the witnesses, but not knowing who they are, he must kill everyone in their village and has 28 minutes in which to do this before the police can arrive.

This west coast-set thriller (shot in various Scottish locations, with a final chase and shoot-out in Slains Castle), is almost a one-man film: Scottish-born Simpson wrote, directed, produced and edited *The Ticking Man*. The premise is a good one, and in the right hands this could have been an exciting, tight film. Ideally of course it would be 28 minutes long. It is – if you set the playback speed to 3.01x. It's marginally better that way. *The Ticking Man* is over-directed, and the premise is wasted. This is how one 150-second scene is constructed: (1) shot of the roof of a dramatically lit brick tunnel. North stands in the middle, motionless, facing one end of the tunnel which is flooded with bright light; (2) his image dissolves into a close-up; (3) the hitman appears walking through the light; (4) cut to a tighter close-up of North; (5) cut back to the hitman, who in a series of dissolves slowly emerges; (6) North in close-up; (7) the hitman in medium shot; (8) North in tighter close-up, his head given a halo by yellow sodium light; (9) the hitman in close-up; (10) North, medium shot, throws an envelope to the hitman; (11) names and numbers are shown in extreme close-up; (12) a bag of money is passed over; (13) the hitman turns and walks away, going out of shot as the focus remains on North, now in long-shot; (14) North kneels down, framed in the light behind him; (15) the image shrinks on the screen, losing focus and becoming one panel of five, of different aspect ratios, all of which are at first out of focus; (16) in one of these the hitman stands beside a police station, and starts his stopwatch. This is exhausting stuff and unnecessarily gimmicky. Later in the film we get to the point where seven split screens are employed. Simpson described the film as 'Terminator meets a Western and a morality tale'. It isn't.

There are few contemporaneous reviews of the film. *Variety* took the following line: 'A decent suspense concept grows more formulaic via hyperbolic execution... writer-helmer Steven Lewis Simpson piles on split-screen effects that distract from the overall tension.' *The Ticking Man* is not a wholly bad film; it is simply a good idea which could have been far better developed. This was not easy to track down. I obtained a German DVD (*28 Minuten bis zum Tod* – '28 Minutes to Death'), with an English-language soundtrack.

Young Adam (2003) S+++ T12

Directed by David Mackenzie
Screenplay by David Mackenzie
Leading cast: Ewan MacGregor (Joe Taylor); Tilda Swinton (Ella Gault); Peter Mullan (Les Gault); Emily Mortimer (Cathie Dimly); Jack McElhone (Jim Gault); Therese Bradley (Gwen)
Colour, 98 minutes, UK

Glasgow: the mid-1950s. Joe, who is trying to write a novel, and Cathie move in together. Joe leaves, telling Cathie he is heading to China. Instead, he becomes a bargee on the Clyde, working with Les, and begins a torrid affair with Ella, Les's wife. Later Joe and Cathie meet in Glasgow and have sex; she becomes pregnant, and after he rejects her, slips and drowns in the Clyde. Her body is recovered, and an innocent man convicted of her murder.

Ewan McGregor and Emily Mortimer in happier times

A web of connections runs through *Young Adam* into Scottish cinema. Director Mackenzie has helmed multiple Scottish films, including *Hallam Foe* and *Outlaw King*. McGregor is in *Shallow Grave, Trainspotting, T2: Trainspotting* and *Perfect Sense* (also directed by Mackenzie). Bradley is in five further films in this book (including *Filth* and *Calibre*), while Mullan has played a central role in Scottish film as both actor and director. McElhone and Mortimer were both in *Dear Frankie. Young Adam* is also one of only two films in this book to feature Swinton, who has Scottish roots, is strongly associated with Scotland, and is one of the finest screen actors working today. *Young Adam* won her the Best Actress award at the BAFTA Scotland Awards in 2004 – contributing to the 70+ other awards she holds. *Young Adam* itself won the award for Best Film, and netted Mackenzie Best Director, and McGregor Best Actor. The London Critics Film Circle mirrored this, giving Mackenzie the Best Newcomer award, along with awards for Swinton, McGregor and the film.

Young Adam is based on the 1954 novel of the same name by Glaswegian author Alexander Trocchi, who had a remarkable and very colourful career, based in part in Paris – where, as editor of the literary journal *Merlin* he published work by some of the leading writers of the 20th century (*his* life would make for a good biopic). There is in fact something very *un*British about the story, and indeed the film. Although Trocchi is often labelled a British Beat writer, there is perhaps more of the French than the American about *Young Adam*. One could easily imagine this being written by authors with whom Trocchi would have empathised, Jean

The incomparable Tilda Swinton

Paul Sartre, Albert Camus, or Jean Genet (or even perhaps Émile Zola – there are definitely shades of *Thérèse Raquin*, 1868) and directed by one of the grittier *nouvelle vague* directors (there are echoes here of Jean Vigo's 1934 classic *L'Atalante*). Trocchi died at the age of 58 in 1984. His work benefited from a resurgence of interest after his death.

It is straightforward to rearrange events such that the story appears simple and linear: the film's structure is complex, not obscure. Joe's life on the barge, and his life off it, are separate but interconnecting strands. His story with Cathie is told largely in flashback, and in both strands we cannot be certain that we are seeing events linearly. This however is *not* baroque and ornate simply for its own sake. There is a power to the fractured narrative. This is particularly the case as the audience only slowly realises that Joe's reactions to finding Cathie's corpse are not simply those to a 'random' death, but to the death of someone who loved him and was carrying his child. It is not clear that he feels guilt, and it is very easy to dislike Joe, although to all the film's women he seems irresistible. He is a *poseur* (or perhaps more generously a *flâneur*), trying and failing to write a novel like none written before, using the excuse of finishing one of his ever-present paperbacks as the cover for his affair with Les's wife, and pretentiously telling Cathie, when she finds him still in Glasgow: 'I *have* gone away. I shed my old skin and merged into the folk'.

The soundtrack, composed by the Talking Heads' David Byrne (who won an Oscar for his work on *The Last Emperor*, Bernardo Bertolucci, 1987), is haunting and lovely. The canal scenes show aspects of Scotland rarely seen on film.

Blinded (2004)   S+++

Directed by Eleanor Yule
Screenplay by Eleanor Yule
Leading cast: Peter Mullan (Francis Black);
  Anders W Berthelsen (Mike Hammershoi);
  Jodhi May (Rachel Black); Samantha Bond
  (Caroline Lamar); Phyllida Law (Bella Black)
Colour, 93 minutes, UK

The Borders: Danish hitchhiker Mike is offered work at the Blacks' farm, where Francis, blinded in a car accident, lives with his wife Rachel and his mother. Mike and Rachel form an attachment, and Francis dies.

In May 2003, *The Scotsman* reported that Mullan was working with Jill Daley, a young woman who became blind at the age of 18, to gain insight into life without sight after a sudden event: Mullan had taken Daley to a screening of *Young Adam* (with which *Blinded* has elements in common)

and was heard describing in some detail its more graphic scenes to her. *Blinded*, made on a budget of £350,000 flowing from an innovative partnership between Scottish Screen, STV and Grampian TV and private investors was premiered the following year, at the Moscow Film Festival, but did not secure a limited UK release until September 2005 (demonstrating the difficulty in securing distribution deals for indigenous Scottish productions).

Yule, who was nominated Best First-time Director at the 2004 BAFTA Scotland Awards (losing out to Bernard MacLaverty for the short, *Bye Child*, 2003), was paid just £5,000 for her work on *Blinded*, leading Mullan to call out the pay disparities between Scotland and England. With a small cast, and a constrained location (which is beautifully photographed by Jerry Kelly and Michael Miles), the film is as much thriller as melodrama; the investigation into Francis' death reveals dark secrets.

The limited scope of *Blinded* did however give rise to criticism: in *Time Out* Dave Calhoun admired the acting but wondered whether the 'mildly interesting rural Scottish thriller... would be better suited to the small screen'. As Steve Rose noted in *The Guardian*, *Blinded* is 'not a million miles away from *Young Adam*: sex and death in an overcast Scottish microcosm'. But *Blinded* does not have the depth of *Young Adam* and its narrow world is far less convincing. For Rose, once Mullan disappears from the film, 'things fall apart in every sense'.

Dear Frankie (2004) S++ T100

Directed by Shona Auerbach
Screenplay by Andrea Gibb
Leading cast: Emily Mortimer (Lizzie); Jack
  McElhone (Frankie); Mary Riggans (Nell);
  Sharon Small (Marie); Gerard Butler (the
  stranger)
Colour, 105 minutes, UK

Emily Mortimer, Jack McElhone and Gerard
Butler form an ersatz family

*'Port Howat', near Glasgow: Lizzie hires a
stranger to pretend to be the father of her
deaf son, Frankie, who believes his dad is
a seaman. His father is, in fact, an abuser
who is the cause of Frankie's deafness. The
stranger and Frankie bond.*

Dear Frankie is a sensitive and clever film,
beautifully made, with a lean script, raising
important questions about families and
their constitution. It was Shona Auerbach's
first feature film and received very positive
critical responses (from Richard Roeper: 'it's
a terrific film'), giving Aeurbach a career-
start which many directors would dream of.
It is surprising that she has made only one
film since, the well-received *Rudy* (2023).

Like any snapshot of life, much in *Dear
Frankie* is left open; information is slowly
revealed through the natural course of
events. It takes time for us to know why
Lizzie is no longer with David, and why
this nuclear family is constituted as it is.
Lizzie exists to protect Frankie, and the
cost is constant moves, social isolation,
and the maintenance by Lizzie of a lie.
This poses the question: which is better,
a real relationship with a bad father, or a
fake relationship with a good one? The
stranger is never named. It's not that he's
an enigmatic man of mystery, but rather
that, at least in the short time he is in
Frankie and Lizzie's life, he is the perfect
man – a blank canvas onto which Frankie
can project an ideal of fatherhood. Lizzie's
friend, Marie, reveals at the end that the
stranger is her brother, offering hope
perhaps to viewers of an optimistic bent
that the relationships formed over the two
days may be continued.

I am unreasonably suspicious of Gerard
Butler's performances and films, but he is
rather good at being a blank canvas. He
was born and partly raised in Paisley, and
before becoming a full-time actor he read
law at Glasgow University. He would
have felt at home for the Glasgow-based
shoot of *Dear Frankie*, which was made
after *One More Kiss*† (Vadim Jean, 1999
– this is set in England, not Scotland),
and before Zach Snyder catapulted him
to the B+ list with the nonsense which
was *300* (2006). Mortimer is *always*
watchable, and the relationship with her
mother Nell, who chain-smokes her way
through life, is vibrant and convincing.

Scottish veteran Riggans had her first credit in 1954, her last in 2006. As Frankie, McElhone is excellent; he was nominated for the Scottish BAFTA for Best First-Time Performance. He also appears in *Young Adam* and *Mrs Brown*.

Devil's Gate (2004)　　S++

Directed by Stuart St Paul
Screenplay by Stuart St Paul and Trevor Todd
Leading cast: Laura Fraser (Rachael); Callum Blue (Rafe); Luke Aikman (Matt); Tom Bell (Jake)
Colour, 95 minutes, UK

Shetland: Jake, Rachael's father, is found injured and ill by island-hopper Matt. Ex-boyfriend Rafe calls Rachael home from her job as a nurse in a Scottish mainland hospital. She intends to stay for only one night, but probes the disappearance of her mother when she was a child, and stays longer. Rachael rejects Rafe's advances and her closeness to Matt invites his envy. Tragedy and dark secrets come to the fore.

Devil's Gate was the first film to be shot in Shetland since *The Edge of the World* in 1936. Logistically there are easier Scottish islands on which to make a movie (but see *Moon Dogs* and *Sacrifice*). That this is true did not prevent Scottish Screen from being strongly criticised when, in a letter rejecting a funding application, it stated: 'There was general bafflement as to why a film which could be shot anywhere should choose to relocate to one of the most inhospitable parts of the UK at one of the most difficult times of the year'. The local MSP promised to take matters up with ministers.

There is no clear reason why the story told in *Devil's Gate* needs to be set in Shetland (the director first intended to make it in the Australian outback), and Glasgow-born Laura Fraser (also in *Nina's Heavenly Delights* and *Beats*) expressed concern that 'the film wasn't set anywhere, which is always worrying'; but a great many stories can be relocated without undue sacrifice (it was originally intended that the Glasgow-set *Postmortem* be set in San Francisco). And here Shetland has something to bring to the table: stunning scenery, remoteness, and a community in which there are many secrets, yet paradoxically everyone knows everyone else's business.

Absent the support sought from Scottish Screen, work went ahead, and *Devil's Gate* became the first film to premiere in Shetland, at the Garrison Theatre in Lerwick. Fraser said later that she was criticised by director St Paul for complaining about the incessant horizontal rain during the shoot and admitted that *Devil's Gate* 'wasn't the best movie ever made.' The Glasgow *Evening Times*' critic agreed with Fraser about the film's quality – noting that 'she does her best but really deserves better than this'. The great twist towards the film's end should surprise no one, and the ludicrous denouement jarringly and disjointedly tilts the tone towards the ridiculous.

In a Man's World (2004)   S+++

Directed by Lee Hutcheon
Screenplay by Lee Hutcheon
Leading cast: Niko Hutcheon (Malki McCann);
   Connor Scully (Jinxsy); Robert McAlpine
   (Mincy); Callum Leiper (Franky); Jimmy Lynch
   (Carmell)
Colour, 75 minutes, UK

*Aberdeen: Malki and his friends, just
entering their teens, are 'four hungry
neighbourhood kids just looking for a
quick pound'. They're drawn into a life of
crime, bringing with it tragic consequences.*

Aberdonian Hutcheon began shooting
films on Super 8mm as a boy, became a
graphic designer, and made his first listed
short film in his mid-20s (*Vendetta*, 1999).
He succeeded in placing a script with
Columbia-Tristar, but that project was
axed, before making this, his first feature,
with a largely unpaid amateur cast (his
son, Nico, and four friends taking the
leads), saying later 'the street kids I used
in the film were absolutely tremendous'.
After the film picked up the Best Feature-
Length Drama award at the New York
International Independent Film and Video
Festival in 2004 distributors expressed
interest, but ultimately the film failed to
secure distribution and was released only
on DVD.

   In a Man's World's laudable ambition
is evident, but the lack of experience and
resource is on display. Shooting in the
Woodside, Tillydrone and Northfield
areas of Aberdeen endows the film with
some authenticity, but a heavy reliance on
voice-over (the story is told by an adult
Malki looking back on a less than rosy
childhood) plasters over deficiencies in
cinematic storytelling; shot before advances
in video technologies radically impacted
filmmaking, a tight, but uncinematic 4:3
aspect ratio is employed. While this creates
a sense of oppression and verisimilitude, it
would undoubtedly have reduced the film's
commercial appeal.

   Hutcheon also directed *The Clan* (2009)
and *My Brother's Keeper* (2012) (at the
time of writing, his last film), both of which
appear to satisfy the criteria for entry
in this book, save for the fact that I was
unable to locate copies. He appears as an
actor in **Attack of the Herbals**.

One Last Chance (2004)   S+++

Directed by Stewart Svaasand
Screenplay by Stewart Svaasand
Leading cast: Kevin McKidd (Seany); Iain
   Robertson (Nellie); Jamie Sives (Fitz)
Colour, 96 minutes, Norway/UK

*'Tullybridge', in the Highlands, is a place
where nothing happens, until, that is,
Fitz believes he has found a gold nugget
clutched in the hands of a dead prospector.
Together with friends Nellie and Seany,
plans are made and gangsters are
contended with.*

Having started out working as a
mechanical fitter in the oil industry,
while being obsessed with cinema,

Edinburgh-born Svaasand retrained by way of night school and a film production course, then worked as a camera assistant, before his script for *One Last Chance* was optioned in 1998; it took nearly six years to move from that point to completion of this slender Scottish comedy, with shades of Bill Forsyth.

On the occasion of *OLC*'s premiere in March 2004, Svaasand was quoted by *The Herald* as saying, 'I think black comedy is really part of the Scottish psyche. Nobody laughs harder than the Scottish if someone is having a bad time and I didn't have to go very far to find that inspiration because I think we're all guilty of that.' The comedy here could be blacker and sharper (as **One Day Removals** achieves) and, as the *Morning Star*'s reviewer put it, the film relies on 'stock cliches about inept criminals and people trying to escape from their miserable small-town existence.' A similar view was reached by *Time Out*'s Wally Hammond, who flagged the 'lame comedic convention', while accepting the film 'oozes warmth for its characters and basks in parochial pride'.

OLC was shot in Tomintoul and around Glasgow, and features James Cosmo playing a vicious gangster (just as he had done in **In a Man's World**), Dougray Scott and Brian Pettifer.

The Rocket Post (2004)   S++

Directed by Stephen Whittaker
Screenplay by James MacInnes and William Morrissey
Leading cast: Ulrich Thomsen (Gerhard Zucher); Shauna Macdonald (Catriona Mackay); Gary Lewis (Jimmy Roach); Eddie Marsan (Heinz Dombrowsky)
Colour, 112 minutes, UK

1938: Europe heads towards war and Zucher, a German rocket scientist, is detained on the Isle of Scarp, Scotland. He is instrumental in developing a rocket used to deliver post between islands, while falling in love. He returns to Germany when his family is arrested and is executed.

Plans for *The Rocket Post* started grandiosely. Producer Mark Shorrock intended to secure stars of the stature of Sean Connery, or Harvey Keitel. Albert Finney turned the film down, because, Shorrock said, he was not willing to travel to the Outer Hebrides. Shorrock talked of the film as a potential Oscar winner. None of this came to pass. The lead actor is the Dane Ulrich Thomsen, who plays the German scientist on whose exploits the film is (very loosely) based, and the film won only one award, the Grand Prize at the Stony Brook Film Festival (nope, me neither). The production was rocked when, only a few days before shooting was due to begin, the American owner of Scarp refused permission to film, necessitating a relocation to neighbouring Hebridean island Taransay, and a doubling of the budget to £10m. In 2001, *The Scotsman*'s James Rampton visited the set: 'The production has the precision and scale of a major military operation. Fifty builders spent four weeks on Taransay constructing a facsimile of a 1930s Highland village complete with jetty and church hall... it was worth it: the results are breathtakingly convincing.' The 'breathtakingly convincing' here refers to the replica village, not the film.

As critics pointed out, *TRP* plays fast and loose with history, notwithstanding the 'based on a true story' tag. In the real world, Zucher was deported to Germany by the British and served in the Luftwaffe. The further the film departs from some semblance of veracity, the worse it gets, with absurdity entering after the 80-minute mark. The result is that a decent cast and a great location have been wasted.

TRP received its premiere in the 'Screen Machine', a mobile cinema, on Harris. Reviews were poor; the film was not shown in a cinema in the UK again until four years later, for the first two nights of the newly opened cinema at Stornoway's An Lanntair Arts Centre. Anna Smith reviewed the film twice. In *S&S* she wrote '*The Rocket Post* aims to fit the [*Whisky Galore!*] mould but falls slightly short of the mark.' In *Empire*, she gave the film two stars (a 'sleepy pre-World War II drama'). For the BBC, Stella Papamichael too was underwhelmed: 'the business of building the rocket... feels incidental. The stakes only get upped once Hitler issues the order for Zucher to return to the motherland with his research... that also means taking a sharp left turn into melodrama.'

Festival (2005)   S++

Directed by Annie Griffin
Screenplay by Annie Griffin
Leading cast: Chris O'Dowd (Tommy O'Dwyer); Billy Carter (Conor Kelly); Stephen Mangan (Sean Sullivan); Lyndsey Marshall (Faith Myers); Daniela Nardini (Joan Gerard); Raquel Cassidy (Petra Loewenberg); Lucy Punch (Nicky Romanowski)
Colour, 107 minutes, UK

Various characters and stories intersect at the Edinburgh Festival.

The BFI website is not alone in drawing a comparison between *Festival* and Robert Altman's masterpiece *Nashville* (1975). Critic Michael Ferraro, for example, wrote that '*Festival* is like the *Nashville* of the fringe scene; a multi-character exercise that shows writer/director Annie Griffin's wonderful ability to juggle a large cast with an enjoyable story and constant laughs.' It is an obvious comparison to make, but the comparison does a disservice to both films and puts an impossible burden on *Festival*. *Nashville* is in part about 'the state of the Union' and stands in for something larger than itself; *Festival* is about the Edinburgh Festival (the focus is on the Fringe) and some of those involved with it and makes no claims to greater ambition. With a strong cast, a sharp script and an on-location shoot, *Festival* authentically captures the chaos of Edinburgh in August. At the very least, writer/director Annie Griffin knew what she was writing about. Having moved to Scotland from her native America, she had already had one 'Scottish' success with her TV series, Glasgow-set *The Book Group* (2002–2003), and had performed at Edinburgh.

The film is unusual in being an 18-rated comedy. Interviewed for *Future Movies*, Griffin explained that pressures were brought to bear by the film's investors: 'we had a really strong producer [Chris Young], who said we are making an 18-certificate film with 16 principal characters, and we're not getting rid of any storylines and we're not getting rid of the sex scenes – those were the big arguments.' More unusual than the 18-rating however is the fact that there are few happy endings here, and in the most disconcerting storyline there is death. Griffin said: 'Life is like that. You can be having a really funny day and then watch someone get hit by a car.' This makes the film more unsettling than a straight comedy, and less laugh-a-minute, but more satisfying.

Happy Go Lovely is also set at the festival, and *Long Shot* is set during EIFF.

GamerZ (2005)   S+++ T100

Directed by Robbie Fraser
Screenplay by Robbie Fraser
Leading cast: Ross Finbow (Ralph); Danielle
   Stewart (Marlyn); Johnny Austin (Davy); Ross
   Sutherland (Hank); James Young (Lennie)
Colour, 101 minutes, UK

At Glasgow University Ralph takes over the fantasy gaming society in a ruthless coup, and falls in lust with beautiful goth Marlyn. Lennie, an unwelcome acquaintance from Ralph's past, joins the games, and sparks fly between he and Marlyn. Events take a dark turn...

Unreasonably, my heart sank when *GamerZ* came to my attention. I'm not a gamer; everything I know about this world comes from watching *The Big Bang Theory* (2007–2019). That being said, I am unreasonably addicted to *Lord of the Rings*, something I share in common with minor drug dealer Lennie. However, watching *GamerZ* was one of the unexpected pleasures in writing this book. The film was funded under the same partnership arrangement between Screen Scotland, STV and Grampian TV which gave rise to *Blinded*: this may be a first film from Glaswegian director Fraser (who has become an accomplished documentarian – see *Final Ascent: The Legend of Hamish MacInnes* and *Hamish*), made with an inexperienced cast, and on a micro-budget, but it is *not* amateurish.

GamerZ premiered at the 63rd World Science Fiction Convention, which was held at Glasgow's SECC in 2005, and received strong reviews, including from Amy Simmons in *S&S*: 'simultaneously charming, idiotic and genuinely witty... Propelled by a buoyant script, laced with quickfire Glaswegian patter'. *GamerZ* is peppered with jokes, right down to ersatz posters displayed at Freshers Week ('The Crustacean Retrieval Society: Don't be selfish – save a shellfish'). Animated sequences following the world of the game by Konstantinos Koutsoliotas and Elizabeth Schuch are excellent (reportedly inspired by Ralph Bakshi's *The Lord of the Rings*, 1978). It is a great shame that after multiple festival screenings *GamerZ* was not able to secure a distribution deal; DVDs are available.

Man to Man (2005) S++

Directed by Régis Wargnier
Screenplay by Michel Fessler and Fred Fougea
Leading cast: Joseph Fiennes (Jamie Dodd);
  Kristin Scott Thomas (Elena van den Ende);
  Iain Glen (Alexander Auchinleck); Hugh
  Bonneville (Fraser McBride); Lomama Boseki
  (Toko); Cécile Bayiha (Likola)
Colour, 122 minutes, France/South Africa/UK

1870, Africa. Dodd captures two pygmies, Toko and Likola, and brings them to Edinburgh as part of a cargo of 'wildlife' collected for den Ende, who supplies zoos. Dodd and his anthropologist friends, Auchinleck and McBride, believe they have discovered the missing link between great apes and humans, but Dodd comes to realise that the pygmies are as much human as he is.

Wargnier's 1992 French epic *Indochine* won the Oscar for Best Foreign Film; starring Catherine Deneuve, the film dealt with the French experience in Vietnam, emphasising – through a white lens – the ills of colonialism. *Man to Man*, Wargnier's first English-language film, similarly deals with issues arising out of colonialism, with the focus squarely on the unacknowledged racism underpinning scientific assumptions at the time, such that the film often makes for uncomfortable viewing. Early on, after

Joseph Fiennes and Lomama Boseki

Toko and Likola are brought to Scotland, where they are to be studied before being housed in a zoo, the staff in the stately home (Drummond Castle was used in the shoot) are told: 'Our guests are savages from the forests of Africa, very dangerous. They're also cannibals.' *Man to Man* spends a heavy two hours making the point that they are just as human (and as humane, if not more so) than their captors.

The cast is exceptional (although French journal *Positif*'s reviewer wrote that Bonneville 'plunges into a madness that is too emotional on screen to be credible'), and little expense is spared in recreating late-19th-century Edinburgh and its world of classism, sexism, and scientific enquiry (the film was budgeted at $28m). But something here does not work; perhaps it is that the film is, notwithstanding its two hours, *too* short to contain all that Wargnier wants to throw at the audience. *The Hollywood Reporter*'s Kirk Honeycutt argued that the film 'falls between the camps of intriguing independent filmmaking and commercially calculated filmmaking', failing to deliver either to full satisfaction. Although it opened the 2005 Berlin Film Festival, *Man to Man* had very limited international distribution, and was not shown in the UK.

Night People (2005)   S+++

Directed by Adrian Mead
Screenplay by Jack Dickson and Adrian Mead
Leading cast: Katrina Bryan (Jane); Lily Waterton (Alison); Alan McCafferty (Stewart); Anthony Martin (David); Kellyanne Farquhar (Mary)
Colour, 95 minutes, UK

Edinburgh: a taxi driver with her young daughter in tow, a homeless teenager, a struggling father of two, a runaway and others get through the night.

Ten years before he directed *Night People*, Adrian Mead, who described himself in *The Herald* as 'more a writer than a director', worked as a nightclub bouncer in Edinburgh, storing up impressions and images which influenced this multi-strand film set over one night in the city. Made for just £300,000 with a shoot of 25 days, *Night People* was well received by those few who were able to watch it on release. It won the BAFTA Scotland audience award (beating the much more widely distributed *On a Clear Day*), along with the approval of Mark Cousins, who in the *Sunday Times* described it as 'a lushly photographed portrait of the night-time ecosystem of a modern city... a gleaming film of real power and insight'. Unfortunately, it struggled to secure a wide release, moving onto DVD after limited showings in Scotland.

The film deserved more. Sitting in the back of her mother's taxi, while her mother explains events in fairy tale terms (a female drug dealer is going to meet Prince Charming; cocaine is 'fairy powder'), Alison blends the images she sees into her own magical version of Edinburgh. As producer Clare Kerr said, there is a 'mystical fantasy element to the story and it is trying to show what the city might be like for people who are up and around at night while everyone else is asleep'. Largely forgotten and overlooked, *Night People* is a wee gem.

On a Clear Day (2005)   S++

Directed by Gaby Dellal
Screenplay by Alex Rose
Leading cast: Peter Mullan (Frank); Billy Boyd (Danny); Brenda Blethyn (Joan); Sean McGinley (Eddie); Benedict Wong (Chan); Ron Cook (Norman); Paul Ritter (Mad Bob)
Colour, 95 minutes, UK

Having been made redundant from his job in a Clyde shipyard, Frank sets out to swim the Channel, aided by a group of friends. Along the way he faces difficulties in his marriage, and the ghosts of his past.

On a Clear Day benefits from both a female director, and the star power of Mullan in the lead role (as does *Blinded*). It is also among a small minority of films in this book to foreground an actor who is not white. The film picked up the BAFTA Scotland awards for Best Film and Best Screenplay. A Best Supporting Actor award went to McGinley in

Peter Mullan, Sean McGinley, Billy Boyd and Benedict Wong take to the water

the *Irish* Film and Television Awards. The film is satisfyingly feelgood. At the start it is closer to Mike Leigh/Ken Loach territory, but in a somewhat awkward tonal shift it becomes clear we are swimming into happier waters.

Mullan's performance was singled out, even by many of the sizeable minority of critics who disliked the film. Thus, for example, in the *San Francisco Chronicle*, Ruthe Stein noted that '[o]ne thing Dellal did right, however, was to cast Mullan, who sinks into the role and acquits himself swimmingly'. *The Guardian's* Peter Bradshaw was sparer in his praise: Mullan gave a 'decent' performance in a 'derivative' and 'pat' film.

On a Clear Day is not without flaws. The writer and director struggle to tie together two strands: one about a man made redundant looking for a new role in life; the other about a man who still has not come to terms with the death of a young son, and as a result has a fractured relationship with the surviving sibling. For Stein, the root of the problem was that *On a Clear Day* was a first feature film, and that the inexperience of both director and screenwriter showed. Dellal was, in fact, making her second feature, although 2003's *The Ride* sank without trace. While the focus is on Mullan, the supporting cast is exceptionally strong. Blethyn came to the film with huge experience; Boyd had completed the *Lord of the Rings* trilogy and was beginning to show that he could play people, as well as a hobbit. Wong, who was born in Eccles, had a cv extending back to the early 1990s but was still relatively unknown when *On a Clear Day* was made. He is now very recognisable, having played a recurring role as Wong (that's not a mistake!) in the Marvel Cinematic Universe franchise. There is extensive location shooting in Glasgow; the swimming pool scenes were filmed at the Whitehill Swimming Pool on Onslow Drive.

Unleashed (aka *Danny the Dog*) (2005)   S+

Directed by Louis Leterrier
Screenplay by Luc Besson
Leading cast: Jet Li (Danny); Morgan Freeman (Sam); Bob Hoskins (Bart); Michael Jenn (Wyeth); Kerry Condon (Victoria)
Colour, 103 minutes, UK/France/US

In Glasgow, gangster Bart keeps Danny chained until his fighting skills are needed. Bart enters Danny into death matches, until Bart escapes, finding refuge with Sam and Victoria.

Unleashed, while set wholly in Glasgow, could be set in any large city in many countries. That we are in Glasgow is explicitly acknowledged: trying to habilitate Danny, Sam takes him shopping to the local Spar, telling him that 'Maddy runs the best supermarket in all of Glasgow'. It is therefore peculiar that *not once* in the film is a Glaswegian (or Scottish) accent heard – even from minor characters (Maddy, for example, is played by London-born Carol Ann Wilson). That *Unleashed* was filmed

Jet Li and Bob Hoskins

in Glasgow flows in part from support provided to the Franco-UK production by the Glasgow Film Office, and the assistance given by the local police. In the closing credits, which are almost exclusively in English, there is some delight to be found in the section thanking '*Strathclyde Police de Glasgow*', and '*La Ville de Glasgow*'.

There is also some delight to be found in the film, although the blend of scenes of intense theatrical violence – which largely consist of Jet Li despatching bad guys in well-choreographed fights (incorporating *wire fu*, popularised by Hong Kong filmmakers, including Li) – with a long central sequence of domestic life is not entirely successful. Hoskins, reprising the gangster role he first played in *The Long Good Friday* (John Mackenzie, 1980), has charisma aplenty, and makes a good sparring partner for Freeman, although they meet only once, as Freeman smashes a flowerpot on his head. Their arena and prize is Danny's soul. While there can be no doubt as to the outcome, the journey to it is entertaining enough.

French director Leterrier started his feature career with three films penned by Besson: *Unleashed* sits between *The Transporter* (2002), which was an unexpected smash hit, elevating Jason

Statham to the A-list, and *Transporter 2* (2005). He also directed the Edward Norton version of *The Incredible Hulk* (2008) and the ridiculously successful, and ridiculous, *Now You See Me* (2013), also starring Freeman. Really though, *Unleashed* belongs to Li *and* to Besson, a writer whose style can shine through more strongly than the director's.

Unleashed did not set the box office alight on release, but more than covered its reported $50m budget. Reviewers were largely positive.

Dood Eind (Dead End) (2006) S+

Directed by Erwin van den Eshof
Screenplay by Erwin van den Eshof
Leading cast: Everon Jackson Hooi (Chris);
    Anniek Pheifer (Barbara)
Colour, 90 minutes, Netherlands, Dutch/English

Seven friends from the Netherlands go on a camping trip in Scotland. Their van breaks down, and they seek refuge in an abandoned house in the woods. Then the 'horror' begins.

A Scottish-set Dutch horror (with some scenes in the Netherlands) with echoes of genre touchstones *The Texas Chainsaw Massacre* (Tobe Hooper, 1974) and *The Evil Dead* (Sam Raimi, 1981), serving up a few jump moments but the horror is weak, and the ending is pathetic. What's most remarkable is that this film won a couple of awards, including one from LA's annual Screamfest. The disjunct between the script

and the actual location is disconcerting, and it is not clear why the filmmakers were wedded to this location. The film was shot in Overveen and Amersfoort in the Netherlands and, as Phil van Tongeren put it in *PreView*, 'it is never credible that we are looking at a house from the eighteenth century situated in Scotland'.

The Flying Scotsman (2006) S+++

Directed by Douglas Mackinnon
Screenplay by John Brown, Simon Rose and
    Declan Hughes
Leading cast: Jonny Lee Miller (Graeme Obree);
    Laura Fraser (Anne Obree); Billy Boyd (Malky);
    Brian Cox (Douglas Baxter)
Colour, 96 minutes, UK

Graeme Obree struggles with depression, and attempts suicide. In flashback he builds a record as one of the world's best competitive cyclists, in constant conflict with the cycling authorities. In 1995 he wins, for the second time, the World Championship 4,000m pursuit.

Graeme Obree, born in Warwickshire, but living his life in Scotland (and identifying as Scottish), disrupted and changed competitive cycling forever, adopting a streamlined position – a variant of which has become standard – and designing and building his own bike ('Old Faithful') to accommodate this. In the film he says 'make do and mend, that's the old way approach', although he apparently regrets letting it be known that he cannibalised the home washing machine for the bike's bearings, as this is something that journalists tend to lean into – as does Mackinnon's straightforward biopic, which is buoyed by an exceptionally strong cast and occasionally thrilling cinematography.

The Flying Scotsman starts on a bleak note, as Obree prepares a suicide attempt (a scene to which the film returns 80 minutes later), then flashes back to school bullying. He is given his first bike as a means of permitting him to outrun the bullies, and his chief tormentor subsequently appears at two other significant points. Later in Glasgow he works as a courier and meets Malky (Billy Boyd – who started his career, in common with many Scottish actors, in *Taggart*; and see *On a Clear Day*). The friendship blossoms, and Malky becomes responsible for seeking the sponsorship required to support Obree's first attempt at the 1hr distance record, before becoming his manager. Obree is also befriended by Baxter (Brian Cox), serving as the surrogate father-figure and counsellor. As his wife, Anne, Laura Fraser (*Small Faces, 16 Years of Alcohol, Beats, Nina's Heavenly Delights* as well as TV's *Breaking Bad*, 2012–2013, and *Better Call Saul*, 2017–2020) is, as always, very watchable.

It is axiomatic that biopics of this kind require conflict, and obstacles to be overcome. In this case there is Obree's internal conflict with his mental health, and a clash with the sport's governing body, the Union Cycliste Internationale ('UCI') – personified in the character of Ernst Hagemann, played by perennial villain Steven Berkoff. The former is foregrounded, but not explored in any depth, with Obree's position at first being 'everyone's a bit down sometimes', and 'I get down… There's nothing really wrong with me'. Later he recognises the nature of his illness and accepts (first from Baxter) the help he needs. Obree has since been open about the nature of his bipolar disorder. The conflict with the UCI is also not well explained, although his wife, Anne, says 'you got to the top the wrong way'. For the most part – at least as far as the record is public – the film sticks closely to the real events but is overly pedestrian in delivery (in *The Guardian* Peter Bradshaw was dismissive, 'a limp underdog sports movie').

→ *Battle Mountain: Graeme Obree's Story* (2015)   DOC

Directed by Dave Street; 104 minutes

A documentary following Obree's attempt to design and build a bike on his way to setting a world record in Nevada's International Human Powered world championship event, with the focus heavily on his homegrown approach to design and engineering. Obree's openness about his mental health issues and sexuality (he came out as gay in 2011) is commendable, but the film does not have enough to lift it out of niche interest. Most of the film is shot in Scotland.

Nina's Heavenly Delights (2006)

S+++

Directed by Pratibha Parmar
Screenplay by Andrea Gibb
Leading cast: Shelley Conn (Nina Shah); Laura
Fraser (Lisa MacKinlay); Veena Sood (Suman
Shah)
Colour, 94 minutes, UK

After her father dies, Nina returns to the family home and restaurant in Glasgow's comfortable suburb of Bearsden. She falls in love, relationships are resolved, and the restaurant's future is secured.

There are only four films discussed in this book which have at their heart a non-white Scottish family: *Ae Fond Kiss*, *Adam Joan*, *Girl*, and *Nina's Heavenly Delights*. Like *Ae Fond Kiss*, *Nina* is set in Glasgow, although in the West End rather than Southside; and like *Ae Fond Kiss* it emphasises the younger generation's relationships formed outside the non-resident Indian ('NRI') community. Atta Yaqub, who played Casim in *Ae Fond Kiss*, is also in *Nina*.

Nina fled to London three years ago on the day of her planned wedding and returns too late for her father's funeral. When cooking, but only in this context, he always encouraged her to follow her heart. In *Nina* however, this translates to the love she finds with Lisa (played by Glaswegian Laura Fraser). Her younger brother has, without telling his mother, married local lass Janice, who has not told her own family as her father is an outright racist. The younger sister, Priya (Zoe Henretty, in her only film appearance), is a champion traditional Scottish dancer, but was prohibited by her father from pursuing her passion. Following the death of her husband, whom she loved, but who was 'not the one', Suman is ultimately accepting of all relationships and choices.

Written by Scot Andrea Gibb (see also *AfterLife* and *Dear Frankie*) *Nina* is a warm-hearted portrayal of inclusion and acceptance, in which a vibrant NRI plays a strong role, adopting, adapting, and influencing Scottish culture. It is, however, predictably formulaic, and did not find favour with critics, or with audiences on a limited release. In *The NYT* Jeanette Catsoulis wrote: 'Tackling the conflict trifecta – race, sex and class – *Nina's Heavenly Delights* groans beneath ethnic stereotypes and half-baked performances'. Catsoulis was not alone, but the film does not deserve its lowly Rotten Tomatoes rating of 16 per cent. *Nina* is discussed by David Martin-Jones in *Scotland: Global Cinema*.

Red Road (2006)   S++ T6

Directed by Andrea Arnold
Screenplay by Andrea Arnold
Leading cast: Kate Dickie (Jackie); Tony Curran
 (Clyde Henderson); Martin Compston (Stevie)
Colour, 113 minutes, UK/Denmark

In Glasgow Jackie works for the police monitoring CCTV. To her alarm she identifies a man released from prison who is responsible for the deaths of her husband and daughter. He now lives in the Red Road flats. She pursues him, both on CCTV and in person, and eventually confronts him. Things do not go as she expected, and a resolution is reached which permits her, finally, to move on.

Andrea Arnold's short film *Wasp* (2003) secured her the Oscar for Best Live Action Short Film in 2005. Glasgow-set and shot *Red Road* became her first feature film on what is now an exceptional list, including *Fish Tank* (2009), *American Honey* (2016) and *Bird* (2024). *Red Road* firmly established Arnold as a major talent, garnering awards and critical praise. Arnold won the Jury Prize at Cannes in 2006, and was Palme d'Or nominated; at the BAFTA Scotland Awards the film secured wins in the Best Director, Best Screenplay, Best Actor, and Best Actress categories. The exceptional Kate Dickie (also in: *Shell; For Those in Peril; Outcast; Tell It to The Bees; Balance, Not Symmetry* and *Our Ladies*, amongst others) additionally won the Best Actress award at the British Independent Film Awards, with Curran (*Outlaw King*, and *Calibre*) winning the actor award.

Dickie's Jackie is more complex than Curran's Clyde, and neither can be dismissed as one-dimensional. Sympathy may lie initially with Jackie, who we see using her Argus-like privileged viewpoints to help people in peril (saving one girl's life), and who is empathetic towards those she watches. But over the course of the film sympathy shifts towards Clyde, who tries to connect with his daughter, and breaks up a fight in the pub before he takes Jackie home.

The 'Red Road' of the title is not just the name of the road in Glasgow's Springburn, but also the metaphorical road on which Jackie embarks once she identifies Clyde: the red road of revenge, or danger. Only late in the film does the audience learn that it was an accident which killed Jackie's family; up to that point we may believe Clyde to be a murderer, and that Jackie faces great danger (beyond the moral) in her pursuit.

Red Road's most interesting aspect is the way it deals with looking – something of interest to filmmakers for years (after all, a film is an exercise in ways of looking). Famously, Alfred Hitchcock emphasised this in *Rear Window* (1954), in which James Stewart's LB, wheelchair bound in his apartment, believes he has seen a murder through the windows opposite. Stewart was an immensely likeable actor, and there was no suspicion in that film that he was a voyeur, or in any way a threat to 'good folk'. While it is common to conceptualise a surveillance society as one of totalitarian threat, the surveillance Jackie engages in is at first also, as noted above, benevolent,

Kate Dickie watches...

and it is she who perverts it. But it is also through surveillance – of Clyde's attempts to reconnect with his own daughter – that she steps back from revenge into, if not forgiveness, at least acceptance. It is significant that in *Red Road* the focus is *not* on a man's gaze, but on a woman's, and that it is a woman who sets out on revenge (a more unusual approach than is the case nearly 20 years later). These feminist perspectives are unusual and refreshing.

The only potentially false note in this exceptional film lies in the ending, which is somewhat more positive, and less psychologically powerful or convincing, than the trajectory to that point would suggest.

True North (2006)   S++

Directed by Steve Hudson
Screenplay by Steve Hudson
Leading cast: Peter Mullan (Riley); Martin Compston (Sean); Gary Lewis (the skipper); Steven Robertson (the cook); Angel Li (the girl)
Colour, 96 minutes, UK/Germany/Ireland

Victims of a people smuggling operation are put on a trawler heading to Scotland, with tragic results.

True North is a morally complex film, which deals with a vital issue in respect of which simple answers are thin on the ground. The opening scenes make it clear that the Chinese who join the boat are (illegal) economic migrants, not refugees in fear of persecution (it's easier to know this if you speak Chinese, as my wife does). The Belgian people-smuggler with whom Sean deals conflates issues when he tells Sean that by transporting the migrants he will be doing something good, and that without someone doing the same for his own mother she would have died in Hitler's holocaust, rather than in her 80s. Mullan's Riley, the most complex character, is shown in a Belgian brothel exploiting two girls from Africa who are almost certainly underage, and who are likely to have been trafficked for the purposes of modern slavery in the sex trade. He is delighted to take the £4,000 offered by Sean but is appalled as events on the boat lead to death, and hands his money to the girl at the film's end.

True North is writer/director Hudson's only feature film as director. His career as an actor began with *Full Metal Jacket* (Stanley Kubrick, 1987) and in 2004 he had acted alongside Compston and Lewis on the film *Niceland (Population 1,000,002)* (Friðrik Þór Friðriksson). *True North* was an ambitious film to start a directorial career with. Of the seven-week shoot, *Variety* reported that five weeks were spent on the decks of the boat – a trawler which had been decommissioned the year before.

True North was released in the UK in the autumn of 2007. In *The List* Eddie Harrison praised the performances of Compston and Mullan but was less comfortable with the film as a whole: 'while *True North* is a worthy attempt at raising awareness of

immigration issues, the impact of Hudson's film is undone by a compromised last act which glibly ducks the important social issues raised'. This is something several critics struggle with, praising the film for its attempt to deal with difficult issues, but less happy with the execution.

Without wishing to get into issues of maritime law, *True North* is included in this book on the basis that the trawler on which almost all the action is set has a Scottish crew, is heading home to Peterhead, and operates as an extension of Scotland.

The Truth (2006) S+

Directed by George Milton
Screenplay by George Milton and Mark Tilton
Leading cast: William Beck (Scott); Elaine Cassidy (Candy); Elizabeth McGovern (Donna); Lea Mornar (Mia); Karl Theobald (Spud)
Colour, 114 minutes, UK

Strangers converge on 'Serenity Lodge' in the Highlands, to attend a course led by Donna. The group swear to 'tell the truth at all times', which gives rise to tensions, although secrets remain. One of the group, Mia, is found murdered; all deny killing her, and Spud suggests they continue with their search for 'truth'...

Like *The Last Great Wilderness*, *The Truth* blends dark humour with mystery in a retreat in the Highlands, but it is much more fun ('a real rollercoaster, alternating deliciously deadpan humour with serious insights, deft satire with dark suspense'

– Geoff Andrew in *Time Out*). As Anna Smith wrote in *Empire*, 'if you're willing to be drawn into its odd, dark little world, it has many pleasures.' Unfortunately, the film disappeared largely without trace.

American McGovern (who is in two films in this book, the other being *Swung*) gets many of the best lines as she spouts what Candy worries is mumbo jumbo, and appears to have great fun with her role. While establishing shots make it clear that the retreat is in the Highlands, and the film was shot there, nothing turns on the Scottish location.

Death Defying Acts (2007) `S+`

Directed by Gillian Armstrong
Screenplay by Tony Grisoni and Brian Ward
Leading cast: Catherine Zeta-Jones (Mary McGarvie); Guy Pearce (Harry Houdini); Saoirse Ronan (Benji McGarvie); Timothy Spall (Sugarman)
Colour, 97 minutes, UK/Australia/US, English

Edinburgh, 1926: Mary, living with her daughter Benji, performs a fraudulent stage act as a clairvoyant. Houdini's latest tour brings him to the city and Mary takes him on when he issues a challenge. The two embark on a passionate affair.

Australian director Gillian Armstrong's second feature, *My Brilliant Career* (1979), is rightly lauded and, like *Death Defying Acts*, it is a period piece, with a strong woman at its heart. But *Death Defying Acts*, notwithstanding a strong cast and

production values, does not recapture the magic of the earlier film, and failed to find either critical approval or box office success.

DDA is a piece of fiction; Houdini did tour Scotland, making over 100 performances in the country, but he last appeared in Edinburgh in 1920. The story is pedestrian, and Zeta-Jones and Pearce, between whom there appears to be little chemistry, are outshone by the 13-year-old Saoirse Ronan in her fourth film (see also *Mary Queen of Scots* and *The Outrun*). Some exteriors were shot in Edinburgh.

Hallam Foe (aka *Mister Foe*) (2007) `S++`

Directed by David Mackenzie
Screenplay by David Mackenzie, Ed Whitmore
Leading cast: Jamie Bell (Hallam); Sophia Myles (Kate); Claire Forlani (Verity); Lucy Holt (Lucy); Ciarán Hinds (Julius)
Colour, 95 minutes, UK

The Borders: Hallam is a troubled young man; his mother died by suicide, and he suspects his stepmother of being complicit. She seduces him, then tells him to leave. In Edinburgh he becomes obsessed with Kate, who reminds him of his mother. Later he confronts his father and stepmother at the family home but is reconciled when his father tells him the truth about his mother's death.

Hallam Foe is one of five films in this book to be directed by David Mackenzie (see also *Young Adam, Perfect Sense, You Instead, Outlaw King*). It opened the Edinburgh

Film Festival in 2007, and won multiple awards at other festivals, along with the Scottish BAFTA Best Actress award for Sophia Myles. The film is based on the 2001 novel of the same name by Peter Jinks, but the story of an obsession with heavy Freudian overtones (Verity, having seen Kate, asks Hallam if he enjoys having sex with his mother) works better on the page than it does in a compressed version on film.

The film walks a fine line between the charming (at places verging on rom-com, although never quite falling into the genre; Mackenzie has said that 'there's some quite strong comedic elements in it – to me it's an ugly duckling story'), the uneasy, and the downright creepy. In *S&S*, Philip Kemp referred to a 'tone of mingled manic obsession and farce'. At times events move too quickly without sufficient explanation, lacking credibility. Verity's rapid recovery, and lack of condemnation after Hallam has attempted to drown her before saving her, are particularly jarring.

Interviewed in *The Scotsman*, Mackenzie explained that his challenge as screenwriter was to collapse the novel's timeframe from four years to the three weeks over which the film is set, which goes some way to explain the abruptness of some of the action. Mackenzie also moved Hallam's family home from Leicestershire to the Borders and gave Hallam a job in the Caledonian, the same hotel Mackenzie had worked in when he first came to Edinburgh, where the interior scenes were shot (the hotel's exterior, with its clocktower from which Hallam spies on Kate at night, belongs to the Balmoral).

While Myles and Bell were both lauded, perhaps the real star of the film is Edinburgh itself, which Mackenzie has described as 'part gothic, and part fairytale'. As AO Scott put it in *The NYT*, *Hallam Foe* is 'a nimble, acrobatic tour of Edinburgh, traipsing through narrow alleyways, up drainpipes and across gables and gutters as it follows Hallam on his pathological way'. Later, in 2021, *The Scotsman* ranked *Hallam Foe* as the 15th best film set in Edinburgh (first place went to *F9: The Fast Saga*† (Justin Lin, 2021), partly shot in Scotland, so the list should not be taken too seriously).

Critical reaction to *Hallam Foe* was very largely positive, although commercially the film may have struggled to break even. AO Scott found much to praise but was not entirely convinced: 'the main problem with *Mister Foe* [the film's US title] is that Hallam's strangeness is a puzzle only to him and those around him. He's more of a mystification than a mystery, and never quite creepy enough to risk our not liking him.' *Variety*'s Derek Elley was more positive: 'Tip-top performances, led by young British thesp Jamie Bell, and a deftly handled tone reflecting all the title teen's confused emotions make *Hallam Foe* a viewing delight'.

One of the awards won by *Hallam Foe* was for its soundtrack. This consists of songs by Scottish artists, including Orange Juice, Franz Ferdinand and James Yorkston, and is worth tracking down.

Mister Lonely (2007)

Directed by Harmony Korine
Screenplay by Harmony Korine, Avi Korine
Leading cast: Diego Luna (Michael Jackson);
    Samantha Morton (Marilyn Monroe); Denis
    Lavant (Charlie Chaplin); James Fox (the Pope);
    Werner Herzog (Father Umbrillo)
Colour, 112 minutes, UK/France/Ireland/US

Samantha Morton (as Marilyn Monroe) and
Diego Luna (as Michael Jackson)

*'Michael Jackson' is a street performer in
Paris, where he meets 'Marilyn Monroe'
who is married to 'Charlie Chaplin' and has
a daughter who 'lives as Shirley Temple'.
He goes to a Highland commune populated
by 'celebrities'. Elsewhere, Father Umbrillo
leads an aid mission, on which nuns develop
the miraculous ability to fly.*

If you really want to watch someone living
their life as Michael Jackson (for opaque
reasons), practicing moves loch-side, or
the wonderful Samantha Morton living as
'Marilyn Monroe' being badly sunburnt
in the Highlands, this is the film for you
(Morton was nominated as Best Actress
at the 2009 *Evening Standard* British Film
Awards). If you prefer narrative films to be
coherent, look away. Harmony Korine is
rarely boring, although his work is not to
everyone's taste, and there is little Scottish,
save for a key location, about *Mister
Lonely* (the film moves to the Scottish
commune after 28 minutes, with scenes
shot around Plockton).

   Mister Lonely appears to be about
identity, self-awareness and performance.
The key to unlocking its mystery might lie
in words spoken by 'the Queen': 'We are

but humble impersonators, regular people
like you, and without you we would be
nothing. Our goal as always in performing
is to try and entertain you and search out
the beauty that is life, the splendour and
poetry of it all'. And what can we make
of an entirely different strand in which
Werner Herzog (see also **Incident at Loch
Ness**) marshals flying nuns? Interviewed in
Indiewire in 2008, Korine said that Herzog
'had no idea about the other story'. Asked
whether people should read the film as an
allegory for his own, turbulent, life, Korine
said: 'I don't think there's any right or
wrong way… I'm sure a big percentage of
the audience won't even care about reading
it. They'll just want to walk out and think
nothing about it. Hopefully, there are
some people out there that will get a good
laugh'. There *are* critics who loved the film;
I do not. In *Filmmaker Magazine* Michael
Tully wrote: 'Korine delivers an achingly
personal and heartfelt meditation on our
quest to find our true selves in such a sad,
indifferent world'. But such praise belongs
to the minority. However, as Roger Ebert
has written: 'there is the temptation to
forgive its trespasses simply because it is
utterly, if pointlessly, original'.

Seachd: The Inaccessible Pinnacle (2007) S+++ T27

Directed by Simon Miller
Screenplay by Jo Cockwell, Iseabail T
  NicDhòmhnaill, Iain F MacLeòid, Aonghas
  MacNeacail, Simon Miller
Leading cast: Padruig Moireasdan (Young
  Aonghas); Coll Domhnallach (Aonghas – aged
  20); Aonghas Pàdraig Caimbeul (seanair)
Colour, 100 minutes, Gaelic and English, UK

The narrator, Aonghas', parents died on a mountain, and he is raised by his grandfather, Seanair, a storyteller. As Seanair dies in hospital, Aonghas visits, and recalls his childhood.

When he visits Seanair in hospital, Aonghas remains angry at the extent to which Seanair takes refuge in stories. For Seanair, to tell a story is to explain the world. The stories are not enough for Aonghas, however, and he argues that now is the time, finally, to tell the truth. The world that Seanair and the young Aonghas live in is the Gaelic-speaking community of Skye, in the mid-1990s. *Seachd* plays with time and adopts a magic-realist approach to the narrative. At the very end, time collapses – a young Aonghas is with the dying Seanair. This is a beautiful end to a complex film. The four stories Seanair tells during the film are fully incorporated visually. Not all deal with loss and tragedy; a truly wonderful episode tells of a Spaniard shipwrecked from the Armada who washes up on an island with an exiled MacDonald – 'a proud and hungry man'. They bond over the Spaniard's 'patatas'

and become firm friends. On their eventual escape, MacDonald founds 'the first fish and chip shop' (MacDonald: 'Do you have any potatoes?… I wonder what they'd be like fried.' 'Fried! Fried! For the love of God. What is it with you people and fried food?')

Seachd was the first Scottish Gaelic film released theatrically (**Hero** was the first produced; **As an Eileann** had limited exhibition). In 2007 *Seachd*'s Scottish producer, Chris Young, resigned from the BAFTA when it refused to nominate the film for the Oscars in the Best Foreign Language category, sparking a debate as to whether Scotland should maintain its own SAFTA with the ability to do so. Shot in widescreen, *Seachd* emphasises the open landscape and the enfolding community in which Aonghas grows up and, sometimes, his estrangement. It is a film well worth spending time with.

Between Above and Below (2008), *Big Gold Dream* (2015), *Teenage Superstars* (2017) DOC

Directed by Grant McPhee; 72 minutes/94
  minutes/107 minutes

These are not the only documentaries about Scottish bands and music directed by McPhee (see also *Your Attention Please: Scars*†, 2013 and *The Glasgow School*†, 2016), but these three have received cinema screenings. McPhee clearly loves his subject, and his passion carries through to the films. *BAB* follows Edinburgh-based folk-rock outfit Jacobs Pillow (who claim to be influenced by The Incredible String Band, so I was sold immediately) and leans heavily into their performances. It's a film fans of the band should love. *Big Gold Dream* focuses on Scottish independent labels Fast Product (about which McPhee has also co-written a book, *Hungry Beat*, 2022) and Postcard Records, both vital in the early post-punk era, the former in Edinburgh, the latter in Glasgow (Postcard put out the first Orange Juice single). The film won the audience award at the 2015 EIFF. *Teenage Superstars* focuses on the Glasgow independent scene in the mid-'80s to mid-'90s (so in a double bill could precede *Lost in France*). For those interested in Scottish music, all of these will be of interest (along with *Lost in France*, *The Possibilities are Endless*, *Where You're Meant to Be*, *The Skids: Revolution*, *Heading West: A Story About a Band Called Shooglenifty* and *Since Yesterday: The Untold Story of Scotland's Girl Bands*; *The Ballad of a Great Disordered Heart†*, 2022, Mark Cousins/Becky Manson/Aidan O'Rourke is also well worth a watch, but at a run time of 64 minutes is below the threshold of 70 minutes required for an entry in this book). McPhee has also directed fiction feature films (see *Sarah's Room*, *Night Kaleidoscope* and *Far from the Apple Tree*).

The Dead Outside (2008) S+++

Directed by Kerry Anne Mullaney
Screenplay by Kerry Anne Mullaney and Kris R Bird
Leading cast: Alton Milne (Daniel); Sandra Louise Douglas (April); Sharon Osdin (Kate)
Colour, 86 minutes, UK

'Braehead Farm', in Scotland, 'six months after the outbreak': Daniel breaks into the farmhouse, occupied by April. The world outside is ruled by zombies, but April is immune. An attempt is made by a nurse, Kate, to seize her for research purposes.

The first, and to date only, feature from Scottish director Mullaney (who had previously directed one short, the Edinburgh-based *Hit*, 2007), *The Dead Outside* is a bleak, terse horror film mining the zombie mythology cinema has embraced since the release of *White Zombie* (Victor Halperin, 1932; this is normally considered the starting point, although the sub-genre received its most significant boost with *Night of the Living Dead*, George A Romero, 1968). My use of the term 'zombie' here is generic; the film does not use the word (neither did the TV series *The Walking Dead*, 2010–2022 – had none of the characters heard of zombies?). Perhaps, unlike 'vampire', 'zombie' is inherently silly; but *The Dead Outside* is not. The film was one of many surveyed by academics researching the portrayal of nurses in zombie films (because that's the sort of thing academics do) (see David Stanley et al, 'Celluloid zombies...'). In *The Dead*

Outside, Kate, who at first appears to be a sympathetic character, is anything but; the authors of the study concluded that 'the film is generally very bleak and does nothing to offer a positive view of nurses'.

Made on a limited budget, and shot in just 15 days, *The Dead Outside* makes the most of its remote location, while letting the imagination run wild as to just how awful things are in the rest of the world. The film was listed as 'one of the six scariest Scottish films ever made' by *The Scotsman* in 2015. Kim Newman – the undisputed guru of horror films – was a fan, describing it as an 'unsettling and evocative little film… an extremely impressive debut'.

The New Ten Commandments (2008) `DOC`

Directed by Doug Aubrey et al; 101 minutes

This portmanteau film – part documentary, part advocacy – opens with the text: 'In 1948 the United Nations adopted the Universal Declaration of Human Rights. 60 years later Scotland reaffirms its faith in fundamental human rights …'. We are shown ten short films, each related to a specific right enshrined in the UN Declaration: the first, 'The Right to Freedom of Assembly' (directed by David Graham Scott) focuses on the experiences of republican activist and protestor Peter Dow, as he is moved to the outer margins of the Queen's state opening of the Scottish Parliament; the last – and for lovers of cinema this is an absolute delight – 'The Right to Freedom of Thought', is a joint work by

Mark Cousins and Tilda Swinton.

The film's segments are structured to provoke reflection and discussion rather than as closed arguments. Each is based firmly around Scottish stories, whether it be enslaved sex workers, the trial of the alleged Lockerbie bomber, or the high-profile lawyer Aamer Anwar facing contempt of court proceedings after his condemnation of a guilty verdict. The film was shown at the EIFF in June 2008, has been widely distributed in Scotland, and was used in schools alongside study materials designed to promote understanding of the Declaration. The whole is greater than the sum of its parts; its parts are intelligent and well-crafted.

Occasional Monsters (2008) S+++

Directed by Sam Addison and Michael Cox
Screenplay by Sam Addison and Michael Cox
Leading cast: Marcus McMillan (Wolfgang Markus); Craig Stewart (Duane Craig)
Colour, 83 minutes, UK

In Aberdeen, Wolfgang and Craig are shadowed by a documentary crew as they attempt to get their monster-hunting business off the ground.

It is a pity that, following a 13-minute short, *Life in Ruins* (2008), *Occasional Monsters* is Addison and Cox's only feature film (indeed, it appears to be the only film of everyone involved in its production), and that it came and went almost without trace (in November 2008 there were at least one-off screenings in Aberdeen's Belmont Cinema, and the Cameo in Edinburgh). The film is far better than many micro-budget independent productions, maintaining a charm throughout. It's important in mockumentaries like this that, however ineptly clueless the protagonists are, they take themselves seriously, and Wolfgang and Duane are nothing if not serious in their lunacy: Wolfgang shouts in outrage early on 'We're proper [effing] monster hunters!' It's also useful to know, should you ever need to kill a cat, that an M60 machine gun will do the job *very* effectively.

One Day Removals (2008) S+++
T100

Directed by Mark Stirton
Screenplay by Mark Stirton
Leading cast: Patrick Wight (Andy); Scott Ironside (Ronnie)
Colour, 85 minutes, Doric, UK

In Aberdeen, two removal men-with-a-van anticipate a straightforward day. They end up with a van load of corpses.

There are some wonderfully inventive independent filmmakers in Scotland. The films of Lawrie Brewster and Sarah Daly (see **White Out** etc), David Ryan Keith (see **Attack of the Herbals** etc) and Graham Hughes (see **The Big Slick** etc) are separately discussed. To them must be added the Aberdeen-based (very) independent auteur Mark Stirton who has made three feature films – *One Day Removals*, *The Planet* (2006), which is not, for the purposes of this book, a Scottish film, and **Dark Highlands**,

discussed below. In *ODR* he also provides the (vigorously profane) screenplay, cinematography, editing, music, and digital effects (the latter as part of a team). He also had the chutzpah to make *ODR* in broad Doric. As if that was not enough, he has written the book *Movie Boy* (2017), the story of his work in film.

The plot of *ODR* is ridiculous, but that is partly the point, and the implausibility is itself a determining plot feature. The first unfortunate event is just that, and plausible. So, to a degree, is every subsequent unfortunate event. But less is usually more, and in combination the film should *not* work. That it does is testimony both to a tight construction, and to ingenuity and wit. Stirton must, surely, have had conversations with friends along the lines of 'how could the next UE happen?'. *ODR* is, if you don't mind bad language, very funny (right down to the mock *Time* cover) and can (as of late March 2025) be watched in high quality on YouTube without guilt – it was uploaded by Stirton's production company.

→ Dark Highlands (2018) S+++

Directed by Mark Stirton
Screenplay by Mark Stirton
Leading cast: Junichi Kajioka (the artist); Steve Campbell (the gamekeeper)
Colour, 85 minutes, UK

The Highlands: a Japanese landscape artist is targeted by a killer, the Gamekeeper, and fights to survive.

Having made the wonderfully inventive *One Day Removals*, Stirton's second feature boasts enhanced production values, and is unique in this book in having a Japanese visitor to Scotland at its heart. Kajioka is himself an award-winning filmmaker based in London; as an actor he has been in, amongst others, *47 Ronin* (Carl Rinsch, 2013) and *Spectre* (Sam Mendes, 2015). Stirton told the *Press and Journal* 'Junichi read the screenplay and said he liked it immediately. We picked the most summery dates and it has still been terrible weather.' The film also features Brian Cox – although in a voice performance only; he donated his time to read the opening prologue, having seen and admired *One Day Removals*.

There's virtually no dialogue in the film – what there is, comes largely incidentally from characters who are at the margins of the film – but Stirton shows that he can build tension with visuals (and a thumping score provided by Jon Brooks). While *Dark Highlands* 'is a slow-burning, suspenseful ordeal horror which implements some interesting visual storytelling techniques to get the narrative across' (*lovehorror.co.uk*), little is done to generate concern, other than as an abstract puzzle of survival, for the artist. We know nothing about him at the start of the film, and not much more, save that he is resilient, at its end.

The film had limited festival engagements, before moving to Blu-ray and DVD.

Stone of Destiny (2008) S+

Directed by Charles Martin Smith
Screenplay by Ian Hamilton, Charles Martin Smith
Leading cast: Charlie Cox (Ian Hamilton); Kate Mara (Kay Matheson); Billy Boyd (Bill Craig); Robert Carlyle (John MacCormick); Stephen McCole (Gavin Vernon); Ciaron Kelly (Alan Stuart)
Colour, 96 minutes, UK/Canada

14 September 1950: Glasgow University. Bill and Ian attend an event promoting a Scottish Covenant to grant Scotland greater autonomy. Ian and his friends liberate the Stone of Destiny from Westminster Abbey and repatriate it to Scotland.

The success of *The Full Monty* (Peter Cattaneo, 1997), which recouped nearly 75 times its budget at the global box office, led to a spate of 'quirky' British films – somewhat in the manner of the Ealing comedies. *Stone of Destiny* is one of the weakest of these. Whether this is because the director, Smith, is an American is a matter of some debate, but liberties are certainly taken that one would hope a director more sensitive to the subject matter would have avoided. I had hoped for better, as he had previously directed a strong episode of *Buffy the Vampire Slayer* ('Welcome to the Hellmouth', 1997), which, as everyone knows, is the second-best TV series ever made. *The Guardian* accorded *Stone* only the shortest of reviews, and Cath Clarke homed in on Smith's nationality: 'which wouldn't matter if this didn't feel so much

The gang toast their success

like a wee-dram-and-bagpipes invitation to a mythical Scotland of yesteryear'. And does it ever! The theft, or repatriation, of the Stone of Destiny, or the Stone of Scone, was an act of Scottish defiance both celebrated and condemned. *Stone* does not labour the history, but it labours 'Scotland' right from the start when it opens with the requisite shot of a Highland glen, to the accompaniment of a bagpiper, and it does not let this bone drop.

When geographical distortions pander to shortbread-tin caricatures of Scotland criticism is justified. The Glenfinnan Viaduct is a wonderful piece of structural engineering but if you, as Ian does, travel by train from Glasgow to London and were to find yourself passing over the viaduct, heading

north-west (meaning you are travelling from Fort William to Mallaig) you would have cause to be seriously alarmed. You might wonder if you were taking this route only because a film director wanted to show you SCOTLAND. In this case, you'd be right.

That the film retains slight charm flows from three factors: its basis in truth (despite inaccuracies added for dramatic effect); its setting in Glasgow's West End and the university (although neither the university's central quad nor Park Circus stand in well for London – particularly when it has already been established that one of these key locations is *not* London); and its strong and likeable cast, who really should have known better.

Trouble Sleeping (2008)   S++

Directed by Eunice Olumide and Robert Rae
Screenplay by Robert Rae, Ghazzi Hussein and
    others
Leading cast: Alia Alzougbi (Halla); Seham Ali
    (Seham); Okan Yahsi (Methi); Hassan Naama
    (Ahmed); Waseem Uboaklain (Khalid)
Colour, 103 minutes, UK, Arabic/English

Edinburgh: members of the Arabic-speaking community, of varying nationalities, live precarious lives. Halla works in a refugee support centre, and is asked to help Ahmed, a Kurd, but this comes at a cost as past tortures are revealed. Mehti is gay and struggles with the conflict between cultural expectations.

Trouble Sleeping premiered at the EIFF in June 2008, and won a Scottish BAFTA award, notwithstanding some weaknesses (*The Hollywood Reporter* called it 'a respectable effort'). It is the first of several films in this book to deal with the plight of refugees and asylum seekers in Scotland (see also *Limbo* and *Girl*), opening with the words 'in 1999 the Government introduced a policy of dispersal which led to some seeking asylum in the UK being transported to Glasgow'. The film then moves to the impact of this decision in Scotland, including the hoops asylum seekers need to go through to establish their status, and the very real risk of deportation. Interlocking stories, the central one of which is harrowing, are told almost entirely through the perspectives of the refugees, centred around the local 'Blue Nile' café/social spot. Arabic dominates, both in dialogue and the soundtrack, which consists almost entirely of Arabic music (and is a little over intrusive).

There is no doubting the sincerity with which the film was made, and we are told the stories 'are based on the experiences of members of Edinburgh's refugee community'; the BBC quoted the film's producer as saying the intention was to challenge 'public perceptions about refugees and their lives in Scotland'. While there is strength in the central story, there are otherwise too many threads which don't weave into a tapestry. A small number of professional actors were involved in the project but the principals were, necessarily (and in the *cinema verité* tradition), amateur; some are relaxed in front of the camera, others stiff. Most were not willing to speak on the film's release, afraid of consequences for their relatives in their home nations.

I was only able to watch this film through the National Library of Scotland Moving Image Archive at Kelvin Hall in Glasgow.

Book of Blood (aka Clive Barker's Book of Blood) (2009)   S+

Directed by John Harrison
Screenplay by John Harrison and Darin
    Silverman
Leading cast: Jonas Armstrong (Simon McNeal);
    Sophie Ward (Mary Florescu); Paul Blair (Reg
    Fuller); Clive Russell (Wyburd)
Colour, 100 minutes, UK/Canada

Edinburgh: Simon, wounded and exhausted, is taken prisoner by Wyburd and offered a quick painless death if he tells his story.

Claiming to be clairvoyant he has assisted writer and academic Mary to investigate a mysterious gruesome death in Tollington House. Throughout the investigation he fakes manifestations, but this angers the dead, who respond. Mary promises to listen to them and tell their stories.

In December 2007, *The Scotsman* ran a piece under the headline 'Horror stories: Scotland now a top location for filmmakers raising hell', referencing, amongst others, the ongoing shoot for *Book of Blood*. A production representative said, 'Edinburgh is an amazing city. Every location we are using elevates this story to such an incredible level' (shooting also took place in Glasgow). *Dog Soldiers*, which was shot largely in Luxembourg, has been credited with kicking off the trend, which gained traction in the late-noughties, and runs through to the time of writing (in 2025 we might be lucky enough to have a horror film potentially called *Midgies*, as momentum for what began as a joke has generated a plan, funding, and a trailer). As Mark Cousins has said, Scotland's Gothic locations provide a great backdrop for this sort of horror, whether the base be urban (as in *Book of Blood*) or whether it be rural (see, eg, *She Will*). Few of these films embed themselves in Scotland, and a significant proportion could be set anywhere: the Edinburgh and Glasgow locations used in *Book of Blood* could readily be substituted by Washington and Baltimore.

Book of Blood has pedigree: it is based on two of Clive Barker's short stories in the 'Books of Blood' cycle, and like his cult classic *Hellraiser* (Clive Barker, 1987) is set largely in a single house-with-a-history. It was intended that the film be the first in a series but, although it was moderately well received by genre critics, *Book* was not the success that *Hellraiser* was, and with a limited release it performed poorly at the box office.

The mantra in the film (repeated three times) is the 'dead have highways that lead to interconnections, that spill into our world, and if you find yourself at one of the intersections you should stop and listen'. This line is repeated by Simon when, after looking at his close to necrotic body, Wyburd says, 'Jesus Christ son, you are a book of blood. Read it to me'. As the director said in an interview ahead of a FrightFest ten-minute teaser screening, 'it is not a gore fest... it is more of a supernatural thriller'. Unfortunately, as is pointed out on *The Kim Newman Website*, 'there's a lot of brooding, uneventful sitting about waiting for things to happen'. When things do happen, the film is moderately effective.

Crying with Laughter (2009) S+++

Directed by Justin Molotnikov
Screenplay by Justin Molotnikov
Leading cast: Stephen McCole (Joey Frisk); Malcolm Shields (Frank Archer); Jo Hartley (Karen); Andrew Neil (Jonathan Meldrick)
Colour, 93 minutes, UK

Portobello beach: stand-up comedian Joey practises a new routine and realises he needs new material. In Edinburgh he runs into an old school friend, Frank, which sparks off the worst week of his life. He delivers a new routine, intercut with the extremely dark events underpinning it.

The 'Scottish noir' (Peter Bradshaw) *Crying with Laughter* played at the EIFF in June 2009 and went on to win the Scottish BAFTA Best Film award (along with the 'Best Indie' award at the Edmonton International Film Festival, and Best Feature Drama at the 31st Celtic Media Festival). Sadly, it is the only feature film from director Molotnikov, who has a strong CV in directing for TV, including episodes of *Doctor Who* and *Outlander*. *Crying* starts strongly, driven by a powerful script, a smart structure, and bravura central performances from Scottish actors McCole (*Rushmore*, Wes Anderson, 1998) and Shields (both actors are in *The Acid House* and *Orphans*).

Glasgow's *Evening Times* reported McCole prepared for the role by performing stand-up gigs across Scotland. *The Express* highlighted the risk involved in McCole's approach: 'Ignoring the advice of producer Claire Mundell and director Justin Molotnikov, who both urged Stephen to let comedians write the material for him, he decided to do the scenes with his own improvised material.' Behind the comedy *Crying* deals with some very serious issues, including child abuse, and even attracted the attention of a Professor of Psychiatry in response to questions of crime, responsibility and punishment.

Not everything comes together, but there is real promise here, and it is a great pity that Molotnikov is one of all too many directors whose work is covered in this book who made only the one film (a film planned for 2012, *Blood or Water*, fell through).

In *The Guardian*, Peter Bradshaw's short review was strong: 'Molotnikov drives his movie forward with real storytelling skill; there's some interesting location work, and the comedy is at all times satisfyingly nasty', with only some reservations about loose plot threads left dangling. *Little White Lies'* Laurence Boyce was struck by *Crying's* 'freshness and bite'. The film secured only a limited UK release notwithstanding its strong reception, and moved to DVD in 2010; a two-disc 'collectors edition' DVD is occasionally available on second-hand websites.

Dark Nature (2009)   S+++

Directed by Marc de Launay
Screenplay by Eddie Harrison
Leading cast: Niall Greg Fulton (McKenzie); Tom Carter (Hayward); Doreen McGillivray (Mrs Petrie)
Colour, 76 minutes, UK

A beautiful house by the shore in the Highlands. Many people are murdered.

In a 'behind the scenes' section on the DVD release of *Dark Nature*, director de Launay says that his ambition for the film was that it would be 'cross genre, in that it will be very well shot arthouse, intellectual values, as well as, "oh, it's a thriller" ... we're trying to subvert the thriller genre'. While the film wears arthouse (Dario Argento, Mario Bava etc) on its sleeve, and secured de Launay a nomination from BAFTA Scotland in its New Talent category (cinematographer Andrew Begg picked up an award from the HD Festival), the result does not live up to the ambition. Carrying an audience score of 4 per cent on Rotten Tomatoes, *Dark Nature* did not attract much attention from critics. Mark Bitel, in *Eye For Film*, was one of the few to trouble himself, reaching the conclusion: 'once the tide of genre trappings… has rushed in and drained away again, we are left only with the film's essential emptiness'. The film had a very limited Cineworld release in the UK and went quickly to DVD. It is, to date, the first and only feature to be directed by de Launay.

The Edge of Dreaming (2009) DOC

Directed by Amy Hardie; 73 minutes

Hardie, at the time head of research at the Scottish Documentary Institute, had a dream: 'I don't really remember my dreams, but one night I woke up in the middle of the night, because I'd had a dream that my horse was dying, and he asked me if I was ready to start filming.' Her horse *had* died. Later she dreamt of her death at the age of 48. She then made this unusual film, exploring dreams and the way they shape our consciousness. A sell-out at the EIFF, and an award winner, the film is now a little hard to track down, although DVD copies exist. Hardie also made *Seven Songs for a Long Life* and, at the time of writing, is very much alive.

Morticia (2009)   S++

Directed by Nabil Shaban
Screenplay by Nabil Shaban
Leading cast: Jenni Young (Morticia/Kylie); Ricky Callan (Malcolm); Karen Douglas (Molly); Sofie Alonzo (Maria/babysitter); Nabil Shaban (Dr Moores)
Colour, 70 minutes, UK

Edinburgh: Kylie is ridiculed by three local women; her bedroom is littered with vampire-related paraphernalia – she aspires to be a vampire and insists her name is 'Morticia'. Her father, Malcolm, has returned from the Gulf War where he killed children, women and unarmed civilians. Neither he nor Kylie's mother have strong parenting skills. After an incident at school, Kylie is required to see a psychiatrist. Later she steals a vampire bat from the Edinburgh Zoo, self-harms, and (in a fantasy?) is carried away by Dracula.

In July 2010, in the St Cuthbert's Church cemetery (just off Lothian Road in Edinburgh), *Morticia* opened the ninth iteration of the now defunct 'People's Festival'. The film was shot entirely in Edinburgh, with a local cast, most of whom, director Shaban aside, are largely unknown to film and TV audiences. Earlier the film had played at a vampire film festival in October 2009, although strictly speaking it is not about a vampire: as Shaban has said, *Morticia* 'is not a genuine vampire movie in the conventional sense', but about a young girl who, in the face of disassociation, wishes to become a vampire, and adopts the name 'Morticia'. The film was not picked up for distribution, nor released on DVD. It is, however, (at the time of writing) available in a fairly poor transfer on YouTube.

Shaban is well known to *Doctor Who* fans (playing the alien Sil in seasons 22 and 23 when Colin Baker was the Doctor), and has a strong resumé, including *Children of Men* (Alfonsó Cuaron, 2006); he also makes a brief appearance in **Trouble Sleeping**. The Jordanian-born, British actor/director (based near Edinburgh for a long time) made *Morticia* for less than £10,000, but the film rises above budgetary limitations (although a rubber vampire bat does somewhat jar), lifted by a clever concept, local authenticity, and a strong script. The young lead actress carries her role well (even if she was, in the view of Shaban, who suggested the film is inappropriate for under-15s, too young to watch the result); Edinburgh actor Ricky Callan whose first role in a feature film was in **The Acid House** is strong as the father struggling with post-war trauma and parenthood.

The film is littered with teasing references to vampire and associated lore – with weight given to Bram Stoker's original source novel, *Dracula* (1897) ('that's not a nice book', and 'this is horrid', says her mum, while Malcolm throws it in the bin). Three local mothers take on a role akin to that of *Macbeth*'s witches (they're billed as such in the credits); a poster of Buffy the Vampire Slayer – at first blush an incongruous picture perhaps for a wannabe vampire to have – has fangs drawn onto Buffy. *Morticia* is certainly better than

any of the four more traditional vampire films covered in this book (see entry for **Night Kaleidoscope**). It is as much about the consequences of (illegal) war as it is about vampires, and the ending is decidedly downbeat (it's noteworthy that of the three Scottish films to deal with the Middle East wars and the involvement of British soldiers – *Morticia*, **The Unkindness of Ravens**, and **Sunshine on Leith**, two are horror-adjacent). Should you choose to watch *Morticia*, you should do so right through the end credits. There's a nice gag buried in the standard tedious copyright infringement warning.

Running in Traffic (2009) S+++

Directed by Dale Corlett
Screenplay by Dale Corlett and Bryan Larkin
Leading cast: Bryan Larkin (Joe Cullen); Kenneth Cranham (Bill Cullen); Anna Kerth (Kayla Golebiowski); Atta Yaqub (Amman); Ross Maxwell (Nick)
Colour, 97 minutes, UK

Glasgow: Kayla and Joe, who are unconnected, mourn: Kayla, for an unborn baby; Joe, for his father. Their lives proceed in parallel towards a possible convergence.

New Zealander director Corlett has made only this one feature; his co-writer on the film, Glasgow-born Larkin, is better known as an actor (see, eg, *Dungeons & Dragons: Honor among Thieves*, John Francis Daley and Jonathan Goldstein, 2023). Larkin, who won a BAFTA Scotland New

Talent Producer award for the film, had worked on the script for some time before developing it further with Cullen. For him, the story was 'semi-autobiographical because it was written after my own experience of losing my father'. On the face of it, Joe and Kayla have nothing in common (he is a part-time drug dealer; she a waitress in a café, and a link between them is purely tangential); but in their grieving and response to death, we see a shared path that all must go through. It's not a structure which would appeal to all, but downbeat and strongly grounded, *Running in Traffic* succeeds.

After premiering at the EIFF in June 2009, *Running in Traffic* performed well on the festival circuit. Following a screening at the Mannheim-Heidelberg International Film Festival, *Film-Dienst*'s reviewer gushed: 'The moving, excitingly told film creates the story in parallel plots that have hardly any connection points, but in the end suggests a possible future in an actually wonderful setting'.

A *Spanking in Paradise* (2010)
S+++ T100

Directed by Wayne Thallon
Screenplay by Wayne Thallon
Leading cast: Andrew Hawley (Justin); Simon Weir (Rab)
Colour, 90 minutes, UK

Edinburgh: Justin, a young human rights lawyer who must stay out of trouble for a month while his US visa is processed, starts working for his uncle in a local brothel, 'Birds of Paradise'.

Spanking, the only film made by its Scottish writer/director, played at the EIFF in 2011 where it went down well: *HeyUGuys*' reviewer clearly loved it – 'a spankin', swind screamer of pure shant lunacy, right from the grubby black heart of Edinburgh's underworld... a dark gem of perverse hilarity'. Locations and accents reek of authenticity, and there is threat and seediness behind the dark comedy. The authenticity goes deeper than a casual viewer might recognise. Thallon's life is fascinating: one side of his family ran a sauna/brothel in Edinburgh, and Thallon has made it clear in interviews that many of the film's specifics were drawn directly from his experiences. Thallon had previously written *Cut-Throat: The Vicious World of Rod McLean* (2005), a real-life account of the life and death of his uncle, a gangster, drug baron, mercenary and, just possibly, an MI6 agent, who was found murdered in a flat in London.

While the focus is on Justin, it is Weir's Rab who dominates the film, constantly telling stories, his forceful personality combining boundless charm underpinned with threat. Perhaps better known for his TV work within Scotland, he is a prolific actor and appears in eight films in this book, ranging from *Postmortem* to *Wigilia*.

While *Spanking* received some exposure after its festival success it did not get a wide release, despite being picked up by IFC films for distribution in the US, and has drifted into modest obscurity, available at the time of writing only through YouTube.

Centurion (2010) S+

Directed by Neil Marshall
Screenplay by Neil Marshall
Leading cast: Michael Fassbender (Centurion
    Quintus Dias); Dominic West (General Titus
    Virilus); Olga Kurylenko (Etain)
Colour, 97 minutes, English and Gaelic, UK/
France/US

Michael Fassbender and Olga Kurylenko, a 'gothic ninja Barbie'

117 AD: General Virilus takes the IXth Roman Legion north of the border to defeat the Picts, led by Gorlacon. The Romans fall victim to effective guerrilla warfare. Most are killed, and the General captured. Having failed to recover him, the survivors attempt to make their way back to Roman Britain.

Having made one Scottish film, **Dog Soldiers**, in Luxembourg, Marshall was determined that *Centurion* be filmed in Scotland, and much, but not all, of the shoot took place in the majestic wilds of the Cairngorms (Marshall also made **Doomsday**). Like **The Eagle**, with which *Centurion* is thematically linked, the argument could be made that this is *not* a Scottish film within the definition adopted in this book. However, as the bulk of the action takes place in what is today Scotland, and as this is positioned as being *beyond* the Roman-occupied territory in Britain (and therefore has a theme in common with so many of the films covered here in which Scotland exists in opposition to, or as something different than, England), it is included here. Andrew Cumming's 2022 film *The Origin*† – shown at the GFF in

March 2023, and winner of a Scottish BAFTA for Best Film in 2024 (as *Out of Darkness*) – is not. *The Origin* is set '45,000 years ago', in the Stone Age, thousands of years before any concept of a nation state had developed.

Centurion is fiction, not history. It is almost certainly influenced by Rosemary Sutcliff's 1954 novel, *The Eagle of the Ninth*, which takes as its basis the disappearance from the record of the IX Legio Hispana (this is explicitly the source for **The Eagle**), although there is no credit to this effect. There is no clear evidence that the legion met its demise in Scotland. The story of the missing legion also underpins *The Last Legion* (Doug Lefler, 2007), which features Peter Mullan, but not Scotland. *Centurion* has just enough history to provide a framework which is – if one does not examine it too closely – plausible. But the Picts weren't Picts at the time, Gaelic was not spoken, naming conventions are flouted, and weapons and armour are exotically diverse. As Alex von Tunzelmann wrote in *The Guardian*'s Reel History series, 'The governor of Britain, Julius Agricola, summons the Ninth Legion. This is very impressive of him, considering that by AD117 he had been dead for 24 years... He orders the commander of the Ninth... to subdue the Picts [and] gives him a Pictish scout, Etain... a kind of gothic ninja Barbie.' In fact, there is something unpleasantly regressive about Kurylenko's role – she plays a woman whose entire life has been dictated by rape and brutalisation; she is the way she is because of the way she has been treated, and lacks agency.

If you treat the film as simply a tale of a small band of warriors making their way through hostile territory and peoples against insurmountable odds, it's not all bad. The cast is very strong: in addition to those named above, David Morrissey, Liam Cunningham, Imogen Poots and Riz Ahmed appear. The plot is – just – slightly more plausible than is the case in respect of *The Eagle*, and Fassbender a more convincing Roman centurion than Channing Tatum.

→ *The Eagle* (2011)   S++

Directed by Kevin Macdonald
Screenplay by Jeremy Brock
Leading cast: Channing Tatum (Marcus); Jamie
    Bell (Esca); Donald Sutherland (Uncle Aquila);
    Mark Strong (Guern)
Colour, 89 minutes, UK, English/Gaelic

'North of the Wall', 140 AD. Marcus, a Roman officer, and his British slave, Esca, head to the Highlands to attempt the retrieval of 'The Eagle', the standard of a 5,000-strong Roman legion, commanded by Marcus' father, which vanished 20 years previously.

The Eagle is set in an area which belongs geographically in modern Scotland, is directed by a Scot (Macdonald also directed the much better *The Last King of Scotland*, 2006, which is set in Uganda), and (erroneously) employs Gaelic once our two intrepid heroes are north of Hadrian's Wall.

Neil Marshall's **Centurion**, which, despite there being no link between the two productions, forms a prequel to *The Eagle*, is the better film. There are problems aplenty with *The Eagle*, but it does, at least – thanks to cinematographer Anthony Dod Mantle (who won an Oscar for his work on *Slumdog Millionaire*, Danny Boyle and Loveleen Tandan, 2008) – look magnificent. Tatum is not magnificent as Marcus; Kyle Smith in the *New York Post* described him as a 'sulky slab'. Sutherland is Sutherland (he was *far* better in *Eye of the Needle*), Strong is wasted, and only Jamie Bell appears to fit his role. Best of all are the 'painted people' of the Seal Tribe. The script is somewhat trite (the closing exchange might as well have been replaced with 'I think this is the beginning of a beautiful friendship') and relies very heavily on coincidence and sheer dumb luck to reach the implausibly satisfactory conclusion.

Donkeys (2010)   S+++   T100

Directed by Morag McKinnon
Screenplay by Colin McLarenn
Leading cast: Martin Compston (Stevie
  Blantyre); James Cosmo (Alfie); Kate Dickie
  (Jackie); Natalie Press (April Hayley); Brian
  Pettifer (Brian Colburn); Natasha Watson
  (Bronwyn Morrison)
Colour, 78 minutes, UK/Denmark

*Elderly friends Alfie and Brian bury Brian's
pet duck and contemplate a trip to Spain,
but Alfie is ill and seeks to rebuild his
broken connection to his daughter, Jackie,
and granddaughter, Bronwyn. Next door
to Jackie, Stevie moves into his mother's
flat, while she is dying of cancer in hospital,
and rebuilds his relationship with her. He
becomes friends with Jackie, and gradually
the five main characters bond – a process
which is interrupted by a revelation from
Alfie, but resumes and is reconfigured after
his death.*

Had *Donkeys* followed its original conception, it would have used the same characters as **Red Road**, as part of a project called 'Advance Party'. Lone Scherfig and Anders Thomas Jensen (see **Wilbur (Wants to Kill Himself)**) created eight characters, who were then going to be worked into films by three different directors, with Arnold's **Red Road** being the first. But the project was adapted when the time came to make *Donkeys* – a film which, given its content, is much more life-affirming than one would expect. When McKinnon asked Lars von Trier (who was involved in the project) what she should do when she found it difficult to work all the characters into her film, his response was 'just have them go by on a bus'. The story behind the production is explained by Jane Graham in *The Guardian*, who wrote in part that 'while **Red Road** was sauntering towards its final edit, *Donkeys* – supposedly being made simultaneously – was trailing behind, struggling with a mismatched writing team and a lead actor whose deteriorating health was causing concern.' The surprising result, wrote Graham, was that the story 'appears to have a happy ending, and this jet-black comedy about an old man coming to terms with his impending death is shaping up as Scotland's underground hit of the year'.

Donkeys was premiered at the EIFF; McKinnon was delighted by how much laughter there was in the audience. It went on to win the Scottish BAFTA award for Best Feature Film in 2011, while James Cosmo was awarded Best Actor (Peter Mullan took the Director award for *Neds*). As Murray acknowledges, the film finds comedy 'in any number of profoundly discomfiting themes: terminal illness, broken families, accidental incest and premeditated betrayal'. At the hub of this chaos is Cosmo's Alfie. Cosmo appears in many films in this book (even more than Peter Mullan), ranging from *Living Apart Together* to **Get Duked!**, and has an extremely extensive list of credits – in excess of 200 – on IMDb. Here he pulls off the extremely neat trick of turning someone who appears to be utterly destructive into a character we can nevertheless care about. It is part of the great irony of the film that his attempts to rebuild a family find fruition only after his funeral, and that his death fulfils the wishes of both of his children. The appearance of an inflatable penguin is one of at least two references in Scottish films to *Gregory's Girl* (see also *Anna and the Apocalypse*).

In *The Herald*, Alison Rowat noted the connection between the film's tone and its location: 'As you might expect from the Glasgow setting, the humour is as snarly as two dogs fighting over a bone'; the story, however, is one which could be readily transposed to any location – a much noted feature of the Dogmac films.

McKinnon also directed 3; more recently she has turned to documentary and short film making.

Golf in the Kingdom (2010)

Directed by Susan Streitfeld
Screenplay by Susan Streitfeld
Leading cast: Mason Gamble (Michael Murphy); David O'Hara (Shivas Irons)
Colour, 86 minutes, US

'The links of Burningbush', 1956: at 'the most famous golf course in the world – where it all began', Michael, a philosophy student on his way to India, stops off to play a round of golf. He falls in with a group of academics obsessed with golf and takes lessons (in both life and golf) from the club professional, Shivas.

If you approach *Golf in the Kingdom* as a proud Scot who loves your golf, you're going to start off outraged and likely stay that way (fortunately the film was not released in the UK). If you approach this simply as someone interested in golf – there's no other reason to watch the film, based on 'the best-selling golf novel of all time', by Michael Murphy (1971) – you might be more forgiving, but only a little. After all, the film boasts a strong supporting cast, including Malcolm McDowell, Julian Sands, Joanne Whalley and, offering at least an additional touch of Scottish authenticity alongside Glasgow-born O'Hara (*Comfort and Joy*, *Braveheart*, *The Near Room*), Tony Curran (see eg *Red Road* and *Calibre*).

Golf in the Kingdom is blighted by its trite faux philosophising, a heretical approach to golfing history and lore, and in the words of *Village Voice*'s Nick Schager, is 'devoid of thematic coherence or consequence'. To make matters worse, the film was shot entirely in Oregon, a mere 4,770 miles from the Old Course at St Andrews. The other golfing film in this book, *Tommy's Honour*, is *far* better.

l'Illusionniste (The Illusionist) (2010) `S+` `T25`

Directed by Sylvain Chomet
Screenplay by Jacques Tati, adapted by Sylvain Chomet
Leading cast: Jean-Claude Donda (illusionist); Eilidh Rankin (Alice)
Colour, 80 minutes, English/French/Gaelic, France/US/UK

Paris 1959: the illusionist's career is in obvious decline. He travels to London and is then offered work in a Highland village inn. Alice, the Gaelic-speaking servant girl, is enraptured and follows him when he leaves for Edinburgh. He secures a residency at the Royal Music Hall and provides for Alice. He is let go and then works for Jenners, before leaving Edinburgh. Alice stays behind with a man she has met.

The Illusionist is an animated film based on a script for an unrealised Jacques Tati project not intended for animation. Sixty-four minutes in, there is a nod to Tati's career in cinema, which spanned five decades, but a relatively small output. He made a sequence of three films in a ten-year period which are considered classics: *Jour de Fête* (1949), *Monsieur Hulot's Holiday* (1953) and *Mon Oncle* (1958). Sylvain Chomet has the illusionist walk past Edinburgh's Cameo cinema, displaying posters for *Mon Oncle*. He then stumbles into the cinema and Jacques Tati is on the screen – the only piece of non-animated action in the film. Chomet has said that:

'you have the animated Tati and then you have the real Tati, like a mirror, and they look at each other and say "Do you want to stay?", but they say "no, no, no" and they leave. I think he needed to be there, if only for a moment.'

In *Jacques Tati* (1999) David Bellos contextualises Tati's script. Tati was working in music halls across Europe, 'a sad occupation for a man in middle age, and it is the pathos of decline and failure that informs the [script]'. Later Bellos writes, 'it is probably just as well that Tati never actually made this film, with its complicated, sentimental, and obviously autobiographical plot.' Bellos was writing before Chomet decided to adapt the script for animation, which is delivered in stunning quality, with Edinburgh beautifully rendered.

The script as it appears on the screen departs from that written by Tati, but it retains a profound sense of pathos. It is spare, and there is no instance of a full conversation. The illusionist speaks only French with a few words of English, and Alice speaks Gaelic. The only times the illusionist really has success are in a small Highland inn (the audience is easily pleased – someone is applauded for flicking the light switch on and off), and as an attraction in the window of Jenners department store. When he first performs in London, he follows a cheesily named rock and roll band, which has the audience on their feet. Once the band leave the stage (after many encores), only two are left in the audience. The same band later displaces the illusionist from his residency in the Royal Music Hall. Alice is fascinated by

Edinburgh is beautifully rendered in *L'Illusionniste*

radio and television sets in an Edinburgh shop window; the old world of music hall and variety is ending.

The relationship between the illusionist and Alice comes to fruition only in the sense that both move on; her position has certainly been improved. We do not know what the future holds for the illusionist. For Chomet, this is 'not sad. It's an evolution... [they] are both going their separate ways. She's young, from a different generation, so she's going to live her own life within her own culture. And he is an old man, but he's also going to carry on and do something else'.

The lights literally go out at the end of *The Illusionist*. In the final scene before the credits (one very short scene is shown after), the last thing we see is the dimming of the lights on the façade of the Royal Music Hall. The illusionist leaves a note on the desk of the hotel when he departs: 'Magicians do not exist'.

Imogène McCarthery (2010) S+

Directed by Alexandre Charlot and Franck Magnier
Screenplay by Alexandre Charlot and Franck Magnier
Leading cast: Catherine Frot (Imogène); Lambert Wilson (Samuel Tyler)
Colour, 82 minutes, France, French

A secretary at the (French-speaking) Admiralty in London is tasked with delivering secret documents to a scientist in 'Falkland', Scotland. She is part of an elaborate plot of which she has no knowledge, the purpose of which is to unmask a Russian mole.

Based on Charles Exbrayat's novel, *Ne vous fâchez pas, Imogène!* (1959; the first of his seven books featuring the intrepid Scot), *Imogène McCarthery* provides a fairly pleasant way to idly pass 80 minutes. The film is slight, ridiculous, and fun. Entertainingly, the spy to be unmasked is Imogène's colleague Nancy, played by a young Sara Giraudeau five years before she took on the role of a French agent in the terrific TV series *The Bureau* (2015–2020). London exterior scenes were shot in Edinburgh, the Scottish scenes elsewhere in Scotland.

Outcast (2010) S+++ T100

Directed by Colm McCarthy
Screenplay by Colm McCarthy and Tom K McCarthy
Leading cast: Kate Dickie (Mary); James Nesbitt (Cathal); Niall Bruton (Fergal); Hanna Stanbridge (Petronella); Josh Whitelaw (Tomatsk)
Colour, 98 minutes, UK/Ireland

Mary, a member of a clan of Irish witches, and her son, Fergal, move into an Edinburgh housing estate. They are being hunted. While Mary uses her powers to protect them, Fergal undergoes a sinister transformation.

Outcast is a strong horror film, made unusual by its approach to social realism. This mix was commented on by *The Scotsman*'s critic Alistair Harkness, who praised the ambition, but noted an 'uneven hybrid of grim social realism and flat-out monster movie theatrics', and a muddled plot. Most critics found more to praise than to condemn. At the time of writing *Outcast*

has a Rotten Tomatoes score of 64 per cent. Dickie in particular garnered praise (eg, 'as in *Red Road*, Dickie is outstanding' – Kim Newman, in *Empire*). Interviewed in *The Guardian* in May 2022, Mark Kermode was asked the question: 'which actor do you think has produced the greatest quality of work across their career?'. His answer was emphatic: 'Kate Dickie. She is the most consistently brilliant actor I can think of'.

It takes time for *Outcast* to establish that it really is a film about the fantastical. Until Mary casts a curse on an officious housing officer, it is not clear whether she and Fergal really are the special people he claims. The curse takes hold, and from this point we are not watching a psychological horror film in which a young woman, protecting from his father the son she conceived at 15, constructs a fantasy to provide the framework for their existence. The result is that *Outcast* is, to summarise Kim Newman, simply a werewolf movie, albeit one that 'takes interesting detours to get there'. But a film about modern-day witches and beasts, set in a housing estate in the Edinburgh suburbs, makes a welcome change from films about witches and beasts set in remote Gothic mansions, although the set designers endow the building which Mary and Fergus move into with *some* of the trappings of a creaky Gothic pile. The estate provides an element of social authenticity, as well as a suitable set of blind alleys, corridors, and abandoned utility rooms in which to hang out, perform magic, be chased down, kill and be killed. James Nesbitt is an effective adversary to Dickie, although his mentor,

Ciarán McMenamin, is required to provide a more balanced performance. Both young leads shine in their first film roles. Edinburgh-born McCarthy, who directed and co-wrote the screenplay, also directed the rather good *The Girl with All the Gifts* (2016). He has an extensive list of credits for work on TV, including *Sherlock, Black Mirror* and *Peaky Blinders*.

A Lonely Place to Die (2011) S++

Directed by Julian Gilbey
Screenplay by Julian Gilbey and William Gilbey
Leading cast: Melissa George (Alison); Alec Newman (Rob); Ed Speelers (Ed); Kate Magowan (Jenny); Garry Sweeney (Alex)
Colour, 89 minutes, English/Serbian, UK

Amidst stunning scenery, five climbers in the Highlands find a girl who has been kidnapped and buried alive. Unable to phone for help, they split up – with two tackling the 'Devil's Drop' cliff face to alert the authorities, while the others attempt to take the girl to a village 15 miles away. They are all hunted.

Made by the Gilbey brothers, whose previous work included the poorly received *Rollin' With the Nines* (2006) and *Rise of the Footsoldier* (2007), *A Lonely Place to Die* is a strong thriller which fared better with both critics and audiences. It carries a Rotten Tomatoes rating of 75 per cent and won several awards at festival screenings. The film is driven by action, not character development; the only surprise

in the trajectory is the high death toll. Ali Asad's cinematography and the on-location shooting lifts the film above the mere humdrum, and the climbing scenes are, for the most part, strong, although there are points at which the joins show a little too clearly. Phillip French praised the execution: 'a heartless film, but an effective one'.

That this is set in Scotland adds little except scenery and remote distance. A kidnapper explains that the girl has been left in 'a location as remote as it is inaccessible'. Those are the requirements here: isolation and lack of contact. A *Wicker Man*- and Up Helly Aa-inspired fire-festival in the village of 'Annan Mor', where all the threads come together, is a somewhat bizarre addition, although it adds chaos, and the sound of fireworks conceals the hail of gunfire. Newman and Sweeney are both Scottish.

Attack of the Herbals (2011) S+++

Directed by David Ryan Keith
Screenplay by Alisdair Cook, Liam Matheson and David Ryan Keith
Leading cast: Calum Booth (Jackson McGregor); Lee Hutcheon (Danny the Pincer); Richard Currie (Stevie, 'The Roadrunner'); Liam Matheson (Bennett Campbell); Claire McCulloch (Jenny Robertson)
Colour, 81 minutes, UK

'Lobster Cove' in Aberdeenshire: Jackson returns home, and times are hard. A cargo of 'herbal tea', jettisoned in WWII by Nazi scientists, washes up. Jackson sells

it in the post office, and it proves to be extremely popular. It has the side effect of turning people into something approaching zombies.

Described in *Screen International* as a zombie comedy (perhaps, in Scottish terms, **Whisky Galore!** meets *World War Z*), *Attack of the Herbals* (marketed in Germany as *Attack of the Nazi Herbals*) was the first feature film from director Keith. He has since, with his producer partner and wife Lorraine, made a further five. The film premiered in Newtonhill, where much of the shoot took place (Stonehaven was used for harbour shots). Later, *Herbals* was shown at the 2012 Loch Ness Independent Film Festival and received a limited release, before moving to DVD and streaming. Surprisingly – and based on thin evidence – the *Aberdeen Evening Journal* later reported the film was 'a big hit in America, Canada and Germany'. The budget was variously reported as being £600 and £15,000. The latter is the more plausible figure. The film was made by volunteers: Liam Matheson said, 'We do this for nothing. There were times during filming when we were standing in the pouring rain that I wondered why I was doing this. But it is a passion and friendship. We want to do this for the love of it.'

While it received limited distribution, and virtually no reviews, as a calling-card *Herbals* was an undoubted success. As entertainment there is some enjoyment to be had, particularly once everything runs riot, but as Dave Gammon puts it on

Horrornews.net, 'one is best recommended to check expectations and inhibitions at the door'. Keith's other Scottish films are discussed below; 2023's *I am Rage* was released straight to streaming.

→ *The Redwood Massacre* (2014) `S+++`

Directed by David Ryan Keith
Screenplay by David Ryan Keith
Leading cast: Mark Wood (Bruce); Lisa Cameron (Pamela); Lisa Livingstone (Kirsty); Rebecca Wilkie (Jessica); Lee Hutcheon (Hunter); Adam Coutts (Mark)
Colour, 82 minutes, UK

'Five people go into the forest to find an old house where a family massacre took place. They soon realise the legends are all true while being stalked by a masked killer' (David Ryan Keith).

Having proved with **Attack of the Herbals** that he knew how to make a feature film and having had some exposure, Keith was able to put in place financing for the more polished *The Redwood Massacre*, which picked up four awards at the Chicago Horror Film Festival in 2014: Best Feature, Director, Writer and Screenplay. On the face of it, *TRM* sounds like it should be American, but *this* Redwood is 'Redwood Farm' in the Aberdeenshire woods. *TRM* is, in fact, as one critic has pointed out, 'the closest thing we're ever likely to see to a Scottish version of *Friday the 13th* [Sean S Cunningham, 1980]' (*Trash Film Guru*), and here, unlike Keith's earlier film, there is no comedy. Ahead of a screening at the Aberdeen Film Festival, the Aberdeen *Evening Express* quoted Keith: 'It's your stereotypical slasher film from the 1980s, we've stuck pretty close to the formulas used back then'.

Horror films often exist in their own ecosystem (for low-budget ones this is especially true) and are overlooked by mainstream reviewers, but there are passionate audiences, and many sites devoted to them. On these, the reception accorded to *TRM* was strong (and there is a sequel – see below). *horrorsociety.com*'s take was that *TRM* was 'the slasher film of the year... brutal and relentless'. I haven't checked how many other slasher films were released in 2014 but am quite prepared to believe that this was among the best of them.

The film begins with a brutal slaying and the pace barely slackens – that there is no CGI used in creating the effects ensures the requisite killings (it's a slasher movie!) remain visceral. The cast is strong; the step up from *Attack of the Herbals* evident. Livingstone for example (who also features in *Ghosts of Darkness*, below), already had professional roles under her belt, and went on to appear in *Run*, as did Wood. Cameron's first role was in *Sawney Flesh of Man* and she has become a Keith regular, appearing in three further films. Aberdeen band DeadFire provided two songs, 'War' and 'Mind On The Kill', for the soundtrack.

→ *Ghosts of Darkness* (aka *House of Ghosts*) (2017)   S++

Directed by David Ryan Keith
Screenplay by David Ryan Keith
Leading cast: Michael Koltes (Jack Donavan);
   Paul Flannery (Jonathan Blazer)
Colour, 82 minutes, UK

'Richmond House' in the Highlands: paranormal debunker Jack, and Jonathan, an acclaimed psychic, are tempted by a $50,000 reward to spend three nights locked together in an allegedly haunted house; if either leaves both forfeit the money. They battle dark forces and a sacrifice must be made.

Ghosts of Darkness was made in part with US backing, and a budget of £50,000. Keith told the *Press and Journal*: 'Having the financial backing has helped us greatly improve on the films we have produced in the past.' This step up in finance probably explains the presence of German-born, US-based Koltes, who has a long CV. This was Flannery's first screen role (he is better known as a live performer/presenter/comedian). The strength of the film lies not in its scares, but in the interaction between the two leads, who, after conflict, work together to survive (*wickedhorror.com*: 'an unexpectedly deep piece that bravely focuses more on the characters of Jack and Jon rather than the goings on at the house'). The dapper Jonathan gets the best lines ('this hapless handyman came round to fix the washing machine; an hour later he hung himself out to dry') – serving as the comic (yet competent) foil to Jack's dour sceptic. The film works because the relationship works.

Ghosts was shot in Aberdeenshire and near Fort William over a three-week period and, like **Lord of Tears**, Ardgour House is the main location.

→ **The Dark Within** (2019) S++

Directed by David Ryan Keith
Screenplay by David Ryan Keith and Paul
  Flannery
Leading cast: Paul Flannery (Blaine/Marcus);
  Kendra Carelli (Sarah Price); Stephanie Lynn
  Styles (Dr Norton)
Colour, 88 minutes, UK

Marcus, who is on parole and in mandated therapy, may be a psychic. His psychiatrist, Dr Norton, persuades him to revisit his childhood home, a derelict cabin, from which his parents went missing in 1981. Marcus takes a serum developed by his father, which enhances psychic abilities.

Like **Ghosts of Darkness**, The Dark Within was produced in part with American backing, and with Americans involved in the film's production. The high proportion of female crew led to the film being accepted for the Los Angeles Femme International Film Festival. The film was, in common with the previous Keith productions, shot largely in the North East of Scotland – the derelict house being in the Aberdeenshire village of Logie Coldstone; the interiors were constructed in

a warehouse in Stonehaven. Paul Flannery, who was so strong in **Ghosts of Darkness**, returns in the lead, and shares a co-writing credit with Keith.

The film's set-up is strong, and echoes of *The Evil Dead* (Sam Raimi, 1981) do no harm. The questions we're asked to consider are good ones, but in the second half the film loses its way, something critics have commented on. For *Film Threat*, Enrique Acosta wrote, 'Keith does an admirable job of creating a creepy, brooding, uncomfortable atmosphere. Unfortunately, any goodwill that was built up in act one is squandered in the rest of the film.' A similar concern is raised by David S Smith in *horrorcultfilms*: 'The core puzzle stays interesting throughout. However, during the second half the hallucinatory parts, along with some of the scares, lose a lot of their dramatic impact'.

→ **Redwood Massacre: Annihilation** (2020)   S+++

Directed by David Ryan Keith
Screenplay by David Ryan Keith
Leading cast: Danielle Harris (Laura Dempsey);
  Damien Puckler (Max); Gary Kasper (Gus); Jon
  Campling (Tom Dempsey); Tevy Poe (Jen); Lisa
  Cameron (Pamela); Benjamin Selway (Burlap Killer)
Colour, 104 minutes, UK

Dempsey has written a book about the Redwood Massacre, and is contacted by a fan, Max, who says he has found the mask used by the killer. A group go to the farm to find out more...

Redwood Massacre: Annihilation played at FrightFest 2020, where it drew the ire of Kim Newman: '… this is resolutely minor fare, and (length apart) among the least ambitious British horror films of recent years'. The original film (see above) had the virtue of being close – deliberately so – to a pastiche of the glory years of the American slasher, but Keith doesn't pull that off twice. Even the presence of horror stalwart Danielle Harris cannot save this.

The Big Slick (2011)   S+++   T100

Directed by Graham Hughes
Screenplay by Keith Grantham, Graham Hughes and Graeme McGeagh
Leading cast: Graeme McGeagh (Gavin); Martin Haig (Daniel); Keith Grantham (Jessie); Scott Cunningham (Shug); Robbie Williams [not that Robbie Williams] (Murray); Graham Hughes (Alex)
Colour, 87 minutes, UK

'Not too long ago, in a small town in Scotland…': Gavin and his friends plan to play poker, but events take over. They survive a chaotic evening, involving a psychotic drug dealer, a party, robbery, mugging, a mother's ashes, and a samurai sword.

Graham Hughes is an independent filmmaker, based in Glasgow, who should be better known and appreciated. He's made four films, three of which are dealt with here (the 2023 film *Hostile Dimensions* deals with alternate dimensions). Alongside a BAFTA Scotland award for the writers in the 'New Talent' category, *The Big Slick* picked up the audience award at the annual Lanarkshire-based 'Deep Fried Film Festival'. There's an element of 'boys will be boys' to *The Big Slick*, but there is charm (particularly in a short discussion as to how much better *Sex and the City* and *Desperate Housewives* would be if they were to include Jack Bauer, guns, explosions and terrorists), some good gags, and the script ties things together extremely neatly. The filmmakers' inexperience shows (particularly in sound recording levels), but it's hard to knock the result. Made on a shoestring budget (IMDb gives the figure of £200), with friends taking on the lead roles, and shot locally around Kirkintilloch, Hughes should be proud of the result. I laughed out loud at least three times and admired the tight plotting. There is wit and intelligence on display here, as well as an acute eye for authenticity. *The Big Slick* was put up on YouTube by Hughes (so there's no need to feel any copyright-theft guilt in watching it this way).

→ *A Practical Guide to a*
Spectacular Suicide (2014) S+++

Directed by Graham Hughes
Screenplay by Keith Grantham, Graham Hughes
and Graeme McGeagh
Leading cast: Graeme McGeagh (Tom Collins);
Ray Crofter (Mr Neilsen); Annabelle Logan
(Eve McKinlay); Patrick O'Brien (Dr Watson)
Colour, 85 minutes, UK

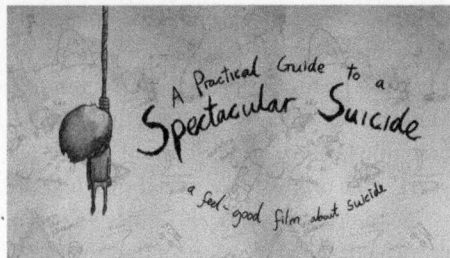

Tom repeatedly tries and fails to die by
suicide. He is required by a court order
to spend time with Mr Neilsen providing
care support, and with a psychiatrist, Dr
Watson. He also forms a relationship with
one of Watson's patients, Eve.

Practical Guide has much in common with
The Big Slick: the writing team is the same,
the lead actor is in both films, and others
from the first film appear. The budget and
aspirations have clearly grown – as has
the film's technical sophistication. This is
a more assured, and ambitious, second
feature, although not without its flaws.
The cast remain largely inexperienced, and
Hughes is a little *too* eager to make the
most of the expanded opportunities open
to him: multiple techniques are used (the
most charming being animation), but the
impression these create is occasionally one
of discord rather than harmony.

There's an element of risk in making
a comedy about a subject as serious as
suicide. It helps here that Tom is inherently
likeable, and that enough of the jokes
land. There is a fundamental problem,
however, with the set-up. Given Tom's

apparent determination to die, and the fact
he lives on a high floor of an apartment
building (in Glasgow, where the film is
set), that he remains alive at the start of the
film suggests an ineptitude verging on the
ridiculous, *or*, and this may be the point
– he does not really wish to end his life at
all. This makes the premise a difficult sell.
This was certainly an issue for Stephen
Neiss, writing for *HeyUGuys* after the
EIFF screening: 'Never for a moment does
[it] capture the imagination, or invite the
necessary suspension of disbelief. You wait
to be swept up in the story… it's just not
going to happen.' I liked the film more than
Neiss. Tom's relationships with Mr Neilsen
and Eve are well-built. Best of all, however,
is his relationship with the improbably
named Dr Watson (although there must
of course be doctors out there with this
resonant surname). This also leads to a
cutely punning book title: 'Watson Your
Mind?'

→ *Death of a Vlogger* (2019) S+++

Directed by Graham Hughes
Screenplay by Graham Hughes
Leading cast: Graham Hughes (Graham Hughes);
    Annabel Logan (Erin); Paddy Kondracki (Steve);
    Joma West (Alice Harper)
Colour, 88 minutes, UK

Graham is a vlogger who fakes a 'livestream' featuring paranormal phenomena. He is exposed, and subject to intensive trolling. He appears to be taken by the very ghost he has been faking.

Death of a Vlogger is the first of Graham Hughes' films in which he takes sole credit for the screenplay. It marks a significant shift in tone from his first two films where the emphasis is on humour. The fakeumentary approach in *Vlogger* treats social media content as found footage, resulting in a high-premise film which is as much a comment on social media and its users, as it is a horror/ghost film. It found favour with reviewers and holds a 100 per cent score on Rotten Tomatoes at the time of writing.

There's a curious meta-approach to *Vlogger*. Graham Hughes plays Graham Hughes, and the film is largely set in his own flat (you can spot on the wall his BAFTA Scotland New Talent Award, for 2011's *The Big Slick*), but this can also be distancing, and the horror element of the film is in danger of being undermined by its own cleverness: we know Hughes is a filmmaker and the director of this work of fiction and are therefore invited to hold on to both this reality and the fiction created by Hughes at the same time. It is also hard to feel sympathy for, and therefore to empathise with, Graham when he is clearly a giant arse (in the film; IRL he is probably delightful).

There is constant questioning through the film as to what is real and what is fake – and here there is layer upon layer of fakery (or is there?). An introductory segment focuses on perception, and how this can be played with (it also introduces the possibility of the paranormal). One result is that while there are effective 'jump' moments (Hughes created his own effects), there is not the build-up of tension which good horror relies on. Another, and perhaps more important result, is that this is an effective commentary on the difficult relationship between social media, truth, reputation, trolling and mental health. Graham is the ultimate victim of the film, and perhaps it does not matter whether he is the victim of trolling or of a spectre. Either way, he is – presumably – dead.

Hughes' 2023 film *Hostile Dimensions*† is linked to *Death of a Vlogger* in that it too is a found footage documentary, shot in part in his flat. This has its leads heading into alternate dimensions on the hunt for a disappeared graffiti artist.

Billionaire Ransom (aka *Take Down*) (2011) S+

Directed by Jim Gillespie
Screenplay by Alexander Ignon
Leading cast: Jeremy Sumpter (Kyle Hartmann);
  Phoebe Tonkin (Amy Tilton); Mark Bonnar
  (Lawrence Close); Robert Cavanah (Tom
  Maxwell)
Colour, 107 minutes, UK

'Island of West Soay', Scotland: an institution designed to rehabilitate the 'spoiled over-privileged offspring of the super rich'. While on a survival course, the youths are threatened with kidnap by a gang seeking the largest pay-off in history and put their newly acquired skills to use.

Scottish director Jim Gillespie's greatest success came with his first feature, the smash hit *I Know What You Did Last Summer* (1997). Sadly, nothing he has done since – it's a relatively short list – has had anything like the same impact (his 2005 film *Venom*, is *not* the first instalment in the DC Tom Hardy series). At the time of writing *Billionaire Ransom* is his most recent feature. This film is set on an invented Scottish island (to guarantee the required remoteness), but was shot on the Isle of Man, and in Wales. Mark Bonnar, playing the head of the 'school', was born in Edinburgh, and has a long list of credits, primarily in television. *Billionaire Ransom* is by-the-numbers filmmaking; while there are a few good moments, overall, it's lacklustre fare.

Blooded (2011) S+

Directed by Edward Boase
Screenplay by James Walker, Edward Boase and
  Nick Clark Windo
Leading cast: Neil McDermott and Nick Clark
  Windo (Lucas Bell); Isabella Calthorpe and
  Cicely Tennant (Liv); Mark Dexter and Oliver
  Boot (Charlie Bell); Sharon Duncan-Brewster
  and Tracy Ifeachor (Eve); Adam Best and Joseph
  Kloska (Ben Fitzpatrick)
Colour, 80 minutes, UK

October 2005, Mull: Lucas Bell, the face of unlawful fox-hunting in the UK, and some friends spend time on Mull to escape the threats he is subject to. A group of anti-hunt activists decide to take robust action. A documentary is constructed after the events.

A mockumentary (one of three in this book, along with *The Incident at Loch Ness* and *Occasional Monsters*), *Blooded* is also one of three films in which people hunt people (*New Town Killers* and *Get Duked!*). It is built on supposed found footage (within the world of the film, video shot by anti-hunt activists), reconstructions, and interviews with the five leads voiced by actors, a combination which gives rise to a clumsy device in which two sets of actors play each role. Rightly, the film fared badly with critics. Philip French in *The Observer* wrote that '*Blooded* centres with something less than total conviction on a quintet of dislikable upper-middle-class blood sports enthusiasts', while Cath Clarke in *The Guardian* was more brutal: 'a hokey idea, and badly botched.'

The Decoy Bride (2011)   S++

Directed by Sheree Folkson
Screenplay by Neil Jaworski and Sally Phillips
Leading cast: Kelly Macdonald (Katie); David
  Tennant (James); Alice Eve (Lara); Maureen
  Beattie (Iseabail)
Colour, 89 minutes, UK

Seeking a private wedding, a Hollywood star and her author fiancé decamp to 'Hegg' in the Outer Hebrides. A 'decoy bride' is employed to thwart resourceful paparazzi. Misunderstandings, farce, and romance follow.

Rom-com *The Decoy Bride* has a strong cast led by two very fine Scottish actors, with plenty of talent familiar from British films (including Dylan Moran and James Fleet) on display. It aims at Ealing-esque whimsy, and was shot in beautiful locations both in Scotland (Glasgow University's cloisters, Caerlaverock Castle, etc) and the Isle of Man. It even has the required happy ending. But the result is deathly dull. The set-up is simple – a 'decoy bride' and her 'groom' fall in love – but takes almost 30 minutes to get into gear. The script is leaden; the best 'joke' comes when a character on 'Hegg' ('the plain Jane of the Hebrides') says 'we don't want them thinking this is the Orkneys where anything goes'. Macdonald and Tennant give it their best, but their task is akin to rolling an improbably large stone up an impossibly steep hill. Although the film

David Tennant and Alice Eve

fared very poorly with the critics, I must acknowledge some were seduced, including *The Guardian*'s Peter Bradshaw and, in *The NYT*, Neil Genzlinger; most were not. As *The Village Voice*'s Michael Atkinson put it, 'If you don't bridle at the pandering, nothing bothers you.'

Fast Romance (2011)   S+++

Directed by Carter Ferguson
Screenplay by Debbie May and James McCreadie
Leading cast: William Ruane (Gordon Boyd); Samantha Mollin (Heather); Lesley Hart (Lorna Kerr); Lawrence Crawford (DC Spencer); Jo Freer (Nadine Catalano); Derek Munn (Kenny Cairns)
Colour, 97 minutes, UK

Glasgow: a story about 'seven very different people who went looking for love and got more than they bargained for'.

After *Fast Romance* won the Cineworld Audience Award at the Scottish BAFTAs, associate producer Alasdair McDougall said, 'Scotland has become known for dark films such as *Trainspotting* and *Neds* and while these are great films, we wanted to make a more light-hearted film in the vein of eighties comedies like *Gregory's Girl* and *Local Hero*'. Made on a budget reported to be between £40,000 to £60,000, partly raised from local businesses wanting to see more positive portrayals of Glasgow, the producers relied on social media to support the Glasgow-set rom-com's distribution. *The Scotsman* later commented in reporting on

the controversy surrounding the following year's award, that '*Fast Romance*, though pilloried by the critics, made full use of the web to court the public vote'.

Described by *The Evening Times* as Scotland's answer to *Love Actually* (Richard Curtis, 2003), an extremely flattering comparison, *Fast Romance* is based around multiple interconnecting lead characters, although few of these are from the smart classes which dominate *Love Actually*. Director Ferguson had played Harry Black in *River City* (2004–2005) and had small roles in *Complicity* and *Women Talking Dirty*. Many of the cast and crew had also spent time on the long-running Glasgow-based soap, the importance of which in nurturing Scottish talent cannot be understated.

Fast Romance found little favour with critics and is no *Love Actually*. In *S&S*, Hannah McGill was dismissive of the clumsy script, but thought the 'biggest problem, however, is not the hoary language but the register of the acting... [The actors] have clearly been directed to make every reaction as big as possible, and the effect is oppressive rather than amusing'. *The Scotsman*'s Alistair Harkness was more direct, lambasting the film as being 'rubbish in a way that only low budget Scottish movies seem able to manage'*. *Fast Romance* remains the only feature to be directed by Ferguson, and to be written by the wife and husband team of May and McCreadie.

* I'm not convinced that there is something uniquely terrible about low-budget Scottish films.

While there are some truly awful films covered in this book, I suspect these appear on Harkness' radar in a way that terrible films from other countries do not, as they would have no traction outwith misguided patriotic distribution.

Graders (2011)　　　　　S+++

Directed by David Hutchison
Screenplay by David Hutchison
Leading cast: Joanna Kaczynska (Ania Krol);
　Greg Drysdale (Lem); Agnieszka Bresler
　(Celina Krol); Janet de Vigne (Mrs Graham)
Colour, 98 minutes, UK

Celina, a young Polish woman busking in Edinburgh, is invited to a job at a fish processing plant in the Highlands, and leaves her pregnant sister, Ania, behind in Edinburgh. Celina falls out of contact and Ania sets off to find her, saying: 'There's something funny going on'. She's right.

Influenced in part by the murders of two central-European women in Scotland, and by his own time working in a fish factory, Scottish filmmaker Hutchison wrote and directed *Graders* on a budget of £4,000, with shooting in part around Lochinver and Assynt in the northwest Highlands. *Graders* received its world premiere at the Inverness Film Festival in November 2011, then went on to generate some faux controversy (the *Scottish Express* reported in August 2012 that a 'horror film inspired by the murders of two Eastern European women living in Scotland has sparked outrage in the communities where their

bodies were found'), but limited interest.

Graders is not alone in being a low-budget horror film set in Scotland, and does not stand out from the crowd. Its trajectory is clearly signalled in the opening scene, and its 'horror', based around illegal organ harvesting, is both unbelievable and dialled down to the point where this is as much thriller as horror, but neither thrilling nor horrific.

Island (2011)　　　　　S+

Directed by Elizabeth Mitchell and Brek Taylor
Screenplay by Elizabeth Mitchell
Leading cast: Natalie Press (Nikki Black); Janet
　McTeer (Phyllis); Colin Morgan (Calum)
Colour, 102 minutes, UK

Twenty-nine-year-old 'Nikki Black' travels from London to a Scottish island, lodging with Phyllis and her son Calum. Dark family secrets are uncovered, and the living are condemned to repeat the past.

The only feature film made by its co-directors, *Island* blends magic-realism with realism to unpick complex and uncertain family relationships. Moving to a limited release after playing at the GFF, it fared poorly with critics. In the *Sunday Times*, Edward Porter had praise for the cast, but some scorn for the 'highly strung tale set on a Hebridean island' noting 'at no point... could I take the film as seriously as it does itself'. Laurence Phelan in *The Independent* found *Island* 'not so much enigmatic and intense as it is opaque and muddled'. The film is at its most muddled in a final confrontation between Phyllis and Nikki, with Phyllis apparently holding simultaneously the beliefs that her daughter, Susan, died aged nine, *and* that Nikki is, as she claims to be, Susan. Much of the dialogue is heavy-handed, signposting that we are meant to peel apart the layers (as Nikki/Susan says in a preface 'don't believe everything you are told... give me the fairy story everyday') but while this may have worked well on the page (the film is based on Jane Rogers' novel of the same name) it does not work well on film (or, at least, in *this* film).

With the magic-realism stripped out, *Island* would become very similar, both tonally and thematically, to the (much better) films of Scott Graham (see *Shell* etc).

Ewan McGregor and Eva Green in a film which resonated through the Covid pandemic

Perfect Sense (2011)   S+++

Directed by David Mackenzie
Screenplay by Kim Fupz Aakeson
Leading cast: Eva Green (Susan); Ewan McGregor (Michael)
Colour, 92 minutes, UK/Sweden/Denmark/Ireland

A pandemic sweeps the world, stripping people of their senses, one by one. Susan, an epidemiologist in Glasgow, and Michael, a chef at a local restaurant, form a relationship as events unfold, and are together at the very end.

A fascinating premise is wasted in this pandemic-leading-to-extinction film. It is a peculiar choice to make one of the lead characters, Susan, an epidemiologist. Normally, this would signal a scientific explanation, a fightback, and the ultimate triumph of human ingenuity. Here, it appears the purpose is to emphasise the inability of humanity to resist the tide, but the consequence is that *Perfect Sense* is a science fiction film without the science. This may be why the *other* pandemic film from 2011, Steven Soderbergh's *Contagion*, became the one to watch during the Covid-19 pandemic (note that **White Out**, below, also deals with a pandemic).

Green and McGregor are quite capable of playing characters who are fundamentally not very pleasant, but it's a hard relationship for the audience to invest in. The pandemic is much more interesting than their coupling. By far the most effective sequences in the film have Michael and his colleagues (including Denis Lawson and Ewen Bremner) designing restaurant meals which are based around colour and texture, rather than around taste and smell.

Susan provides the final line of the film in voice-over: 'And if there had been anybody left to see them then they would look like normal lovers, caressing each other's faces, bodies close together, eyes closed, oblivious to the world around them, because that is how life goes on, like that.' The problem with *Perfect Sense* is that life will not go on, like that. There is no way back at this point: there will be a global collapse of society, and almost everyone will die, probably quite horribly and slowly. As Andrew Lapin says in his review for NPR, the film 'continually, wrongly insists that Susan and Michael's defeatist romance is the real story'. The downbeat final trajectory renders everything that has happened so far somewhat pointless.

The Space Between (2011) S+++

Directed by Tim Barrow
Screenplay by Tim Barrow
Leading cast: Vivien Reid (Lisa); Tim Barrow
  (Steven)
Colour, 85 minutes, UK

London: Steven lives alone, after the death of a child. Edinburgh: Lisa leads a lonely, largely silent existence after being left by her married lover; she too has lost a child. Arriving back home, Steven is mugged on Anchor Close; he loses his wallet, and is helped by Lisa. Slowly, they come together.

Writer/director/lead actor/producer (perhaps the use of the word *auteur* here would be fully justified) Tim Barrow shot *The Space Between* in just 17 days in the summer of 2010 with a budget of £15,000.

He'd previously written and appeared in *The Inheritance* (Charles Henri Belleville, 2007), also a Lyre Production (see too, **Riptide**, below), and has a significant CV in film and theatre as an actor on both stage and screen (he has a very small role in **New Town Killers**; and is credited with stunt work on **Anna and the Apocalypse**). Tim is also, based on my experience, generous with his time and encouragement. Vivien Reid was in her first film, moving across from the stage. Made at a time where there were still not that many films set in Edinburgh, *The Space Between* was described in the *Stirling Observer* as an 'anti-Trainspotting' film. It isn't, but here Edinburgh is a city which permits recovery.

The space between London and Edinburgh, the physical space between Lisa and Steven at the start of the spare story, is just a little over 330 miles. Mentally, the space appears to be unbridgeable, with both locked in self-absorbed grief. But in Edinburgh ('Set against a sumptuously-filmed series of famous Auld Reekie landmarks' – *News of the World*), they come together, not through a contrived 'meet-cute' (this is not that sort of film), but so slowly and plausibly that it almost seems rightly inevitable.

The film is slow – it is a *long* time before the first words are spoken – and this is not to everyone's taste (at *the wee review.com* Amy Taylor wrote the 'film is simply too heavy, too bogged down by innumerable side stories and issues'). But the pacing *has* to be a deliberate choice, and it largely works, buoyed by strong performances and Chris Martin's camera work. If there is a problem here it is that, in the words of *Screen Daily*'s Allan Hunter (generally strongly supportive of Scottish cinema), 'the film fails to generate a significant emotional investment in the anguish of the central characters. The decision to keep their backstory to a minimum means that we never gain a full sense of who they really are'.

The Space Between remains available on DVD from Lyre Productions.

→ *Riptide* (2020)   S+++ T100

Directed by Tim Barrow
Screenplay by Tim Barrow
Leading cast: Tim Barrow (Jacob); David Tudor (Jonathan); Elspeth Turner (Eva); David Whitney (Dr Lloyd)
Colour, 90 minutes, UK

Edinburgh, autumn: Jacob returns home after treatment for schizophrenia. He's employed as a street cleaner, spends time at a boxing gym, and receives support from a community practice nurse and Dr Lloyd. On a road trip he saves Eva from what he believes to be a suicide attempt. She has her own struggles with mental health, but a relationship develops to the benefit of both.

Scottish-born Tim Barrow (see also *The Space Between*) produces, directs, writes, and takes the lead role in *Riptide*. Any severe criticism of the film is therefore unavoidably a direct criticism of his work, a sincere attempt to (as he put it to me) 'bust the stigma around mental health'. As someone who has been bipolar for much of my life that's an aim I'm fully on board with, and it's a relief that my response to *Riptide* is one of praise, rather than condemnation.

Riptide has been made with proper respect to its difficult subject matter after extensive careful research, and – perhaps to the point for those more interested in cinema than causes – has been made well, budgetary limitations notwithstanding. Barrow's experience shines through; cinematographer Robbie Jones (**Night Kaleidoscope** and **Wigilia** amongst many others) has a great eye both for relevant small details, and for wide expanses when these are called for; the intelligent screenplay neither patronises nor preaches.

On the festival circuit, and in targeted screenings (to healthcare professionals for example), *Riptide* has benefited from strong feedback and has picked up awards. There have been a fair number of screenings in Scottish cinemas, but at the time of writing the film is disappointingly hard to watch (I'm grateful to Barrow for providing me with access to a copy). Barrow has told me he intends to make it available on Lyre's website.

Two Years at Sea (2011) and *Bogancloch* (2024)   DOC

Directed by Ben Rivers; both 85 minutes

Black and white documentaries (with limited colour in *Bogancloch*) focusing on Jake Williams' life as a hermit in the Cairngorms, with arresting imagery. Little is offered in terms of explanation and there is neither a narration nor explanatory titles; at the EIFF screening of *Bogancloch*, Rivers said 'we live in a world where there's so much explanation; it's good to leave some room for the viewer's imagination'. *Two Years at Sea* was a winner of a CPH:DOX (Copenhagen International Documentary Film Festival) award. *Bogancloch* was well received at its EIFF 2024 screening and has more lyricism than *Two Years*. In the films Jake says nothing; in person (I had the pleasure of chatting with him at the EIFF), he is soft-spoken and charmingly candid. The richly textured films have a subtle and slow power.

White Out (2011)   S+++

Directed by Lawrie Brewster
Screenplay by Sarah Daly
Leading cast: Jon Finnegan (John Hanson); Mike McEvoy (Ben); Dougie Clark (Doug); Nancy Joy Page (Nancy McIntyre)
Colour, 85 minutes, UK

In Dysart, Fife, snow lies on the ground, and John helps residents to complete questionnaires for the Health Service. In his flat, he watches 'The Trojan Horse' website. The winter does not end, and a pandemic sweeps the world. Society breaks down. Dysart, like everywhere, descends into violence and chaos. In a final shot, alone, John walks out of Dysart in the snow.

Five films directed by Lawrie Brewster, all written by his partner Sarah Daly (who also wrote the award-winning short comedy film *Ransom* (Halfdan Hallfest, 2021),

and is an accomplished singer/songwriter, providing some of the soundtrack for *White Out*) are covered in this book. Brewster and Daly should be more widely known and celebrated – in Scotland, and beyond.

Interviewed on *Buddy's House of Horror*, Brewster described his output as 'weird-ass horror films'. His mission is 'making serious, alternative horror films that aim to tell genuine, emotionally-driven stories with intriguing characters set against backgrounds filled with mysterious lore and mythology'. He is from Fife and trained to be a Minister of the Church of Scotland, studying at St Andrews University. He has said that 'where I'm from in Scotland... the idea of working in film would just be insane'. *White Out* however, is *not* a horror film; like *Perfect Sense* (see above) it is apocalyptic sci-fi.

White Out is available on YouTube, with an introduction by Brewster. He explains that it barely even hit the micro-budget level. Yet, relying on a tiny crew (many of whom multi-task), and local people helping out, it deals with 'the collapse of Western civilisation... a dystopian and apocalyptic film which imagines what would happen if winter never ended'. Add to the mix a pandemic, and you've got 'a combination of every paranoid idea about the collapse of civilisation, all brought together in one film'. The *really* clever element here was the inveigling of contributors around the world to provide vlogs, which are watched by John on The Trojan Horse. This allows the film to ground the local in the global, at minimal cost. It's this sort of invention which distinguishes Brewster and Daly's work. Given the resources available, it is remarkably good.

→ *Lord of Tears* (2013) S+++ T100

Directed by Lawrie Brewster
Screenplay by Sarah Daly
Leading cast: Euan Douglas (James Finlay); David Schofield (Moloch/The Owlman); Lexy Hulme (Evie Turner)
Colour, 85 minutes, UK

Schoolteacher James Finlay inherits a large Highlands house, Baldurrock, which he associates with childhood trauma. He visits the house, where past, present and future mingle, orchestrated by Moloch (the Owlman). After leaving the house, James' friend, Allen, sacrifices James to Moloch to save his own father (events foretold in visions James had at Baldurrock).

Brewster and Daly's second feature, and their first pure horror film, *Lord of Tears*, was produced by their own, Scotland-based, production company, Hex Media. A 13-person crew shot the film in 2012, much of it at Ardgour House, north of Loch Linnhe (also the location for *Ghosts of Darkness*). Like the later *The Unkindness of Ravens*, it has roots in folk-horror and mythology and, perhaps unsurprisingly given Brewster's background, in the Bible (Old Testament, not New). Asked about the source of his inspiration, Brewster has said that he and Daly's 'first port of call is folklore and legend, something Scotland is rich in!'

The Owlman

Genre reviewers were kind to the film. *BloodyDisgusting*'s Patrick Cooper wrote that the 'Scottish film blends the classic Hammer sensibilities with strong storytelling and an atmosphere of thick dread not easily shaken off after it's over... The film's low-budget is given a tremendous boost thanks to the creepy old mansion in the Scottish Highlands where it was shot. Who needs CGI when you're shooting in the fog-drenched landscape of Scotland?' Bernice Murphy, in *The Green Book*, described *Lord of Tears* as 'an ambitious, likably old-school supernatural horror film with a promising sense of style'. The only review listed on Rotten Tomatoes is positive, although it must be recognised that the audience review rating is an undeserved 35 per cent.

Moloch/the Owlman (who reappears in *The Black Gloves*, below) is a remarkable invention and has attracted something of a cult following (there's a Living Dead Doll, and a plush version available; while Hex produced a series of prank videos featuring the character). Daly's script has the Owlman describe himself in splendidly florid gothic terms: 'I am the immortal owl... I am of oblivion. I am the almighty misanthrope, the rope that tightens with the ticking of the clock, the grit that sits in the bellies of believers forcing bile to the throats of gloating hordes...' He is given magnificent voice by Schofield. A sidenote: the late-Giallo film *Stagefright* (*Deliria*) (Michele Soavi, 1987) features a psychopathic serial killer sporting a giant owl mask.

→ *The Unkindness of Ravens* (2016) S+++

Directed by Lawrie Brewster
Screenplay by Sarah Daly
Leading cast: Jamie Scott Gordon (Andrew)
Colour, 85 minutes, UK

Andrew, a veteran who fought in Afghanistan, is in counselling and suffering from PTSD. He spends time at an artists' retreat cottage in the Highlands, where he confronts his demons and begins to heal.

There are elements shared between *Unkindness* and the earlier *Lord of Tears* – in both films a man confronts past trauma in the Highlands, and in both birds are central to the imagery. *Lord of Tears* and *Unkindness* share a folk-horror vibe, but *Unkindness* is more optimistic in its outcome.

In *Unkindness* Brewster and Daly have something interesting to say, and a strong grasp of the horror conventions within which to say it. *Unkindness* had its premiere at FrightFest 2016. It has not had a general release in any territory but is easily available on streaming services and on DVD. Leading horror critic Kim Newman suggests that the film might benefit from repeat viewings. As Andrew's flashbacks become stronger it is not clear whether what we see is an event which has fed into his illness, or an internalised attempt to make sense of things. The nightmares in *Unkindness* – the phantastical horror – are well executed. Sinister raven-like figures, wearing flowing black cloaks and medieval doctors' black plague masks, hunt Andrew. He is then able literally to kill his demons. This is a rich metaphor, and the grounding of it in the longevity of folk culture, including the use of the haunting traditional song 'The Three Ravens', works well. Gordon is strong in the central role – as he carries the entire film, he needs to be convincing; the scenes in which he confronts himself are excellent.

→ *The Black Gloves* (2017) S+++

Directed by Lawrie Brewster
Screenplay by Sarah Daly
Leading cast: Jamie Scott Gordon (Finn Galloway); Macarena Gómez (Lorena Velasco); Alexandra Hulme (Elisa Grey)
B&W/Colour, 93 minutes, UK

In 1948, psychologist Finn Galloway investigates a recurring myth referenced by his patients, and spends time with star ballerina Elisa Grey, who was dancing in a production of Swan Lake when a fire ripped through the theatre. She lives at former orphanage, Baldurrock House, with Lorena Velasco, her teacher. Recurring visions of the Owlman plague

Finn, and haunt Elisa. Attempts to leave fail, until Lorena sacrifices herself. Later, Elisa returns to Baldurrock, the Owlman returns, and Finn dies.

A prequel of sorts to **Lord of Tears**, *The Black Gloves* sees the reappearance of the Owlman – although if watched in the order in which the films are set, this would be his first appearance. The Owlman remains a figure of terror, but the mythology is stronger if the films are watched in the order of their production. In this version the Owlman is not gifted the gloriously baroque language used in **Lord of Tears** – in fact, he has no voice (and is not played by David Schofield; Keith Robson stepping in). Brewster and Daly do not position this as an Owlman origin story (such heavy lifting as there is, is done by manuscript pages shown on screen). There's also linkage through to Tchaikovsky's *Swan Lake*, with Elisa dancing the black swan role (*The Black Gloves* was made six years after *Black Swan*, Darren Aronofsky, 2010), which along with the orphanage backstory compounds doubts as to whether we are in a psychological, or supernatural horror. In *Starburst*, John Higgins opted for the former: 'a strikingly shot in black-and-white psychological horror' – although it would be hard to read the films in their entirety as presenting anything other than a literal story of an ancient and demanding god exacting a heavy toll for bargains made. Lexy Hulme, here credited as Alexandra Hulme, is also back, as Elisa, and in the last shot of the film remains at Baldurrock (again, Ardgour House). It

might be possible to construct an otherworldly narrative in which Elisa becomes Evie in the first (and chronologically later) film.

The black gloves of the title are worn by Lorena, her hands badly disfigured in the catastrophic fire. Gómez, a Spanish actor with a strong genre credits list, plays Lorena as a highly stylised (almost to the point of caricature) gothic villainess – her manipulation/protection of Elisa blending Svengali with Grand Guignol. Anton Bitel in *S&S* enjoyed this: 'The shrill hysteria of Gómez's performance perfectly modulates the tone here, which is knowingly funny, but still always unnerving'. This feeds into the impression that the film draws on 1940s/1950s gothic horror through to *The Innocents* (Jack Clayton, 1961), a reference point that several critics have picked up. In *Horrified*, Mark Anthony Ayling wrote: 'The Black Gloves is a nostalgic callback to the classic Goth melodramas... there is a mystery that must be solved, a haunted stately home gone to seed, ripe dialogue, a terrifically overwrought central romance, moments of gloomy foreshadowing, and increasingly unhinged central protagonist, some supernatural stuff, and a veritable stew of sexual repression'.

The Black Gloves was first released in black and white, in 2017. A colour version (the one I have watched) was later released in 2020. A three-disc box set is available from Hex Media.

→ *The Devil's Machine* (aka *Automata*) (2019) S+++

Directed by Lawrie Brewster
Screenplay by Sarah Daly
Leading cast: Jamie Scott Gordon (Dr Brendan Cole); Alexandra Hulme (Talia); Victoria Lucie (Rose)
Colour, 95 minutes, UK

Dr Brendan Cole, the leading authority on the fabled 'infernal princess' automaton, spends a week at a remote mansion with his stepdaughter, Rose, evaluating the automaton which, after 300 years, has been found. Cole finds a document in which its maker confesses it 'is not a mechanical marvel, but an abomination', consisting of a mutilated and imprisoned Talia (the daughter of the General who commissioned its construction). Rose and Cole are beset by the past, crowding in on them.

The last film by Brewster and Daly to be covered here, *Automata* is also perhaps the most accomplished. It retains the gothic patina of *Lord of Tears* and *The Black Gloves* and is set in an isolated stately house (in reality, the Georgian House of Dun, near Montrose). Inspiration for the film may also be found in Ovid's *Pygmalion*. Daly has said that 'aside from the obvious superficial similarities the tale has with ours, there are also thematic commonalities. For example, how it concerns the objectification of women, and of the notion of the narcissistic creator'.

Filmmakers know all too well the power dolls and puppets have to be deeply creepy.

But when the 'doll' is a life-size facsimile of a living person we plunge headfirst into the uncanny valley, and things get intense. To this already potent mix Daly's script adds incest, abuse, murders, mutilation, and a bizarre form of imprisonment (apparently in perpetuity) as Talia *becomes* the automaton. The result is a strong genre film which opened the GFF in 2019 and won Brewster the Best Director award at the Starburst Media City Fantasy Film Festival in 2019. Both Jamie Scott Gordon and Alexandra Hulme are back, with Hulme's movement skills working well when she plays the automaton. The third lead in *The Devil's Machine* is Victoria Lucie, an English actor making her second feature film; she won the Best Actress jury prize at the Unrestricted View Film Festival.

Reviewers have been very positive about *The Devil's Machine* (most of these are writing for genre outlets, and don't get picked up by Rotten Tomatoes, which leads to a false impression of indifference on the review aggregator). I'll stick to one example: *Pop Culture Uncovered*'s take was that 'Brewster outdoes himself... whereas previous films were mostly creepy, *The Devil's Machine* has some great scares in it. Moments of dread and sudden figures add a new style of terror that delights and frights.'

Hex's more recent films do not hit the criteria for inclusion in this book, but the company's prolific output continues to attract praise from genre critics.

You've Been Trumped (2011) and You've Been Trumped Too (2016)   DOC

Directed by Anthony Baxter; 100/79 minutes

YBT focuses on the initial stages of the development of a new golf course complex on the Menie estate in Aberdeenshire, starting in 2010, placing particular emphasis on a group of residents adjacent to the estate, whose properties and way of life were threatened by the development. YBTT, made five years later, returns to the residents, focusing on Molly and Michael Forbes. In the second film, Baxter seeks to find out whether American supporters of Donald Trump's presidential gambit would be swayed if they knew of his actions in Scotland.

You've Been Trumped is a textbook example of how time and events can change the way in which a film is read. It is impossible now not to watch this through a political lens. When the film was released, it was as the story of a powerful corporation's destructive impact on the environment and its co-option of those with local political and legal power to facilitate this. It won awards at the Sheffield International Documentary Festival and the Sedona International Film Festival for its environmental credentials.

The Menie estate, which was purchased by the Trump Organisation in 2006, incorporated a unique Site of Special Scientific Interest, the highest protection designation the UK accords to the natural environment. The grandiose plans for development, which claimed substantial economic benefits, were rejected by Aberdeenshire Council, and were then 'called-in' by the Scottish Government, led at the time by First Minister, and the development's local MSP, Alex Salmond. The Government overturned the local authority's decision, granting permission to proceed. Salmond is quoted early on in the film: 'we can see the social and economic benefits; 6,000 jobs across Scotland, and 1,400 local and permanent jobs here in the Northeast... and that outweighs the environmental concerns'. Later, Professor Paul Cheshire, of the London School of Economics examines the impact report prepared for the development: 'There's not been enough caution in interpreting those numbers... I do find it more surprising that the Scottish Government, which I thought was quite canny, has fallen for it in the way that they have'.

Kenneth Tynan, of the *Los Angeles Times*, wrote that the film was 'a potent study of the intimidating power of money not in theory but on the ground, an examination of how a wealthy man with a boundless sense of entitlement can strong-arm all opposition without really breaking a sweat.' What is most remarkable is not, in fact, how opposition was strong-armed – we might expect that of a large, foreign, corporation. The real story here (at least before Trump's Presidential run) is the extent to which the Trump Organisation was aided, abetted, and validated, by the Scottish Government, the local police force, local media (an issue discussed in *YBTT*), and a local university. Few come out of this film with reputations enhanced. Dr David Kennedy, former Principal of Robert Gordon University (RGU) stands out. In support of the residents of the Menie estate he handed back his RGU honorary doctorate when the university decided to award one to Trump. The moral vacuity of RGU's position was exposed when in 2015 it stripped Trump of the award following his racist comments on the campaign trail in the US.

Donald Trump's arrogance comes through early on. Speaking of Michael's property: 'I happen to be a very truthful person. His property is terribly maintained, it's slum-like, it's disgusting. He's got stuff thrown all over the place, he lives like a pig. And I did say that, I'm an honest guy, and I speak honestly. And I think that's why some people like me, and some people probably don't like me'. These words are repeated through both films. Michael responds: 'he's nothing but a compulsive liar'. The arrogance and ignorance on display is breath taking.

YBT makes use of two external film sources. The first is Bill Forsyth's *Local Hero*, which has resonance although its use is perhaps a little facile. Better use is made of archive film, including of Molly's father participating in a ploughing contest, and of local salmon fishing, which support a convincing portrayal of a deeply rooted local community and way of life. This contrasts strongly with the 'values' espoused by the Trump Organisation.

There were critics who disliked the film, finding it one-sided and simplistic – this

was the approach taken in *Time Out*, and in the *New York Daily News* – but they are in a minority. Baxter sides with the locals, and the influence of Michael Moore is clear but, except when he is arrested, Baxter does not insert himself into the narrative as Moore does. Viewed as a film about a small community's response to environmentally damaging development perpetrated by the powerful, *YBT* is a clever and engaging documentary. Viewed as a description of the methods of a man who would later convince first a large enough minority of US voters, then a majority of voters to put him in the White House twice, it is terrifying.

YBTT was produced when Trump was running for President for the first time and was made freely available in the US on Facebook. While Molly and her family remain at the centre of the film, the focus is on the US election, with Baxter asking the question whether 'Americans would vote for him if they knew how he had short-changed the people of Scotland?' As Mark Kermode says, 'it's more of a political intervention than a satisfying movie'. It is a polemical work, lacking the sophistication of *YBT*. The interactions we are shown clearly demonstrate the extent to which Trump's supporters were concerned with placing America first. There is one powerful moment late on, when Trump's acceptance of the Republican nomination ('I have joined the political arena so that the powerful can no longer beat up on the people who cannot defend themselves') is presented in a montage alongside Molly collecting water in a bucket, her supply having been cut off for five years by the development works, and Michael's look of aghast incomprehension.

You Instead (aka Tonight You're Mine) (2011) S++

Directed by David Mackenzie
Screenplay by Thomas Leveritt
Leading cast: Luke Treadaway (Adam); Natalia Tena (Morello); Rebecca Benson (Lucie); Mat Baynton (Tyko)
Colour, 80 minutes, UK

T in the Park: Adam and Morello, who play with different bands, and who argue when they first meet, find themselves handcuffed together for the duration of the festival, and are forced to perform together.

Most rom-coms ask the question, 'how do they get together?' It's a nice twist that here the question Adam and Morello are confronted with is 'how do we separate?' Appropriately, 'Tainted Love' is the first song they perform together. But this twist, and the festival setting aside (which is entirely authentic, dropping in cameos and performance clips), there is little to commend *You Instead*, which was shot quickly by Mackenzie, and ranks well below his best work. The two leads are likeable enough (although Tena was nominated for the Irina Palm d'Or worst British actress 'award') but are given nothing of substance to work with. Peter Bradshaw was not at all impressed: 'a jaw-droppingly self-indulgent, shallow, smug if mercifully brief feature with

a plot that looks like the outline for a pop video... lazy and pointless'. A small number of critics were charmed (Leslie Felperin in *Variety*: 'this hipster romantic comedy should prove a crowdpleaser at youth-skewed film fests'); the majority were not.

Brave (2012) S++ T100

Directed by Mark Andrews, Brenda Chapman, Steve Purcell
Screenplay by Mark Andrews, Steve Purcell, Brenda Chapman, Irene Mecchi
Leading cast: Kelly Macdonald (Merida); Billy Connolly (Fergus); Emma Thompson (Elinor)
Colour, 93 minutes, US/UK

For her birthday, Merida, Princess of Dun Broch, is given a bow and arrow set, and becomes an expert archer. Later, when suitors from the clans compete for her hand in marriage she sets, and wins, an archery challenge, before fleeing. When a spell backfires, her resilience and skill save her family.

Like much of Pixar's output, *Brave* is based on an original story, according greater freedom to subvert genre and reflect contemporary sensibilities. Ostensibly, *Brave* is a straightforward fairy tale, and even builds into its own fabric a story which is believed to be merely a legend; but as Merida says (echoing her mother, Elinor), 'legends are lessons; they ring with truths'. *Brave* focuses on a mother and daughter relationship and offers a modern, feminist twist on the fairy tale, although it

does not push this nearly as far as it could, and the ending is conventional.

For most of the film Merida struggles to establish her own identity, and to live life the way she wants to. Her petty rebellions in the castle, and her bickering with Elinor, are entertaining, and both Macdonald and Thompson give strong voice performances. More thrilling is the scene where Merida is free to ride through the forest, practicing her archery; but while her skill with the bow and arrow remains a significant plot point, more could be made of this. As Merida says, her brothers 'can get away with murder. I can never get away with anything. I'm the princess. I'm the example. I've got duties, responsibilities, expectations. My whole life is planned out, preparing for the day I become – well, my mother'. By the film's end Merida strengthens her relationship with her mother, and they have better mutual understanding. She also has

success in changing tradition, such that people can follow their hearts in love and marriage, rather than being dictated to by clan requirements, and she saves Elinor/ bear from being slaughtered, but all this is undercut by the fact that her final destiny is to become, well, her mother: she remains a princess to be wooed. *Brave*'s engaging portrait of a tomboy princess lacks the subtlety and scope of, for example, the *Toy Story* quartet, *Soul* (Pete Docter and Kemp Powers, 2020), or *Inside Out* (Pete Docter and Ronnie Del Carmen, 2015). However, even a moderately good Pixar movie remains good, and there are enough jokes for adults to give them something to laugh at while the kids are being entertained.

Technically, *Brave* is a masterpiece. Many films covered in this book are set or shot, in part, in the Highlands, but rarely has the region looked as beautiful as it does in Pixar CGI. The animation in *Brave* is stunning. This is best demonstrated in two scenes involving water, which always presents challenges for animators: one where Merida stands in the spray of a mountain waterfall, dipping her hands in the flow for a drink; another when Elinor/ bear catches salmon.

Brave also pays proper respect to its Scottish setting. It *could* have been set pretty much anywhere in a rural past, but having opted for Scotland, the writers have gone all in. The soundtrack, by Patrick Doyle, who was born in Scotland, is authentic without being twee (and benefits from the ethereal singing of Julie Fowlis); there is use of Scots dialect ('jings crivens help ma boab', 'tumshie' etc) sufficient to provide colour, yet not enough to give rise to complaint from uncomprehending audiences; there is even some use of Doric (albeit played for humour) and Gaelic; and riffing presumably on *Braveheart* and gently mocking it (*Brave* is a much better film), there are bare bums.

Citadel (2012) S+

Directed by Ciarán Foy
Screenplay by Ciarán Foy
Leading cast: Aneurin Barnard (Tommy); James Cosmo (Priest); Wunmi Mosaku (Marie)
Colour, 84 minutes, Ireland/UK

A run-down housing estate in Glasgow: Tommy, the young father to a baby, whose pregnant wife was killed by a gang of hooded children, is permanently fearful. The children return to take his child.

The clunky horror film *Citadel*, which has nothing to do with AJ Cronin's novel of the same name, left the festival circuit with a clutch of awards and nominations, but failed to gain traction on a limited release. As **Urban Ghost Story** and **Outcast** had proved earlier, city housing estates can be home to just as much threat as remote Gothic houses, or woodland cabins. In *Citadel* everything conspires to hold Tommy captive while the threats close in – the only person sympathetic to his plight is a friendly nurse, Marie; the local vigilante priest (Cosmo, who features in many films in this book) appears to be as much of a threat as the hooded children.

Until the priest moves to centre stage, *Citadel* is interesting: perhaps Tommy suffers post-traumatic stress disorder, perhaps his fears are unreasonable. But then the film descends into the silly, not helped by a vapid lead actor. Alistair Harkness, who noted that the film's first planned release was pulled, was bluntly dismissive, describing *Citadel* as an 'inauspicious feature debut for [Foy], who fails to give the film the kick needed to make its fanciful plot... work'.

Electric Man (2012)   S++

Directed by David Barras
Screenplay by David Barras and Scott MacKay
Leading cast: Toby Manley (Jason Archer); Mark
   McKirdy (Wolf); Fish (Uncle Jimmy); Jennifer
   Ewing (Lauren McCall)
Colour, 100 minutes, UK

Glasgow: a comic collector is murdered, leaving behind the extremely valuable first issue of 'Electric Man'. Jason (Jazz) and Wolf, the owner of the Deadhead comics shop in Edinburgh, need to raise £5,000 to keep the shop open. A series of implausible events and coincidences connect Jason and Wolf to the comic.

Shot in Edinburgh over three weeks on a tiny budget (close to £50,000), after being written in first draft in three days ('out of boredom', according to Scott MacKay at a GFF Q&A), *Electric Man* is Armadale-born David Barras' only feature. In July 2012 it became the first Scottish film to play the San Diego Comic-Con International Festival – Barras is quoted in the Edinburgh *Evening News* saying 'San Diego was the holy grail for us'.

I wanted very much to like *Electric Man*, but, in common with most reviewers, couldn't. Alistair Harkness hated it; Peter Bradshaw was a little more sympathetic ('one or two nice moments and performances'); but Jennie Kermode (*Eye For Film*) is spot on: 'it's a good 25-minute short padded out to an hour and a half'. This is a pity: the film was clearly made with enthusiasm but still labours negative 'comic book geeks' tropes, is too convoluted for its own good, and in bad need of a tighter script edit. The result lacks the wit and spark the subject matter requires (something pulled off in, for example, *Chasing Amy* (Kevin Smith, 1997) or in the culturally adjacent *GamerZ*.

Night is Day (aka *Night is Day: The Movie*) (2012)   S+++

Directed by Fraser Coull
Screenplay by Fraser Coull
Leading cast: Chris Summers (Jason Mackenzie);
   Kirsty Anderson (Lina); John Gaffney
   (Superintendent Charles Sloan); Nicki Fleming
   (Lexi); Tam Toye (Mr Philips)
Colour, 103 minutes, English/Gaelic, UK

Glasgow: an electrically charged superhero, Jason, fights crime. A demon, 'the Caillech Bheur', rises and threatens the end of the world in three days. Mackenzie works with a special police unit to resolve matters.

Night is Day is as ropey as the synopsis suggests. There's no doubting the enthusiastic commitment required to bring this to the screen, and on a budget of £5,000 and a shoot of less than nine weeks, the result is probably as good as could be expected – which is to say, not good at all. The film picked up the Best Low Budget Film gold award at the Los Angeles Film Festival in 2020 (a surprising eight years after the film's completion, although later revisions were made). It feels churlish to disparage a film made on such limited resources, but there are moments when *Night is Day* approaches the films of Neil Breen (see, eg, *Double Down*, 2005 and *Twisted Pair*, 2018 – although, really, don't) in the size of the gap between aspiration and delivery.

Sawney: Flesh of Man (aka *Lord of Darkness*) (2012)　S+++

Directed by Ricky Wood
Screenplay by Ricky Wood
Leading cast: David Hayman (Sawney Bean);
　Gavin Mitchell (Bill Munro); Samuel Feeney
　(Hamish MacDonald)
Colour, 90 minutes, UK

Aberdeen: Sawney, a descendant of a clan of cannibals, drives a taxi, but his passengers are as liable to end up back in his lair in the Highlands, where very bad things happen, as they are at their destination. A journalist, Hamish, begins writing about the disappearances, and Detective Munro is on the case...

Whether Sawney Bean and his family really existed in 16th-century Ayrshire is a matter of debate. The legend is that a cannibal clan (its growth fuelled by incest), led by Sawney, was responsible for upwards of 1,000 deaths (the figures vary hugely depending on the source), before being hunted down and publicly executed. True or not – the DVD cover is emphatic that it is – it's the sort of story which fuels horror films, and it is reported to have been a key

David Hayman goes full throttle in Sawney

influence on Wes Craven in making his seminal US horror *The Hills Have Eyes* (1977). It is perhaps surprising it took until 2012 for a Scottish version of the story to appear, written and directed by Rick Wood, whose only feature this is (like several other directors whose work is covered in this book, he is engaged primarily in corporate film work).

Cinematographer Ranald Wood was BAFTA Scotland nominated for his work (he lost out to Alan C McLaughlin for the 15-minute short, *Lost Serenity*, Ben Sharrock, 2013), saying at the time that while he had spotted some mistakes, it was 'not bad for a first try' (not exactly a ringing endorsement). Lead actor Hayman was more enthusiastic: 'It was an incredibly powerful piece and done on a shoestring budget... Having never played a serial killer before, it was great fun, really something to get your teeth stuck into.' When Hayman is on-screen, *Sawney* is, as *thisishorror.co.uk* put it, 'gruesome, visceral, blackly funny, harrowing [with] a savage brio that makes it hugely enjoyable.' When he's not, some of the air goes out.

The open landscape dominates Shell

Shell (2012)   S+++ T40

Directed by Scott Graham
Screenplay by Scott Graham
Leading cast: Chloe Pirrie (Shell); Joseph
   Mawle (Pete); Michael Smiley (Hugh); Iain De
   Caestecker (Adam)
Colour, 91 minutes, UK

A remote garage and petrol station in the western Highlands, and snow is on the ground. Seventeen-year-old Shell serves a regular customer, Hugh. Shell lives with, and cares for, her father, and the relationship is ambiguous. He dies by suicide after making sexual overtures to her. Shell leaves, accepting a lift in a lorry. She does not know where she is going.

Scott Graham made his first short film, also called *Shell*, in 2007. He followed that with another short, *Native Son*, in 2010, before being able to expand *Shell* to the full-length feature released in 2012. This led to multiple award nominations, including Outstanding Debut by a British writer, director or producer at the BAFTAS in 2014, while Scottish actor Pirrie (who is terrific in *Shell*) won the Most Promising Newcomer award at the British Independent Film Awards in 2013. She had previously been in a short, *Solstice* (David Stoddart, 2010), which Graham had seen. *Shell*, like Graham's later films **Iona** and **Run** puts parent/child and transgressive relationships at the centre of the film. In *Shell* that relationship is disturbing. Loneliness and isolation bring with them the spectre of incest, although it is not clear whether desires (held by both father and daughter) are acted on beyond a kiss – which drives Pete to suicide.

Many of the films covered in this book which are not based in history or myth are set in Glasgow or Edinburgh (the balance is in Glasgow's favour). In an interview with Samuel Wigley for the BFI Graham was explicit about his motivations for setting his first film in the Highlands: 'I like a lot of urban storytelling, but I did keep thinking of that line by Morrissey: "It says nothing to me about my life." If I have some experience of what I'm writing about I think my writing is a little stronger, more honest maybe. Scotland's not a big country but it seemed like the balance was off.' It is telling that Claire (Kate Dickie), whose car hits a deer early on, forcing a stop at the garage, is from Edinburgh, but has never seen the Highlands until her one-day road trip ends badly. In this respect *Shell* is an antidote to the more clichéd representations of Scotland, in which *everyone's* life appears to intersect with, or be lived in, the Highlands.

Shell is shot in widescreen 2.35:1 ratio, which is unusual for an intense and intimate low-budget independent film; the scale emphasising the isolation Shell and Pete are subject to. The one constant in *Shell* is the sound of the wind, something that Xan Brooks noted in his review for *The Guardian*:

'a hushed and haunting coming-of-age drama, pungently played out in the remote Scottish Highlands, where the wind boings off the microphone'. The sense of remote distance is reinforced by the petrol station itself, which was constructed by the film's set designers, and demolished at the film's completion (thwarting location tourists who ask, online, where the station is).

The majority of those who reviewed the film on the festival circuit or on release were positive, with most praising Pirrie. Allan Hunter spoke for many when, in *The Express*, he called the film a 'sensitive, unflinching exploration of bleak lives [marking] the emergence of a distinctive new voice in British cinema and a striking young performer in Chloe Pirrie'. A 2024 Sam Minghella film, *Shell*, starring Elisabeth Moss and Kate Hudson has nothing to do with Graham's film, but is more prominent in internet searches.

→ *Iona* (2015)　S+++

Directed by Scott Graham
Screenplay by Scott Graham
Leading cast: Ruth Negga (Iona); Ben Gallagher (Billy/Bull); Douglas Henshall (Daniel); Sorcha Groundsell (Sarah); Michelle Duncan (Elizabeth); Tom Brooke (Matthew)
Colour, 85 minutes, UK

After Iona and her son, Billy, return to her place of birth – Iona – following a violent incident in Glasgow, familial and relationship tensions are to the fore. They stay with Daniel, with whose family Iona lived when she was 15. Unknown to Billy, he is Daniel's son. Daniel later dies. When the police come to Iona looking for Billy, he dies by suicide, and in the last shot Iona cradles his body.

Graham's second film, *Iona*, is more expansive than *Shell*, but retains a strong focus on familial relationships within an isolated community. In all three of Graham's films what is not said is as important as what is ('Graham employs silence effectively' – Charlotte Keeys in *Little White Lies*). It is also striking that in all three Graham explores complex transgressional relationships which cast ripples and are potentially destructive: in *Shell* incest; in *Iona* Elizabeth describes Iona as her 'sister', yet her father is the father of Billy, which also means that Billy and Sarah, Elizabeth's daughter, are uncle and niece (although they do not know this when they have sex); and in *Run* Finnie contemplates escape with his son's girlfriend.

Iona is the only film in which Graham explores religion – it would be all but impossible to set a film on the island and *not* do so. But where others have portrayed religiosity in the Scottish islands as oppressive and exclusionary (**Breaking the Waves, Nobody Has to Know, The Silent Storm**), or in the extreme, murderous (**The Wicker Man, Consecration**), Graham is more subtle. Religion here is simply a part of life. The church is welcoming, and Billy tells Iona that he feels better when he prays;

Iona, however, has turned her back on the church. Interviewed by Wendy Mitchell for *Screen Daily* before *Iona*'s Edinburgh Festival premiere, Graham said: 'As I was developing *Shell* someone asked me about conflict within families and the parent-child relationship, and I thought that might be something I'd continue to explore. Then I came to this idea of someone going [to Iona] who doesn't feel close to God. She has a sense of anger about being there. It is a very peaceful place, but not for her.'

Iona is not as forceful as *Shell* or *Run*. After it was shown at Edinburgh, Graham decided to re-edit the film: 25 minutes were cut. Graham said that it was his own decision to do this, telling Charles Gant: 'I was setting up one thing, and then delivering another... Although the film is very much Iona's story, we are giving the perspective of each of the six characters, seven if you count the island. By beginning in Glasgow, we lost some of that shared perspective.' In *The National* there was praise for the cast, but not for the film: 'undoubtedly a step down... to an allusive, less sure-footed directorial follow-up'. However, a rating on Rotten Tomatoes of 63 per cent at the time of writing indicates that, on the whole, critics had more good than bad to say about the film, and it would be a pity to watch only two of Graham's films: it is worth completing the set.

→ *Run* (2019) S+++ T100

Directed by Scott Graham
Screenplay by Scott Graham
Leading cast: Mark Stanley (Finnie); Amy Manson
(Katie); Marli Siu (Kelly); Anders Hayward (Kid)
Colour, 78 minutes, UK

Mark Stanley wrestles with temptation

Fraserburgh, on the north-east Scottish coast. Finnie works in a fish processing plant, from which his elder son, Kid, is sacked. Kid's girlfriend, Kelly, is pregnant. Finnie's wife, Katie, works at a hair salon. After a tense family dinner, Finnie takes Kid's high-performance car, meets Kelly, and races other drivers. Finnie wants to 'get out of here', and Kelly offers to go with him. But they don't leave, and fences are mended the following day.

Run opens with an on-screen quote from Bruce Springsteen's 'Born to Run' (1975) and Finnie has 'Born To Run' tattooed on his left chest, Katie on her right calf. Yet after his return home, Finnie has to say to Katie 'we didnae run very far, did we?' Finnie and Katie failed to get out while they were young and end the film where they started 24 hours earlier. Yet Finnie's life is not a 'death trap'. He has a job, a loving wife, has raised a family, and is shortly to be a grandfather. 'Born to Run' is not on the film's soundtrack; the closing credits play out over a different, and in the context more optimistic, Springsteen track, 'She's The One' (also from the album, *Born to Run*).

Graham is from Fraserburgh and, in an interview with *The Skinny* in 2020,

explained that at one point he was researching a short film about boy racers there, when he heard a story about 'a fishwife leaving her husband because he was listening to too much Bruce Springsteen'. As he put it, this percolated over the years, eventually becoming his third feature film, *Run*.

Run was award nominated at the 2019 Tribeca Film Festival, and was well received by critics. *The Guardian*'s Cath Clarke gave *Run* three stars: 'a film with echoes of Andrea Arnold and perhaps Ken Loach – but Graham is a local boy, and brings a sense of place and character that is all his own. And Stanley is terrific'. For *Variety* Guy Lodge wrote that 'it's a celebration of the open road that nonetheless hits the breaks at the city limits, engine idling with should-I-stay-or-should-I-go uncertainty. That's the tension that powers *Run* through a bare-bones 76 minutes'.

Most critics zoned in on the strong sense of locality, and the remarkable performances from the ensemble cast, all of whom are exceptional.

Sir Billi (aka *Sir Billi the Vet,* aka *Guardian of the Highlands*) (2012)   S++ W2

Directed by Sascha Hartmann
Screenplay by Tessa Hartmann
Leading cast: Sir Sean Connery (Sir Billi); Alan
   Cumming (Gordon); Ruby Wax (Patty Turner)
Colour, 76 minutes, UK/US

A lone beaver escapes deportation to Norway and is taken in by rabbits; Billi sets out to save it. But really, who cares?

Sir Billi is noteworthy for three reasons: it was the last film in which Sean Connery appeared (providing a voice performance); it was the first, and to date only, Scottish-produced animated CGI feature; and it is horrendously, cataclysmically, atrocious. *The Scotsman's* review is representative: 'Rubbish in ways that seem unimaginable'. In *The Guardian*, Peter Bradshaw described it as a 'tedious, crudely animated, bafflingly conceived cartoon feature… so cheaply and unimaginatively made it would hardly pass muster on children's TV'. It leaves 'so bad it's good' gasping for breath in the rear-view mirror. It has a well-deserved 0 per cent score on Rotten Tomatoes. Under no circumstances should you watch it.

In the first edition of this book, I labelled *Sir Billi* the worst Scottish film. *Deti protiv volshebnikov*, which at that point I had not come across, is even worse.

La Traversée (The Crossing) (2012)

Directed by Jérôme Cornuau
Screenplay by Jérôme Cornuau and Alexandra
   Deman
Leading cast: Michaël Youn (Martin Arendt);
   Pauline Haugness (Lola Arendt); Fanny Valette
   (Norah Kross); Émilie Dequenne (Sarah
   Arendt); Jules Werner (Clément)
Colour, 97 minutes, France/Luxembourg/
   Belgium, French/minimal English

'Bac Mòr' island, Scotland: on holiday, Lola, the young daughter of Martin and Sarah Arendt, disappears without trace. Two years later, Martin is told she has been found exactly where she went missing. He travels to Bac Mòr to bring her home.

French director Jérôme Cornuau's *La Traverseé* is, and is not, set very largely in Scotland, on an unnamed island of some size and distance from the mainland, requiring an overnight ferry crossing. None of the principal photography took place in Scotland. In the context of the film however, it makes sense that Scotland is not authentically drawn.

I make clear in the introduction that these entries contain plot-spoilers, but am here being somewhat careful, given you are unlikely to have seen *La Traverseé* and it is a psychological mystery (at one particularly unsatisfactory point it hints at heading down the sci-fi route, but swerves). Not all of what we are shown makes sense but, with strong echoes of *The Sixth Sense* (M Night Shyamalan, 1999) and faint echoes of *Inception,* (Christopher Nolan,

2010) that too makes sense. Don't let the reference to two classic films mislead: *La Traversée* is a long way from being in their class. French reviews were not kind. *Le Parisien* is representative: 'this agonising thriller is so empty, the story so tightly constructed that at no point do you get hooked the direction doesn't help.' At one point Sarah says to Clément 'c'est la folie' ('it's crazy'); she's right. *La Traversée* is not a total failure, but it is a one-trick pony which feels like a weaker, overly languorous, episode of TV's *Black Mirror*.

Blackbird (2013)   S+++

Directed by Jamie Chambers
Screenplay by Robyn Pete
Leading cast: Andrew Rothney (Ruadhan);
 Scarlett Mack (Amy); Patrick Wallace (Callum);
 Norman Maclean (Alec)
Colour, 90 minutes, UK

The Machars, Dumfries and Galloway: Ruadhan, a young man living on an abandoned boat, is fascinated by the precarious local culture expressed in song. He forms a tentative relationship with Amy, who lives in Glasgow, but his behaviour becomes erratic. Separately, Amy and Ruadhan determine to leave the town; Ruadhan drives off with his friend Callum.

Blackbird received its world premiere at the 2013 EIFF where it was named one of the 'Best of the Fest'. Producer James Barrett, who met Chambers when they were both students at the London Film School, has said, 'our motivation came from wanting to give a voice to a culture which felt under threat in some way and to dramatise that for film.' The threatened culture in *Blackbird* is that of traditional Scottish singing. Ruadhan, who loves these songs, and the people who sing them, is determined that the songs at least shall not die. If the film has a flaw, it is that Ruadhan is not strongly fleshed out; we don't know why he is, in essence, squatting, or unable to find work, or why he appears to be so solitary. There are hints that he is a tortured soul, but the nature of the torture remains obscure.

Director Chambers (a lecturer in film at the Edinburgh College of Art) is committed to the preservation of Scottish oral traditions. The title song for the film was taken from Martyn Bennett's album *Grit* (2003). In *The Guardian*, Chambers said that 'I was listening to Goldie and Leftfield and Orbital, but it was thrilling to realise that Martyn's music could stand alongside those things. As a young Scot I'd been looking for a long time for something that I felt was authentic within my culture… Now here was something that was deep and important and still alive in Scotland.'

Scottish legend Maclean, who plays the role of Alec, was interviewed in *The Scotsman* when *Blackbird* was premiered in Edinburgh. He said, '*Blackbird* is about falling in love with the past… It reminds me of the tag line for *Heaven's Gate*, which was "What one loves in life, are the things that fade"… but maybe there's a degree of hope in the future for our Scottish culture.'

The film, however, did not attract a wide audience and was not released outside of the festival circuit.

Blackbird was shot on location in the Machars in Dumfries and Galloway. This was also the location for Chambers' earlier short film *When the Song Dies* (2013). *Blackbird* is not readily available to stream but is available on DVD. It would be disappointing if this lovingly made film were to be consigned to obscurity.

The Dying Eye (2013)   S++

Directed by Shiphrah Meditz
Screenplay by Shiphrah Meditz
Leading cast: Hugh Burgess (Robert Drigson);
  Gary Lind (Ward Johnson); Chloe Ann Taylor
  (Mary Michaels)
Colour, 97 minutes, UK/New Zealand/US

In Edinburgh, Robert, a student, is a member of 'the Company' in thrall to Ward, and spends his time stalking people, determining whether they are to be executed or initiated into the Company. He falls in love with fellow student Mary.

The Dying Eye is the only feature film from director Meditz, who had previously made one short. She has said she was given the opportunity to study in Edinburgh and wanted to set a story there. The film had limited screenings at festivals and has left little footprint (even the version on YouTube – placed there by Meditz – had less than 100 viewings when I watched it). This is not surprising as, although

competently made, it has little to offer. Ostensibly a story about response to trauma, it's somewhat incoherent, and as Meditz has said, 'descends into mayhem'.

Dying Light (aka *Darkness Comes*) (2013)   S+++

Directed by David Newbigging
Screenplay by Gordon Mclean
Leading cast: Owen Whitelaw (Eddie Bowen);
  Kelly Wenham (Suze); James Cosmo
  (policeman)
Colour, 72 minutes, UK

Eddie is taken home by Suze. He is drugged and trapped in a bare room. Suze begins a dark ritual...

That *Dying Light* exists at all is remarkable. It was filmed in Greenbank over 11 days, with a crew of 20 unemployed youngsters who had attended workshops on filmmaking, on a budget of £50,000 and resources donated by local businesses. Mclean, who in 2008 had, along with Newbigging, won a Scotland BAFTA New Talent award for a short film, donated the screenplay. Cosmo's appearance is literally dialled in – he is the voice of a police officer whom Eddie speaks to when, for a short time, he has taken over in Suze's room. Results should therefore be measured not in terms of awards, artistic success, or box office, but in the impact the film had on the lives of those involved. If you were to stumble across this on a random trawl of horror films (which,

315

frankly, would take some doing – the film is *not* easy to track down or to find material about), and did not know the background, dissatisfaction would be the most likely result. The film is very short on answers, and (obviously) its production values are low.

Fire in the Night (2013)   DOC

Directed by Anthony Wonke; 90 minutes

On the night of 6 July 1988, an explosion and fire on the Piper Alpha North Sea oil rig led to the deaths of 167 people. This powerful documentary, made for the BBC by BAFTA- and Emmy-award-winner Wonke, tells the story through interviews, contemporaneous footage, and dramatic reconstructions. The film won the BAFTA Scotland award for Best Documentary, and the audience award at the EIFF.

For Those in Peril (2013) S+++ T100

Directed by Paul Wright
Screenplay by Paul Wright
Leading cast: George MacKay (Aaron); Kate Dickie (Cathy); Michael Smiley (Frank); Nichola Burley (Jane)
Colour, 92 minutes, UK

A small Scottish fishing town. A boating accident results in the deaths of five young men. The only survivor is Aaron, whose mental health deteriorates. He is wracked with guilt and is convinced that his brother is held by the Devil in the sea. He sets out to rescue him and dies. In the final shot his mother, Cathy, stands by a monstrous beast which has been washed up on shore.

For Those in Peril is a remarkably assured film from first-time writer/director Wright; to date this is his only feature. It is a complex interrogation of grief in the wake of tragedy, in which Wright's work is supported by exceptional performances from Dickie (who features in 14 films in this book) and MacKay, who was also in *Sunshine on Leith* in the same year. Prior to *Peril*, Wright had made only three short films (one of which, 2010's *Until the River Runs Red*, won the BAFTA for Best Short Film in 2011); following it he has directed a single episode of the TV series, *Murder*, in 2016, and the documentary *Arcadia* in 2017. At the BAFTA Scotland Awards in 2013 MacKay secured Best Actor, and *Peril* was recognised as Best Film. The jury of the Stockholm Film Festival also awarded MacKay Best Actor, the nomination being the following (in part): 'this actor expresses what it is like to be forced to the outer limits of human pain and sorrow. His complete vulnerability, isolation and despair are just as frightening for us as viewers as for his character and is very accurately portrayed'. *Peril* was shown in the Cannes Festival Critics' Week before moving onto the festival circuit, and then securing a limited UK release.

Peril is riddled with ambiguities. One possible interpretation is that we are watching something akin to horror, in which Aaron is responsible for the deaths of the missing five, and is now living with guilt, but on a path to commit more harm. Another interpretation is that he is the survivor of a tragic accident, is suffering from post-traumatic stress disorder, and losing his mental health. Yet another is that we live in a world of myth, in which stories told by mothers to their children have a basis in truth. It is this interpretation that the film's closing scene most closely clings to. As Stephen Dalton wrote in *The Hollywood Reporter*: 'To Wright's credit, this sorrow-soaked psychodrama never descends into the bloodthirsty revenge thriller that seems to be lurking behind every corner... *For Those in Peril* proves that creeping grief and guilt can deliver just as much dread-filled dramatic tension as a straight horror movie.'

Shot largely in the Aberdeenshire coastal village of Gourdon, *Peril* provides 'an evocative depiction of place, where young teens flee from adult supervision and danger lies in wait' (Charles Gant, in *Variety*). The film's multiple textures, combining what appears to be TV coverage of the initial tragedy, home video and mobile phone footage of the past, and lyrical/magical underwater shooting enhance the sense of this being a place with its local histories and tradition. The result is a very good film which rewards the attention it requires.

The Happy Lands (2013)   S++

Directed by Robert Rae
Screenplay by Peter Cox and Robert Rae
Leading cast: Kevin Clarke (Michael Brogan);
  Jokie Wallace (Dan Guthrie); Aaron Jones
  (Wee Baxie); Kevin Adair (Davey King);
  Farah Ahmed (Mary Miller); Stevie Allan (Pug
  Henderson)
Colour, 108 minutes, UK

1926, Carhill: the Fife mining community struggles through the General Strike.

Developed as a community project by Theatre Workshop Scotland, with some cast members playing their own (deceased) relatives, *The Happy Lands* is based on true stories from the mining community during the General Strike, blending interviews with descendants and reconstructed action (flirting with the boundaries between documentary and fiction). Jokie Wallace's family had worked in the pits, and he had heard stories about the strike; he told UNISON: 'I saw an advert in the paper and I'd always been interested in politics and trade unions but I'd never done anything like this before. The professionals were brand new and would take you through the process. There was a great spirit with the crew.' Rae had previously, working with refugees in Scotland, made *Trouble Sleeping* (2008). After producing a community play with Staffordshire miners, he spent some years developing the script for *The Happy Lands* with the support of Creative Scotland.

Interviewed by Roger Crow for *Bakewell Today*, Rae said reaction to the film had been very positive: 'I've done lots and lots of screenings up and down the country and people afterwards don't feel the need to be Barry Norman [the noted TV film critic]. They're more likely to come and say, "Well, this is my family's story, this is what the film meant to me"'. *The Happy Lands* was screened at the GFF, the inaugural Kelty Community Cinema Festival, and at the Scottish Parliament (and elsewhere), before moving to TV. A DVD is available. It is a strong piece of socially conscious cinema and, sadly, one which now would probably struggle to attract funding.

Jack and the Cuckoo-Clock Heart (*Jack et la mécanique du cœur*) (2013)

Directed by Stéphane Berla and Mathias Malzieu
Screenplay by Mathias Malzieu
Colour, 94 minutes, English and French versions,
France/Belgium

1874, Edinburgh: Jack is born on a bitterly cold winter's night. The midwife finds his heart is 'hard as a rock', and replaces it with a cuckoo-clock. Jack is told he must never fall in love; if he does, the clock will break.

The animated (not quite a musical) feature *Jack* only just makes it into this book. Almost half the film is set in Edinburgh, where Jack's story begins and ends but, unlike *L'Illusionniste*, there is no attempt to animate Edinburgh: we have to be told we are in the city, which could be substituted for anywhere else. It would have been a pity however to omit such a strong film.

Mathias Malzieu's novel *La mécanique du cœur* was published in 2007, becoming a bestseller in his native France. Previously, Malzieu was better known as one of the leads of the quirky band Dionysos. Lead songwriter Malzieu links his fiction and his music: a concept album featuring the songs which later became part of the film's soundtrack was released in 2007. In the French-language release of the film Malzieu provides Jack's voice (I watched the English-language version, with different actors voicing the characters).

The film, which was César-nominated in the Best Animated Feature category, is tonally close to Tim Burton's animated features (above all to *Edward Scissorhands*, 1990). This is certainly not for young children – the language is complex; the themes mature. For fans of film history there is much pleasure to be found in the central section, set in France and then Spain, where Jack hooks up with early film pioneer and illusionist Georges Méliès who uses his mechanical skills to cannibalise parts from his camera to mend Jack's broken heart; several scenes are based on Méliès' imagery. English-language reviews are thin on the ground. In France the reaction was positive, one critic describing *Jack* as a 'journey of intoxicating visual and musical poetry [which] touches and bewitches thanks to very beautiful moments'.

Not Another Happy Ending (2013) S+++ W10

Directed by John McKay
Screenplay by David Solomons
Leading cast: Karen Gillan (Jane Lockhart);
   Stanley Webber (Tom Duvall); Gary Lewis
   (Benny Lockhart); Henry Ian Cusick (Willie Scott)
Colour, 102 minutes, UK

Karen Gillan and Stanley Webber lack chemistry

In Glasgow, Jane's first novel, published by Tom, is a success. She struggles with the second, and Tom resorts to extreme measures to push her. The book is eventually published; Jane and Tom kiss.

NAHE is an annoying film. It could have been so much better had it *not* betrayed the promise of its title, and were it not packed to the gunnels with rom-com clichés and irritating quirkiness – the film clearly aims for cute, but overshoots: a female author called Jane (who models her look on Annie Hall), writes a novel in which the lead character is called Darcie! The strong cast deserve better. Screenwriter Solomons has said that Scottish culture can fall into 'miserabilism'*, but his efforts to liven things up fall flat (and he ignores his own advice, as voiced by Jane, 'why is it the saddest endings always seem the truest?'). Karen Gillan plays the lead with gusto verging on desperation, but cannot win out over the script, and Kate Dickie and Gary Lewis are wasted. Following a screening at the EIFF, *The Scotsman*'s Alistair Harkness wrote that NAHE was a 'weird amalgam of broad-strokes comedy and try-hard kookiness [that] barely works on any level'.

* This word is used far too often to describe Scottish films – even by Scottish filmmakers represented in this book; it has become a truism that there is a tendency in Scottish films towards 'miserabilism' – represented by films such as *The Gorbals Story, The Bill Douglas Childhood Trilogy, Ratcatcher, Neds, My Name is Joe* etc. When such films are set in England they are praised for their 'social realism'; when set in Scotland they are condemned as 'miserable'.

Sarah's Room (aka *To Here Knows When*) (2013) S+++

Directed by Grant McPhee
Screenplay by Chris Purnell
Leading cast: Patrick O'Brien (Joe); Kitty
   Colquhoun (Emma); Hanna Stanbridge (Sarah)
Colour, 85 minutes, UK

Edinburgh: Joe returns home after an absence to find that Emma, his partner, has taken a lodger, Sarah. He resents the intrusion, although is fascinated by Sarah. His mental health is fragile to begin with, and further deteriorates.

Sarah's Room, made on a micro-budget, with a small cast and limited locations, is one of six films in this book by Grant McPhee, who has an extensive credits list in digital imaging and cinematography (see **Wigilia**) in addition to his directing. The other two feature films are dealt with below; see **Between Above and Below** for three films about the Scottish independent music scene. *Sarah's Room* had limited exposure at film festivals but did not secure a cinema release. Irish actor Patrick O'Brien can also be seen in Graham Hughes' films **A Practical Guide to a Spectacular Suicide** and **Death of a Vlogger**, where he plays the engaging Dr Watson, and is also in **Night Kaleidoscope**, below, as is Scottish actor Kitty Colquhoun. Hanna Stanbridge appears in several films in this book, including **Prey for Us**. The real star here is McPhee's own cinematography, for which he won an award at the Bootleg Film Festival of New York. *Sarah's Room* is not driven by conventional narrative (not much actually 'happens') but by the depiction of a slow mental disintegration, in which the striking imagery does much of the heavy lifting as the film builds to a strong conclusion. However, as Jennie Kermode notes in *Eye For Film*, the subject matter 'is difficult territory for someone with limited experience [McPhee] and sometimes deliberately confused imagery becomes too distancing, so the film's grip slackens'.

→ *Night Kaleidoscope* (2017)
S+++

Directed by Grant McPhee
Screenplay by Megan Gretchen and Chris Purnell
Leading cast: Patrick O'Brien (Fion); Kitty Colquhoun (Carrie); Mariel McAllan (Isobel); Jason Harvey (Lewis)
Colour, 83 minutes, UK

In Edinburgh, vampires are tracked down by Fion, a drug-taking investigator with psychic powers.

Four films in this book feature vampires directly, and none are strong, although *Night Kaleidoscope*, which saw McPhee move into full-blown genre filmmaking, at least offers more menace than *The Little Vampire* (and was made for a tiny fraction of the older film's budget) and less nonsense than *Night is Day* and *The Slayers* (the best 'vampire' film covered here is *Morticia*, which is not, strictly, a vampire film at all). The threat however is refracted through Fion's drug-addled state. In common with *Sarah's Room*, strong visuals – *Night Kaleidoscope* is very thin on dialogue – are not able fully to compensate for a lack of narrative drive. As Nick Rocco Scalia puts it in *Film Threat*, the film has 'style to burn, but its problems mostly arise in the story department. Too often, *Night Kaleidoscope* seems torn between pursuing the psychedelic abstraction conjured up by its title and telling a standard, if pulpy, good-versus-evil tale'. This did not prevent the film from picking up several awards on the genre festival circuit, including the delightfully named Carnage Award from the 2017 Diabolical Film Festival.

→ *Far from the Apple Tree* (2019) `S+++`

Directed by Grant McPhee
Screenplay by Ben Soper
Leading cast: Sorcha Groundsell (Judith); Victoria
  Liddelle (Roberta Roslyn)
Colour, 89 minutes, UK

Aspiring artist Judith secures a placement with the well-established Roberta and moves into Dern Hall. Images of Maddy, Roberta's daughter who died by suicide, remind Judith of herself and she begins to construct art from Maddy's images. Witchcraft raises its head as Judith merges into Maddy.

The fantasy/horror *Far from the Apple Tree* played at the Dundead Horror Film Festival in May 2019, and at a Toronto film festival (not *the* Toronto International Film Festival) won Sorcha Groundsell (who was born on Lewis and can also be seen in *Iona*) the Best Performance award. Scottish actor Liddelle is also in *Outlaw King*. As with *Sarah's Room* and *Night Kaleidoscope*, much of what happens is internalised and fractured, but here the result is more accomplished, eliciting admiration from genre critics: *Horrified* described it as 'a dazzling film with shades of the occult and folk horror'. McPhee himself has described it as a 'Pop Art fairytale'. The budget was very small,

but McPhee has said that he turned this to his advantage: 'I don't think many people now actually use the fantastic opportunity and freedom offered by working independently... I wanted something which looked cool, played around with structure and form and was a bit trippy' (DCA, April 2019).

Sunshine on Leith (2013) `S+++` `T44`

Directed by Dexter Fletcher
Screenplay by Stephen Greenhorn
Leading cast: George MacKay (Davy); Kevin
  Guthrie (Ally); Jane Horrocks (Jean); Peter
  Mullan (Rab); Freya Mavor (Liz); Antonia
  Thomas (Yvonne)
Colour, 100 minutes, UK

Davy and Ally return to Edinburgh after serving in Afghanistan. Ally is dating Davy's sister, Liz, who introduces Davy to Yvonne. Davy's parents, Jean and Rab, face difficulties when Rab becomes aware he has an adult child and then has a heart attack. Ally and Liz break up, and Ally rejoins the army; Davy and Yvonne break up, and he wins her back.

Even before sitting down to rewatch *Sunshine on Leith* for this entry, I had seen it on multiple occasions, first at a cinema in Cardiff on a Sunday morning when my wife and I were the only two people at the screening. I like The Proclaimers; this obviously matters, as if you have no time for their music then you are unlikely to enjoy a film version of a stage musical built around The Proclaimers' songs. If you do like The Proclaimers (who make a fleeting appearance about five minutes and 30 seconds in), and know their material, there's a fun guessing game to play: which songs are going to be in, and who is going to do what? It is likely that there will be a woman called Jean and that someone will propose marriage; it is *certain* that someone is going to go to America, and that someone else will promise to walk 500 miles. These opportunities, and their realisation, are engaging Easter eggs, rather than annoyingly predictable.

Director Dexter Fletcher has had a fascinating career and showed with *Rocketman* (2019), also a film with music, that he could achieve brilliance. There are hints in *Sunshine* (his second film) of what would come later. He has 'officially' directed only four films, but it is no secret that he stepped in to rescue *Bohemian Rhapsody* (Bryan Singer, 2018) when Singer was removed from the production, although Fletcher did not receive a directorial credit. As an actor he started young, appearing in *Bugsy Malone* (Alan Parker, 1976) when he was ten years old. In Derek Jarman's stunning *Caravaggio* (1986) he played the artist as a young man. He continues to accumulate acting credits. For the most part *Sunshine* is conventionally made, but there are moments when the light really shines through – for example in the utterly joyous final scene, as a flash mob join in with Yvonne and Davy's rendition of '500 Miles' on the Edinburgh Mound.

The six leads are very strong. Mullan

George MacKay, Kevin Guthrie, Antonia Thomas and Freya Mavor break into song

is perfect as Rab – he is unlikely to be releasing an album of classic ballads any time soon but is certainly no Rex Harrison (he also sings in *Young Adam*). Horrocks shot to fame with *Little Voice* (Mark Herman, 1998) proving then that she could *really* sing, and gets the lion's share of the stronger songs in *Sunshine*. MacKay has built an impressive CV (most prominently *1917*, Sam Mendes, 2019 – he is also in *For Those in Peril*), and convinces as a Scot. Neilston-born Guthrie is also in, amongst others, *Sunset Song*. Mavor and Thomas (who has the stronger voice of the two) are probably better known for roles in TV series; Mavor (who is also in *Balance, Not Symmetry*) for *Skins* (2011–2012) and Thomas for *Misfits* (2009–2011).

There are some contrarians who appear not to like *Sunshine on Leith,* but fortunately they are in a minority. It holds an impressive 90 per cent score on Rotten Tomatoes and was Mark Kermode's film of the week for *The Observer*; like him, I shed a tear (or several) but spent most of the film 'beaming like a gibbering, love-struck fool.'

Under the Skin (2013)   S+ T4

Directed by Jonathan Glazer
Screenplay by Walter Campbell, Jonathan Glazer
Leading cast: Scarlett Johansson (the female)
Colour, 108 minutes, UK/Switzerland

Glasgow: The Female, an alien passing as human, cruises the streets at night, and takes men home where they are in some way processed. Eventually she releases a potential victim and is then herself hunted. She flees to the Highlands, and is attacked by a logger, doused with petrol, and set on fire. Her corpse is burnt to ashes.

Under the Skin is one of the best films covered in this book – in 2022 it was voted the best British film of the 21st century in a critics' poll conducted by MASSIVE Cinema. It is also divisive, significantly splitting audiences from critics. On Rotten Tomatoes it has an 84 per cent score from critics, but a lowly 55 per cent from audiences. At the time I began writing this entry, the 'top review' on IMDb dismissed *UTS* as 'incoherent garbage trying to pass itself off as style'. *UTS* is perhaps one of those films which is easier to *admire* than to *like*. Whether you like or hate it probably depends on your tolerance for weird, and for films which depart significantly from the book on which they are based; *UTS* is true to the spirit of the disturbing source novel, but radically departs from it in both detail and vision. It has a *very* sparse script, and relies heavily on the power of the camera, and design, in its storytelling.

When *UTS* was released Scarlett Johansson's more recent work included *Iron Man 2* (Jon Favreau, 2010), *We*

Scarlett Johannson is riveting as The Female

Bought a Zoo (Cameron Crowe, 2011) and *The Avengers* (Joss Whedon, 2012). She was (and still is) best known as the Black Widow (Natasha Romanoff) in the Marvel Cinematic Universe. But she had also made *Ghost World* (Terry Zwigoff, 2001) and *Lost in Translation* (Sofia Coppola, 2003) before she was 20. *UTS* reminded anyone who had been foolish enough to forget it that she is an *extremely* fine actor. Since *UTS* she has starred in, amongst others, *Her* (Spike Jonze, 2013), *Hail, Caesar!* (Ethan Coen and Joel Coen, 2016), *Jojo Rabbit* (Taika Waititi, 2019) and *Marriage Story* (Noah Baumbach, 2019). It is a list of films many actors would kill for. In *UTS* Johansson plays an unnamed – in a departure from the book – alien disguised and engineered to appear human, permitting her to operate amongst humans, harvesting them for consumption by her own race. The film is based on Michel Faber's extremely unsettling and quite brilliant 2000 novel of the same name. The film is *slightly* less disturbing: significantly, its focus is entirely on The Female whereas the book spends time also with her victims and co-workers.

The shooting of *UTS* attracted significant media attention in Scotland – it is not every day that a film star as elevated and fetishised as Johansson, sporting a black wig and wearing a faux-fur jacket, is required to, as *The Scotsman* reported, 'drive a van around the city's dodgier areas, giving the come-on to random men who had no idea they were being filmed'. She was only once recognised, but the risks were obvious. Glazer said: 'in those moments you just use your common sense', and security was always on hand. I suspect that more men now claim to have been propositioned by Johansson than were.

Glazer started his professional life, like many filmmakers, with pop videos; in his case for cool bands such as Massive Attack, Radiohead and Blur. His breakout film success came with 2000's *Sexy Beast*, which was followed up with the controversial *Birth* (2004) with Lauren Bacall and Nicole Kidman – a neat trick for a director making his sophomore movie. After *UTS*, it took Glazer ten years to release his next film, 2023's *The Zone of Interest*, which won the Grand Prix at Cannes, Oscars, and plaudits galore.

In *The Herald*'s review of *UTS* Alison Rowat wrote: 'With barely any dialogue, a plot as thin and taut as a piano wire, and not a lot in the way of budget, *Under the Skin* is reliant for success on its A-list star, and its director's ability to conjure up an other-worldly atmosphere from the mundane. Both parties, with the help of a brilliant score by Mica Levi, triumph in bringing Michel Faber's novel to the screen in the fashion it deserves... it is Scotland on screen as you have never seen it before.' Levi's exceptional score garnered several of the film's many awards. On the film's tenth anniversary, the GFF mounted a screening with a full live orchestral performance of the soundtrack.

We are Northern Lights (2013) DOC

Directed by Nick Higgins and David Graham
Scott; 98 minutes

The filmic equivalent of a patchwork quilt, built from hundreds of contributions submitted by the Scottish public (some showing great wit). Made as part of the Year of Creative Scotland 2012, the film toured the Highlands and west coast by way of the mobile Screen Machine and was also shown in Scotland's Cineworlds.

Alasdair Gray: A Life in Progress (2014; re-edit, 2024) DOC

Directed by Kevin Cameron; 94 minutes (re-edit
106 minutes)

If anyone in recent Scottish cultural life merits a feature-length documentary it is artist, author and *agent provocateur* Alasdair Gray (1934–2019). If you live in the West End of Glasgow his art is easily seen in Òran Mór, the Ubiquitous Chip and the Hillhead subway station; if you read 20th-century fiction, his magnum opus *Lanark: A Life in Four Books* (1981) is essential. He also advocated consistently for republicanism and an independent Scotland.

Notoriously irascible and resistant to interviews, Gray allowed himself to be filmed over a period of 15 years for Cameron's documentary, first released in 2014, which develops into a fitting tribute to an exceptional man. Yorgos Lanthimos'

2023 terrific adaptation of Gray's *Poor Things* (1992) drew significant coverage in Scotland. While it was the most high-profile push for Gray's profile outside of Scotland, it also effaced the Glasgow setting of the novel, sparking strong reactions within Scotland, and speculation that Gray would have hated it. Cameron's re-edit of *A Life in Progress* adds new material, dealing in part with *Poor Things*, and including interviews with people Gray did not want filmed when he was still alive.

Beyond (2014) S++

Directed by Joseph Baker and Tom Large
Screenplay by Joseph Baker and Tom Large
Leading cast: Richard J Danum (Cole); Gillian
MacGregor (Maya); Paul Brannigan (Michael)
Colour, 89 minutes, UK

Cole and Maya meet at a party two years and 291 days before an 'asteroid' may hit Earth. Later they struggle to survive after an apocalyptic alien attack.

Many films have been made with the basic premise of 'Oh my God, we're all going to die!' The genre can be great fun, notwithstanding the death toll, or profound, spectacular or mundane. *Beyond* definitely lies on the side of mundanity, and offers little in the way of profundity. Set in Scotland because the exteriors were largely filmed here.

En tierra extraña (In a Foreign Land) (2014) DOC

Directed by Icíar Bollaín; 72 minutes

A Spanish production exploring the lives of (mostly) young Spanish migrants in Edinburgh, and the circumstances behind their migration.

In response to what is now known as the 'Great Spanish Depression' of 2008–2014, it is estimated that up to 700,000 Spanish workers took advantage of the EU's right to freedom of movement. Many of these were young and highly qualified. As many as 20,000 ended up in Edinburgh, where, as participants in this intelligent and engaging documentary make clear, some felt more valued as kitchen porters, or shop assistants, than they did as teachers or engineers in Spain.

Bollaín, Spain's leading female director, intercuts the Scottish experiences with a recording of actor Alberto San Juan delivering a scathing, and witty, monologue on the injustices of the Spanish (and global) economic system to a theatre audience in Spain, and archive footage. While *En tierra extraña*'s target is the Spanish political economy, it also provides an interesting window into the reception in Scotland of economic migrants (something dealt with in fiction in, eg, *Graders* and *On Falling*), which in the experience of the film's participants is broadly, but not universally, positive.

Everybody's Child (2014) DOC

Directed by Garry Fraser; 75 minutes

Fraser, a drug addict in recovery and a filmmaker (he worked on *T2: Trainspotting*), grew up in Muirhouse in Edinburgh, and spent ten years in the care system. In the late 1980s Muirhouse became the centre of Edinburgh's HIV/AIDS epidemic. Fraser presents a powerful portrait of the damage done to the community and a searingly honest self-examination.

From Scotland with Love (2014) DOC

Directed by Virginia Heath; 76 minutes

Covering nearly 100 years of footage, the film shows Scots at work, at leisure, at rest, in protest, and living with war. Heath has brilliantly edited together archive footage from material held in the Scottish Screen Archive, without narration, but with a soundtrack consisting of King Creosote songs (spawning an album with the same name). *From Scotland with Love* is mesmerising; to quote Mark Braxton (*RadioTimes.com*), 'it's like a new kind of history programme: immersive, lyrical and, in its way, beautiful.'

Garnet's Gold (2014)   DOC

Directed by Ed Perkins; 75 minutes

Made by accomplished documentarian Perkins for the excellent BBC Storyville series, with festival screenings and awards. Garnet Frost, a Londoner described by a friend as a 'romantic idealist', who lives with his feisty octogenarian mother, determines to find the 40,000 gold coins brought to Scotland in 1746 to fund (too late) Bonnie Prince Charlie's campaign – allegedly hidden on the shores of Loch Arkaig. He fails, but there is warm storytelling here. In *The Scotsman*, Alistair Harkness noted the balance drawn between portraying 'a dreamer coming to terms with the fact that life might have passed him by', and 'a windbag'. But as he recognises, the 'beautiful and expressionistic' film is 'oddly compelling'.

God Help the Girl (2014)   S++

Directed by Stuart Murdoch
Screenplay by Stuart Murdoch
Leading cast: Emily Browning (Eve); Olly
   Alexander (James); Hannah Murray (Cassie);
   Pierre Boulanger (Anton)
Colour, 112 minutes, UK

Eve, who has left an eating disorders clinic, hooks up with James, an aspiring musician. They hang out in Glasgow, and form a band, 'God Help the Girl'. After a successful gig, Eve heads to London.

At the outset, this entry requires a declaration of interest. Writer/director Stuart Murdoch is a key figure in one of my favourite bands, Belle and Sebastian. Add to that the presence of musician/actor Olly Alexander, who was terrific in Russell T Davies' 2021 TV series *It's a Sin*, and the result is that I was predestined to like the film (which I missed on its release).

GHTG started life as a music project, leading to an album of the same name, released in 2009. Struggling to turn the project into a film, Murdoch was unable to raise funding from producers and resorted to a Kickstarter campaign. The result was that GHTG was made on a shoestring budget (this does not really show). As Murdoch said in an interview with *The Guardian* in 2014 'It was pretty manic… We were a small crew, we passed silently through the night, we didn't have much lighting, there wasn't much razzmatazz. You wouldn't have even known we were there. Sometimes we'd even move from scene to scene without putting anything in a truck or a car, we'd just push our trolleys around the West End.' Murdoch would have preferred the cast be Scottish: 'James was definitely meant to be Mr Glasgow, and I always imagined Eve coming from a small town in Fife. Cassie was supposed to be the only odd one out' (Elle Fanning was originally cast as Cassie). Given the diversity of Glasgow's West End population it is not wholly unreasonable that we have instead two English actors, and the Australian Browning (*Sucker Punch*, Zack Snyder, 2011; *Sleeping Beauty*, Julia Leigh, 2011).

There should be a simple rule: like Belle and Sebastian, like *GHTG*. But Leslie Felperin, in *The Guardian*, described herself as a longstanding fan; her review of the film includes the following: 'this musical layers swinging-60s pastiche upon Gallic-style pop pastiche upon indie-kid angst to build a teetering tower of fey posturing that takes 112 excruciating minutes to topple into a smeary mess of twee'. That's overly harsh, and she is in the minority. Reporting from the Berlin Film Festival, Ryan Gilbey was much kinder: recognising some flaws he nevertheless found *GHTG* 'polished, poised and endearingly confident, driven by editing and performances every bit as precise as the wordplay in Murdoch's lyrics'.

GHTG is inconsequential but charming, although at nearly two hours the charm occasionally is stretched thin.

Let us Prey (2014) S++ T100

Directed by Brian O'Malley
Screenplay by Fiona Watson and David Cairns
Leading cast: Liam Cunningham (Six); Pollyanna McIntosh (PC Rachel Heggie); Hanna Stanbridge (PC Jennifer Mundie); Bryan Larkin (PC Jack Warnock); Douglas Russell (Sgt MacReady)
Colour, 92 minutes, UK

'Inveree': Rachel arrives for the first night shift at her new police station. A stranger appears and is placed in the cells. Hell descends and the body count rises.

Douglas Russell dials it up to 11

For horror fans there is much to enjoy in *Let us Prey*, which manages to build to an effectively violent climax, ratcheting up the craziness (in the *Irish Times* Tara Brady wrote, 'Just when the viewer thinks things can't get any more baroque, they do. Just when you imagine the people onscreen couldn't be more evil, they are'), despite having, for those steeped in the genre at least, clearly signposted the journey. If the set-up is not obvious from the very start, it certainly should be by the point the stranger references Revelations 6:8 ('And I looked and beheld a pale horse: and his name that sat on him was death'). Scottish actor McIntosh (also in *Burke and Hare, Filth* and *White Settlers*) has fun with her strong action role and the path to something more than survival, while Stanbridge (*Outcast*, and 25 episodes of *River City*, 2015–2020) wallows in sleaze. Most florid of all is Russell (*Neds* and *The Wee Man*) who descends into full-blown twisted religious mania. Critical reaction was broadly positive.

Northmen: A Viking Saga (2014)

Directed by Claudio Fäh
Screenplay by Bastian Zach and Matthias Bauer
Leading cast: Tom Hopper (Asbjörn); Ryan
  Kwanten (Conall); James Norton (Bjorn); Charlie
  Murphy (Inghean); Ken Duken (Thorald)
Colour, 97 minutes, Switzerland/Germany/South
  Africa

*Eight Vikings are washed ashore on the
coast of Scotland, and battle their way
through to a Viking settlement in Northern
England. Early on they seize the local
King's daughter, Inghean, as a hostage.*

Filmed on location in South Africa and
Ireland, but explicitly set in 'Scotland'
(which is just plausible if we are near the
very end of the Viking presence in what
is now the UK, by which time 'Scotland'
had entered usage), *Northmen*'s action
credentials are undoubted; its ability to
grip is not. The film is at best, to quote
Dennis Harvey in *Variety*, 'uninventive but
diverting'. It's a by-the-numbers heroes-
in-peril tale, in which the plucky Viking
band's numbers are slowly whittled down
as the group moves south.

The Possibilities are Endless (2014)   DOC

Directed by James Hall and Edward Lovelace; 83
  minutes

In February 2006, Edwyn Collins, who
co-founded Orange Juice in the late 1970s
and continued with a solo career after the
band's split, had a stroke leading to aphasia
(difficulties with language recognition and
speech). The lyrical documentary deals
with the period of recovery up to a live
performance, and Collins' relationship
with his wife, Grace Maxwell, whose
name was one of the only things he was
able to say after the stroke – another
being 'the possibilities are endless'. Mark
Kermode described the well-received
film as a 'gorgeously poetic tale of the
redemptive power of love'. The visually
poetic extended opening section may test
the patience of some viewers.

The Pull (2014)   S++

Directed by Jenni Townsend
Screenplay by Jenni Townsend
Leading cast: Jenni Townsend (Olivia); Tony
  Townsend (Ian); Martin Haddow (Sean)
Colour, 89 minutes, UK/US/Australia

*Olivia, a modern nomad from Melbourne,
arrives in Glasgow to stay with her father,
Ian. She meets Sean, and they hang out. In
the face of Sean's stability, Olivia questions
her lifestyle, but when her father returns to
Melbourne, she moves on.*

'It's a nice little town, takes a little while
to grow on you, but you'll love it'. This
is the description of Glasgow given by
Ian, an Australian working in the city, to
his daughter early on in her stay. Little
happens in *The Pull*, yet the film has
substance and charm. Olivia might be

described as a 'citizen of the World' and struggles to answer the question 'where are you from?'; while Sean is firmly grounded in place and has never left Scotland – seeing no need to. When asked by Olivia to name the most exotic place he's ever been, the answer is Inverness; and he's not being sarcastic. It's unlikely that the two could have a future together – *The Pull* is then about the fleeting friendship, and the questions it forces Olivia to face.

The Pull won the Best Foreign Feature award at the Toronto Female Eye Film Festival. It is Townsend's only feature and, in what seems a total swerve, her most recent directing work has been all 30 episodes of the animated series *Akedo: Ultimate Arcade Warriors* (2021–2023). *The Pull* is available on YouTube.

The Silent Storm (2014) S+ W4

Directed by Corinna McFarlane
Screenplay by Corinna McFarlane
Leading cast: Damian Lewis (Balor McNeil); Andrea Riseborough (Aislin McNeil); Ross Anderson (Fionn); Kate Dickie (Mrs McKinnon)
Colour, 102 minutes, UK

Balor, the minister, lives in an isolated island manse after WWII with his oppressed wife, Aislin. The Glasgow Rehabilitation Mission places Fionn, a young 'sinner', with the McNeils. God speaks to Balor, and he determines to move his kirk to the mainland, stone by stone.

In 2014, writer/director McFarlane travelled to Scotland to 'discover her roots' and stayed on Mull. She was interested in the excessive zeal with which some of the Protestant churches were run on the Western Isles, and is quoted in the *Radio Times* (Claire Webb, 2016): 'I went to some islands in the Outer Hebrides where the women I spoke to weren't allowed to go to their husband's or father's funerals because the minister decided it wasn't appropriate. So the women would have to watch from nearby hills – and this is only going back 55 years.' Her response was *The Silent Storm*, shot on Mull, but set on an anonymous island. This is, thankfully, the director's only feature film.

The result is heavy-handed, allegory-bedecked, cliché-riddled nonsense. It is risible and is one of the few films in this book that should simply be avoided. I am compelled to point out that not everyone agrees with me. Most reviews are scathing, but Mark Kermode, in *The Observer*, rated it 3/5, and Anna Smith in *Empire* and Kate Muir in the *Times* both rated it 4/5. Mike McCahill catches the more prevalent mood in *The Guardian*: 'McFarlane's gibbering Highland melodrama huffs and puffs… it rapidly ascends to the kingdom of heaven-help-us'. In the *Irish Independent* Paul Whittington wrote that, 'The high winds of hamminess roar through the rafters'.

Lewis, who has been in *Homeland* (2011–2014 – when it was still good), *Wolf Hall* (2015) and *Billions* (2016–2021), is given no respite by the director or by the script. For most of the film he is required to look as if he is experiencing the Passion

Damien Lewis hams it up

and declaims lines such as: 'God has spoken to me!' The nadir in the 'just in case they haven't got it let's ram the point home' school of directing that McFarlane adopts comes when Balor struggles along the strand, dragging behind him a pew: Mull as the Via Dolorosa! Anderson gets to be the Glasgow docks thug who is at heart a sensitive soul and reads Yeats (aloud), while Riseborough spends most of the film as a repressed victim – ending it with an oh-so-long look of ecstasy. The viewer too is likely to end the film with a similar look, glad that, like Aislin's wretched existence with Balor, it's finally over.

Skeletons (2014)   S+++

Directed by Craig-James Moncur
Screenplay by Craig-James Moncur
Leading cast: Gareth Morrison (Tom); Rachael
  Keillor (Rachel); Michael Daviot (Vincent)
Colour, 80 minutes, UK/US

In Edinburgh, Tom, Rachel and Vincent are all struggling with life. Rachel takes on sex work, Tom becomes obsessed with murder, and Vincent contemplates suicide. Their lives intersect to mutual benefit.

Scottish actor/writer/director Craig-James Moncur has directed several shorts. IMDb is not alone in suggesting that *Skeletons* is his only feature, although Moncur has, in interviews, referenced a first film called *Walter*, which may never have been exhibited (a version of this is available on YouTube). As an actor he appeared in many episodes of the CBBC Scottish series *Jeopardy* (2002–2005) (note that on IMDb there are separate entries for Craig Moncur, and Craig-James Moncur). As Craig-James Moncur he also appears in *Night Kaleidoscope*.

Skeletons was made on a minimal budget, with contributors donating their time. Moncur explained that it 'was a much more ambitious project than I had originally set out to make. I had next to no budget and as such I was working as Producer, Director and Shooter. In all honesty, it was too much.' Matching its minimal budget, the film has a minimalist script, with the leads having virtually no lines. Moncur explained he 'wanted to make the film all about tone and observation. I wanted the audience to build a picture in their heads about who the characters were, even though they knew nothing about them, before completely smashing their perception at the end of it all'. *Skeletons* is a lean and stylish work, which merits more exposure than the limited screenings it has been able to obtain. Fortunately, a good quality version is available on YouTube.

What We Did on Our Holiday (2014)   S++ T100

Directed by Andy Hamilton and Guy Jenkin
Screenplay by Andy Hamilton and Guy Jenkin
Leading cast: Rosamund Pike (Abi); David Tennant (Doug); Billy Connolly (Gordie); Emilia Jones (Lottie); Bobby Smalldridge (Mickey); Harriett Turnbull (Jess)
Colour, 95 minutes, UK

Abi and Doug, who are separating, and their three children, Lottie, Jess and Mickey, head to the Highlands for the 75th birthday of Gordie, Doug's father. He dies while on a beach with the children, who give him a spectacular funeral.

It's a reasonable expectation that any film called *What We Did on Our Holiday* is likely to be lazy, unoriginal, and awful. But this film is written and directed by the key creative team behind *Drop the Dead Donkey* (1990–2008), and *Outnumbered* (2007–2016), with which it has a great deal in common. It has a strong cast, and is smart, funny, and occasionally affecting. The title is revisited as the children make the preparations for warrior Gordie's funeral – he has died in a battle, against cancer. Mickey says: 'I can't wait to go back to school, when we write about "What I did on our half-term". But I bet Shona's done something more interesting, like she always has'.

This is one of two films in this book (the other being *Mary Queen of Scots*, 2018), to feature Scottish-born David Tennant, still best known as Doctor Who

David Tennant and Emilia Jones

(2005–2013). Pike plays his icy blonde soon-to-be-ex-wife (having played in a similar tone before: *Gone Girl*, David Fincher, 2014; *I Care a Lot*, J Blakeson, 2020). Doug and Abi convincingly walk the razor line between domestic warfare and maintaining appearances for the sake of the children and Gordie. Connolly is strong as the kindly grandfather who is accepting of his impending death and has learnt the lessons that this new perspective brings. If anything, Gordie is a little *too* perfect. All three children are excellent. While Jess has some of the best lines, the more important role is Jones' Lottie, often framed as the most mature person in the film. Buffeted by the tos and fros of her parents' relationship, she keeps track in a notebook. As the disintegrating family prepares to leave London she says archly, 'I need a list... of the lies we're going to tell. In case I forget one'. One of the better scenes is a conversation between her and Gordie on the value of lies when delivered in the appropriate circumstances. Jones went on to play the lead in the 2022 Oscar-winning *CODA* (Sian Heder, 2021).

What We Did performed moderately well at the UK box office. Although not released in the US, it recouped over $10m globally. Critical response was strong, with a Rotten Tomatoes score of 73 per cent at the time of writing. Much of the film was shot in Wester Ross, although scenes involving ostriches (because, why not?) were shot at the Blair Drummond Safari Park.

White Settlers (aka *The Blood Lands*) (2014)   S+

Directed by Simeon Halligan
Screenplay by Ian Fenton
Leading cast: Pollyanna McIntosh (Sarah Chapman); Lee Williams (Ed Chapman)
Colour, 79 minutes, UK

The Borders: English couple Sarah and Ed Chapman move into a farmhouse which is too expensive for local people to afford. On their first night, they are subject to a home invasion.

White Settlers was released in the UK on 5 September 2014 (moving very quickly to streaming), almost exactly two weeks before the Scottish independence referendum. Halligan described this as a 'happy coincidence' but said also of Fenton's script that it 'had come up a few years ago, and those issues were always at the back of the film. That was what he wanted to write his script about… primarily, it's a suspense thriller, it's more like a horror film. But the background to why it's going on has a political context.' The timing was not lost on critics, who recognised the film's potential political subtext. Home invasion films are a tried and tested horror trope, but maybe *White Settlers* had something to add to the horror (just as *Calibre* has more to say than *Deliverance*). Unfortunately, as Alistair Harkness wrote, the filmmakers 'fail to make these tropes scary or tense enough within a Scottish context. Consequently, they can't capitalise on the film's blatant political subtexts in any meaningful way. The end result is fairly mediocre, boringly executed stuff'. Indeed, the handling of the 'subtext' is so blunt and obvious as to rob it of any deep significance.

Whatever the filmmakers may have intended, it is the remoteness which matters in *White Settlers*, and certainly not Scottish authenticity (the film was shot in England's Peak District and around Manchester). It's why we are told twice in the first four minutes that there is no mobile phone reception. Ed is not surprised: 'welcome to Scotland' is his rejoinder, and he's clearly not enamoured with the country: 'the weather is shit, the food is shit, the football is shit'. We are, I suspect, *meant* to find the Chapmans irritating. But there must be *some* sympathy for the victims, or the film would simply not work at all. By far the best thing here is McIntosh (also in *Filth*, *Burke and Hare* and *Let us Prey*), who was born in Scotland and who plays Sarah – somewhat less irritating than her husband – with a cut-glass English accent. Although Ed had earlier dismissed her practicality, it is she who is resourceful and who leads the fightback. Some critics *were* impressed (the film carries a Rotten Tomatoes rating of 50 per cent). Given the unsatisfying and faintly ridiculous ending, that's a little hard to fathom.

Wigilia (aka *Wigilia: A Christmas Eve Story*) (2014) S+++

Directed by Graham Drysdale
Screenplay by Graham Drysdale, Iwona
  Glowinska and Duglas T Stewart
Leading cast: Iwona Glowinska (Agata); Duglas T
  Stewart (Robbie)
Colour, 72 minutes, English/Polish, UK

Christmas Eve, Glasgow: in a flat which she cleans, left vacant while the owner is on holiday, Agata prepares a traditional Polish Wigilia dinner. To her surprise, Robbie, the owner's brother, arrives.

An intimate chamber piece, *Wigilia* is set over two Christmas Eves, a year apart, in two different flats. Three of the four key figures in its production, producer/director/ writer Drysdale (at the time a lecturer in screenwriting and film production at QMU, Edinburgh), and co-stars/writers Glowinska (who also prepared the 12-course dinner served in the first act) and Stewart, have no other film credits. Only producer/ cinematographer Grant McPhee has gone on to further work in film (see *Sarah's Room* etc and *Between Above and Below*). McPhee picked up a couple of awards from festival screenings for his cinematography.

  Wigilia was self-funded by the producers on a micro-budget and shot over just five days. Co-producer Steven Moore has said 'the way we now consume content makes these types of productions even more attractive... a voice can now be found by having it available on Amazon and Netflix... I think audiences will be much more susceptible to less polished perhaps more authentic films.' It is the authenticity and intimacy of the film that provide its strengths – and the fact that a Christmas miracle (of a sort) *does* happen feels not at all out of place. Following a screening at the Wisconsin Film Festival, Rob Thomas wrote in the *Cap Times* that the 'understated performances and spare dialogue make for a film that's charming and humane'.

Anna Unbound (2015) S++

Directed by Bernd Porr
Screenplay by Martin Brocklebank
Leading cast: Vasso Georgiadou (Anna); Martin
  Sweeney (Josh); James Robson (Robert);
  Sharon Osdin (Ruth)
Colour, 89 minutes, UK/Greece

Anna, a young woman from Athens, moves to live with her Scottish boyfriend, Martin, in Glasgow. She secures a job, but one of her colleagues, Robert, prompts memories of trauma in Greece. As Anna's mental health disintegrates the boundary between imagination and reality becomes fluid.

Anna Unbound is the only feature film from director Porr who, when not making films, is a senior lecturer in Biomedical Engineering at the University of Glasgow, with an earlier background as a sound engineer for radio and live performance. The film was a spin-off from the short *Cut Free* (2013), also featuring Georgiadou. Most of the shoot took place in Glasgow.

  Anna Unbound deals with how people

move on geographically and psychologically, specifically from trauma, but in a fluid world of migration there is wider resonance. On the site *Onefilmfan.com* Porr said there were 'two main motivations in this film: to tell a story about trauma and how one deals with such flashbacks and to tell a story about immigration, but in a way that it's not a gritty drama, but rather in a softer way which also reflects experiences of Europeans moving from one place to another.'

Anna Unbound was never going to be a film with a commercial footprint, but it performed well on the festival circuit, with both Georgiadou and Scottish actor Osdin (also in *Cleek*), who plays Anna's colleague, picking up awards. Georgiadou was described in *The National* as having 'a terrifically captivating presence'.

The Closer We Get (2015) DOC

Directed by Karen Guthrie; 87 minutes

Karen returns to her hometown of Largs, where three generations of the family live. Her elderly mother has had a stroke and needs constant care at home. A sensitive, but candid, portrait of a family in which Karen's father leads a double life (with a second family in Djibouti) follows.

Con Men (2015) S++

Directed by R Paul Wilson
Screenplay by R Paul Wilson
Leading cast: Paul Comrie (Rob); Tom Moriarty (Tom)
Colour, 90 minutes, UK/US

Following the murder of Joe, a con man, the experienced Rob takes Tom under his wing to assist him with Joe's planned big score, involving a major card game in Glasgow; but who is conning whom?

R Paul Wilson's Glasgow-set micro-budget film *Con Men* was made for less than £5,000 and shot in 12 days. This was his first feature, flowing from his background in magic and illusion, and his work on the BBC series *The Real Hustle* (2006–2012) in which professional tricksters perpetrated scams on unsuspecting members of the public (returning any monies taken at the end of the show). Wilson then set out to put his knowledge to use in making the fictional *Con Men*, saying the 'main objective was to try and make a con movie that recognised that the audience would be trying to get ahead of the scam from the first frame and still maintain the mystery until the end but without cheating!'

Con Men has the old hand coaching the tyro (and by proxy the audience) and relies heavily on dialogue. Its jaunty soundtrack is not matched by the action, and it lacks the wit and sparkle of better-known films based around the intellectual game of the con trick. This limitation is underscored by a shoehorned reference to *The Sting* (George

Roy Hill, 1972), which has a verve *Con Men* lacks. That being said, for the size of its budget the film is a remarkable achievement. Wilson has accepted the 'scams in *Con Men* are all real but used for dramatic purposes and perhaps, if I'm honest, I wish I'd made those scams a little more prominent.'

The film makes good use of Glasgow locations, and features, in a smaller role, Atta Yaqub (*Ae Fond Kiss*). Wilson's second film, *Isolani*, is covered below.

→ *Isolani* (2017) S+++ T100

Directed by R Paul Wilson
Screenplay by R Paul Wilson
Leading cast: Kate McLaughlin (Isla); Catriona Evans (procurator fiscal); Jim Sweeney (Brian Ross); Gianni Capaldi (Tom)
Colour, 107 minutes, UK

In Glasgow, young single mother Isla witnesses a murder, and is compelled to navigate her way through multiple threats.

Isolani opens with a quote from former world chess champion Gary Kasparov: 'women by their nature are not great chess players. They are not great fighters.' An isolani is an isolated queen's pawn which is unprotected on its flanks, but in the hands of a strong player on the right board the piece can have power, as Isla – a strong performance from McLaughlin in her first feature – does here.

Late on, Isla asks Evans' Procurator Fiscal what, if she were in her shoes, she would do: the answer is 'whatever it takes'. Wilson,

making his second Glasgow-based feature, throws aside stereotypes of young single mothers as Isla, under constant threat from abusive parents, a corrupt police officer, a local gang lord and a largely unsupportive bureaucracy, does whatever it takes and outplays them all to protect her son and herself. In meetings with social services determined to place her son with her parents, she is assertive and well-informed; to the surprise of an overbearing and impatient social worker, she *has* read, and understood, all the material, and knows her rights. She dances on a knife edge to save herself and her son from being used, or sacrificed, as pawns in others' criminal games.

Although slow paced, Wilson's second film is a strong and effective thriller, which was nominated for the Best UK Film award at the Raindance Film Festival, and the Discovery award at the British Independent Film Awards. The film was not picked up for distribution but is available on some streaming services.

Demon Baby (aka *Wandering Rose*) (2015) S+

Directed by Corrie (Coz) Greenop
Screenplay by Corrie (Coz) Greenop and Lee Phillips
Leading cast: Carina Birrell (Rose); David Wayman (Theo)
Colour, 70 minutes, UK

Rose, who is pregnant, and Theo, are staying in their camper van in the Highlands when Rose is tormented by nightmares and confronts her demons.

The title under which this mercifully short first feature from English director Coz Greenop won three awards at the British Horror Film Festival, *Wandering Rose*, is less likely to disappoint than the sensationalised *Demon Baby*. This is because while there is a pregnancy, there is no baby – demon or otherwise. This marketing slip however can only partially explain many viewers' negative comments on review sites; a more comprehensive explanation lies in the fact that *Demon Baby* isn't good, and don't let the great shots of the Cairngorms fool you into thinking otherwise.

Robert Carlyle and his 'mum', Emma Thompson

The Legend of Barney Thomson (aka *Barney Thomson*) (2015)

S+++ T41

Directed by Robert Carlyle
Screenplay by Richard Cowan
Leading cast: Robert Carlyle (Barney Thomson);
 Emma Thompson (Cemolina); Ray Winstone
 (DI Holdall); Tom Courtenay (Chief
 Superintendent McManaman); Brian Pettifer
 (Charlie Taylor)
Colour, 96 minutes, UK/Canada

A barbershop in Bridgeton in the East End of Glasgow: Barney is a 50-year-old barber, who has 'nae patter, nae sparkle', but who – through little fault of his own – ends up killing people. A more serious serial killer is at work, and Thomson is suspected of all killings.

This black comedy is one of several films covered in this book from Scottish actors who have turned to directing. As of March 2025, this is Glasgow-born Carlyle's only film as director. The script, based on Douglas Lindsay's first novel, *The Long Midnight of Barney Thomson* (1999), is sharp. It is also often vulgar. The result is that some of the cast, Emma Thompson and Tom Courtenay in particular, look as if they are having the time of their lives. It is unlikely that British cinema goers (*Barney Thomson* was not distributed in the US) would have anticipated Emma Thompson's appearance as a line-ravaged mother to a 50-year-old (she is, in real life, only two years older than Carlyle), as a former sex worker, and as a hard-as-nails serial killer. Until a bitter scene just before her death, Thompson plays the role deadpan. Winstone is not asked to be anything other than a brash cockney – at which he excels. Here he is on the phone: 'Do you mind saying that again in English sir? I can't understand a word you're saying... I realise you're Scottish... I know I'm up here.'

Shot in Glasgow by cinematographer Fabian Wagner, *Barney Thomson* is rich in local colour: bingo at the Barrowlands; greyhound racing at Shawfield Stadium;

the Central Station; Thomas Hays Pet and Aquarium Corner in Osborne Street; and the Sarry Heid (Saracen's Head) in Gallowgate are among the many locations used. Lindsay went on to write further novels featuring Scotland's 'most unlikely serial killer' Barney Thomson. The film is elegantly self-contained and great fun.

Scottish Mussel (2015)   S++ W3

Directed by Talulah Riley
Screenplay by Talulah Riley
Leading cast: Martin Compston (Ritchie); Talulah Riley (Beth); Morgan Watkins (Ethan); Joe Thomas (Danny); Paul Brannigan (Fraser); Steven O'Donnell (Gavin); Marianna Palka (Fiona)
Colour, 96 minutes, UK

Three Glaswegian chancers, Ritchie, Danny and Fraser, become involved in a scheme to steal freshwater mussels for their valuable pearls. Ritchie falls for a conservationist, Beth. A petty crime boss, Gavin, bullies his way into the operation. After inevitable tensions and complications, all works out for the best.

'The worst film ever made in Scotland' – these are the words of *The Scotsman*'s Alistair Harkness, not me. My view is that this is merely *one* of the worst films made in Scotland; it is irredeemably awful, although perhaps a die-hard rom-com fan might take some pleasure in the all-too-predictable happy ending. That *Scottish Mussel* is going to be terrible should be

obvious from the get-go, simply from the badly punning title. The full horror of what is to come is exposed, literally, when, ten minutes in, Beth returns a mussel to the river. This involves her stripping down to a red bikini, while ogled by Ritchie's friends, and diving into the river – permitting a lingering sensuous shot of her underwater. The film includes a gross caricature of a gay ethical jeweller (who gets a line about 'pearl necklaces'), while Watkins appears to have been instructed that the way to play American is to perform a bad impersonation of Matthew McConaughey. His accent is risible, as is – as Harkness points out – Thomas's Glaswegian.

With a different director, as was intended, things might not have turned out quite so dire. As Riley (who as an actress has appeared in *Pride and Prejudice*, Joe Wright, 2005 and *Inception*, Christopher Nolan, 2010, amongst others; she is possibly better known for being twice married to Elon Musk) told *The Scotsman* in 2015: 'I didn't plan to direct it but it's so hard to get a film made it seemed the only way to get it done was to champion it myself as my own project. It took six months to a year to write it and three years to get it made. It was an arduous process. I made several attempts to get someone else to do it, but in the end had to do it myself.' It's hard to credit that this piece of tosh took over six months to write. On the plus side, freshwater mussel pearls are a real thing – in August 2024 the BBC reported the 'Abernethy Pearl' sold for £94,000.

The Slayers (2015)   S++ T100

Directed by John Williams
Screenplay by John Williams
Leading cast: Darren McAree (Nigel); Matthew
   Sandland (Job); George Newton (Reg)
Colour, 101 minutes, UK

Ducking out of a mass cult suicide,
brothers Nigel and Job decide to make the
most of their last two weeks before the
anticipated destruction of the Earth, setting
out to complete a bucket list. They buy a
camper van, and head for Scotland where,
with Reg, they take on a vampire coven.

The Slayers, a comedy/horror with
the emphasis firmly on the comedy ('it
generates more laughs than terror',
LoveHorror.co.uk), is the second feature
from Stoke-on-Trent-based Williams. His
first film, *The Mothertown* (2014) was
made for just £500; for *The Slayers* the
budget increased to £15,000.

Having chosen not to participate in
the mass suicide of the members of the
Big Scary Comet Cult, brothers Nigel and
Job arrive in Scotland shortly after the
20-minute mark, quickly establishing their
cultural bearings:

NIGEL: Are Scottish people English?
JOB: No, they're Scottish.
NIGEL: So where are The Krankies then?
JOB: Not sure mate, they're probably
   around here somewhere.

There are multiple pop-culture
references running through the film,
and some nice playing with these – the
brothers' dog is called Buffy, but they don't

... even the poster tagline is witty...

recognise an obvious vampire; although,
inconsistently, they've seen *Blade* (Stephen
Norrington, 1998). There is also a very
strong soundtrack.

Digital shooting, drone technology, and
streaming have democratised filmmaking.
On a very tight budget, filmmakers
can now bring to audiences results that
previously would have been unachievable.
Williams and his cinematographer, Will
Price, make the most of this, and while
Graham Taylor's special effects are low-
tech, they are fun, and will be appreciated
by genre fans. Where the budget does not
stretch, the wit does (at its very best in a
cracking WWII flashback, and in a later
breaking of the fourth wall). I'm even

prepared to accept, as purely a gag, naming a character Jock McBasterd. As Sean Evans, of *backtothemovies.com* writes, the film 'oozes comedy and class'. *The Slayers* played at several festivals, winning Williams the Best Director audience award at the Bram Stoker International Film Festival.

Sunset Song (2015) S++ T19

Directed by Terence Davies
Screenplay by Terence Davies
Leading cast: Agyness Deyn (Chris Guthrie);
  Peter Mullan (John Guthrie); Kevin Guthrie
  (Ewan Tavendale)
Colour, 135 minutes, UK/Luxembourg

Scotland, the early 1900s. Chris takes over the family farm after the death of her mother and tyrannical father. She marries and has a child; her husband dies in World War I, and she is left on the farm with her son Ewan.

In early 2016 I met two friends to catch up after the Christmas and New Year break, and recommended they see *Sunset Song*, which at that point was still playing in some Scottish cinemas (it had received a general release, after appearing at many film festivals, in December 2015). To my astonishment they told me that they had already done so and were bored to tears by it. *Sunset Song* is close to being a masterpiece, and although it moves in a slow rhythm, keeping in pace with the seasons and agricultural cycles, it is *never*

boring. It is also at times a film of stunning lambent beauty.

Davies had been trying to film *Sunset Song* since 2000, when he was turned down for funding assistance by the UK Film Council on the grounds that 'it hasn't got legs' (see Jonathan Romney, 'Hearth and Home' in *Film Comment*, 2016). The novel of the same name, first published in 1932, is the first of Lewis Grassic Gibbon's *A Scots Quair* trilogy (followed by *Cloud Howe*, 1933 and *Grey Granite*, 1934). It is one of the most loved Scottish books; in 2016 it headed a BBC poll to find Scotland's favourite novel. The fact that Davies was going to direct the film inspired confidence, notwithstanding that he is English; it would indeed be hard to think of anyone better. The fact that Chris, loved by readers as much as the novel, was to be played by Deyn, a former high-profile model who had appeared on the cover of American *Vogue* in her mid-teens, did not inspire as much confidence. These fears proved to be unfounded. Deyn, who had by then appeared in just three feature films, is sensationally good as Chris. Davies told Romney he was looking for an actor who 'could look old and young at the same time' and that the performance 'is truly innocent and pure, because she is'.

There are three stars of the film: Deyn, the land, and the cinematography by Paisley-born Michael McDonough (who had previously been director of photography on the similarly rural-set *Winter's Bone*, Debra Granik, 2010). In its earlier scenes, notwithstanding its independent literary source, *Sunset Song*

Agnes Deyn is magnificent as Chris

carries echoes of Davies' masterpiece *Distant Voices, Still Lives* (1988) – surely one of the very best British films – in which a family is held in thrall to a tyrannical father (in that case Pete Postlethwaite). But it also has similarities to a line of 'slow' films rooted in agricultural communities, particularly to Ermanno Olmi's *The Tree of Wooden Clogs* (*L'albero degli zoccoli*, 1978), in which the relationship between people and the land on which they live and toil is emphasised. Indeed, the occasional voice-over tells us at one point that Chris 'felt in that gloaming she was with the land'. The land we see in Scotland is lush and fertile (although the summer scenes were largely shot in New Zealand). In the

flashback scene towards the film's end, we see a different land on the Western Front: one of mud, craters, barbed wire, and death.

Most critics praised the film, but its release was sadly limited. It deserved a far bigger audience than it attracted. Older readers may remember that in 1971 BBC Scotland produced a six-part TV series of *Sunset Song*, with Vivien Heilbron (see *Kidnapped*, 1971) taking the role of Chris (the series has since appeared on the BBC again). This was followed by *Cloud Howe* and *Grey Granite*, completing, on TV at least, the *Scots Quair* trilogy.

Swung (2015)   S+++

Directed by Colin Kennedy
Screenplay by Ewan Morrison
Leading cast: Elena Anaya (Alice); Owen
  McDonnell (David); Elizabeth McGovern
  (Dolly)
Colour, 87 minutes, UK/US

*Glasgow: Alice begins a journalistic
'investigation' into the world of sex clubs,
partly in the hope that it will restore her
boyfriend David's interest in sex. 'Erotic'
nonsense follows.*

'On a scale of 1–10 what angle would
you say your erection was at this point?',
is one of the first lines in *Swung* (spoken
by a therapist to David). From the outset
the film thrusts us into issues of sex,
which become increasingly fevered as the
film progresses. Ewan Morrison's 2007
Glasgow-set novel, *Swung*, attracted
significant media attention on publication,
but the film – directed by Sigma alumnus
Kennedy – did not. In February 2015,
Fifty Shades of Grey (Sam Taylor-Johnson,
2015) was released (it went on to gross
$569,651,467 worldwide). *Swung* was
released three months later, and there
was only room for one bad erotic film
masquerading as art.

  Not everyone hated the film. Leslie
Felperin in *The Guardian* wrote that
Swung 'takes an admirable risk in
trying to make a serious film about the
contemporary swinging scene without
resorting to either juvenile sniggering or
censoriousness'. Alistair Harkness in *The*

Scotsman is closer to the mark: 'a dull and
mostly dour affair... The dialogue is risible
too, as are the performances'.

Where Do We Go from Here? (2015)   S++

Directed by John McPhail
Screenplay by John McPhail
Leading cast: Tyler Collins (James); Lucy-
  Jane Quinlan (Jen); Maryam Hamidi (Miss
  Thompson); Alison Peebles (Joan); Richard
  Addison (Malcolm)
Colour, 82 minutes, UK

*Jen takes a job at the 'Easy Love Care
Home' in Glasgow, and is surprised to meet
James, a 25-year-old who enjoys spending
time with older people. James persuades
Jen to provide the necessary medical cover
on a three-day trip to Fort Augustus for
three of the residents. Romance blossoms.*

Shot over just 16 days, *Where Do We Go
from Here?* is the first feature from Glasgow-
born John McPhail. Finance was partly
raised through crowdfunding. The film
played at multiple festivals (including the
GFF, where it had to be moved to a larger
venue to accommodate demand), and was
richly rewarded with prizes, including Best
Actor *and* Best Score awards for Alaskan-
born Collins (who had met McPhail while
studying at the Glasgow Conservatoire);
Peebles (also in *Fast Romance* and *The
Road Dance* amongst others), who has also
directed (*AfterLife*), was nominated for the
BAFTA Scotland Best Actress award.

McPhail said that with *Where Do We Go from Here?* he wanted to make a film 'that was going to leave audiences with that feelgood factor', and that he was influenced by films such as *Gregory's Girl*, *Cocoon* (Ron Howard, 1985) and *Garden State* (Zach Braff, 2004). The characters may be a little one-note and the trajectory obvious, but there's no denying the feelgood factor and it is refreshing to find a film which so ably bridges age gaps with love and humour. The success of *Where Do We Go from Here?* led directly to McPhail being given the opportunity to direct **Anna and the Apocalypse**.

Deti protiv volshebnikov (Дети против волшебнико) (*Kids Against the Sorcerers*) (2016) W1

Directed by Georgiy Skomorovskiy
Screenplay by Georgiy Skomorovskiy and Nikos Zervas
There's no 'acting' here worthy of mention
Colour, 88 minutes, Russia, Russian

The world in general, and Russia in particular, is under threat from 'wizards, mages and seers', taught at, and controlled through, the High Academy of Occult Sciences in Scotland. Five young Russians are at the HAOS; a patriotic cadet soldier and his friend are sent to retrieve them.

Early on in *KATS*, a trainee soldier asks his commander 'Did we mess it up? Is something wrong?' The right answer is obvious: 'we all messed up by being in this totally crap film'. Online opprobrium directed at *KATS* is rife, and occasionally funny. On IMDb the film carries a uniquely low rating of 1.1, although with insufficient user reviews to make it onto IMDb's 'Bottom 100' list, on which no film has a score below 1.2 (even *Sir Billi*, which sucks big time, has a score of 2.8).

Combining live 'action' with some of the shoddiest CG animation ever to grace a screen, this piece of garbage, of which almost exactly half is set in Scotland (in a castle which clearly is intended to remind us of Hogwarts*) is at heart propaganda for the worst aspects of a Putinesque Russia, replete with 'traditional' morality and nationalism. David Leask wrote about the film in *The Herald*, quoting a former colleague of mine at the University of Glasgow, Ammon Cheskin: 'this looks like a crass film... This sounds Stalinist'; Ammon had seen only the trailer, and while I would normally question a judgement made on such a slim basis, occasionally one must accept that taking an instant dislike to something simply saves time.

I've watched it so you don't have the displeasure of doing so – although I appreciate that some will find it irresistible. A good copy is available online with subtitles. You have been warned!

* The reason I deal with this film here, and not with the *Harry Potter* franchise, is that in *Deti* Scotland is expressly named, and there are strategic maps on a wall explaining where the Hogwartsish castle is.

Hamish (2016) `DOC`

Directed by Robbie Fraser; 86 minutes

Premiering at the GFF in February 2016, *Hamish* celebrates the life and work of Hamish Henderson (1919–2002), a Scottish writer, songwriter, folklorist, makar, soldier and campaigner. An early clip of a documentary made for Italian TV channel RAI claimed that Scots rarely travelled abroad, but that Italy was now being visited by one of the most illustrious Scots, Hamish Henderson – a true internationalist. Fraser's homage, incorporating a wide range of footage and interviews, lovingly brings Henderson to life, presenting a strong case for his place in the canon of Scottish culture, and better recognition domestically of his life's work. Although it has been broadcast on BBC Alba, the film is a little hard to track down. Fraser had previously directed the fiction feature *GamerZ*, and later directed another documentary about a Scot called Hamish – *Final Ascent: The Legend of Hamish MacInnes*.

Lost in France (2016) `DOC`

Directed by Niall McCann; 100 minutes

In 1997 a group of Scottish musicians, drawn from Glasgow's vibrant music scene – as best exemplified in the success of the Chemikal Records label – played at a festival in Mauron, France. Eighteen years later, at the urging of filmmaker Niall McCann, six of them returned. McCann

said, 'this allowed me to draw parallels easily between the mid-90s and the present. A lot has changed. Changed utterly and this was a great way to highlight and discuss that change.' Stewart Henderson, founder of Chemikal and formerly of The Delgados, says at the end of the film (having clearly been sceptical of the project), 'sometimes it's important to look back at certain things within a very specific context'. *Lost's* participants are engaging, erudite, and passionate about what they do. They have interesting things to say about themselves, each other, and the state of the music scene in a changing post-industrial city, and in the wider UK. The film also reminds us just how remarkable the music scene was in Glasgow in the late 1990s, with over 20 venues, and hundreds of bands (Alex Kapranos suggests as many as 500) playing in them.

Moon Dogs (2016) `S++`

Directed by Philip John
Screenplay by Derek Boyle and Raymond Friel
Leading cast: Jack Parry-Jones (Michael); Christy
    O'Donnell (Thor); Tara Lee (Caitlin)
Colour, 93 minutes, UK

Stepbrothers Michael and Thor undertake a road trip from Shetland to Glasgow, teaming up with Caitlin along the way...

Most road trips in this book head north (from England to remote Scotland); it makes a refreshing change then to see the journey taken in the other direction, from Shetland to Glasgow via Orkney (where the brothers

Jack Parry-Jones, Tara Lee and
Christy O'Donnell

Sacrifice (2016) S+

Directed by Peter A Dowling
Screenplay by Peter A Dowling
Leading cast: Radha Mitchell (Dr Tora Hamilton);
  Rupert Graves (Duncan Guthrie); Ian
  McElhinney (DI McKie); David Robb (Richard
  Guthrie)
Colour, 91 minutes, Ireland/Germany/US

fall in with Caitlin), Wick, the Highlands and Stirling. The route is better than the film, which has its moments, but tries a little too hard to charm. The meet-cute with Caitlin has an air of predictability, as does her assumption of the tired manic pixie dream girl trope. As Peter Bradshaw puts it, 'there is something forced, contrived and a bit clichéd about this fey British indie in the road-movie style'. A similar view was taken by Josh Slater-Williams in *The Skinny*, who suggested *Moon Dogs* suffers from 'a screenplay rife with humour that very rarely lands and lacking in much invention to elevate its cookie-cutter narrative'. Glaswegian O'Donnell and the Irish Lee are both musicians, and the soundtrack is the strongest component of the film. As in **Wild Rose**, there is a life-affirming Celtic Connections performance as the three travellers manage to coalesce into a functioning band.

Moon Dogs is the only feature by Welsh director John. It played at the EIFF and picked up some awards from others; Parry-Jones was awarded Best Actor by BAFTA Cymru.

Tora and Duncan, her husband, move to Shetland. She discovers a mutilated body buried in peat. Against the advice of her husband, and the local police, Tora is determined to unravel the mystery.

This multinational production was shot in small part in Shetland, but also in Ireland and New York (from where Tora and Duncan have moved following a miscarriage). Dowling is better known as a screenwriter, notably for the Jodie Foster thriller, *Flightplan* (Robert Schwentke, 2005). For *Sacrifice*, he adapted Sharon Bolton's 2009 novel of the same name. Australian actor Mitchell plays the outsider who refuses to follow local expectations; her husband (played by Somerset-born Graves) is a Shetlander, but has spent years away.

The most surprising thing about *Sacrifice* is that anyone ever thought there was a feature film to be made from this thin material. The film carries a big green splat on Rotten Tomatoes with a rating of 35 per cent. Glenn Kenny in *The NYT* could barely contain his exasperation with a film the likes of which he had far too often previously seen, noting that

Sacrifice 'trades heavily on a hoary genre convention', containing 'every cliché that a 90-minute movie can contain'. That a film has a premium Blu-ray/DVD dual release is no guarantee of quality.

Seat in Shadow (2016) S+++

Directed by Henry Coombes
Screenplay by Henry Coombes and David Sillars
Leading cast: David Sillars (Albert); Jonathan
  Leslie (Ben)
Colour, 82 minutes, UK

Glasgow: Albert, a psychiatrist, agrees to see Ben, a young gay man who feels depressed.

Seat in Shadow, a micro-budget production which is the only feature credit for most of those involved with it, was shown at the EIFF in 2016, following which critic Scott Clark described it as 'a studied and emotional look at artist and muse, a close-up look at alienation, and an uplifting expose of life and love through the prism of gay experience'. The early scenes in which Albert seeks to understand Ben are engaging but lop-sided; Sillars is an arresting performer, but Leslie appears out of his depth. As the film moves beyond the boundaries of Albert's home it loses focus.

Seven Songs for a Long Life (2016) DOC

Directed by Amy Hardie; 83 minutes

A life-affirming doc focusing on the day-care patients and the amazing staff at Strathcarron Hospice at Denny. Made for the BBC by Amy Hardie while she was filmmaker in residence.

Tommy's Honour (2016) S+++ T100

Directed by Jason Connery
Screenplay by Pamela Marin, Kevin Cook
Leading cast: Peter Mullan (Tom Morris); Jack
  Lowden (Tommy Morris); Ophelia Lovibond
  (Meg Drinnen); Sam Neill (Alexander Boothby)
Colour, 112 minutes, UK/US

The life of 'young' Tom Morris (Tommy), from learning to play golf with his father, to being the greatest golfer of his time.

It is perhaps inevitable that a book about Scottish films is going to feature at least one film about golf, the modern version of which was developed in Scotland. In fact, it features two, this and *Golf in the Kingdom* (which is very poor). 'Old Tom Morris' was influential in setting up the Open in 1860 and won the title four times between 1861–1867. His son, 'Young Tom Morris', was the first man to win the Open three years running, beating his father to his first title in 1868, and remains the youngest ever winner, being 17 at the time. The film is based on the book of the same name by

Kevin Cook (2011). Lowden (who is terrific in *Calibre*, and who is also in *Mary Queen of Scots*, 2018) is excellent as Tommy, and Peter Mullan strong as his father.

Tommy's Honour features a *lot* of golf, but it is not *about* golf – or rather, if golf is not your thing there is another, more important story being told. This is one about class and social (im)mobility in Victorian Britain. In the world of the film, golf clubs are the preserve of gentlemen (no women of course, although there is a reference to the first tournament played by women in England, with concerns expressed that their bosoms might get in the way). Tom Morris may have designed 70 courses, but he was not permitted to join the club. Matches were arranged by gentlemen, wagers would be laid, and the winning golfer would be capriciously and inconsistently rewarded by his 'backers'. While Tom knows his place (and earned what was at the time a comfortable wage), Tommy's aspirations are greater, creating tension between father and son, and between Tommy and the gentlemen club owners. This is never more clearly enunciated than in the confrontation between Tommy and the club captain, Boothby, who makes his position clear: 'Your station in life was set before you were born, young Morris… never think putting on a gentleman's suit makes you a gentleman.'

The accuracy of *Tommy's Honour* has been picked over, but even golf experts are satisfied. Rick Young of *ScoreGolf* writes: 'the director has been deeply respectful of [the] story while wanting to be genuinely authentic, right down to the details, in how it was portrayed. That included seeking out the Royal & Ancient Heritage Society to lend an historical assist.' It was clearly a project about which Connery was passionate: 'I had many, many doors slammed in my face with people telling me that I'd never get it made and if I did no one would ever go watch it'. The result is a much better film than might be feared.

Den ofrivillige golfaren† (*The Accidental Golfer*) (Lasse Åberg, 1991) is a delightfully goofy Swedish film with some scenes involving golf in Scotland, but insufficient time is spent in the country for the film to make it into this book as a separate entry.

Waterboys (2016) S+

Directed by Robert Jan Westdijk
Screenplay by Robert Jan Westdijk
Leading cast: Leopold Witte (Victor); Tim Linde (Zack)
Colour, 89 minutes, Netherlands/UK, Dutch/English

Successful author and philanderer Victor, and his son, Zack, a musician, are both kicked out by their partners, and undertake a road trip of discovery and self-growth to Edinburgh.

The music of the Waterboys is central to this film, for which they played two concerts in a Netherlands venue to facilitate the shoot. Victor is obsessed by the Waterboys and Mike Scott, whose songs provide the soundtrack. On the drive to Edinburgh, Victor and Zach hear on the radio that the band are to play while they are there; the music is an integral part of the film, the songs clearly influencing the screenplay and directorial choices. The result is charming, but slender. A region 1 DVD is available.

Where You're Meant to Be (2016) DOC

Directed by Paul Fegan; 76 minutes

Aidan Moffat (sometime of Arab Strap) 'just wanted to take old songs from Scotland that made me giggle and rewrite them for fun'. Sheila Stewart, a 79-year-old folk singer, who espoused purity in the form, was not amused. Moffat has said it 'wasn't even an argument or a disagreement, just two completely opposed ideas'. This sets the basis for a compassionate and warm analysis of whether anyone may be said to 'own' folk music, and whether it is a record of the past, or a living thing, constantly adapting. Fegan's film, buoyed along by Moffat's charm ('endearing and game throughout… providing the film with a lilting, self-reflective narration that nimbly explores these questions of custodianship', Tom Grieve in *The Skinny*), is a delight that deservedly won multiple awards.

Adam Joan (2017) S++

Directed by Jinu Abraham
Screenplay by Jinu Abraham
Leading cast: Prithviraj Sukumaran (Adam Joan Pothen); Narain (Cyriac); Rahul Madhav (Alan Pothen); Bhavana (Swetha); Mishti Chakravarty (Amy Adam Joan); Lenaa (Daisy)
Colour, 160 minutes, India, Malayalam/Tegulu

Satanists in North Berwick, led by an Edinburgh University professor, kidnap Adam Joan's child (murdering granny in the process). Her father sets out to rescue the girl before she can be sacrificed to Satan on Good Friday. Really…

If I had been warned before I started this project that I would have to watch a 160-minute-long Malayalam film in which Scotland is depicted as a hotbed of satanic devil cults I am not certain whether I would have been invigorated, or deterred. But here we are, and *Adam Joan* is set and shot almost entirely in Scotland. The film is (far, far) too long, although its representation of Scotland is refreshingly off-the-wall. The country 'has a kind of mystic beauty… it is no wonder that JK Rowling stayed here and wrote the Harry Potter series'. The police and satanists aside there is little interaction with Scots. Available (behind a pay wall) on YouTube with subtitles.

And Violet (2017) S+++

Directed by Paul Gray
Screenplay by Paul Gray
Leading cast: Hana Mackenzie (Violet, 'V'); Kirsty
  Strain (Zoe); Liz Strange (Louisa)
Colour, 105 minutes, UK

*Violet, who has been adopted after
spending time in several foster homes,
unexpectedly runs into her birth mother,
Zoe. This puts strain on Violet and her
relationship with her adoptive family.
Violet, Louisa (her adoptive mother) and
Zoe work to resolve issues.*

And Violet, which won the festival prize
for Best Dramatic Feature at the Arizona
International Film Festival, received
publicity in Scotland for its strong
treatment of issues surrounding adoption,
with local councils, and at least one MSP,
putting on free screenings. The festival
circuit and these screenings aside, the film
has had little exposure (although at the
time of writing it is available to stream
on Amazon). Scottish writer/director/
producer Gray, whose only feature this is,
has made an intelligent film in which strong
performances create a believable coming-
of-age dynamic.

Anna and the Apocalypse (2017) S+++ T100

Directed by John McPhail
Screenplay by Alan McDonald, Ryan McHenry
Leading cast: Ella Hunt (Anna Shepherd);
  Malcolm Cumming (John); Sarah Swire (Steph
  North); Marli Siu (Lisa); Ben Wiggins (Nick);
  Paul Kaye (Arthur Savage)
Colour, 93 minutes, UK

*In 'Little Haven', high-school students Anna
and her friends attempt to survive a zombie
apocalypse while bursting into song.*

In 2011 Ryan McHenry wrote and directed
a 16-minute short film, *Zombie Musical*,
in which two school students sing while
killing and evading zombies. It's easy to
find online and is included with a DVD
release of *Anna*. McHenry died of cancer,
aged 27, in 2015. He is co-credited, along
with McDonald, for the script for *Anna
and the Apocalypse*, which received its
premiere at Fantastic Fest in the US in
September 2017. Over the following
year it was shown at festivals around the
world, including the EIFF in June 2018,
before receiving a very limited UK release in
November 2018. If Box Office Mojo is to
be believed, its global box office amounted
to less than £500,000. And that's a
travesty. There *are* other zombie musicals
(notably *The Incredibly Strange Creatures
Who Stopped Living and Became Mixed-
up Zombies!!?*, Ray Dennis Steckler, 1964),
but how many other films hit the musical/
zombie/Christmas sweet spot? I regret
turning down the chance to be an extra in

Anna walks to school, oblivious to the zombies

Anna; it is ridiculously good fun.

I'm not alone in enjoying *Anna*. At the time of writing, it holds a 'certified fresh' score of 77 per cent on Rotten Tomatoes, and it made its way onto at least one critic's top 10 of the year. Of course, there are detractors. Manohla Dargis, in *The NYT*, dismissed the film as a 'Scottish novelty item', and Port Glasgow ('Little Haven') as 'so generic it might as well be in a Disney movie', but as John sings in 'Hollywood ending', 'this isnae Disney'! It certainly isn't. The film merits its 15-certificate rating, not so much for its violence, which is to be taken with a pinch of salt (the BBFC describes this in part as 'zombie's head exploding with sight of blood and brain matter'), but for its language.

The songs are written and composed by Roddy Hart and Tommy Reilly (who also provided the songs for *Our Ladies*), and are integral to the film, moving it forward, fleshing out the characters, and even commenting on the film itself. Best of all, surely, is Siu's rendition of 'It's that time of year' at the Christmas show. Following two inept breakdancing penguins (a sly nod to *Gregory's Girl*), she receives a standing ovation. And it is utter filth (and, unlike the disapproving headmaster, I mean that in an entirely positive way), ending with the line 'Come on Santa – give it to me'. In *Film Comment* Sragow wrote of Siu, also excellent in *Run* and *Our Ladies*, that she 'is such a balmy performer that she can examine the phallic potential of her microphone and mike stand and obliterate the distinction between "naughty" and "nice"'. She has gone on to significant roles in two TV series: *Alex Rider* (2020–2024) and *Everything I Know About Love* (2022).

The largely young cast are strong, and those who are required to sing actually can. *Anna* was the first feature film for Siu and Cumming. For Hunt, Swire and Wiggins it was the second; Swire also appeared in *God Help the Girl* (she also choreographed the routines in *Anna*). Director McPhail had previously made the feature **Where Do We Go from Here?**

An 83-minute documentary, *The Making of Anna and the Apocalypse*, was produced in 2019, directed by Phillip Escott.

Ayat-Ayat Cinta 2 (Verses of Love 2, aka Second Verses of Love) (2017) `S+`

> Directed by Guntur Soeharjanto
> Screenplay by Ifan Ismail and Alim Sudio
> Leading cast: Fedi Nuril (Fahri); Pandji Pragiwaksono (Hulusi)
> Colour, 125 minutes, Indonesia, Indonesian and English

Following Ayat-Ayat Cinta [not a Scottish film], Farhi has become a lecturer and researcher at the University of Edinburgh (teaching in Indonesian), and budding entrepreneur. He pines for his lost love (who, after the first film, one has reason to believe to be dead), while wafting through the strongly multicultural city buffeted by anti-Muslim sentiment and performing acts of random virtue. A new romance leads to complications as the past intrudes on the present...

The romantic drama *Ayat-Ayat Cinta* (Hanung Bramantyo and Iqbal Rais, 2008) was stupendously successful in Indonesia, outperforming even *Titanic* (James Cameron, 1997) at the local box office. Cinematic success inexorably leads to sequels, in this case to one set almost entirely in Edinburgh, and largely shot on location (albeit with exteriors at the University of Glasgow purporting to be its Edinburgh counterpart).

You'd need to be an enthusiastic watcher of Scotland on screen to track this down. It is aimed very much at a domestic market (it was commercially successful in both Indonesia and Malaysia), is overlong, and follows on directly from the events in *Ayat-Ayat Cinta*, so for this to make any sense you'd really need to commit to both films. Given that the film consists predominantly of Fahri performing random acts of kindness, demonstrating his commitment to his Muslim ideals, with virtue and location being the only strong connecting threads, even if you watch both films you might find *Ayat-Ayat Cinta 2* somewhat incoherent. The stereotyping of ethnicities and religions is facile, and some plot elements are beyond ridiculous.

Cleek (2017) `S+++`

> Directed by Gary J Hewitt
> Screenplay by Gary J Hewitt
> Leading cast: Mark Barrett (Jacob Cleek); Sharon Osdin (Norma); Simon Weir (Sam McBride)
> Colour, 112 minutes, UK

Jacob Cleek is a smoothly presented artist, and an addicted serial killer. As media interest in missing women mounts, Cleek offers a room to Norma while she sorts her life out.

Ahead of a screening of *Cleek*, set and shot around Glasgow's Southside and Paisley, at the Strasburg Film Festival, Hewitt said, 'I wanted to do a film about addiction [but many] Scottish films are filled with Scottish miserabilism... In these types of films most people are either addicted to drink or drugs and I knew I had to find something different'. He also said that he was influenced by TV series *Desperate Housewives* (2004–2012), in which smart veneers hide dark secrets. *Cleek* is framed therefore as a film about addiction (Cleek says, 'I have it under control', and 'just once a week, on Tuesday' when challenged by a fellow AA attendee), but adds to the screen pantheon of serial killers; his closest antecedent is perhaps Christian Bale's Patrick Bateman (*American Psycho*, Mary Harron, 2000). It's a well-worn route and one *Cleek* competently follows, even if the pacing should be tighter, although the film had very little impact.

Hewitt's follow-up film, *The Defender* (2024), a thin revenge/vigilante 'thriller' set in Glasgow, is, at the time of writing, available on the STV Player. While some online sources, and *The Glasgow Guardian* suggest that this had a run at film festivals, and won awards*, it is not clear that the film was ever screened other than for cast and crew, and IMDb suggests it went straight to streaming.

* Not all awards are equal, and not all awards are the result of film festival screenings. In its IMDb entry *The Defender*'s awards section starts with the Sweden Film Awards (it holds Best Feature Film and Best Actor awards from 2023). If you check out *swedenfilmawards.se* you will find that for the very reasonable price of $175.00 you can purchase one of these, and have *your* interview, and *your* review of

your film published on the website. 'Awards' are made monthly. There are other 'awards' following a similar model. Enterprises such as this can lead to ill-informed journalists and online commentators reporting that films have festival runs and awards, an impression that producers may do little to dispel. I was tempted to see whether I could obtain a Sweden Film Award for this book...

Edie (2017)　S+

Directed by Simon Hunter
Screenplay by Elizabeth O'Halloran
Leading cast: Sheila Hancock (Edie); Kevin Guthrie (Jonny); Paul Brannigan (McLaughlin)
Colour, 102 minutes, UK

When Edie's abusive husband dies, she heads to Scotland to walk to the top of Mount Suilven, which she does with the assistance of Jonny.

Near Lochinver in Sutherland, Mount Suilven, at 2,389 ft, is a 'Marilyn' – being over 492 ft, the profile and location of which make for a striking aspect, which cinematographer August Jakobsson makes the most of. That the film does not fake Hancock's ascent – at the age of 85 she was fit enough to do this herself – is admirable. In *The Guardian*, Hancock suggested it was probably the mere fact that she *could* do this which led to her being cast: 'I thought: That's why I've been asked, because I'm fit for my age.' As she explained, even getting to the mountain was demanding. There were '[t]errible snaky things. Scottish

Sheila Hancock as Edie

The Gaelic King (2017) S+++

Directed by Philip Todd
Screenplay by Matthew Todd and Philip Todd
Leading cast: Jake McGarry (Alpin); Noah Irvine
(Finn)
Colour, 87 minutes, UK

froggy things jumping at you. Awful. You fall all the time, you go down a great hole.' This was not Hancock's first experience of working in Scotland – she also features in *Hold Back the Night*.

Beautiful landscape aside, *Edie* is a slight film. Critics were split between those who found *Edie* saccharine and trite, and those who found it empowering and optimistic (on Rotten Tomatoes its score stood at a healthy – I would argue overly generous – 67 per cent at the time of writing). In the former camp, for example, see Jeannette Catsoulis of *The NYT*: 'The result is a scenic saccharin bomb that Edie's long-simmering anger can't defuse. Hancock is wasted here...' Jamie Neish, in *Little White Lies* took the alternative approach: 'Elizabeth O'Halloran's script works best as a character study... for that, plus the undeniably empowering message of a woman reclaiming her life at its core, Edie is worth the time and investment.'

Guthrie is in *Sunshine on Leith, Sunset Song, Connect* and *Get Duked!* On 14 May 2021, he was sentenced to three years' imprisonment for breaches of the Sexual Offences (Scotland) Act 2009. An appeal was rejected.

790AD, Scotland: Alpin McEchdach's family, the rulers of Dál Riata, are attacked. He and his brother, Finn, are the only survivors. Ten years later Finn is captured by 'shadows' under the control of a sorceress; Alpin uses King's magic to save him, and returns to Dál Riata to take up his rightful place as King.

Few films inspire Scottish Parliamentary motions, but on 6 July 2017, Angus MacDonald MSP submitted one to celebrate the release of *The Gaelic King*. Described, occasionally, as 'the budget *Braveheart*', *The Gaelic King* was made on a wing and a prayer (supported by a strong dose of goodwill and crowdfunding) by 'Fellowship Films', consisting of three Glaswegian brothers, Philip, Matthew and Nathan Todd, and two of their cousins. The director said: 'We brought together more than 200 people whose creativity, talent and energy helped us achieve the impossible. All in all, this is a fantastic Scottish project, a film made in Scotland in every way.' It was reported that all involved in the production waived their fees but would be paid once the film returned a profit. Shown as a work in progress at the EIFF, the completed film was screened at Glasgow's CCA, before moving to online and DVD distribution. The low budget shows, but given the necessary limitations, *The Gaelic King* is very well done, although don't look to it for a history lesson. The language is modern (as are the sentiments), and on the film's official Facebook page it is, accurately, described as a 'Scottish historical fantasy'; however, it is *very* Scottish.

Fellowship Films also made, again with Philip Todd directing, *Jessie and the Elf Boy* (2022), a children's film which has had several good reviews, but which – as far as I can determine – has had no cinema screenings.

I Am Anna (2017) S+++

Directed by Timo Langer
Screenplay by Laura Anne Anderson and Timo Langer
Leading cast: Laura Anne Anderson (Anna); Eveliina Honkanen (Anna); Dechlan Donnell Nicoll (Benjamin); Calum Barbour (Euan)
Colour, 84 minutes, UK

In Edinburgh, Anna is followed as she navigates a difficult time in a relationship with her boyfriend, Benjamin, during which she is unsure what to believe.

I Am Anna is Edinburgh-based Langer's only feature film as director; as an editor he has worked more extensively, including on Mark Cousins' *I Am Belfast* (2015). Cousins called *I Am Anna* 'an understated and beautiful piece of indie modernism'. It's a challenging film, in which the fierce

direction of the gaze on Anna verges on the invasive. The film lies firmly in the art-cinema category and includes scenes of a strongly sexual nature. Winner of several festival awards, but with no distribution otherwise, *I Am Anna* is available to watch on the film's dedicated website (which maintains the fictional world of the film, presenting it as a documentary).

Abroad: Finding Faith (2018) S+++

Directed by John-William Noble
Screenplay by Binglin Luo and John-William Noble
Leading cast: Serena Luo (Michelle)
Colour, 111 minutes, UK

Michelle, a Chinese student, arrives in Edinburgh to study at the university, where she struggles with the cultural adaptation; she is socially isolated and finds the hedonism of Scottish students difficult. Things take a turn for the better when she finds God.

In the US, Christian faith-based movies find a robust market and cannot be dismissed as niche. UK equivalents are rare, and when made they do not have traction outwith the target audience. John-William Noble, a Christian filmmaker born in Peterhead, and at the time of writing a Pastor in Aberdeen, has 'an enthusiasm for creating Christian films to portray Christian living in the Western world in a realistic and challenging way'. He also produced *The Hope Within* (2009), another Christian film set in

Scotland directed by his brother Graeme Noble, which I have been unable to locate. *Abroad* has been shown at film festivals, and merits inclusion in this book. The film is competently made, although production values are low, and clear as a cudgel to the head with its message.

Calibre (2018) S+++ T29

Directed by Matthew Palmer
Screenplay by Matthew Palmer
Leading cast: Jack Lowden (Vaughn); Martin McCann (Marcus); Tony Curran (Logan McClay); Ian Pirie (Brian McClay)
Colour, 101 minutes, UK

Marcus and Vaughn stay in the village of 'Culcarran' in the Highlands, from which they go hunting. There are some tensions with locals. Vaughn accidentally shoots a young boy, and events spiral horrifically out of control.

Calibre is terrific. When Stephen King signals his approval of a low-key, taut horror/thriller things are definitely going well. This was the case when, in July 2018, King tweeted: '*Calibre*, on Netflix: This one is a genuine nail-biter. It's got a Hitchcock vibe with a little bit of *The Wicker Man* tossed in for good measure.' This in turn led on to inevitable press coverage (the *Scottish Sun*, *The NYT* etc). *Calibre* had by that point already won the Michael Powell Award for Best British Feature Film at the 2018 EIFF and been nominated for a slew of BAFTA Scotland (the three leads winning joint Best Actor) and British Independent Film Awards.

Twenty minutes into *Calibre* the descent into horror is complete, and the rest of the film wades through it, although we have been heading in this direction from the start. There is menace in the pub the night before the hunting trip, but this does not coalesce – in much the same way that in John Boorman's *Deliverance* (1972), an obvious progenitor of *Calibre* (*The Wicker Man* also casts a pall), the early tensions only come alive later. It is not the accidental shooting of the boy, Sam, which turns the world upside down, but Marcus' murder of Sam's father and his immediate attempt at concealment. Even on the drive to Culcarran there are hints of Marcus' potential danger, as he questions Vaughn's ability to shoot a deer: 'Reckon you can take down a deer?… Not everyone can do it. Trick is you have to switch off your emotions and let instinct kick in.' There is an awful, inexorable, inevitability to the action in *Calibre*, with a constant drip of cause and effect; like the venison served at dinner, the script is lean and bloody.

Calibre has garnered strong critical praise – how could it not? – and holds a 95 per cent score on Rotten Tomatoes. Here's Glenn Kenny in *The NYT*: 'The first "holy crap!" moment of the movie occurs not even 20 minutes in, and at that point it's don't-get-up-from-the-sofa time… the details provided in the writing, and by the two leads' performances, add distinctive details and dimension here. This makes the film's harrowing action all the more believable.' *The Guardian*'s Leslie Felperin

Jack Lowden and Martin McCann

was also bowled over: 'On a beat-by-beat basis, writer-director Matt Palmer's feature debut skates close to the edge of cliché – only to swerve suddenly in an interesting new direction almost every time.' Ryan Lambie continued with the praise in *Den of Geek*: 'Told with a brutal efficiency... *Calibre* is a terrific drama-thriller about suspicion and gnawing guilt... be prepared for a movie that rewards patience and a close attention to small details.'

Everything about this film is excellent. Edinburgh-based, first-time feature director Palmer pulls the strings with focused precision, the cast are uniformly superb, and the cinematography and sound design are exceptional. *Calibre* is one of the best films covered here.

The Isle (2018)   S+

Directed by Matthew Butler-Hart
Screenplay by Matthew Butler-Hart, Tori Butler-Hart
Leading cast: Alex Hassell (Oliver Gosling); Fisayo Akinade (Cailean Ferris); Graham Butler (Jim Bickley); Conleth Hill (Douglas Innis); Tori Butler-Hart (Lanthe Innis); Dickon Tyrell (Fingal MacLeod); Alix Wilton Regan (Korrigan MacLeod); Emma King (Lorna/Persephone)
Colour, 96 minutes, UK

1846: three sailors, Oliver, Jim and Cailean, are shipwrecked on an island off the west coast of Scotland, where they are ensnared until a curse is broken.

Alix Wilton Regan, Tori Butler-Hart and Emma King in one of the much better 'weird stuff in Scotland' films

The Isle opens with a quote from the 19th-century classicist and barrister, Walter Copland Perry: 'The siren's song "though irresistibly sweet, was no less sad than sweet and lapped both body and soul in a fatal lethargy, the forerunner of death and corruption"'. We are immediately pitched into the world of gothic/folk/myth/horror which the film inhabits, building on the Greek myth of Persephone and the sirens (in this respect following Ovid's version of the stories). This well-made film is, for the most part, successful in delivering on its ambition. Location shooting took place on the privately-owned Eilean Shona in Loch Moidart on the Scottish west coast (see also *The Burning Baby*); some interiors were shot in England. *The Isle* played well at festivals and won a handful of awards (including the jury prize for Best Sci-fi/ Horror Film at the London Independent Film Festival). I would argue the film only *just* makes it into the horror category, although US marketing emphasised the horror element. It received limited commercial releases in the UK and the US.

Reviews were more positive than not. Peter Bradshaw's review in *The Guardian* is selectively quoted on the DVD cover: 'a well-made, forcefully acted film... an intriguing work, modestly and intelligently conceived, a supernatural melodrama characterised by an eerie sort of restraint. There are hints of Shakespeare and classical and Scots mythology.'

The Isle is also the name of a very good Korean film from 2000 (*Seom*, Kim-ki Duk). This too has a pervading air of strangeness; they'd make an interesting, if unusual, double bill.

Malevolent (2018)   S+

Directed by Olaf de Fleur (Olaf de Fleur Johannesson)
Screenplay by Ben Ketai and Eva Konstantopoulos
Leading cast: Florence Pugh (Angela); Ben Lloyd-Hughes (Jackson); Celia Imrie (Mrs Green); Scott Chambers (Elliot)
Colour, 89 minutes, UK

Glasgow, 1986: Jackson, working with his sister, Angela, runs a scam 'cleaning' houses of unwelcome spirits. Events spiral murderously out of control at a former foster home in which young girls were serially killed.

Produced in part by Sigma Films, with funding from Creative Scotland, *Malevolent* is set in and around Glasgow, starring two English actors playing Americans (albeit gifted with Scottish heritage – James Cosmo has one scene as the grandfather), and Celia Imrie occasionally moderating her accent with a Scottish twist. Ever since *Poltergeist* (Tobe Hooper, 1982) raised the bar for haunted house set-ups, filmmakers have, with varying degrees of success, repeatedly turned to a genre which permits tight unity of time and space (in *Malevolent*'s case much of the film is set in one suitably large Gothic pile – Hunterston House in Ayrshire). *Malevolent*, based on Konstantopoulos' novella *Hush* (2011), relies heavily on Florence Pugh (see also ***Outlaw King***) for its success but she alone cannot lift this from the humdrum. The novella, set in the US, is told in the first person and offers a livelier treatment than the film, although on basic narrative beats the two align well. Most disappointing is the 1980s setting. Little is made of this: TV series *Stranger Things* (2016–) has shown the value of creating a world rich in period detail, but in *Malevolent* one is left with the impression that the sole reason for the period setting is to eliminate modern communication.

Dumbarton schoolgirl, 15-year-old Anna Coote, plays one of the ghosts/victims in the film. She told the *Dumbarton Reporter* she enjoyed her time on the set; her 'favourite part was getting the make-up done because it was really interesting, and it didn't even take too long' – florid tortures being *de rigueur,* she has had her lips sewn shut, a fate which also befalls others. Critical response to the film was justifiably lukewarm.

Matriarch (2018) S+

Directed by Scott Vickers
Screenplay by Scott Vickers
Leading cast: Charlie Blackwood (Rachel Hopkins); Scott Vickers (Matt Hopkins); Julie Hannan (Agnes Fairbairn); Alan Cuthbert (Bob Fairbairn); Briony Monroe (Faith Fairbairn/Ellie Adams)
Colour, 119 minutes, UK

In Scotland, on a break to get away from it all, Matt and Rachel seek refuge at a local farm after crashing their car. Rachel is heavily pregnant, a fact which seems to secure them a welcome. There's no mobile reception, the phone lines are down, and the place reminds them of the 1950s. The baby is all that the farmers want...

It would be possible to watch *Matriarch* (not *Matriarch*, Ben Steiner, 2022, which features Kate Dickie) without immediately realising it is a Scottish film. But it was filmed and set in Balfron, and Vickers has said, 'I wrote this film based [partly] on the location'. This was because Alan Cuthbert, who appears in the film, had turned part of his farm into the 'Cuthbert Farms' TV and film studio. Shot in 12 days, *Matriarch* was made for just £35,000, with first-time director Vickers (who had appeared in over 300 episodes of TV's *River City*) leveraging his house to raise funds.

Matriarch won the Best Film award at the Glasgow Horror Fest in October 2018, and was shown in Glasgow's Cineworld, but in the UK did not secure further theatrical distribution. Its horror is effective and sidesteps anticipations; the ending is a twist. Rotten Tomatoes reports no reviews, but on genre sites there are several. *Horrorfuel.com*'s take was that *Matriarch* 'is sinister, atmospheric, and full to the brim with seat squirming menace'.

Nae Pasaran (2018)   DOC

Directed by Felipe Bustos Sierra; 96 minutes

In March 1974, workers at the Rolls-Royce plant in East Kilbride, in solidarity with victims of the Chilean junta, refused to work on equipment destined for the Chilean Air Force. The story of their resistance to tyranny is constructed by Chilean director Sierra, who said in 2018: 'I'd been told that many of the original guys had passed on, so I was intending the film to be fiction not documentary. Then, when I met them, I realised they're natural born storytellers.'

Of Fish and Foe (2018)   DOC

Directed by Andy Heathcote and Heike Bachelier; 91 minutes

Charts the running tensions between one of the last groups of 'netsmen' (wild salmon fishers) off Angus, animal rights activists and regulators. Leslie Felperin in *The Guardian* wrote that it 'makes for surprisingly gripping viewing'. Eschewing voice-over narration, *Of Fish and Foe* balances finely on a tight line between the opposing forces.

Only You (2018)   S+

Directed by Harry Wootliff
Screenplay by Harry Wootliff
Leading cast: Laia Costa (Elena Aldana); Josh O'Connor (Jake)
Colour, 119 minutes, UK

Glasgow: at New Year a chance encounter propels Jake, 25, and Elena, 35, into a passionate relationship. They try and fail to conceive a child.

Funded in part by Creative Scotland, and set and shot in Glasgow, multiple-award-winning *Only You*, the first feature by writer/director Wootliff, is driven by powerful central performances. While their friends seemingly produce babies at will, Jake and Elena fail to conceive. Their distress and frustration grow, and recriminations fly, leading to a break-up and a redemptive reconciliation. Glasgow (particularly the West End) provides a constant backdrop, but the location is of little significance.

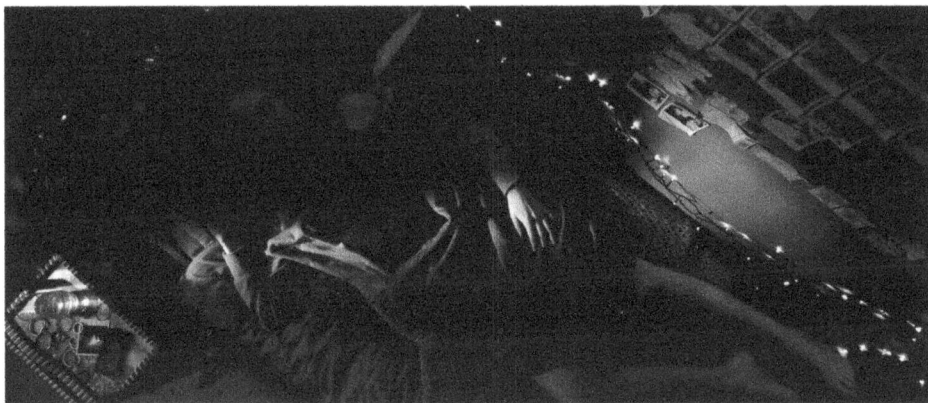

Director, writer and lead, Karen Gillan

The Party's Just Beginning (2018)   S+++ T50

Directed by Karen Gillan
Screenplay by Karen Gillan
Leading cast: Karen Gillan (Liusaidh); Lee Pace
  (Dale); Matthew Beard (Alistair); Rachel
  Jackson (Donna)
Colour, 91 minutes, UK

Inverness, 2018. Liusaidh lives with her parents and works in a supermarket. A friend, Alistair, dies by suicide, as does a neighbour, and an elderly man she talks to after he dials the wrong number for a helpline. She forms a tentative relationship with Dale, but he leaves. Liusaidh attempts to regain control of her life, reaching out to friend Donna for support.

The Party's Just Beginning is an admirable first film from writer/director Gillan, who anchors it with her strongest performance yet. *TPJB* has, at the time of writing, a critics' score of 78 per cent and an audience

score of 73 per cent on Rotten Tomatoes. Gillan, whose role as Amy Pond in *Doctor Who* made her recognisable internationally, had previously appeared in two films set in Scotland, **New Town Killers** and the irritating **Not Another Happy Ending**.

The first draft of *TPJB*, which was originally going to be called *Tupperware Party*, was written by Gillan at the age of 24, after finding out 'the suicide rate in the Highlands of Scotland was higher among young men than anywhere else in Scotland. And then I was like, why, when it's such an idyllic place to live?' Gillan was born in Inverness, where *TPJB* is set and was partly filmed. This was something she had to push for. In an interview with *The Guardian* in 2018 she said there was pressure to film in Glasgow, where most of the crew came from: 'It was important to me to shoot the exteriors in Inverness... Any Scottish person watching the movie will know that [it's wrong] if it's Glasgow'. Almost the first thing we hear Liusaidh say (although this is towards the end of the

361

timeline) is: 'Now a town like this tends to lend itself to an overactive imagination'. Although *TPJB* is firmly grounded in the city, beautifully shot by cinematographer Edd Lukas (the youngest ever London Film School graduate), the issues it explores have relevance wider than the local.

Two suicides are shown in the film: that of Alistair repeatedly; one is heard over the telephone; and Liusaidh prevents Dale from taking his own life in precisely the same way as Alistair. Luisaidh's own mental health is fragile and in the hardest scene to watch she is raped (although she later says, wrongly, she was not, as she 'chose to go' with the three men). *TPJB* is not, as described in several places, a comedy/ drama, although there are some sharp lines, and some nice touches of detail. It may be that the dark subject matter reduced its commercial appeal. After festival screenings it did not move to general release in the UK and had only limited screenings in the US. The later film **Connect** also deals with the issue of male suicide rates but does not pack the punch of *TPJB*.

Super November (2018) S+++

Directed by Douglas King
Screenplay by Josie Long
Leading cast: Josie Long (Josie); Sean Biggerstaff (Mikey); James Allenby-Kirk (Roddy); Darren Osborne (Darren); Matt Winning (Steven)
Colour, 77 minutes, UK

Glasgow: Josie, politically engaged on the Left, begins a relationship with Mikey just after the ousting of a Conservative government. By November, Mikey is off the scene, and a right-wing coup has led to fascist-like policies, including curfews, registration requirements and mass arrests.

Glaswegian director King's micro-budget feature *Super November* starts as a rom-com and ends in dystopian drama. The budget was so limited the *Scottish Daily Mail* reported that when the script required the actors to drink a bottle of Prosecco, the best route was simply to buy one from the local petrol station and drink it for real. The film was written by stand-up comedienne Long (also in **God Help the Girl**), who had previously worked with King on two Glasgow-set shorts (*Let's Go Swimming*, 2012 and *Romance & Adventure*, 2013), and who, by the Covid-19 lockdowns, had moved to Glasgow.

The structure of *Super November* is ambitious, particularly on a low budget (Long accepted that the 'story really did stretch resources'). Prior to a screening at the GFF, King said: 'We wanted to explore how we don't recognise the political impact on our lives because we're so wrapped up in personal day-to-day stuff'. Although the focus is on a change for the worse in the political climate in the UK, the film 'was a response to seeing a lot of people's complacency in the face of the refugee crisis'. *Super November* is a strong reminder that oppressive authoritarian regimes rarely emerge overnight but grow in a culture of acceptance and passivity. The change in tone certainly packs a punch, and if the film is trying to do too much, that is preferable to a film not trying hard enough. Peter Bradshaw was one admirer: 'the dawnings of this new police state are disturbing in ways they might not have been in a conventional thriller... This is a creatively open-minded film.' This one is worth watching.

Tell It to the Bees (2018)   S+

> Directed by Annabel Jankel
> Screenplay by Henrietta Ashworth, Jessica Ashworth
> Leading cast: Anna Paquin (Dr Jean Markham); Holliday Grainger (Lydia Weekes); Gregor Selkirk (Charlie Weekes); Kate Dickie (Pam Stock); Emun Elliott (Robert Weekes)
> Colour, 108 minutes, UK/Sweden

Charlie remembers a summer as a child in Scotland 1952, during which his mother began a lesbian relationship with local doctor, Jean.

Based on Fiona Shaw's 2009 novel (the author Fiona Shaw and the actor of the same name are different people), *Tell It to*

Holliday Grainger in 'mid-century' Doune

the Bees is one of only a very small number of films in this book to foreground the experiences of LGBTQ+ characters (see also *Seat in Shadow*, *Limbo* and *Our Ladies*). Unfortunately, it is poor, offering a laboured metaphor which does not work well, and in which in a key scene is wholly unconvincing. The depiction of the central (and in context, transgressive) love affair is anodyne: 'the shorthand of suppressed yearning, sideways glances and secretive gestures feels overfamiliar and a little tedious' (Christina Newland, in *Empire*). The ending is overly trite, and implausibly optimistic.

The film had its world premiere at the 2018 Toronto International Film Festival, and its UK premiere the same year at the BFI London Film Festival, later receiving a limited UK release. At the GFF Scottish premiere, Bearsden's Gregor Selkirk attended the red carpet but was required to leave the cinema before the film started. He was 11; the film had a 15-certificate. The *Daily Record* reports that he was instead taken for a chocolate milkshake. *Tell It to the Bees* had a rather poor critical reception, currently holding a score of 54 per cent on Rotten Tomatoes.

The film does capture well the look of mid-20th-century small-town Scotland. There was substantial location shooting in

Scotland, centred around Doune, including at the historic Morton Young and Borland Ltd lace factory in the Irvine Valley.

The Vanishing (2018) S++

Directed by Kristoffer Nyholm
Screenplay by Celyn Jones and Joe Bone
Leading cast: Peter Mullan (Thomas); Gerard
  Butler (James); Connor Swindells (Donald)
Colour, 107 minutes, UK

Gerard Butler, Peter Mullan and Colin Swindell

Three lighthouse keepers on a remote station find gold, defend themselves against those who wish to take it back, and commit murder. One survives.

In December 1900, the remote lighthouse on the Flannan Isles (in the Outer Hebrides), manned by three keepers, was found abandoned. An investigation by the Northern Lighthouse Board's Superintendent, who knew the men well, found nothing suspicious. It was presumed that a large storm (of which there was evidence) had washed supplies out to sea, that two had attempted to recover them, and an attempt at rescue by the third ended with the death of all. The official report has not stopped incessant speculation, amplified in *The Vanishing*, which claims in the opening titles to be 'inspired by a true story' (ie, with potentially only a thin relationship to the truth – although two of the keepers' names are retained).

Danish director Nyholm's first (and to date only) feature film received its UK premiere at the GFF in February 2019 but

has had limited exposure in the UK. Three months later, in May 2019, Robert Eggers' very different, but much better known film, *The Lighthouse* (2019), received its premiere at Cannes. Both films fared well critically (*The Lighthouse* just pips *The Vanishing*'s high 85 per cent Rotten Tomatoes rating), but *The Vanishing* was not lionised in the way that the later film was. *The Vanishing's* speculative explanation for the keepers' disappearance is outlandish; there are early hints that we might be heading into territory occupied by *The Treasure of the Sierra Madre* (John Huston, 1948), but these are abandoned as the conflict becomes more conventional. What *The Lighthouse* did exceptionally well was to capture the claustrophobia of the keepers' existence. *The Vanishing* has some of this – the keepers cannot avoid conflict given the possibility of retreat is extremely limited (the film was shot in part at the Galloway Mull Lighthouse) – but to nothing like the same degree. As Alistair Harkness noted in *The Scotsman*, the 'biggest surprise... is the rare but welcome sight of Gerard Butler being good in a half-decent film... [he] digs deep to get beyond the gruff action-man machismo that's become his default setting'.

Wild Rose (2018)   S+

Directed by Tom Harper
Screenplay by Nicole Taylor
Leading cast: Jessie Buckley (Rose-Lynn); Julie
  Walters (Marion); Sophie Okonedo (Susannah)
Colour, 101 minutes, UK/US/Canada

Released from prison, single mother Rose-Lynn pursues her dream of becoming a country singer, while bonding with her children, and rebuilding her life.

Rose-Lynn has a tattoo on her arm, 'Three chords and the truth', a line she uses to explain her love of country music. It is, then, somewhat predictable that confronting uncomfortable truths is central to *Wild Rose*'s salvation narrative. Halfway through the film it appears that the dream of being a country singer will be set aside to permit family bonds to be restored. But her mother (Walters) opts to support Rose-Lynn's dream. True to some extent to its country roots, *Wild Rose* takes an extremely conventional path. It may be its very conventionality that led to the success of *Wild Rose*, which won awards galore, holds a Rotten Tomatoes score of 92 per cent, and performed well at the UK box office.

Wild Rose stands firmly on the shoulders of Jessie Buckley. As she proved in *Beast* (Michael Pearce, 2017) she is a very fine actor; *Wild Rose* reminds us she is also a very fine singer (this was established in the 2008 reality TV series *I'd Do Anything*). The film is at its best when Buckley sings – the stand-out moments being her rendition of 'Peace In This House' (better in the film than on the soundtrack album), and 'When I Reach The Place I Am Going'.

The film is grounded in Glasgow, making use of authentic locations. The Glasgow Grand Ole Opry on Govan Road is one of Europe's more significant country

Jessie Buckley dreams of being a country music star

music venues. Some scenes are shot there, but more could be made of this; there is a strong country (and western) music scene in Glasgow. Given Rose-Lynn is a convicted drug offender, works as a cleaner, and that we move from gaol to a working-class estate to local venues, *Wild Rose* is a very *polite* film (Rose-Lynn's frequent swearing aside); everything feels overly sanitised and neat. This criticism extends to the direction, which, one scene aside, is solid and conventional. During her first stint in Susannah's large house, Rose-Lynn dances and sings along to a country song; a drummer appears on the stairs, and other musicians appear in rooms off the corridor. This happens early enough to offer hope that Harper will creatively exploit the licence that films with music (*Wild Rose* cannot be called a musical) offer – something spectacularly shown by Dexter Fletcher, director of *Sunshine on Leith* (which is a more exciting film than *Wild Rose*), in *Rocketman* (2019). *Wild Rose* is good, and reliably upbeat. But it could have been much more exciting.

The Amber Light (2019) DOC

Directed by Adam Park; 93 minutes

A gentle but slender documentary about the relationship between Scotland, its people and whisky ('Scotch's story isn't linear, it's discursive').

Balance, Not Symmetry (2019) S+++

Directed by Jamie Adams
Screenplay by Jamie Adams, Simon Neil
Leading cast: Laura Harrier (Caitlin Walker); Kate Dickie (Mary Walker); Bria Vinaite (Hannah); Scott Miller (Rory); Shauna Macdonald (Catherine Hendricks)
Colour, 87 minutes, UK

Caitlin struggles with personal tragedy while pursuing her studies at the Glasgow School of Art. She pulls her life together, and the end of year show is a success.

BNS was clearly a deeply personal (if ultimately shared) project. Adams' mother died when he was at university, and he had wanted to make a film based around this for some 20 years. He had always anticipated this would involve music, and it is this element which has attracted most attention, thanks to the involvement of Scottish band Biffy Clyro. But the relationship between the screenplay, soundtrack, and on-set improvisational approach is ultimately unsatisfactory. The film and music do not appear to support each other in any meaningful way. *BNS* works neither as a musical, nor a series of extended music videos, nor as drama. In an interview with *The Guardian*, Biffy Clyro's Simon Neil may provide the explanation for what is a bigger problem for the film than for the album: 'I wanted the record to be its own thing. It had to exist by itself'. In his very positive *NME* review of the album, James McMahon points to the discrepancy: 'The movie... reportedly deals with the concept of grief.... It's somewhat strange, then, that the accompanying album sounds so full of life.' Such dialogue as there is tends to the jejune and vacuous: simply discussing art in a museum – even one as striking as Glasgow's Kelvingrove – does not make a scene, or the film, profound. A great backdrop is not a substitute for intelligent and meaningful conversation.

The album was generally very well received. The film was not. In *The Times* Ed Potton highlighted problems with the screenplay: 'Everyone in the film is annoying — variously self-obsessed, pseudy, theatrically needy or hopelessly drippy, while the dialogue veers between excruciating… and cheesy'. Peter Bradshaw was similarly critical: 'you may have to bite your lip very hard to stifle harrumphs of exasperation watching this drifty on-the-fly Glaswegian indie drama… the whole thing has the tentative, incomplete feel of an improv actors' project.'

This is not to say that there is nothing good at all about *BNS*, although the pickings are slim, and there is a lot to wade through to get them. Lithuanian-born Vinaite, who shone in *The Florida Project* (Sean Baker, 2017), is likeable, and Macdonald is excellent as Catherine.

Beats (2019)   S+++ T30

Directed by Brian Welsh
Screenplay by Kieran Hurley, Brian Welsh
Leading cast: Cristian Ortega (Johnno); Lorn Macdonald (Spanner); Laura Fraser (Alison); Neil Leiper (Fido); Ross Mann (D-Man); Brian Ferguson (Robert)
B&W/Colour, 101 minutes, UK

West Lothian, 1994: as the Criminal Justice and Public Order Bill threatens the rave scene, and Johnno's family plans to move, Johnno and Spanner make the most of what is left of their time.

Cristian Ortega and Lorn Macdonald

I loved *Beats* when I first saw it, putting it well within my top ten films for 2019. Watching it later, it remains vibrant. Rightly, it won awards and plaudits aplenty. Adapted from a stage play by Kieran Hurley, *Beats* is set at the time the Conservative government, unopposed by Tony Blair's Labour, was clamping down on rave culture. This provides an ever-present backdrop, but the real heart of the film lies in the relationship between unlikely friends Johnno and Spanner, as they engage in a last hurrah, knowing that they are going to move on, and likely part ways. Because of their youth, Spanner and Johnno come late to the rave scene, and here it is not just the friendship which is coming to an end, but also the scene itself, not only because of the oppressive new legislation, but because, as Spanner recognises, 'it's a fag-end scene anyway all this, it's been done, washed up'. But as Johnno says, 'it's not been done by us, pal'. They get to the last big local rave, but, to the sounds of Human Resource's 'Dominator', the police violently break it up. After being released from a night in the cells Johnno is still able to describe the experience as 'fucking fantastic'. Macdonald's performance is exceptional – he won the BAFTA Scotland Best Actor award in 2019 and was nominated as Best Newcomer at the British Independent Film Awards.

It's hard in places not to think of *Trainspotting* when watching *Beats*. The echoes of Renton's most famous lines are strong when D-Man's protest pirate broadcasts reach a staccato climax: 'to be governed is to be at every operation noted, registered, stamped, measured, numbered, assessed, authorised, admonished, prevented, forbidden, reformed, corrected, watched, inspected, spied-upon, directed, enrolled, indoctrinated, preached at, controlled, checked. In other words, listeners, sisters, brothers, fuck these fucking motherfuckers right to absolute fuck.' Inter-generational conflict, and conflict between youth culture and 'the system' (D-Man: 'The only good system is a sound system') is a well-used trope, in cinema at least stretching back to *Rebel Without a Cause* (Nicholas

Ray, 1955). *Beats* recognises its place in this tradition when D-Man references Timothy Leary's famous words in 1967 at San Francisco's 'Human Be-In' gathering, and urges his listeners to 'turn on, tune in, and drop the fuck out'.

Apart from some sequences at the rave, and material just prior to the closing credits, *Beats* is shot entirely in black and white. The cinematography by Benjamin Kračun is superb (he won the cinematographer award at the British Independent Film Awards). So too is the soundtrack, and sound design, and this is a film to watch loud.

Inconsequential trivia is occasionally fun: the old estate car driven to the rave was also driven by Anna's father in *Anna and the Apocalypse*; the hula girl on the dashboard is there in both films.

Bend Don't Break (2019)   DOC

Directed by Alex Harron; 83 minutes

There's pathos in listening to someone committed to their sport – in this case American Football – saying 'I hate losing', when he's a member of a team which never wins. This is the case for the Dundee Hurricanes at the time the film was shot (a downturn from the glory days a decade previously when the team won divisional championships). *Bend Don't Break* is more likely to generate *schadenfreude* than joy, and is perhaps only of parochial interest, but there is something special here: triumphs are to be found not in winning results, but in the smaller victories such as simply being able to field a team or to find the funds to turn up to an away match.

Blood's a Rover (2019)   S+++

Directed by Tim Fraser-Granados
Screenplay by Tim Fraser-Granados
Leading cast: Cameron Brown (David Boyd);
George McWilliam (Alan Torrance); Jacqueline
Gilbride (Eileen Ballantyne); Gordon Holliday
(Blair Eadie)
Colour, 100 minutes, UK

Edinburgh: Detective Chief Inspector Boyd becomes involved in the hunt for a missing person, and a labyrinthine set of connections link corruption, paedophilia and murder (including the death, five years previously, of his father).

Fraser-Granados describes himself as a 'German born Scottish filmmaker' (who at the time of writing is based in the US), and his film as a neo-noir (the one screening I have been able to track down was at an LA Neo Noir festival). That apart there is no obvious public recognition of the film. *Blood's a Rover* is Fraser-Granados' only feature film and followed a short, *The Poet Dreaming of the City of Light* (2012), which was a cinematic prose poem to Edinburgh. *Blood*'s low budget was raised in part through a crowdfunding campaign. The film has no relationship with the 2009 James Ellroy novel of the same name; the title comes from AE Housman's poem, 'A Shropshire Lad' ('Clay lies still, but blood's

a rover.') The plotting is overly complicated, and some of the acting clumsy around the edges, but the essential trappings of noir are here (including voice-over), although much of the film is shot indoors in well-lit rooms, somewhat jarring with the noir vibe.

Connect (2019)   S+++

Directed by Marilyn Edmond
Screenplay by Marilyn Edmond
Leading cast: Kevin Guthrie (Brian); Siobhan
Reilly (Sam); Stephen McCole (Jeff)
Colour, 97 minutes, UK

In North Berwick, in the lead-up to Christmas, Brian contemplates suicide. An intervention by Jeff, owner of a day-centre for the elderly, sets Brian on a new path.

Connect sets out to deal with the issue of suicide and its incidence in men in the UK under 45 (previously foregrounded in 2018's *The Party's Just Beginning*). The film premiered at the GFF and went on to play in other festivals but had little mainstream exposure. This may be the result of the impact of the Covid-19 pandemic on distribution, or because its lead, Kevin Guthrie, was convicted of sexual assault in 2021 and imprisoned. It may also be because the issue the film deals with merits a far better response than *Connect* provides.

Set at Christmastime, *Connect* is nearly crushed by the weight of its cinematic influence: Brian is saved from possible suicide and comes to value human connections, rediscovering pleasure in his music and writing a song dedicated to his other 'angel' (Sam). Early on, an incidental character quotes directly from *It's a Wonderful Life* (Frank Capra, 1946). The result is a film whose beats are too metronymic, and whose characters are anodyne ciphers ('sketchy characters who are little more than clusters of symptoms' – Leslie Felperin, in *The Guardian*).

Convergence (2019)   S++

Directed by Steve Johnson
Screenplay by Steve Johnson
Leading cast: Jeremy Theobald (Martin);
  Nicolette McKeown (Lily)
Colour, 97 minutes, UK

In Glasgow, Martin, a successful author, struggles to come to terms with the death of his wife and young child. He joins a bereavement support group, meeting Lily, whose abusive partner caused her to miscarry.

Winner of a slew of awards at film festivals, *Convergence* was the second feature from English director Johnson, who said of the film: 'I feel it breaks with a familiar type of Scottish film that centres around zombies*, drugs, gangsters, deprived housing etc, and concentrates on the emotional connection between two individuals'.

The film is set in Glasgow (it does not go out of its way to make this obvious) and premiered at the British Independent Film Festival in 2019 where it won, amongst others, the Best Feature Film award.

Convergence is carried along by the two leads (Glaswegian McKeown appears also in *Lost at Christmas*) and the central relationship works, but Johnson chooses to distance us from emotional engagement, in part by disrupting the image, and in part by relating the characters to pieces on a chess board manipulated by someone Johnson has called 'the strategist' (God?). These devices are not entirely successful.

* Of the 427 films covered in this book only three, *The Dead Outside*, *Attack of the Herbals* and *Anna and the Apocalypse*, deal with zombies; two of these are not overly serious.

Dark Sense (2019)   S+++

Directed by Magnus Wake
Screenplay by Geoff Dupuy-Holder and Alistair
  Rutherford
Leading cast: Shane O'Meara (Simon Eildon); Jim
  Sturgeon (Steve Brennus)
Colour, 93 minutes, UK

Edinburgh: Simon's formidable psychic powers lead to him attempting to track down a serial killer, working with an ex-SAS corporal, Steve, to do so, while he comes to the attention of MI5.

After a hesitant start, *Dark Sense*, the first feature from Scottish director Magnus Wake (based on Peter A Flannery's novel *First and Only*, 2012) builds strongly to an effective, if predictable, conclusion. The film played at one festival in the US in the summer of 2019, and FrightFest, before moving to DVD and streaming. The result is that reviews are sparse. The central pairing of O'Meara (an Irish actor who was in 46 episodes of *Waterloo Road*, 2012–2014), and Scottish actor Sturgeon (*A Shot at Glory*, *AfterLife* and *Iona* amongst others) works well: after an uncertain start both help each other. In *thehollywoodnews* there was praise for a 'strong debut', and Wake's 'keen eye, and an ear for setting up tone and atmosphere'. Set and filmed in Edinburgh; a strong supporting cast includes Siobhan Redmond.

Final Ascent: The Legend of Hamish MacInnes (2019)   DOC

Directed by Robbie Fraser; 81 minutes

At the age of 84, against his will, legendary climber/explorer Hamish MacInnes was hospitalised, suffering from physical debilitation and cognitive degeneration, as a result of illness. His life story and attempt to recover is told through interviews (including with MacInnes), clips, and stills.

Michael Palin's opening words to *Final Ascent* are: 'There's something about Hamish's presence; he had this aura about him that made him feel you were going to be OK. He would get you down if anyone could'. Chris Bonnington states that the only reason he and MacInnes, who had been left for dead several times, were both still alive (at the time of filming; MacInnes died in 2020) was that they 'were both very very lucky'. The materials used in Fraser's documentary, which sets out to be as much about memory and identity as mountaineering, include those relied on by MacInnes to help him recover his memories. It is disappointing, given MacInnes' influence on the development of mountaineering, and his filmmaking and writing that he gives away very little of himself in the interviews on which Fraser relies, and we must rely on Palin's description of his 'presence'. *Final Ascent* received festival screenings and has been shown on the BBC.

Get Duked! (aka Boyz in the Wood) (2019)   S+++ T100

Directed by Ninian Doff
Screenplay by Ninian Doff
Leading cast: Lewis Gribben (Duncan); Rian Gordon (Dean); Viraj Juneja (DJ Beatroot); Samuel Bottomley (Ian); Eddie Izzard (the duke); Kate Dickie (Sgt. Morag)
Colour, 100 minutes, UK

Three 'young delinquents' and a virtuous pupil at the same school, taking the Duke of Edinburgh Award, head from the city to the Highlands. They become the objects of a deadly hunt mounted by a crazed, psychopathic Duke, and are mistaken by the local police for terrorists.

If *Calibre* and *Restless Natives* had a love child, and raised it on hip-hop, *Get Duked!* would be the result (although the closest film in this book to *Get Duked!* thematically would be Richard Jobson's *New Town Killers*). Scottish director

Ninian Goff, who responded to the closure of the Edinburgh Filmhouse late in 2022 by tweeting 'it's not an exaggeration to say I grew up in the building', established a strong reputation for directing music videos before making this, his first feature. *Get Duked!* opened the EIFF in 2019, but its distribution was hit by the Covid-19 pandemic, which is a pity, as this one is a gem. As *American Cousins* had done 16 years earlier, *Get Duked!* crosses genres, blending (in this case) horror and comedy into a delightful cocktail. Without the comedy we might as well be in *Calibre* territory, but the comedy *never* goes away, even at the most intense moments of threat; even the nod to *The Texas Chainsaw Massacre* (Tobe Hooper, 1974) works as humour when Eddie Izzard and Georgie Glen adopt Leatherface's signature look.

The film won the Midnighters Audience Award at the SXSW film festival and was very well received by critics (it's 'Certified Fresh' on Rotten Tomatoes), who praised its sharp humour. In *The Scotsman*, Alistair Harkness noted the 'raucous, irreverent tone', of this 'entertainingly crude and surreal coming-of-age movie, with a surprisingly pointed bit of streets-vs-the-elites social commentary running through it'. Simran Hans in *The Observer* singled out the ever-excellent Katie Dickie: 'drily funny as a sergeant who abandons her search for the local bread thief in the hope of catching an influx of "hip-hop" terrorists'.

Although there are better-known actors in the film (including Kevin Guthrie, Brian Pettifer and James Cosmo, all of whom appear to be having a blast), the real stars are

Samuel Bottomley, Viraj Juneja, Lewis Gribben and Rian Gordon

the four young men. Gribben and Gordon are both Scottish: Gribben had previously had only a small role in *T2: Trainspotting*, and has since built a strong CV, including *Our Ladies* and *Limbo*; Gordon has worked extensively in film and TV.

Last Breath (2019)　DOC

Directed by Richard da Costa and Alex Parkinson; 90 minutes

The remarkable story of the survival and rescue of Chris Lemons when an accident left him 100 metres below the surface of the North Sea with only five minutes of heliox supply. He was recovered 40 minutes later, unharmed. This BBC film, containing original footage, reconstructions, and interviews, brilliantly captures the claustrophobia of diving at depth. Parkinson later directed a dramatised version of the story – also filmed as *Last Breath* (see below).

→ *Last Breath* (2025)   S+

Directed by Alex Parkinson
Screenplay by Mitchell LaFortune, Alex
  Parkinson and David Brooks
Leading cast: Woody Harrelson (Duncan
  Allcock); Finn Cole (Chris Lemons); Simu Liu
  (Dave Uasa); Bobby Rainsbury (Morag)
Colour, 93 minutes, US/UK

*After its positional system fails, the crew
of a support vessel battle to rescue a diver
running out of oxygen, trapped 100 metres
below the surface of the North Sea.*

Last Breath, released in March 2025, is
one of the most recent films covered in this
book. At the time of writing, the film was
rated 'fresh' on Rotten Tomatoes, with a
score of 79 per cent. It's easy to see why
critics were broadly positive as everything
done in the film is done well. It's less
easy to see *why* it was done, and while
Parkinson, who directed the documentary
on which this feature is based, has chosen
to emphasise veracity ('this is a true story'
rather than the glib 'based on a true story'),
the story has cinematic limitations. The
central issue of the film is Lemons' highly
improbable survival; the emotional heart
lies with Harrelson's Allcock (the BBC
reported Harrelson told Allcock he would
not try to replicate his Yorkshire accent);
and the action – a technical solution to a
technical problem – lies on the bridge of
the ship, where functions matter more than
characters.

The cinematography options are
limited in *Last Breath*: the dive site is pitch
black, and all interiors are confined. The
soundtrack does a lot of the heavy lifting;
the score is by my former neighbour,
BAFTA-nominated composer Paul
Leonard-Morgan.

Far more people watch drama
than documentaries. If you do watch
documentaries, the better telling of
Lemons' story probably lies there; if you
don't, this dramatised version does the job
very well.

Our Ladies (2019)   S+++

Directed by Michael Caton-Jones
Screenplay by Michael Caton-Jones, Alan Sharp
Leading cast: Abigail Lawrie (Finnoula); Rona
  Morrison (Chell); Marli Siu (Kylah); Tallulah
  Greive (Orla); Sally Messham (Manda); Eve
  Austin (Kay); Kate Dickie (Sister Condron);
  David Hasselhoff (David Hasselhoff)
Colour, 106 minutes, UK

*Fort William, 1996: Kylah rehearses with
a band; Orla has had leukaemia; Manda
pours vodka into a large cola bottle; Chell
snogs a guy. The girls go to Edinburgh for
a choir contest, representing their Catholic
school, and take the opportunity to expand
their experience.*

Our Ladies is based on Alan Warner's
award-winning novel *The Sopranos* (1998)
– a title that, for obvious reasons, was
never going to be used for the film. The
book had previously been adapted into a
2015 play, by Lee Hall, bearing the longer
title *Our Ladies of Perpetual Succour*. It

The ladies misbehaving in Edinburgh

was performed by the National Theatre of Scotland and transferred to London's West End. The play has a raucous energy and intensity lacking in the more expansive film adaptation (the closest the film comes to matching this is in the performance of 'Tainted Love' in the Pillbox, with Marli Sui – see *Anna and the Apocalypse* and *Run* – again demonstrating her strong voice). The film however tells us more about the characters and makes effective use of location shooting. It is particularly sharp in its depictions of the limits on the girls' world. The biggest divide between the characters is not sexual experience and class; it is between those who are going to move on, and those who will stay.

After directing *Rob Roy* in 1995, Scottish-born Michael Caton-Jones spent time in Hollywood, before returning to Scotland for *Our Ladies*. This is one of the better films to have had its prospects severely damaged by the Covid-19 pandemic. The critical response to *Our Ladies* was positive (the film holds a 93 per cent score on Rotten Tomatoes), but few reviews were wholly unqualified. Recurring concerns are that the film was dated before it was even made – which is partially acknowledged in the opening voice-over; and that Caton-Jones tries *too* hard to get the tone right. This point is well made by Simran Hans in *The Observer*: 'As a male director, Caton-Jones knows better than to let the film become a pre-#MeToo sleazy fantasy, yet his tentativeness feels ill-suited to the uninhibited teenage sexuality the source material celebrates.' The film was nominated in the Best Film category at the 2022 Scottish BAFTAs, with Sui nominated for Best Actress.

There is a good reason to watch the film through the closing credits, which include not only a final song from the ensemble cast, but also a cameo from the Hoff himself.

Runrig: The Last Dance (2019) DOC

Directed by Marcus Viner; 94 minutes

This curiosity is one of only two films in this book to have no IMDb entry; it does not even appear in the list of works from director Viner. Neither does the three-hour-plus original final concert documentary (released on DVD and screened on BBC Alba several times) on which this cut-down cinema version is based. The copyright line at the end of the credits states the date as being 2019, although I was not aware of the film's existence until the GFT screened it at the year's end in 2024. One result of the editing is that the tagline that plays across the screen at the start, 'A success story of a band and its audience that never conformed to rock's norms' is not, for this shortened version, entirely true. There is very little story, and while there are plenty of shots of members of the 50,000+ audience at Runrig's farewell concert (in front of the stunning backdrop of Stirling Castle) in August 2018, none of their stories of fandom are told. What we are left with is a well-made concert film, enhanced by this being the band's emotional final performance, and a strong set list, ending, of course, with 'Hearts of Olden Glory'. The editorial choice means this is a film for fans, which has no wider story to tell.

Scheme Birds (2019) DOC T24

Directed by Ellen Fiske, Ellinor Hallin; 90 minutes

The documentary charts the progress of 18-year-old Gemma through to her early 20s. She lives in a Motherwell housing estate, in an area once labelled Steelopolis. She hasn't met her mum since she was a baby, becomes pregnant, has a child herself, and eventually leaves.

Filmed over four years, *Scheme Birds* is a remarkable piece of work, and not always an easy watch. It is perhaps not so curious that a Swedish team has made a great documentary about modern Scotland. Interviewed for the Swedish Film Institute, Fiske suggested being outsiders helped in gaining the trust of the film's subjects: 'it's because we came from outside. Had we come from the BBC or been a local film crew, they would probably have felt more vulnerable. Since we came from Sweden and felt harmless, it became easier to let us in.' It was Gemma herself who pitched the idea to Fiske and Hallin, while Fiske was working on a short documentary, also set in Motherwell, about single fathers.

Motherwell does not come off well in *Scheme Birds* – for which Gemma blames

Margaret Thatcher; the local steel works was shut down towards the end of her time as Prime Minister. *Variety* describes it as 'a deprived, lustreless Scottish town'. That's the only negative comment in a glowing review of a 'superb documentary, an alternately lyrical and gut-punching coming-of-age study'. Closer to home, *The Skinny* too was full of praise: 'the visually raw and unfiltered footage highlights the profound reality of the bleak post-industrial setting... Delving with a respectful intimacy into the lives of their subjects, the directors skilfully draw out the nuances of their subject matter.'

The filmmakers do not interpose themselves directly into the film. There are no titles, and no voice-over. Instead, those shown are allowed to talk for themselves, with Gemma providing a framework and narrative voice-over. This guarantees authenticity, but limits the scope of the film, and left me wanting to know more – Gemma's perspective is necessarily limited; but the approach does speak to *her* experience in a raw and powerful text. The access obtained by Fiske and Hallin is remarkable, with cameras very close to the participants, but invisible in their impact. Scheme Birds could almost be mistaken for scripted drama (a 'top' user review on IMDb makes that mistake) – there is a thin line between this and films like *Sweet Sixteen* and *Neds*. What distinguishes *Scheme Birds* is its searing honesty.

Schemers (2019) S+++

Directed by Dave Mclean
Screenplay by Dave Mclean
Leading cast: Conor Berry (Davie); Sean Connor (Scot); Grant Robert Keelan (John); Tara Lee (Shona); Mingus Johnston (Kenny); Alastair Thomson Mills (Fergie)
Colour, 91 minutes, UK

Dundee, 1979. Davie's rise to being a gig/concert promoter is charted as he navigates financial woes, local gangsters, and the demands of bands.

Schemers is based in truth and is unusual in being set in Dundee (the opening titles proclaim: 'Proudly made in Dundee', making this the only film in this book to be set almost entirely in the city). Its focus on a city in the east of Scotland, a long way from London (there is a gag in which Davie and a London manager tussle over how much bands should be paid based on travel distance – this after the manager has asked his PA, 'Annabelle, where the fuck is Dundee?') could have been a real strength, but not nearly enough is made of this such that, accents aside, little is distinctively local.

Culturally, the short time over which the film is set was an exciting one – there is a strong soundtrack (although, puzzlingly for a film based around the music industry, there are anachronisms – The Proclaimers' 'I'm On My Way', was not released until 1988). The opening sequence positions the film against the backdrop of the election of Margaret Thatcher's Conservative government, and in many ways Davie and his friends epitomise the Thatcherite spirit of assertive entrepreneurship. But the result is disappointingly thin. *Schemers* ends up as another 'here's a homespun folksy story of Brits doing something eccentric and winning through' film. It is a simple tale of three likeable chancers, a beautiful girl, and their circle, getting involved with gangsters, putting on a gig, paying off their debts, and moving on.

The end credits, which tell the subsequent fates of the three central characters, suggest that there is a better story to be told. In the *New Musical Express* Rhian Daly picked up on this: 'Frustratingly, we're told the fates of each of the trio via a series of title screens and it's hard not to feel short-changed. It's important to tell the beginning of any story, but you'll come to question if it needed a whole film dedicated to it when you read some of the tales that followed.'

The Burning Baby (2020) S+

Directed by Paul Kindersley
Screenplay by Paul Kindersley
Leading cast: Jenny Runacre (Mother); Nick Patrick (Baby); Tamara MacArthur (visitor/the wife)
Colour, 95 minutes, UK

'Baby' is an adult male treated as a baby by his 'ugly sisters' and overbearing mother on a wooded island. 'Wood dwellers' also live on the island and are invited to Baby's 'second' birthday party at which a visitor shows interest in him. After a Bacchanalian night in the woods, Baby is taken by the visitor and they marry; Mother is devastated. Baby kills his wife and crawls back to Mother.*

Eilean Shona provides a stunning backdrop to Burning Baby

Shot entirely on Eilean Shona (which, thanks in part to Oscar Oldershaw's cinematography, looks stunning), a location linked with JM Barrie and *Peter Pan* (1904) in particular, *The Burning Baby* makes the island's landscape a leading character while on a deep dive into folk-weird. *The Burning Baby* was completed just before Covid-19 hit, and Kindersley has struggled to find a distributor, although the film has had several one-off screenings.

But don't expect *The Burning Baby* to turn up at your local multiplex; this is not mainstream narrative cinema and in fact is one of the most distinctive films covered in this book, falling somewhere between art and queer cinema – imagine a film made collaboratively by Derek Jarman and Ken Russell, with each having full rein, and then throw in a splash of Peter Greenaway just for fun. The crucial point however is that nothing here is an accident, and that the result reflects a singular vision which has been fully realised (with extremely high production values); if it is off-the-wall bonkers, it's *meant to be so*. Jonathan Sisson gets it right in *We Are Cult*: 'the film would suffer if it weren't so impenetrable. Often, when an interviewer asks David Lynch why he chose to do something in a particular way, he'll answer by saying something like "It felt correct." Whilst nothing about *The Burning Baby* remotely resembles a David Lynch film… everything about [it] feels absolutely correct'. Realistically, most readers of this book would probably hate *The Burning Baby* with a passion; equally realistically, they would not seek it out and would not accidentally come across it. I loved it; make of that what you will.

The commitment from the ten-member cast to the project is considerable; Kindersley himself is one of the ugly sisters; producer Ellie Pole plays a 'Wood Dweller'; and Jenny Runacre shines. She had worked with Kindersley and Pole previously, while her long career includes roles for directors such as Jarman (*Derek Jarman's Jubilee*, 1978), John Cassavetes (*Husbands*, 1979) and Pier Paolo Pasolini (*The Canterbury Tales*, 1972). For Patrick, the role of 'Baby' must have been extremely physically demanding. Kindersley told me 'Shona is really a magical place… and as we were all on the island living together for the duration of the intense shoot – it really was a main character – there were no cars etc, so all the locations were about two/three hr hikes!'

It would be possible to watch *The Burning Baby* without identifying the setting as Scottish (although where else in the UK could offer such scenery?). The family's accents are cut-glass English (leading us into fairy tale/pantomime territory perhaps), so its inclusion here might be a slight cheat. I was able to watch it only because Kindersley generously enabled this. But the film is so distinctive that it would be a great shame to have ignored it.

Falling for Figaro (2020)   S+

Directed by Ben Lewin
Screenplay by Ben Lewin and Allen Palmer
Leading cast: Danielle Macdonald (Millie Cantwell); Joanna Lumley (Meghan Geoffrey-Bishop); Hugh Skinner (Max Thistlewaite)
Colour, 104 minutes, Australia/UK/US

Giving up her job in London, 20-something Millie determines to become an opera singer. In the Highland village of 'Drumbuchan', she trains under Meghan. She fails to win the prestigious 'Singer of Renown' competition. Three years later she is an up-and-coming performer.

It is not by design that Joanna Lumley's acerbic Meghan lives in a quaint farmhouse in the Highlands. She is there only because an admirer once gifted her the property in Drumbuchan. Nevertheless, this is where Millie must go, and so from the 11th minute (after she leaves her comfortable but unsatisfying London life) the clichés pile on – snow-capped hills, Highland cattle, loch-side encounters, and Ramsay (Gary Lewis), a grumpy/grasping publican running a barely-getting-by pub (Millie is told at one point that she *is* the local economy). Unsurprisingly, Ramsay warms to Millie, as does Meghan's only other pupil, Max. Millie's path can never really be in doubt, although there are plenty of arias to sing on the way. But the strong performances, and the bite in the script, are *just* sufficient to overpower the cliché and saccharine (although citizens of Edinburgh might not forgive the outdoor scenes set in the city being filmed in Glasgow). As David Stratton put it in *The Australian*, 'Falling *for Figaro* gets by thanks to the excellent actors and a quietly subversive sense of humour. Lumley steals the show, but that comes as no surprise'.

Limbo (2020)   S++ T20

Directed by Ben Sharrock
Screenplay by Ben Sharrock
Leading cast: Amir El-Masry (Omar); Sidse
  Babett Knudsen (Helga); Kenneth Collard
  (Boris); Vikash Bhai (Farhad); Ola Orebiyi
  (Wasef); Kwabena Ansah (Abedi)
Colour, 104 minutes, UK

Asylum claimants housed in a dispersal centre on North Uist struggle to cope with the uncertainty surrounding their futures, and with their pasts.

With *Limbo* (the second film in this book to deal with the plight of asylum seekers in Scotland – see also *Trouble Sleeping*), Scottish screenwriter and second-time director Ben Sharrock has made a marvellous film in which Scotland is not so much the *other*, as the *nowhere*.

Cultural theorists refer to liminal spaces – areas of transition which lie between two geographic, or metaphorical, zones. Those passing through liminal spaces may find that reliable conventions reflected in laws, norms, or behaviour break down and characters emerge transformed (think of Dorothy's journey through the land of Oz – perhaps the ultimate liminal space in cinema). In this respect, Scotland as an area in which characters may be changed or challenged has rarely been employed so perfectly, or with such good intent. The central characters in *Limbo* are in a liminal space, both physically and legally. Their situation is one of (in the proper meaning of an overused word) existential jeopardy, suspended between powerful oppositions: acceptance or rejection; asylum or deportation; safety or danger; life or death. While awaiting the outcome of very lengthy procedures (Farhad, a Syrian refugee and acclaimed musician, has been waiting '32 months and 5 days'), in which they may be barely able to participate, asylum seekers are in limbo. As Lorenzo Codelli wrote in French film magazine *Positif*, Sharrock's 'sad reflection, neither desperate nor neutral, on immigration which affects the whole world, is worth one thousand true reports, or the heavy reprimands of Ai Weiwei'.

In a wonderful opening scene, Danish actor Sidse Babett Knudsen dances to Hot Chocolate's 'It Started with a Kiss'. She invites a man to dance with her: he behaves inappropriately and is slapped. We are in a classroom; the lesson is 'Cultural Awareness 101: Sex: Is A Smile

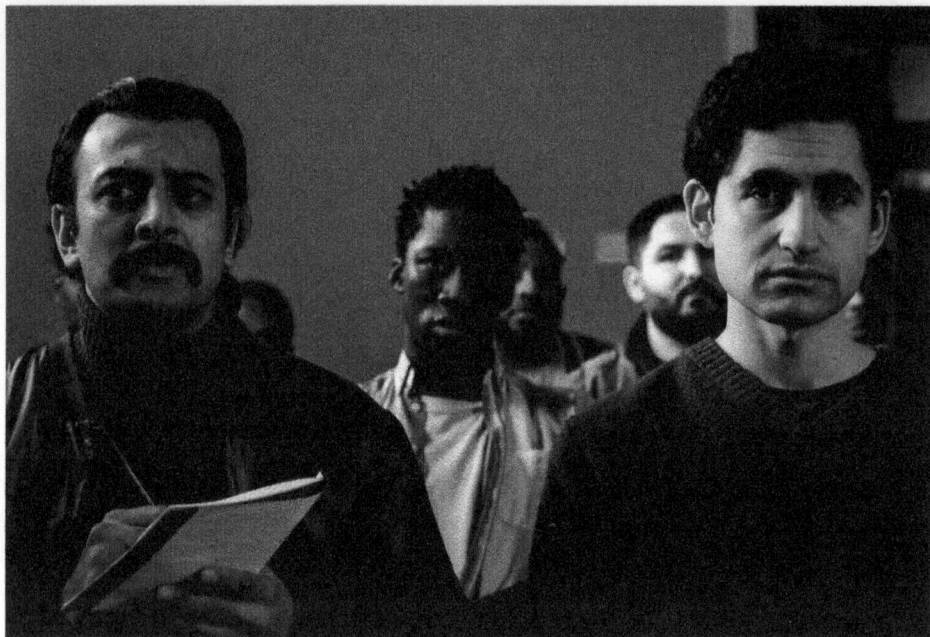

Vikash Bhai, Amir El Masry

An Invitation?' After nearly four and a half minutes the first word is spoken, and it is a shouted, angry 'No' – the possibility of rejection is raised. There are many moments of silence in *Limbo*, and where there is communication much of it is awkward – a result of both linguistic difficulties, but also of failures of comprehension. Even in its awkwardness there is real humour here; *Limbo* is not a comedy, but it is, frequently, very funny. Small kindnesses abound, although there is hostility in the landscape, the process, and occasionally the local population (at one point a sign 'Refugees welcome' is defaced to read 'Refugees NOT welcome'). Omar, played with absolute mastery by Egyptian-born El-Masry (who later had a small role in Kenneth Branagh's *A Haunting in Venice* (2023)), does not directly encounter hostility from the islanders, but lack of understanding is prevalent. He is instructed by one young islander: 'Don't, like, blow up shite, or rape anyone right?', as a prelude to being offered a kindly lift.

Omar is cocooned in silence, and there are hints that he may be suffering PTSD, although we are not told the full backstories of any of the refugees. He carries his oud in almost every shot but does not play it until the last five minutes of the film, at which point the screen aspect ratio pans out from a tight 4:3 to 1.85:1

widescreen. It's a stunning moment. The Western Isles are continually shown as bleak, open, and windswept, but Nick Cooke's cinematography makes them appear austerely beautiful, nonetheless. The later Glasgow-set film *Girl* deals with integration into society after asylum is granted.

In the UK, the 1999 *Immigration and Asylum Act* was followed by the introduction of a policy of dispersal to ensure that asylum seekers were distributed across the UK. As of 2022, the only designated dispersal area in Scotland was Glasgow, although the then Home Secretary was considering plans to use Scottish islands. It turned out that she thought Rwanda was a better bet.

later into this feature-length Christmas rom-com/drama. *Lost at Christmas* has the strength of not being as twee as many of its American counterparts (the relationships are more complex, the language more sweary), and benefits from a strong cast, which includes ex-Doctor Who Sylvester McCoy (playing alongside Frazer Hines, who appeared as Doctor Who's assistant Jamie, in 116 episodes between 1966 and 1985) and Scottish national treasure Clare Grogan. But it sticks perilously close to the Christmas movie formula. Cinematography is by John Rhodes, who lensed *16 Years of Alcohol*. Natalie Clark had also worked with Hendrick on *Minds of Glass* (2011), which meets the criteria for entry in this book, but which I have not been able to track down. Hendrick later directed *Mercy Falls*.

Lost at Christmas (aka *Perfect Strangers*) (2020)   S+++

Directed by Ryan Hendrick
Screenplay by Ryan Hendrick and Clare Sheppard
Leading cast: Natalie Clark (Jen); Kenny Boyle (Rob)
Colour, 100 minutes, UK

Fort William, Christmas Eve. Jen and Rob, both heartbroken, meet while trying to get back to Glasgow. They travel together, and are stranded in the snow at a lodge in Glencoe.

In 2015, Scottish writer/director Ryan Hendrick made the short film *Perfect Strangers*, which was expanded five years

→ Mercy Falls (2023)   S+++

Directed by Ryan Hendrick
Screenplay by Meliá Grasska and Ryan Hendrick
Leading cast: Lauren Lyle (Rhona), Nicolette McKeown (Carla), Layla Kirk (Heather), James Watterson (Scott), Joe Rising (Donnie), Eoin Sweeney (Andy)
Colour, 103 minutes, UK

In Scotland, five friends trek to find a 'long lost cabin in the woods'. They are joined by Carla, who acts as a guide. Things go horribly wrong.

Hendrick's follow-up to *Lost at Christmas* is overly formulaic in its approach to the perils and horror implicit in a trek to a 'cabin in the woods'. As anyone who has watched the Joss Whedon-penned *The Cabin in the Woods* (Drew Goddard, 2011), or *The Evil Dead* (Sam Raimi, 1981) well knows, cabins in the woods are *not* ideal destinations for groups of young adults. This is particularly the case when tensions simmer within the party, and when two have complex backstories of trauma, nightmares, and PTSD. The film suffers from a disjunctive combination of predictability and improbability. Widely referenced as being set in the Highlands, the group begin their trek at the delightful Rowardennan Hotel, on the east shore of Loch Lomond, and never reach the Highlands.

Mercy Falls was shown at the cut-back 2023 version of the EIFF, from where it attracted mixed reviews, before moving on to streaming platforms.

Playhouse (2020)   S++

Directed by Fionn Watts and Toby Watts
Screenplay by Fionn Watts and Toby Watts
Leading cast: William Holstead (Jack Travis);
   Grace Courtney (Bee Travis); Helen Mackay
   (Jenny Andrews); James Rottger (Callum
   Andrews); Rebecca Calienda (Kathryn)
Colour, 87 minutes, UK

'Horrorpreneur' author Jack, and his daughter, Bee, have moved into a 'castle' in Caithness in the north of Scotland against Bee's wishes. Bee makes friends locally, but falls victim to an ancient curse.

The first feature film from the Watts brothers, who founded the production company 'Far North Film' in 2011, is a gothic horror heavily reliant on the genre tropes, set where the brothers, originally from Sheffield, grew up. *Playhouse* was filmed over 13 days in their father's house, Freswick Castle, on a micro-budget of £65,000. The film received its premiere at FrightFest in 2020, won an award at the Hot Springs Festival, and secured a theatrical release in Russia (but not in the UK).

William Holstead and Grace Courtney are both English actors at the start of their careers – this was the first film for Courtney (the real-life age gap between them is close to five years, making the father/daughter relationship a difficult sell); Glaswegian James Rottger had previously been in *Going Green* and *Our Ladies*. The real stars of the film, however, are Freswick Castle, and the Caithness scenery. The plot is ambitious, attempting to tie together gothic horror *and* the process of artistic creation, as Jack's writing and the supernatural intertwine. Limited reviews are broadly positive, with most focusing on the strength of the location. As Jennie Kermode in *Eye For Film* puts it, *Playhouse* 'is strong on atmosphere, with an instinctive understanding of the possibilities offered by the location. For all its difficulties, it's a bold first feature, and its stronger moments will stay with you'.

A second film from the brothers, *Black Daruma* (2023), is *not* Scottish.

Then Came You (2020)   S++

Directed by Adriana Trigiani
Screenplay by Kathie Lee Gifford
Leading cast: Kathie Lee Gifford (Annabelle
  Wilson); Craig Ferguson (Howard); Elizabeth
  Hurley (Clare Hollings)
Colour, 97 minutes, US

Recently widowed Annabelle begins a
world tour to scatter her husband's ashes.
Her first, and last, stop is the 'Awd Inn' on
the shores of Loch Fyne.

Gifford, who both wrote and produced
Then Came You (in addition to taking the
co-lead role), and Ferguson had previously
worked together on the *Today* show, and
Ferguson said in one interview that he
had suggested they do a film together. The
result is somewhat lacklustre. If there is
joy to be found in *Then Came You* it lies
in the setting (starting with the drive from
the Arrochar and Tarbet train station to
Ardkinglas House – 'Awd Inn'), and in
Ferguson's performance. Reports suggest
that he was given free rein to improvise,
which is fortunate as Gifford's script is
otherwise tired and overly reliant on a
standard formula (as Carla Hay puts it in
Culture Mix, the film 'panders to the worst
rom-com stereotypes'). There are better
Scottish rom-com films, including the same
year's **Falling for Figaro**.

Iorram (aka *Boat Song*) (2021) DOC

Directed by Alastair Cole; 98 minutes

A 'gentle and ruminative, if slightly placid'
(Peter Bradshaw, *The Guardian*) Gaelic
language documentary about fishing in
the Western Isles, which played at the GFF
in 2021 and has had screenings across
Scotland. *Iorram* provides recollections,
extending back to before World War II, and
contemporary voices, but the use of voice-
over without direct-to-camera interview,
and contemporary footage only, results
in uncertainty as to when a particular
description or recollection relates. Aidan
O'Rourke's score is a delight.

Nobody Has to Know (2021)   S+

Directed by Bouli Lanners
Screenplay by Bouli Lanners
Leading cast: Michelle Fairley (Millie); Bouli
  Lanners (Phil); Julian Glover (Angus); Andrew
  Still (Brian)
Colour, 99 minutes, UK

The Western Isles: Phil, a Belgian migrant,
works on a farm. He has a stroke and has
amnesia when he returns. Millie tells him
they are in a relationship. His memory
returns, and he realises Millie lied. Invited
to return home, Phil decides to stay with
Millie, but a second stroke kills him.

Nobody Has to Know is clearly set in the
Western Isles (although no specific location
is named in the film) and was shot on

383

Harris and Lewis (Frank van den Eden's cinematography is magnificent). As Allan Hunter put it in *Screen Daily*, this is 'a windswept, God-fearing community where life revolves around hard graft, Sunday worship and nights at the pub. People tend not to ask awkward questions'. Phil's brother puts it a little differently, describing it as 'the World's arse' (the English subtitling renders this as 'a shithole'). In *Nobody* we are in a remote community, physically and culturally distanced from the mainland. Phil is one step further removed in that he is an immigrant. Phil's brother says that Phil has made running away a habit. This then places *Nobody* amongst those many films in which Scotland, and above all its islands, is a place to escape to, providing a remoteness that few places in Europe can match.

At the heart of the film is a love story, in which the love flourishes only because of a lie (the French title, *L'Ombre d'un Mensonge*, might be translated as 'In a Lie's Shadow'). There is a difficulty – or at least a challenge – in the film's construction. I have no doubt that the audience is intended to find the film uplifting (certainly critics have). Its focus on love and sex in late middle age is very much to be welcomed; the relationship is rewarding for both; and Phil forgives Millie the lie because he had wanted the relationship all along (it was a 'good' lie). Yet Phil's consent to the sexual relationship was certainly not an informed one – however eager it was. This in turn takes us into the question of the relationship between memory and self, which the film fascinatingly teases out.

Michelle Fairley and Bouli Lanners

Critical response to Lanners' film was very positive. It won both he and Fairley Silver Bear awards at the 2021 Chicago International Film Festival. From the Toronto International Film Festival, Diana Sanchez described *Nobody* as 'a deeply endearing film that asks us to consider who we are and what we want regardless of the stories we tell – or are told'. That's a pretty good summation.

Prince of Muck (2021) DOC

Directed by Cindy Jansen; 77 minutes

Lawrence McEwen's family has owned the island of Muck since 1896, but at the time of filming the family is riven with tensions, and an ongoing commitment to Muck looks precarious. Throughout *Prince of Muck* Lawrence McEwen provides his own narration, direct to camera, as he goes about his daily life. Added depth is provided by extracts, read by Lawrence, from family diaries going back to 1964, and his reflections on the future as he ages. A clip from an earlier film, when he was in his prime, has him saying, 'we want evolution, not revolution'.

Lawrence remains reluctant to abandon the family's connection to the island, but family discussions reveal tensions, and his relationship with his son is strained. *Prince* deserved to receive more attention when it came out. The limited reviews are glowing – the *Daily Telegraph*'s Benji Wilson noted its 'Shakespearean depths' and 'elegiac brilliance'. *Prince* received its world premiere at the EIFF in 2021, at a time when the shadow of Covid-19 loomed large, with documentary audiences, which skew older, being reluctant to return to cinemas.

This is the second film in this book (see also *Scheme Birds*) in which a foreign documentary maker has cast a keen lens on Scotland.

The Road Dance (2021) S+

Directed by Richie Adams
Screenplay by Richie Adams
Leading cast: Hermione Corfield (Kirsty Macleod); Will Fletcher (Murdo MacAuley); Morven Christie (Mairi Macleod); Ali Fumiko Whitney (Annie Macleod); Mark Gatiss (Dr Maclean); Ian Pirie (Constable McRae)
Colour, 116 minutes, UK

Lewis, 1904: Kirsty is taught to swim by her father, who dies of cancer. 1916: Kirsty dreams of emigrating to America. She has a relationship with Murdo, a soldier. A road dance is held after which Kirsty is raped. She hides a pregnancy; the baby dies shortly after its birth. The concealed body is discovered, and the local constable investigates. A year later, Kirsty moves to America…

The Road Dance was shot entirely on Lewis. It is based on John MacKay's 2002 novel of the same name and directed by American Richie Adams. After winning the audience award at the EIFF in 2021, it received a limited UK release in May 2022. *The Road Dance* is at heart a conventional melodrama, albeit one with modern sensibilities – a young woman who is the victim of sexual assault survives and fulfils her dreams. As Cath Clarke put it in *The Guardian*, 'it's sentimental, though the way Kirsty is helped by women boiling with fury at the injustice does feel modern'. These modern themes are played out in a claustrophobic village community (from which Kirsty seeks to escape), at a time when different judgements might be made, and when the 'Great' War was shattering not only lives, but also social conventions. The mix is not entirely successful, and the film works best when the focus is on Kirsty and her aspirations, although there is effective poignancy in a scene in which the postman delivers a telegram notifying parents of their soldier-son's death.

Too much in *The Road Dance* is resolved too neatly. Kirsty's rapist (Mark Gatiss) is helpfully quick to remove himself from the scene once threatened with exposure. The village elder ('Old Peggy', played by Alison Peebles) acts as *Deus ex machina* when she instructs the constable to take no further action against Kirsty. Credibility is certainly stretched in the 'spurious' (Alistair Harkness, *The*

Scotsman), ending scene – a cynical viewer is likely to let out a cry of exasperation.

The strengths of *The Road Dance* are its cinematography, by Petra Korner, and the performance of Hermione Corfield, who is excellent (Wendy Ide in *The Observer*: 'keep an eye on this one, she'll go far').

Alice Krige is wasted in *She Will*

She Will (2021)   S+

Directed by Charlotte Colbert
Screenplay by Kitty Percy and Charlotte Colbert
Leading cast: Alice Krige (Veronica); Kota Eberhardt (Desi); Rupert Everett (Tirador); Malcolm McDowell (Hathbourne)
Colour, 95 minutes, UK

Veronica, a retired film star whose best-known film was shot when she was 13, recovers from a double mastectomy at a retreat in the Highlands with her carer, Desi. In a place where witches were once burnt to death, they both draw strength from the soil, and bond.

She Will (which legendary *Giallo* director Dario Argento liked so much that he came on board as an executive producer) is largely set and shot on the edge of the Cairngorms, around Loch Garten. According to Colbert, quoted by *Bloody Disgusting*'s Meagan Navarro, this location was significant: 'It's so, so, so beautiful. It's also where the last women to be burnt for witchcraft in [the UK] were from… It's always so stunning how people are afraid of witches and not the people who burned them. It's just completely crazy.' It

is, however, disappointing that after over 100 years of films being set in Scotland, the country remains the place where weird stuff happens. This persistent othering of Scotland, which refuses to go away, clearly irritates *The Scotsman*'s film critic, Alistair Harkness: 'the dramatically inert script and the use of a generic Scottish setting as an off-the-peg signifier of folkloric dread all leave a lot to be desired.'

She Will fuses folk-horror and toxic masculinity with #MeToo (in a way similar to that achieved by the superior film, *Men*, Alex Garland, 2022). By the time of its eventual UK release the film had garnered a Rotten Tomatoes rating of 86 per cent, although its approach was not to everyone's taste (see Jennifer Heaton in *Alternative Lens*: 'Oh no she won't!… it's a meandering and confusing horror film that teases cool concepts but is either too self-assured or too conceited to actually explore them'). More typical, however, is Navarro: '*She Will* eschews a conventional narrative and instead casts an atmospheric spell through tactile, dreamy visuals. It's less of a nightmare and more like a darkly magical dream'. An excellent cast, with Eberhardt particularly strong in her third film, is somewhat let down by an all-too-predictable story. There can be very little doubt, after the initial set-up, as to how *every* element of *She Will* is going to play out.

Angry Young Men (2022)   S+++

Directed by Paul Morris
Screenplay by Paul Morris
Leading cast: Paul Morris (Jimmy); Alexander
  Hamilton (Charlie Miller); Nathan Boland
  (Raymond McMurray)
Colour, 85 minutes, UK

'Mauchton': gangs battle for territory as the Bramble Boys take on newcomers The Campbell Group.

Angry Young Men, a no-budget independent film, received its world premiere at the GFF in 2022 – and played at the GFT again – before moving onto YouTube. Director (and writer, cinematographer, editor, and co-composer) Paul Morris said that the film cost less than £5,000 to make and was shot in Hamilton over a period of three years, some of it during the Covid-19 pandemic restrictions. As Amber Wilkinson wrote in *Screen Daily*, 'If, in the end, he has bitten off rather more than he can successfully chew, you still have to admire the ambition and commitment it took to bring something like this together with just £5,000 of filming gear and props'. Interviewed in the *Daily Record*, Morris said he had wanted to make films ever since leaving school, and *Angry Young Men* 'came about through my love of film and when I was younger

my friend and I used to shoot short movies using our phones.'

Filmed on a shoestring, reliant entirely on location shooting, and with an inexperienced cast (Morris noted the scheduling difficulties arising from working with some 70 actors, who weren't being paid), the legacy of Bill Forsyth is clear in *Angry Young Men*, but the film doesn't match *That Sinking Feeling*'s strong sense of place. In *The Skinny*, Rory Doherty noted the 'ensemble cast is game, and all bring a lot of singular Scottish weirdness to the erratic characters, but you never get the sense of a town beyond the gang members.' The film would benefit too from even tighter editing than that leading to the current 85-minute running time – there is an uneasy balance between comedy and drama, and although some scenes are excellent, others lag. At the time of writing, Morris was working on a script for a feature film and seeking financial backing.

Heading West: A Story About a Band Called Shooglenifty (2022)   DOC

Directed by Don Coutts; 86 minutes

Coutts (who also directed *American Cousins*) has made in *Heading West* a warm-hearted and compassionate film about the Scottish 'acid-croft' band Shooglenifty (which appears to operate as much as a family as a group of musicians), responding to the death of founder-member Angus R Grant in 2016 at the age of 49.

Heading West was planned while Grant was still alive, but became something quite different after his death. The film focuses on a Celtic Connections gig celebrating Grant's music, and later work in Galicia with Tanxugueiras, and in Rajasthan with traditional Indian musicians. Good use is made of found footage, although sources were limited. As is said in the film, long may Shooglenifty continue 'fighting the fight against the bland'. The film received its world premiere at the EIFF in 2022, and toured Scotland in February 2023.

The Hermit of Treig (2022) DOC

Directed by Lizzie MacKenzie; 79 minutes

Like *Two Years at Sea* and *Bogancloch*, *Hermit*'s focus is on the life of someone living off-grid in remote Scotland; in this case, Ken Smith, who has lived in isolation for 40 years. The film is warmer than *Two Years*. The relationship between director and subject is affectionate as Smith explains his life. When the film played at the GFF in 2022, Smith's attendance attracted significant interest.

My Old School (2022) DOC T42

Directed by Jono McLeod; 102 minutes

The hugely engaging (and slightly disconcerting) dramatised documentary *My Old School* fits into the category of 'you couldn't make this up' storytelling, in which truth really is stranger than fiction. The story of Brian MacKinnon, *aka* Brandon Lee, who in 1995 as a 30-year-old, returned to the school from which he had graduated, telling his classmates he was just 16, and very nearly pulled it off, is well known in Scotland, and attracted national media attention when the plan unravelled. McLeod, a pupil at Bearsden Academy and a classmate of Lee at the time, is perfectly positioned to bring this ridiculous story to the screen.

My Old School was shown at Sundance in 2022 and received its European premiere at the GFF in March 2022 – a screening which (based on knowing howls of laughter) clearly included a number of those who'd been at the Bearsden Academy at the time. Critics have been overwhelmingly positive. From Sundance, *Cineuropa*'s reviewer wrote: '*My Old School* is a unique account of identity, deceit and unhealthy ambition, even though these three aspects do not necessarily come from the same place, making it all the more complex and perplexing.' Laughter dominated both the screenings of the film I have been to, but there is within the jauntiness (emphasised by period-influenced animation, directed by Rory Lowe) a dark undercurrent. MacKinnon's words are at times chilling. He says, 'you can get round the impossible', claims to have the power to mesmerise, and dismisses his classmates, some of whom benefited from what they believed to be genuine friendship: 'to me they were just ciphers'.

MacKinnon/Lee is 'played' by Alan Cumming, although it is MacKinnon's words we hear. Having agreed to cooperate with McLeod he later refused to appear in front of the camera (leading to some speculation at the end as to why this might be). Interviewed in *The Guardian* on the film's release Cumming hit on the central fascination of the film: 'People pretend to be different things all the time, but as Scots we think of ourselves as canny. "You can't pull the wool over my eyes." So for that to happen here... that's why it was such a huge story.' The film dances through this quandary, with McLeod, whose voice is occasionally heard but who stays in the background, proving himself a skilful puppet master. He permits his interviewees to tell the story as they 'know' it, before peeling back the layers. We then get the joy of watching their reactions to the true – and even more bizarre – story. With hindsight of course it is clear that Lee was *not* a teenager; but who expects their 16-year-old awkward schoolmate to be a grown man in his 30s – even when he attracted the nickname '30-something'? Clearly this plays well in Glasgow, but the widespread 4- and 5-star reviews show the film has wider appeal. The story is so ridiculous, and the film so deftly handled, how could it not?

There are points at which a little more clarification would help, and MacKinnon/ Lee is perhaps let off the hook, particularly in relation to whether his mother/ grandmother was aware of, and actively took part in, the deception. It seems clear she was/did, but MacKinnon denies this, and is not pressed. McLeod stated at the Q&A following the GFF screening that it

was not his intention to make a 'takedown' of MacKinnon, but rather to tell the story of a bizarre event, at which he happened to be one of the witnesses. In this respect the film is wholly successful. McLeod was awarded 'Best Director Factual' for the film at the 2023 Scottish BAFTAS.

Stella (2022)   S+++

Directed by Jessica Fox
Screenplay by Jessica Fox
Leading cast: Oli Fyne (Stella); Gary Lewis (Lord Rig); Susan Vidler (Lady Rig); Louis Hall (Will)
Colour, 119 minutes, UK

In the late 1930s, Jewish-German Stella, an Oxford student, becomes a tutor working for Lord Rig in Galloway. He is a fascist sympathiser, eagerly anticipating a visit by Oswald Mosley, and Stella conceals her identity. She falls in love with Will.

Award-winning *Stella*, produced by the female-led Innerwell Media, was shown on the festival circuit and at selected cinemas in Scotland, before moving onto the STV player. Writer/director Jessica Fox, whose memoir *Three Things You Need to Know About Rockets* (2013) details her move from a high-pressured job at NASA to working in a second-hand bookshop in Wigtown (where part of the action of *Stella* is located), is the descendant of grandparents who survived the Holocaust. She had previously made two short films in the US, before completing this, her first feature film.

Parallels with the modern world in which displaced refugees struggle to find safety and acceptance are clear, and although *Stella* is a period drama, its sensibilities are thoroughly modern. It was this which attracted Edinburgh-based Oli Fyne to the role, telling *The Scotsman* 'the way that Stella was written, she breaks every archetype of what you would expect a young woman to be like at that time'. While the story has some punch, the restricted production values diminish the impact of *Stella* as a feature film. Shooting was on location, but there are very clear limitations in terms of cast size and set decoration; Galloway House, which serves as the Rig family home, is strangely bare, run-down and under-decorated. The script is occasionally clunky, its wish-fulfilment strains credulity, and the editing could have been more ruthless.

Consecration (2023) S+

Directed by Christopher Smith
Screenplay by Christopher Smith and Laurie Cook
Leading cast: Jena Malone (Grace); Danny Huston (Father Romero); Steffan Cennydd (Michael); Janet Suzman (Mother Superior)
Colour, 91 minutes, UK/US

Following the death of her brother, Michael, at the 'Mount Saviour Convent' on Skye, Grace attempts to find out what happened. Religious horror/mystery/nonsense follows...

The Wicker Man has much to answer for. Here we are, 50 years later, and *still* Scotland (its islands in particular) is the go-to destination for British weird, particularly religious/folk weird. *Consecration* is yet another horror film in which strange and sinister stuff (which could happen anywhere) happens in Scotland – this time on Skye. Speaking ahead of a GFF screening, Malone said of Skye, it 'has all the right elements of isolation, the really beautiful mountains, the cliffs and the bleak oceanside', to all of these undeniable attractions English director/writer Smith (responsible for the effective horror *Creep*, 2004) has added a Catholic convent occupied by members of an 'extreme sect' where secrets lurk. Malone has said she enjoyed her time in Scotland, probably far more than I enjoyed this by-the-numbers religious horror.

When *Consecration* screened as part of FrightFest at the 2023 GFF, I asked Smith about this persistent casting of Scotland as the place of all weirdness. His position was that the film needed a remote setting, and that Scotland, above all, offered 'a scale' which was unmatched in the UK. A Scottish viewer, however, is likely to struggle with the set-up: that there is a Catholic convent on Skye which has been there for centuries. Of course, Grace (the not-so-subtle name matters!), having driven up from London after being told of the death of her brother, arrives by ferry; the simpler option of taking the bridge would *not* flag 'remote' in quite the same way. There's a nice sequence of her driving across the island, and isolation is moderately established (even though the local police station seems accessible, modern, and professionally run – although there is some nonsense about having no jurisdiction over the convent on the ridiculous basis that it is Vatican territory). But nothing turns on this isolation, and there is no reason why St Albans, where the real convent building is and where much of the shoot took place (the crew was on Skye for a week), would not function equally well in carrying the plot – which does *not* depend on remoteness. A viewer who is not invested in representations of Scotland is more likely to struggle with the *entire* premise. By the end, suggested Owen Gleiberman in *Variety*, 'you may just feel like casting out the demon of sketchy pretentious sensationalist filmmaking'.

Girl (2023)

S++ T37

Directed by Adura Onashile
Screenplay by Adura Onashile
Leading cast: Déborah Lukumuena (Grace);
  Le'Shantey Bonsu (Ama); Liana Turner (Fiona)
Colour, 91 minutes, UK/US

Glasgow: Grace, a 26-year-old woman who has been granted asylum, is fiercely protective of her 11-year-old daughter, Ama, telling her they must trust no one. Grace struggles to adapt to her new life while Ama begins to make friends.

Having premiered at Sundance (a work-in-progress screening took place at the London Film Festival the previous November),

Le'Shantey Bonsu and the remarkable Déborah Lukumuena

Girl opened the GFF in 2023, playing in the city where it is set and was shot. Like Ben Sharrock's ***Limbo***, the film focuses on refugees, although Grace must contend not with the bureaucracy of the asylum process (she is working lawfully, so has navigated that minefield), but with bureaucracy and the development of the social skills required to function in any modern society. French actress Lukumuena (who won the César for *Divines*, Houda Benyamina, 2016) plays Grace as being simultaneously ferocious in her protection of Ama, and utterly broken by the horrors perpetrated on her in Africa (she 'functions predominantly in a mode of muted watchfulness and mounting unease, her physicality suggesting a woman with the weight of the world, and of her past, on her shoulders' – Jonathan Romney in *Screen Daily*).

The world created by Onashile, who had previously directed only one short film, *Expensive Shit* (2020), based on her own play, is constrained and closed – the only open vista is one which reaches across the city from a high Gorbals' window. Ama's gaze is constrained to the flats opposite her, which she watches through binoculars, permitting her to save lives, including that of Fiona who then befriends her, when a fire breaks out unseen by all but Ama. As Guy Lodge wrote in *Variety*, 'the wary, vulnerable mother and daughter [make] their world as small as possible — barely stretching beyond the front door of their shabby council apartment'. *Girl*'s visuals, driven by Tasha Back's cinematography, are strong, and while the drama occasionally lags, the central performances offer more than enough. Reviews were extremely positive: on its eventual release in November 2023, *Girl*'s Rotten Tomatoes 'score' stood at 95 per cent.

Kill (aka *Betrayal*) (2023) S++ T39

Directed by Rodger Griffiths
Screenplay by Rodger Griffiths and Robert Drummond
Leading cast: Brian Vernel (John); Daniel Portman (Henry); Calum Ross (Vince); Paul Higgins (Don); James Harkness (Miller); Joanne Thomson (Annie); Anita Vettesse (Kate)
Colour, 94 minutes, UK

In a remote Scottish forest, three brothers, Jonn, Henry and Vince, and their father, Don, are hunting. Following a well-laid plan, Don is shot and buried. The remaining 89 minutes explain the lead-up to the shooting, and its consequences.

Kill, a smart genre film, is one of the few entries in this book in which I have given the entire cast in the credits above – all seven characters are heavily involved, willingly or otherwise, in the maelstrom

The brothers have acted …

that surrounds the shooting. This is symptomatic of a film in which English director Griffiths, with his first feature, makes the most of a tight, well-structured script, and of limited resources. Shot on location in only 21 days, *Kill* serves as 'both a calling card for its cast and crew, and a fun exercise in plotting' (Fionnuala Halligan in *Screen Daily*).

Where *Calibre*, a film with which *Kill* has commonality (both on and behind the screen), draws from social inequalities and deprivations, *Kill* draws from domestic abuse and coercive control. Following the shooting, the brothers return to the family farmhouse, and open a bottle of their father's whisky. One says, 'he was saving this for a special occasion. D'you think we found one?' It's a good line, punctuating the tension, and serving as a pivot around which the film whips, plunging us into the past, explaining why Don has been shot. He was a brutal tyrant, emotionally and physically abusive to the entire family; the brothers' mother is dead, and action has been taken. From this point, *Kill* alternates between a present in which the consequences of the shooting, tensely and bloodily, play out, and a past which continues to deliver unexpected twists. Throughout, the legacy and impact of abuse, cascading through generations, is ever-present and an essential plot-driver.

After premiering at the EIFF in August 2024, *Kill* was acquired for distribution in the UK. Unfortunately, the generic title means the film gets lost in searches (on IMDb and Rotten Tomatoes it is listed as *Betrayal*).

Silent Roar (2023) S++

Directed by Johnny Barrington
Screenplay by Johnny Barrington
Leading cast: Louis McCartney (Dondo); Ella
Lily Highland (Sas); Fiona Bell (Norma); Mark
Lockyer (Paddy the Priest)
Colour, 90 minutes, UK

Lewis: Dondo, a young man taking his Advanced Highers, surfs. His father, Willy, has been missing for nearly a year, after 'fishing on the Sabbath'. Dondo struggles to accept his father's death, while his mother, Norma, has. At school, Dondo forms a loose friendship with Sas, whose mother is determined she move on to study medicine at Oxford. Under the influence of a new priest, Paddy, Dondo appears to embrace religion.

Silent Roar opened the cut-down 2023 EIFF, from which reviews were positive. *The Guardian*'s Peter Bradshaw liked the film: 'a whimsical coming of age drama with a touch of Bill Forsyth' (it's a very small touch, but Forsyth remains one of the lodestones in the assessment of Scottish films). In *Variety*, Catherine Bray was similarly won over: 'coming-of-age films [are] ten a penny... but the good ones make it count, and this... is one of the good ones'. *The Scotsman*'s Alistair Harkness was a notable dissenter from general praise. It's a pity then that the film has had so little exposure following its run on the festival circuit. It has no BBFC certificate but is a BBC production made with the support of Screen Scotland. I was able to watch the film at a screening at Glasgow's Arlington Baths, which was also attended by members of the crew.

Barrington wrote most of *Silent Roar* during the Covid lockdown and has explained how he spent significant time connecting with nature by watching sunsets on YouTube; he was also influenced by Éric Rohmer's *Le rayon vert* (*The Green Ray*, 1986 – which lingers on a sunset). *Silent Roar* was shot on film, Barrington saying 'I love the way film interacts with bright sunlight', introducing a tactility he believes digital lacks. The cinematography by Ruben Woodin Dechamps is terrific (underwater and surfing sequences were shot by Jon Frank).

The BBC's description of the film is: 'a contemporary adolescent tale of surfing, sex and Hellfire...', and such media comment as there has been has often focused on the surfing. But *Silent Roar* is no more about surfing than *The Old Man and the Sea* (Ernest Hemingway, 1952) is about fishing. The film is closer in theme to *For Those in Peril* (also incorporating magical realism) and while it is about coming to terms with loss and death it is also about a few too many things: coming-of-age and establishing identity; sexual curiosity (there is very little sex, and none between the leads); and faith, doubt and disbelief. Dondo appears to be reconciled to his father's death at the film's end, but the path he has followed is obscure, and the significance of four characters, including a black, female 'Swiss Jesus' (Chinenye Ezeudu), who come to him in dreams/visions/reveries, remains unclear.

What the film should do is help build the careers of its two Irish leads: McCartney is strong and possesses charm in abundance. Ella Lily Hyland, playing well below her years, is outstanding, and gets many of the stronger and funnier scenes, creating a slight imbalance pulling focus from Dondo; in late 2024 she made a big impact as an assassin in the TV series *Black Doves*. *Silent Roar* will presumably find its way onto the BBC and streaming options should open. It deserves better than to slip into obscurity.

The Skids: Revolution (2023) DOC

Directed by Colin Graham and Laura Graham; 76 minutes

A documentary tracing the story of The Skids, who enjoyed chart success in the 1980s, from the band's working-class roots in 'a culture soaked in alcohol' (to quote Jobson in the film) through to the later reunion. It's an interesting story of outsiders to the mainstream struggling to make an impact, and told with some verve.

The Strange Case of Dr Jekyll and Mr Hyde (2023)   S+++

Directed by Hope Dickson Leach
Screenplay by Vlad Butucea, Hope Dickson Leach and Robert Louis Stevenson
Leading cast: Henry Pettigrew (Dr Jekyll); Lorn Macdonald (Utterson); Alison Peebles (Poole); David Hayman (Sir Danvers Carew)
B&W, 84 minutes, UK

In Victorian Edinburgh, lawyer Gabriel Utterson, worried by the behaviour of his friend, Dr Jekyll, seeks to uncover the nature of Jekyll's relationship with the mysterious Mr Hyde, while himself plunging headfirst into moral degradation.

Having premiered at the 2023 cut-back, but extremely welcome, EIFF, and later screened at selected cinemas, *Dr Jekyll* moved onto Sky Arts. Stevenson's novella, a seminal work in the British Gothic literature of the late 19th century, was written in Bournemouth and set in Victorian London, which is where almost all the 20 or so screen adaptations place the action. Leach's version is unique in moving the setting to Edinburgh (Stevenson may have been, in part, inspired by a notorious Edinburgh episode in which a seemingly normal teacher – a friend of Stevenson – was sentenced to death after murdering his wife in 1878).

The film flowed from a collaboration between Hong Kong-born British director Leach and the National Theatre of Scotland, which first staged the hybrid production of which this film is an adaptation at Edinburgh's historic Leith Theatre, in early 2022, the audience watching a screened version of a live performance. At a GFT Q&A, lead actor Macdonald described the process as 'a very strange experience', and 'a proper adrenaline rush'. The footage broadcast during the three live performances was then edited into this film, with additional inserts expanding the vista away from the stage sets into a murky Edinburgh, ruled over by unscrupulous businessmen and corrupt councillors. As Leach has said in an introduction to the film, the city was at the time somewhere where 'enormous wealth was being generated, by using and exploiting others'. This is a masculine world, in which the only visible women are servants, and young girls are victims of violence.

The result feels more like a film than a recording of a theatrical performance, and Leach has said that she always 'came at this film first'. Where the theatrical origins are clear is in the text ('screenplay' does not feel like the right word to use here). While the feel of Victorian Edinburgh is strong, the gothic horror relies for the most part on the implicit, given the limitations of what could be achieved in a live performance (although there is one genuinely stomach-churning scene involving David Hayman and liquorice). An emphasis on the moral slide of Utterson – a very strong performance from Macdonald (also in *Beats*) – through the film gives weight and symmetry to the story, leading to an effective modern twist on a Scottish gothic classic.

To See Ourselves (2023)   DOC

Directed by Jane McAllister; 121 minutes

To See Ourselves tells one side of the 2014 Scottish independence referendum through the microcosm of the activism of Fraser McAllister, a campaigning councillor in Musselburgh devoted to the cause. Shot by his daughter, filmmaker Jane McAllister, the film is an affectionate portrait of her father, and a reflection on the difficulties of persuading sufficient Scots that 'better together' was a fallacy. With no pretence of neutral objectivity, the film wears its clear biases lightly, although it is likely to find more success with supporters of the 'Yes' option. That viewers will know 'the ending' adds a bittersweet element to the night of the vote, when Fraser's emotions are buffeted by the roller coaster of results. Although he has been consistently exasperated at the failures of the Yes campaign, he expresses anger only in the immediate aftermath: 'I feel let down. I feel kicked. I feel lied to', and 'people are stupid'. One suspects this is not a sentiment generally held by Fraser, whose warmth and humour enliven the film. The two-hour running time may deter some: the story could be told, and the argument made, more economically.

The film has been widely shown and is available to watch online.

True Sickness (2023) S+++

Directed by Alan Main
Screenplay by Alan Main and Cameron Blyth
Leading cast: Alan Main (the dreamer); David
  McKnight (Black Balaclava)
B&W, 72 minutes, UK

A young man runs through snow in a local park. Waking alone in his Coatbridge flat, he plunges into psychological trauma in which he is menaced by a man wearing a balaclava – was the dream a warning, and how much of what follows is objective reality?

Alan Main's no-budget *True Sickness*, a reflection on mental health and illness, received a world premiere screening (not counting screenings in Main's house) at the GFT in May 2023. The 23-year-old director, who was inspired to make films after watching Sergio Leone's masterpiece *Once Upon a Time in America* (1984) (which is to say, he has very good taste), sold his car to raise the money for this. After starting out as a short, *True Sickness* had morphed into a feature made by Main and three friends. Main targeted entry into the GFF, but the finished film was accepted neither for that, nor for any other festivals to which it was submitted. While it is perhaps regrettable that the GFF, with its extensive schedule, was unable to find the space for a local film, *True Sickness* would have been a hard sell. A lot is asked of the viewer: there's virtually no dialogue, few clear signposts, and it's 25 minutes before The Dreamer's first monologue sets things out with any clarity. Main has said *True Sickness* deals with 'challenging and provocative aspects of mental illness, which I thought would be an interesting story to write about', but the 'story' is hard to penetrate.

Main has made the film available online, and *True Sickness* is a perfect example of the possibility of making a truly independent film, and finding outlets for its dissemination, in the digital age. In April 2023, Main told *Lanarkshire Live* that he and his collaborators planned 'on making another film in the future so any further success with *True Sickness* can only support that ambition'. There are altogether far too many instances in this book of a single-film directorial career. He has told me he is working on a new film, but this may take some time to appear.

A Sudden Glimpse to Deeper Things (2024) DOC

Directed by Mark Cousins; 78 minutes

Receiving its premiere at the 2024 EIFF, Mark Cousins' *Sudden Glimpse*, narrated by his friend Tilda Swinton (the two collaborated on the closing segment of the portmanteau film *The New Ten Commandments*), focuses on the Scottish artist Wilhelmina Barns-Graham (1912–2004). Although strongly associated with the modernist St Ives school of artists, Barns-Graham was born and died in St Andrews. In 1949 she had something of an epiphany while overlooking the Grindelwald glacier in Switzerland, and it's this pivotal event which forms the locus of Cousins' deeply poetic exploration of her work. In *Dear Orson Wells and Other Essays* (2023) Cousins explains that his relationship with words is as vital as his relationship to images (something that becomes very clear if one both watches his epic 2011 documentary *The Story of Film: An Odyssey*, in my view the best survey of film history available, and reads the accompanying book *The Story of Film*). The 'intricate and fiercely intelligent' *Sudden Glimpse* (Wendy Ide, *The Observer*) might be better described as a filmic essay. And it is, for art lovers, an excellent one.

The Bench (2024)   S+++

Directed by Sean Wilkie
Screenplay by Sean Wilkie
Leading cast: Jennifer Byrne (Alex); Matt
    McClure (Aidan); Ilaria Nardini (Lauren); Sean
    Wilkie (Steve)
Colour, 75 minutes, UK

Summer 2007, Renfrewshire ('the Scottish wilderness'): Alex's car breaks down and she is assisted by a group of students. To thank them, she offers to let them stay with her in a cabin in the woods she has recently inherited from her grandmother. They discover a blood-drenched bench in the cellar...

The Bench received a very brief mention in the first edition of this book, in the appendix of films I believed to exist, but was unable to track down (see appendix 2 to this edition for an updated version). Thankfully, the problem here lay not in my lack of persistence, but in the fact that it took *17 years* for Sean Wilkie, a Glaswegian who has also directed *PondLife* (2006) (which sadly remains unavailable to watch), to complete the film, which only saw the projector's light in 2024. With extremely limited cinema exposure (a single screening in a Cineworld), and otherwise having a straight-to-streaming release, *The Bench* just makes it into this book.

On the film's eventual appearance Wilkie told the BBC that, in making this 'grisly slasher', he was inspired by some of his favourite genre films: the influential trifecta, *Halloween* (John Carpenter, 1978), *The Hills Have Eyes* (Wes Craven, 1977) and *The Texas Chainsaw Massacre* (Tobe Hooper, 1974), to which *The Bench* serves as an homage. The film's long gestation was explained by factors including 'badly misjudging the Scottish weather' (this from a Glaswegian!), and the perennial issue facing independent filmmakers – running out of money. But persistence has paid off, although one consequence was that some nifty editing was required to deal with continuity issues (such as actors' hairstyles radically changing over the 17-year period).

In a bold move, *The Bench* starts with the murders of Alex and Aidan (so this is not a plot spoiler), then loops back to the first meeting. We know from the outset that we're in slasher-land and the only real question is whether the ride is a good one. It is if you enjoy the influences cited by Wilkie: as *Film Threat*'s reviewer puts it, 'a sense of dread is palpable' and 'the kills, when they occur, are brutal and brought to life by some excellent effects'. What more do you need?

Billy & Molly: An Otter Love Story (2024) DOC T100

Directed by Charlie Hamilton-James; 77 minutes

A documentary exploring the relationship between Billy Mail, a middle-aged man on Shetland, and Molly, a young otter whom he cared for.

Susan Mail gets the first words in Billy: 'Let me tell you a story about a man, my man, Billy and how he was lost for a while, until beauty found him'. This gentle tone is maintained throughout an otterly delightful documentary which, at the time of writing, carried a 100 per cent critics' rating on Rotten Tomatoes, with a 96 per cent audience rating. In one sense, however, Susan's first introduction is misleading: the film is as much her story as it is Billy's.

Shetland – in the words of Susan, 'Britain's last outpost before the Arctic' – has never looked as good on film or TV as it does here. National Geographic documentary maker Hamilton-James has captured shots of stunning beauty, whether in the long light of summer, gentle autumn, or the harsh days of winter, including spectacular shots of the northern lights and the Up Helly Aa festival. Given the film, after securing multiple award nominations at festivals, and lashings of media attention in Scotland, made it onto

Disney+ one might expect an uptick in visitors to Shetland (where this book was conceived on the day my wife and I spent time otter-watching).

Damaged (2024) S++

Directed by Terry McDonough
Screenplay by Koji Steven Sakai, Gianni Capaldi and Paul Aniello
Leading cast: Samuel L Jackson (Den Lawson); Vincent Cassel (Walker Bravo); Gianni Capaldi (DCI Glen Boyd); Kate Dickie (Laura Kessler); John Hannah (Colin McGreggor)
Colour, 97 minutes, US/UK

Hunting a serial killer across continents, ageing Chicago detective Lawson teams up with Edinburgh police officers Boyd and Bravo.

One would hope that a film with a cast as strong as *Damaged*, set and shot in Scotland, would be good. Regrettably, the screenplay is poor and performances perfunctory: the result is *Damaged* by name and by nature.

Mogwai: If the Stars had a Sound (2024) DOC

Directed by Antony Crook; 92 minutes

We are told in *Mogwai* that John Peel, who grew to love the Glaswegian band, once said he thought it would be one only the weirdos would like, but in February

2021, roughly 25 years after the the band's formation, their tenth album, 'As the Love Continues', toppped the UK album charts. This is the fulcrum around which a formulaic, but well made, documentary revolves. With a mix of archive recording and concert footage, interviews, celebrity talking heads (Ian Rankin is the most insightful), and fan testimonials, *If the Stars had a Sound* will likely be loved by existing fans, but is unlikely to garner many new ones.

Harvest (2024)   S+

Directed by Athina Rachel Tsangari
Screenplay by Joslyn Barnes and Athina Rachel Tsangari
Leading cast: Caleb Landry Jones (Walter Thirsk); Harry Melling (Master Kent); Frank Dillane (Master Jordan); Arinzé Kene (Quill)
Colour, 131 minutes, UK/Germany/France/US/Greece

The Village, Scotland: the late 18th century (?). The village, in which life is lived moderately well, albeit with a shortage of men for labour, is threatened by a new owner intent on the profit to be made from wool.

The novel *Harvest*, by English author Jim Crace, was published in 2013, and tells the story of the impact of the enclosure of its common land on a remote English medieval village. In *Tsangari*'s film adaptation, shot largely on location in the Highlands, the village is somewhere in Scotland (the language used throughout leaves no room for doubt), two days' ride to the nearest market town. While Crace's novel showed the impact of policies which ran from the medieval period onwards, the relocation to Scotland places the focus more specifically on the Clearances. This is the reason I take a stab at the dating in the synopsis above, although the film gives none; what clues the film offers are certainly not consistent with a medieval setting. Perhaps only Scotland's subjugation to England and the industrial revolution caused as much permanent change in the fabric of the nation as the Clearances. Running for approximately a century from the 1750s onwards, they changed the pattern of land ownership and usage, displaced communities, and fuelled an international Scottish diaspora. *Harvest* is the only film covered in this book to tackle the subject.

Harvest is an immensely ambitious film, with outstanding cinematography by Sean Price-Williams, a long runtime, and a strong cast headed by the American Caleb Landry Jones (who struggles with the Scottish accent), with support from UK-based and international actors. Greek director Athina Rachel Tsangari is experienced (her first feature, *The Slow Business of Going*, was made in 2000; her 2015 film *Chevalier* won awards aplenty), and the subject remains pregnant with significance. Yet the film does not work as it should. The main beats of the novel are preserved, save for the change in setting, but there is something oddly askew in the mix. Perhaps it is that Tsangari's approach gives rise to tropes which are too redolent of folk-horror (strangers to the village are blamed for a fire and set in the stocks; a female stranger has her hair shorn and is outcast), such that we are waiting for a shoe to drop that never falls. Reviewing the film after its screening at the Venice Film Festival, Peter Bradshaw alluded to this: 'it's a tiresome folk non-horror'.

Perhaps there is a structural reason for the film's failure. Thirsk, who serves as our narrator, is distanced from the villagers early on. While the time he spends with Quill, who draws the maps facilitating the enclosure of common lands, makes clear the wider picture, the villagers themselves become passive and unknown ciphers (in *Variety* Guy Lodge noted they 'are compelling as a mass but never fully articulated as individuals'). They barely respond to the local manager's vision of flocks of sheep replacing food crops; while they resist abuses carried out by retainers of the true owner of the land, they are bought off easily with a casual promise. When they leave the village, it is with barely a whimper (see Peter Bradshaw again, 'when the story builds to a melodramatic confrontation, a hideous display of patriarchy, cruelty and sexual violence, everyone seems bored and half asleep'). It is a pity that the one film to deal with such a vital part of Scottish history is, ultimately, anodyne and dull.

On Falling (2024) S+ T100

Directed by Laura Carreira
Screenplay by Laura Carreira
Leading cast: Joana Santos (Aurora)
Colour, 104 minutes, UK/Portugal

Aurora, a Portuguese migrant, works as a picker in a warehouse. The work is monotonous and dull, and Aurora just about gets by, but is isolated and lonely.

By the time Portuguese-born, Edinburgh-based director Laura Carreira's *On Falling* received its Scottish premiere at the GFF in March 2025, it had won awards at the London Film Festival (the Sutherland Award in the Best First Feature category) and the Spanish San Sebastián International Film Festival. Although it is set and shot in Scotland (although it would take a very eagle-eyed viewer to pin a more specific location to *On Falling*) it is not surprising that the film has had an international reach. While Aurora works at a warehouse (unbranded) as a picker in a Scottish city (unnamed), her plight is not wedded to a locale, but rather to a class of itinerant workers in places far from home, searching and hoping for something better. Laura's flatmates, with whom interaction is limited, come from (at least) Ukraine, Poland and Romania; no time frame is specified for *On Falling*, but it is surely set pre-Brexit. Paula's interactions with Scots are limited: in shops, at a job interview, and with managers at the warehouse.

While the Scottish location is not effaced, what matters most here is the economic precarity of Laura, her flatmates, and her fellow pickers: serving the local economy and its inhabitants, but shoved to the sidelines. Laura herself is a blank page but, thanks in part to the precision with which Santos plays her, she is a person entire to herself, even though we know virtually nothing about her, beyond her nationality, her job and her living circumstances. Asked at an interview to say something about *herself*, Laura is left speechless. When she does respond, it is with lies: she claims to have enjoyed a holiday in the Bahamas, when we know that this destination was offered up simply because she had earlier picked a guidebook to the country as part of her day's drudgery. It is not that Laura is an inveterate fabulist, but rather that the grind of work and poverty have left her hollowed out; in her world, the question 'what do you like to do outside work?' simply has no resonance. We do not know why Laura has moved to Scotland; what, if any, obligations remain in Portugal, or what her long term aspirations are; we don't even know her age or education, atlhough we can make a decent guess at the former based on her physical appearance. We do know that her economic life is *extremely* precarious, and that every decision comes at a cost: the breaking of her mobile phone (which is the gateway to most of her interaction with the world) comes with a £99 repair bill which pushes her over the edge: her response is to starve herself and steal food from her flatmates.

The warehouse work itself is shown with a cold objectivity. This is an environment in which workers are valued only for their shift-by-shift economic utility. One day Laura is praised for being one of the fastest pickers (her reward is to be offered one of a selection of cheap chocolate bars); on another she is interrupted early on by a manager asking why her work rate has fallen, and instructed to pick up the pace. A school-group shown around the warehouse is told that items of the same nature are deliberately not placed together: 'it's kind of like a treasure hunt: it keeps them [the pickers] on their toes, makes the day more interesting' – the arrangement of this scene places Laura in the position of an animal being watched in a zoo. One of Laura's workmates tells her the highlight of his day came when he 'swapped a book for a dildo'. At a superficial level, these oppressive economic outcomes are no one person's fault: they are simply the result of the way modern economies are organised. But *On Falling* forces us to challenge that lazy shibboleth. As Guy Lodge wrote in *Variety*, *On Falling* 'turns warehouse-picking from an ignorable abstract process into a human routine of vivid, slowly erosive despair'. Given a random drug test, Laura and her colleagues are told by the woman administering the process 'this has got nothing to do with me. I'm only doing my job' – surely one of the most depressing phrases in the English language, the use of which is only exceptionally rarely a sign of virtue or positivity.

Other films have trod similar territory. It is a testimony to the strength of *On Falling* that it merits comparison with the

Oscar-winning *Nomadland* (Chloé Zhao, 2020). In the Scottish context, the 2014 documentary *En tierra extraña*, would make a very good double bill with *On Falling*.

The Outrun (2024)   S+ T13

Directed by Nora Fingscheidt
Screenplay by Nora Fingscheidt, Amy Liptrot and Daisy Lewis
Leading cast: Saoirse Ronan (Rona); Paapa Essiedu (Daynin); Saskia Reeves (Annie); Stephen Dillane (Andrew)
Colour, 118 minutes, UK/Germany

[Chronological order] Rona grows up on an Orcadian farm on a piece of land known as 'the outrun'; her father is bipolar and her mother seeks solace in her Christianity. Rona moves to London to pursue a PhD in biology. She is an alcoholic, losing control of her life. After completing a zero-tolerance rehab programme Rona returns to Orkney where she is able to rebuild her life.

A few months before the release of *The Outrun* I overheard a conversation between four young Scottish women on a late evening train from Edinburgh to Glasgow; one of them, at least, was a university student. They discussed a mutual friend from Orkney, but were confused as to where that was. The best one of them could come up with was, pointing at the carriage ceiling, 'Isn't it up, like way up?'. I confess that, having

been to Orkney a fair few times, I simply assumed that every Scot knew where the archipelago was. If any of those young ladies get to see *The Outrun*, they will be given a wee geography lesson. After she moves out for some months to Papay (the locals' name for Papa Westray), Rona explains in voice-over: 'Britain is an island off Europe; Orkney is an island off Britain; Westray is an island off Orkney; Papay is an island off Westray'. You couldn't get much more remote...

As German director Nora Fingsheidt, who hadn't been to Orkney before preparing for the film, has said, 'the islands are a character', and Orkney, shown in all its widescreen beauty, is a co-star of *The Outrun*. The vistas here are more expansive than they are in *Venus Peter*, although the relationship of islanders to the sea is there in both films, as it is too in *Blue Black Permanent*, both also set and shot (at least in part) in Orkney. This was something forgotten on the popular film podcast 'Kermode and Mayo' when it was suggested *The Outrun* was the first film to be shot on Orkney (a correction was made in the following episode). Orkney will not win awards for its appearance, but its co-star Saoirse Ronan, who received four Oscar nominations by the age of 24, received her first Best Actress award for the film in early November 2024 at the Evolution Mallorca International Film Festival, and later won the London Critics' Film Circle Award for Best British or Irish Actor (this was given for the combination of her performances in *The Outrun* and *Blitz*,

Award-winning Saoirse Ronan in *The Outrun*

Steve McQueen, 2024), and the Irish Film and Television Award for Best Actress (she also won the Best Supporting Actress award for *Blitz* at the same ceremony). Ronan dominates the film, based on Amy Liptrot's award-winning memoir of the same name published in 2016. Liptrot (who makes a fleeting appearance in the film) is co-credited with both the 'screenstory' and the screenplay for the film, much of which is grounded firmly in reality.

The Outrun is clear as to the destructive impact of alcoholism, a topic which Ronan has said she has 'been very familiar with most of my life', and was something she wanted to explore, but does not wallow in it. A non-linear structure emphasises the causes and impact of Rona's behaviour, and breaks things up so we swing between addiction and recovery,

self-destruction and healing. A particularly strong scene occurs when, in rehab, Rona says, of alcohol, 'I miss it; I miss how good it makes me feel'; while Fingsheidt's direction has the dialogue playing over earlier behaviour shocking in its self-destruction and injury.

Arguably the weather is the film's third star, particularly the wind ('our most defining weather' Rona says at one point). The wind that drives across Papay during Rona's stay is a cleansing force. Following a chillingly tragic relapse on her father's farm while his depression leaves him unresponsive, Rona moves away from the family pressures to the community of 60 on Papay. Immersing herself in the landscape and the sea (the latter literally), she stays sober, and refinds enthusiasm for research. In rehab in London she said 'I can't be happy sober', but there are at least some moments of joy for Rona on Papay and (even if one does not know Liptrot's story), there is hope at the film's end.

The Orcadian shooting took place in four stages, timed to coincide with natural events, including lambing (a skill Ronan had to learn, leaving her 'completely terrified'; she told the BBC it was 'one of the biggest acting challenges I've ever faced'), bird nesting, and for the seals, which play a prominent role in the film's mythology. For a Papa Westray festival the director simply turned things over to the islanders, who 'all came together, friends and family, from other islands too. They danced and the local band played and we became more like a documentary unit to film it'.

At the time of writing, *The Outrun* was smashing box office records in Kirkwall's Phoenix Cinema which scheduled nearly 40 screenings. Critically the film has been a success, with Ronan's performance rightly lauded.

Silent Men (2024)   DOC

Directed by Duncan Cowles; 88 minutes

How hard is it to say 'I love you'? For some men, as award-winning Scottish documentarian Cowles shows, it is extremely hard. Towards the beginning of *Silent Men*, Cowles says, 'I'm meant to be making a film about men and how we struggle emotionally', the voice-over puncturing a cinematically charming attempt at prevarication. Cowles spends

a lot of the film prevaricating, but this is largely the point. How is it, Cowles asks, that he can feel love for his friends and family, but struggle to express that. The film is described often as a 'road trip', but really the trip here is a personal voyage, assisted in part by a small number of other men (one a friend of Cowles), his family, and his then girlfriend (now wife).

The remarkable thing about Cowles (and *Silent Men*) is that someone who is so bad at expressing their feelings in person can so eloquently express them through film. As Cowles says, while talking to his friend Ainslee, he had the fear that making the film would serve an excuse for *not* expressing his love to his family and girlfriend in person. Towards the end of the film he says 'filming is my way of expressing and dealing with things'. His use of the medium is charming, skilled, and effective. In the screening I attended there was, nowtihstanding the difficult subject matter (a key interviewee failed in a suicide attempt during the four-year process of making the film), plenty of laughter alongside the reflection. From me, and I suspect I was not alone, there was also a tear or two.

Covering some of the same ground as *The Party's Just Beginning* and *Connect*, in response to the same harsh statistics, but with a more personal and more authentic punch, *Silent Men* is one of the better documentaries covered in this book. After a premiere at the Sheffield International Documentary Festival, where it won a special mention in the first feature awards, *Silent Men* has been widely screened, and has been used to promote the brilliant work of Andy's Man Club generally, and in Scotland the Scottish Men's Sheds Association.

Since Yesterday: The Untold Story of Scotland's Girl Bands (2024) DOC T23

Directed by Blair Young and Carla J Easton; 94 minutes

There is a plenitude of Scottish documentaries about music: *Since Yesterday* is the best of them. Blair Young and Carla J Easton (the latter of TeenCanteen and The Vaselines amongst others) have produced a film which is both a superb run-through of their subject matter, and a manifesto. Don't let the use of that word put you off; any criticisms of the way the music industry works are entirely justified and in need of addressing. Easton also provides and wrote the narration.

When I watch a film for the first time for this book I take notes, which normally run to a couple of pages; for *Since Yesterday*, scribbling in the darkened screen 3 at the GFT, my notes ran to just over nine pages, and recommendation emails were later pinged out to friends. I count myself as being moderately music literate, and at 60+ years old, have been around for all of the bands covered in the film, but was astonished at what I *did not* know. I was even more surprised that musically literate Scottish friends – including one who was in a real band, with a record and everything

– knew of so few of the artists referenced in *Since Yesterday*.

Since Yesterday chronologically starts with The McKinlay Sisters, hailing from Edinburgh, who opened for the Rolling Stones at the revamped Wembley Arena in 1964, and in the process became the first girl band to play Wembley. They were the first Scottish girl band to break into the charts, were signed to Columbia, but dropped by the label in 1965 after their single 'Give Him My Love' failed to chart. As Easton's narration puts it, they were 'the first girl band from Scotland [and are] forgotten today'.

Using multiple interviews and original footage (in some cases only very limited material is available), *Since Yesterday* takes us from The McKinlay Sisters to The Hedrons, Pink Kross, Sally Skull and Melody Dog, with plenty in between. These are bands which knew how to play, were successful on the vibrant Scottish music scene, and in some cases managed the step up from a small independent label to one of the majors, and (in the case of Strawberry Switchblade) to international chart success and touring. Yet until The Hedrons reformed and released a second album in 2023, none released more than one album. Time and again the story is of vibrant creativity but no resources or money in the independent sector, versus control, direction and, in some cases, still only a little money for the majors. As one of the members of Strawberry Switchblade (the only Scottish girl band to break into the UK top 30) puts it, 'all this electric shit's been forced on us'; the band split up under the pressures imposed on them by their label.

Male voices are almost entirely absent from *Since Yesterday*, short clips from radio and TV shows aside (John Peel is enthusiastically supportive; Jools Holland interested; Frank Bough patronisingly dismissive) and that is how it should be. At the film's start, Easton discusses being asked the question 'what do you want to be?' as a child. The film's argument is that without visible role models ('we don't normalise women making music together'), it's hard for a girl to say 'I want to make music'. Again and again we are told of sexism and sexist behaviour directed at the musicians, ranging from outright

assault and career-ending discrimination, to patronising dismissiveness, and of a dominant narrative from which the successes of girl bands are largely omitted. *Since Yesterday* goes at least some way to redressing the imbalance. By itself it cannot of course change the industry, but in what is a coda to the main story, we hear from Scottish activists and collectives seeking to make effective change.

The film is likely to have you searching for new music to listen to, although as Easton makes clear, finding the material can be a challenge; thankfully, for those with access to Spotify, this has been simplified.

Appendix 1

The 100 best and the 10 worst

IT IS WITH slight reluctance that I include these two lists. 'Best' and 'worst' imply some objective criteria at play – and here I am ranking artistic output, not 100 metre sprinters. Clearly there can be *some* objectivity. Objectively, *L'Illusionniste* is a better film than *Sir Billi*: the animation is more accomplished; the script coherent. Yet there will be somewhere a little boy whose favourite film is *Sir Billi*, and who am I to say he's wrong (it's OK – he'll grow out of it). But above a certain level of incompetence, subjective criteria take over. In 2022, *S&S* published its ten-year list of 'the greatest films of all time', as selected by filmmakers and critics. *Jeanne Dielman* (Chantal Akerman, 1975) topped the list; the 50th slot was shared by *The Piano* (Jane Campion, 1993) and *The 400 Blows* (François Truffaut, 1959). I've seen all three films and could make an argument for the position of each, but I could probably justify any random rearrangement of the list. My favourite film, *Blade Runner* (Ridley Scott, 1982) came in at number 54 – I could certainly make a case for it to be ranked in the top five. The lists below are therefore purely personal. On a different day I am sure I would rearrange, at least in part, the top 50. I am moderately content that if you were to watch the entire top 100 you'd have completed a pretty good survey of Scottish cinema.

The bottom ten are arranged from worst to less awful (ie, the worst film in this book – one of the worst films I have ever seen – sits at 1). I take the view that in judging a film to be awful, some account must be taken of its aspirations (this is why *Star Wars: Episode 1 – The Phantom Menace*, George Lucas, 1999, may reasonably be classed as one of the worst films ever made). Had, for example, *The Silent Storm* been made with no pretension (although I am not sure that is possible), and with a cast of unknowns, it might not have merited its fourth worst place on the list below. There are micro-budget films in this book which are, all things being equal, worse than it, but all things are *not* equal.

The best 100 (1 – 50)

1. *I Know Where I'm Going*
2. *The Bill Douglas Childhood Trilogy*
3. *Trainspotting* and *T2: Trainspotting*
4. *Under the Skin*
5. *The Wicker Man*
6. *Red Road*
7. *Ratcatcher*
8. *The Prime of Miss Jean Brodie*
9. *Breaking the Waves*
10. *Gregory's Girl*
11. *La Mort en Direct*
12. *Young Adam*
13. *The Outrun*
14. *The Ballad of Tam Lin*
15. *The 39 Steps* (1935)
16. *That Sinking Feeling*
17. *The Ghost Goes West*
18. *The Angels' Share*
19. *Sunset Song*
20. *Limbo*
21. *Ae Fond Kiss*
22. *Orphans*
23. *Since Yesterday: The Untold Story of Scotland's Girl Bands*
24. *Scheme Birds*
25. *L'Illusionniste*
26. *The Body Snatcher*
27. *Seachd: The Inaccessible Pinnacle*
28. *Dog Soldiers*
29. *Calibre*
30. *Beats*
31. *Small Faces*
32. *Filth*
33. *The Spy in Black*
34. *Tunes of Glory*
35. *Whisky Galore!*
36. *Devil Girl from Mars*
37. *Girl*
38. *Macbeth* (1971)
39. *Kill*
40. *Shell*
41. *The Legend of Barney Thomson*
42. *My Old School*
43. *Silent Scream*
44. *Sunshine on Leith*
45. *Mary, Queen of Scots* (1971)
46. *The Edge of the World*
47. *Kidnapped* (1917)
48. *On Approval*
49. *Macbeth* (2015)
50. *The Party's Just Beginning*

51 – 100 (alphabetical order)

16 Years of Alcohol
A Spanking in Paradise
American Cousins
The Amorous Prawn
Anna and the Apocalypse
Another Time, Another Place
Big Slick, The
Billy & Molly: An Otter Love Story
Blue Black Permanent
Brave
Country Dance
Dear Frankie
Donkeys
Flesh and the Fiend, The
For Those in Peril
GamerZ
Get Duked!
Greyfriars Bobby: The True Story of a Dog (1961)
Isolani
Late Night Shopping
Laxdale Hall

Let us Prey
Local Hero
Long Shot
Lord of Tears
Maggie, The
McKenzie Break, The
Morvern Callar
My Name is Joe
Neds
On Falling
One Day Removals
Outcast
Outlaw King
Private Life of Sherlock Holme, The
Restless Natives
Riptide
Rob Roy (1995)
Run
Said O'Reilly to McNab
Slab Boys, The
The Slayers
Sweet Sixteen
Tommy's Honour
Urban Ghost Story
Venus Peter
What We Did on Our Holiday
Wilbur (Wants to Kill Himself)
Winter Guest, The
You're Only Young Twice

The worst 10

1. *Kids Against the Sorcerers*
2. *Sir Billi*
3. *Scottish Mussel*
4. *The Silent Storm*
5. *Gregory's Two Girls*
6. *The Match*
7. *Cycle*
8. *The Brothers* (although this might, just possibly, be so bad it's good)
9. *Nessie, das verrückteste Monster der Welt*
10. *Not Another Happy Ending*

Appendix 2

Potentially Scottish films unavailable at time of writing

The following films would appear to be Scottish within the definition I have consistently adopted, but I have not been able to obtain access to a copy at the time of writing. Given I have not watched these, my identification of them as 'Scottish' remains speculative. This list is up to date as of 30 June 2025; films which I know to be in the pipeline or scheduled for release later in 2025 and onwards are not included here.

A Woman's Triumph (1914) J Searle Dawley

Peggy (1916) Charles Giblin, Thomas H Ince

Bonnie Mary (1918) AV Bramble

Kilties Three (1918) Maurice Sandground

Patriotism (1918) Raymond B West

The Fair Maid of Perth (1923) Edwin Greenwood

Little Miss Nobody (1923) Wilfred Noy

The Loves of Mary, Queen of Scots (1923) Denison Clift

The Cohens and the Kellys in Scotland (1930) William James Craft

Give me the Stars (1945) Maclean Rogers

The Priest and the Pirate (1994) Hugh Farrell

Daybreak (2000) Bernard Rudden

Just Around the Corner (2002) Uisdean Murray

PondLife (2006) Sean Wilkie

An Act of Terror (2009) Shahid Nadeem

The Clan (2009) Lee Hutcheon

The Dungeon Moor Killings (2009) Jim Hickey

The Hope Within (2009) Graeme Noble

Kirk (2009) Michael J Ferns

Ouija Board (2009) Matt Stone

Wasted (2009) Stuart Davids

In Search of La Che (2011) Mark D Ferguson

Minds of Glass (2011) Ryan Hendrick

Revenge (2011) Bill Little

Daddy Issues (2012) Benny Brice

A Mug's Game (2012) Joe McArdle

My Brother's Keeper (2012) Lee Hutcheon

Pub Crawl (2012) Ian Gueden

TimeLock (2013) David Griffith

The House of Him (2014) Rab Florence

Nowhere (2014) Tez Palmer

What's the Score (2014) Justin Smith

The Dark Mile (2017) Gary Love

It's Complicated (2017) Torkjell Stromme

The Confessions of Aleister Crowley (2020) Nick Faust

The Brexit Tree (2021) Jan Martinec and Clemens Wilhelm

Choose Irvine (2023) Ian Jefferies

Kim Carnie Out Loud (2024) Maureen MacLeod

Image Credits

All images reproduced in this book are in accordance with the terms of s 30 of the Copyright, Designs and Patents Act 1988 in the context of review and criticism. All practical efforts have been made to acknowledge copyright holders. Any omissions or errors will be rectified, if notified to the publisher, in future editions of this book.

P10 Moviestore Collection Ltd/Alamy stock photo
P20 No credit available
P23 Moviestore Collection Ltd/Alamy stock photo
P24 Universal Images Group North America LLC/Alamy stock photo
P25 Everett Collection Inc/Alamy stock photo
P26 No credit available
P27 Entertainment Pictures/Alamy stock photo
P30 Cinematic Collection/Alamy stock photo
P31 Alamy stock photo
P35 United Archives GmbH/Alamy stock photo
P36 Pictorial Press Ltd/Alamy stock photo
P37 United Archives GmbH/Alamy stock photo
P40 Photo 12/Alamy stock photo
P43 Alamy stock photo
P45 Cinematic Collection/Alamy stock photo
P46 Pictorial Press Ltd/Alamy stock photo
P48 Moviestore Collection Ltd/Alamy stock photo
P50 Allstar Picture Library Ltd/Alamy stock photo
P51 Associated Press/Alamy photo
P53 Lifestyle Pictures/Alamy stock photo
P56 Masheter Movie Archive/Alamy stock photo
P61 Alamy stock photo
P63 Moviestore Collection Ltd/Alamy stock photo
P68 Everett Collection Inc/Alamy stock photo
P70 Shawshots/Alamy stock photo
P72 Cinematic/Alamy stock photo
P77 Mary Evans/Studiocanal Films Ltd/Alamy stock photo

P79 United Archives GMbH/Alamy stock photo
P80 Allstar Picture Library/Alamy stock photo
P81 TCP/Prod.DB/Alamy stock photo
P83 DMC Film/Cinematic/Alamy stock photo
P85 Disney/Allstar Picture Library/Alamy stock photo
P89 Ealing Studios/Sam Novak/Alamy stock photo
P91 Everett Collection Inc/Alamy stock photo
P95 Entertainment Pictures/Alamy stock photo
P97 Moviestore Collection Ltd/Alamy stock photo
P101 Everett Collection Inc/Alamy stock photo
P102 Masheter Movie Archive/Alamy stock photo
P103 Pictorial Press Ltd/Alamy stock photo
P106 No credit available
P108 Mary Evans/Studiocanal Films Ltd/Alamy stock photo
P112 Alamy stock photo
P115 British Lion Film Corp/Cinematic/Alamy stock photo
P117 United Artists/Cinematic/Alamy stock photo
P121 A7A Collection/Alamy stock photo
P122 Disney/Moviestore Collection Ltd/Alamy stock photo
P127 20th Century Fox/Landmark Media/Alamy stock photo
P130 No credit available
P133 British Film Institute/Photo 12/Alamy stock photo
P136 No credit available
P137 Rank Film Distributors/Cinematic/Alamy stock photo

P138 BFA/Alamy stock photo

P139 BFA/British Lion Film Corporation/Alamy stock photo

P145 Everett Collection Inc/Alamy stock photo

P146 RetroAd Archives/Alamy stock photo

P150 United Archives GmbH/Alamy stock photo

P153 No credit available

P154 Everett Collection Inc/Alamy stock photo

P156 United Archives GmbH/Alamy stock photo

P159 Moviestore Collection Ltd/Alamy stock photo

P163 MGM Studiocanal/Mary Evans/Alamy stock photo

P164 Columbia/Cannon/Waner/Alamy stock photo

P165 Columbia/Cannon/Warner/Alamy stock photo

P169 Photo 12/Alamy stock photo

P175 Pictorial Press Ltd/Alamy stock photo

P176 BFA/Paramount Pictures/Alamy stock photo

P177 ScreenProd/Photononstop/Alamy stock photo

P179 colaimages/Alamy stock photo

P181 Moviestore Collection Ltd/Alamy stock photo

P184 Pictorial Press Ltd/Alamy stock photo

P186 Channel Four Films/Cinematic/Alamy stock photo

P187 Channel Four Films/FlixPix/Alamy stock photo

P188 Pictorial Press Ltd/Alamy stock photo

P191 Moviestore Collection Ltd/Alamy stock photo

P196 BBC/AJ Pics/Alamy stock photo

P197 Channel Four Film/Maximum Film/Alamy stock photo

P201 Entertainment One/AJ Pics/Alamy stock photo

P206 Moviestore Collection Ltd/Alamy stock photo

P210 Moviestore Collection Ltd/Alamy stock photo

P213 DNA Films/Cinematic Collection/Alamy stock photo

P225 FilmFour/Ideal World Productions

P227 TCD/Prod.DB/Alamy stock photo

P228 Rogue Pictures/Intrepid Pictures/Crystal Sky Pictures

P230 Scottish Screen/Cinematic Collection/Alamy stock photo

P234 Moviestore Collection Ltd/Alamy stock photo

P240 KPA Publicity Stills/United Archives GmbH/Alamy stock photo

P242 Hanway Films/Cinematic Collection/Alamy stock photo

P243 Hanway Films/Cinematic Collection/Alamy stock photo

P245 Visual Icon/Miramax/Album/Alamy stock photo

P251 Album/Alamy stock photo

P253 Entertainment Pictures/Alamy stock photo

P254 Canal+/AJ Pics/Alamy stock photo

P259 Holly Horner/BBC Films/Cinematic Collection/Alamy stock photo

P263 Dreamachine

P269 Infinity Features Entertainment/The Mob Film Company/Alliance

P276 Pathé/Cinematic Collection/Alamy stock photo

P281 Pathé

P288 Graham Hughes

P291 Écosse Films/Cinematic Collection/Alamy stock photo

P294 Neil Davidson/Zentropa Entertainments/AJ Pics/Alamy stock photo

P298 Hex Media

P305 Disney/Cinematic/Alamy stock photo

P306 TVP Film and Multimedia

P307 BFI/Creative Scotland

P312 BBC/BFI/Bard Entertainments/Barry Crerar

P319 Synchronicity Films/British Film Company

P322 Entertainment Film Distributors/Cinematic Collection/Alamy stock photo

P323 Film4/Cinematic Collection/Alamy stock photo

P328 Fantastic Films

P331 Alastair Caplin/Neon Films

P333 BBC/Moviestore Collection Ltd/Alamy stock photo

P338 Icon Film Distribution/Cinematic Collection/Alamy stock photo

Acknowledgements

I AM EXTREMELY grateful to Gavin MacDougall of Luath Press who asked if I would be interested in preparing this edition for Luath. Working with his colleagues at Luath has been a pleasure. I thank all filmmakers who have responded to questions from me, or who have generously given me access to their films. I'm grateful to the staff at the BFI Mediatheque in London and the Scottish National Library, Moving Image Archive who facilitated viewings of otherwise impossible-to-watch films. I greatly appreciate the emails I have received from readers of the first version of this book, particularly those suggesting titles for inclusion, in which respect Stephen Souter above all has been immensely helpful (he maintains a brilliantly comprehensive list of Scottish films on Letterboxd, albeit with different inclusion criteria to this book). James Chalmers has, throughout this project, been indispensable; my wife has offered occasional encouragement. Other friends who should be thanked know who they are.

Mark Furse
markfursescottishfilm@gmail.com

Index

Luath Press Limited

committed to publishing well written books worth reading

LUATH PRESS takes its name from Robert Burns, whose little collie Luath (*Gael.*, swift or nimble) tripped up Jean Armour at a wedding and gave him the chance to speak to the woman who was to be his wife and the abiding love of his life. Burns called one of the 'Twa Dogs' Luath after Cuchullin's hunting dog in Ossian's *Fingal*. Luath Press was established in 1981 in the heart of Burns country, and is now based a few steps up the road from Burns' first lodgings on Edinburgh's Royal Mile. Luath offers you distinctive writing with a hint of unexpected pleasures.

Most bookshops in the UK, the US, Canada, Australia, New Zealand and parts of Europe, either carry our books in stock or can order them for you. To order direct from us, please send a £sterling cheque, postal order, international money order or your credit card details (number, address of cardholder and expiry date) to us at the address below. Please add post and packing as follows: UK – £1.00 per delivery address; overseas surface mail – £2.50 per delivery address; overseas airmail – £3.50 for the first book to each delivery address, plus £1.00 for each additional book by airmail to the same address. If your order is a gift, we will happily enclose your card or message at no extra charge.

Luath Press Limited
543/2 Castlehill
The Royal Mile
Edinburgh EH1 2ND
Scotland
Telephone: 0131 225 4326 (24 hours)
Email: sales@luath.co.uk
Website: www.luath.co.uk